George Washington's Indispensable Men

GEORGE WASHINGTON'S INDISPENSABLE MEN

*The 32 Aides-de-Camp
Who Helped Win
American Independence*

Arthur S. Lefkowitz

STACKPOLE
BOOKS

Guilford, Connecticut

Published by Stackpole Books
An imprint of The Rowman & Littlefield Publishing Group, Inc.
4501 Forbes Blvd., Ste. 200
Lanham, MD 20706
www.rowman.com

Distributed by NATIONAL BOOK NETWORK
800-462-6420

British Library Cataloguing in Publication Information Available

Library of Congress Cataloging-in-Publication Data Available

ISBN 978-0-8117-3791-3 (paperback)
ISBN 978-0-8117-6808-5 (e-book)
ISBN 978-0-8117-1646-8 (hardback)

∞™ The paper used in this publication meets the minimum requirements of American
National Standard for Information Sciences—Permanence of Paper for Printed
Library Materials, ANSI/NISO Z39.48-1992.

Printed in the United States of America

This book is dedicated to my uncle
Pfc. David Lefkowitz
killed in action in the Philippines, May 7, 1945

My father served on the battleship *Missouri* during World War II and I found a letter he wrote home from Tokyo Bay the day Japan surrendered, in which he spoke of his younger brother David:

When the flag was raised then we knew the war was finally over. We waited for hours for this event and when it did happen, I said a silent prayer for my brother Dave. Not only did I lose a brother but a true friend. Whenever I think of him my head greaves heavy. I guess that is the way of life, some have to go before their time and I will never forget him as long as I live.

The science or art of War, requires a freedom of thought and leisure to reflect upon the Various incidents that dayly occur, which cannot be had where the whole of ones times is engrossed in Clerical employments . . . It is like a merchandise of small Wares.[1]
Gen. Nathanael Greene to George Washington,
July 25, 1776

COVER ILLUSTRATION

The painting shown on the cover of this book is titled *The Capture of the Hessians at Trenton* by John Trumbull. It was started by Trumbull in London in 1786 and completed following his return to America in 1789. The artist's imagined composition is based on the American victory at Trenton, New Jersey, on December 26, 1776. The town's garrison consisted of 1,600 Hessian troops under the command of Col. Johann Rall, who was mortally wounded in the battle.

Trumbull's painting is appropriate for this book as several of Washington's aides-de-camp are depicted in his work. They are Tench Tilghman, who is shown on horseback immediately behind Washington. Behind Tilghman is Robert Hanson Harrison, who served as an aide to the Commander-in-Chief for more than six years. Holding the severely wounded Rall is William Stephens Smith. Smith was an aide to Gen. John Sullivan at the time but joined Washington's staff later in the war.

The artist, John Trumbull, was also one of Washington's aides. Trumbull capitalized on his close association with Washington throughout his life— despite the fact that he served as one of the general's aides for only nineteen days. Trumbull died in 1843. By then there were few people alive who knew of his brief tenure on Washington's staff.

Painting reproduced courtesy of the Yale University Art Gallery.

CONTENTS

Photo Section appears between pages 174 and 175.

LIST OF MAPS

PREFACE

One of the pleasures of studying history is that you are always meeting new and interesting people. I was introduced to George Washington's Revolutionary War aides-de-camp while I was researching my book about the 1776 retreat of Washington's army across New Jersey. My study showed that Washington had a personal staff who reported directly to him. They had different titles including aide-de-camp, military secretary, extra aide-de-camp, assistant military secretary, recording secretary, and volunteer aide-de-camp, and I wondered what the different titles meant. I got to read some of their letters and orders, which made me curious to know who these men were and what they did for Washington, especially since they sometimes seemed to be operating independently of him. Further investigation showed that most of them had been lawyers, doctors, or businessmen before the war. This unplanned introduction to Washington's aides-de-camp made me curious to learn more about who they were and exactly what they did at headquarters.

My inquiry into the subject led me to the two books that had been written about Washington's aides-de-camp. Both were obscure and long out-of-print. One was authored by Emily Stone Whiteley and entitled *Washington and His Aides-de-Camp.*[2] It was published in 1936. The other was *With Pen and Sword,* dating from 1952. I was able to locate copies of both books and read them. The Whiteley book was the better of the two, which is the kindest thing I can say about it. Ms. Whiteley naively reported stories about Washington and his aides without questioning their basis of fact. She told her gossipy stories in a fantasy Revolutionary War backdrop devoid of the grim realities, which included avarice, mismanagement, mutinies, starvation, and petty jealousies over rank and promotion. In one regard, however, I found Ms. Whiteley's book not far from the mark. It was her portrayal of Washington and his aides as a Revolutionary War version of King Arthur and his Knights of the Round Table. I came to agree with her appraisal that Washington and his aides were a close-knit group of courageous and honorable men. But Washington's aides lived through a very complicated and difficult time, and I wanted to look beyond the simplistic yarns spun out by Ms. Whiteley. As a result I decided to embark upon my own voyage of historical discovery.

As I began researching Washington's aides, I soon realized why this interesting subject had been neglected by historians. One reason for it, is that it is a complicated topic due to the numerous men identified as being Washington's aides-de-camp. Unraveling who was an aide to Washington and who was not was challenging, and when I finished I still had thirty-two names. This is a large number of people to write about in a single volume, and I wanted to include all of them without confusing or boring my readers. I hope this book accomplishes my goals. Another reason the subject has received little attention is that many of the men who served in the position are obscure figures in American history, so that researching them was a problem. I wanted to do more than just record the basic facts of their lives, and I felt that the key to understanding them was to find their personal letters. But I was frustrated to find that their correspondence had been scattered all over the world, and locating their remaining letters was going to be a difficult task. I was also interested in writing about how Washington's headquarters operated during the Revolutionary War. For example, could a gentleman simply walk into army headquarters and talk to General Washington? Perhaps they were first referred to one of his aides whose job included screening visitors. In the course of my research I uncovered only two well documented sources of information about Washington's aides. They were a chapter in a 1924 book entitled *The Spirit of the Revolution: New Light from Some of the Original Sources of American History* by John C. Fitzpatrick and a 1997 master's thesis entitled *Gentlemen of the Family* written by Gerald Edward Kahler.[3]

What my research into the subject of Washington aides found was a laudable group of men whose workhorse contributions to the winning of American independence have been largely overlooked. As a group, they were much older and better educated than I had expected. My curiosity about finding out what happened to them after the Revolutionary War ended led me well into the nineteenth century as I unearthed their postwar accomplishments and misfortunes, many of which are included in this narrative.

Historians have only recently been able to break through the camouflage created by Fourth of July orators to realize that the American Revolution was often a half-hearted effort by men who drifted in and out of active participation in the conflict. But some men stayed the course and they are the ones who made independence possible. It was gratifying to conclude that Washington's aides-de-camp were among these dedicated American patriots.

As hard as I tried to write this book about Washington's aides-de-camp, I found that I kept writing about George Washington. He dominates this book, as he reigned over his family of aides-de-camp and the American Revolution at large. It is impossible to separate Washington from his aides. The affectionate link between them is one of the great stories of the war.

Arthur S. Lefkowitz
Piscataway, New Jersey

ACKNOWLEDGMENTS

This book is the story of thirty-two men who, with the exception of Alexander Hamilton, are obscure figures in American history. It was a challenging project and if this book informs and entertains it is due to the encouragement and help of many outstanding historians. My thanks are due first to Philander D. Chase, editor-in-chief of *The Papers of George Washington.* Phil Chase was an early supporter of this project and he gave me advice and encouragement throughout the research and writing of this book. I also take this opportunity to acknowledge the help of other staff members of *The Papers of George Washington* who are associate editor Frank E. Grizzard, Jr., assistant editors Edward G. Lengel and David Hoth, and research assistant Daniel Boyd Smith. Mr. Chase and his staff are true scholars because they are ready to share their considerable knowledge with researchers like myself.

I am also indebted to my artist/historian friend George C. Woodbridge who finally defined his area of expertise as "*the clothing, arms, and accoutrements used in the American Revolution.*" One meeting with George stands out in my mind. I went to visit him at his home one summer day eager to talk about my manuscript only to find him on his roof repairing his rain gutters. Rather than miss the opportunity of talking to him, I stood on the ground reading excerpts from my book while George scampered about his roof banging away at his rain gutters with a rubber mallet. He would stop me when he wanted to discuss some point or suggest a change. This went on for several hours in what we fondly look back on today as the *Rooftop Lecture.*

A number of National Park Service historians were also very helpful to me and I am pleased to have this opportunity to acknowledge their help. They were Joseph Lee Boyle at Valley Forge, John Frayler at Salem (Massachusetts), Eric Olsen and David J. Vecchioli at Morristown, and Diane Depew at Yorktown. Also Andrew B. Chamberlain and William Brown from the National Park Service center at Harpers Ferry, West Virginia. A number of people from the New Jersey State Park Service also gave me valuable assistance. They were Margaret Carlsen and Jennifer Saar at Rockingham (Washington's headquarters near Princeton, New Jersey), John Mills at Princeton Battlefield, W. James Kurzenberger at the Wallace house (Washington's headquarters during the winter of 1779–80), and Dr. Garry Wheeler Stone, historian at Monmouth Battlefield State Park. One visit with Garry Stone was memorable. Monmouth is the best preserved battlefield of the American Revolution and the view is spectacular in all directions except for a modern water tower, which reminds visitors that they are in the twenty-first century. Garry was pointing out terrain features to help me understand the movements of the armies during this complicated day-long battle. We were walking along paths between fields of corn, beans, and wheat stubble on a hot July day and even though we were both wearing comfortable, lightweight clothing, we became uncomfortable in the heat. On the day of the battle, the temperature soared to almost 100 degrees with high humidity. It was incredible to believe that soldiers fought for this ground in appalling heat and humidity for an entire day wearing heavy woolen uniforms, carrying sixty pounds of equipment, and charging across these farmed fields. "The Continental soldiers left their coats and packs in Englishtown," Dr. Stone said, "but most of the British troops went into action in their woolen regimentals carrying packs, haversacks, canteens, cartridge boxes, and muskets." As we continued to walk along, Garry suddenly turned to me and said, "I wish someone would tear down that water tower." I got a firsthand lesson on what preservationists call a historic view shed.

I also visited a number of historic buildings that are associated with Washington's aides-de-camp. At each place I received a warm welcome, and assistance with information and reference materials. These sites were the birthplace of Samuel B. Webb in Wethersfield, Connecticut, the Mount Vernon Hotel and Gardens (formerly called the Abigail Adams Smith House) in New York City, the birthplace of David Humphreys in Derby, Connecticut, the Morris-Jumel Mansion in New York City, the New Windsor Cantonment in Vails Gate, New York, the Schuyler Mansion in Albany, New York, and the Hasbrouck House in Newburgh, New York. It was during a research trip to Newburgh that a local restaurateur told me why the town was in an economic slump. Unaware that I was a Revolutionary War historian, he related that George Washington had his headquarters in Newburgh towards the end of the Revolution. According to the restaurant owner, as Washington was leaving Newburgh, for what proved to be the last time, the general stuck his head out of the window of his coach as it was pulling away and yelled back to the town's burghers, "don't do anything until I get back."

I also want to acknowledge the assistance of Ms. Dorothy Twohig, the retired editor-in-chief of *The Papers of George Washington* and an associate editor of *The Papers of Alexander Hamilton.* When I began this project I asked Ms. Twohig to recommend two Hamilton biographies for me to read. Her suggestions were Jacob Cooke's *Alexander Hamilton* and John C. Miller's *Alexander Hamilton: Portrait in Paradox.* I took these suggestions to Clarence Wolf , the proprietor of the George S. MacManus Co. Mr. Wolf is a leading rare book dealer specializing in colonial Americana. To my delight, Clarence pulled both Hamilton biographies from his shelves.

Joseph Rubinfine also shared his considerable knowledge of Revolutionary War manuscripts with me. Joe is a document dealer specializing in George Washington letters and while editing some copy for me he pointed out a typographical error that I had made. In listing the types of documents that were filed at Washington's headquarters I wrote, "these included troop returns, reports, *roosters* and inventories." Joe noted that I meant rosters, however on the margin he added, "I did have a letter once where George Washington ordered some poultry as a present for Admiral D'Estaing."

I also have the pleasant task of acknowledging some other people who helped me with this book. They are my friend Mike Leonard, commander USNR, who assisted me with nautical terms. Mike taught me, for example, that the navy of Great Britain is always referred to as the Royal Navy. Another friend, George C. Neumann, helped me with information about Revolutionary War weapons. My friend and fellow extreme Revolutionary War hobbyist, Raymond Andrews, assisted me with information about Revolutionary War uniforms. Richard Walling shared his expert knowledge of the battle of Monmouth with me. Professor Richard Buel, Jr., from Wesleyan University was another active supporter. Professor Buel was my toughest critic and I lived in fear of his e-mail critiques. But I am grateful to him because he gave me constructive advice and I feel honored to have his valuable input in this project. My special thanks also go to Associate Professor Gregory D. Massey at Freed-Hardeman University who generously read my manuscript, and saved me from making some embarrassing errors. Professor Massey is the author of an important new biography about John Laurens, one of Washington's aides-de-camp. Additional help came from Marko Zlatich, an independent researcher and consultant to the Smithsonian. The distinguished historian Thomas Fleming also encouraged me throughout the long process of writing this book. He is the author of many outstanding books about the American Revolution but my favorite (so far) remains *The Forgotten Victory: The Battle for New Jersey, 1780,* which was published in 1973. Tom Fleming helped me create a readable book without sacrificing scholarship.

Research for this book was done at a number of institutions. They were The David Library of the American Revolution at Washington Crossing, Pennsylvania; Yorktown Victory Center, Yorktown, Virginia; the Family History Library of the Church of Jesus Christ of Latter-Day Saints in Salt Lake City; The Pierpont Morgan Library in New York City; The Society of the Cincinnati Library (special thanks to Ellen McCallister Clark, library director) in Washington, D.C.; The Massachusetts Historical Society in Boston; The New Haven Colony Historical Society; The New York Historical Society; The New York Public Library; Rutgers University Library in New Brunswick, New Jersey; The Library of Congress and Jim Hobson's antique shop in Annapolis, Maryland. Mr. Hobson's contribution concerns a letter George Washington wrote about one of his aides-de-camp in which the general used the term "Hobson's choice." I knew it meant the appearance of a choice where none actually existed, but I did not know the origin of the term. I decided an explanation of "Hobson's choice" was beyond the subject of my book and I dropped the idea of including it as a footnote. Months later I was window shopping in Annapolis, Maryland, when I walked by an antique shop named Hobson's Choice. Upon inquiry I learned that it was owned by Mr. Jim Hobson who was an expert on the term. He shared his extensive collection of printed information on the subject with me. I felt that fate had brought me to Mr. Hobson's doorstep and I had to include the origin of the term, which appears as a foot-note at the appropriate place in this book.

I believe that it is important to visit historic sites to help understand the events that took place there. I was fortunate to have the good company and insightful comments of my friend, Dr. Richard Prouty, on many of my excursions. One of our outings was to look at the places along the lower Hudson River connected with the treason of Benedict Arnold. Our guide for this excursion was local historian David Whieldon who, at one point, led us through a thickly wooded area across the Hudson River from West Point. Richard Prouty is a retired doctor and he is always neatly dressed in a tailored business suit with an immaculate white shirt, tie, and classic hat. It was interesting to watch the good doctor climbing over rocks and navigating streams while historian Whieldon, leading the way in his rugged outdoor clothing, was chatting away about General Arnold unaware of Dr. Prouty's plight.

The good doctor and I had another memorable excursion, this time to learn the technical details of writing with a quill pen and ink. Our instructor was John Muller, director of the Fort Lee, New Jersey, historic site, who has made a study of the subject. Dr. Prouty and I walked away from the experience agreeing that a handful of ballpoint pens could have shortened the American Revolution by several months.

I must also thank my wife Susan for her patience and understanding during the long process of creating this book. She critiqued drafts and was especially patient in explaining the recipe for Alexander Hamilton's wedding cake, which is included in my book. I am also proud to acknowledge that my friend Col. Lance Betros, Ph.D., who wrote the introduction to this book, has been appointed Professor and Deputy Head of the Department of History at the United States Military Academy, West Point.

INTRODUCTION

Shortly before assuming my duties as an aide-de-camp, I asked a currently serving aide how he was enjoying the experience. He cracked a wry smile and responded, "It's a great job to have *had*."

His terse commentary reflected the ambivalence that goes with being an aide. On the one hand, the work is exciting and developmental, a stepping-stone to advancement in one's career. Constantly at the side of a military leader of high rank and responsibility, the aide is privy to the most important and sensitive issues within an organization. He is at the epicenter of power, albeit as an observer, and gains a sophisticated understanding of high-level politics and policy making. He is familiar with the leader's personality, habits, and priorities and has frequent contact with him. Consequently, the aide assumes a mantle of power out of proportion to his rank, as persons seeking access to or preferment from the leader often curry his favor. In the process, he is able to meet important people and develop a network of personal contacts—no small advantage to the talented and ambitious officers typically chosen to be aides. Perhaps most important, the aide gains a powerful mentor whose potential value to the young officer far exceeds the service rendered by the aide to the leader.

On the other hand, the job has its drawbacks. An aide works long hours performing myriad tasks that are tedious and thankless. He travels often and can easily end up spending more time with his boss than with family and friends. Though chosen for his competence and professionalism, he stays in the background and defers to the priorities of another. He is constantly at the leader's beck and call, expected to do jobs that a prideful person might consider demeaning. A strong personal friendship with the leader helps mitigate these irritants; the lack of one compounds them.

In several illuminating passages of *George Washington's Indispensable Men,* Arthur Lefkowitz reminds us that the life of an aide has not changed much since the Revolution. The thirty-two men appointed to the position during the war were talented and dedicated subordinates who exhibited the same natural ambivalence of modern aides. As part of Washington's "military family," they relished being near the pinnacle of power and enjoyed the prestige of their association with the commander in chief. Nonetheless, the unrelenting demands of the job, exacerbated by the general's exacting standards, weighed heavily on them. None of Washington's aides would have traded the experience, but in the end they probably would have agreed that it was a great job to have *had*.

The duties of an aide have remained fairly constant over the years. As part of the leader's personal staff, he takes care of the mundane tasks that otherwise would consume the leader's time and distract his attention from the pressing issues of command. He attends to the leader's personal needs—health, safety, welfare, social obligations—and provides routine administrative services. The aide focuses less on the operational mission than on the immediate environment in which the leader works; nonetheless, he must understand the big picture and anticipate changes that could influence the leader's ability to function effectively.

From day to day, the aide stays busy with many and diverse duties. He keeps the leader's appointment schedule and manages confidential files. He prepares correspondence for the leader's signature and occasionally acts as a courier for sensitive or personal messages. Prior to meetings, official functions, and social gatherings, the aide visits the site and reviews the agenda with event organizers; he then briefs the leader and accompanies him to the event to ensure that everything goes smoothly. On official trips he coordinates for travel and lodging, insures the security and delivery of baggage, records expenses, and navigates the leader through every activity on the itinerary. The moment the leader has to ask about these mundane issues, the chances are good that the aide has fallen down on the job. It is no wonder that the aide is always in motion, rising early to be ready for the day, retiring late after preparing for the next.

Because the aide accompanies the leader to official functions and many social events, one of his most visible duties is to be a paragon of military professionalism. The aide is a reflection of the leader almost as a child is a reflection of the parent. Of course, a parent will tolerate lapses in behavior far more than a military leader; hence, the aide must be quick to master his duties and avoid mistakes that could embarrass or inconvenience his boss. He must exhibit outstanding military bearing, appearance, and attitude. He should be resourceful, yet unobtrusive; forceful yet discreet. In sum, his job is to be an officer and a gentleman.

Despite the commonality of most aide duties past and present, Washington's aides faced challenges unknown to their modern counterparts. The principal reason was the embryonic organization of the Continental Army. Washington did not have the benefit of a professional general staff, which evolved in the United States during the last decades of the nineteenth century. By way of contrast, a general commanding an American army today would have at his disposal the talents of hundreds of staff officers and soldiers working within discrete functional areas and monitored by an experienced chief of staff. The primary staff would handle the most pressing tasks—personnel administration, intelligence, operations, and logistics. A secondary staff, tailored to the peculiarities of each mission, would provide support in such areas as civil affairs, combat engineering, communications, media relations, and liaison with adjacent units, foreign armies, and civilian agencies.

Washington had all of these concerns, but not nearly enough people on his staff to address them. He therefore relied on a small cadre of trusted subordinates—primarily his aides—to help him manage the affairs of the army, and these men quickly found themselves enmeshed in a multitude of critical issues. Washington's aides, in addition to the tasks traditionally associated with the job, were constantly busy transcribing the commander in chief's verbal guidance and written notes into clear, concise directives for execution by the army in the field. The prodigious quantity of correspondence that left the headquarters reflected the essential mission they performed. Constantly with the commander, constantly in touch with the most important issues of the day, the aides were truly Washington's indispensable men. No one worked more closely with Washington than his aides and, except for Martha, no one knew him better.

Historians who have studied Washington's voluminous writings have yet to uncover evidence that his aides played a formal role in formulating policy. Given the talents of the men he picked as aides, however, one might reasonably surmise that they served in this capacity. Lefkowitz cogently argues the point based on his study of the operational rhythm of the headquarters and the proximity of the aides to every substantive issue. It would be hard to imagine men of such high caliber not having well-reasoned opinions on the key issues facing the Continental Army. It is equally unlikely that Washington would have wasted the opportunity to benefit from the perspectives of his trusted aides, especially when there were relatively few others in whom he could confide. In the following pages, readers can judge for themselves the persuasiveness of Lefkowitz's argument.

What is the purpose of studying the men who served as Washington's aides? First, they were a fascinating group of Americans who reflected the spirit and character of the new nation. Upwardly mobile and dedicated to the cause of liberty and equality, they demonstrated in their own lives faith in republican virtues and the benefits of a merit-based society. Several of them would rise to cabinet positions during Washington's presidency, and many others would distinguish themselves in state and local government. Lefkowitz provides riveting accounts of their individual stories, with emphasis on Washington's profound legacy on their lives after the war. To a man, the aides viewed their association with the commander in chief as a life-shaping experience and a source of great pride—in some cases, even mentioned in their epitaphs.

Second, the aides' close association with Washington gave them unique insights into virtually every aspect of the War for Independence. They shared Washington's anguish during the long retreat into New Jersey, the difficult winter encampments, and the discovery of Benedict Arnold's treason; likewise, they rejoiced with him after the victories at Trenton, Princeton, and Yorktown. Since Washington selected his aides in large part based on their writing skills, it should come as no surprise that some of the best accounts of key military events were penned by the aides-de-camp.

Third, there has been little historical interest in Washington's aides, despite their close relationship with the commander in chief throughout the Revolutionary War. Although biographies have appeared on a few of them, Lefkowitz is the first to systematically study the group as a collective entity. The job was not easy because the personal records of most of the officers were widely scattered and poorly catalogued. As he collected the information, however, thirty-two individual stories evolved into a rich and coherent history. The result of his scholarship is a fascinating account of life within Washington's military family and a fresh look at the commander in chief himself.

Finally, if Lefkowitz is correct about the role of the aides in helping Washington formulate policy, then they assume an importance hitherto unknown and unappreciated by historians of the Revolution. His work is an invitation for further study into the lives of the aides as a means of better understanding Washington and the influence of the aides on his thoughts and actions. This line of inquiry represents uncharted territory in an area otherwise well traveled by students of American history.

It is said that the character of a man can be judged by the company of the people he keeps. If the adage is true, then Lefkowitz has given us thirty-two more reasons to revere the Father of our Country.

Lance Betros, Ph.D.
Colonel, U.S. Army, and Senior Aide-de-Camp
to the Secretary of the Army, 1998–99

PART ONE

THE FIRST YEARS
OF THE REVOLUTION

1775–77

In 1775, at the beginning of the American Revolution, Washington was forced to recruit his aides-de-camp from men with little military experience. They were Joseph Reed, Thomas Mifflin, John Trumbull, Edmund Randolph, Robert Hanson Harrison, Stephen Moylan, William Grayson, and George Baylor. Several of them lasted on the job for a short time, for various reasons that are explained in the text that follows. However, as the war entered its second year, Washington was able to replace part of his original staff with officers from the Continental Army who had excellent writing skills as well as military experience. This second generation of aides included Samuel B. Webb, William Palfrey, Richard Kidder Meade, and Tench Tilghman. By the decisive battles of Trenton (December 26, 1776) and Princeton (January 3, 1777), Washington's personal staff had developed into a professional organization.

CHAPTER ONE

Washington Reinvents the Aide-De-Camp, 1775

At present, my time is so much taken up at my Desk, that I am obliged to neglect many other essential parts of my Duty; it is absolutely necessary therefore for me to have person's that can think for me, as well as execute Orders . . .

George Washington to Joseph Reed,
January 23, 1776[1]

George Washington was a great horseman but he did not ride through the American Revolution, he wrote through it. As commander in chief of the Continental Army, he was repeatedly forced to take responsibility for coordinating the military efforts of the infant nation. The civilian government was befuddled by military problems and repeatedly abdicated its responsibilities to Washington, who proved to be an expert administrator with practical wisdom. The war effort centered on Washington because he was a capable executive, patient conciliator, and in the words of John Adams—a person of "excellent universal character."

Historians like to add drama to their narratives of the American Revolution by pointing out that Washington had little military experience when the war began. They are assisted in their appraisal by Washington's own words, which include a possible conversation he had with Patrick Henry about his lack of training to lead the army: "Remember, Mr. Henry what I now tell you; from the day I enter upon the command of the American armies, I date my fall and the ruin of my reputation."[2] However, while it is correct that Washington never commanded a large army prior to the Revolution, he was an experienced and competent army administrator. Washington learned how to run an army from two renowned British military administrators: Gen. Edward Braddock and Gen. John Forbes. He served under these two officers during the French and Indian War (1754–63), and he was a keen observer of their administrative techniques to the point of copying their orders into notebooks that he kept for future reference.

As commander in chief of the Continental Army, Washington used the skills he learned from Braddock and Forbes, to which he added his expertise of running a large plantation and his experience of a dozen years sitting in the Virginia House of Burgesses. Washington's administrative skills were important because the American Revolution proved to be a war where solving logistical problems often made the difference between victory and defeat.

Effective communication was the key to Washington's management style. His letters were often motivational, and his themes included appealing to patriotism, bemoaning the suffering of the army, or inducing fear that, for example, the Continental Army was on the verge of collapse. He tended to give gloomy descriptions of situations as a means of prodding his recipients into action. With his emphasis on effective communication, Washington wrote, or had written at his instructions, about 12,000 letters and orders during the eight years that he served as commander in chief. To understand how much writing this involved, consider the exhaustive project undertaken by historian John C. Fitzpatrick and a team of researchers to publish every known letter written by Washington. Although Washington was a prolific writer with a wide circle of correspondents and a lifetime of public service including eight years as president of the United States, when Fitzpatrick and his team published their findings from 1931–44 as *The Writings of George Washington,* twenty-four of the thirty-seven thick volumes in the set dealt exclusively with letters and orders written by Washington during the American Revolution. It was more correspondence than any one person could possibly have written himself during this relatively short period of time.

How did Washington manage to write 12,000 letters and orders during the Revolution? If he had commanded a modern army, he could have turned to the officers on his headquarters staff for help. Today's modern day staff officers deal with four major administrative functions: personnel, military intelligence, operations (planning), and logistics (supply, transportation, maintenance, and record keeping). However, when Washington took command of the Continental Army the creation of a headquarters staff was still 100 years in the future. The American army had some rudimentary elements of a professional staff, notably in copying the office of the adjutant general from the British. Perhaps the adjutant general helped Washington write his letters and orders? Let's look at his function.

The adjutant general's job was to organize the day-to-day operations of the army. The 1779 *Universal Military Dictionary* specified some of his duties,

> the Adjutant General is an officer of distinction, who aids and assists the general in his laborious duty…and keeps an exact state of each brigade and regiment…He every day at headquarters receives orders from the general officer of the day, and distributes them to the majors of brigades, from whom he receives the number of men they are to

furnish for the duty of the army, and informs them of any detail which may concern them.[3]

In other words, all orders, instructions, and assignments were recorded and transmitted to the army through the adjutant general. Washington placed particular stress on this office to provide him with regular and accurate strength reports on the number of soldiers in the army. Washington had a capable and experienced adjutant general at the start of the war in the person of Horatio Gates, a former British major who proved to be an expert administrator.[4] Gates, however, was absorbed in the great responsibilities of his own office and was unable to offer Washington much assistance in drafting correspondence.

Another possible source for help to Washington might have been the men who ran the various departments established by Congress. As with the office of the adjutant general, the Continental Congress copied the organization of the British Army by establishing various departments. Almost everything that the army needed was purchased, transported, and distributed by a department. These departments included the Quartermaster Corps, Artillery Corps, and Clothier Department. The head of each department was appointed by Congress, and they were sometimes more of a burden than a source of help to Washington.[5] The problem was that many department heads were inexperienced or incompetent. They were often overwhelmed by their own responsibilities with no time available to help Washington at headquarters. In fact, the departments became a drain on Washington's time. Adding to the problem was that Congress suspected that the various departments were corrupt and were suspicious of every recommendation to reform them.[6] As a result the army suffered, requiring Washington to spend part of his working day trying to make the infant department system work.

The officers in the various regiments, called line officers, were another potential source of help to Washington. However, the line officers were frequently too absorbed in the operation of their commands to render any real assistance to their commander. This potential source of help at headquarters was further distanced because there was frequently a shortage of officers to fill the line commands.[7] Painfully aware of the limited talent pool available to him, Washington relied almost exclusively on the small staff authorized by Congress to assist him. He took this perquisite and staffed it with a group of brilliant men that one Washington scholar called "the most remarkable group of young men to be found in the history of the United States."[8]

At the beginning of the Revolution, Congress authorized Washington to have a personal staff composed of one military secretary and three aides-de-camp.[9] The military secretary's job was to compose letters and orders. He was selected for his writing skills and discretion since he frequently had access to confidential information. He might be asked, for example, to attend councils of war and keep minutes. Only Washington, as commander in chief of the army, was authorized by the Continental Congress to have a military secretary.[10] The other members of Washington's personal staff were called aides-de-camp. An aide is an administrative assistant and personal representative of a general officer. The position was already an established prerogative in the eighteenth century, and the privilege continues to this day. Congress authorized three aides for Washington and two for all other generals. The duties of an aide were undefined and they were expected to do whatever was asked of them by their commanding general. However, aides were generally entrusted to deliver important dispatches and other privileged information in camp, on the march, and in battle. During a battle, if there was no time to write a note or dispatch, a general would use one of his aides to deliver verbal orders. The *Universal Military Dictionary* emphasized the function of an aide as a messenger,

> An aid-de-camp is an officer appointed to attend a general officer . . . he receives and carries their orders, as occasion requires. He is seldom under the degree [rank] of a captain . . . This employment is of greater importance than is generally believed, it is, however, often entrusted to young officers of little experience, and of as little capacity; but in most foreign services, they give great attention to this article.[11]

A military secretary or aide-de-camp did not necessarily have to be a soldier. Washington stated this point in a letter to a Congressional Committee: "They ought to be men of abilities . . . constantly calling for talents and abilities of the first rate: men who possess them ought to be taken wherever they can be found."[12] Note that Washington wanted *men of abilities* as his aides and was not interested in appointing someone because of his political connections, family pedigree, or battlefield experience.

Because the duties of an aide-de-camp were unspecified, what they did was largely dependent on the personality and character of their boss. Washington was a dedicated hard worker and his headquarters was a serious workplace. One of his opponents during the war, Gen. Sir Henry Clinton, in comparison, used his aides to indulge his passion for giving military instructions, and telling military anecdotes of his campaigns.[13] Clinton had an interesting experience when, as a young officer, he served as an aide-de-camp to Gen. Sir John Ligonier. General Ligonier was seventy-seven at the time with a string of young mistresses. The aged general maintained that no woman past the age of fourteen was worth the trouble of pursuing and he kept four mistresses whose combined ages were less than sixty. Ligonier expected Clinton to enter into the spirit of his frolics and spend money on women and other entertainments along with him.[14]

There was no shortage of job seekers for a position as a general's aide-de-camp in the Continental Army. It was looked upon as a means of social mobility. Some applicants were even ready to serve on a general's staff as gentlemen volunteers without any rank or pay because they hoped it would lead to a permanent assignment.[15] While a position as an aide-de-camp to Washington was particularly desirable, the general set high standards for his aides and the position was beyond the reach of most men. The individuals Washington sought for his staff were urbane and intelligent men who sometimes preferred a commission in a line regiment or a prominent post in the new national or state governments rather than work in the shadows at headquarters. Washington still had a large pool of outstanding applicants to choose from, especially as his reputation grew during the course of the war. He was aware that the men serving in his *military family* were capable of holding more prestigious offices and he appreciated their unselfish devotion to the cause.[16]

In almost every instance Washington selected men who possessed unassailable family credentials for his staff, not because he was a snob but because the men he needed could only be found among the wealthy and genteel class of colonial America. The eighteenth-century term for the men who were recruited by Washington for his staff was *gentlemen.* Washington often referred to his personal staff during the Revolution, both officially and unofficially as "the gentlemen of the family."[17] In the strictest eighteenth-century definition, "gentlemen" were men of independent means who did not have to work for a living. However, this was a European idea. In America, gentlemen were distinguished by the success of their work and not by their leisure. But gentlemen on both continents were recognized by their fine clothing, good manners, and elegant lifestyles all of which required money.

Washington also wanted what he called "confidential" men as his aides-de-camp. In letters and speeches he mentioned his aides as his "Confidential Officers."[18] What Washington meant was that he wanted trustworthy men around him. His aides had access to important information that was of value to the enemy or could adversely affect the discipline of his army. Washington expected his aides not to gossip or innocently repeat anything they heard or saw at headquarters. He also wanted "confidential men" as his aides because he had no intelligence staff and probably employed his aides to assist him in directing various spy rings and other clandestine operations. It is possible that Washington wanted his aides and other intermediaries to deal with spies for security reasons (their role as spy masters was disguised by their routine duties) and to protect Washington who could claim ignorance of covert activities when the situation suited him. Washington may have also used his aides to examine deserters and prisoners of war as a means of obtaining information. Historians have only recently begun to recognize the importance both sides put on questioning prisoners and deserters, and Washington's aides may have been at the center of this intelligence gathering for the Americans. The general's aides remained discreet about their involvement in spy activities to the ends of their lives; despite the fact that they were accomplished writers, not one of them is known to have written an account of what they did at headquarters during the Revolutionary War.

The educational level of the aides-de-camp is another clue to their importance to Washington. There were few college graduates on the eve of the
American Revolution. Only 830 American college degrees can be confirmed as
having been awarded between 1769–75. In comparison, the population of the
thirteen colonies was 2,500,000. However, the majority of Washington's thirty-
two aides-de-camp had college degrees or attended college for at least one
year. Some of his other aides may also have had some higher education. Harvard produced the largest number of college graduates between the years 1769
and 1775. It awarded 308 degrees, followed by Yale with 188 and the College
of New Jersey (today's Princeton University) with 150.[19] Graduates from these
colleges were aides to Washington, along with alumni from The College of
William and Mary, the University of Pennsylvania (at the time called the College, Academy, and Charitable School of Philadelphia), and the University of
Delaware (known as Newark Academy).

Even rarer in colonial society than an American college degree were men
who had been educated in Europe. Seven of Washington's aides are known to
have been educated abroad. It is also possible that one of the general's aides,
William Grayson, attended Oxford University in England. Another of his
aides, John Laurens, was arguably the best educated young American of his
day with private tutoring at home followed by schooling in Switzerland and
England. It is interesting that George Washington who had little formal education of his own, spoke no foreign languages, and had never traveled outside the
thirteen colonies (except for a visit as a teenager to the island of Barbados)
sought out educated, worldly men to serve as his aides and seemed comfortable in their presence.

As we have already seen, Washington used specific words to describe the
men he wanted as his aides-de-camp: *ability, gentlemen,* and *confidential.*
Another term he frequently used to describe the kind of men he sought was
"pen-men." Writing to a fellow officer in February 1776, Washington said, "It is
unnecessary for me to observe to you, the multiplicity of business I am
Involved In . . . call loudly for Aids that are ready Pen-men."[20] What Washington meant by *pen-men* was the skill of being able to write intelligently, clearly,
quickly, and endlessly. All of the men who served as Washington's aides had
the essential quality of being good writers. While his military secretary's function was to assist him with his communications and his aides were his administrative and personal assistants, Washington made no distinction between the
two positions: everyone wrote well or they were useless to him. Because
Washington made no differentiation between his military secretary and his
aides-de-camp, I will generally do the same and refer to them all, regardless of
their official designation, as aides-de-camp. It is generally believed that Washington selected his aides based on either their "riding" or "writing" abilities.
This is incorrect. Good writing skills were a prerequisite to be Washington's
aide. He had one aide who can be classified as a "riding aide." His name was

George Baylor and he was appointed to Washington's staff early in the war. Baylor proved to be an excellent horseman and reliable courier but he was incapable of composing a letter or order. Washington liked Baylor but discreetly got rid of him at the first opportunity.

With the help of his aides, Washington was able to carry on an extensive, detailed, and persistent correspondence that pulled the limited resources of the colonies together to make independence possible. The ready pens of his aides also made it possible for him to address a variety of major issues throughout the Revolution, including campaign and battle plans, supplies of food and clothing, financial problems, reorganization of the army, defensive measures, raids on British positions, military intelligence, mutinies, affairs of the Northern and Southern armies, defense of the frontier, and foreign relations. After 1777 he took responsibility for coordinating military activities with his French allies, which led to the combined French-American victory at Yorktown in 1781. Only a handful of the French officers spoke English so Washington was fortunate to have men on his staff—including Tench Tilghman, Alexander Hamilton, John Laurens, and Benjamin Walker—who were fluent in French. It is also possible that aides Stephen Moylan and David Humphreys could read and write Spanish.

In addition to the 12,000 letters and orders drafted for Washington's signature, his aides-de-camp produced another 5,000 official documents on their own consisting of letters, orders, troop returns, reports, rosters, inventories, lists, estimates, vouchers, warrants, invoices, receipts, payrolls, ledger accounts, commissions, oaths of allegiance, passes, leaves of absence, and discharges.

When Washington said he wanted *pen-men,* he meant not only men who could write, but who could write well. While recent scholarship has been in favor of an upward revision of the literacy rate in colonial America, literate proficiency was a scarce commodity at the time. To illustrate this point, here is an excerpt from a letter written by Lt. Col. Experience Storrs to General Washington:

> Cambridge, 30 October 1775. Ens. Isaac Farewell wishes to be discharged from the army on account of Indisposition of Body. . . . I have no more to Say to your Excelencey than that when he has been able he has Done his Duty with Cherfullness, but for Some Time past ben Troubled with the Rumitis & unable to Doe Duty, That in Case your Exelencey Sould Think best to Release him, so rather Think it would not be any Disadvantage to the Service.[21]

Storrs's spelling and grammar are actually not bad in comparison with that of other Americans at the time. For example, here is an excerpt from a letter written by Lt. Joseph Hodgkins to his wife. Hodgkins wrote this letter from Valley Forge:

I am in grate hast as the Barer is wating I must just inform you that what our soliders have suffered this Winter is Beyond Expression as one half has Ben Bare foot & all most Naked all winter the other half Very Badly on it for Clothes of all sorts and to ComPleat our misery Very shorte on it for Provison not Long since our Brigade drue But an half Days aLownce of Meat in Eight Day But these Defeltis the men Bore with a Degree of fortitude Becoming soldiers.[22]

By comparison, excerpts from personal letters and diaries written by Washington's aides-de-camp demonstrate that they were talented writers with excellent literate proficiency.

Writing to his future wife, Elizabeth Schuyler, Alexander Hamilton said, "I meet you in every dream and when I wake I cannot close my eyes again for ruminating on your sweetness. 'Tis a pretty story indeed that I am to be thus monopolized by a little nut brown maid like you and from a soldier metamorphosed into a puny lover."[23]

Aide Samuel B. Webb wrote his brother-in-law following the death of Webb's wife:

This world truly appears a mighty void, nor have I the least relish for its greatest enjoyments. Time, no doubt, will soften my affliction, otherwise nature could not support the shock; but to Forget my dear Eliza is as impossible as it is for me ever to enjoy her company here on earth again . . . A day ere long will come, I hope, when I may sit down with you, when, in the bosom of friendship, it will be pleasing to relate my misfortunes and to laud the innumerable virtues of my dear Eliza.[24]

Tench Tilghman wrote to his fellow aide-de-camp James McHenry:

Does not the Republic go on charmingly? By the Body of my father as honest Sancho used to swear, we have advanced as far in luxury in the third year of our Indepeny. as the old musty Republics of Greece and Rome did in twice as many hundreds: But we Americans are a sharp people. And we are in more senses than one: and if we do not keep a sharp look out we shall be little the better for the profusion of money and no small quantity of Blood that has been spent. All cry out that nothing but economy can save us, and yet no one allows that he or she is extravagant. You shall hear much when we fill the sociable bunks, where all is under the secure lock and key of Friendship.[25]

Aide James McHenry kept a wartime diary. Here is an excerpt from his entry for June 21, 1778:

A rainy evening . . . Let me see, what company have we got within doors.—A pretty, full-faced, youthful, playfull lass.—The family quakers, meek and unsuspicious. . . . —The pretty girl gives me some excellent milk, and sits and chats with me till bedtime.—She was too innocent a subject for gallantry, so I kissed her hand—telling her that we should be all gone before she got up—but not to forget that one man is often more dangerous to a woman than a whole army.[26]

Besides their literary proficiency the aides tended to have neat and clear handwriting. Their letters are easy to read and sometimes beautiful to look at. Good penmanship was implied when Washington used the term *pen-men* and clear handwriting was another prerequisite to be appointed as one of his aides-de-camp. Washington cared about presentation, and he wanted his letters to look impressive, especially if he was corresponding with the enemy, which he did on numerous occasions, regarding issues such as prisoner exchange and the return of personal property.

Some nineteenth-century historians believed that Washington's wartime letters were written for him by his aides-de-camp. They argue that many of them had excellent educations, that included studying in Europe and training as doctors. They correctly show that almost all of his wartime letters are in the handwriting of one of his aides and only signed by him. They also argue that Washington's meager education made it impossible for him to have written letters of remarkable clarity with good spelling and grammar for the standards of the time. However the notion that Washington's letters were written by his aides is incorrect. If it were true, the letters would show the different writing styles of his aides. But that is not the case; all of Washington's wartime letters read as if they were written by the same person. Commenting on this point, John C. Fitzpatrick, who edited the thirty-nine volume *Writings of George Washington,* noted in his introduction, "it is necessary only to read a few dozen of the letters here printed to catch their undeviating swing and mannerisms, regardless of which aide drafted them. . . . Sufficient examples are found among the letters of his ability to condense and improve his aides' drafts with simple, more forceful English."[27]

The contention that Washington's aides authored his letters, however, refuses to die. A recent example involves a biography of aide Tench Tilghman, which claims that Tilghman authored finished letters (called fair copies) for Washington. Tilghman's biographer states, "Often Washington would simply sign what Tilghman had written."[28] Philander D. Chase, editor-in-chief of *The Papers of George Washington* believes otherwise. "I don't believe," Mr. Chase said, "that Washington ever signed any significant letter or other document without having considerable input and checking it to see that it accorded with both his intentions and style."[29]

Washington's letters were his own no matter who composed them for him. He was sensitive about his image and his aides became adept at sublimating their own writing styles in favor of imitating his. The general's writing style was consistently respectful (especially to members of the Continental Congress), tactful, and businesslike. Washington edited the drafts written for him by his aides. As an example, General Gates once countermanded an order from Washington to ship some muskets to Valley Forge. One of Washington's aides drafted a response to Gates that included, "This countermand has greatly disappointed and exceedingly distressed me." Washington changed the focus of this phrase from his own disappointment to the good of the army: "This countermand has greatly disappointed and exceedingly distressed and injured the service."[30]

Although Washington kept tight control on what was written, the process by which letters and orders were produced at his wartime headquarters remains a matter of speculation. Considerations include the amount of correspondence that had to be written and their importance. Another factor was whether Washington was in the midst of a tense military campaign or sitting quietly in his office. Other variables are the number of aides available and their writing expertise.

One of Washington's aides, James McHenry, left us a clue to the writing process at headquarters. He wrote that the general's usual mode of writing a letter was to give an aide notes on what he wanted to be written. "Having made out a letter from such notes," wrote McHenry, "it was submitted to the General for his approbation and correction—afterwards copied fair . . . and signed by him."[31] Washington probably dictated some or all of the text for short letters or orders. In some instances he wrote outlines, which he gave to his aides who wrote letter drafts that he edited. He also wrote complete drafts of letters that his aides *copied fair* for his final review and signature. Some of the longer letters are in the handwriting of two or three aides as one after another of them were apparently called away for more important work. No matter how many men were involved in drafting a letter, they all read as if they were written by Washington.

In considering the process by which letters may have been produced at Washington's headquarters, it is important to understand that letter writing was a serious activity in the eighteenth century, and educated people took great pride in the content and appearance of their letters. Any permanent writing was done in ink using a quill pen—a writing instrument made from a large feather with a tip that was cut to a sharp point. The quill pen could only hold a small amount of ink on its tip, which had to be replenished after writing a few words. It took skill and concentration using this "dip and scratch" method to write neatly and clearly.[32] To ease the process, whenever possible, letters were written sitting at a desk that was often covered with a cheap woolen cloth called baize.[33] This soft material, frequently green in color, cushioned the quill pen making it easier to write. Most letters at the time of the Revolutionary War were written in an alphabet style called English Roundhand. It was the standard alphabet style used by businesspeople at the time. The letters of this alphabet were clear and it was easy to write fast. Every known document emanating from Washington's headquarters was written in English Roundhand. A person was taught to write Roundhand at school or could learn it himself by tracing the letters from a copybook, the most popular of which at the time was *The Universal Penman* written by George Bickham. As a young man Washington had poor penmanship, but he used copybooks to teach himself the gentlemanly art of writing neatly, clearly, and elegantly.

There is a possibility that some headquarters correspondence was drafted in pencil. Pencils were widely used at the time because one could write much faster with a pencil than with a quill pen and ink. The explanation why there are no known examples of letters or orders drafted in pencil is that anything written in pencil was not intended to survive. Another reason why pencil might have been used is that shorthand was in use at the time. Thomas Jefferson, for example, knew shorthand. In order to take shorthand quickly it was necessary to write with a pencil. There is no evidence that Washington knew shorthand but it is likely that some of his aides did, especially the businessmen among them. Washington could have dictated letters, which were taken down in shorthand, and these notes were eventually scrapped.[34] No aspect of this book created as much discussion among my advisors as the possibility that Washington's aides wrote preliminary drafts in pencil and/or in shorthand. The most compelling argument against the use of pencil drafts and shorthand is that paper was expensive and hard to get during the war. Valuable paper would not have been wasted to write pencil or shorthand drafts.

Washington had no formal system for selecting his aides-de-camp. Some candidates arrived at headquarters with letters of recommendation, but were otherwise unknown to him. An impressive letter of introduction was a good start, as attested by a statement Washington made in a December 1775 note written to a friend in Philadelphia from army headquarters: "Indeed no Gentleman that is not well known, ought to come here without Letters of Introduction, as it puts me in an awkward Situation with respect to my Conduct towards them."[35] Washington relied upon letters of recommendation, inquiries to his trusted friends, and his own innate skill in sizing up people to help him find suitable men for his staff. If he was unsure, he invited the candidate to work for him as a volunteer. One of the candidates who failed to get a job was Anthony Walton White from New Brunswick, New Jersey. White is particularly interesting to this narrative because he is sometimes mentioned as being one of Washington's aides.

White arrived unexpectedly at headquarters on July 25, 1775, armed with a letter of recommendation from New York congressman George Clinton. Congressman Clinton wrote: "Inspired with Love for our injured Country he now visits your Camp to offer his Services as a Vollenteer in the Army under your Command."[36] Washington also received at least two letters from White's father, Anthony White, Sr., asking the general to appoint his son as an aide-de-camp.[37] Washington could not ignore the request, because Anthony White, Sr., was a man of great wealth and the holder of several important offices in New Jersey. Moreover, White's mother was the daughter of New Jersey governor Lewis Morris. Washington apparently decided to put young White to work at headquarters on a trial basis. The general was disappointed with his performance and privately expressed his displeasure to his associate Joseph Reed: "I find it is absolutely necessary that the Aids to the Commander in Chief should be ready at their Pen (which I believe he is not) to give that ready assistance that is expected of them."[38] But Washington was too savvy a politician to openly voice his real opinion of White. Instead he made excuses in flattering letters to White's father, which included this undertaking: "may believe me sincere, when I assure you, that it will give me pleasure to shew any kind of Civility in my power to your Son, whose modest deportment richly entitles him to it."[39] Frustrated in his efforts at headquarters, White eventually returned home in late October 1775 to seek a commission in one of the Continental regiments being raised by New Jersey.[40]

Washington spoke of White many years later saying he was "never celebrated for anything . . . but frivolity and empty shew."[41]

When the workload at headquarters became overwhelming, Washington often pressed anyone who could write a decent letter into service. Other men were recruited to copy letters, especially if numerous copies of the same letters or orders were required for circulation to various military commands or government functionaries. These multiple letters were called circular letters and each had to be clearly and neatly written by hand. Even Martha Washington helped her husband in his office during her frequent visits to army headquarters.[42]

Many men have been cited over the years as having served as aides-de-camp to Washington. Some of them, however, are not correct. They include Light-Horse Harry Lee, Aaron Burr, the marquis de Lafayette, Jackie Custis (Washington's stepson), and a Lenape Indian named Simon Simon. Who were the genuine members of Washington's personal staff? We are fortunate to have an authoritative list of Washington's aides and secretaries compiled by Worthington Chauncey Ford in 1906. He was the chief of the Manuscripts Division of the Library of Congress at the time. Ford listed thirty-two men plus Martha Washington as aides-de-camp and military secretaries to George Washington. Martha's inclusion on the list is an honorary title to acknowledge that she worked at her husband's headquarters office. Ford established excellent guidelines for inclusion on his list. His criteria were (1) an appointment as Washington's aide in the general orders of the Continental Army, or (2) a citation in the journals of the Continental Congress as being appointed or serving as an aide to Washington, or (3) a definite statement from the commander in chief that a particular individual was his aide-de-camp.[43] The following is Ford's list, which is the cornerstone of this book:

GEORGE WASHINGTON'S REVOLUTIONARY WAR AIDES-DE-CAMP AND MILITARY SECRETARIES AND THE DATE THEY JOINED WASHINGTON'S STAFF, AS COMPILED BY WORTHINGTON CHAUNCEY FORD.

Thomas Mifflin, July 4, 1775
Joseph Reed, July 4, 1775
John Trumbull, July 27, 1775
George Baylor, August 15, 1775
Edmund Randolph, August 15, 1775
Robert Hanson Harrison, November 5, 1775
Stephen Moylan, March 5, 1776
William Palfrey, March 6, 1776
Caleb Gibbs, May 16, 1776
George Lewis, May 16, 1776
Richard Cary, June 21, 1776
Samuel Blachley Webb, June 21, 1776
Alexander Contee Hanson, June 21, 1776
William Grayson, June 21, 1776
Pierre Penet, October 14, 1776
John Fitzgerald, November —, 1776
George Johnston, January 20, 1777
John Walker, February 19, 1777
Alexander Hamilton, March 1, 1777
Richard Kidder Meade, March 12, 1777
Peter Presley Thornton, September 6, 1777
John Laurens, September 6, 1777
James McHenry, May 15, 1778
Tench Tilghman, June 21, 1780 (served as a volunteer aide
    from August 1776)
David Humphreys, June 23, 1780
Richard Varick, May 25, 1781
Jonathan Trumbull, Jr., June 8, 1781
David Cobb, June 15, 1781
Peregrine Fitzhugh, July 2, 1781
William Stephens Smith, July 6, 1781
Benjamin Walker, January 25, 1782
Hodijah Baylies, May 14, 1782
Martha Washington[44]

Some who did not make Ford's list, including Aaron Burr and the marquis de Lafayette, will also be discussed in the course of this narrative. We will see that some of them were invited to join Washington's staff but refused the offer.

Others were rejected after a trial period or were simply taken to be aides by historians because of their close association with Washington or because they were known to have done some work at headquarters.

With the exception of Alexander Hamilton, most of Washington's wartime aides are obscure figures in American history. The narrative that follows hopefully raises the veil of obscurity that surrounds them. What emerges are some of the brightest and most dedicated officers in the Continental Army. Their service on Washington's headquarters staff also made them among the best informed officers of the army. Washington probably had a polite working relationship with most of them; a general officer to his personal assistants. However, I believe that there were exceptions and that Washington enjoyed a close association with some of his aides. These warm associations developed from the ability of these men to assist Washington in expertly and quickly handling the tremendous volume of work that was necessary to keep the army functioning. The possible influence that these exceptional men had in Washington's wartime decisions is a fascinating subject which will be explored as this narrative unfolds.

CHAPTER TWO

The Siege of Boston
July 1775–March 1776

*My Head & Times are so much engaged here in very important
matters . . . Every Day preparing & expecting an Engagement.*
Thomas Mifflin in a letter to his cousin
Jonathan Mifflin, July 20, 1775[1]

The delegates to the Second Continental Congress gave considerable
thought to whom they wanted as leader of their new army. John Hancock,
the prince of merchant activists and president of the Continental Congress,
wanted the job, but he had no military experience and all his political cajoling
failed to get his fellow delegates to seriously consider him. Among the leading
candidates to command the army was Artemas Ward, the aged politician and
sometime soldier from Massachusetts. Ward, who commanded the New
England troops encircling Boston had many admirers in Congress. Other congressmen favored Lt. Col. Charles Lee, a half-pay British Army officer who
had joined the revolutionary movement.[2] Lee was the most experienced soldier
available to the colonists and an expert on partisan warfare. There were several
other British officers available, the most impressive of whom was Maj. Horatio Gates. But Lee and Gates were Englishmen by birth, and the rebels wanted
an American to lead their army. The men in Congress also wanted tight control
over the army. They were afraid that professional soldiers like Lee and Gates
might use the army to overthrow the weak civilian government and set themselves up as military dictators. The delegates knew history and remembered
that Oliver Cromwell had used his popularity with the army to seize power following the English Civil War barely 100 years before.

The influential Massachusetts delegation, headed by Samuel Adams and
his cousin John Adams, favored Col. George Washington to command the
army. Washington was a Virginia delegate to the Continental Congress who
had impressed his fellow delegates with his performance on congressional

committees dealing with financial forecasting for the army, military preparations, and regulations for the new Continental Army. In committee meetings
and social gatherings with his colleagues, the forty-three-year-old Virginian
had kindled their confidence in him for his military knowledge, combined with
his soldierlike bearing and self-assurance. Washington also became a favorite
in Congress because he was a wealthy man with a serious financial stake in the
successful outcome of the rebellion.[3] But perhaps the most decisive factor in
Washington's favor was that he was a Virginian. The Revolution had started in
Massachusetts and its congressional delegates wanted to be sure that the war
was *continental* in its scope. The Northerners reasoned that a politically
dependable and respected Southerner at the head of the army would help unite
the colonies in their insurrection.

On June 15, 1775, the members of the Continental Congress unanimously
elected their fellow delegate, George Washington, "to command all the continental forces, raised, or to be raised, for the defence of American Liberty." In
the days that followed, other appointments were made by Congress. Artemas
Ward, who commanded the Massachusetts troops, was named second in command to appease the New England colonies. Charles Lee, the rebellious British
lieutenant colonel, was named third in command. Lee was promised compensation for any financial loss he might incur (such as seizure of his property in
England) by joining the rebellion. Horatio Gates, the half-pay British major,
was among the other men appointed generals in the new Continental Army.
Each region or colony was satisfied, in turn, by having a favorite local politician or popular militia officer appointed as a general in the new army. New
York, for example, was placated by the appointment of Philip Schuyler, a rich
and influential landowner who had served as a colonial auxiliary during the
French and Indian War. Schuyler was an experienced and capable military
administrator in his own right, and had served with Washington on several
military committees while a delegate to the Continental Congress.

Congress also specified the new commander's military staff, authorizing
him to have one military secretary and three aides-de-camp. His military secretary was voted a salary of $66 per month and his aides were authorized $33
per month.[4] There was no military rank assigned to either position. On June
21, Congress voted that each of the major generals were to have two aides-de-
camp at the same salary authorized for the commander in chief's aides.[5]

Following British Army precedent, Washington was permitted to make his
own selections for his personal staff. As the newly elected commander in chief,
Washington was immediately approached by a number of politicians and
friends each of whom had a favorite that he wanted the general to appoint as his
aide or secretary.[6] As a courtesy, Washington also asked several New England
delegates for recommendations. But he knew from the start whom he wanted
on his staff and offered the post of aide-de-camp to a thirty-one-year-old
Quaker from Philadelphia named Thomas Mifflin. Mifflin was a successful
businessman and Pennsylvania delegate to the Continental Congress. He and

Washington had worked together on a congressional committee dealing with ammunition and military stores. Washington was impressed by the young merchant who he felt was a person of outstanding abilities. Despite the fact that Mifflin was a major in the Philadelphia area militia (known as the Associators) he actually had little military experience at the time of his appointment to Washington's staff, but he was intelligent and a fast learner. Even the usually critical John Adams felt Washington had made a good choice in Mifflin. Adams wrote to a Massachusetts friend from Philadelphia, "Major Mifflin goes in the Character of Aid de Camp to General Washington. I wish You to be acquainted with him, because, he has great Spirit, Activity and Abilities, both in civil and military Life. He is a gentleman of Education, Family and Fortune."[7]

Washington asked another Philadelphian, Joseph Reed to be his military secretary. Reed was a popular young lawyer who was active in local politics. Washington had known Reed prior to the outbreak of the Revolution, although where and when they first met is unknown. There is a note, for instance, in the journal of Samuel Curwen for May 9, 1775, "passed the evening at Joseph Reed's in company with Colonel Washington."[8] Reed was a lieutenant colonel in the militia, but he joined Washington's staff with little actual military experience and a serious personal problem; namely the large family he had to support in style through his law practice and speculative business deals. Reed agreed to accompany Washington only as far as New York City while he thought about his personal obligations.

Washington departed Philadelphia for Boston on June 23, 1775, accompanied by Gens. Charles Lee and Philip Schuyler. Washington, Lee, and Schuyler were seated in a small four-wheeled coach (called a phaeton), while Mifflin and Reed accompanied them on horseback. Washington, his officers, and staff were ceremoniously escorted to the outskirts of the Quaker City by a company of the splendidly appointed Philadelphia Light Horse.[9] The journey across New Jersey took two days as Washington's entourage was stopped at every crossroads and hamlet to inspect local militia companies or listen to speeches. Their slow journey had one advantage; it gave Washington time to court Reed into accepting the position as his permanent military secretary. Washington was probably supported by Charles Lee, who was a brilliant and heady talker. There would also have been Philip Schuyler, an unsmiling man with impeccable manners, a scion of a great New York family, who possessed manor houses and vast land holdings in the Hudson River Valley. Reed must have been impressed with Schuyler and Washington. Charles Lee was a professional soldier while Washington and Schuyler were men of great wealth who were risking everything they owned, as well as their very lives, by taking up arms against their king. Reed believed that he also was a patriotic American who was prepared to accept danger and make sacrifices for his political beliefs. The patriotic zeal of the moment must have overwhelmed the young Philadelphia lawyer because by the time they reached New York City he had agreed to accept a permanent position as Washington's military secretary. Reed commented later in a letter to a friend about what happened on the two-day trip between Philadelphia and New York City, saying that Washington "expressed himself to me in such Terms that I thought myself bound by every Tye of Duty and Honour to comply with his Request to help him through the Sea of Difficulties."[10] Reed added, "I have no intention of being hanged for half treason."[11]

The new commander in chief arrived at headquarters at Cambridge, Massachusetts, on July 2, 1775, and made an inspection tour of his new command the following day. The general was appalled to find that discipline was lax or nonexistent and that the army was composed of one-year enlisted men and militia. The New England troops were the most frustrating for Washington to command because they were composed of independently minded farmers and tradesmen who elected their own officers, including generals. These officers were reluctant to give unpopular orders that might get them voted out of office. Washington's frustrations with militia dated back to the French and Indian War, when he unsuccessfully attempted to defend the Virginia frontier with militia men pressed into active service.

Washington remained discreet in public about the problems he faced with the army, but was candid in his private letters. He described his army of New Englanders in a personal letter written to his distant cousin Lund Washington (1737–96) soon after he took command, "their Officers generally speaking are the most indifferent kind of People I ever saw. I have already broke one Colo. and five Captain's for Cowardice & for drawing more Pay & Provisions than they had Men in their Companies." Confiding further, he told his cousin, "in short they are by no means such Troops, in any respect, as you are led to believe of them from the Accts which are published," calling them "an exceeding dirty & nasty people."[12] Despite this very frank view of his problems, Washington had amazing perseverance in the face of his difficulties.

Charles Lee was also unimpressed with the army he found at Boston. He called Gen. Artemas Ward, who commanded all the troops at Cambridge, "a fat gentleman, who had been a popular church warden but had no acquaintance what ever with military affairs."[13] The contentious Lee was also quick to observe that Washington was being referred to as His Excellency shortly after he assumed command of the army. The origins of this pretentious designation are unknown, but probably were started by Reed or Mifflin at headquarters. "I cannot conceive who the Devil first devis'd the bauble of Excellency for their Commander in Chief," wrote Lee in the private letter, "or the more ridiculous of His Honour for me—Upon my Soul They make me spew."[14] Regardless of Lee's opinion, Washington was referred to as His Excellency throughout the war as a mark of respect.[15]

From the moment of his arrival at Cambridge, Washington took action to improve organization and tighten discipline. With the possible assistance of Reed and Mifflin, he wrote the first general orders of the army on July 3, 1775, the day following his arrival in Cambridge. The first general orders are quoted below almost in their entirety to show their scope of reference. General orders were frequently issued from Washington's headquarters. The process by which the general orders were created is unknown but Washington's aides seem to be the most likely men to have drafted them under the general's direction.

General Orders
Head Quarters, Cambridge, July 3rd 1775
Parole, Lookout.　　　　　　　　Counter Sign, Sharp.
The Colonels or commanding Officers of each Regt are ordered forthwith, to make two Returns of the Number of men in their respective Regiments; distinguishing such as are sick, wounded or absent on furlough: And also the quantity of ammunition each Regimt now has.

It appears by the Report of Henry Woods, the Officer of the main guard, that one William Alfred is confin'd for taking two horses, belonging to some Persons in Connecticut; but that he has made Satisfaction to the injured parties, who request that they may not be longer detain'd as witnesses: It is ordered that he be discharged, and after receiving a severe reprimand, be turned out of camp.

After Orders. 4 oClock. P:M:
It is ordered that Col. Glovers Regiment be ready this evening, with all their Accoutrements, to march at a minutes warning to support General Falsam of the New Hampshire forces, in case his Lines should be attack'd . . .[16]

As the Continental Army continued its siege of Boston, Joseph Reed was struggling between his family and business obligations and his valuable service as Washington's military secretary. Reed is frequently associated with Philadelphia but he was born and grew up in Trenton, New Jersey, where his father was a prosperous merchant. He earned a bachelor of arts degree from the College of New Jersey (now Princeton University) in 1757. Young Reed remained at the college where he undertook a self-directed course of study that earned him a master of arts degree in 1760, when he was nineteen years old.[17] Following his graduation, he decided to become a lawyer and he obtained a position as a clerk in the law office of Richard Stockton, one of New Jersey's most distinguished attorneys.[18] After reading law with Stockton for three years, Reed was made a member of the New Jersey Bar in May 1763. Encouraged to further his law studies in England, he departed for London in October 1763, where he studied law at the Inns of Court, Middle Temple, London from 1763 to 1765.

While studying in England, Reed met Esther De Berdt, a descendant from a Flemish family that had fled to England seeking religious toleration. Esther was seventeen years old at the time. Joseph and Esther fell in love, and young Reed wrote Esther's father a letter asking permission to marry his daughter.

Esther's wealthy merchant father, Dennys De Berdt, refused his proposal because he felt Reed was an upstart colonial with little money who would be largely dependent upon his earnings as a lawyer. Despite Reed's pleadings and assurances, De Berdt forbade his daughter to see or correspond with Reed again. The two lovers carried on a clandestine correspondence with the help of a friend and the young couple became secretly engaged. Esther's mother saw that her daughter was hopelessly in love with Reed and prevailed upon her husband to allow the two young people to see each other again, with the understanding that Dennys De Berdt would reconsider Reed's marriage proposal after the young lawyer had permanently settled in England.

During the same period, Reed's young brother begged him to return to America to help save their father Andrew's failing business. Alarming letters also reached Joseph from his father's business partner, to the effect that Andrew Reed had become erratic and quarrelsome. Joseph was told that his father was drinking excessively and was unwilling to reduce his spending habits during the business depression that followed the end of the French and Indian War. Young Reed was asked to cut short his law studies in London and return to Trenton while the chance remained to liquidate the family business and save something from his father's creditors. Although passionately in love with Esther, Joseph returned to America. Before departing, he promised her that he would quickly return to England to marry her.

Reed arrived at his father's Trenton home in May 1765 to find a gloomy situation. His father prevailed upon his oldest son to save the family business. Upon Joseph's shoulders also lay the burden of supporting three younger brothers and sisters. His father's faithful business partner (and Joseph's brother-in-law) Charles Petit was also destitute and looked to Joseph to support him, his wife, and their three children. At the time, Joseph Reed was only twenty-four years old. He went to work as a lawyer to earn money quickly, making his first appearance in the May 1765 term of the Hunterdon County (New Jersey) Court of Common Pleas. His reputation as a competent lawyer quickly spread and he built an impressive law practice. Reed rarely accepted a criminal case; the bulk of his practice was civil. All through this period, Joseph exchanged letters with Esther De Berdt in London. He told her of his growing law practice and wealth. Joseph concocted a complicated business arrangement that would allow him to return to England to marry her. He arrived in London in 1770 to find that Dennys De Berdt had suddenly died leaving considerable debts and few assets. Joseph tried to unravel the family's complicated business affairs, but with little success (partially because he could not legally practice law in England). In the midst of this chaotic situation, Reed married Esther on May 31, 1770. He packed up his new wife and her mother and took them back to America. They arrived in New Jersey to find that, as a result of his absence, his law practice had vanished.

Reed decided to make a new start in Philadelphia, a city that offered greater business opportunities than Trenton. He rented a house in Philadelphia and moved in with his new bride and mother-in-law in December 1770. Reed's experience, talent, and education paid off in Philadelphia, for his law business flourished and he became moderately wealthy. He invested in land but had to work continuously as a lawyer to maintain an upper middle-class standard of living. The Reed's first child, Martha, was born in May 1771, followed quickly by the birth of two more children, Joseph Jr., in 1772 and Esther in July 1774. Reed was a devoted husband and father. He particularly doted upon his oldest daughter, Martha, or Patty, as he called her. She was a sickly girl who came close to dying several times during 1772 and 1773. Despite her parent's fears, Martha outlived them both and died in 1821.

After a stormy beginning, Joseph Reed settled into a happy life in Philadelphia as a successful lawyer with a loving wife and family. His brother-in-law, Charles Petit, became his closest friend. Reed was active among the alumni of the College of New Jersey. In the midst of this satisfying scene, the American Revolution exploded into Reed's life. He had no military experience prior to becoming Washington's military secretary, which he confessed in a letter to his adoring wife from the American siege lines surrounding Boston: "I do not pretend to much or any military knowledge, but with you I may venture an opinion that the enemy never will attempt a passage through this place."[19]

Within days of his arrival in Massachusetts, Washington realized that he had made an outstanding choice in his selection of Joseph Reed as his military secretary. The young lawyer was a seasoned letter writer accustomed to corresponding with men in high station. He also had a great knowledge of the law and was a gentleman of "distinguished courtesy," which impressed the stodgy New England soldiers and politicians.[20] Reed proved an efficient and capable administrator and quickly became Washington's indispensable assistant, intimate friend, and advisor.

From the start of their long and bumpy relationship, Washington realized that Reed would be a difficult person to manage. He had been born into a wealthy family, but his high lifestyle and social climbing depended on a steady income from his lucrative Philadelphia law practice. His rich clients and loving wife wanted him back home. His Philadelphia friends added to his restlessness at army headquarters, by whispering to him that a position as Washington's military secretary was a trivial job and a waste of his considerable talents. A position on Washington's staff was immensely desirable to some middling officer or civilian volunteer but of little interest to a social climber and politician of Joseph Reed's caliber, who could best serve his own interests and those of the rebellion at the center of political action in Philadelphia. Reed was torn between his desire to serve Washington, his own political ambitions, and his constant need for money.

For the moment at least, Reed became immersed in helping Washington solve the problems of the army. The shortage of gunpowder was a major problem and Reed wrote to a friend on August 21, shortly after the arrival of a supply of gunpowder to alleviate the crisis: "I can hardly look back without shuddering at our situation before this increase of our stock. Stock, did I say? It was next to nothing. Almost the whole powder of the army was in the cartridge-boxes and there not twenty rounds a man."[21]

Thomas Mifflin was also very busy at headquarters at this time, apparently using his proximity to the general to advance his military career. He served as Washington's aide for six weeks before moving on to a more prestigious position. Mifflin was thirty-one years old when he was appointed Washington's first aide-de-camp. He was a Quaker but apparently did not subscribe to his religion's doctrine of pacifism and opposition to war. Mifflin was a 1760 graduate from the Philadelphia Academy (which later burgeoned into today's University of Pennsylvania). Following his graduation, he spent four years preparing for a mercantile career in the countinghouse of William Coleman. He then went to Europe and upon his return started his own business in partnership with his brother George. On March 4, 1767, Mifflin married his cousin Sarah Morris (1747?–90), described by John Adams as "a charming Quaker Girl."[22] The Mifflins were popular in Philadelphia high society, and Washington dined at their home on several occasions. Although the Continental Congress had authorized Washington to have three aides-de-camp, Mifflin was his only aide at the start of the war.

Mifflin's official appointment to Washington's military family appeared in the general orders of the Continental Army for July 4, 1775: "Thomas Mifflin Esqr. Is appointed by the Gen one of his Aid-de-Camps and . . . in future to be consider'd and regarded as such."[23] If Reed was a great pen-man, then Mifflin was a great orator. He apparently did a creditable job as Washington's aide but he had higher ambitions; his immediate goal was to be named as the quartermaster general of the army.[24] Congress allowed Washington to fill this plum job, and Mifflin must have approached the general requesting the position. The quartermaster's duties were being temporarily handled by Joseph Pearse Palmer who wanted his son named to the post. Palmer was a respected businessman whose activities included the manufacture of chocolate. Palmer was also a prominent member of the Massachusetts provincial congress. Mifflin enjoyed a good reputation as a businessman and was well liked by Washington. He also had the advantage of working at headquarters, which gave him easy access to His Excellency. Washington wrote favorably of appointing Mifflin to the position "from a thorough perswation of his Integrity—my own experience of his activity—and finally, because he stands unconnected with either Governments; or with this, that, or t'other Man."[25] Mifflin was appointed quartermaster general on August 14, 1775.

Within weeks of his taking command, Washington's little personal staff was falling apart. Mifflin was preparing to leave for his new post as quartermaster general and Reed was restless to return to his Philadelphia law practice and family. Always a planner, Washington quickly cast about for other qualified men to serve on his staff. He took great pains to avoid any sort of significant partiality or favoritism, especially during this early period of the war. But despite his wishes to be "unbyass'd by any private attachments," Washington was forced out of necessity to turn to his family, friends, and political connections to find the able men he wanted as his aides-de-camp.[26] A listing of the men who served on Washington's Revolutionary War staff reveals significant favoritism in the selection process. The general's wartime aides included one relative, several sons of important political leaders, and a number of his prewar Virginia social and business acquaintances. In addition, although eight of the thirteen colonies were represented on his staff, eleven Virginians were selected by Washington to be his aides-de-camp. Five of the aides were affiliated with Massachusetts, four each were from New York and Connecticut, three each from Maryland and Pennsylvania, and one each from South Carolina and France. How can it be claimed, based on these statistics, that Washington was objective when it came to appoint an aide-de-camp if eleven of his aides were from his home state or were his prewar acquaintances, relatives, or sons of friends and politicians? The answer is that Washington showed bias in filling what he knew were secondary and frequently short-term positions. Only a handful of Washington's aides were critical to the operations of his headquarters. These important aides were selected on merit and they kept their jobs because they were productive. Also, despite the large number of Virginians who served as aides-de-camp to Washington, they never dominated or controlled the operations of headquarters.

Washington showed the high standards required to be appointed to his personal staff in his choice of John Trumbull as his next aide-de-camp. Trumbull was a Harvard graduate, class of 1773, and the youngest son of Connecticut's governor Jonathan Trumbull. The governor was a passionate advocate of the insurrection and one of Washington's greatest admirers. He was also the only colonial governor who sided with the rebels.

Young John Trumbull was teaching school when the Revolution broke out. He promptly joined the First Connecticut Regiment as its adjutant and marched off with them to the fighting around Boston. One of his older brothers, Joseph, was appointed commissary general of the army. He wanted to help advance his younger brother's military career by getting him an appointment as Washington's aide-de-camp. Joseph, who was frequently at headquarters, saw his chance when he learned that Washington wanted a plan of the British fortifications on Boston Neck. From childhood, John had been fond of drawing and was a talented artist, despite the fact that he had lost the vision in one eye when one of his brothers threw him down a flight of steps as a child. But Gov. Jonathan Trumbull regarded painting as an unsuitable profession and discouraged his son from pursuing his passion. Trumbull, the amateur artist, decided to volunteer for the dangerous mission of drawing a plan of the British fortifications for Washington "as a means of introducing myself to the favorable notice of the general." Hiding in the high grass and creeping slowly forward, he got close enough to the enemy fortifications to make a drawing of the works. Washington, who had been a surveyor in his youth, admired Trumbull's illustration, which proved to be accurate, and invited the intrepid young man to be his aide-de-camp.[27] Trumbull was nineteen years old when he was appointed an aide on July 27, 1775. The General Orders for the Army for that date mentioned his appointment: "John Trumbull Esqr. being appointed Aid: D. Camp to his Excellency the Commander in Chief; He is to be obeyed as such."[28] Trumbull was the youngest person to be appointed as Washington's aide-de-camp.

Shortly after his appointment, Trumbull wrote that "The scene at headquarters was altogether new and strange to me." Trumbull found himself "in the family of one of the most distinguished and dignified men of the age" and he soon felt himself "unequal to the elegant duties of my situation." The problem was that despite his Harvard education, young Trumbull had led a sheltered life because his father was a man of modest means and simple tastes. Trumbull felt intimidated at headquarters and found the work load greater than he expected. He resigned after only nineteen days as Washington's aide, but as one of his biographers said, "he traded on that exalted position all his life."

Trumbull and Mifflin left Washington's military family on August 14, 1775, leaving only Reed, who was on the verge of decamping for home. But Washington had not been idle. The following day, he announced the appointment of two new aides-de-camp. The new men were Edmund Randolph and George Baylor, both from Virginia. Their appointment was mentioned in the general orders on August 15, 1775: "Edmund Randolph and George Baylor Esqrs. Are appointed Aide-de-Camp, to the Commander in Chief."[29]

Edmund Jennings Randolph was born on August 10, 1753, at his father's home in Williamsburg, Virginia. His parents were Arianna and John Randolph. John Randolph (1728–84), one of the most accomplished members of the Virginia Bar, was appointed the King's attorney general for the colony in 1766. Edmund grew up in Williamsburg, and when his two sisters became oppressive he could take refuge in the home of his aunt and uncle, Elizabeth and Peyton Randolph, who lived a few blocks away. Uncle Peyton was also an attorney. The highlight of Edmund's education was his enrollment at William and Mary College. However, he cut short his college education, deciding instead to clerk for his father in preparation for a career as a lawyer. Edmund became a lawyer and entered the elite of his profession when he qualified to practice before the Virginia General Court, the colony's highest court. In August 1774 his fellow attorney Thomas Jefferson transferred his General Court cases to young Randolph. Jefferson was ill at the time and was unable to travel to the General Court, which met in Williamsburg. The coming of the Revolution changed the peaceful and happy lives of the Randolph clan. John Randolph sided with the Crown while his brother Peyton joined the rebel cause. After much soul searching Edmund decided to support the rebellion. Because his father was a leading Virginia Loyalist it was suggested that Edmund apply for a position as General Washington's aide-de-camp to prove his commitment to the rebellion. Young Randolph did not dare approach the commander in chief directly.

A place on Washington's staff was secured by letters of recommendation or an invitation from the general to join his staff. Randolph got help in his bid for a post as an aide-de-camp from his uncle Peyton who was the former speaker of the Virginia House of Burgesses and president of the Continental Congress. Uncle Peyton recruited the help of his brother-in-law Benjamin Harrison to help his nephew Edmund. Harrison was another Virginia delegate to Congress a well as General Washington's good friend. Harrison wrote his old friend on July 21, 1775, on behalf of young Randolph, "I am sure our good old Speaker [Peyton Randolph] will be much Obliged for any favor you shew him . . . that a most valuable Young Man, and one that I love, without some Step of this sort may from the Misconduct of his Parent, be lost to his Country, which now Stands much in need of Men of his Abilities."[30]

Young Randolph had other weighty supporters and General Washington received endorsements for his "patronage and favor" on behalf of Edmund from Patrick Henry, Thomas Jefferson, and Richard Henry Lee. The general was impressed and wrote Richard Henry Lee, "the merits of this young Gentleman, added to your recommendation & my own knowledge of his character, induced me to take him into my Family as an Aide de Camp."[31] Randolph was appointed Washington's aide-de-camp on August 15, 1775. He was twenty-two years old at the time. Ironically the September 9, 1775, edition of one of the Virginia *Gazettes,* published in Williamsburg, reported on Edmund Randolph's appointment as General Washington's aide-de-camp as well as the departure of John Randolph for England. The newspaper story said, "Yesterday morning John Randolph, Esq. his Majesty's Attorney General for this colony, with his lady and daughters, set out from this city, for Norfolk, to embark for Great Britain."[32] John Randolph wrote his only son a final letter a month earlier entreating him to join his family in exile: "For God's Sake, return to your Family & indeed to yourself." Edmund never saw his parents alive again. His father died in England but his wish was to be buried in Virginia. Edmund made the arrangements and John Randolph was brought back to Williamsburg and interred in the chapel at William and Mary College.

Randolph apparently did an outstanding job as Washington's aide but he left after a few months. The reason for his departure was the sudden death of Peyton Randolph on October 22, 1775. Peyton's wife Elizabeth wanted Edmund to arrange for her husband's funeral and to settle his estate. Edmund took a leave of absence from headquarters and never returned.[33] He was in Virginia for his uncle's burial as reported in a local newspaper, "Williamsburg, November 29 [1775] . . . The remains of this worthy man were brought thither from Philadelphia by Edmund Randolph, Esq., at the earnest request of his uncle's afflicted and inconsolable widow."[34]

Once back in Williamsburg, Randolph was swept into Virginia politics and, despite his best intentions, never returned to Washington's headquarters. Technically he remained a member of the general's military family, on a leave of absence, until March 1776 when Congress appointed him the deputy muster master general for the Southern Department of the Continental Army.[35] However, his actual active service as Washington's aide-de-camp lasted only two months.

The second man appointed as Washington's aide-de-camp on August 15, 1775, was a very different kind of person than Randolph. George Baylor was twenty-three years old when he was appointed Washington's aide. Before the war he was a planter in Caroline County, Virginia. Little is known about his childhood or education. Washington's ties with Virginia and his friends are evident in Baylor's appointment. He was the son of Col. John Baylor (1705–72), Washington's longtime friend and comrade during the French and Indian War. Young Baylor came with a recommendation from Virginia congressman Edmund Pendleton who wrote to Washington from Philadelphia on July 12, 1775, on Baylor's behalf, "My friend Mr. George Baylor will be the bearer of this, who has caught such a Military Ardor as to travel to the Camp for instruction in that Art, I beg to recommend him to your Countenance & Favor, not only on Account of his worthy Father, but from my Opinion of his own Merit."[36] Baylor received a further recommendation from several members of the Virginia delegation to Congress, which included this oratorical phrase, "His Ardor in the noble cause has drawn him to your school for instruction & employment as far as his services may be required."[37]

Baylor was a disappointment to Washington because the young man was not a good writer. On February 10, 1776, the general expressed his dissatisfaction in a letter to General Lee who was in New York City at the time: "Mr. Baylor is as good, and as obliging a young Man, as any in the World, and as far as he can be Serviceable in Riding, & delivering verbal Orders as useful; but the duties of an Aid de Camp at Head Quarters cannot be properly discharged by any but Pen-men."[38] Lee responded on February 19, comparing his own aides-de-camp with Baylor, "Messrs Griffin and Byrd are very good young Men, but pretty much in the predicament of your Baylor—They can ride, understand and deliver verbal orders—but you might as well set them the task of translating an Arabick or Irish Manuscript as expect that They shou'd in half a day copy a half sheet of orders."[39] The general found other things for Baylor to do. Typical was a task in November 1775, when His Excellency ordered Baylor to go to Norwalk, Connecticut, to meet Martha Washington and escort her on the remaining part of her journey to Cambridge where she would spend the winter with her husband.[40]

Washington was not idle during these early months of the war despite the deadlock at Boston. One of his projects in the summer of 1775 was snagging unescorted enemy merchant ships sailing in New England waters. Washington eventually assigned this task to his secretary Joseph Reed and expected him to carry out the project in addition to his other duties. The general launched the scheme when he became aware that the enemy were convinced of their naval supremacy and were allowing unescorted merchant ships to sail from England,

Nova Scotia, and the West Indies with food and munitions for the besieged Boston garrison. The British held Boston, the most important seaport in New England, but the rebels occupied a number of smaller port towns nearby including Salem, Beverly, and Gloucester. In addition, the Americans had a superior knowledge of the local waters and small, fast ships that could be converted into warships. Impatient with waiting for Congress to outfit men-of-war, Washington decided to experiment on his own by dispatching a ship to attack the enemy's seaborne supply line to Boston.[41] Washington brought in Col. John Glover, an energetic Marblehead, Massachusetts, shipowner turned soldier to assist Reed. Working together, Glover and Reed supervised the arming of the coasting schooner *Hannah* (owned by Glover and named after his wife) to intercept enemy shipping. The *Hannah* put to sea on September 5, 1775, only to be chased by a British warship. The *Hannah* evaded capture and later succeeded in capturing an enemy merchantman. The project showed promise, and Washington wanted to expand it. Additional men with naval experience were needed so the general added the services of Stephen Moylan, a shrewd Philadelphia merchant shipmaster with extensive experience in the purchasing and outfitting of vessels. Moylan proved to be an intelligent and dedicated workhorse. He impressed Washington, who later appointed him as one of his aides-de-camp.

Moylan was thirty-eight years old when the Revolution began. He was born in 1737 in Cork, Ireland, where his family were rich and successful merchants. Facing limited educational opportunities in Ireland, his family smuggled young Stephen out of the country to Paris to be educated. Following his schooling in Paris, Moylan went to Lisbon, Portugal, for additional education. He remained in Lisbon to manage a branch of his family's shipping business. After three years in Lisbon, Moylan moved to Philadelphia (in 1768) where he established a new branch of his family's business. The brigantine *Richard Penn* of 30 tons, built at Philadelphia, was registered as being owned by him. In 1769 the brigantine *Minerva,* 120 tons, was also registered and listed "Stephen Moylan of Philadelphia" as its owner. His far-reaching business connections are evident in the listing of the ship *Don Carlos* (a British-built vessel of 100 tons) recorded as owned by Edward Forrest, a British subject residing in Lisbon, John and David Moylan of Cork, Ireland, and Stephen Moylan of Philadelphia, Pennsylvania.

Moylan was a prominent merchant in Philadelphia by the eve of the Revolution, and was an organizer and the first president of the Friendly Sons of St. Patrick, which was started in Philadelphia in 1771. The Friendly Sons was composed mainly of prosperous merchants engaged in the shipping and import business in Philadelphia, and many of its original members were neither Irish nor Catholic. Washington knew Moylan who was a guest at Mount Vernon at least once before the start of the war. John Adams mentioned meeting him while attending the first Continental Congress in Philadelphia. Moylan also knew Charles Carroll, a wealthy landowner and member of Congress who wrote in June 1776: "Waited on General Washington; saw Generals Gates and Putnam and my old acquaintance and friend Mr. Moylan."[42]

The French officer, the marquis de Chastellux, traveled with Moylan during the war and recorded his impression of the young man. Chastellux said that he enjoyed riding in silence, but felt obliged to strike up a conversation with Moylan with surprising results: "I began to question him," Chastellux said, "he to answer me, and the conversation gradually becoming more interesting, I found I had to do with a very gallant and intelligent man, who had lived long in Europe, and who has traveled through the greatest part of America. I found him perfectly polite; for his politeness was not troublesome, and I soon conceived a great friendship for him. Mr. Moylan is an Irish Catholic; one of his brothers is Catholic Bishop of Cork, he has four others, two of whom are merchants, one at Cadiz, the other at L'Orient; the third is in Ireland with his family; and the fourth is intended for the priesthood. As for himself, he came to settle in America some years ago, where he was first engaged in commerce."[43]

When the Revolution started, Moylan wanted a post in the army and asked his friend John Dickinson who was a Pennsylvania politician to help him. Dickinson wrote Washington on his friend's behalf on July 25, 1775, and His Excellency responded by appointing Moylan as continental muster master. The general wrote Dickinson confirming the appointment: "Your favor of the 25th Ulto recommendatory of Mr Moylan, came duely to hand & I have the pleasure to inform you that he is now appointed Commissary General of Musters—one of the Offices which the Congress was pleased to leave to my disposal."[44] Washington soon put Moylan's prewar knowledge of the shipping business to good use by involving him with Reed and Glover in expanding his naval project, which modern historians call "Washington's Navy." Encouraged by the early success of the armed schooner *Hannah,* Washington wanted to outfit and send more American ships to sea to snag unescorted enemy merchant ships. On October 4, 1775, Washington ordered Moylan to join Reed and Glover in outfitting two additional armed vessels.[45] Besides Moylan's knowledge in the ways of shipwrights and chandlers, Washington probably wanted him working alongside Glover, who had many friends and relatives in the Massachusetts seaport towns who might prove inclined to softheartedness in doing business with kith and kin.[46] Moylan was soon writing Reed from the seaport town of Marblehead, Massachusetts: "You Cannot Conceive the difficulty, the trouble & the delay there is in procuring the thousand things necessary for one of these vessels. I dare say one of them might be fitted in Philadelphia or New York in three days . . . But here you must Search all over Salem, Marblehead, Danvers & Beverly for every Little thing is wanting."[47] Reed responded unsympathetically, "Lose no time, Everything depends on Expedition."[48] Washington's naval enterprise became more important when headquarters received intelligence from John Hancock in Philadelphia that two British merchantmen had sailed from England with valuable cargoes: "The Congress having this day Rec'd certain Intelligence of the Sailing of Two North Country built Brigantines, of no Force, from England on the 11th of August last, loaded with Six Thousand Stand of Arms, a large Quantity of Powder & other Stores for Quebec, without Convoy, and . . . it is of great importance if possible to intercept them."[49]

Reed informed Moylan and Glover of the secret intelligence on October 11, 1775, and ordered them to speed up the preparation of the two armed vessels: "we have just received very important Advices respecting the Dispatch of a Number of Transports from England which may be hourly expected on the Coast . . . you will immediately set every Hand to Work that Can be Procured & not a Moment of Time be lost in getting them ready."[50]

The ships of Washington's Navy went to sea flying a white ensign with a picture of a pine tree and the motto, "An Appeal to Heaven." Joseph Reed recommended the design of this flag in a letter to Moylan and Glover dated October 20, 1775: "Please fix upon some particular color for a flag, and a signal by which our vessels may be know one another. What do you think of a flag with a white ground and a tree in the middle, the motto, AN APPEAL TO HEAVEN—this is the flag of our floating batteries."[51] The Americans were flying this flag on two floating gun batteries they had recently launched on the Charles River. Reed saw the flag and recommended its use to Moylan and Glover. The design was adopted and the flag is remembered to this day as the Washington Cruiser Flag. Probably flying this ensign, the armed schooner *Lee* made a spectacular capture on November 28, 1775, when it seized one of the ships that had been reported to Congress. The ship was the unarmed brigantine *Nancy* heavily laden with enough arms and military supplies to equip over 2,000 troops.

Washington showed his skill at improvising and stretching his resources when he created his makeshift navy in August 1775. This incident also highlighted other impressive characteristics such as his skill in identifying and promoting talented subordinates and in delegating responsibility. The little cruisers of Washington's Navy captured thirty-one prizes with cargoes valued at over $600,000. Washington's resourcefulness in this situation was not unique. He sought to maximize every resource and person at his disposal. Men like Reed and Moylan were too valuable for him to use solely to draft his letters and shuffle papers at headquarters. Washington used them in more important ways including seeking their advice and opinions on a variety of subjects.

Joseph Reed finally broke free of Washington's grip in late October 1775. Reed took a leave of absence to return to Philadelphia to look after his law practice, particularly a number of important cases that were about to come to trial before the Pennsylvania Supreme Court. Since Reed was a volunteer, Washington could not stop him but vowed to keep the military secretary's post open until his reappearance. Washington tried to hasten Reed's return by writing Richard Henry Lee to put pressure on the court to postpone the cases because of the war. Washington wrote Lee on October 29, 1775, suggesting that his cases be postponed, "if some of you Gentn of the Congress in the course of Conversation with the Chief Justice & others would represent the disadvantages wch must result to him in case his causes should be hurried to tryal." Washington then told Lee how important Reed was at headquarters: "That Colo. Reed is clever in his business and useful to me, is too apparent to mention; I should do equal injustice, therefore, to his abilities and merit, were I not to add that his Services here are too important to be lost."[52] The idea of postponing the cases actually came from Reed who wanted to use it as a tactic to delay bringing his cases to trial. Reed returned to headquarters the following year but not as Washington's military secretary. The engaging nineteenth-century historian and novelist Washington Irving summarized Reed's role in the successful start of Washington's tenure as commander in chief: "His fluent pen had been of great assistance to Washington in the despatch of his multifarious correspondence, and his judicious counsels and cordial sympathies had been still more appreciated by the commander in chief, amid the multiplied difficulties of his situation."[53]

As Reed was finishing up his work at headquarters in late October in preparation for his return to Philadelphia, Edmund Randolph, as we have already seen, unexpectedly left to attend to his uncle Peyton's funeral and estate. Washington was desperate for help and asked Moylan to step in and act as his secretary *pro tem*. Moylan agreed and took up the post in addition to his duties as muster master general. He apparently only handled both positions for a short time because by January 23, 1776, Washington wrote Reed of "Mr. Moylan, whose time must now be solely Imployed in his department of Commissary."[54] Moylan was a competent administrator and a ready pen-man and Washington would shortly invite him to join his military family as a full-time aide-de-camp.

Back home in Philadelphia Reed was trying to make up his mind what to do next. After returning to Philadelphia in late October 1775 he worked to repair his damaged law practice and leaped into politics on behalf of the patriot cause. The months rolled along and assurances were given that he planned to return to headquarters. Reed's extended absence did not mean that Washington did not call upon him for assistance. During this period, His Excellency entrusted his absent military secretary with several tasks, including hosting Martha Washington as she passed through Philadelphia in November. He also asked Reed to help him with other matters, one of which was mentioned in a letter dated November 27, 1775: "If any Waggon should be coming this way, Pray order a qty of good writing Paper to head Quarters; & Sealg Wax."[55]

In February 1776 Reed was elected a member of the Pennsylvania general assembly, where he worked to raise troops for the defense of the colony and to liberalize the assembly's instructions to its delegates in the Continental Congress to permit them to vote for independence. He appeared intent on finishing up his business in Philadelphia and returning to the army, but his plans seemed to be disrupted by one circumstance or another. It is difficult to decide if Reed really wanted to return to Washington or was simply making excuses to remain in Philadelphia to tend to his law practice and be with his family. Fearing that Philadelphia would be attacked by the British, in March 1776 he rented a house in Burlington, New Jersey, which had been built by William Franklin, the colony's last Royal governor.

Washington wrote Reed a number of personal letters during this period asking him to return to headquarters. The general's letter of April 23, 1776, says for example, "My extreme hurry, with one kind of business and engagement or another, leaves me little more than time to express my concern for your Indisposition, and the interposition of other obstacles to prevent me from receiving that aid from you which I have been wishing for & hourly expecting."[56]

Washington's personal letters to Reed during this period included some candid expressions of his feelings. The general trusted Reed and told him how he felt about a number of issues. In some instances we can compare what Washington wrote publicly on a subject and what he said privately on the same topic to Reed. Toward the end of 1775, for example, Washington was faced with expiring enlistments and the need to recruit a new army while the British, commanded by Gen. William Howe, continued to occupy Boston. Washington begged his troops to remain until replacements could be found, but they refused and were preparing to march home. The general wrote to Congress on November 28, 1775, concerning this serious problem. His letter to Congress is in the handwriting of Stephen Moylan:

> I am sorry to be necessitated to mention to you the egregious want of publick spirit which reigns here, instead of pressing to be engaged in the Cause of their Country which I vainly flattered myself would be the Case, I find we are likely to be deserted, at a Most Critical time, those that have inlisted must have a furlough, which I have been obligd to grant to 50 at a time from each Regiment, the Connecticut troops, upon whom I reckoned are as backward, indeed if possible more So, than the people of this Colony, our Situation is truly alarming, and of this General Howe is well apprised.[57]

On the same day Washington wrote privately to Reed regarding the same subject:

> Such a dearth of Publick Spirit & want of Virtue: such stock jobbing, and fertility in all the low Arts to obtain advantages, of one kind or another, in this great change of Military arrangement I never saw before, and I pray God I may never be Witness to again . . . We have been till this time Enlisting about 3500 Men—To engage these I have been obliged to allow Furloughs as far as 50 Men a Regiment; & the Officers, I am persuaded, indulge as many more—The Connecticut

Troops will not be prevail'd upon to stay longer than their term and such a dirty, mercenary Spirit pervades the whole, that I should not be at all surprizd at any disaster that may happen . . . could I have foreseen what I have, & am like to experience, no consideration upon Earth should have induced me to accept this Command. A Regiment, or any subordinate department would have been accompanied with ten times the satisfaction—perhaps the honour.[58]

On January 14, 1776, a frustrated Washington wrote privately to Reed what would turn out to be one of his most frequently quoted wartime letters: "I have often thought, how much happier I should have been, if, instead of accepting of a command under such Circumstances I had taken my Musket upon my Shoulder & enterd the Ranks, or, if I could have justified the Measure to Posterity, & my own Conscience, had retir'd to the back County and livd in a Wig-wam."[59]

By early November, Mifflin, Trumbull, and Randolph had left Washington's staff for one reason or another, leaving him with the eager but inept Baylor. The general also had Moylan, who was capable enough but serving on a temporary basis as Washington's military secretary in addition to his duties as muster master general of the army. Reed who was still listed as military secretary was making himself useful in Philadelphia and probably unsure if he should return to headquarters. But help was on the way! Washington's lawyer was coming to headquarters to bail out his client.

As previously mentioned, Washington could not risk being unbiased in selecting men to fill important positions on his personal staff. However he was remarkably objective and based his selection on merit. It was only natural for him to call upon his own experiences in prewar Virginia and to invite qualified acquaintances and business associates to become his aides-de-camp. Robert Hanson Harrison was the first of Washington's Virginia contacts to join his personal staff. Harrison was also the only Virginian to play an important role on Washington's headquarters staff.

Harrison was Washington's principal lawyer before the war and involved in a number of the general's complicated prewar business transactions. It is known, for instance, that Harrison accompanied Washington each day from October 23–25, 1769, to the foreclosure sale of the property of Capt. John Posey.[60] Posey was in debt to Washington who wanted to collect what was owed him from the sale of Posey's property. Harrison, his lawyer, attended the proceedings to make sure that Washington's legal rights were upheld.[61] Washington's prewar relationship with Harrison was mostly business. But the general also invited him to a few social occasions at Mount Vernon. Harrison, for example, was a guest at Mount Vernon during mid-September 1769. Washington's diary entry for September 15 mentions Harrison, "Mr. Grayson & Mr. Robt. Harrison came down in the afternoon." On the following day Washington wrote, "we all went fox huntg. Started one & run him into a hollow tree, in an hour & 20 minutes," and on September 17 the diary entry includes, "At home all day. Mr. Harrison went away in the morning before breakfast."

Washington began cultivating Harrison to join his military family in late August 1775, just two months after he assumed command of the Continental Army. At that time Washington wrote his cousin Lund Washington, who was managing Mount Vernon in his absence, to contact Harrison in nearby Alexandria and inquire if he would be interested in becoming Washington's aide-de-camp. Washington's expectation of a favorable reply from Harrison probably accounts for the fact that although Washington was authorized three aides-de-camps, he was slow in filling one vacancy. Because of the disruptions caused by the war, the general's letter did not reach cousin Lund until early October, and a few more days were lost until Lund was able to visit Harrison. Harrison promptly accepted Washington's offer and quickly settled his personal affairs.[62]

Although Harrison is often referred to as a Virginian, he was actually born and raised in Maryland. He was the oldest of three sons born to Richard and Dorothy Harrison. His mother was born Dorothy Hanson, a member of one of the leading families of Maryland. His father, Richard, was a rich landowner who was also active in politics and the local militia. An English traveler who stopped at Richard Harrison's home, which was situated on the Maryland side of the Potomac River, wrote this impression of him: "June 2nd, 1774. Spent the afternoon at Colonel Harrison's. Find him a very intelligent man and seems to take pleasure in communicating the customs and manners of his countrymen."[63]

Robert Hanson Harrison was educated for the law, although the details of his education are unknown. By 1769 he was established in his profession in the busy seaport of Alexandria, Virginia, where he met Col. George Washington who lived nearby. Both Harrison and Washington were gentlemen from the upper class of colonial society so it was only natural for them to meet, especially since both were active in local politics. Another of Harrison's clients was George Johnston, Sr., of Fairfax County, Virginia. Harrison was a regular visitor to the Johnston plantation (called Belvale) where he courted and married one of Johnston's daughters, Sarah. Sarah died a few years after their marriage, leaving Harrison to raise their two daughters, Sarah and Dorothy. There was a link between Harrison and another man who was appointed Washington's aide: George Johnston, Jr., who was the brother of Harrison's wife Sarah and Harrison's brother-in-law, who was appointed an aide in 1777.[64]

Harrison's prewar circle of acquaintances, including Col. George Washington, swept him into the revolutionary cause. He is listed as a member of Alexandria's Committee of Correspondence and an officer in the town's militia company. When Harrison received Washington's request to join his military staff, he had several concerns, the most important of which was the care of his two young daughters. This problem was solved when his sister-in-law agreed to care for his children during his absence. Harrison's poor health was another consideration, as evidenced by his frequent illnesses during the Revolution and his death at a young age. However, at the age of thirty, the young widower—

despite two small children, a thriving law practice, and not being in the best of health—was determined to help the revolutionary cause, and set off as quickly as possible for Washington's headquarters in Cambridge.

Harrison apparently began working as one of Washington's aides-de-camp during October 1775. His appointment is mentioned in the general orders for November 6, 1775: "Robert Hanson Harrison Esqr. is appointed Aid-de-Camp to his Excellency the Commander in Chief, and all orders, whether written or verbal, coming from the General, through Mr. Harrison are to be punctually obeyed."[65] Harrison served for six years on Washington's staff, the second longest serving aide among the thirty-two men who were appointed to that post. He was affectionately called the "Old Secretary" by his fellow aides, and he enjoyed their lifelong friendship.

At first Washington was apprehensive about Harrison's ability to handle the job. He mentioned of his new aide in a letter dated November 20, 1775, just two weeks after the appointment, "that Mr. Harrison, though sensible, clever & perfectly confidential, has never yet moved upon so large a Scale as to comprehend at one view, the diversity of matter which comes before me."[66] By January 1776, Washington wrote more enthusiastically, "Mr. Harrison is the only Gentleman of my Family that can afford me the least assistance in writing . . . If he should go, I shall really be distressed beyond Measure."[67] Harrison became one of the most valuable members of Washington's personal staff.

As 1776 began, Washington's military family consisted of only two aides-de-camp, George Baylor and Robert Hanson Harrison. Stephen Moylan helped when he could break away from his duties as muster master general. Washington was operating with a thin staff since Harrison had little military experience and Baylor was willing but incapable of helping Washington beyond riding around the countryside to deliver orders. Edmund Randolph had been away on leave for several months with little possibility that he would return to resume his duties at headquarters. Washington mentioned Randolph's situation in a letter dated February 10, 1776: "Randolph who was also ready at his Pen, leaves me little room to expect him."[68]

On another front, in January 1776, Congress finally got around to considering what military rank to give to the Continental Army's aides-de-camp. An aide-de-camp was a function without an assigned military rank. If one of Washington's aides was referred to as major or captain during this early period in the war it was because he held that rank in a militia or Continental line regiment prior to joining Washington's staff. On January 5, 1776, Congress resolved that John Hancock should write Washington, "and desire him to inform Congress, what rank the aids-de-camp of the general officers should have in the army of the United Colonies."[69] Washington responded on January 30, 1776, explaining that he did not know of any particular rank associated with aides-de-camp, but generally they were ranked as captains. He went on to explain that "higher rank is often given on account of particular merit, & particular circumstances." The general further explained that aides to the king of England had the rank of colonel and that he felt that the commander in chief's aides should have a higher rank than those of other generals.[70] However, despite Washington's detailed response, Congress apparently did nothing further on the subject of military rank for the army's aides-de-camp for another six months.

With his small staff, Washington had to deal with some large problems. The British, while continuing to hold Boston and its surrounding waterways, still lacked sufficient manpower to attack the rebel positions. Washington and his army had them bottled up on the land side but did not have enough heavy artillery to lay siege to the city and force a showdown. Adding to Washington's problems was the idealistic—but unrealistic policy of Congress that men should agree to volunteer to serve in the Continental Army for one year only. The soldiers who had enlisted in 1775 had departed camp for their homes, and were replaced by new, untrained men who had just joined. It was a tense period for Washington as he worked frantically to train his new recruits in the face of the enemy.

As Washington did during the first half of 1776, we must turn our attention again to Joseph Reed, who was still in Philadelphia with his family and lucrative law practice. Washington was seriously understaffed and longed for Reed's extraordinary writing, legal, administrative, and diplomatic skills. The general repeatedly wrote his intimate and capable friend, entreating him to return to headquarters. As an example, Washington wrote Reed in late November 1775, saying, "I can truly assure you that I miss you exceedingly."[71] In another letter dated January 23, 1776, Washington told the recalcitrant Reed, "Real necessity, compels me to ask you whether I may entertain any hopes of your returning to my Family?" Aware of Reed's need for money, Washington tempted him in this same letter, "I dare venture to say that Congress will make it agreeable to you in every shape they can—My business Increases very fast, and my distresses for want of you, along with it."[72] While Washington continued to implore Reed to return to headquarters, he took an unusual move in another direction to get pen-men: he raided the staff of his fellow officer, Maj. Gen. Charles Lee, for his competent aide-de-camp, William Palfrey.

Washington first met Palfrey in early July 1775, while en route to Cambridge to take command of the army. He was a member of the delegation of gentlemen who rode out to greet the new commander at Worcester, Massachusetts. Palfrey was a thirty-four-year-old businessman when the Revolution began. He was born on February 24, 1741, in Boston, the son, grandson, and great-grandson of New England sail makers. Young Palfrey was educated for a mercantile career and worked in the countinghouse room of Nathaniel Wheelwright, one of the great Boston merchants of the period. Palfrey established his own small mercantile business in 1762, when he came of age, but when his business failed in the depression that followed the end of the French and Indian War, he went to work for John Hancock, who was another Boston-based merchant. His first assignment from Hancock was to manage a retail store in which imported goods were sold. The shop had to be closed during one of the nonimportation protests against Great Britain that took place prior to the outbreak of war. Apparently Hancock thought Palfrey was a competent man of business because he next appointed him as his clerk.

Eventually Palfrey and another man named William Bant managed Hancock's business interests while their boss became more infatuated with politics and the protests against Britain. Palfrey and Bant became Hancock's "painstaking but uninspired lieutenants." They purchased his goods, wrote many of his letters, and paid his bills.[73]

Palfrey was married and had two young children when the war began. His wife was Susanna Cazneau, whom he married in February 1765, and they had two sons named William, Jr. (born in December 1765), and John (born in October 1768). In 1771 Palfrey made a business trip to London on behalf of his employer. There is an intriguing entry in his memorandum book from his trip. Palfrey went to St. James's Palace on Sunday, February 17, 1771, and, "staid in the antechamber about an hour in the midst of a genteel mob" to get a view of the king. He wrote in his memorandum book, "drest myself in a clergyman's habit" for the occasion. This comment was intriguing because Palfrey may have had some religious training and had been ordained as a clergyman, although he earned his living as a businessman. Nonpracticing clergymen were not uncommon in America at the time. Palfrey was also entrusted with great sums of money later in the war and it was usual in eighteenth-century America to have clergymen handle money.[74]

Palfrey became an aide-de-camp to Maj. Gen. Charles Lee sometime during July 1775. Lee was the third highest-ranking officer in the Continental Army and an important advisor to Washington. It was only natural for Palfrey, as one of Lee's aides, to come in contact with the commander in chief. Sometime in late November or early December 1775 Palfrey's civilian experience as a businessman was put to use when he was commandeered by Washington to oversee the offloading of two British merchant ships that had just been captured in the waters around Boston. These prizes, the *Concord* and the *Nancy,* contained valuable cargoes that had to be quickly moved inland before the Royal Navy could launch a raid to recapture them.

Palfrey did a creditable job, especially in moving the windfall of cannon and ordnance supplies captured on the brig *Nancy*. From the Massachusetts seaport of Salem, he wrote a report directly to Washington on December 3, 1775. In his report, Palfrey told Washington that he was procuring a number of horses "to carry the Baggage Waggons & Gun Carriages to Cambridge & intend to begin upon that Business to-morrow Morning." Commenting further, Palfrey said, "I hope General Lee will not be uneasy at my long stay."[75] A few days later he wrote to Washington again to update him on the movement of the ships' cargoes to safety. In this letter Palfrey told Washington that a large quantity of potatoes were found aboard the prizes, "which if not speedily dispos'd of will perish & be of no Service to any one." There is nothing further known about the captured potatoes, but this incident shows the enterprise and zeal with which Palfrey went about his business.[76] As a fellow businessman, Washington was apparently impressed with Palfrey and wanted him as his aide-de-camp. He made the request to General Lee in a letter dated February 10, 1776. At the time, Lee and Palfrey were in New York City surveying the city's defenses. Washington admired Lee and, like many Americans, considered the renegade former British officer a brilliant soldier, which is probably why His Excellency requested Palfrey's services rather than giving his subordinate a direct order. Washington began his letter tactfully: "I am going my Dear Sir to propose a matter to you, which, if it should not meet with your approbation, will give no offence, as none is intended." Washington then described his predicament as a further preliminary leading up to asking Lee to give him Palfrey: "It is unnecessary for me to observe to you, the multiplicy of business I am Involved In—the number of Letters, Orders & Instruction's I have to write—with many other matters which call loudly for Aids that are ready Penmen." The general finally got to the point later in his letter: "If you could part with Mr. Palfrey & he is willing to come to me, it would be a great relief; & I shall thank you both, as I really do not know where to meet with a Man so much to my liking. If it should not prove agreeable to you both, the matter rests—& nothing more need be said about it."[77]

Lee graciously agreed to release Palfrey, replying to Washington on February 19, 1776, "I am extremely happy that there is any open(ing) for a more comfortable establishment for poor Palfrey than his present—He is a valuable and capable Man, and the pittance of a simple Aide de Campship is wretched for a Man who has a family to support—on this principle and in obedience to your commands I shall send him to Head Quarters without delay—I must at the same time confess that the loss will be irreparable to me, particularly if I am detach'd to Canada."[78]

Palfrey joined Washington's staff on March 6, 1776, and his appointment was mentioned in the general orders for that date. It is unfortunate that we do not know more about Palfrey because he appears to have been a likable and accomplished person. In fact, several normally fractious people including Charles Lee and Horatio Gates were kind to him during his short lifetime.[79] There is constant reference to him in correspondence as "poor Palfrey" and his need for money to support his family. For instance, General Gates wrote his friend Charles Lee on February 10, 1776, "The General [Washington] writes to you about poor Palfrey, you will unless you are certain of providing better for him, send him of course to Head Quarters."[80]

Palfrey served as Washington's aide for only six weeks, from March 6 to April 27, 1776. One of the interesting aspects of his brief service was that he was the first person to join Washington's staff with experience as an aide-de-camp. His service was cut short when he was elected by Congress as paymaster general of the Continental Army. Palfrey's fortuitous promotion was not coincidental. It came about when his business mentor John Hancock got early news that the current paymaster was about to resign and he lobbied to get Palfrey appointed in his place. Hancock felt his former clerk should be in Philadelphia to help promote his election as paymaster. He wrote Washington on April 20, 1776, requesting Palfrey's presence without mentioning the reason: "if Mr. Palfrey could, consistent with the Service, be permitted to pass two or three Days with me in this City, on Business of Importance to me, I shall esteem it a particular Favour."[81] Apparently, Palfrey did not know about Hancock's politicking on his behalf either because, on the same day that Hancock wrote Washington, he also wrote Palfrey confidentially explaining that he was a candidate for the lucrative and prestigious position of paymaster: "I think you may Depend on being promoted, you stand well, and any Additions of mine will not be wanting."[82] Palfrey got the appointment and resigned as Washington's aide to assume his new position.

From his surviving correspondence, we can see that Palfrey was an accomplished writer with a charming sense of humor. Here is an example of his writing style: he penned the following to his former boss General Lee on May 6, 1776, soon after his appointment as paymaster general:

> If apologies would make any atonement for my long neglect of you, I could fill this and another sheet with a list of the many engagements which have hitherto prevented my paying you that respect which my duty as well as my inclination exacts from me. Ever since I left you have I been kept so tightly at it from morning 'till night that I have scarce had time to satisfy the cravings of Nature, which is rather hard upon one, who, you well know, is so often called upon by that insatiable Dame.
>
> The Public papers have doubtless announc'd to you that I have retir'd from delivering of Messages & writing of orders, to thrumming of pounds, shillings and pence in the character of a Pay Master General . . . I beg my compliments to Byrd, and acknowledge the receipt of a Letter from him since we parted. His saddle, that I bought of Thompson, turn'd out a damn'd hard Bargain.[83]

Charles Lee was critical of almost everybody but he seemed to be fond of his former aide-de-camp. Lee wrote Palfrey in July 1776, "We often long to laugh with the gallant Palfrey—but you wou'd only afford us half the Amusement you did formerly—for you must remember that not only the quantity of good things which came out of your mouth but the quantity of good things which went into your mouth furnish'd us with matter of wonder and pleasure."[84]

Palfrey served as paymaster general until 1780 when he resigned to accept another appointment from Congress as the United States consul in France. Congress voted to send Palfrey to France to assist Benjamin Franklin, especially with mercantile concerns. On December 20, 1780, Palfrey embarked on board the armed ship *Shillaha,* carrying sixteen guns, sailing from the Delaware River port of Chester, Pennsylvania. His ship stopped briefly downriver at Wilmington where he sent a letter ashore addressed to his wife and two sons. From Wilmington, the *Shillaha* put out to sea for France and was seen clearing the Capes. The ship never arrived in France and its fate remains unknown to this day. Thus William Palfrey, "a fiery son of Liberty," was taken by the sea and disappears from history and this narrative at the age of thirty-nine.[85]

When Palfrey was named as Washington's aide on March 6, 1776, another man was named as an aide alongside him, and his identity should come as no surprise. The March 6, 1776, general orders read, "Stephen Moylan & William Palfrey Esqrs. are appointed Aids-De-Camp, to his Excellency the Commander in Chief; they are to be obeyed as such."[86] Moylan was finally a fully fledged aide to Washington, who was happy to have the full-time services of this competent businessman and ardent American patriot.

Washington finally broke the stalemate at Boston in March 1776, when Col. Henry Knox arrived at Cambridge with artillery from Fort Ticonderoga. The story is that Washington needed artillery to force the British out of Boston. He only had a few cannons, but there was a considerable arsenal at Fort Ticonderoga, 350 miles away across mountains, rivers, and lakes. Knox, a former Boston bookseller, masterminded the operation of getting the artillery from Ticonderoga to Boston. He waited until winter, when the rivers and lakes froze, and moved the artillery from the fort on sleds pulled by oxen across the frozen rivers and lakes and along the snow-covered dirt roads. The plan worked beautifully and Knox's "noble train of artillery" was one of the greatest exploits of the Revolution. After their safe arrival at the American camp, the cannons were secretly moved into position on Dorchester Heights where they could fire into the enemy-held city.

John Trumbull, Washington's former aide-de-camp, left an eyewitness account of what happened when the British woke up to find themselves looking down the barrels of American artillery. "Our position, on the summits of two smooth, steep hills, were strong by nature, and well fortified. We had at least twenty pieces of artillery mounted on them, amply supplied with ammunition . . . We waited with impatience for the attack . . . Within a few days the enemy abandoned Boston, and we entered it on St. Patrick's day, the 17th of March. It was a magnificent and beautiful sight."[87]

Washington proudly wrote to John Hancock with the news: "It is with the greatest pleasure I inform you that on Sunday last, the 17th Instant . . . The Ministerial Army evacuated the Town of Boston, and that the Force of the United Colonies are now in actual possession thereof. I beg leave to congratulate you Sir, & the honorable Congress."[88] The British evacuation of Boston on March 17, 1776, ended the opening phase of the American Revolution. This is a good point to return to John Trumbull, the young Yale graduate who served as one of Washington's aides-de-camp during this early period of the war. It will be remembered that Trumbull served on Washington's staff for only nineteen days, resigning on August 14, 1775. Trumbull continued to serve in the army in various administrative positions until April 19, 1777, when he resigned his commission to pursue his love of painting. Trumbull never returned to active military service despite his close association with the Revolution. He studied art in wartime Boston after leaving the army but he craved more advanced artistic training, which he could only get in Europe. Trumbull decided to go to London to study with the great American-born artist Benjamin West. As a former American officer and aide-de-camp to Washington, Trumbull took an enormous risk by going to London in the midst of the war. The inevitable happened in November 1780, when he was arrested in London as part of the public outrage over the execution, by Washington's order, of British major John André as a spy. Loyalists (Americans who sided with the British) who were living in England in exile at the time were probably responsible for Trumbull's arrest and internment in Bridewell prison on suspicion of treason. Trumbull was freed eight months later, largely through the efforts of West, who got him released from prison on the condition that Trumbull leave England immediately. Commenting on this incident, historian John Fitzpatrick wrote: "The calmness with which this ex-aide of the rebel Commander-in-Cief walked into the lion's mouth merely because he wished to study art was regarded, probably, by the British as the act of a lunatic."

Trumbull decided to go home following his harrowing experience in England. But his flirtations with death were not over. Trumbull arranged for passage to America on the frigate *South Carolina* sailing from Holland. The ship was blown off course and almost floundered on the rugged coast of the Shetland Islands. After three months at sea the *South Carolina* reached the friendly port of Corunna, Spain, to make repairs. Trumbull was impatient to reach home and learned that there was an American privateer in port named the *Cicero,* sailing soon for Beverly, Massachusetts. He took passage on her, finally reaching America in January 1782, six months after leaving Holland. He was physically and mentally exhausted after his two-year absence from home with little to show for his efforts. The soldier-artist went to work for his brother David, who had an army supply contract, while his father urged him to abandon painting and study law. But young Trumbull refused, and the moment peace was declared he returned to Benjamin West's studio in London.

Trumbull resumed his studies in England with periodic visits to the European mainland, notably Paris, to study and paint. In 1785 he began his life's greatest work—a series of paintings depicting events from the American Revolution. He was encouraged in his efforts by Thomas Jefferson, who was the American minister to France at the time. The best known painting in his series of Revolutionary War events is *The Declaration of Independence,* which he began in July 1786 in Paris. Jefferson supplied him with a first-hand account of the event, and the soldier-artist was able to paint Thomas Jefferson, Benjamin Franklin, and John Adams from life directly onto the canvas. Trumbull's technique was to paint the backgrounds and figures leaving the faces blank. As he found the people in his paintings he added their portraits from life. Jefferson and Trumbull became good friends. Trumbull periodically visited Paris where he was Jefferson's guest. Jefferson, in turn, called upon Trumbull to act as his purchasing agent for works of art, books, and on one occasion a coach that he wanted from London. Typical of their exchange of letters regarding Jefferson's purchases is one from Trumbull, dated London, May 23, 1788, in which the young artist advised his friend about the design of a vase:

> The Tea Vase . . . They all agree that the projection of the robinet [french for spigot or spout] is of absolute necessity:—and that whatever form is substituted to the present straight one, still the projection must be preserved: so that all they can do is to exchange the present form for a serpent or something of that kind, which vomiting the water from his mouth, is rather more than less offensive, and at best is not your Idea. The only form, or the least objectionable to my mind is the Elephants Head and Trunk: if you think well of it I will try to have it executed.[89]

Trumbull returned to America in 1789 to pursue his career as the premier artist of the Revolution. In 1794 a position that appealed to Trumbull's pride and pocketbook was offered to him by John Jay. Jay had been appointed by President Washington to negotiate a treaty with England that would, among other things, establish America's northern border. Special envoy Jay invited Trumbull to be his secretary.[90] Trumbull accepted the post and until 1804 he remained in Europe where he continued his painting and various commercial schemes. While living in England he fell in love with Sarah Hope Harvey, whom he married. Trumbull returned to America with his English-born wife, settling in New York where he continued to paint. The greatest commission of his lifetime came as a result of the British burning the Capitol during the War of 1812. In 1817 Congress agreed to pay the artist what was then the enormous sum of $32,000 to enlarge four of his popular Revolutionary War paintings for the new rotunda of the Capitol. Trumbull's four murals were installed in 1826 and include his well known *Surrender of Lord Cornwallis at Yorktown.*[91] President Madison wanted the paintings to be "as large as life" but Trumbull was used to painting "in the little." As a result, his 12 feet by 18 feet copies for the restored Capitol rotunda were correctly criticized for not being the same quality as the originals. The originals, which are only 24 inches by 36 inches in size, are considered Trumbull's best paintings and are on exhibit at the Yale University Art Gallery in New Haven, Connecticut.

Trumbull published his autobiography in 1837. In it, he boasted of his service as Washington's aide-de-camp but was purposely vague about the length of time he served in this position. The truth was that he was Washington's aide for only nineteen days. By that time, however, there were not many people alive who could dispute his claim. Trumbull died on November 10,

1843, in New York City, an old, rather cantankerous man in the Jacksonian era. He was America's first college-educated artist and the last of Washington's aides to die. Trumbull was a self promoter to the end. He left instructions that he be buried in a vault in the Yale University Art Gallery beneath the portrait he painted of George Washington. His wishes were honored, and his tomb can be viewed today with the inscription he specified: "Col. John Trumbull . . . Patriot and Artist, Friend and Aid of Washington. . . . To His Country He Gave His Sword and His Pencil."

CHAPTER THREE

In Defense of New York
March–December 1776

Life at Headquarters was an exciting one; the aides were a hard-riding, hard-working little group, and it was oftentimes due to the driving energy with which they delivered the Commander-in-Chief's orders that Washington's plans were successfully carried through.
Historian John C. Fitzpatrick[1]

Following their hasty evacuation of Boston in March 1776, the British garrison commanded by Gen. William Howe went to the Royal Navy base at Halifax, Nova Scotia. Through spies and sympathizers in England, the Americans knew that the British government was rushing reinforcements to America including hired mercenaries from six German principalities. Once his reinforcements arrived, Howe could take the offensive.

At this point in the Revolution there was not a single British soldier in the American colonies. This meant the British were free to select their targets, and the Americans were certain that their first objective would be to seize New York City. Their conclusion was based on the fact that the British needed a seaport. New York was the logical choice because of its strategic location, protected harbor, and easy access into the interior of New England via the Hudson River. The British Army used New York as their base of operations during the French and Indian War (1754–63), and there was every reason for them to use it again. It was therefore no surprise that the following story appeared in the *Pennsylvania Evening Post* less than a month after the British Army evacuated Boston, "Last Saturday [April 13], His Excellency General Washington arrived at New York from Cambridge, attended by William Palfrey, Esq. His aid-de-camp, Horatio Gates, Esq. Adjutant General, and several other gentlemen of distinction."[2]

Prior to his arrival in New York, Washington sent his most experienced officer, Maj. Gen. Charles Lee, to look at the city and prepare its defenses. Writing from New York on February 19, 1776, Lee told Washington, "what to do with the City, I own puzzles me, it is so encircle'd with deep navigable water, that whoever commands the Sea must command the Town."[3] The Americans had no navy to defend New York, and the British could attack it from any number of directions using their naval superiority. Washington faced a staggering organizational and administrative job to get New York ready for the enemy attack. Every aspect of the city's defense required detailed planning, written orders, reports, memoranda, and follow-up. Even before his arrival at New York City from Boston, Washington realized that hopes were fading for a quick reconciliation with Britain. He had to take steps to make his Continental Army a "respectable army" that was organized to fight a long and difficult war.[4] Washington's genius for organization touched almost every aspect of military life, and this is a good opportunity to look at some of the things he did that are of special interest to our story.

Realizing that he faced a protracted struggle with Britain, he wanted his aides-de-camp to be properly compensated for their hard work. Washington wrote John Hancock, the president of the Continental Congress, on April 23, 1776, concerning this matter: "I take the liberty unsollicited [sic] by, and unknown to my aid de Camps to inform your Honble body, that their pay is not, by any means, equal to their trouble and confinement. . . . No person wishes more to save money to the public than I do—nor no person has aim'd more at it—but there are some cases in which parsimony may be ill placed; and this I take to be one." Washington went on to repeat his ideas about the qualities of the individuals whom he needed on his personal staff: "It requires Men of abilities to execute the duties with propriety and dispatch where there is such a multiplicity of business as must attend the Commander in chief of such an army as our's." He told Hancock how hard his staff worked: "I give into no kind of amusements myself; consequently those about me can have none, but are confined from morn till Eve."[5]

Washington's letter met with only limited success because Congress only approved a modest salary increase for his aides-de-camp on April 26, 1776, from $33 to $40 per month.[6] A little over a month later, on June 5, 1776, Congress finally reached a decision concerning the military rank of aides-de-camp. They decided that the commander in chief's aides would be lieutenant colonels while the aides to other generals would be majors. Congress mentioned Robert Hanson Harrison by name (the only acting military secretary in the army) and also appointed him a lieutenant colonel.[7] In the following year, Congress decided that the pay of all aides-de-camp should be equal to that of other officers of the same rank.[8]

Another of Washington's actions in early 1776 was the establishment of a special military unit that was called the Commander in Chief's Guard or simply the Life Guard. In his typical enterprising fashion, Washington tapped its officers to act as his aides-de-camp. The mission of the Commander in Chief's Guard was to provide security for headquarters, which included questioning anyone trying to approach the area and protecting the headquarters property. They also guarded the army's cash and the personal baggage of Washington and the members of his military family. The detachment was organized in the general orders of the army dated March 11, 1776.[9] It was a considerable force originally consisting of 180 picked men. The number of men serving in the unit varied during the war from as few as 50 men to as many as 250. Detachments from the Commander in Chief's Guard were used for special missions at various times during the war. For instance, one 1778 report states that "100 men from the Guard were out with their Captain & Covered the retreat of the Marquis [Lafayette] the other day. These are consequently equal in numbers to three Companies & indeed to some of our Regiments."[10]

Washington selected Capt. Caleb Gibbs from Massachusetts to command the Life Guard, and George Lewis of Virginia was appointed a lieutenant and named second in command. Caleb Gibbs was born in Newport, Rhode Island, on September 25, 1748. His education and prewar activities are unknown. He was probably living in Massachusetts at the outbreak of the war because his first post was adjutant in Col. John Glover's Massachusetts regiment. Glover appointed Gibbs to the post on April 21, 1775, just a few days after the start of the war. Gibbs continued to serve as Glover's adjutant when his Marblehead, Massachusetts, regiment was reorganized as the 14th Continental Infantry on January 1, 1776. Gibbs was named captain and senior officer in the Life Guard two months later.

The second and junior officer of the Life Guard was George Lewis, Washington's favorite nephew. Lewis was born on March 14, 1757. His father, Col. Fielding Lewis, was a member of the House of Burgesses and his plantation, called Kenmore, was one of the showplaces of Virginia. His mother, Elizabeth (Betty) Washington Fielding, was George Washington's sister. George Lewis was a Princeton graduate, class of 1775. When the war broke out his father was appointed a commissioner for the construction and management of a Virginia state arsenal for the manufacture of weapons. Working behind the scenes, Colonel Lewis devoted his time and ultimately much of his money to the wartime production of firearms for the American army. In November 1775, George Lewis escorted his aunt Martha on her journey north to join her husband for the winter. Upon reaching headquarters, young Lewis apparently sought a commission in the army through his uncle's influence, because Col. Fielding Lewis wrote Washington on February 4, 1776, expressing his approval of his brother-in-law's "caution in bestowing commissions, more especially on a Relation." In the same letter Colonel Lewis suggested that his son "may be servicible to you in some other way, as you must have occasion for some person to do some little things that you can confide inn [in]."[11] Uncle George probably felt duty bound to take care of his nephew and on March 12, 1776, George Lewis was appointed as the junior officer in the Commander in Chief's Guard. Lewis was nineteen years old at the time. Washington promptly commandeered both Captain Gibbs and Lewis to compose letters for him. Letters written by Gibbs start to appear in March 1776. Both Gibbs and Lewis were acknowledged as performing the function of aides-de-camp without ever being appointed as such. The general orders dated May 15, 1776 state this fact: "Any orders delivered by Caleb Gibbs, and George Lewis Esquires (Officers of the General's guard) are to be attended to, in the same manner, as if sent by an Aid-de-Camp."[12] Captain Gibbs was also appointed Washington's steward when Ebenezer Austin left that post in April 1776.[13] The steward was responsible for overall supervision of the general's household. Gibbs was promoted to major on July 29, 1778, and transferred to a line command (the 2nd Massachusetts Regiment) on January 1, 1781. He participated in the siege of Yorktown (1781) where he was wounded in the ankle. He was breveted lieutenant colonel on September 30, 1783, and remained in the army until June 20, 1784.[14] Robert Morris wrote a letter of recommendation on Gibbs's behalf, which gives additional information about his military service: "This Gentleman commenced Soldier with the Battle of Lexington and has continued in the army ever since without absenting himself from Duty one Single day since that time."[15] Washington's nephew, George Lewis, left headquarters on December 14, 1776, to recruit a troop of horse that became part of the 3rd Continental Dragoons. He returned to headquarters with some troopers drawn from the 3rd to function as a mounted unit within the Life Guard sometime in May 1777.[16] Lewis's detachment was dubbed the "cavalry of the Life Guard."[17] He resigned from the army during the summer of 1779 to get married.

In a letter to Captain Gibbs in 1777, Washington stated the purpose of the Commander-in-Chief's Guard was "for the security of my baggage and papers, &c."[18] The unit was never intended to be a personal bodyguard for Washington. Some historians have asserted that whenever Washington rode, he was escorted by a heavily armed squadron of his Life Guard.[19]

This is incorrect. Washington tended to ride accompanied only by two or three of his aides-de-camp who, at best, were armed with swords and pistols. Washington's slave Billy (or Will or William) Lee probably also accompanied his master in the field. Billy begins to be mentioned in Washington's diary as his companion on his periodic prewar trips to Williamsburg, and other cross-country journeys. Billy was an excellent horseman and one of the few men capable of keeping up with his master. Washington gave him his freedom in his will: "And to my Mulatto man William (calling himself William Lee) I give immediate freedom . . . and this I give him as a testimony of my sense of his attachment to me, and for his faithful services during the Revolutionary War."[20]

As time went on, Washington realized that a protracted war would mean that he would need tents for himself and his aides-de-camp for field operations with the army. No ordinary tents would do for Washington's military rank, social position, and standards of personal comfort. He wanted spacious and comfortable tents, especially when they were a legitimate expense. Washington decided he needed three large tents from which he could operate his headquarters and provide for his personal comfort. The ability to live well in the woods was part of being a gentleman. The gentlemanly "better sort" were expected to be intelligent enough to know how to live comfortably under imperfect conditions. But how did his aides-de-camp, who were also gentlemen, operate when the army was in the field? Let's look at some of the things we know about Washington's camping style first.

Early in 1776, Washington contacted his friend Joseph Reed and asked him to obtain, "a Sett of Camp Equipage—Tents—and a Baggage Waggon made at Philadelphia under his own Inspection."[21] Reed promptly complied with His Excellency's request and contracted with the Philadelphia firm of Plunkett Fleeson for three tents and tent equipage. By March 15, 1776, Reed was able to write his friend with good news:

> Most of your Camp Equipage will be completed this Week or the Beginning of next . . . I hope when you see them they will prove agreeable I have consulted Oeconomy [economy] as much as I thought consistent with your Rank & Station . . . I am never happier than when I am on your Business so that you may depend upon it that I shall spare no Pains to have them done in the best Manner, & forwarded with the greatest Expedition.[22]

The three finished tents were impressive and deserving of the name marquees.[23] Each had two layers of fabric that made them more resistant to rain and cold than a standard (and cheaper) one-layer design. Of the three tents, one was a large dining marquee, which probably doubled as a work area for the aides-de-camp. Another was a two-room sleeping tent for Washington's personal use. The third was a baggage tent to safely store the headquarters baggage and personal belongings of Washington and almost certainly the personal items belonging to his aides.[24] The cost for Washington's tents and everything that went with them was charged to the government.

Each of Washington's aides-de-camp probably had at least one tent of his own. Despite the fact that they had to buy their own tents and equipment, like every other officer during the war, there is no known record of their purchases. Like their chief, the aides traveled in the field with folding beds, food, and at least one servant to attend to their personal needs and take care of their horse or horses. Their camping gear was probably transported from place to place in government wagons as part of the headquarters baggage. When the army camped even for one night at a place, everything was unpacked and set up. Washington's field headquarters was a large and busy place. There were numerous tents, including the general's three marquees and the tents belonging to his aides-de-camp. The perimeter of the headquarters encampment was patrolled by the Life Guards. Additional sentries were posted nearer to His Excellency's sleeping tent. The Guards were also responsible for erecting and dismantling the headquarters encampment including the aides' personal tents. The headquarters encampment was a conscious display of wealth and intelligent planning by Washington and his aides to provide for their own comfort and to impress visitors.

While Washington was having his tents made in Philadelphia, his former aide-de-camp Thomas Mifflin was in trouble. Congress was aghast at the cost of running the army and it was convinced that almost everyone involved in feeding and clothing its troops was incompetent or a crook. Rumors of mismanagement and scandal swept up everyone involved, including the popular Thomas Mifflin, the quartermaster general of the army. Reed wrote Washington on March 7, 1776, to warn him of rumors that were circulating in the Quaker City about Mifflin,

> It is no Secret in this Town that Persons are constantly employed in purchasing up Goods here which do not all go to the publick Stores as the Parties concerned have boasted of their great Profits amounting in some Cases to 200%. Persons who come from the Camp seem to be well acquainted with the Mode in which it is carried on & are not sparing of their Remarks.[25]

Washington replied on March 25, being discreet not to mention Mifflin by name. Apparently Mifflin was at headquarters at the time because the general wrote, "He protests most solemnly that he is not, directly or indirectly; & derives no other profit than the Congress allows him for defraying the expenses, to wit 5 p. Ct [percent] on the Goods purchased."[26] Mifflin was removed from office by Congress who persuaded His Excellency's aide-de-camp Stephen Moylan to take over the job. Moylan was appointed on June 5, 1776, and lasted only a short time as quartermaster general. He also proved unsatisfactory to the capricious Continental Congress who reinstated Mifflin on October 1, 1776.[27] Moylan's reputation seems to have survived his short tenure as quartermaster general because he returned to Washington's staff as a volunteer aide-de-camp. Meanwhile Mifflin resumed his quartermaster duties but was unhappy in the position. He wanted to command troops, and participate in high-level war councils. But Washington needed him as quartermaster general, a job which required all of his attention. Mifflin focused his growing dissatisfaction with his situation in the army on Washington.[28]

The crisis in the Quartermaster Department lay in the future as Washington absorbed himself in the details of organizing his army, which included the selection of uniforms. A detailed study of Washington's uniform is important to this narrative because his aides dressed like their commander. Washington took an interest in uniforms because they helped to create the image of a professional army and encouraged esprit de corps. He believed that it was important to show the public a functioning army, part of which was the wearing of uniforms along with at least the illusion of military pomp and splendor. The general expected that his officers, especially the members of his military family, would wear well-tailored uniforms. When Washington attended the Second Continental Congress in Philadelphia in 1775, he arrived wearing a new and unpretentious uniform consisting of a blue regimental coat with buff-colored collar, lapels, and cuffs (collectively called facings) and plain yellow metal buttons. His waistcoat and breeches were also buff. This was the modest uniform with which he was to be associated in both fact and legend. The origins of his uniform date from 1774 when a number of Virginia gentlemen organized themselves into the Fairfax Independent Company of Volunteers and elected Washington as their field commander. They probably conferred with him about their uniforms before deciding that they should be blue and buff, "the ancient Whig Colours of England," the Whigs being the opposition party to the Tory government then in power. Washington had a blue and buff uniform made for him at Mount Vernon by his indentured tailor in November 1774.[29]

In keeping with the republican attitudes of the time, Washington's Revolutionary War uniform was simple and austere. He was a gentleman, however, so his uniforms, although plain, were elegantly tailored and made from fine fabrics. A portrait of him wearing his uniform painted in 1776 by Charles Willson Peale shows him wearing a simple buff waistcoat but with elegantly embroidered edging. Washington also displayed his status as a high ranking officer and a person of wealth by wearing gilt buttons on his uniform coat. In the absence of any regulations about officers' uniforms until later in the war, Washington's simple blue and buff uniform was quickly adopted by his senior officers and aides-de-camp.[30] Washington's aides in particular wanted to wear the same distinctive uniform to mark their association with the commander in chief. They had the money to have simple but good quality blue and buff uniforms made for them when they were appointed to Washington's staff.

One aide wrote a letter home soon after his appointment ordering a new uniform, "agreeable to Gen'l Washington's new form."[31] Another wrote asking for "a coat, blue turned up and faced with buff, white lining and plain white buttons."[32] John Laurens, who joined Washington's military family in the spring of 1777, wrote to his wealthy father from Valley Forge on February 9, 1778, asking him to send him materials to make a new uniform. Laurens wrote that he needed "blue and buff cloth, lining, twist, yellow flat double gilt buttons sufficient to make me a uniform suit . . . besides, corded dimity for waistcoats and breeches against the opening of the campaign . . . A pair of gold epaulettes and a saddle cloth may be added, if not too expensive."[33]

A plain but well-tailored blue and buff uniform worn by Washington's aide Tench Tilghman, on display at the Maryland Historical Society, is the most complete Revolutionary War uniform known today.[34]

Another detail that Washington addressed was to provide for a system to recognize rank and function. Washington decided that he would wear a light blue riband to identify himself as commander in chief. He authorized all aides-de-camp to wear a green riband (not a ribbon) as a badge of their office.[35] There is a receipt dated July 10, 1775, in Washington's expense account for a riband. The voucher reads: "By Ribband to distinguish myself [By is an archaic accounting term used on the credit side of a ledger or statement, meaning, *for the purpose of*]."[36] Washington is depicted in paintings executed during the Revolution wearing his distinctive blue riband, while a miniature of one of Washington's aides, Alexander Hamilton, painted by Charles Willson Peale in 1777, shows Hamilton wearing a green riband with a uniform that is almost identical to Washington's.[37]

A charming reference to the aides-de-camp's green riband is included in a letter written by John Laurens to his father. Young Laurens was wounded in the shoulder by a musket ball at the battle of Germantown (October 4, 1777). He wrote his father a month later asking him to get him a green riband, "If James (his father's clerk) can purchase a broad Green Ribband to serve as the Ensign of my Office, and will keep an account of what he lays out for me in this way I shall be obliged to him."[38]

Various colors of cockades and ribands were used to identify rank during the first years of the war. However, they were generally phased out in favor of epaulets. Epaulets were slow in making an appearance in the American army because they had to be imported from Europe. Most of Washington's aides-de-camp were ranked as lieutenant colonels and as epaulets were phased into use, they wore an epaulet on each shoulder as a symbol of their rank.

During the latter part of the war the Americans started to wear feathers in their hats to denote rank and functions. Just when feathers began to replace ribands to identify an aide-de-camp is a matter of speculation: however their use was officially authorized by the general orders of the army dated June 18, 1780.[39] Washington's aides were authorized to wear a white feather with a green tip in their hats. Aides to brigadiers and major generals wore only a green feather in their caps. Nothing was mentioned concerning the size or shape of the feather and there was a wide variation in style and shape, according to personal taste, from a single ostrich feather to a modest plume of feathers.

Washington and his aides-de-camp were not expected to fight. They usually wore a sword, however, as a symbol of their status as officers. Washington, his aides-de-camp, and senior army officers tended to own several different types of swords, each of which served a different purpose. They typically owned a type of sword called a "small sword." This weapon had a graceful silver-mounted rapierlike straight blade and was usually worn on formal occasions. They might also own a short-bladed sword called a "cuttoe" or "hunting sword," which they tended to wear in the field. Another type of sword they typically counted among their personal possessions was a heavy weapon called a "horseman saber." This was worn when they were mounted. Many lower ranking American officers were armed by economic necessity or preference with a single small and light curved all-purpose sword called a "short saber."

Washington continued to face staffing problems as the size of his army grew and additional responsibilities were given to him by Congress. The titles "acting," "temporary," "volunteer," "extra," and "assistant" aides-de-camp began to identify some of the men who were working at headquarters. The explanation for these new titles is that the Americans were trying to fight a war while they created the administrative machinery to do so. Washington was improvising as he went along including new titles and levels of management within his growing staff.

By June 1776 New York City was a sea of swinging shovels and flying dirt as the Americans dug fortifications and watched for the first signs of the enemy invasion fleet. As the work progressed, Washington's aides wrote out the orders, letters, notes, and memoranda that transformed the city from an international seaport into a fortress. There were rebel fortifications on western Long Island (Brooklyn Heights) and up and down Manhattan Island including a big fortress (Fort Washington) on upper Manhattan whose purpose was to prevent the Royal Navy from sailing up the Hudson River. Washington was encouraged in his work by the members of the Continental Congress who insisted that New York City was to be defended. However, some knowledgeable soldiers and civilians believed that a defense of the city was impossible and that it should be burned and abandoned.

It was in the midst of furious efforts to prepare New York City that William Palfrey was appointed paymaster general and Stephen Moylan was named quartermaster general. This reduced Washington's staff to George Baylor and Robert Hanson Harrison. Caleb Gibbs and George Lewis, the officers of the Commander in Chief's Guard, were special aides.[40]

Washington needed replacements quickly and he found them. In one swoop, Washington added three capable men to his staff: Samuel Blachley Webb and Richard Cary, who replaced Palfrey and Moylan, and Alexander Contee Hanson who was added as an assistant secretary to help Harrison. Their appointments were mentioned in the general orders of June 21, 1776: "The General has been pleased to appoint Richard Cary and Samuel Webb Esquires, his Aid-du-Camps—and Alexander Counter Harrison Esqr: assistant Secretary, who are to be obeyed and regarded as such."[41]

It was Washington's friend and wayward military secretary, Joseph Reed, who suggested Samuel Blachley Webb as a candidate for the general's family.[42] Reed wrote Washington on March 3, 1776, with news from Philadelphia mentioning "Mr. Webb has long had an Inclination to be in your Family, if the Post should be agreeable to him & he is agreeable to you I believe I should prefer him to any other."[43]

Samuel Blachley Webb was born in Wethersfield, Connecticut, a thriving commercial town in the interior of the colony near Hartford. Despite its seemingly landlocked location, Wethersfield was a cosmopolitan seaport that lay at the head of navigation on the Connecticut River. Young Webb's father was Joseph Webb, described as "a eminent merchant in Wethersfield whose application and industry were equalled only by his ability and integrity in business."[44]

Webb was born on December 15, 1753. His father, Joseph, died in 1761 when Samuel was eight years old. His mother, Mehitabel Nott Webb, was left a fortune by her merchant husband. She married Silas Deane, a socially prominent lawyer and merchant, in 1763. Mehitabel Nott Webb Deane died in 1767 and Deane remarried in 1769. He apparently treated his stepson kindly. We do not know what formal education, if any, was given to young Webb by his step-father. Webb is frequently described as being educated by Deane, who was a Yale graduate and a former schoolteacher. At the outbreak of the Revolution, Deane was a Connecticut delegate to the Continental Congress. Through his influence, his stepson was appointed a lieutenant in the Continental Army and was at the battle of Bunker Hill, where he was wounded. Webb's leadership qualities and bravery were noted, and he was promoted to major and aide-de-camp to Israel Putnam, Connecticut's famous senior general and folk hero. Webb was twenty-two years old at the time of his appointment as "Old Put's" aide.

Webb came into contact with Washington as a result of his appointment as Putnam's aide-de-camp. Apparently Washington took an interest in having Webb join his headquarters staff. Webb's family ties were of the first order, and a recommendation from Joseph Reed was impressive. Washington wrote back to Reed on March 25, 1776, concerning Webb as a possible assistant for Reed, who might return to headquarters at any moment. Washington's comments are enlightening because they give us more insight into the qualities that he looked for in the men he wanted on his personal staff:

> You mention Mr. Webb in one of your Letters as Assistant— . . . what kind of a hand he writes I know not—I believe but a crampt one; lat-terly [lately] none at all, as he has either the Gout or Rhumatism in both—He is a Man fond of Company—of gaiety—and of a tender Constitution; whether therefore, such a person would answer yr pur-pose so well as a plodding, methodical Person, whose sole business shd be to arrange his Papers &ca in such order as to produce any one, at any Instant it is called for, & capable at the sametime of composing a Letter, is what you have to consider.[45]

Webb was ultimately invited to headquarters as an aide-de-camp to Wash-ington. He had the distinction of being one of the three aides who were wounded while serving on Washington's staff. He was in fact, shot three times during the war; the first time was at Bunker Hill (June 17, 1775), the second at White Plains (October 28, 1776), and the third time at Trenton (January 2, 1777). With Washington's approval, Webb resigned as his aide to organize a regiment in January 1777: "Colonel Webb's Additional Regiment." He had the worst luck of any of Washington's aides: He was wounded three times, and then he was captured by the British and held in captivity for several years (December 1777 to December 1780). By chance some of his wartime letters were saved and ultimately published. Webb started off by carefully preserving all his letters and a wartime diary. His son remembered what happened to them—he said that his father kept all his papers stored away in two large chests, "as accurately and carefully filed as are the archives of any court of record." The papers were carefully preserved between the pages of bound books of blotting paper. Unknown to the colonel, his seven children tore out the blotting paper for drawing and scribbling. "We tore out those journals," his son recalled, "and destroyed all the written manuscript contained in them, and presented the pretty little books of blotting paper to our school friends." Most of Webb's correspondence and diary were destroyed by his children, however what remained was collected and published by his grandson in 1893.[46]

Another of the three men to join Washington's staff in June 1776 had the imposing name of Alexander Contee Hanson. He was born in Annapolis, Maryland, on October 22, 1749, and was a lawyer by profession. Hanson arrived at headquarters with a formidable pedigree; he was the son of John Hanson (1721–83) who was a Maryland delegate to Congress at the time and was elected as president of that body in 1781. John Hanson served as president of Congress until 1782.

Hanson joined Washington's family as an assistant secretary. Congress authorized the position and provided a salary in a resolution dated May 22, 1776: "That General Washington be empowered to appoint an assistant clerk to his secretary, with the pay of 40 dollars per month."[47] Note that the position had no military rank. Hanson was Washington's first assistant clerk (secretary), and he worked under the supervision of Robert Hanson Harrison who also happened to be the young man's cousin. At the time of his appointment to Washington's staff, Alexander Contee Hanson was twenty-seven years old and a graduate of the College of Philadelphia. After college he studied law and was admitted to the Maryland Bar in 1772. Hanson served in Washington's military family for only a few months, from June to September 1776. He apparently resigned because of ill-health and returned home.

Hanson went on to an impressive career as a Maryland lawyer, clerk of the Maryland Senate (1777), and an associate judge of the general court of Maryland from 1778 to 1781. He was a fiery American patriot who apparently went overboard in his patriotic zeal when he presided over a special court in June 1781. The story is that the Americans had uncovered a plot by some local Loyalists to release a number of British prisoners held in jail in Frederick County, Maryland. The seven leaders of the plot were arrested and tried before a special court presided over by Judge Hanson. They were found guilty, and Hanson ruled that "they ought to suffer to the full, the penalty for high treason." He sentenced all seven to be hanged, drawn, and quartered; a medieval form of punishment unknown in America and extreme in relation to the crime. The sentence was carried out, but Maryland passed a law the following year limiting the penalty for anyone found guilty of a similar crime.[48] Hanson's career, however, seemed to be undamaged by the incident because he was appointed chancellor of Maryland in 1789, and served in that capacity until his death in 1806.

The third person to join Washington's staff in June 1776 was Richard Cary. Cary is sometimes mentioned as being a Virginian because he spent some time in the South, including some business contacts with George Washington, just before the start of the Revolution.[49] He was from an old New

England family, having descended from James Cary, a draper from Bristol, England, who came to America and settled in Massachusetts sometime before 1647. Richard Cary was probably born in Charlestown, Massachusetts, where his father was a distiller and a prosperous merchant. Young Cary was born in 1746 and graduated from Harvard College, class of 1763. We do not know what he did following his Harvard education, but there is a record of his marrying Anna Phillips on July 12, 1771, with the groom described as "being of the 14th Regiment."[50] The interpretation is that Cary's rich father probably purchased his son a commission in the British Army. The length of Cary's military service is unknown, but we know that by 1772 he was employed in his father's business.[51] There are records of him traveling on business to New York City, Philadelphia, and Baltimore, as well as what is today the state of Maine. He made a business trip through the South early in 1775, just before the start of the Revolution. During his southern trip, he probably met Washington. Cary's wealth, business, and personal contacts, and possible service as a British army officer would have assured him a warm reception at Mount Vernon from Colonel Washington. Apparently Cary was still in British-occupied Boston a few weeks after the start of the Revolution because he wrote a letter to a friend from the embattled city on May 3, 1775: "My daughter Nancy is in the country, which I wish was with you. The rest of the family are with me. I shall continue in town until I apprehend danger. I am of some little service to my distressed friends that come out of Boston, who give me pleasure in coming freely to my house . . . It looks as if the horrors and distresss of a civil war will soon take place."[52]

The Cary family were friends with John Adams, who probably paved the way for young Cary to get a good appointment in the army. Adams wrote the influential Massachusetts scion, James Warren, from Philadelphia on July 27, 1775, mentioning that several young gentlemen were bound for the American army camp: "Mr. Cary is with them son of Mr. Cary of Charlestown—neither Father nor son want Letters."[53] Adams meant that Cary was well known and respected and needed no letters of introduction. On the following day, Congressman Adams wrote another of his Massachusetts cronies on Richard Cary's behalf. This letter was written to William Tudor, judge advocate to the Continental Army.[54] Cary was promptly appointed a brigade major. He served in this position until his appointment as Washington's aide-de-camp in June 1776. Cary was thirty years old at the time of his appointment to Washington's staff.

Richard Cary resigned from Washington's military family in December 1776 to get married, although he probably left headquarters sometime prior to that date. Webb mentions Cary's marriage plans in a letter to a friend: "Head Quarters Pennsylvania in Bucks County on Delaware, Dec. 16th, 1776, Poor Cary has got into the Limboo's, and will in all probably be Married in ten days to a Miss Low."[55] The "Miss Low" referred to in Webb's letter was Anna Low, the daughter of a wealthy New York merchant named Cornelius P. Low. It was

Cary's second marriage. Cary was in Philadelphia when he wrote a farewell letter to his comrades that gives a glimpse of the fellowship existing among Washington's staff:

Phila. 22d Dec. 1776.

Dear Boys:

I hardly know whom to address particularly & therefore you may take it all together. . . . it may possibly be worth while to tell you that I am a very happy fellow & have been really so since the night before last. . . . Mr. Harrison, I have taken all possible pains to get your Breeches & Stockings, but as yet have no prospects of success . . . Mr. Webb, you have no chance at present for your Boots, but don't despair—dear Sam [Samuel Webb]—don't loose sight of your matrimonial intentions . . . Capt Gibbs your letter went forward before I arrived here—hope it got safe to hand . . . God bless you all my dear Boys health & happiness ever attend you [,] my most dutiful Respects to our worthy General.[56]

Richard Cary saw some limited military service following his resignation from Washington's staff. He eventually went to the Caribbean island of St. Croix where he set himself up in the dangerous but potentially very profitable business of running goods past the Royal Navy ships that were patrolling American waters. At the end of the Revolution Cary returned to America and settled in New York City, where he continued his mercantile business. He next moved to upstate New York where there was a land boom. Cary did not prosper, however, as shown by a letter he wrote his friend and former fellow aide-de-camp Col. Benjamin Walker in 1796, which included, "My Mill dam has turned out a much more expensive and tedious jobb that I had any idea of & is not near completed for want of money."[57] Cary's enterprises failed, and he was forced to declare bankruptcy. He died at Cooperstown, New York, in 1806. His daughter, Anne Cary (1784–1851) married Richard Fenimore Cooper, a brother of the author James Fenimore Cooper and son of William Cooper, the founder of Cooperstown.

Washington's aides came from different parts of the colonies. The mercantile backgrounds of New Englanders like Webb and Cary clashed with the Southern aristocratic plantation upbringing of Harrison and Baylor. They also had different abilities, experiences, and shortcomings. However, close friendships developed between them; they were fellow soldiers sharing a common experience. They depended on each other, sharing a heavy workload from a demanding taskmaster, and sometimes they risked their lives in battle.

There apparently was a tryout period for some of the men who were invited to join Washington's staff. It gave a candidate the opportunity to work alongside Washington as a volunteer. This tryout was a test of a man's abilities but it was also a two-way situation: the general wanted to be sure that a man understood what was expected of him and was prepared to stay on. Aaron Burr was probably the most famous tryout for Washington's staff. The young man had the qualifications to be on the commander in chief's staff: Graduation with honors from the College of New Jersey, study of law until the outbreak of the Revolution, and distinguished service as a volunteer in the ill-fated 1775 expedition against Canada.[58] Burr is frequently but erroneously listed as one of Washington's aides-de-camp. The facts are that he was invited by Washington to work at headquarters sometime during the middle of June 1776. He worked at headquarters only briefly, perhaps for just one week. The explanation for Burr's departure include a story that Washington discovered him going through his private papers. Another yarn is that Washington fired Burr when he found out about his preoccupation with women. A more creditable explanation for Burr's departure is that he left to accept a better job working for Gen. Israel Putnam. Putnam was a popular war hero in Connecticut, and Burr may have decided that he could do better working as a senior aide-de-camp for Putnam rather than serving as a junior member on Washington's staff.[59] Burr's subsequent career included a successful law practice, a period as a United States senator, and appointment as the third vice president of the United States. He had numerous love affairs, mortally wounded Alexander Hamilton in a duel in 1804 and led a conspiracy to establish a separate nation in the American West.

Washington had a substantive personal staff during the spring of 1776 composed of Harrison, Baylor, Webb, Cary, Hanson, Gibbs, and Lewis. But the general still longed for the talented and smooth talking Joseph Reed to return to headquarters. Unlike the situation in New England, which wholeheartedly supported the Revolution, Washington was confronted with a much more complicated and delicate political situation in New York, where there was strong Loyalist sentiment. He wanted Reed's finesse to help him maneuver through the politics. He bluntly stated his need for his old military secretary in a letter to Reed dated April 15, 1776: "When my good Sir will you be with me? I fear I shall have a difficult card to play in this Government & could wish for your Assistance and advice to manage it."[60] Reed's kindest biographer, John F. Roche, said that Reed delayed returning to headquarters when he learned of Washington's success in getting the British to abandon Boston: "the British evacuation of Boston removed the necessity for great haste in rejoining Washington."[61] Reed had also been swept into Pennsylvania politics following his return home and was making important contributions to the rebel cause in Philadelphia. He seemed sincerely interested in returning to Washington's military family, but knew he was accomplishing great things on the home front. He wrote Washington in this vein on March 7, 1776: "an Affair of great Importance in the Assembly will detain me some Time tho I hope not long."[62]

Reed was evaluating his options during this period as shown by a letter he wrote to his brother-in-law, Charles Petit, on March 30, 1776. Reed confided to Petit, "I never felt so much puzzled to know how to act . . . I think a little time must give us more light. What with the Assembly, the little business of my own, and extra avocations, I have scarce an hour I can call my own. If I stay here I shall be ruined by devoting my whole time to the public for nothing. In the other case, I shall at least bear my own weight."[63]

Financial concerns probably played an important part in Reed's decision to stay in Philadelphia rather than return to army headquarters. While Washington doggedly tried to get Reed to come back, he could not ignore the unselfish dedication and growing competency of his aide and prewar lawyer acquaintance Robert Hanson Harrison. In a show of support, Washington announced Harrison's appointment as his military secretary in the general orders of the army on May 16, 1776: "Robert Hanson Harrison Esqr. is appointed secretary to the Commander in Chief, in the room of Joseph Reed Esqr., whose private concerns will not permit him to continue in that office."[64] If Reed decided to return, it would have to be in some other capacity than military secretary.

Washington soon found another opportunity to snare Reed. On May 23, 1776, the general arrived in Philadelphia to "advise and consult" with Congress on the present state of affairs. He remained in the Quaker City until June 6 and used the opportunity of his visit to meet with Reed. He surprised his friend by offering him the post of adjutant general of the Continental Army, which became available when Horatio Gates was promoted. The adjutant's job had more prestige and pay than the position as the commander in chief's military secretary. Reed asked the general for a day to think the offer over. One of his concerns was that he had no experience in the adjutant's duties. Washington agreed to let his friend consider the offer but buttonholed several of his friends in Congress, asking them to help him convince Reed to take the job.

Washington would have preferred Reed to come back as his secretary, but he was willing to give him the adjutant general's post if that was what was needed to get him to return to headquarters. Washington must have also felt that Reed was competent to handle this important position in the army. He hoped the adjutant's position carried sufficient prestige and compensation to persuade Reed to accept the post. Reed informed Washington on June 4, 1776, that he would take the job. On the following day the Continental Congress confirmed Washington's appointment, naming Reed the adjutant general of the army with the rank of colonel and the considerable salary of $125 per month.[65]

Before returning to headquarters in New York City, Reed visited his wife and family in Burlington, New Jersey, a quiet town up the Delaware River from Philadelphia. He moved them to Burlington for fear that Philadelphia would be captured by the British. While he was there Reed drew up an inventory of his personal estate and made a will. He bade his family farewell on June 15, 1776, and spent the following night at Charles Petit's home in Perth Amboy, New Jersey. He arrived at Washington's headquarters in New York City the following day and his appointment as adjutant was announced in the general orders of June 18, 1776: "Joseph Reed Esqr: is appointed Adjutant General of all the Continental Forces with the Rank of Colonel, and is to be regarded and obeyed accordingly."[66]

Seemingly right on schedule, the first Royal Navy warships appeared off New York harbor on June 25.[67] The American defenders counted 130 warships and transports.[68] This proved to be only the vanguard of the British task force, and more ships kept arriving. Gen. William Howe, who had left Boston so ignominiously the previous March, commanded the formidable British army being conveyed to capture New York City. Howe landed unopposed on the south shore of Staten Island and took possession of the island. His older brother, Adm. Lord Richard Howe, arrived on July 12 with additional warships. When assembled, the British force totaled over 30,000 professional soldiers supported by a fleet of thirty warships and hundreds of transports against 19,000 largely untrained Americans who did not have a single warship.[69] The battle for control of New York City was about to begin.

In the midst of the frenzy to get New York City ready for the British attack, an event took place that would change the character of the war. On July 4, 1776, the Declaration of Independence was adopted. Henceforth, the Americans were fighting for independence and not reconciliation with Britain. On July 9, 1776, the Declaration was read with "an audible voice" to the various brigades of the Grand Army at New York.[70] A celebration followed that included the toppling of a statue of King George III, and aide Samuel Blachley Webb wrote about this incident in his journal the following day: "Last night the statue of George 3d was tumbled down and beheaded, the troops having long had an inclination to do so, thought the time of publishing a declaration of independence a favorable opportunity."[71]

After arraying their formidable army and navy across the harbor from New York City, the British commanders made an overture to end the war peacefully. On July 14, 1776, a Royal Navy officer carrying a flag of truce came across the harbor in a barge. His barge was intercepted by three American boats commanded by Lt. Col. Benjamin Tupper. The American officer demanded to know the British officer's business. The British officer, who turned out to be Lt. Philip Brown of HMS *Eagle,* said he had a communication from Adm. Lord Richard Howe for the American commander. Tupper ordered Brown's barge to lay to while he sent a boat to shore for instructions.

Upon hearing the news, Washington directed his best man for this job, Joseph Reed, to meet the British envoy. Washington warned Reed not to accept any communication from the enemy that was not properly addressed; the British would not be allowed to denigrate the American cause. Reed took aide Samuel Blachley Webb and Col. Henry Knox of the artillery with him. The three American officers were rowed out into the harbor in a barge, meeting Lieutenant Brown's boat about halfway between Governor's Island and Staten Island. As the two boats lay bobbing in the water, Lieutenant Brown rose in his barge, removed his hat and bowed ceremoniously to the American officers. He said that he had an important letter from Adm. Lord Richard Howe for their commander. Reed yelled across to Brown to tell him to whom the letter was addressed. Brown replied that the letter was addressed to "George Washington, Esquire."

Reed described what happened next in a letter he wrote to his brother-in-law. Reed said, "I told him we knew no such person in the army." Brown then showed Lord Howe's letter to Reed and attempted to hand it to him. Reed replied, "No, sir, I cannot receive that letter."[72] The British officer became agitated explaining that the letter he wanted to deliver was of a civil nature, explaining to Reed "that Lord Howe regretted he had not come sooner, that he had great powers, and it was much to be wished the letter could be received."[73] Reed reaffirmed that he could not receive such a letter. "Here we parted," Reed told his brother-in-law.

The two parties exchanged letters from prisoners of war, after which the officers saluted each other and Brown began to be rowed back to his ship. However, Reed said, "After he had got some distance he put about, and we again met him. He then asked me under what title General,—but catching himself, Mr. Washington chose to be addressed. I told him the General's station in the army was well known . . . He then expressed his sorrow at the disappointment, and here we parted."[74]

Admiral Howe's younger brother, Gen. William Howe, attempted to have his letter delivered to the American commander two days later. His communiqué was refused for the same reason. Upon hearing the news, Admiral Howe's secretary, Ambrose Searle, angrily wrote in his diary, "it seems, to be beneath a little paltry Colonel of Militia at the Head of a Banditti or Rebels to treat with the Representative of His lawful Sovereign, because 'tis impossible for him to give all the Titles which the poor Creature requires."[75]

The flag of truce returned on July 19, this time in the person of one of General Howe's aides-de-camp. Joseph Reed was again dispatched to meet the enemy flag. Howe's aide asked if the adjutant general of the British army might be admitted to an interview "with his Excellency General Washington." Finally, the acknowledgment Reed and Washington were waiting for! "On which Colonel Reed, in the name of General Washington, consented and pledg'd his honor for his being safe returned." They agreed to the interview for the following day.[76]

At noon the following day, Reed and Webb met General Howe's acting adjutant, Lt. Col. James Paterson of the 63rd Regiment of Foot. Colonel Paterson transferred to Reed's barge and was rowed to New York City. He was escorted to the interview without the usual formality of having his eyes blindfolded. Once landed in New York, Paterson had a one-hour interview with Washington. His Excellency was joined by his aides and several senior officers for this meeting. The Commander in Chief's Guard provided appropriate stateliness to the occasion. Colonel Paterson was resplendent in his scarlet coat with green facings and silver buttons. He attempted to open peace negotiations with the rebels. Nothing purposeful happened during the meeting, especially since the Americans had declared their independence from Great Britain earlier that month. Paterson was safely returned to his barge by Reed and Webb. He was sociable and chatty with them and thanked them for not blindfolding him. The British would have to regain their colonies by force of arms.

The British buildup on Staten Island intensified and it seemed that each day brought additional enemy ships and reinforcements, eventually totaling 32,000 men. Reed looked out across the harbor one day and wrote his wife, "The enemy have received a reinforcement of one hundred sail within these ten days; they make a very formidable appearance. When I consider the force and preparations against us, I cannot but admire the spirit of the country, and the inequality of the contest. The whole world seems leagued against us."[77]

Across the harbor, 20,000 American troops continued to strengthen their defenses. Washington and his aides were overwhelmed with the administrative details necessary to operate the army as well as prepare the defenses of New York City. Having pushed himself and his staff to their limits, on July 25, 1776, Washington wrote to John Hancock requesting an additional aide-de-camp. Washington said,

> I find myself under the unavoidable necessity of asking an Increase of my Aid de Camps . . .The business of so many different departments, centering with me, & by me to be handed on to Congress for their information, added to the Intercourse I am obliged to keep up with the adjacent States and incidental occurrences, all of which requiring confidential (& not hack) writers to execute, renders it impossible in the present state of things for my family to discharge the several duties expected of me with that precission and dispatch that I could wish.[78]

It seems that Washington was always open with Congress about his staff needs, and his civilian bosses were reasonably cooperative. On July 29 Washington's request for an additional aide was read aloud in Congress which promptly resolved that "the General be empowered to appoint another aid-de-camp."[79] Washington filled this important new addition to his staff with another lawyer. As previously mentioned, it was only logical for Washington to draw upon his own prewar experiences when he needed men of merit to serve on his headquarters staff. Washington's bias, however, was directed to appointing qualified men as his aides, decisions unswayed by regional connections, blood relationships, or influence. The new man Washington invited to join his staff was his Virginia neighbor and acquaintance William Grayson. Grayson's appointment was included in the general orders dated New York, August 24, 1776: "The General has appointed William Grayson Esqr. one of his Aide-de-Camps; he is to be obeyed and respected accordingly."[80]

Grayson's early life is clouded by family traditions and legends that found their way into an 1890 book written by Hugh Blair Grigsby entitled *History of the Virginia Federal Convention of 1788.*[81] Grigsby's book is the source for some of what we know about Grayson's childhood and education. Grigsby reported that Grayson was born in 1736, the son of a Scottish immigrant. According to Grigsby, Grayson graduated from the College of Philadelphia after which he went to England for additional training at Oxford University and the Inns of Court, Middle Temple, in London where he studied law. He returned to Virginia where he launched his career as a lawyer at the age of thirty. Grigsby's information is probably incorrect. William Grayson was born in Prince William County, Virginia, in 1742, not 1736, which made him thirty-four years old at the time of his appointment as Washington's aide. The Grayson family was of English origin and well established in Virginia society by the time of William's birth. His father, Col. Benjamin Grayson was one of the most successful members of the American branch of the family. His title came from his rank of colonel in the Virginia militia. From his Belle Air plantation, Benjamin Grayson managed a commercial empire that included plantations, speculation in western lands, and town lots, stores, mills, and warehouses. William's mother was the former Susanna Monroe, who bore Benjamin three sons and a daughter: Benjamin, Jr., Spence, William, and Susanna.[82] She died in 1752 after which Benjamin Grayson married Sarah Ewell but they had no children. When Colonel Grayson died in 1758, his eldest son, Benjamin, Jr., was his principal heir. But Colonel Grayson provided handsomely for his other children, leaving William (aged sixteen) 2,800 acres of land in Prince William and Loudoun counties, twenty slaves, and a considerable sum of money.

With his elder brother Benjamin, Jr., acting as his guardian and custodian of his funds, young William Grayson traveled to Philadelphia in the late summer of 1759 to enroll in the College of Philadelphia. He was accompanied on this trip by two servants and given a large allowance, which he spent freely. William attended the college for only one term. He dropped out of school and next turned up in London. The best estimates are that he sailed for London in February 1760. There is no evidence to support the story that Grayson attended Oxford University or studied law at the Inns of Court during his time in England. He probably returned to Virginia in July 1762 after learning that much of his inheritance had been lost by his older brother: Apparently Benjamin, Jr., did not have the same aptitude for business or the luck of his father. Young William seems to have buckled down when he returned home and began what proved to be a three-year clerkship as a lawyer. In 1766 he was qualified in four northern Virginia counties to practice law. His family background and connections helped him establish himself as a successful lawyer in Dumfries, which was the county seat of Prince William County. The town is near Washington's estate at Mount Vernon, and these two Virginia gentlemen, who had much in common, became friends. William Grayson was one of Washington's prewar card-playing, fox-hunting, and business cronies. Grayson was active in local politics and was named a member of the Prince William County Committee of Safety and was appointed captain of its military arm,

The Prince William County Independent Company. He was subsequently chosen colonel of the county's battalion of minutemen. Grayson was described as
a tall and remarkably handsome man of noble appearance and manners.
George Washington's cousin, Lund, knew Grayson, calling him, "among the
most amiable, respectable men of the day in which he lived and very popular."[83] The usually derisive Gen. Charles Lee met Grayson early in the war and
was favorably impressed, calling him "a Man of extraordinary merit."[84]
Another glowing endorsement of Grayson was written by John Page to his
friend Thomas Jefferson. Page's recommendation was written on April 6,
1776, when Jefferson was a Virginia delegate to the Continental Congress:

> Col. Grayson who behaved admirably well at Hampton and who has
> taken great Pains to improve himself in the Military Science intends
> to offer his Service to the Congress. He is highly deserving of
> Encouragement. Do introduce him and recommend him to your
> Friends. He will make a Figure at the Head of a Regiment. He dis-
> played Spirit and Conduct at Hampton. For God's sake declare the
> Colonies independant at once, and save us from ruin.[85]

Grayson was also noted for his "almost unrivaled play of the intellectual
powers."[86] He was a skilled lawyer and debater who ended his long public
career as a United States senator. His wife was Eleanor Smallwood, the sister
of William Smallwood (Revolutionary War major general and elected three
times as the governor of Maryland). The Graysons had four children: William,
George, Robert, and Alfred. A daughter of William Grayson's brother Spence
(Susannah Monroe Grayson) married General Washington's cousin and Mount
Vernon wartime manager, Lund Washington.[87]

Another important addition was made to Washington's military family
during the summer of 1776 when Tench Tilghman was named a volunteer
aide-de-camp. Tilghman was born on Christmas Day 1744 at his family's
Fausley estate in Maryland. It was located along the banks of the Wye River in
Talbot County, Maryland. Tench was the eldest of six sons born to James and
Ann Tilghman. He spent his youth on the eastern shore of Maryland before
being sent to Philadelphia to attend college under the supervision of his grandfather Tench Francis. Tilghman graduated from the College of Philadelphia in
1761. After college he went into business with his uncle Tench Francis, Jr., and
their firm prospered, no doubt in part due to their influential and widespread
family connections. Both men signed the Non-Importation Resolutions of
October 25, 1765, and continued to support early commercial protests against
Britain including compliance with the 1774 prohibition of importation of all
goods from Britain and Ireland.[88]

In April 1775 war broke out between Britain and her colonists. In August
of the same year young Tilghman accepted an appointment as secretary to a
committee of Congress appointed to secure a neutrality treaty with the power-

ful Indian tribes along the New York state frontier. His appointment undoubt-
edly came about through the influence of his uncles Turbutt Francis, who was
appointed one of the members of the commission, and Matthew Tilghman
(1718–90), who was a Maryland delegate to the Continental Congress (serving
from September 1774 to December 1776).[89] Tench's assignment lasted one
month, during which he traveled to upstate New York with the commissioners.
When he returned to Philadelphia he and his uncle decided to dissolve their
business. Tench wrote about it years later, saying, "I Made as hasty a close of
my commercial affairs . . . to begin the World in a manner anew."[90] Tilghman's
"manner anew" was his decision to become more active in the revolutionary
struggle. He joined a Philadelphia militia company called the Ladies Light
Infantry and was elected a lieutenant. The troop was a social as well as a military organization, "consisting of the flower of the city" and branded by some,
"as an aristocratic assemblage," nevertheless the unit drilled and prepared for
action.[91] In July 1776 Tench went on active duty when he was named a captain
in the Pennsylvania battalion of the Flying Camp.[92] This appointment brought
him to New York City and closer to Washington's headquarters. Washington
knew Tench's father, James Tilghman, Sr., Tench's brother James Tilghman,
Jr., and Tench's uncle Matthew Tilghman before the war. James Tilghman, Sr.,
moved from Talbot County, Maryland, to Philadelphia, sometime before the
start of the Revolution, where he established himself as one of the prominent
lawyers in that city. James, Sr., also held some local appointments including
secretary of the Pennsylvania Land Office. As a man prominent in Philadelphia
society, James Sr., hosted Washington on several ocasions before the war.[93]
The general was also friendly with James Tilghman, Jr., a lawyer who lived in
Alexandria, Virginia, during the 1770s.[94] Washington also knew Tench's uncle
Matthew who was active in Maryland politics and served with him in the Continental Congress in 1774 and 1775. We can assume that Washington's association with the Tilghman family brought Tench's presence in the Flying Camp
to his attention. Because Washington was always desirous to recruit gentlemen
for his staff who could write well, in August 1776, Tench Tilghman joined his
staff as a volunteer aide-de-camp, which meant he agreed to serve without any
rank or pay.[95] He stayed with Washington almost until the end of the war.[96] He
was one of Washington's principal aides-de-camp and he was probably the
general's best all-round wartime assistant. Others may have been better at
drafting letters, office work, French translations, or conveying orders in the
field, but Tilghman did *all* of those things reasonably well. Nor was he the
brightest of Washington's aides, though he was intelligent, dependable, and
apparently got along well with his boss. Washington liked Tilghman and the
two men formed a lasting friendship. I especially like a personal letter Washington wrote him late in the war. Tilghman had taken a leave of absence to
court a young lady whom he wanted to marry. After several months of silence,
Tilghman apparently wrote Washington that his courtship was making
progress. Washington replied, "so believe me sincere, when I request you to

take your own time to accomplish it, or any other business you may have on hand. At the same time permit me to assure you, that you have no friend that wishes more to see you than I do."[97]

During the summer of 1776, however, Tench Tilghman's thoughts of marriage lay in the future. He and everyone else in the American army were preoccupied with the defense of New York. Joseph Reed felt the inevitable British invasion was fast approaching. He wrote his wife from New York on August 9, 1776,

> When I look down and see the prodigious fleet they have collected, the preparations they have made, and consider the vast expense, I cannot help being astonished that a people should come three thousand miles, at so much risk, trouble, and expense, to rob, plunder, and destroy, another people because they will not lay their lives and fortunes at their feet . . . Providence, my dearest love, has cast our lot in a most unhappy period.[98]

After spending the summer gathering men and equipment, Gen. William Howe began his campaign to capture New York City. On the eve of battle, a review of General Washington's military family would show Joseph Reed as adjutant general of the Continental Army and a close advisor to Washington. Robert Hanson Harrison was the general's military secretary with Alexander Contee Hanson listed as an assistant military secretary and working for Harrison. Washington's aides-de-camp were George Baylor, Samuel B. Webb, Richard Cary, and William Grayson. Capt. Caleb Gibbs and Lt. George Lewis, officers in the Commander in Chief's Guard, were listed as special aides. Tench Tilghman, formerly of the Pennsylvania Flying Camp, was a volunteer aide.

Howe landed troops on the western tip of Long Island (today's Gravesend Bay, Brooklyn) on August 22. There was only minor skirmishing for the next four days. But on the morning of the twenty-seventh, British troops commanded by Gen. James Grant made a noisy demonstration in front of the well-entrenched Grand Army while 10,000 more British soldiers with artillery, commanded by Gen. Henry Clinton, made a wide encircling move. When Clinton's force got behind the American lines, a cannon shot signaled that his corps was in position. At this signal, General Grant's troops suddenly stopped diddling with the rebels and assaulted them from the front while Clinton attacked from behind. What followed was a disaster for the Americans and Washington's first lesson in soldiering from Gen. William Howe.

Washington's Grand Army spent the rest of the morning fighting their way out of the British trap with terrible losses. By noon, the survivors had retreated to the immediate safety of the substantial rebel fortifications on Brooklyn Heights, just across the East River from Manhattan Island. Washington and Reed came over from Manhattan about an hour before the battle began. They took no part in the battle, but helped rally the troops on Brooklyn Heights. This was Reed's first taste of fighting. Several Pennsylvania regiments had taken part in the engagement and Reed counted numerous friends and neighbors among the American killed, wounded, or captured. Harrison was also with the general who apparently ordered him to return to Manhattan Island and send a dispatch to Congress telling them what had happened. Washington was very sensitive about his relations with Congress and authorizing Harrison to write the dispatch shows that the general had confidence in his new military secretary. Harrison began the letter, addressed to John Hancock:

> New York Augt 27. 1776 Eight Oclock P.M.
> I this minute returned from our Lines on Long Island where I left his Excellency the General. [Harrison then explained how the enemy had landed on Long Island and the placement of the American troops.] This being done, [he went on,] early this Morning a Smart engagement ensued between the Enemy and our Detachments, which being unequal to the force they had to contend with, have sustained a pretty considerable loss—At least many of our Men are missing, among those that have not returned are Genls Sullivan & Lord Stirling . . .[99] While These Detachments were engaged, a Column of the Enemy descended from the Woods and marched towards the Center of our Lines . . . and his Excellency Inclines to think they mean to attack and force us from our Lines by way of regular approaches [a siege] rather than in any other manner.[100]

Harrison left Long Island before the end of the day's fighting and did not know the extent of the American disaster when he wrote his report to Congress. By the evening of August 27, General Howe's army had routed the American troops on Long Island and surrounded them on the land side in their fortifications on Brooklyn Heights. It was only a matter of time before a favorable shift in the wind would allow the Royal Navy to block their only escape route, which lay across the East River to American-held Manhattan Island. Realizing his precarious situation, Washington took advantage of the bad weather and abandoned Brooklyn Heights on the night of August 29. He managed to get his troops across the East River to the immediate safety of Manhattan before the British army facing him knew what was happening. Tradition has it that Tench Tilghman assisted Washington throughout the desperate evacuation and was among the last men to leave the American fortifications in Brooklyn. Following his safe arrival in Manhattan, Tilghman proudly wrote his father, "Our Retreat before an Enemy much superior in Numbers, over a wide River, and not very well furnished with boats certainly does credit to our Generals."[101] Reed wrote the next morning that he had not taken his uniform off for four days and had not slept for two nights.[102] He wrote his wife a few days later,

When I look round, and see how few of the numbers who talked so largely of death and honor are around me, and that those who are here are those from whom it was least expected, (as the Tilghmans, &c.,) [a complimentary reference to Tench Tilghman] I am lost in wonder and surprise. Some of our Philadelphia gentlemen who came over on visits, upon the first cannon, went off in a most violent hurry. Your noisy sons of liberty are, I find, the quietest in the field.[103]

On September 15, 1776, General Howe resumed military operations against the rebels. He conducted a textbook-perfect amphibious landing against the weakly defended Kips Bay portion of mid–Manhattan Island. In this engagement, the inexperienced Connecticut militia defending the area were easily routed by Howe's professionals. Washington was at Harlem when the shooting started; when he heard the sounds of gunfire, he galloped to the scene with several of his aides. He probably took Baylor and Grayson, who were the best horsemen. Washington got as far as a wheat field (at the present site of Lexington Avenue and 42nd Street) where he found everything in chaos. He later described what he saw in a letter, "the Troops that had been posted in the Lines retreating with the utmost precipitation . . . [and those ordered to support them] . . . flying in every direction and in the greatest confusion."[104] The panic-stricken militiamen were running towards the safety of the strong rebel positions on upper Manhattan. Washington screamed at them to halt and form a line. An American officer heard him cry out, "Take to the walls! Take the corn field," but it was impossible to restore order.[105] According to Tilghman, who may also have been present, Washington "laid his Cane over many of the Officers who shewed their men the Example of running."[106] Unable to restore discipline, Washington, his aides, and several other senior officers on the scene (Brig. Gen. Samuel Parson and Massachusetts militia general John Fellows are most frequently cited as being present) began to cane and whip the fleeing militia, screaming at them to stop and form ranks.[107] The frightened soldiers ignored their entreaties and kept running. According to one account, Washington then "threw his hat on the ground and exclaimed, 'Are these the men with which I am to defend America.'"[108] Another version has Washington so "distressed and enraged" at the conduct of the troops "that he drew his sword and snapped his pistols to check them."[109] At this moment British Redcoats came into view. A second-hand account claims that as the British reached the crest of the hill coming up from Kips Bay, Washington was sitting motionless on his horse blinded with rage and unable to move, "that he sought Death rather than life."[110] At that moment, according to historian Washington Irving, one of the general's aides-de-camp seized the bridle of his horse and hurried him away.[111]

Meanwhile, at the bottom of Manhattan Island, the American troops defending New York City were about to be cut off from the rest of the army gathering at Harlem Heights. The troops in the city were commanded by Gen. Israel Putnam. An eyewitness account of Putnam's escape with his troops was written by his aide-de-camp David Humphreys. This young officer would join Washington's military family as an aide-de-camp later in the war. Humphreys was interested in writing and poetry and here is his dramatic account of the events of September 15, 1776, as Putnam's troops narrowly escaped capture and rejoined the rest of the army, after dark, on the heights of Harlem:

> Before our brigades came in, we were given up for lost by all our friends. So critical indeed was our situation, and so narrow the gap by which we escaped, that the instant we had passed, the enemy closed it by extending their line from river to river. Our men, who had been fifteen hours under arms, harassed by marching and counter-marching, in consequence of incessant alarms, exhausted as they were by heat and thirst, if attacked, could have made but feeble resistance.
>
> —That night our soldiers, excessively fatigued by the sultry march of the day, their clothes wet by a severe shower of rain that succeeded towards the evening, their blood chilled by the cold wind that produced a sudden change in the temperature of the air, and their hearts sunk within them by the loss of baggage, artillery, and works in which they had been taught to put great confidence, lay upon their arms, covered only by the clouds of an uncomfortable sky.[112]

As Putnam was herding his men north to Harlem Heights, the British moved troops south and seized New York City, establishing it as their headquarters until the end of the war. The following day, September 16, the British tested the American lines at Harlem Heights on upper Manhattan Island. The Redcoats blew fox horns as they advanced to mock the flighty rebels. A small-scale battle ensued as each side poured more men into the melee. After intense fighting, the British withdrew. The battle of Harlem Heights was only a small victory for the Americans, but at least they had finally beaten the British. Joseph Reed took part in the day's fighting, and he wrote his wife a few days later telling her about the battle: "It hardly deserves the Name of a Battle, but as it was a Scene so different from what had happened the Day before it elevated our Troops very much & in that Respect has been of great Service." Reed explained that a report was brought to headquarters that morning that the enemy was advancing against the American defenses at Harlem Heights. "I went out to see what Truth there was in it," Reed told her, and gave the details of the battle. He finished his letter with a story that must have frightened her:

> But the greatest [danger] was from one of our own Rascals who was running away, upon my driving him back a second Time he presented his Piece & snapp'd at me at about a Rod Distance—I seized a Piece from another Soldier & snapp'd at him—but he had the same good Luck. He has been since tried & is now under Sentence of Death—

but I believe I must beg him off as after I found I could not get the Gun off, I wounded him in the Head & cut off his thumb with my Hanger—I suppose many Persons will think it was rash & imprudent for Officers of our Rank to go into such an action (Gen Putnam, Gen. Green, many of the General's family—Mr. Tilghman & etc were in it) but it was really done to animate the Troops who were quite dispirited & would not go into Danger unless their officers led the Way.[113]

The Grand Army continued to occupy Harlem Heights into October 1776. Washington established his headquarters at the estate of Lt. Col. Roger Morris, a retired British Army officer who had fled America at the start of the war. His wife, Mary occupied the house until June 1776, when she too vacated it for safer territory. Washington and his staff occupied Colonel Morris's mansion from the evening of September 15, following the battle of Kips Bay and their loss of New York City, until October 20. The house survived the Revolutionary War and is known today as the Morris-Jumel Mansion.

Despite the tension of the moment, Washington and his aides-de-camp continued their daily routine during their occupation of the Morris mansion.[114] Washington was a wealthy Virginia gentleman and he did his best to make his life as comfortable as possible during the eight years he served as commander in chief of the Continental Army. He traveled throughout the war with his clothing, toiletries, bedding, tents, dinnerware, silverware, wine, liquor, and food. The taste for living well was partially a behavior learned from his experience as a young officer attached to the British Army; he demanded the best of everything as commander in chief. It helped maintain the dignity of his office and thus discipline throughout the army. But Washington was frugal in comparison with some British officers who were famous for traveling in style during the Revolution. In 1777, for example, Gen. John Burgoyne led an army through the dense forests of upstate New York accompanied by his mistress, a considerable entourage of servants, some splendid wine and brandy, and thirty wagons carrying his personal baggage and that of his aides-de-camp.

Officers of means, like George Washington, had servants to attend to their grooming, clothing, and feeding. These servants would have included a personal body servant, a hostler (horse tender), a coachman, a cook, and a washerwoman.[115] We know that Washington's body servant throughout the war was a slave named Billy Lee. Billy was purchased by Washington in 1768 from the widow of Col. John Lee. His usual job was to dress his master's hair, lay out his clothes, and assist him in washing and dressing.

Washington took pride in setting a handsome table for his guests at Mount Vernon and he continued this practice as commander in chief. This required a separate staff of cooks, cooks' helpers, and a steward whose job it was to purchase everything consumed by the large household and to keep expense records. The steward was also in charge of all the male servants in Washington's household with the exception of Washington's slave Billy Lee. Capt.

Caleb Gibbs, commander of the Life Guard, managed the household during part of the war.[116] Washington also had a housekeeper throughout the war to oversee the domestic operations of his headquarters. His housekeeper during his stay at the Morris mansion was a "very worthy Irish woman" named Mrs. Elizabeth Thompson. She supervised all the female servants and probably also served as cook during her period of employment.[117] She may have been illiterate because her household records had to be kept for her. Legend has it that Mrs. Thompson was making pickles for Washington in the cellar kitchen of the Morris mansion while the battle of Harlem Heights was raging nearby.[118] Washington and his military family had plenty of dirty laundry so there was a full-time washerwoman to attend to this household chore. From 1776 to 1778, the headquarters washerwoman was Margaret Thomas. She probably had an assistant. The household linens and tablecloths were washed once a week. Besides the servants already mentioned, there were a number of housemaids, houseboys, and assistant hostlers. Some of them are identified as free blacks. Records for the period include wages paid to "Negro Hannah and Negro Isaac," cash paid to "Negro wench for washing Linnen &c.," and "Cloas washed by Marther the Negro wench."[119]

Washington's aides-de-camp were also members of the gentry who left behind comfortable homes with servants and house slaves. This is particularly the case with Harrison and Baylor who were Southern gentlemen. Despite the hardships of war, the general's aides had the private means to make things as comfortable for themselves as circumstances would allow. The aides may have brought one or more of their male servants and/or slaves with them to headquarters or hired servants after their arrival. Their servants attended to their personal needs as well as taking care of their horses. As men of means, the aides also probably traveled with a wagon or several wagons filled with their personal belongings. There is a brief eyewitness account that mentions the headquarters baggage train. It was written by Dr. James Thacher who accompanied the Grand Army as it marched through Philadelphia in 1781 en route to Yorktown. Thacher said, "Our line of march, including appendages and attendants, extended nearly two miles. The general officers and their aids, in rich military uniform, mounted on noble steeds elegantly caparisoned, were followed by their servants and baggage."[120]

Another category of servants, which Fourth of July orators prefer that we forget, were the common soldiers who were commandeered to be personal servants. The American officer corps believed that they were entitled to military attendants as one of the perks of their rank. They based their demands on the tradition of European armies, including the British Army in America, whose officers used common soldiers as personal servants whom they called waiters or batmen. British officers in America also employed paid servants and runaway slaves as personal servants. Continental Army officers also wanted to be gentlemen with servants and the expedient was to use common soldiers as personal servants.[121] Washington did not like to see his army's manpower diminished in this manner, but the practice was popular and difficult to control. As a clue to the extensive use of enlisted men as personal servants in the national army, Washington issued a general orders late in the war to try to control the practice. His order specified how many soldier-servants an officer could have. Included in the orders was an assertion that aides-de-camps were allowed to have one servant taken "from the Army."[122] The soldiers themselves did not object because being a personal servant was a welcome relief from combat and the harder work of felling trees and digging fortifications. Washington preferred that his officers follow his example and hire civilian personal servants whenever possible. However, the general's officers were often not as wealthy as he was and did not own slaves or could not afford to pay for personal servants.[123] It is likely that Washington's aides-de-camp, who had money and lived in close proximity to their chief, followed his example and did not commandeer common soldiers as personal servants.

The Morris mansion looks today much like it did when it was occupied by Washington and his military family. The interior of the mansion is quiet as visitors tour its uninhabited rooms. How different this house must have been during September and October 1776 when it served as Washington's headquarters. The house would have been filled with traffic and sounds during the day: dispatch riders, scouts, civilian and military functionaries, and officers and enlisted men on a variety of official business.

In the running of the army, Washington and his aides prepared the general orders. How these orders were disseminated from headquarters down to the common soldiers is interesting: Each day a major general was detailed as the major general of the day. He was responsible for giving the adjutant general the general orders of the army and other instructions. After conferring with the major general of the day, the adjutant general held a daily meeting at headquarters at 11:00 A.M. attended by the aides-de-camp of major generals and the brigade majors of brigadier generals (a brigadier general commanded an unspecified number of regiments). The adjutant general gave his orders to the army at this daily gathering. The brigade majors returned to their brigades and assembled the regimental adjutants and gave them the necessary orders. The adjutants returned to their regiments, assembled the orderly or first sergeants, and gave the orders for the companies. All important orders were registered in orderly books kept by organizations down as far as companies.[124] Thus did the general orders and other instructions created by Washington and his aides trickle down to the common soldier.

Washington also conferred regularly at his Morris mansion headquarters with his general officers. There was also a stream of visitors at headquarters, including a delegation from the Continental Congress, consisting of Elbridge Gerry, Roger Sherman, and Francis Lewis. The congressmen arrived at the mansion on September 24 and probably stayed until September 30. Other visitors to headquarters at this time included two Indian chiefs from the Caughnawagas tribe, along with an interpreter. In addition to visiting Indian chiefs, politicians, and generals, it was thought that courts-martial hearings were also held in the mansion. But despite the large size of the Morris mansion, there was no spare room to conduct them. It is now believed that courts-martial proceedings were conducted in a nearby house.

The personal baggage belonging to Washington and his aides was stored in some secure area in the mansion or in the nearby two-story stable and coach house. The baggage was guarded night and day by the Commander in Chief's Guard. During nighttime hours, the house provided sleeping quarters for many people. There were servants as well as soldiers from the Guard sleeping in the basement and hallways, on the kitchen floors, and crammed into the attic or in the nearby large stable. Servants sleeping in the hallways of homes was a common practice in colonial America. They slept on stuffed mats that were rolled up and stored during the day. Washington usually had one room reserved for his personal use. At the Morris mansion, it is believed that he used an upstairs room as a combination bedroom and office. It is small in comparison with the other upstairs rooms, but Washington liked privacy and the room he selected was in a quiet back section of the house with views of both the Hudson and Harlem Rivers. It is believed that the commander in chief's personal body servant, Billy Lee, slept in an alcove adjacent to his master's room. Washington's aides-de-camp shared other rooms in the mansion. Each probably had a folding bed that he purchased at his own expense. If there were visitors, such as the congressional delegation that visited Washington in September, they would have joined the general's aides in the bedrooms, finding sleeping space wherever they could. Countless travelers' accounts of the eighteenth century record sleeping two or three to a bed with strangers, so sharing a room or bed with one's fellow officers or guests was not unusual. No matter what the sleeping arrangements were, the general's aides were nearby both day and night to handle any summons or emergency.

Washington and his staff were fortunate because they arrived at the Morris mansion to find it filled with furniture that its former occupants had left behind in their haste to reach safety. Washington and his aides used what they found along with an assortment of folding tables, stools, chairs, trunks, and portable bookcases that they carried with them as part of the headquarters baggage.

Colonel Morris's mansion at Harlem Heights was probably the most elegant house occupied by Washington and his staff during war. It had large rooms suitable for entertaining, and Washington made the most of his stay there despite the vicissitudes of the war. His wife Martha did not join her husband during his stay at the Morris mansion because the house was too close to enemy lines. Washington was a man of regular habits at his Mount Vernon plantation, and part of his daily routine was maintained, when possible, throughout his tenure as commander in chief during the Revolution. In civilian life, the general was a farmer whose day started before sunrise and ended early in the evening. Washington seemed to try to follow this pattern as commander of the army. His day may have started as early as 4:00 A.M., when he got out of bed and was shaved and dressed by his slave Billy. He then began working in his office. It is probable that one or more of his aides joined him for this pre-dawn work session. He stopped for a small breakfast, which was served to him around 7:00 A.M. Washington then returned to work in his office, assisted by his aides-de-camp, who worked in nearby rooms until 3:00 P.M. when the dinner meal was served.

The rooms in the Morris mansion served multiple functions during Washington's stay: Offices during the day and sleeping quarters at night. Distinctions between public and private space were not strict in the eighteenth century, and there are numerous references to officers holding staff meetings in their bedrooms. However, one room in the Morris mansion had only one important purpose. It was the first floor dining room. This room was used for the dinner meal, which started at 3:00 P.M. and lasted, depending on circumstances, from two to three hours.

Dinner was an important part of Washington's management style. He was a very busy man and the dinner meal gave him an opportunity to talk business and socialize with anyone interesting or important who was in camp. All of his aides-de-camp were present for dinner. One of them acted as the host and was responsible for introductions and toasts. The officer of the day was frequently invited. Women were regular guests at dinner, including His Excellency's wife Martha, who joined her husband for the dinner meal when she was at headquarters. Other women at the general's dinner table would have included the wives or daughters of senior officers who were visiting camp. Visiting members of the Continental Congress and other government functionaries would also be dinner guests. The number of people seated at Washington's dinner table varied, but twelve was typical. One guest mentioned that twenty people were seated at the dinner he attended.[125]

Despite "calm and agreeable conversation," business was probably discussed at dinner as Washington worked to give his opinion on various subjects and get the viewpoints of his guests. It was important for his aides-de-camp to be intelligent men of "social ease" who could assist Washington in making a point to a visiting congressional delegation or foreign observer. An indication that business was discussed at the dinner table is shown by some of the invitations that went out from headquarters. As an example, Col. Alexander Scammell received a dinner invitation that read, "His Excellency requests the favor of your Company at dinner tomorrow if you are not engaged. At any rate he wishes to see you some time tomorrow without fail, and that you will bring with you, an accurate state of the Troops under your command, and also of Major Porter's Detachment."[126] The dinner meal was also a good opportunity for Washington to get information. Visitors were encouraged to update His Excellency and his staff on outside events. It was critical for Washington's aides to listen and observe everything that was discussed at the dinner table, and at headquarters at large, since they were expected to compose accurate correspondence for Washington, and they needed to understand what was going on.

From various diaries and letters we can see who received an invitation to dinner at Washington's headquarters. As examples, Dr. James Clitherall received an invitation for dinner on July 5, 1776. The doctor wrote in his diary, "We dined with him [Washington] in company with Gen Wadsworth [Jeremiah Wadsworth—commissary of Connecticut forces and a pioneer in American business] and Mercer [Gen. Hugh Mercer, who was a doctor before the war], Col. Read, adjutant general of the army [Col. Joseph Reed], Major—, and the gentlemen of his household [Washington's aides-de-camp and military secretaries]. The General seemed a little unbent at his table, was very affable and requested our company to King's Bridge the next morning."[127]

Dinner was served on fine china and silverware. The silverware was described as ivory-handled knives and forks. From contemporary accounts we know that the dinner was served in the English style, with many dishes set on the table at once, arranged in a geometrical pattern.[128] Sometimes soup or some meats were served first, followed by a large display of dishes consisting of meat, poultry, or fish, with seasonable vegetables and assorted pastries. From purchase receipts from the time of Washington's stay at the Morris mansion, we know that a great deal of poultry was served; chicken, turkey, duck, and goose. Other food items purchased for Washington and his staff during their occupation of the mansion were bread (anywhere from six to eleven six-pound loaves were ordered daily), apples (the only fruit in season at the time), and limes, which were probably eaten to prevent scurvy. All this food was consumed with green tea, cider, rum, and great quantities of Madeira wine.

Following dinner Washington may have relaxed with his guests if there was no pressing business. There apparently were no rules concerning the length of the workday at headquarters. I will venture to make a generalization that the hardest part of the work day took place from early morning until the 3:00 P.M. dinner meal. Also, there was more of an opportunity to find some moments to relax when the army was encamped and under no immediate threat from the enemy. But the sudden arrival of a courier at any time, with an urgent dispatch, could send Washington and his staff scurrying back to their office. There is evidence that some letters were drafted by Washington and his aides late at night.[129] But, if circumstances allowed, at about 7:30 in the evening the general and his aides returned to the dining room where a small supper was served. Supper was a modest meal consisting of three to four light dishes, usually leftovers from dinner, along with fruit and nuts.

The French officer Marquis de Chastellux was invited to supper with Washington and recorded the details. "I am informed," wrote Chastellux, "that his Excellency expected me at supper. I returned to the dining-room, protesting against this supper; but the General told me he was accustomed to take something in the evening; that if I would be seated, I should only eat some fruit, and assist in the conversation. I desired nothing better, for there were then no

strangers, and nobody remained but the General's family." Following this simple meal, the cloth was removed and a few bottles of good claret and Madeira
were placed on the table, and toasts were given "without order or ceremony."
Everything was done tastefully but simply; George Washington valued privacy
over grandeur.

Supper guests were probably infrequent because the general enjoyed
spending quiet evenings in the company of his military family whenever possible. There is no detailed record of what transpired between Washington and
his aides at these informal gatherings. At the time of his stay at the Morris
mansion Washington had an inner circle of aides who were Tench Tilghman,
Robert Hanson Harrison, and his former aide Joseph Reed. There are hints to
the close relationship that Washington had with these men. Tench Tilghman,
for example, wrote to his father during this period, "The General has treated
me in a Manner the most confidential, he has intrusted me and one other gentleman of his Family, his Secretary [Robert Hanson Harrison], with his most
private Opinions on more Occasions than one."[130] The conventional story is
that Washington relaxed with his aides-de-camp in the evening engaging them
in polite conversation of family, friends, and home. His aides were intelligent,
tight-lipped, and well informed about what was happening throughout the
army, and small talk with them is inconsistent with Washington's work habits,
dedication to duty, and the well-being of the Continental Army. In addition, the
general's talented and well-educated family were likely candidates for serious
discussions because they shared Washington's esprit de corps, and dedication
to the American patriot cause. What then did Washington talk about when he
got together to share a quiet moment with his personal staff? It is difficult to
know exactly what transpired among the general and his aides because Washington was tactfully silent about military matters, and his staff were as secretive as their boss. Three subjects appear most likely to have been topics of
conversation between these men: Strategy, politics, and army administration. I
think we can eliminate strategy because the general had a cadre of talented
senior line officers like Greene and Knox who he could turn to for advice on
this subject. It is also doubtful that Washington discussed politics with his
aides as he had a number of well-informed advisors in Congress (Richard
Henry Lee for example) and state government (Jonathan Trumbull, the governor of Connecticut). However, Washington's aides are at the forefront when we
turn to the administration and management of the Continental Army. They
were probably the best informed, and most knowledgeable officers regarding
the overall organization of the army, what we refer to today as "the big picture." The management decisions made by Washington during the course of
the war played a key role in its successful outcome. To illustrate the importance of good organization in winning the war, I will focus on a letter that
Washington wrote Congress from the Morris mansion on September 25, 1776.
The subject of this letter was the reorganization of the Continental Army.
Washington believed from the outset of the war that victory could only be won

with a professional army rather than reliance on one-year enlistments and militia. Congress favored the latter because they feared that a professional army would be a potential threat to the civilian government, while from a financial point of view calling up short term militia was cheaper than maintaining an army of professional soldiers. Washington, however, decided that he had to have what he termed "a respectable army" of professionals especially after the American defeats at the battles of Long Island and Kips Bay. His September 25, 1776, letter expressed his opinion, and pressured Congress to adopt his reforms.[131] Washington's letter included the following passages: "To place any dependance upon Militia, is assuredly, resting upon a broken staff. Men just dragged from the tender Scenes of domestick life—unaccustomed to the din of Arms—totally unacquainted with every kind of Military skill, which being followed by a want of confidence in themselves when opposed to Troops regularly traind . . . makes them timid, and ready to fly from their own Shadows." Washingon addressed Congress's fear of a professional army later in his letter: "The Jealousies of a standing Army, and the Evils to be apprehended from one, are remote; and in my judgement, situated & circumstanced as we are, not at all to be dreaded; but the consequence of wanting one, according to my Ideas; formed from the present view of things, is certain, and inevitable Ruin." The need to reorganize the Continental Army as a professional fighting force must have been on Washington's mind when he arrived at the Morris mansion, and he probably discussed the subject prior to writing his persuasive letter to Congress. There is no record of his discussing the need for a professional army in the minutes of the councils of war attended by Washington's senior line officers prior to his writing Congress on the subject.[132] I believe, however, that he discussed the reorganization of the army with his personal staff, especially Reed, Tilghman, and Harrison before taking pen in hand. Congress adopted Washington's recommendations, which contributed to the successful outcome of the war. There are other similar examples throughout the Revolution where I sense the influence of Washington's personal staff in the overall management of the Continental Army.

The workday at headquarters was long and Washington preferred to retire early, at about 9:00 P.M., perhaps to read before he went to sleep. His aides might linger on in the dining room to socialize among themselves until around 11:00.[133] Among the numerous items that were thrust upon Washington to solve during his stay at the Morris mansion was the strange case of Pierre Penet. The story is important because the Continental Congress eventually appointed the Frenchman as Washington's honorary aide-de-camp.

Pierre Penet was a French businessman who first came to Washington's attention when he arrived from Europe to Providence, Rhode Island, on December 10, 1775. Penet arrived in America accompanied by his new business partner, Emanuel de Pilarne. The two Frenchmen brought proposals "to supply the United Colonies with arms and warlike stores."[134] A detailed letter from the Massachusetts Board of War shows why the rebels needed the goodwill of

merchants like Pierre Penet. It was early in the Revolution and the New Englanders wanted to sell their raw materials "for warlike stores we yet stand in need
of." Part of the letter to the firm of Louis Penet & Son, merchants at Bordeaux,
reads, "Having an opportunity from Newburyport to ship a small interest by a
chance vessel, we consign it to your house for sale. There may be some small
furs and oil, or perhaps oil only. Whatever effects may come to you for our
account, please to sell them to the best advantage, and return us the proceeds,
freight and all other charges being deducted, in good effective fire-arms, with
bayonets, such as are used in the King of France his army." The Massachusetts
Board of War also wanted gun locks, flints, "borax purifcata," brass cannons, and
"good raven's duck fit for soldiers' tents."[135] The rebels were dependent on European merchants, like Penet, to help them secure these war materials.

Washington met with Penet, was interested in what he had to say, and
referred the matter to Congress. In time, the Frenchman negotiated a contract
to supply arms with the Secret Committee of Congress. Eventually the news
reached the French government, which was clandestinely helping the Americans and was interested in Penet's activities in America. The French foreign
minister Charles Gravier, comte de Vergennes, made some inquiries about him
to one of his operatives, a Dr. Barbeu Dubourg, who responded to the inquiry,
"Permit me to impart to you my uneasiness with regard to our great affair,
[secret French efforts to aid the Americans] and, above all, as to the man who
has the charge of it . . . Mr. Penet was born in Alsace the son of an artillery
store keeper who, having many children, could give them but a mediocre education."[136] Vergennes responded to Dr. Dubourg, "The most favorable judgement one can pass upon the man in question is that he is one of those
fortune-seekers who are willing to enrich themselves at any cost."[137]

The story becomes interesting to this narrative when Penet wrote a letter
to Washington from France on August 3, 1776. His letter was in French and
was translated by Tench Tilghman. In it Penet asked Washington to appoint
him as an aide-de-camp. "I have, my General," Penet wrote, "a demand to
make of you for a favor which I desire to obtain, and which I hope to merit; I
have wrote concerning it to Docr Franklin, it is that you would grant me the
Honour of the Title of your First Aid de Camp and that you would permit me
to wear the Uniform and also the Ribbon. I ask no Pay, but the honor only of
being in your Service."[138]

Washington received Penet's letter on October 6, and promptly endorsed
his request to be named an honorary aide-de-camp. He forwarded the recommendation to the Continental Congress who cooperated by voting Penet a
brevet commission as an aide-de-camp to Washington on October 14, 1776:
"Resolved, That General Washington be informed the Congress approve of his
appointing Monsr. P. Penet his aid de camp by brevet, and that a commission
of aid de camp be accordingly transmitted to him."[139]

The appointment of Pierre Penet is one of the more curious incidents associated with Washington in his role of commander in chief of the Continental Army. This scheme has Washington's imaginative flair associated with it. He probably felt that Penet would be more effective in buying arms and ammunition for the patriot cause if he could parade around in France wearing a Continental Army uniform with the green riband of an aide-de-camp to the commander in chief.

Penet's business went bankrupt in 1782, and he immigrated the following year to America, where he became a land speculator and traded with the Oneida Indians in upstate New York. The Frenchman eventually settled on the Carribean island of Saint Dominique around 1790 and was lost at sea in 1812. Historian John Fitzpatrick commented that there is no documented evidence available to place a value on the services provided by Penet and Pilarne, "but it must have been actual and substantial or Washington would hardly have granted so unusual an honor."[140] The war materials that Pierre Penet supplied may have been the first trickle in the flood of military aid that France would provide the Americans in the Revolutionary War. His appointment as an aide-de-camp was just one of the numerous items handled by Washington and his busy staff while they occupied the Morris mansion.

To complete the picture of how the Morris mansion appeared in October 1776, there is the possibility that Washington had a flag flying from the house. A letter written by a British officer on July 10, 1776, mentions that he saw a flag flying from Washington's New York City headquarters.[141] The Valley Forge Historical Society claims they own a "headquarters flag" used by Washington. However, it is doubtful that the general had a personal or headquarters flag because, while he kept meticulous records of even the smallest purchases in his expense account, there is no reference to the purchase of a headquarters flag or the materials and labor to make one.

In mid-October Washington learned that his adversary, General Howe, had finally secured a beachhead in the Bronx and was moving into Westchester County, New York. If Howe succeeded, his army would cut off Washington's line of retreat from Manhattan Island to the interior of New York state. Washington called together a conference of his officers on October 16 to determine what they should do. There was great excitement at this meeting, because the popular Gen. Charles Lee had returned after organizing the successful defense of Charleston, South Carolina. Lee, for one, advocated the immediate evacuation of Manhattan. Washington agreed and retreated from Manhattan with his army toward the crossroads village of White Plains, New York. The general apparently was too busy to send a dispatch to Congress to update them on the situation so he entrusted Harrison to write one on his behalf. Harrison wrote John Hancock from northern Manhattan Island at 1:30 P.M. on October 20, 1776:

I have it in command from his Excellency, to transmit you the inclosed Copies of dispatches which just now came to Hand & which contain Intelligence . . . His Excellency would have wrote himself, but was going to our Several posts . . . The Enemy are pursuing with great Industry their plan of penetrating the Country from the Sound [Long Island Sound] & of forming a Line in our Rear. They are now extended from Frogs point [the modern Throgs Neck section of the Bronx] to New Rochelle. [Apparently trying to give Congress some good news, Harrison ended his dispatch on a positive note.] On Friday One of their Advanced parties near East Chester fell in with part of Colo. Glovers Brigade & a smart & close Skirmish ensued, in which I have the pleasure to inform you our Men behaved with great coolness & Intrepidity and drove the Enemy back to their Main body.

> I have the Honor to be in hast with great
> esteem Sir Yr Most Obdt St
> Rob. H. Harrison.[142]

The Americans left behind almost 2,000 soldiers when they abandoned upper Manhattan Island. These troops were posted at a fortification called Fort Washington, which sat on a hilltop overlooking the Hudson River. The fort was considered impregnable (at least by the American standards of the time) and continued to be held at the insistence of the Continental Congress. Washington left behind almost 2,000 Pennsylvania troops at Fort Washington. They were commanded by Col. Robert Magaw, who was a lawyer in Carlisle, Pennsylvania before the war. Magaw and his men were in high spirits and ready to defend their post. They were in an excellent defensive position on high ground, surrounded by rough terrain. Gen. Nathanael Greene also favored holding Fort Washington. He was one of the young officers who had become Washington's principal advisors during Reed's absence in Philadelphia. Greene, the son of a Rhode Island anchor maker, had a talent for organization. Another new member of Washington's inner circle was Col. Henry Knox, the corpulent former Boston bookseller with a passion for artillery. Some men did not think much of Greene or Knox and looked to Charles Lee, the educated, professional soldier who remained a bright star against George Washington's fading reputation. While Joseph Reed befriended Nathanael Greene, he was spellbound by Charles Lee, whom he began to look upon as the savior of the American cause. Tilghman mentioned Lee's popularity with the army in an October 17, 1776, letter to the New York state Committee of Correspondence. Tilghman said,

If we can but foil Gen Howe again, I think we knock him up for the Campaign. You ask if Gen Lee is in Health and our people feel bold? I answer both in the affirmative. His appearance among us has not contributed a little to the latter. We are sinking the ships as fast as possible; 200 men are daily employed, but they take an immense quantity of stone for the purpose.[143]

Washington and his staff evacuated the Morris mansion on October 21, 1776.[144] As a man of wealth, the general tended to respect other people's property and possessions. He did not damage or remove anything from the Morris mansion during his stay and left everything just as he had found it. Washington's Grand Army escaped the British encirclement on upper Manhattan only to be pursed by the enemy to White Plains. An indecisive battle was fought there in late October, after which Washington used the cover of a rainstorm to slip away with his army to a stronger position deeper in Westchester County at North Castle. Harrison wrote Congress with several updates on the situation including a dispatch dated November 3, 1776, informing them that nothing had changed for several days except "in the number of our Troops, which is every day decreasing by their most scandalous desertion and return Home."[145]

General Howe and his army followed Washington's forces, but American scouts reported that the British had broken camp during the night of November 5 and were moving west toward Dobbs Ferry on the Hudson River. Washington was convinced from the interrogation of prisoners and deserters that Howe's plan was to cross the Hudson River and invade New Jersey. The Hackensack Valley of northern New Jersey, in particular, had productive farms and Howe would soon need food for his men and horses. Washington called his senior officers together; Joseph Reed and Charles Lee were among those present. As a result of this council Washington decided to split his army into three unequal parts. He would move with 3,000 men into New Jersey to link up with the troops at Fort Lee under the command of Gen. Nathanael Greene. Greene also commanded the troops at Fort Washington, almost directly across the river from Fort Lee. The second part of the army was put under the command of William Heath, one of his undistinguished workhorse generals. Heath would defend the Hudson River at Peekskill, New York. The third and largest portion of the army, composed of 7,500 men including many of the best troops, was put under the command of Gen. Charles Lee, who was ordered to sit tight in Westchester County and await developments. There was the possibility that General Howe had finished campaigning for the season and was marching his army south from Dobbs Ferry into winter quarters in New York City. Washington's final orders to Lee were clear: "If the Enemy should remove the whole, or the greatest part of their Force to the West side of Hudsons River, I have no doubt of your following with all possible dispatch."[146]

It was during this critical part of the war that Washington's prewar acquaintance, business associate, and neighbor, John Fitzgerald, joined the headquarters staff as an aide-de-camp. Fitzgerald replaced Richard Cary who apparently resigned in November 1776 to get married. We do not know the date of Fitzgerald's birth or anything about his family or education. Our knowledge of him begins when he emigrated to America from Ireland in 1769 and settled in

Alexandria, Virginia, as a partner in a successful mercantile business named Fitzgerald & Peers. Fitzgerald arrived in New York in the summer of 1776 as a captain in the 3rd Virginia Regiment. He was promoted to major on October 3, 1776, and joined Washington's staff as an aide-de-camp sometime in November 1776. The first letter he is known to have drafted for Washington was written on December 2, 1776.

Washington moved across the Hudson and reached Fort Lee on the night of November 13, 1776. He promptly met with General Greene who had disturbing news for him; Howe's army had marched south from Dobbs Ferry and added his troops to those of Gen. Wilhelm von Knyphausen, who had already surrounded Fort Washington. Greene assured Washington that the fort atop the rocky terrain of northern Manhattan was in no danger and could withstand a long siege. Besides, Greene reasoned, the 2,000 Pennsylvania troops at Fort Washington could be quickly evacuated across the river to the safety of Fort Lee if the enemy threatened to overrun it. Joseph Reed was aware of the situation at Fort Washington. He was especially concerned because Fort Washington was manned by Pennsylvania troops, including some of his Philadelphia friends. However, neither Colonel Reed nor General Washington were aware of the fort's weaknesses. The problem was that Fort Washington was built by amateur American engineers who piled dirt on the rock of northern Manhattan Island to create a seemingly impressive fortification. But the rocky terrain made it impossible to build a safe place to store gunpowder or secure a source of water. Washington visited the fortress on the night of November 15, but did not order it evacuated since he was assured by the post's commander, Colonel Magaw, that the place was impregnable.[147] Greene secretly reinforced Magaw that night by sending additional troops from Fort Lee. One result of this move was that Fort Washington would be too small to hold its garrison if its outer defensive works were overrun.

On the morning of November 16, 1776, 2,700 American troops were at Fort Washington. They did not know it at the time but General Howe was not planning to engage them in a siege. Instead he ordered his 13,000 British and German troops supported by artillery to storm Fort Washington's outer works simultaneously from all sides, in an all-out assault. Washington and his staff watched the action from the safety of Fort Lee, but gun smoke and dust quickly obscured their view. Suddenly, in the early afternoon, the rocky tree-covered terrain across the river fell silent. Washington sent an intrepid volunteer named Capt. John Gooch across the river to find out what had happened. Washington told Gooch to tell Magaw to hold out until nightfall when a rescue expedition would be organized. Gooch got into Fort Washington and reported back to Washington that the British forces had captured the outer works and the American defenders were jammed into the main fort. The enemy was threatening to lob mortar shells into the crowded fort if Colonel Magaw did not surrender immediately. At Washington's instructions, Reed rushed off a note to General Lee with the dreadful news:

This Morning the Attack was made upon Mount Washington by the whole of Gen. Howes Army in three Divisions—our Troops kept the Lines as long as could have been expected but were at length obliged to yield to superior Numbers—They retired under the Guns of the Fort which stopp'd the Approach of the Enemy—soon after this a Flag went in from the Enemy & since that there appears such an Intercourse that we suppose the Fort has or will soon capitulate. The General has thought it proper you should have the earliest Advice of this Event that you may regulate yourself accordingly.[148]

The silence from across the river was broken when wild cheering broke out from thousands of voices. A moment later, Washington and his officers watched in horror as the rebel standard was lowered from Fort Washington, to be replaced by the British Union flag. Fort Washington had surrendered and its entire garrison was made prisoner. Washington's prestige had suffered a staggering blow. Joseph Reed was angered by the awesome loss and the realization that many of his friends were now dead or prisoners. Reed blamed Nathanael Greene for the disaster and faulted Washington for not acting decisively by ordering the evacuation of the fort while there was still time. Reed read a letter his new intimate Charles Lee had written him: "I cannot conceive what circumstances give to Fort Washington so great a degree of value and importance as to counterbalance the probability or almost certainty of losing 1400 of our best Troops."[149] Like some officers in the American army and members of Congress, including John Adams and Benjamin Rush, Reed had fallen prey to the intrigue of the smooth talking Charles Lee. Lee used the opportunity of the loss of Fort Washington to criticize Washington and enhance his own reputation. Reed, however, did not reveal his feelings to his chief as further calamities befell Washington's Grand Army.

General Howe quickly followed up his victory at Fort Washington with an invasion of New Jersey. The assault on New Jersey came on the night of November 19, just three days after the disaster at Fort Washington, when Howe launched an amphibious assault across the Hudson River, commanded by Gen. Charles Cornwallis. Cornwallis's force crossed the river with Fort Lee as its objective. The British invasion was discovered, and a dispatch rider arrived with the news at Washington's headquarters at the Zabriskie house in Hackensack, New Jersey. Hackensack was six miles inland from Fort Lee. The general immediately mounted his horse and rode off toward Fort Lee with two of his aides, leaving the rest of his staff behind. We know he took Grayson, and the second aide, whose name is not known, was probably Baylor who was the other skilled horseman on his staff. Not surprisingly, Harrison, Washington's dependable secretary remained behind to operate headquarters.

Reed was also left at the Zabriskie mansion as Washington raced off with his small suite. The situation at Fort Lee was confusing, and no one knew exactly what was happening. Reed was agitated by the news of this latest catastrophe. A cavalryman arrived at headquarters earlier that morning with some routine dispatches from an American outpost across the Hudson River near Lee's headquarters. The courier was about to return to his post when Reed ordered him to wait a moment for an important message that he had to deliver without delay to General Lee. Reed hurriedly looked for a piece of paper on which to write the note. The cavalryman found a rough piece of wrapping paper in his pocket and gave it to him. Reed had an old pencil and wrote his champion Lee, "Dear General, we are flying before the British. I pray . . ." and the pencil broke. With no time to lose, Reed ordered the rider to carry the half-written note to Lee and to verbally add, "you are to push and join us." The courier raced off toward General Lee's headquarters with Reed's frantic message.[150]

Meanwhile, a few miles away, Washington calmly helped shepherd the troops from Fort Lee toward the immediate safety of Hackensack. The Fort Lee troops were on the verge of panicking, but the presence of Washington and his aides helped to steady them. In the midst of the turmoil, Washington instructed Grayson to quickly ride back to headquarters and send a message to Lee. Unaware of Reed's distraught message that was already en route, Washington told Grayson to send a dispatch to Lee telling him that the British had invaded New Jersey and that he should cross the Hudson River without delay with his 7,500 men, as previously arranged. Grayson rode back to headquarters and hurriedly wrote his message. Here are the highlights of Grayson's dispatch:

> Hackensack, November 20th, 1776. His Excellency has directed me to write to you, and acquaint you of the late movements of the enemy. They landed this morning between Dobbs's Ferry and Fort Lee . . . His Excellency thinks it would be advisable in you to remove the troops under your command on this side of the North River [Hudson River] and there wait for further orders.[151]

Following the American losses at Fort Washington, Lee's corps represented the largest number and most experienced troops left to Washington. His corps was desperately needed in New Jersey. Grayson also sent a dispatch to General Heath, informing him of the situation. In addition, he sent an express rider to General Mercer, who commanded some troops guarding the New Jersey coastline, telling Mercer, "You will be pleased to hold yourself in readiness to march at a moment's warning."[152]

Harrison was writing a letter to Gen. Philip Schuyler that morning at headquarters prior to the arrival of the courier with the news of the British attack on New Jersey. Schuyler commanded the Northern Army headquartered at Fort Ticonderoga. Harrison's letter contained various matters of business. He interrupted his letter with urgent news: "Ten o'clock.—This minute an express from Orange-Town [today's Orangetown, New York, on the Hudson River] advises that some of the enemy have landed below Dobb's Ferry."[153]

Before proceeding further with the story, it is interesting to look back and document the sequence of events to see how Washington's staff functioned in such a crisis. Washington rode toward Fort Lee to investigate, accompanied by two of his aides. The only other person known to be accompanying him was Gen. Israel Putnam. Washington purposely left most of his staff at headquarters. As Washington galloped towards the Hudson, he met the retreating garrison from Fort Lee at a strategic village crossroads named Liberty Corner (today Englewood, New Jersey). Washington quickly apprised himself of the situation and sent Grayson back to headquarters with instructions to send an immediate dispatch to General Lee. Grayson, who may have attended Oxford University in England and was known for his command of the language, rode back to Hackensack where he composed a clear and intelligent dispatch on his own, which he promptly sent by express rider to Lee. Several other aides were available at headquarters should Washington have needed them for other assignments, including personally delivering orders. Another interesting aspect of the story of the British invasion of New Jersey was that Washington apparently rode toward Fort Lee and unknown danger, accompanied only by General Putnam and two aides-de-camp. The military situation was confusing, and enemy horsemen could have been lurking anywhere. But Washington apparently preferred to move with a small entourage no matter what the circumstances. Even when he was president of the United States, Washington did not like to have all the dust and commotion of a large escort. During the Revolutionary War he rode out to reconnoiter with as small an escort as possible so as to be able to move fast and avoid detection. However, he always rode during the war with one or two of his aides-de-camp. He needed them to carry messages for him or to return to headquarters with his orders.

Until now, we have skimmed over the character of Gen. Charles Lee, one of the most colorful and interesting personalities of the American Revolution. As he is about to become a central figure in the events that are about to unfold, we should take a closer look at this unique eighteenth-century individual. Lee was forty-four years old at the start of the Revolution. He stood about five feet eight inches in height and was unusually thin. He seemed deliberately careless in his dress and manners. Lee was purposely blunt, crude, and rude. Typical of his strange and shocking habits was that he was always accompanied by a pack of dirty howling hounds. The acidulous Lee quipped that he preferred the company of dogs to that of men. He said of his devotion to his dogs, "when my honest quadruped Friends are equal'd by the bipeds in fidelity, gratitude, or even good sense . . . to say the truth I think the strongest proof of a good heart is to love dogs and dislike Mankind."[154] But Lee was an experienced and enterprising officer. John Adams probably made the most perceptive observation of Lee, describing him privately as "a queer creature. But you must love his dogs if you love him and forgive a thousand whims for the sake of the soldier and the scholar."[155] Lee was a favorite of the radical members of the Continental Congress, including Benjamin Rush and John Adams. His reputation had grown since the start of the Revolution and his circle of admirers had expanded to include Washington's confidant and friend Joseph Reed.

Miraculously, Washington led the troops from Fort Lee to the immediate safety of Hackensack. But while the garrison had been saved by quick action, everything else had been left behind. The road from Fort Lee to Hackensack was littered with with American muskets and equipment. Washington expected the British to drive deeper into New Jersey and he prepared for the hasty evacuation of Hackensack for a better defensive position further into the state. Before leaving he wrote a long letter to Charles Lee. The draft of Washington's letter is in the Library of Congress and is in the handwriting of Joseph Reed. In his letter, Washington told his senior lieutenant, "It must be painful to you as well as to us to have no News to send you but of a melancholy Nature. Yesterday Morning the Enemy landed a large Body of Troops below Dobb's Ferry." His Excellency went on to describe the evacuation of the Fort Lee garrison, the enormous material losses sustained by the hasty withdrawal, and his weak position at Hackensack. "I have resolved to avoid any Attack," wrote Washington, "tho by so doing I must leave a very fine Country open to their Ravages." The commander in chief then asked Lee to cross the Hudson with his corps, "by the easiest & best Passage."[156]

Immediately after writing Washington's letter to Lee, Reed secretly wrote Lee a personal communiqué. In this private letter, Reed lamented Washington's poor judgment during the New York campaign and the calamity at Fort Washington. Reed told the self-assured Lee,

> I do not mean to flatter or praise you at the expense of any other, but I confess I do think it is entirely owing to you that this army . . . are not totally cut off. You have decision, a quality often wanted in minds other wise valuable; and I ascribe to this our escape from York Island [Manhattan] . . . and I have no doubt, had you been here, the garrison of Mount Washington would now have composed a part of this army. . . . Oh! General! an indecisive mind is one of the greatest misfortunes that can befall an army: how often have I lamented it this campaign.[157]

An express rider was given Washington's letter to deliver to Lee. A moment later he was on his way to Lee's headquarters in Westchester County with Washington's letter safely tucked into his dispatch case. The courier was also carrying Reed's letter to Lee, which Reed had slipped into the courier's dispatch case when no one was looking. Reed's letter was critical of Washington and begged Lee to cross the Hudson quickly.

Washington abandoned Hackensack and fell back to Newark to await reinforcements from General Lee and the arrival of the New Jersey militia. But help never arrived. From Newark, aide Samuel Blachley Webb wrote his friend Joseph Trumbull with a description of the situation: "Fatal necessity has obliged Us to give up to the Enemy much of a fine country, well Wooded, Watered and Stock'd; not only that, but our Cannon, Mortars, Ordinance Stores &c are mostly gone."[158] Washington sent Reed to Burlington to pressure the New Jersey legislature to rally its militia to help defend the state. When scouts reported that the British were advancing toward Newark, Washington retreated farther into the countryside, arriving at New Brunswick on the Raritan River on November 29. Washington's brief stay at New Brunswick was the darkest moment of the American Revolution. Scouts reported that the enemy were nearby and their strength was estimated at 10,000 troops. They would have to cross the Raritan, but it was a shallow river with numerous fords. To defend the Raritan, Washington's Grand Army mustered 4,000 exhausted troops. The Americans only had one battery of artillery, commanded by Capt. Alexander Hamilton. Half of the rebel army planned to leave the following day (December 1) when their enlistments expired. Despite appeals from Washington and his officers, the eligible soldiers were determined to leave. They said they had done their duty and it was time for others to take their place. Everything depended on the swift arrival of General Lee with his corps of 7,500 experienced troops. But Lee, intoxicated by the flattery of his friends, including Reed, was reluctant to give up his independent command. When Washington reached New Brunswick, Lee was still dallying in Westchester County, New York.

Washington was elated when an express rider arrived in New Brunswick on November 30, with a letter from Lee addressed to Reed. In Reed's absence and certain the dispatch contained the long awaited news that Lee was marching to reinforce him, Washington unfolded the letter and began to read it. His hope turned to despair as he realized that what he was accidentally reading was the latest installment of a private correspondence between Reed and Lee. Washington was aghast to read that both men believed he was befuddled and unable to make decisions:

> My Dr. Reed, I receiv'd your most obliging flattering letter—lament with you that fatal indecision of mind which in war is a much greater disqualification than stupidity or even want of personal courage— accident may put a decisive Blunderer in the right—but eternal defeat and miscarriage must attend the man of the best parts if curs'd with indecision.[159]

Washington apparently said nothing. He quietly refolded the letter and wrote Reed an apologetic note:

> The inclosed was put into my hands by an express from the White Plains. Having no idea of its being a private letter, much less suspecting the tendency of the correspondence, I opened it, as I had done all other letters to you, from the same place and Peekskill, upon the

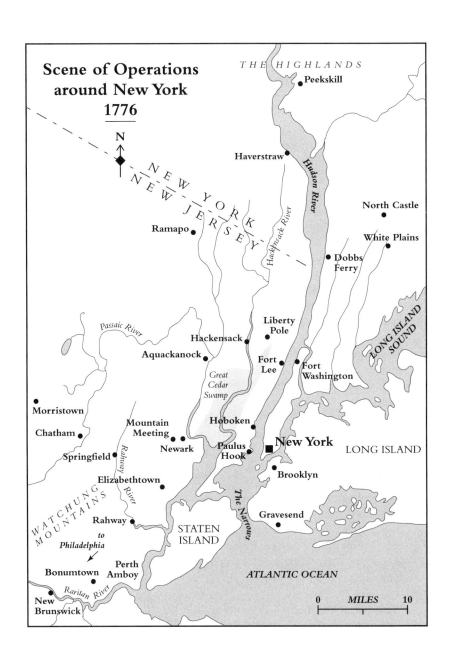

**Scene of Operations
around New York
1776**

N

THE HIGHLANDS

Peekskill

Haverstraw

Hudson River

Hackensack River

North Castle

White Plains

NEW YORK
NEW JERSEY

Ramapo

Dobbs
Ferry

Liberty
Pole

Passaic River

Hackensack

Aquackanock

Fort
Lee

Fort
Washington

LONG ISLAND SOUND

*Great
Cedar
Swamp*

Morristown

Chatham

Mountain
Meeting

Newark

Hoboken

Paulus
Hook

New York

LONG ISLAND

Springfield

Rahway River

Brooklyn

Elizabethtown

*WATCHUNG
MOUNTAINS*

Rahway

The Narrows

Gravesend

*to
Philadelphia*

STATEN
ISLAND

Bonumtown

Perth
Amboy

ATLANTIC OCEAN

New
Brunswick

Raritan River

0   MILES   10

business of your office. . . . [With his emotions in check, Washington continued:] This, as it is the truth, must be my excuse for seeing the contents of a letter which neither inclination or intention would have prompted me to. [The general quickly ended his note to Reed,] I thank you for the trouble and fatigue you have undergone in your journey to Burlington, and sincerely wish that your labors may be crowned with the desired success. My best respects to Mrs. Reed.[160]

With the enemy approaching, Washington had no time to think about his misplaced trust in Reed. The British reached the east shore of the Raritan on December 1 as half of Washington's army marched off, their period of enlistment having expired. The British failed to press their attack, and as soon as it was dark, Washington abandoned New Brunswick and eventually escaped across the Delaware River to the relative safety of Pennsylvania. Aide Samuel Webb wrote about the overly cautious British pursuit of the Grand Army in New Jersey, "'Tis a sacred truth they never yet have ventured to Attack Us but with great Advantages; they pursue no faster than their heavy Artillery can be brought up. With this they Scour every piece of Wood, Stone Walls &c, before they approach."[161]

The British fumbled their best chance to end the American Revolution at New Brunswick. Writing shortly after the event, an unidentified British officer had this to say about the military situation in New Jersey at the time:

> We had every thing to encourage our progress; the enemy was depressed, and drove from every quarter, their principal force was flying before us: the country people eagerly assisting our advances, by repairing the bridges and guiding the pursuit; —yet for want of vigor and decisiveness, we . . . neglected to follow the blow, which would have finally crowned us with success and crushed the rebellion.[162]

General Lee finally crossed the Hudson River on December 2, and in the days that followed, he made his way leisurely toward Washington's main army, which had already crossed the Delaware into Pennsylvania. In one of the strangest twists of fortune in the war, Lee was captured on December 13 by a British cavalry patrol as he lounged with two volunteer French officers at the Widow White's tavern in Basking Ridge, New Jersey. Lee had strayed from the protection of his army "seeking the company of women."[163] Guided by Loyalists, the British cavalry found Lee and carried him away to captivity in New York. Lee's sudden capture must have been a shock to his friend Joseph Reed. Reed busied himself in helping gather reinforcements to defend Philadelphia against a possible British attack. The Americans remained in Pennsylvania until Christmas night when Washington and his little army counterattacked by returning across the Delaware River to surprise the Hessian garrison at Trenton, New Jersey. One reason for selecting Trenton was that its commander,

Col. Johann Rall, had no respect for the fighting abilities of the Americans. For example, when a subordinate asked Rall's permission to construct redoubts to defend the town, the Colonel roared, *"Lasst sie nur kommen! Keine Schanzen! Mit dem Bajonet wollen wir an sie!"* ("Let them come! We want no trenches! We'll at them with the bayonet!").[164]

Washington's surprise raid on Trenton was a riveting success. At one critical point in the battle, he suddenly appeared to rally his troops. George Johnston, Jr. (Robert Hanson Harrison's brother-in-law), was a major at the time in the 5th Virginia Regiment. He later became one of Washington's aides-de-camp. Johnston wrote a famous account of Washington leaping into the firing line to inspire his troops: "Our noble countryman, the Gen'l at the head of the Virginia Brigades, exposed to the utmost danger, bid us follow. We cheerfully did so in a long trot, till he ordered us to form, that the cannon might play."[165]

Two days after the battle, Tench Tilghman wrote his father with an account of the victory at Trenton: "I have the pleasure to inform you that I am safe and well after a most successful Enterprise against three Regiments of Hessians consisting of about 1500 Men lying in Trenton . . . the Enemy had scarce time to form, our people advanced up the Mouths of their Field pieces, shot down their Horses and brought off the Cannon."[166]

The news of Washington's success at Trenton was electrifying and the population of New Jersey rose up against their invaders. Historian David Ramsay said, "The whole country became instantly hostile to the invaders. Sufferers of all parties rose as one man, to revenge their personal injuries."[167] From his headquarters in New York City, Howe ordered Cornwallis to retake Trenton. Cornwallis was confident that he had Washington's army trapped at Trenton on January 2, 1777, but Washington gave him the slip and emerged at Princeton the following morning. Washington surprised three British regiments in the town, along with some light dragoons and he deployed his troops to attack them.[168] When the general observed his troops retreating in confusion, he rode forward waving his hat and calling for them to rally. The soldiers were inspired by Washington's example, as Col. Daniel Hitchcock's New England Brigade suddenly burst forth from the woods and joined the fight. At the same moment, American artillery maintained a smart fire from a ridge to the south. The general was in the midst of the fighting, in danger of being shot by his own infantry or artillery as much as by the enemy's fire.

Aide John Fitzgerald was on the battlefield with the general. Recalling the event years later, Fitzgerald said His Excellency ordered him to ride off to order up some reinforcements from the rear. When Fitzgerald returned he could not find his commander. He looked around for Washington and finally caught sight of him in the midst of the battle. A moment later, he saw Washington riding at the head of his advancing regiments. Both sides then leveled their muskets, with Washington right between them. Horror stricken, Fitzgerald dropped the reins of his horse and drew his hat down to cover his eyes, certain he would open them to find his chief and friend dead on the battlefield.

Fitzgerald recalled that he next heard the roar of musketry exploding followed by shouting. He looked to see the enemy flying from the scene as the American troops advanced. Then Washington suddenly emerged from a cloud of smoke, waving his hat and cheering his soldiers on. Fitzgerald galloped to Washington's side, screaming over the din of the battle, "Thank god your Excellency is safe." He broke out in excited tears as his commander grasped him reassuringly by the hand, "Away, my dear colonel and bring-up the troops. The day is our own!"[169]

Is Fitzgerald's story true? Did George Washington ride into the midst of the battle of Princeton alone? Washington tried to rally some of his troops at Princeton, and in doing so he was exposed to considerable fire for a time, apparently cannon fire for the most part. Although Washington's staff were all nearby, he probably rode into the battle with only one or two of his aides. "Washington was naturally courageous under fire and wanted to convey that sense of courage and calmness to his officers and men."[170] Whatever happened at Princeton, Washington could only operate alone and without his aides-de-camp for a short time. He had to have members of his staff close by during a battle to convey commands to his field officers as well as provide him with reliable reconnaissance.

Not only did the general possess great personal courage but he also seems to have led a charmed life. He did, in fact, survive the war without ever being touched by a bullet or sword. One chronicler of the war explained that Washington was protected by an Indian spirit. This whimsical story appears in George Washington Parke Custis's book about the Revolution. Custis's tale begins the night before the battle of Monmouth in 1778, when Washington's aides-de-camp wrote their chief a memorial, "praying that he would not expose his person in the approaching conflict." They asked Dr. James Craik (1730–1814), the general's friend and companion from his early days on the frontier, to present their petition. Craik told them that they did not have to fear for the general's life because an Indian prophet claimed that Washington was protected by a spirit, "that the enemy could not kill him." Doctor Craik told his audience that "while Washington lived the glorious cause of American Independence would never die." Custis's tale goes on; the morning of the battle of Monmouth, Washington and some of his senior officers and aides-de-camp were reconnoitering the enemy positions from a elevated part of the field, when,

> a round-shot from the British artillery struck but a little way from his horse's feet, throwing up the earth over his person, and then bounding harmlessly away. The Baron Steuben, shrugging up his shoulders, explained, "Dat wash very near," which Doctor Craik, pleased with this confirmation of his faith in the Indian prophecy, nodded to the officers composed the party of the preceding evening, and then, pointing to Heaven, seemed to say, in the words of the savage prophet, "The Great Spirit protects him; he can not die in battle."[171]

Returning to the final phase of the battle of Princeton, British infantry took refuge inside Nassau Hall, the building that housed the College of New Jersey. American artillery commanded by Capt. Alexander Hamilton was brought to bear on the college building. One of Hamilton's biographers quipped, "Although Hamilton had been denied admission to Princeton, he left his mark upon that institution: he put a cannon ball through Nassau Hall where some British troops were holed up."[172] Washington was on the scene and noticed this young artillery officer who skillfully commanded his gun battery. The general would soon invite Hamilton to become one of his aides-de-camp.

Following the battle of Princeton, the main army quickly moved north toward the safety of the village of Morristown, New Jersey, which Washington had previously established as a military base. Gen. Hugh Mercer had been badly wounded during the fighting at Princeton. He was too weak to move and had to be left behind to become a British prisoner of war. According to tradition, when Washington learned that Mercer was still alive, he sent his nephew and special aide-de-camp George Lewis back to Princeton under a flag of truce to attend to Mercer. Mercer lived only long enough to die in Lewis's arms.[173]

Captain Gibbs had been left behind to guard the headquarters baggage at Newtown, Pennsylvania, where rumors reached him of an American defeat and the death of several of his friends. Webb wrote him on January 5 with an accurate account of the battle of Princeton and the army's subsequent dash to Morristown, Gibbs was elated to get the letter and quickly wrote back to his friend Webb,

> Dear Webb,
> I received your agreeable favor of the 5th Instant, and was exceedingly glad to hear our Dear General and all the rest of the family was alive and well, and I heartily congratulate you all on the happiness of your good success. It is utterly impossible for you to conceive the anxiety we were in till we heard that you were all well and in the land of the living, for various were the accounts we received, and the most dreadful. We heard that our dear General was wounded, & Col. Fitzgerald was either killed or taken prisoner. . . . If you should providentially fall in near Paramus, remember me to you know whom. Tell her just as you would if it were your own case, and be serious with her. You know more than any one else does, the particulars between us, & if you should be so happy I shall depend on your friendship & sincerity. Make mention of my letter and tell her to write.
> Tell her I love her; If she asks how well,
> Tell her I love her more than tongue can tell.
> I hope, if matters turn to expectation, to see her not long hence. My greatest love and respect to our dear General, giving him meet joy for his happy success. Regards to all the Lads. I have sent a keg of the

old wine and two loaves of sugar, and should have sent some spirits, but could not get anything to put it in. If you want anything let me know it. Tell Harrison I don't think his horse grows much better. Adieu & believe me to be yours sincerely,

C. Gibbs.

P.S. If you should see a certain Miss B. at Millstone, I make my best regards. I have sent some letters which were left here for you and several others.[174]

Thus ended the dramatic year of 1776. The British failed to crush the rebellion, and Washington's army remained in the field as a dangerous adversary. Subsequent events would prove that although the American Revolution continued for six more years, the British had only one more year, 1777, to defeat the rebels in battle. Once the French came into the war on the American side in 1778, a British military victory was practically unattainable. The year 1777 would also see Joseph Reed try to mend his fractured relationship with George Washington.

PART TWO

THE BATTLE FOR
THE MIDDLE COLONIES

1777–78

As the Revolution entered its third year, Washington was able to select his new aides-de-camp from a pool of experienced officers. At the same time Robert Hanson Harrison and Tench Tilghman emerged as two of his most capable assistants. The best known of Washington's aides, Alexander Hamilton, joined the general's staff during this middle phase of the war along with a young South Carolinian named John Laurens who became Hamilton's idol and intimate friend.

Washington's personal staff reached a new peak of professionalism during this period of the war. They were at Washington's side through the 1777–78, winter encampment at Valley Forge and the epic 1778 battle of Monmouth.

CHAPTER FOUR

The Defense of Philadelphia
January–October 1777

These are the Generals family all polite sociable gentlemen who
make the day pass with a great deal of satisfaction to the Visitors.
Martha Daingerfield Bland,
Morristown, New Jersey, May 12, 1777[1]

In response to the American victories at Trenton (December 26, 1776) and
Princeton (January 3, 1777), Gen. William Howe withdrew his troops from
western New Jersey. He consolidated his New Jersey holdings to a few isolated
towns in the eastern part of the colony: New Brunswick, Perth Amboy, and
Elizabethtown (today's Elizabeth). These towns lay closer than Trenton and
Princeton to the main British encampments around New York City. The Crown
troops who wintered in these New Jersey towns were on the front lines of a
miserable war of around-the-clock skirmishing with the rebels.

In marked contrast with the British, Washington's Grand Army spent the
winter in relative safety in an isolated mountainous region of northern New Jersey. Washington established his headquarters in the farming village of Morristown, which consisted of a few buildings clustered around a village green. It
was in an ideal defensive position that Washington Irving described as "Washington and his handful of men castled among the heights of Morristown."[2] A
friendly population gave the American troops further security from surprise
attack and a blanket of winter snow completed the picture. The peacefulness of
Morristown was a welcome change from the tensions of the long campaign of
1776. Washington's victories at Trenton and Princeton had rekindled patriot
resistance, and the British troops wintering in New Jersey faced constant
harassment from local rebel militia and raids organized from Morristown.

I introduced David Humphreys briefly when I quoted from his account of
the American retreat from New York City during the September 1776 battle
of Kips Bay. Humphreys is important to our story because he became one of

97

Washington's aides-de-camp later in the war. He also wrote an account of the British occupation of New Jersey and how that colony's militia rose up to defend their homes. Here is another example of Humphreys's ponderous, patriotic writing style as he describes the situation in New Jersey in late 1776,

> If we add, to the black catalogue of provocations already enumerated, their insatiable rapacity in plundering friends and foes indiscriminately; their libidinous brutality in violating the chastity of the female sex, their more than Gothic rage in defacing private Writings, public Records, Libraries of learning, Dwellings of individuals, Edifices for education and Temples of the Deity; together with their insufferable ferocity (unprecedented indeed among civilized nations) in murdering on the field of battle the wounded while begging for mercy, in causing their prisoners to famish with hunger and cold in Prisons and Prison-Ships, and in carrying their malice beyond death itself by denying the decent rites of sepulture to the dead,—we shall not be astonished that the Yeomanry [militia] in the two Jerseys [New Jersey was originally two colonies known as East and West Jersey], when the first glimmering of hope began to break in upon them, rose as one man, with the unalterable resolution to perish in the generous cause or expel their merciless invaders.[3]

Washington established his headquarters in Morristown at Arnold's Tavern, which lay on the northwest side of the village green. When Washington arrived at Morristown, his military family consisted of his military secretary, Robert Hanson Harrison, aides-de-camp John Fitzgerald, George Baylor, Samuel Blachley Webb, and William Grayson, special aide Caleb Gibbs, and volunteer aides Tench Tilghman and Stephen Moylan, who was back at headquarters following his brief stint as quartermaster general.

The first weeks at Morristown witnessed an important change in the structure of the Continental Army. Five months earlier, in September 1776, Congress authorized Washington to reorganize the Continental Army and enlist men "for three years or the duration of the war." At the same time the army was expanded to eighty-eight regiments. Congress later authorized an additional sixteen regiments to be raised. Samuel Blachley Webb, William Grayson, Stephen Moylan, and George Baylor all sought line commands in the newly established regiments and Washington accommodated their wishes. Washington's decision depleted his personal staff, which he had to rebuild almost from scratch. However, his decision to promote his assistants to command regiments of troops fitted into his management style, which was to selectively recruit, train, recognize accomplishments, and promote deserving officers, including the men who served as his aides-de-camp. Here are the stories of the four aides-de-camp who were rewarded by their chief with coveted line regiment commands.

William Grayson was absent from headquarters in early January 1777, and Washington wrote to him from Morristown on January 11, 1777, with an offer to command one of the sixteen new regiments, "which the Congress have been pleased to leave me to raise, and appoint the Officers of."[4]

Grayson accepted Washington's generous invitation and returned to Virginia to raise his regiment. He turned out to be a lucid and prolific correspondent who wrote Washington frequently reporting on his recruiting efforts and requesting advice. Their amiable exchange of correspondence is valuable because it shows the difficulty of recruiting troops for the American army during the Revolutionary War. The system was that a worthy, experienced officer was given a regiment and appointed its colonel and commander. However, the regiment only existed on paper. The new regimental colonel had to recruit men for his unit. He would first select his junior officers, which was not difficult because many men wanted the prestige and pay of a regimental line officer. Once the regimental officers were appointed, all the officers would go out to sign up common soldiers and noncommissioned officers. Officers for new regiments were often commissioned because they were popular among the local people and able to convince their neighbors to enlist in the regiment.

Recruiting was not easy, and Grayson's frustrations were evident when he wrote Washington shortly after his return to Virginia on January 29, 1777:

> With respect to the recruiting business, you may depend that every thing in my power shall be done to get the regiment completed in a short time; though I am sorry to inform you that we labor under a very great disadvantages; in every part of this state, there is nothing to be seen but recruiting parties & a number of the best officers have been already engag'd . . . We shall set out immedy & continue to ride through the Country until we have finished the appointments.[5]

On April 1, 1777, Grayson wrote Washington, "I am sorry to inform you that the recruiting service in that quarter does not by any means answer my expectations or wishes."[6] On April 8 Grayson wrote Washington from his home in Dumfries, "I heartily wish it was in my power to give satisfaction in this business, but if men will not enlist it is not in our power to force them."[7] Then on April 29, Grayson wrote his chief, "I have nothing new to inform you of relative to this regiment, since my last, except the resignation of some of the officers, from their inability to raise men."[8] Grayson finally managed to raise his regiment from Virginia, Maryland, and Delaware. His regiment took to the field in the spring of 1777 as Grayson's Additional Continental Regiment and was assigned to the 4th Virginia Brigade, an element of Washington's Grand Army.

The circumstances in which the general's intrepid "riding aide" George Baylor was given command of one of the new regiments were unique and arranged by Washington. It started when the general gave Baylor the honor of presenting Congress with his official report and a captured flag from the victory at Trenton. Included in Washington's report was a kind word for Baylor, "Colo. Baylor, my first Aid de Camp, will have the honor of delivering this to you, and from him you may be made acquainted with many other particulars; his spirited Behavior upon every Occasion, requires me to recommend him to your particular Notice."[9] The delegates understood the message and voted Baylor a horse and a promotion.[10] Congress named the general's aide-de-camp commander of the newly organized 3rd Continental Dragoons.

It is interesting to speculate why Washington picked Baylor to bring his official dispatch of the Trenton victory to Congress. Officers selected to bring news of great victories were sometimes rewarded with promotions. Washington liked Baylor who was also an excellent horseman, but the young Virginian was useless as a letter writer. I believe that Washington used the good fortune of the Trenton victory to ease Baylor from headquarters. Baylor's father and Washington's old friend, Col. John Baylor (1705–72), was dead but Washington did not want to treat the young man disrespectfully. Orchestrating young Baylor's coveted appointment as commander of one of the newly formed light dragoon units was a polite way of easing him out of headquarters.

Although Baylor's small regiment of light horse was officially called the 3rd Continental Dragoons, it was better known as "Baylor's Dragoons." Historians also call Baylor's regiment "Lady Washington's Horse" or "Mrs. Washington's Guards"; however, there is no evidence that these romantic nicknames were used to identify the regiment during the war. Washington's famous attention to detail is evident in his instructions to Baylor concerning the purchase of horses. Included in the precise instructions that Washington wrote to his former aide-de-camp were,

> In purchasing these Horses you are not restricted to price on the one hand, nor by any means to launch into Acts of extravagance on the other; good Horses are wanting, and for such the customary prices must be given; take none less than a quarter blooded, nor under fourteen and a half hands high, sound and clean made; they are not to exceed twelve years old, nor be under five, this Spring.[11]

George Baylor was a nice young man and an excellent horseman who was well liked by Washington. But unfortunately for the men in his regiment, Baylor proved to be an incautious officer whose carelessness was responsible for the horrible deaths of many of the men he commanded.

Baylor's Dragoons saw some action during the campaigns of 1777 and 1778. In late September 1778, 6,000 British troops crossed the Hudson River from their New York City stronghold into northern New Jersey. It was harvest time and the British were on a foraging expedition. They swarmed over the rich New Jersey farms, gathering the freshly harvested crops and fattened cattle. Baylor's Dragoons were ordered into the area to report on the activities of the enemy and help drive cattle out of the reach of the foragers. In late September Baylor and his men were operating in an old Dutch area of northern New Jersey known as the Overkill Neighborhood (today a part of River Vale, New Jersey). We do not know exactly how many troopers were with Baylor but 120 officers and men is the usually accepted number.[12] Baylor and his troops camped for the fatal night of September 27-28 in six barns and a farmhouse owned by Cornelius A. Haring along the Overkill Road (today's River Vale Road). It was a dangerous place for a small regiment of isolated American troops to bivouac because the area was swarming with Loyalists, informers, and British Army foragers. Baylor personally fixed a guard of a sergeant and twelve men about a half mile away from the Haring farmhouse near a strategic bridge that crossed the Hackensack River with orders to "Patrole a Mile below the Bridge, & at some Distance from the Roads—the Patroles were to be relieved every hour."[13] It is believed that the guards occupied a farmhouse and barn near the bridge. He allowed the rest of his command to remove the saddles from their mounts and to undress, which was ill advised with the enemy known to be in the area. The self-confident Baylor then joined his officers who bedded down at the Haring house. Historian Washington Irving wrote that Baylor had selected "careless quarters" for the night.[14] In addition, the guard at the bridge was too small and more casual in performing its duty than the situation required.

The enemy forging party was commanded by General Cornwallis and with him was Gen. Charles "No-flint" Grey, a senior officer with a bloodthirsty reputation. Grey got his nickname from his order that his men remove the flints from their muskets before a planned surprise attack. Grey used this trick to prevent any of his men from prematurely firing their muskets to warn the enemy. Loyalists came into Cornwallis's camp and told him that Baylor and his men "lay very negligently and unguarded in barns."[15] Cornwallis quickly laid a plan to cut off Baylor's detachment. He ordered Loyalist guides to lead No-flint Grey to the Haring farm.

Grey's soldiers were led through fields and byways to a position behind the Haring farmhouse and barns where Baylor and his men lay sleeping. Cornwallis benefited from another local British sympathizer who, according to tradition, took it upon himself to drive a herd of cows down Overkill Road in front of Haring's farmhouse. He observed the American positions minutely as he trudged slowly behind the cattle, passing the picket guard posing as an indifferent cowherder. He waited until he was out of sight to abandon the cattle in a nearby field and dash madly to Cornwallis and Grey with the exact positions of the Americans. As a result the location of Baylor's sentries was known. They were cut off, captured, or killed before they could give the alarm to their fellow troopers. After silencing the sentries, Grey's Redcoats burst into Haring's house and barns at about 3:00 in the morning with their bayonets fixed "and immediately commenced the horrid work of slaughter."[16] A few shots were fired from pistols and a feeble defense with sabers was made. Some of the dragoons attempted to hide under the hay in the barns but were bayoneted until their blood was seen running on the floorboards. The British killed about forty of the troopers in what quickly was dubbed by the Americans as "Baylor's Massacre." Baylor himself was surrounded in the Haring farmhouse with his officers. They tried to escape up a Dutch oven chimney but were caught by Grey's men. Baylor was bayoneted through the lungs and captured along with thirty-nine other men who were hurried off to prison in New York. Many of the Americans who surrendered were clubbed and bayoneted. Some men who escaped returned the next day and counted among the dead a fellow dragoon with eighteen bayonet wounds.[17] Even British historians were horrified by what had happened. Writing about the event, a Loyalist named Thomas Jones spoke of Baylor "as an amiable young Virginian, of a fair character, reputable family, and large estate." Jones gave his grim account of the cutthroat attack:

> the whole corps were massacred in cold blood, and to the disgrace of Britons many of them were stabbed while upon their knees humbly imploring and submissively begging for mercy. A merciful mind must shudder at the bare mention of so barbarous, so inhuman, and so unchristian an act. An act inconsistent with the dignity of honor of a British General, and disgraceful to the name of a soldier.[18]

Baylor was held prisoner in New York City where his wounds were tended to by his regimental surgeon, also taken prisoner during the raid. Baylor was ultimately exchanged and returned to duty, but he never recovered from the wounds he had received. On September 30, 1783, Baylor was breveted brigadier general but his health was failing. He went to the island of Barbados, at the close of the war, where he hoped the climate would help him recover his health. His condition only worsened and he died in Bridgetown, Barbados, in March 1784 from complications of the wounds he received in the 1778 massacre. Apparently Baylor was buried in Barbados, because a servant returned to Virginia after his death with his will and personal effects. Baylor was thirty-two years old when he died. He was married to Lucy Page but there is no record that they had any children.

Washington also gave a line command to his aide Stephen Moylan. The general was happy to help Moylan who had served as muster master general, *pro tem* military secretary, aide-de-camp, and quartermaster general of the army. Washington gave Moylan one of the new light dragoon regiments authorized by Congress.[19] He served with distinction until ill health forced him to resign from the army after the 1781 siege of Yorktown.

Samuel Blachley Webb was also rewarded by Washington with the command of one of the new regiments, designated Webb's Additional Regiment, Continental Line.[20] Webb was recovering from the wound he received a month earlier at Trenton when he learned that he had been honored by Washington with the command of one of the new regiments. He was more successful than Grayson in quickly enlisting men for his new command. Webb filled his ranks with men from Hartford, New Haven, and New London, Connecticut. Except for the blue and buff uniform worn by Washington, his senior officers and aides-de-camp, no uniform of the American Revolution has attracted more interest than the scarlet uniforms of Webb's regiment. From this fact some historians have created the myth that Webb's unit was known as the "Decoy Regiment."[21] Webb's men wore scarlet uniforms exactly like those of the British, however, for purely practical reasons. The Americans captured a cargo of military clothing when they seized the armed ship *Mellish* off the coast of Canada in November 1776. Uniforms were hard to come by for the Americans, and it was difficult to clothe an entire regiment with new uniforms at the same time. Word of the cache of captured uniforms reached Webb before he left Morristown to organize his regiment. Webb secured Washington's reluctant permission to take the captured uniforms, which had been transported to Connecticut, for his men. Webb arrived in Connecticut armed with an order from General Mifflin authorizing him to take possession of the British uniforms.[22] His regiment proved to be one of the best in the Continental Army.

Thus we have explored the lives of the four aides (Moylan, Grayson, Baylor, and Webb) who left Washington's military family in early 1777 to command their own regiments. However, we must return to General Washington at Morristown in early 1777 who was in urgent need of new "pen-men" to replace the four who had left his service. Washington thought of asking Major George Johnston of the 5th Virginia Regiment to join his staff. The general wrote his military secretary, Robert Hanson Harrison, on January 9, 1777, inquiring about Johnston who was Harrison's brother-in-law. Harrison was not at headquarters at the time. He had apparently gone to Philadelphia to get immunized against the smallpox when he received Washington's letter:

> My dear Harrison: I often intended, but before I had it in my power forgot, to ask you whether your Brother in law Majr Johnston would not, in your opinion, make a good Aid de Camp to me, I know it is a question that will involve you in some difficulty, but I beg you will not consider the Connexion between you in answering of it. I have heard that Majr Johnston is a Man of Education. I believe him to be a Man of Sense—these are two very necessary qualification's; but how is his temper? As to Military knowledge, I do not expect to find Gentlemen much skilled in it. If they can write a good Letter—write quick—are methodical, & diligent, it is all I expect to find in my Aids. [D]o not therefore if Mr. Johnston posses these qualities, and a good disposition, refrain (from a false modesty) to withhold your recommendation; because in that case you will do him in justice and me a disservice.[23]

George Johnston, Jr., was the son of George Johnston, Sr. (deceased by the time of the Revolution), who had been Washington's friend. Johnston, Sr., was an attorney and a member of the Virginia House of Burgesses. George, Jr., was born at the family plantation, "Belle Vale," in Fairfax County, Virginia, in 1750. We do not know anything about his education or profession. It is believed that he never married. Young Johnston was appointed a captain in the 2nd Virginia Regiment on September 21, 1775, and promoted to major in the 5th Virginia on August 13, 1776. He marched north with his regiment and arrived in Bucks County, Pennsylvania, in time to participate in the American raid on Trenton, New Jersey, on Christmas Day 1776. His appointment as one of Washington's aides-de-camp was announced in the general orders on January 20, 1777: "George Johnston Esqr. is appointed Aide-De-Camp to the Commander in Chief, and is to be regarded and obeyed as such."[24] Johnston died of a fever in October 1777. He was the only one of Washington's aides who died of illness during the war.

The second replacement to join Washington's staff in early 1777 was appointed under strange circumstances. The new aide was a thirty-three-year-old planter from Virginia named John Walker. His appointment was mentioned in the general orders for February 19, 1777: "John Walker Esqr. is appointed an extra Aide-De-Camp, to the Commander in Chief, and is to be considered and respected as such by the Army."[25] Walker was actually an agent for the Virginia Executive Council.

John Walker was born on February 13, 1744, at Castle Hill, his father's estate in western Virginia. He was the son of Dr. Thomas Walker, who was George Washington's distant cousin. Dr. Walker played a prominent role in Virginia's early history, and some information about his life is valuable before we move on to study his son. Dr. Walker spent the early part of his life in Fredericksburg. From Fredericksburg he moved west as a pioneer into what would become Albemarle County, Virginia. In 1750 Walker went further west, leading five explorers into modern Kentucky where he staked a land claim on behalf of the Loyal Land Company. Dr. Walker built the first cabin west of the Alleghenies and ranks with Alexander Spotswood, George Washington, and Daniel Boone as one of the explorers of western Virginia. His son John (our subject) graduated from the College of William and Mary in 1764 where he studied law. He married Elizabeth (Betsy) Moore on June 6, 1764. The couple were married at "Chelsea," the home of the bride's father, Col. Bernard Moore. Thomas Jefferson served as an attendant at their wedding. His participation in Walker's wedding was predictable because the two young men had known each other since childhood. They were also classmates at William and Mary College. Their fathers, Peter Jefferson and Dr. Thomas Walker, had also been friends as well as neighbors and business associates. Jefferson attended John Walker's wedding when he was twenty-one years old and a bachelor. He watched the newlyweds at an estate in Albarmarle County named "Belvoir," which was about five or six miles from his home at "Shadwell." Young Jefferson was a frequent visitor to "Belvoir," sometimes stopping by when John Walker was away. Years later Betsy Walker confided to her husband that Jefferson had tried to seduce her on several occasions. Jefferson's political enemies got hold of this juicy story many years later and used it to embarrass him. Jefferson was president at the time and privately admitted to the imbroglio, "that whn young and single I offered love to a handsome lady. I acknowledge its incorrectness."[26]

The highlights of John Walker's pre–Revolutionary War career were his election to his father's seat in the Virginia House of Burgesses in 1771 and his appointment as continental commissioner of Indian affairs for the Southern Department in July 1775. In 1776 the Virginia Executive Council (Virginia legislature) decided that they wanted an observer at army headquarters who could report to them on the situation of the Continental Army on a regular basis. Washington did not have the time or manpower to satisfy their request. The legislature selected John Walker for the job.[27] Their journal for January 16, 1777, gives the details:

> Resolved that a Gentleman of discernment, discretion, Veracity, and inviolable Attachment to the American Cause, ought forwith to be appointed Agent of correspondence for the purpose aforementioned to reside at or convenient to General Washingtons head Quarters. Resolved that Jn Walker esquire of Albermarle County be appointed to that Office.[28]

Washington agreed to Walker's mission but did not want to set a precedent that might lead to other states demanding the same privilege. His solution was to appoint Walker as his aide-de-camp and keep his real mission a secret. Walker's appointment appears in the general orders dated Morristown, February 19, 1777: "John Walker Esqr: is appointed an extra Aide-De-Camp, to the Commander in Chief, and is to be considered and respected as such by the Army."[29] Washington wrote to Virginia's governor, Patrick Henry, on February 24, 1777, explaining the situation:

> Mr. Walker has, I doubt not, informed you of the situation in which I have placed him, in Order that he may obtain the best information; and, at the same time, have his real design hid from the World; thereby avoiding the evils which might otherwise result from such Appointments, if adopted by other States. [Washington warned Governor Henry to keep Walker's real purpose for being at headquarters a secret.] If Mr. Walker's Commission [instructions], therefore, from the Commonwealth of Virginia, should be known, it would, I am persuaded, be followed by others of the like nature from other States, and be no better than so many marplots. [The general then spoke of Walker] . . . the high Opinion I myself entertain of his abilities, Honour, and prudence, I have taken him into my Family as an Extra Aid de Camp, and shall be happy, if in this Character, he can answer your expectations.[30]

Walker apparently served at headquarters only very briefly. He left Morristown in early March 1777 to deliver letters from Washington to Congress, which was meeting in Baltimore and there is no record that he ever returned to headquarters.[31] The Virginia legislature voted on September 8, 1777, to replace him as their representative at headquarters with Capt. William Pierce.[32] Pierce, however, never received an invitation to join Washington's staff. He served instead as an aide to Gen. John Sullivan and later to Gen. Nathanael Greene.[33] Colonel Walker next turns up in January 1778 when he is appointed by the Continental Congress as a "commissioner to the westward" (one of three Indian commissioners at Fort Pitt).[34] Walker declined the appointment. On June 18, 1778, he was appointed by the Virginia legislature as one of two commissioners "for the purpose of holding a Treaty with the Delaware, Shawanese & other Indians who may assemble at Fort Pitt." He declined this appointment as well, claiming "the Indisposition of his Family."[35] His excuse appears to be valid because he wrote to his friend Thomas Jefferson in 1780 mentioning that members of his family had survived smallpox. On December 14, 1779, Walker was chosen as a Virginia delegate to the Continental Congress. He served in Congress from March to November 1780.[36] Walker returned to military service shortly afterward when Governor Jefferson wrote him on January 18, 1781, asking him to help defend Virginia. Baron von Steuben had been put in charge of the state's defenses but he was, as Jefferson said in his letter, "very much unacquainted with its laws, customs, resources, and organization while he has hourly cause to apply them."[37] Walker apparently agreed and served on von Steuben's staff during much of 1781. Glimpses of Walker's activities during this period include a letter written to Jefferson on March 9, 1781, complaining of a shortage of men and equipment: "The difficulties and embarrassment, that have been thrown into the Baron's way in the course of this Business, have perhaps transported him beyond the bounds of moderation."[38]

Walker completed his law studies after the war ended and was admitted to the Virginia Bar. We get another peek into Walker's life from a letter he wrote Jefferson on February 4, 1786. Jefferson was in France when Walker wrote him that his only child had died, "Long ago should I have written you, My Dear Friend, but for a Tale of sorrow which I feared I should not have had the Fortitude to tell. I suppose you know what I allude to, having heard before this time, that I have lost my Dear Daughter. She died in Carolina Oct. the 17th 1784, leaving us one only Pledge, a sweet little pratling grand Daughter."[39] Walker served briefly as a member of the United States Senate (March 31–November 1, 1790) filling the seat made vacant by his former fellow Revolutionary War aide-de-camp William Grayson who died in office. After leaving the Senate, Walker resumed his law practice and agricultural pursuits. His brother Francis Walker (1764–1806) served as a colonel in the Virginia militia during the Revolutionary War and was elected to the United States House of Representatives for a single term (1793–95).[40]

The scandal concerning Jefferson's advances to Walker's wife was first published in 1805 when Jefferson was president. It was part of a vicious campaign waged by Jefferson's political enemies to embarrass and discredit him. Walker apparently went public with the story because he was angry at Jefferson who had supported James Monroe over him for the United States Senate. Walker asserted that Jefferson's first attempt to seduce his wife happened in 1768 and continued at various times until 1779. In one incident reported by Walker, Jefferson quietly slipped a piece of paper into Mrs. Walker's dress cuff, "tending to convince her of the innocence of promiscuous love. This Mrs W on the first glance tore to pieces."[41] In another instance Walker described how he and his wife and Jefferson and his wife were the overnight house guests of a mutual acquaintance: "On the ladys retiring to bed he pretended to be sick, complained of a headache & left the gentlemen among whom I was. Instead of going to bed as his sickness authorized a belief, he stole into my room where my wife was undressing or in bed. He was repulsed with indignation & menaces of alarm & ran off."[42] Walker claimed that his wife told him about her one-sided love affair in 1784, while Jefferson was in France. There apparently was some truth that Jefferson made overtures to Mrs. Walker when he was a bachelor. What actually happened, however, was swollen by gossipmongers and Jefferson's political enemies. Jefferson scholar Dumas Malone summarized the scandal, "In the absence of other testimony, such an incredible story cannot be accepted in detail. All we can be sure of is that Jefferson made advances of some sort to his friend's wife while he himself was single, that he deeply regretted his actions afterwards, and that he accepted all the blame."[43] Jefferson's friend John Page later attacked Walker's allegations, writing, "Curses on the Tongue of Slander! Perdition seize the wretches who would open the scars of wounded Friendship, to gratify private resnting & party spirit."[44] John Walker died on December 2, 1809, after a brief illness. Jefferson lived nearby but refused to visit his dying childhood friend. He sent a fruit basket instead.

From his headquarters at Morristown, Washington wrote his military secretary, Robert Hanson Harrison, a letter on January 20, 1777, which included the following: "Be so good as to forward the Inclosed to Captn. Hamilton [Capt. Alexander Hamilton of the New York Independent Artillery Company]." Washington's letter to Hamilton no longer exists, but it is believed to be his invitation to join the general's military family.[45] The young artillery officer accepted Washington's invitation and became his aide-de-camp. This was the start of the relationship between Washington and Hamilton, one of the most important and creative associations in American history. A decade later, Washington, as the first president of the United States and Hamilton, as secretary of the treasury, worked together to establish the fiscal policies under which the United States still functions.

The traditional story is that Washington first met Hamilton during the Grand Army's retreat across New Jersey in late 1776. The origin of this legend is George Washington Parke Custis's 1860 book, *Recollections and Private*

Memoirs of Washington. Hamilton was the captain and commanding officer of the Independent New York Artillery Company during the retreat, the only artillery Washington had during his desperate march through the Jersies. According to Custis, the retreating rebels reached New Brunswick, New Jersey, on the west bank of the Raritan River on the afternoon of November 30, 1776, with British troops in hot pursuit. Only the shallow Raritan separated the two armies. An artillery duel followed with Hamilton's battery preventing the enemy from crossing the river. Custis said that General Washington was "charmed by the brilliant courage and admirable skill displayed by a young officer of artillery who directed his battery against the enemy's advanced columns that pressed upon the Americans. The general ordered Lieutenant-Colonel Fitzgerald, his aid-de-camp, to ascertain who this young officer was, and bid him repair to headquarters at the first halt of the army." Custis's imaginative narrative continues with Washington interviewing Hamilton who, "quickly marked him for his own."[46] This charming story has no basis of truth. Washington knew about Hamilton months before the artillery duel along the banks of the Raritan River.

Some historians have speculated that Gen. Henry Knox was behind Hamilton's invitation to join Washington's family. Hamilton had already turned down an invitation to become an aide-de-camp to Knox and another offer from Maj. Gen. Nathanael Greene.[47] Washington's invitation came at a critical moment in Hamilton's fortunes since his artillery company had been reduced to two officers and thirty men as a result of battle casualties, desertions, and expiration of terms of enlistment.[48] His artillery company, which was a New York state outfit, could have been dissolved at any moment.

We are fortunate to have several good descriptions of Hamilton's appearance at the time. One account described him as "under middle size, thin in person, but remarkably erect and dignified in his deportment. His hair was turned back from his forehead, powdered, and collected in a club behind. His complexion was exceedingly fair, and varying from this only by the almost feminine rosiness of his cheeks. His might be considered, as to figure and color, an uncommonly handsome face . . . When he entered a room it was apparent, from the respectful attention of the company, that he was a distinguished person."[49]

Capt. Alexander Graydon recalled meeting Hamilton at Morristown during the spring of 1777 and left us this description: "I had the pleasure of knowing Colonel Hamilton. He presided at the General's table, where we dined; and in a large company in which there were several ladies, among whom I recollect one or two of the Miss Livingstons [daughters of William Livingston, the governor of New Jersey] and a Miss Brown, he acquitted himself with an ease, propriety and vivacity, which gave me the most favorable impression of his talents and accomplishments."[50]

Hamilton rarely mentioned anything about his parents and childhood but his later political enemies were quick to provide the information. John Adams, for one, despised Hamilton, calling him "the Creole" and "that bastard son of an Irish peddler." Adams was correct about Hamilton's origins; he was an illegitimate child. He was born in a modest waterfront house in Charlestown on the Caribbean island of Nevis. In Hamilton's day, Nevis had a population of some 700 white settlers and 10,000 blacks, who were held in slavery under barbarous conditions. Hamilton's date of birth is believed to be January 11, 1755.[51] His mother was Rachel Faucett, who was born on the island of St. Croix, probably of Huguenot extraction. Alexander's father, James Hamilton, was about ten years older than Rachel and described as a charming, ne'er-do-well Scotsman; a drifter who was seeking his fortune in the Caribbean. James deserted Rachel shortly after the birth of Alexander. He was the second of two boys Rachel had with James Hamilton. To complicate matters further, at the time of Alexander's birth, his mother was still legally married to a small-time businessman named John Michael Lavien, who resided in St. Croix.[52] Lavien instituted divorce proceedings against Rachael in February 1759, claiming his wife was "shameless, rude and ungodly." He produced three witnesses who said she had "given herself up to whoring with everyone."[53]

Rachel raised her sons until her death in 1768 from yellow fever, leaving her children with no money and a scant education. Her oldest son, James, became a carpenter's apprentice and young Alexander found work in the offices of the island's merchants. In time a group of St. Croix businessmen were impressed with young Alexander's intelligence and sponsored his further education in America. Hamilton arrived in New York in 1772. He prepared for college by studying under Dr. Francis Barber, who was the principal of the Elizabethtown Academy located in Elizabethtown, New Jersey.[54] Hamilton was accepted at the College of New Jersey but he preferred to attend King's College (a nonsectarian school founded in 1754 and renamed Columbia College in 1784) in New York City.[55] Hamilton probably decided to attend King's College because he loved city life and the isolated village of Princeton held little appeal to him. Hamilton was either sixteen or seventeen years old when he entered college. His original intent was to study medicine, but he soon abandoned his plans to become a doctor.[56]

Hamilton entered college burning with ambition and determined to leave behind his blighted childhood. He found a perfect outlet for his ambition and desire to make new and powerful friends in the growing controversy between the thirteen colonies and Great Britain. Hamilton was brilliant and, as a young college student, he wrote pamphlets espousing the rights of the colonists. His writings brought him to the attention of the leaders of the protests against Britain especially in his adopted New York State. When some of the students at King's College organized themselves into a military company, young Hamilton joined them. They made the transition from students to soldiers with the help of their commander, Capt. Thomas Fleming, a former adjutant in the British Army.[57] Hamilton and his fellow college students drilled every morning in St. George's churchyard, where they maneuvered among the graves for "a considerable time."[58] At the outbreak of the war, Hamilton left school and joined the Independent New York Artillery Company where he was named a captain. He never returned to college and is referred to as Columbia University's most famous dropout.

Hamilton was named aide-de-camp on March 1, 1777. The traditional view is that he was the most important of Washington's Revolutionary War aides. This is incorrect. Hamilton was Washington's best known aide, and he probably was the most intelligent and dynamic person to work at headquarters. His fellow aide, Robert Hanson Harrison, recognized his great energy and skills and nicknamed him, "the little lion."[59] Hamilton's arrival on the scene in 1777 marked the beginning of a diverse and brilliant headquarters team that was of immense help to Washington throughout much of the rest of the war. This brilliant cadre worked together with Washington from 1777 until 1781. It consisted of Robert Hanson Harrison, Tench Tilghman, and Alexander Hamilton. These three men were the cornerstones of Washington's personal staff. They served the longest of any of the aides. Other good men worked alongside them at headquarters, but these three were the most important and probably hardest working men on Washington's staff. Harrison's specialty was administration. He could be counted on to keep the routine functions of the army operating smoothly if Washington was away. Harrison was also the best of all of the aides at communicating Washington's ideas. The general frequently entrusted Harrison to write to Congress on his behalf. Hamilton's strengths included initiative. He did his share of routine headquarters work, but Washington tended to use him more for important military and political missions where superior intelligence, quick thinking, and aggressiveness were necessary. Washington recognized Hamilton's superior intelligence and kept him at headquarters long after the young man wanted to command troops in battle. The third member of the team was Tilghman. He was probably the best all-round aide that Washington had during the war. Congressman James Duane said, "he had a penetrating intellect that flies like an arrow from a bow."[60] Washington respected Tilghman, and they enjoyed an excellent working relationship and a close friendship. Washington also seemed to be on friendly terms with Harrison. However he had a different kind of relationship with Hamilton. Washington respected Hamilton's intelligence and abilities, and entrusted him with tasks that he would give few others. The two men worked closely together but they never had the same warm and congenial relationship that Washington had with Tilghman and Harrison.

Some misconceptions have evolved around Hamilton because he is believed to be representative of Washington's staff. For example, Hamilton's youth at the time of his appointment as an aide has resulted in the assumption by historians that all of Washington's aides were young men. This is not correct. Although Washington's aides were sometimes referred to as "the beardless boys," the majority of them were established, mature men when they joined the staff. Hamilton was the youngest person to be appointed as an aide-de-camp. Because of the uncertainty of his year of birth, Hamilton could have been as young as nineteen years old when he joined Washington's staff. More probably, he was twenty-one. The average age of Washington's aides at the time of their appointments, however, was older. Harrison, who was thirty when he joined the headquarters, was the subject of much teasing by the other aides because of his age. They called him the "old secretary" or the "ancient secretary." They also made fun of him because they knew that he was often troubled with hemorrhoids aggravated by the long workday.[61]

Harrison, however, was not the oldest of Washington's aides, Tench Tilghman was thirty-two when he arrived at headquarters, John Fitzgerald (whose date of birth is unknown) was probably about thirty-four, William Grayson and Joseph Reed were thirty-four, and John Moylan was thirty-eight. By comparison, Washington was forty-three years old when he was appointed commander in chief in 1775.

Hamilton was fluent in French, which was helpful at headquarters. There is evidence, however, that at least one other member of Washington's staff at the time, Tench Tilghman, was also conversant in French though his level of translating the language seems to have been well below that of Hamilton's.[62] There was little need for Washington to have someone who understood French during the early part of the war. But by 1777 Washington needed someone who spoke fluent French because French officers began arriving in America seeking commissions in the Continental Army. Some of them even arrived with promises of high rank from Silas Deane, who was one of the American commissioners to France.[63] Most of these French officers spoke little or no English, and Congress, bewildered by these foreign officers, forwarded them to Washington's headquarters for disposition. Washington had to sort through these men and decide which of them could be of real service to his novice army. The commander in chief must have been happy to have Hamilton and perhaps Tilghman on hand to communicate with these French officers who were invading his headquarters.

Another of young Hamilton's characteristics was that he was ambitious. Unlike Washington's other aides, Hamilton had no wide circle of family, friends, and business acquaintances to help his career. Harrison and Tilghman, for example, were from distinguished, wealthy families and already established in their careers when they joined Washington's staff. As a result, Hamilton probably was more ambitious than any of Washington's other aides. An excellent opportunity arose for Hamilton to build his reputation soon after he joined Washington's staff.

The story begins when the New York State Provincial Convention appointed a committee of correspondence that was instructed to get regular news reports from Washington's headquarters. The committee needed someone at headquarters who was well informed and willing to cooperate with them. One of Washington's aides-de-camp was the logical choice for the job and with His Excellency's blessing, the New Yorkers approached Tench Tilghman. The

Marylander agreed to help but he was very busy and was only able to write them sporadically. However, the reports Tilghman submitted included some remarkable details. In October 1776, for example, the British tried to surround Washington's army by landing troops in the Bronx. Washington countered by abandoning his positions on Manhattan Island (with the exception of Fort Washington) and moving his forces into Westchester County, New York, to meet the threat. Tilghman wrote the New York committee a report dealing with these maneuvers. Here is an excerpt from his letter which is dated October 22, 1776:

> We are so constantly on the move that I am obliged to write when I can find an opportunity. We shall take up our lodging at White Plains this evening, which the General intends to make his headquarters for the present. The enemy are endeavoring still to outflank us, and we are moving rather ahead of them. Early yesterday morning an advanced party, consisting of Rogers Rangers, took possession of Mamaroneck, which our militia abandoned with the utmost precipitation as usual. The General rode up to White Plains to take a view of the country and hearing of this party laid a plan to cut them off. He accordingly detached Major Green of Virginia with one hundred and fifty men of the First and Third Virginia Regiments, and Colonel Hazlet of Delaware, with six hundred men to support them. They attacked Rogers about daybreak, put the party to flight, brought in thirty-six prisoners, sixty arms, and a good many blankets, and had not the guides undertook to alter the first disposition, Major Rogers and his party of four hundred, would in all probability have fallen into our hands.[64]

Tilghman's most dramatic letter to the New York committee was written on November 17, 1776. It reported on the calumnious loss of Fort Washington the previous day and the capture of over 2,700 American troops. Note that Tilghman held his boss blameless for the catastrophe, naming Gen. Nathanael Greene responsible for the disaster:

> I wish I had better news to communicate, but we suffered a heavy stroke yesterday in the loss of Fort Washington and its garrison, consisting of about two thousand men, [Tilghman was either misinformed about the American losses or purposely reduced the number] who chiefly were made prisoners of war; what were not, fell in the action. The lines were bravely defended; but what could a few thousand men do against General Howe's whole Army, who poured in upon them from every quarter? The loss of the post is nothing compared to the loss of men and arms, and the damp it will strike upon the minds of many. We were in a fair way of finishing the campaign

with credit to ourselves, and I think to the disgrace of Mr. Howe, and had the General followed his own opinion, the garrison would have been withdrawn immediately upon the enemy's failing down from Dobbs Ferry. But General Greene was positive that our forces might at any time be drawn off under the guns of Fort Lee [Tilghman is showing his loyalty to Washington who could have overruled Greene and evacuated Fort Washington before it was surrounded by the British]. Fatal experience has evinced the contrary. Whether the enemy will make any other move this season, is matter of speculation. We are posting the Army on this side the river [New Jersey], along from Newark to Amboy [modern Perth Amboy, New Jersey] as places easy of communication with each other, and through which the enemy must pass, if Philadelphia or any place southward is their aim. . . . I shall continue to write to you as I find opportunity.

> . . . I am, dear sir, yours,
> Tench Tilghman[65]

Once the New York Committee of Safety learned of Hamilton's appointment, they approached him to replace Tilghman as their army correspondent. They considered Hamilton to be a New Yorker because of his tenure at King's College and service as a captain in their Independent Artillery Company. Hamilton was busy but accepted their offer. He was happy with the arrangement because it gave him access to the political leaders of New York State. Hamilton wrote them on March 20, 1777, accepting their offer:

With cheerfulness, I embrace the proposal of corresponding with your convention, through you: and shall from time to time as far as my leisure will permit, and my duty warrant, communicate such transactions as shall happen, such pieces of intelligence as shall be received and such comments upon them as shall appear necessary, to convey a true idea of what is going on in the military line.[66]

Hamilton's energy seemed endless because he sent the New York committee frequent reports from headquarters while performing his regular duties as Washington's aide-de-camp. For example, writing from Morristown, Hamilton began a report to the committee by saying, "Extreme hurry of business puts it out of my power to say but very little." He went on, however, to give his correspondents a lengthy news report from headquarters:

Your information concerning a piece of ordnance lately constructed at Philadelphia is true. There is such a piece at Head Quarters . . . As to the ships opposite Fort Washington, The General first supposed they might be intended to make a descent on the Jersey side and come by surprise on our left flank; but he now considers it wholly as an amusement . . .Troops coming on from the southward. We are told there are 2000 Carolinians, far on the way to Philadelphia—a part arrived.[67]

Washington made another important addition to his staff during the first months of 1777 to replace the men who had left to command the newly established regiments. The addition was Richard Kidder Meade, who joined the general's family in March 1777. His appointment was mentioned in the general orders dated, "Head-Quarters, Morristown, March 12, 1777, . . . Richard Kidder Meade Esqr. appointed Aide-De-Camp to the Commander in Chief, and is to be respected and obeyed as such."[68]

Meade was born in Nansemond County, Virginia, and was thirty-one years old at the time of his appointment. He was the son of David Meade and his wife Susannah, daughter of Richard Everard, the governor of North Carolina. Meade was educated in England at Harrow School, Harrow, Middlesex. This school is, with Eton and Winchester, one of the oldest and most famous schools in England. Meade probably studied elsewhere in England as well. A school at Dalston and/or a small private school at Drafton in Hackney parish are mentioned as the two most likely locations.[69] This young Virginian was not a scholar, but a strong and rugged outdoorsman and an excellent horseman. His previous military service was as a captain in the 2nd Virginia Regiment with his commission dating from October 24, 1775.[70] Meade was intelligent and resourceful and was accomplished at composing letters or orders for Washington. Because Meade was an expert horseman, he was frequently used by Washington to deliver important dispatches and orders. Meade was married twice. His first wife was Jane Randolph of "Curles," aunt of John Randolph of Roanoke. She died sometime before 1780. Meade's second wife was Mary Fitzhugh Grymes Randolph, the widow of William Randolph of "Chatsworth." Meade was particularly friendly with his fellow aide Alexander Hamilton who wrote him toward the end of the war when he lived in New York and Meade in Virginia, "Truly My Dear Meade, I often regret that fortune has cast our residence at such a distance from each other. It would be a serious addition to my happiness if we lived where I could see you every day but fate has determined it otherwise."[71]

With the addition of Hamilton and Meade in early 1777 stability returned to the headquarters staff and there would be no changes of personnel until the fall of that year. Washington's staff reached its authorized complement of one military secretary (Harrison) and four aides-de-camp (Fitzgerald, Hamilton, Meade, and Johnston). In addition there was Captain Gibbs of the Commander in Chief's Guard and one volunteer aide (Tilghman). Historian Washington Irving described the general's military family at the time. He called Richard Kidder Meade and Tench Tilghman, "gentlemen of gallant spirit, amiable tempers, and cultivated manners." Washington's secretary, Robert Hanson Harrison, he called "the 'old secretary'" as he was familiarly called among his associates, and by whom he was described as 'one in whom every man had confidence, and by whom no man was deceived.'"[72]

We have an excellent eyewitness account of Washington's staff at the time. The account was written by Mrs. Theodorick Bland who spent two months at Morristown in the spring of 1777. She often saw Washington's aides during her stay at Morristown and described them in a letter to her sister:

> his aid de camps . . . are Col. Fitzgerald, an agreeable broad-shouldered Irishman—Col. Johnston . . . who is exceedingly witty at everybody's expense but can't allow other people to be so at his own, though they often take the liberty—Col. Hamilton, a sensible, genteel, polite young fellow, a West Indian—Col. Meade—Col. Tilghman, a modest worthy man who, from his attachment to the General lives in his family and acts in any capacity that is uppermost, without fee or reward—Col. Harrison, brother of Billy Harrison that kept store in Petersburg and as much like him as possible, a worthy man— Capt. Gibbs of the General's Guard, a good natured Yankee who makes a thousand blunders in the Yankee style and keeps the dinner table in constant laughter.[73]

Mrs. Bland told her sister that if there was no pressing business at headquarters, the dinner meal was followed by riding parties in the late afternoon. Washington enjoyed these excursions and participated in them whenever possible. The general was a physically active person and there is one eyewitness account of him throwing around a leather ball with some of his aides-de-camp for exercise.[74] The aides also had some time for socializing during this lull in the fighting. Capt. Alexander Graydon, for example, mentioned being entertained by Tilghman and Hamilton who took him to drink tea with some of the ladies of the village.[75]

There was also time at the Morristown encampment to pursue romantic interests. Hamilton in particular was noted as a ladies' man. A glimpse into his reputation is reflected in the fact that Martha Washington named a large, lusty tomcat that lived at headquarters "Hamilton."[76] Colonel Hamilton courted Catharine Livingston during the winter at Morristown. She was the daughter of William Livingston, the popular governor of New Jersey. Hamilton lived with the Livingstons at their Elizabethtown home soon after he arrived in America, and knew the family well. He recalled that Catharine was interested in politics and he began his letter to her of April 11, 1777, offering to be her "political correspondent." Hamilton's letter to Miss Livingston is a beautiful example of his writing style:

> Though I am perfectly willing to harmonize with your inclination, in this respect, without making the cynical inquiry, whether it proceed from sympathy in the concerns of the public, or merely from female

curiosity, yet I will not consent to be limited to any particular subject. I challenge you to meet me in whatever path you dare; and if you have no objection, for variety and amusement, we will even sometimes make excursions in the flowery walks, and roseate bowers of Cupid. You know, I am renowned for gallantry, and shall always be able to entertain you with a choice collection of the prettiest things imaginable.

But amidst my amorous transports, let me not forget, that I am also to perform the part of a politician and intelligence. This however will not take up much time, as the present situation of things gives birth to very little worth notice, though it seems pregnant with something of importance. The enemy, from some late movements, appear to be brooding mischief, which must soon break out.[77]

From his position at headquarters Hamilton knew what was happening. He was informed about reports from American spies operating in New York City that the British were planning a big offensive for the spring, probably aimed at capturing the rebel capital at Philadelphia. There were also reports that a second British army under Gen. John Burgoyne was preparing to move south from British-held Canada. Washington wanted to move his army where he could watch the British closer and be in a better position to defend either Philadelphia or the Hudson River. With this in mind on May 28, 1777, the main army marched south from Morristown to Middlebrook, New Jersey, where it established itself in an excellent defensive position atop the ridges of the Watchung Mountains. The flat plains of central New Jersey lay below them. The British were reluctant to move across New Jersey to attack Philadelphia because Washington could swoop down from the mountains to cut their communications and supply lines. In mid-June 1777 General Howe marched his army out of New Brunswick to get closer to Washington's forces. The British general was looking for a decisive battle. An early historian of the American Revolution, Mercy Otis Warren, described how Washington declined to accept Howe's invitation to a battle:

> Confident of his success from his superior numbers in the field, general Howe for a time, exercised all the artifices of an experienced commander, to bring general Washington to a decisive engagement: but, from a perfect command of his temper, and a judicious arrangement of the few continental troops, and militia . . . the American chieftain defeated every measure practiced to bring him to a general action.[78]

Joseph Reed apparently kept a low profile following Washington's accidental discovery of his clandestine correspondence with Gen. Charles Lee. Reed resigned as adjutant general on January 13, 1777, and his replacement

(Col. George Weedon) was named the same day. Reed quickly realized his poor judgment in criticizing Washington and taking up with the busybody Charles Lee. Adding to his predicament was Washington's growing reputation following his stunning victories at Trenton and Princeton as opposed to Lee's ignominious capture by British cavalry at a New Jersey brothel. Reed tried to mend his damaged relationship with Washington and wrote him several apologetic letters, including one written on March 8, 1777: "I could have wish'd to have had one Hour of private Conversation with you on the Subject of a Letter wrote me by General Lee before his Captivity . . . I most solemnly assure you that you would see nothing in it inconsistent with the Respect & Affection which I have & ever shall bear to your Person and Character."[79]

His letters to Washington culminated in the following plea on June 4, 1777, which was delivered to the general in the field. Reed's letter was a far cry from his aloofness of the previous year:

> I am sensible, my dear Sir, how difficult it is to regain lost Friendship . . . let me intreat you to judge of me by Realities not by Appearances . . . A late Perusal of the Letters you honoured me with at Cambridge & New York, last Year, afforded me a melancholy Pleasure. I cannot help acknowledging myself deeply affected, in a Comparison with those which I have since received . . . May God Almighty crown your Virtue my dr & much respected General with deserved Success & make your Life as happy & honorable to yourself as it has been useful to your Country.[80]

With the enemy nearby there was little time to spare to answer Reed's letter. But Washington told the courier who brought the letter to wait while he composed a hasty reply. The general told his former military secretary and confidant,

> True it is, I felt myself hurt by a certain letter, which appeared at that time to be the echo of one from you. I was hurt, not because I thought my judgement wronged by the expressions contained in it, but because the same sentiments were not communicated immediately to myself. The favorable manner in which your opinion, upon all occasions, had been received, the impressions they made, and the unreserved manner in which I wished and required them to be given, entitled me, I thought, to your advice upon any point in which I appeared to be wanting . . . However, I am perfectly satisfied that matters were not as they appeared from the letter alluded to.[81]

Washington was a seasoned politician and he remained on friendly terms with Reed, who was active in politics. However, their relationship was never the same. Reed served as a volunteer aide-de-camp to Washington at various times during 1777 and 1778. Apparently Reed saw action at the battle of Monmouth because his wife wrote a friend on July 6, 1778, from Flemington, New Jersey, "I must also congratulate you on our success at Monmouth, and that our state is free from our cruel enemy . . . My dear Mr. Reed was in the action, and had his horse again shot; this is the third time the same circumstance has happened, and himself unhurt."[82] Reed went on to become a member of the Continental Congress and governor of Pennsylvania. In 1781, following his term as governor, he retired from public life and returned to his law practice. Perhaps his sudden departure from public life was because of the untimely death of his beloved wife Esther who died on September 18, 1780, at the age of thirty-four.[83] Reed had a creditable career but who knows what he would have achieved had he been loyal to Washington.[84] Reed was actually right; Washington had blundered at Fort Washington. The post should have been evacuated long before the British overran it, but Reed did a poor job in directing his feelings. Reed sought to make amends, but he remained somewhat critical of Washington and their relationship was cool and formal for the rest of the war.

Having finished his letter to Reed, Washington returned to the tense military situation in New Jersey. General Howe broke contact with Washington's Grand Army and returned to his base at New Brunswick. After some additional maneuvering in central New Jersey, which failed to bring Washington out of his mountain stronghold, Howe embarked his army onto ships and sailed out into the Atlantic. We turn again to Mrs. Mercy Warren to continue the story. She explained that there was a general anxiety until the later part of August, "when the fleet appeared in the Chesapeak, and the army soon after landed at the head of the river Elk [Maryland]. . . . It was now obvious, that the possession of the city of Philadelphia was the stake for which both armies played."[85] Hamilton reported the British landing to the New York committee of correspondence: "General Howes . . . has landed his whole army within about four miles from the head of Elk." Hamilton went on to explain why Howe's army seemed motionless following their embarkation from their ships: "He still lies there in a state of inactivity; in a great measure I believe from the want of horses, to transport his baggage and stores. It seems he sailed with only about three weeks provender and was six at sea. This has occasioned the death of a great number of his horses, and has made skeletons of the rest."[86]

Washington marched his army through Philadelphia on August 24, 1777, to take a defensive position south of the capital. A knowledgeable onlooker would have noticed a new member in Washington's suite as it marched through Philadelphia—Col. Peter Presley Thornton. Thornton is first mentioned as an aide in a private letter that the general wrote to his brother John Augustine dated August 5, 1777: "I have taken Colo. P.P. Thornton into my Family as an extra Aid; this, I dare say his own merit, as well as the great worth of his Father, well entitles him to."[87] Peter Presley Thornton's father was Presley Thornton another of Washington's prewar friends and a fellow member of the Virginia House of Burgesses. Thornton is the most confusing of Washington's aides-de-camp to accurately delineate. This is because he is often mistaken for his father whose name was Presley Thornton and his brother, who was also named Presley Thornton.

Peter Presley Thornton was born in Northumberland County, Virginia, and was twenty-six years old when he joined Washington's staff. Nothing is known about his education. He represented Northumberland County in the House of Burgesses in 1772 and 1774. He was also a delegate to the Virginia Convention in July 1775. Thornton married Sarah Throckmorton in 1771 and they had at least three children. His credentials for being appointed to Washington's staff were his political and family connections in Virginia. He had some military experience as well. At the start of the Revolution, Thornton joined the Lancaster (Virginia) District Battalion of militia, and he was named a cornet in the 3rd Continental Dragoons in February 1777. Thornton's appointment as Washington's aide, together with John Laurens, is included in the general orders for September 6, 1777: "John Laurens and Peter Presly Thornton Esqrs. are appointed Extra Aids du Camp to the Commander in Chief; all orders therefore thro' them in writing, or otherwise, are to be regarding in the same light as if proceeding from any other of his Aides due Camp."[88]

It is at this point in the war that some historians incorrectly state that Col. Charles Cotesworth Pinckney (1745–1825) joined Washington's staff as an aide-de-camp.[89] Pinckney had all the credentials to be on Washington's staff including family pedigree, European education followed by a successful law practice in South Carolina, and military service from the outset of the war. No documentation has been found, however, to support the claim that he was ever appointed as one of Washington's aides.

On September 6, 1777, however, another South Carolinian did join Washington's family as a volunteer aide-de-camp. His name was John Laurens, and his background and European education rivaled Pinckney's.[90] Laurens proved to be as passionate and reckless as another of Washington's young aides, Alexander Hamilton. Hamilton and Laurens quickly became intimate friends. Hamilton saw Laurens as his role model. Despite the conservative temperament of the other thirty men who served as Washington's aides during the Revolution, Laurens and Hamilton offset them with their impulsive swashbuckling deeds and ancient code of honor. Young Laurens told his father, for example, in a letter, "You ask me, my Dear Father what bounds I have set to my desire of serving my Country in the Military Line—I answer glorious Death, or the Triumph of the Cause in which I am engaged."[91]

John Laurens was the son of Henry and Eleanor Laurens of Charleston, South Carolina. His mother Eleanor was a member of the distinguished Ball family of South Carolina. She married Henry Laurens in 1750, when she was nineteen years old. Henry Laurens was twenty-six years old at the time of his marriage and on his way to becoming one of the richest men in America. His self-made fortune came from plantations cultivated by large numbers of black slaves. Their marriage produced twelve children but only two sons and two daughters reached adulthood. John was their fourth child and the first to reach maturity.[92] He was born on October 28, 1754, and his early education was by private tutors employed under his father's watchful eye. Young Laurens was tutored in French, classical literature, mathematics, surveying, mechanics, and drawing. John was sixteen years old when his mother died in 1771. She was forty years old when she died and Henry thought constantly of his wife's dying words, "I know you Love me, I know you will take care of your Children."[93] Eleanor wanted her children to have a good education and heeding his wife's last wishes, Henry decided to accompany his eldest son to Europe to personally arrange for his higher education. They lived for a while in London where John was privately tutored by the Reverend Richard Clark, the former pastor of St. Philip's Church in Charleston. Henry subsequently settled upon Geneva, Switzerland, for the education of his son. Geneva was the world's greatest center of learning at the time and its superior education system attracted students from many countries. Henry returned to South Carolina while his eldest son remained in Geneva and was soon moving in the city's highest social circles. John spent more than two years in school in Geneva, and it is ironic that Henry Laurens, whose fortune was built on slave labor, chose to give his son the most progressive and liberal education then available. Influenced by the humanitarian ideas he was exposed to in Geneva, John Laurens became an ardent opponent to slavery. Young Laurens next returned to London where he was admitted to the Inns of Court, Middle Temple, on September 16, 1772, and began to read law.

The start of the American Revolution found Laurens studying law in London. He passionately wanted to return to America and join the Continental Army especially after reading Thomas Paine's pamphlet *Common Sense,* which had been published in England. War news and reports from home excited him, including a letter from his father announcing that the colonists had declared their independence from Great Britain. Henry wrote his son from Charleston, "On the 2d of August—A Courier arrived from Philadelphia & brought a Declaration of the 4th July by the Representatives of the 13 United Colonies in Congress, that the Colonies should be 'Free & Independent States.'"[94] Henry, however, was fearful for his son's life should he return home and join the army. He instructed John to continue his law education in London. The next event in young Laurens's life was his marriage in October 1776, but he was strangely secretive about the event. In 1846 historian and storyteller G. W. Parke Custis gave his account of Laurens's marriage in response to an inquiry by a publisher:

> Colonel Laurens was educated in England, as were most of the young Carolinians of fortune and family in the olden time, and had married a Miss Manning, the daughter of the Lieutenant Governor of the Bank of England, when the troubles between the Mother Country and the Colonies, commenced. Knowing the ardor of young Laurens in the cause of liberty and his native land, his English friends and

connections were very desirous of preventing his return to America, well knowing the part that he would take in the approaching contest. His father-in-law offered him a check for 10,000 guineas, if he would give his word of honor, not to leave British shores. Laurens rejected the offer with disdain, and though closely watched, succeeded in concealing himself among the ballast of a ship bound to America, and safely reached his native land.[95]

This was the romantic nineteenth-century explanation of Laurens's sudden marriage. The truth, however, was much less charming; Laurens led an active social life while he was in London and he got a young woman named Martha Manning pregnant and agreed to marry her. John finally prevailed in his quest to return home and left England in December 1776, leaving his pregnant wife behind. She gave birth to a daughter whom Laurens may have seen when he traveled to France later in the war. We are not certain that he ever saw his wife again; she died at Lille, France, in 1781. His comment on the whole sordid affair was, "Pity obliged me to marry."[96]

Laurens set out for America accompanied by a young Pennsylvanian named John White who also wanted to return home to join the Continental Army. Because of the war, the two Americans were unable to sail directly home from England. They went to France in early January 1777 to find a ship that would take them across the Atlantic. They stopped briefly in Paris where they met Benjamin Franklin. Their odyssey next took them to the port city of Bordeaux where they were able to get passage on a ship bound for the French West Indies. From there they were certain they would find a ship that would take them to an American port. When two days out of Bordeaux, off Cape Ortegal, their neutral French ship was stopped and her papers searched by a boarding party from the Royal Navy frigate *Thetis*. The British officers plainly recognized Laurens and White as Americans, but took no further notice of them while the two young men remained silent and apprehensive throughout the ordeal. Their ship was allowed to continue on its way. From Cape François in the French West Indies Laurens and White decided to travel the rest of the way on the *Rattle Snake,* a schooner belonging to South Carolina's navy. Once at sea the *Rattle Snake* was chased by two Royal Navy brigantines. But the fast American schooner evaded capture and arrived at Charleston on April 15, 1777, without further incident. After an absence of almost six years, John Laurens had returned home.[97] John White immediately joined the Continental Army as a volunteer aide-de-camp to Gen. John Sullivan and was killed in action before the year was over.[98] Henry Laurens believed that an appointment as Washington's aide-de-camp was a place of safety and honor for his eldest son. He reasoned that John would be satisfied working at army headquarters and arranged for him to be recommended to General Washington by John Rutledge, president of the South Carolina General Assembly. Young Laurens promptly received an invitation from Washington to join his staff as a volunteer aide-de-camp. Washington's cordial letter of invitation to Laurens was written from the City Tavern in Philadelphia, August 5, 1777, and reads in part,

> For reasons unnecessary to mention, I mean to delay the actual Appointment of my fourth Aide de Camp a while longer; but if you will do me the honor to become a member of my Family, you will make me very happy, by your Company and assistance in that Line as an Extra Aid, and I shall be glad to receive you in that capacity whenever it is convenient to you.[99]

The "reasons unnecessary to mention" was probably Washington's sensitivity to the grave illness of his aide George Johnston, who was Harrison's brother-in-law. Washington did not want to make it appear that he felt Johnston was already dead by appointing Laurens as his replacement.

John Laurens's father, Henry, was a delegate to the Continental Congress at the time of his son's appointment to Washington's staff. Apparently Henry did not know Washington at the time because he wrote John Rutledge, who was the president of the South Carolina assembly, thanking him for getting his son the appointment. The elder Laurens wrote Rutledge from Philadelphia on August 12, 1777, "My Son is now of the General's family & has I presume acknowledged his obligation to your Excellency in the Letter which will accompany this." Henry went on to express his disappointment in his son's decision to join the army: "I wish he had made a choice for his outset in Life in a sphere in which he might have been more extensively useful to his Country."[100] Henry Laurens also expressed his disappointment with his son's decision in a letter to John Lewis Gervais from Philadelphia on August 5, 1777. Laurens's comments are included here to show the high expectation he had for his son and to mark the beginning of an important association among John Laurens, Henry Laurens, and George Washington:

> This morning Mr. John Laurens . . . joined Gen.~ Washington at head Quarters near German Town as one of his family. . . . My heart was too full at parting & would not allow me to enquire into particulars . . . to tell you truly my Sense of this matter—although I believe the Young Man will acquit himSelf well any where, yet I am persuaded he has made an indiscreet choice for his outset in life . . . his Talents & his diligence would have enabled him to have been much more extensively & essentially useful to his Country in a different line at the same time to have been the Cement of mine & the builder of a new family. . . . As a Soldier One Man can act only as one (very few Cases excepted) & in point of real usefulness will often be excelled by Men of moderate abilities & better nerves . . . from this persuasion you will know that I am not perfectly happy under this event, but tis Man's part to bear disappointment with patience.[101]

The first known letter that John Laurens composed for Washington appears a few days after he arrived at headquarters. The letter is dated August 13, 1777, and it is addressed to Gov. George Clinton of New York. Laurens must have spent a few days training at headquarters, or the letter was dictated to him by Washington, because his first letter has the same characteristics as all of the general's official correspondence; respectfulness, good organization, in a clearly worded style. To illustrate the point, here is an excerpt from Laurens's first letter: "You are the best Judge with respect to the length of service to be required from the Militia; however as their assistance is a Resource which must be sparingly employed I would have them detained no longer than is absolutely necessary."[102]

Once at headquarters, he met his fellow member of Washington's military family, Alexander Hamilton. They had similar personalities and quickly became close friends. Hamilton admired Laurens for his wealth, education, polished manners, and European travels. Both were romantics who viewed the Revolution as a mission to defend the liberties of mankind and as a way of attaining personal glory.

Henry Laurens was sadly mistaken if he thought that a staff position in General Washington's military family would keep his son out of danger. Laurens and Hamilton operated as a team. Together they got into the thick of battles, fought duels, defended Washington against his political enemies, and worked to enlist black slaves into the Continental Army.

The summer of 1777 also witnessed the addition of an officer who would become a household name in America: Marie-Joseph-Paul-Yves-Roch-Gilbert du Motier, marquis de Lafayette. Lafayette was born in France on September 6, 1757. His father was killed in the battle of Minden two years later. His mother died in 1770, after which the young nobleman inherited a large fortune from his grandfather. Lafayette wanted to be a soldier like his father, and his military career started at the age of fourteen when he was appointed a junior officer in the King's Musketeers. He was stationed with his regiment at Metz, France, where he attended a dinner in 1775 at which the duke of Gloucester spoke about the revolt of the American colonists. The young Lafayette became interested in the rebellion, and on December 7 he signed an agreement with Silas Deane in Paris to serve as a major general in the Continental Army. Lafayette bought a ship named *La Victoire* and on April 20, 1776, sailed for America in the company of fifteen other European officers, arriving in Charleston, South Carolina, on June 13. He traveled overland to Philadelphia, where he arrived on July 27, and promptly reported to the president of the Continental Congress.

A few days later, on July 31, 1777, the Continental Congress confirmed his appointment stating,

> Whereas, the marquis de la Fayette, out of his great zeal to the cause
> of liberty, in which the United States are engaged, has left his family
> and connexions, and, at his own expense, come over to offer his service

to the United States, without pension or particular allowance, and is anxious to risque his life in our cause: Resolved, That his service be accepted, and that, in consideration of his zeal, illustrious family and connexions, he have the rank and commission of major general in the army of the United States.[103]

Lafayette was never an aide-de-camp to Washington. His appointment, as stated in his commission from Congress, was as a line officer commanding troops in the field. Lafayette served as a volunteer at headquarters until a division of Virginia troops was assigned to him in December 1777.[104] At the time that Lafayette is supposed to have been an aide-de-camp to Washington, he had his own aides-de-camp working for him![105] He became good friends with several of Washington's aides especially Tilghman, Hamilton, and Laurens, all of whom spoke French and helped Lafayette improve his English.

Despite the fondness that Washington had for a number of his aides-de-camp, none came close to the general's special relationship with Lafayette. The young Frenchman was in Washington's inner circle and he become the general's confidant. If Joseph Reed's friendship with Washington was cut short early, Washington's relationship with Lafayette grew and blossomed through the balance of the war and beyond.

After arriving south of Philadelphia, Washington undertook his own reconnaissance of the enemy on August 26, accompanied only by Generals Greene and Lafayette and their aides-de-camp. Washington got within two miles of the enemy camp near Cecil Courthouse, Maryland. From a hilltop he could see the British tents. A severe storm prevented the American scouting party from returning to the safety of their army. Washington took refuge in a farmhouse where he decided to spend the night. It was a dangerous place, close to the enemy, in a house known to be owned by a British sympathizer. His suite stood on guard through the night and they returned to the American camp the next morning. When he departed at dawn, Washington admitted that a single traitor could have betrayed him.[106]

On August 28, Howe broke camp and began to advance cautiously toward the rebel capital at Philadelphia. The two armies maneuvered for some days until two o'clock on the morning of September 9, when Washington began to move to Chadds Ford on Brandywine Creek. Howe assembled his forces at nearby Kennett Square, Pennsylvania, on September 10. The scene was set for the battle of Brandywine.

The battle of Brandywine, fought on September 11, 1777, was another defeat for Washington as his adversary, General Howe, successfully used the same strategy he had used the previous year at the battle of Long Island. Howe ordered part of his army to make a demonstration in front of the Americans while a powerful force secretly moved north along Brandywine Creek, crossed the stream, marched back downriver, and struck the American right flank. After fierce fighting Washington's forces withdrew with most of their units disorganized. Washington's newly appointed aide John Laurens was on the battlefield. Lafayette saw young Laurens and wrote his father about him, "it was not his fault that he was not killed or wounded[,] he did every thing that was necessary to procure one or t'other."[107]

Washington reorganized his army the following day and continued his efforts to defend Philadelphia. He maneuvered his army about ten miles west of Philadelphia and began skirmishing with the British on the morning of September 16. A general engagement was in the making when the clouds erupted in a torrential rainstorm that flooded roads, reduced visibility, and rendered rain-soaked weapons and ammunition useless. General Howe ordered his army to make camp while Washington decided to withdraw to Yellow Springs, Pennsylvania. John Laurens later wrote his father about the incident, which includes references to his uniform: "My old Sash [riband of office] rather disfigur'd by the heavy Rain which half drown'd us on our march to the Yellow Springs, (and which by the bye spoilt me a waistcoat and breeches of white Cloth and my uniform Coat, clouding them with the dye wash'd out of my hat)."[108]

Two days later, on September 18, the general ordered Hamilton to take a small party to assist in removing valuable stores, which included flour, horseshoes, and several thousand tomahawks from the depot at Valley Forge, which lay along the Schuylkill River above Philadelphia. While carrying out his assignment, Hamilton and his detachment were attacked by a large party of British horsemen and light infantry. Hamilton escaped and believed that the British troops that attacked him were part of a larger force en route to occupy Philadelphia. He immediately scribbled a hastily written note to John Hancock, "If Congress have not yet left Philadelphia, they ought to do it immediately without fail, for the enemy have the means of throwing a party this night into the city. I just now crossed the valley-ford [Valley Forge], in doing which a party of the enemy came down & fired upon us."[109] Hancock got Hamilton's message around midnight and panicked. He and the other members of Congress ignominiously fled the city at dawn the following day.[110] Here, for instance is what happened to delegate John Adams: "At 3 this Morning was waked by Mr. Lovell, and told that the Members of Congress were gone, some of them, a little after Midnight. That there was a Letter from Mr. Hamilton Aid de Camp to the General, informing that the Enemy were in Possession of the Ford and the Boats, and had it in their Power to be in Philadelphia, before Morning. Mr. Merchant and myself rose, sent for our Horses, and, after collecting our Things, rode off after the others."[111] Hamilton's warning quickly spread causing pandemonium among the civilian population of the city. But the young aide's assessment of British intentions was wrong, and Hamilton's impulsively scribbled note started a stampede from Philadelphia and "the greatest consternation, fright & terror that can be imagined."[112] Hamilton had merely run into an enemy patrol on the night of September 18. The British had no immediate intention of making a move to seize the rebel capital.

The embarrassed members of Congress, who had vaulted from Philadelphia when they got Hamilton's message, soon realized that the city was in no immediate danger. Their anger was evident in the letters they wrote on the days that followed their degrading midnight departures from the city. Delegate James Duane wrote his wife on September 21, "Our Removal from Philad. Was owning to information that General Howe was crossing Schuylkill . . . However tho' this Intelligence was from one of the General's family (Alexander Hamilton) it was not well founded & we wish we had not left Philad."[113] There is no record of Washington's reaction to his aide's rash behavior and the havoc it caused. The British Army finally seized Philadelphia on September 26, eight days after Hamilton's false alarm.

Having failed to prevent the British from capturing Philadelphia, Washington attempted to defeat the British at Germantown on October 4; but his strategy was too complicated for his army to carry out. As the attack commenced, a dense fog added to the confusion as some American brigades collided with one another in the haze, sometimes mistaking each other for the enemy. At the height of the American attack, part of the British 40th Regiment occupied Cliveden, a two-and-a-half-story stone mansion owned by the Chew family. One of the great chroniclers of the Revolution, the marquis de Chastellux described what happened next. Chastellux said that the Americans were unable to demolish the walls of the Chew mansion with their cannons when a young French volunteer serving with the rebels, the chevalier Duplessis-Mauduit stepped forward with an idea. He proposed to John Laurens that they take some determined men and burn down a door to the mansion. The two intrepid officers agreed and went to get some straw from a nearby barn, which they planned to pile up against the front door of the mansion and set on fire. "M. de Mauduit," related Chastellux, "having no doubt that they were following him with all the straw in the barn, went straight to a window on the ground floor, broke it open and climbed up onto it. He was received, in truth, much like the lover mounting a ladder to see his mistress, who found the husband waiting for him on the balcony." The audacious Frenchman faced a British officer with a pistol in hand who ordered him to surrender. At this moment, a Redcoat briskly entered the room and fired a musket shot that killed not M. de Mauduit, but the officer who was trying to capture him! The Frenchman returned safely, while young Laurens was slightly wounded in the shoulder during the engagement.[114]

Capt. Alexander Graydon tells the story differently in his memoirs. In Graydon's version of events, John Laurens single-handedly attacked the mansion. "At the battle of Germantown, he rushed up to the door of Chew's House, which he forced partly open, and fighting with his sword with one hand, with the other he applied to the wood work a flaming brand, and what is very remarkable, retired from under the tremendous fire of the house, with but a very slight wound."[115]

George Washington Parke Custis also gives a similar account as Graydon of this episode in his *Private Memoirs of Washington,* published in 1860, adding some details: "Laurens clothes were repeatedly torn by the enemy's shot." Custis says that another and equally daring attempt was made by a Major White. "This gallant officer ran under a window with a fire-brand," he was discovered, and "a British soldier shot him dead from a basement window."[116]

Laurens was wounded at the battle of Germantown by a musket ball that went through the fleshy part of his right shoulder. He received what was described as "a blow on his side from a spent ball as he was coming from Chew's House, to the very Door of which he went up Sword in hand; the flow however only occasioned a Swelling in the part Struck."[117] Laurens used his sash (riband) "as a sling for his wounded arm. He wrote his father a month later, explaining that his old sash, "served me as a Sling in our retreat from German Town and was render'd unfit for farther Service."[118]

Henry Laurens knew that John had taken part in a battle at Germantown in which many American officers had been killed or wounded, and was frantic for news about his son. A letter arrived on October 8 from John Laurens written on October 5, saying he had been slightly wounded at Germantown but was safe. His father wrote him back instantly when he saw his son's handwriting on a letter, "the well known inscription instantly dissipated every gloomy Idea, but a sudden revulsion of joy which as instantly followed costing a Tear & brought such a fit of trembling." Henry Laurens was suffering with the gout at York, Pennsylvania, at the time, and he told his son, "My own duty commands my presence upon this spot, if I were free, I would at all hazards lame & incapable as I am of alert traveling fly to assist as your Nurse until you should be able to take the field again at this distance I can only help you with prayers & good wishes & thank you for the honour you have done me." Henry Laurens then warned his son to be careful and that it was his duty to "preserve your own health & strength as it is to destroy an Enemy."[119]

John Laurens established his reputation for courage and temerity at the battle of Germantown. However, he also made a name for himself among some officers as a rash young man who treated prudent soldiers as cowards. Young Laurens was too ready to risk the lives of other men along with his own on his impulsive schemes. How Washington managed to keep him cooped up in an office for much of the war was a miracle. The general appreciated Laurens's courage at Germantown and usefulness as a pen-man at headquarters and rewarded him with a promotion. There is a detailed record of Laurens's military career, which we can study to learn more about the unique status of Washington's aides in the Continental Army.

Laurens joined the headquarters staff as an extra aide-de-camp in the summer of 1777. Washington promoted him in the general orders of October 6, 1777, as follows: "John Laurens Esqr. appointed on the 6th of September extra Aid de Camp to the Commander in Chief, is now appointed Aid de Camp to him, and is to be respected and obeyed as such."[120] Laurens mentioned this change in a letter to his father written on December 3: "Since the battle of German Town, I have no longer been a supernumerary."[121]

Note that while Washington changed Laurens's position from volunteer aide-de-camp to aide-de-camp, there was no mention of his military rank in the general orders of October 6. The inclusion of rank was not necessary in the general orders because, in its resolution of June 5, 1776, Congress said "That the aids de camp of the commander in chief rank as lieutenant colonels."[122] The Journals of the Continental Congress for July 20, 1778, state, "a letter of [July] 18, from Lieutenant Colonel Laurens, one of General Washington's aids, was read."[123]

This makes sense until we come to a Congressional resolution dated March 29, 1779, which read: "Whereas John Laurens, Esq. who has heretofore acted aid de camp to the Commander in Chief, is desirous of repairing to South Carolina, with a design to assist in defence of the southern states: Resolved, That a commission of lieutenant colonel be granted to the said John Laurens, Esq."[124] Why did Congress vote to commission Laurens as a lieutenant colonel if he already held that rank as one of the commander in chief's aides-de-camp? Part of the answer can be found in a letter his friend Hamilton wrote to congratulate him after learning about his commission. Hamilton's letter, dated April 1779 helps explain the situation: "By your appointment as Aide De Camp to the Commander in Chief, you had as much the rank of Lieutenant Colonel, as any officer in the line . . . Congress by their conduct . . . appear to have intended to confer a privilege, an honor, a mark of distinction, a something upon you; which they withhold from other Gentlemen in the family."[125] Note that Hamilton made a distinction between lieutenant colonels who were aides to Washington and those who were line officers. Washington's aides-de-camp were ranked as lieutenant colonels as a practical matter. The rank gave them the prestige and authority necessary for them to fulfill the duties of their office. Their authority, however, did not extend beyond their office. They could not, for example, lead troops in combat. Laurens's commission from the Continental Congress made him equal to other lieutenant colonels in the Continental Army.

Washington's unsuccessful but tenacious attack on Germantown and Gates's victory over Burgoyne at Saratoga impressed the French government. They formed an alliance with the rebellious American colonists and declared war on Great Britain. Victory was still a long way off, but everything changed in favor of the Americans with the entry of France into the war.

This is a good opportunity to explain what happened to Washington's aide Samuel Blachley Webb who was given command of a line regiment in early 1777. Webb was captured by the British in December 1777 and was relatively inactive for the rest of the conflict. It will be recalled that he had been wounded three times by the time Washington gave him command of a line regiment. Webb's bad luck continued when his regiment took part in a surprise attack launched from the Connecticut coast, across Long Island Sound, to destroy military stores on British-held Long Island. Several American boats were involved in the raid. Colonel Webb was aboard the armed sloop *Schuyler*, which was convoying three other vessels, containing a landing party of about 400 men. Rough seas and high winds delayed the expedition, but it was finally launched on the night of December 10, 1777. The night was dark and blustering, and the four vessels lost each other as they made their way across Long Island Sound. Daybreak found Webb and those with him on the *Schuyler* near the shore of Setauket, Long Island, with a Royal Navy sloop bearing down upon them. The *Schuyler* made a run for the shore but ran aground some 200 yards from the beach. The frightened crew launched their boat but it was sunk in the high surf as the enemy warship drew near enough to rake the stranded *Schuyler.* The captain of the Royal Navy vessel *Falcon* yelled across for the *Schuyler* to surrender. With no alternative, the American ship complied and struck her colors as a sign of capitulation. Colonel Webb was taken with the other prisoners of war to British-held Newport, Rhode Island, where he was eventually released on parole. He hoped for an early exchange, but that did not happen and he was ordered by the British to confine himself to the Flatbush area of Long Island (today part of Brooklyn).

Webb remained a prisoner of war for three years. He was a wealthy man despite the war and his service in the army. His wealth came from his mercantile business, which was operated by his brother Joseph.[126] Samuel corresponded with his brother in code concerning their business. This was a common practice at the time but it is particularly interesting because Webb was involved in his business even while he was a British prisoner of war. Here is an example of a coded business letter that Joseph wrote Samuel during the war. In the letter, "324" probably means cargo, the phrase, "376 a 207 thing" in line four apparently identifies a venture in which the Webbs had outfitted a privateer to intercept British merchant ships.

> The 264 is arrived but 408 90 her 324's has about hrrr wt of sugar, some coffee, etc, but no great things to brag of. Her 324 will 197 us hrr Pounds and she's now coming up the river. The 455 is gone down. —in h 214.690 375 448 568 are 366ed One htd. 376 a 207 thing. Your baggage is yet at the store.[127]

Webb's business ventures provided him with money that he used to try to arrange for his exchange. He was given parole by his captors to travel to New Jersey several times to expedite his exchange by lobbying Congress and visiting headquarters to make personal appeals to Washington. He lodged with the Bancker family on one of these trips. They were of Dutch ancestry living in central New Jersey. Webb fell in love with the Bancker's daughter, Eliza, whom he married on October 20, 1779. He was exchanged a few months later. Following his exchange, he returned to his old regiment, which was designated the 9th Connecticut. He left his young wife behind in New Jersey while he was busy reorganizing and training his troops. Within a few months of their marriage, Webb received word that his wife was ill with their first child. Alarmed by this news, he decided to move her to his family's home in Wethersfield, Connecticut, where the climate was considered healthy and he would be nearby. Eliza was too ill to be moved by land and Webb secured a pass from the British to bring her by boat to Connecticut. With considerable effort, Webb managed to get his twenty-three-year-old wife almost within sight of Wethersfield, when she died on November 18, 1781. Colonel Webb was heartbroken, but remained at his post until the end of the war.

With the coming of peace, Webb returned to his mercantile pursuits. He moved to New York City, where his business met with moderate success. He was breveted a brigadier general at the end of the war and "General Webb" was a well-known figure in New York society, helping ladies into their carriages with an old-time courtesy and taking his daily walk at noon on Wall Street. Webb loved New York, where he led an active social life and was friendly with several of his fellow former aides-de-camp including Alexander Hamilton and Benjamin Walker. He was especially fond of the theater and was a regular "first nighter" at many performances. Webb was offered several government positions by President Washington, but declined them all because they would require him to move from New York City. One of his reasons for staying in New York was romantic; he was in love with another young Dutch woman, Catherine Hogeboom (1768–1805), the third daughter of Judge Stephen Hogeboom from Claverack, New York. Webb wrote her on May 3, 1789, describing the inauguration of Washington as the first president of the United States. Webb participated in the inauguration as one of the masters of ceremony.

> To Miss Hogeboom,
> . . . on Thursday last the President-General was publicly sworn, & announced from the Balcony of the Federal Hall,—I had the honor of being appointed, by the Committee of Congress, one of the Masters of Ceremony. I accompanied the President from his lodgings to the Senate room, from thence to St. Paul's Church and back to his House, through the surrounding shouts of Joy, of the greatest concourse of Citizens, that I ever beheld.[128]

General Webb married Catherine on September 2, 1790. Meanwhile, his health was failing (it was said to be a result of his arduous military service) and he decided to retire with his new wife near his father-in-law's home in Claverack. Webb devoted his time to managing a farm and apparently was otherwise active because his wife bore him ten children in fifteen years. Catherine died giving birth to their tenth child in 1805. Webb died on December 3, 1807, in Claverack and was buried beside his second wife. One of his grandsons was Alexander Stewart Webb (1835–1911), who was an outstanding Union general in the Civil War and president of City College of New York from 1869 to 1902.

Samuel B. Webb made a contribution to American independence both on the battlefield and at headquarters where he served as one of Washington's aides. He participated in many of the great events of the American Revolution including the reading of the Declaration of Independence to the Continental Army. Webb described the event in his journal: "July 9, 1776 . . . the Declaration of Independence was read at the Head of each Brigade; and was received by three Huzzas from the Troops—every one seeming highly pleased that we were separated from a King who was endeavoring to enslave his once loyal subjects. God Grant us success in this our new character."[129]

CHAPTER FIVE

Valley Forge
December 1777–May 1778

*Winter Quarters is to us, what a stoppage of Navigation used to be
to you. Rather an increase of Business in the way of Paper, Pens
and Ink—.*

Tench Tilghman to Robert Morris[1]

When the 12,000 soldiers of Washington's tired, ill-clad, and hungry army reached Valley Forge, Pennsylvania, they looked upon an inhospitable countryside.[2] One American officer wrote that the place must have been selected "at the instance of a speculator, or on the advice of a traitor, or by a council of ignoramuses."[3] However, despite its bleak appearance, Valley Forge offered numerous advantages to the Americans, including terrain that favored defense. The area was dry, near an abundant water supply, and had nearby forests that would provide fuel and building materials. But perhaps most important, Valley Forge lay between British-held Philadelphia and the important Continental Army depots and hospitals at Lancaster, Reading, and York, Pennsylvania.

Washington and his Grand Army arrived at Valley Forge on December 19, 1777. It was late to be going into winter quarters; Washington had campaigned into the early winter looking for some favorable opportunity to defeat the enemy. The year 1777 had not been a successful one for Washington. His defeats at Brandywine and Germantown earlier in the year were in sharp contrast with the spectacular victory won by his subordinate, Maj. Gen. Horatio Gates, in the Saratoga campaign. Commanding the Northern Army, Gates had captured Gen. John Burgoyne and 5,791 Crown troops on October 17 in upstate New York. Gates was being acclaimed a hero and challenged Washington's authority by sending notification of his victory directly to Congress. Proper protocol mandated that he first inform the commander in chief of Burgoyne's defeat.

Valley Forge was the first winter encampment of troops serving under the newly instituted enlistment of three years "or for the duration of the war." As such, this was the first winter that the Grand Army enjoyed a continuity of manpower and did not have to scramble to completely reinvent itself in the spring.

Washington's immediate concern was to get his soldiers into huts for the winter. His army had never built a complete cantonment that included soldiers' huts, hospitals, and latrines (called "vaults" at the time of the Revolution). Their December arrival at Valley Forge added to the problem. In the general orders dated December 20, 1777, just one day after the army's arrival, General Washington issued orders that would begin the construction of a military city: "The Major Generals accompanied by the Engineers are to view the ground attentively, and fix upon the proper spot and mode for hutting."[4]

The general orders on the following day stated that the officers who were to supervise the building of the huts were to call upon Washington's aide Richard Kidder Meade, who would show them a model of the hut and point out where they were to be constructed.[5] Some of the huts were hastily built and were cold and drafty. However, many soldiers at Valley Forge had construction experience; they had built their own homes and barns. Contrary to popular opinion, many of the huts at Valley Forge were well-built and warm. We have numerous reports that confirm this, including comments from Washington's aides. Laurens wrote his father, "The Soldiers are nearly cover'd with good huts."[6] Tilghman wrote from Valley Forge on January 16, 1778, "Our Men have all got comfortably covered in their Huts and better quarters are not in the World."[7]

Legend has it that Washington and his military family occupied tents until most of the army had been housed in huts. Then, with the majority of the soldiers housed, Washington and his aides moved into the Isaac Potts house in the midst of a raging snowstorm on Christmas Day 1777. As the fable goes, Washington and his aides celebrated Christmas with a modest dinner to which they invited some of the senior officers. This is an inspiring story but there is no evidence to support it, nor do comments and diary entries about the weather for December 25 mention a snowstorm.[8]

There was little written about life at the Potts house, but years later Washington mentioned that he and his staff lived in tight quarters at Valley Forge. Writing in 1780 from New Windsor, New York, Washington said, "I am in very confined Quarters, little better than those of Valley Forge."[9] Timothy Pickering, who was at Valley Forge for part of the winter wrote, "I might have told you, that, since our arrival at this place, which was on the 20th instant, I have been at my own quarters, separate from the General's family, at whose quarters they are exceedingly pinched for room."[10]

The traditional story is that Washington and his aides shared the Potts house during the Valley Forge encampment, living as one big happy family.[11] This yarn becomes difficult to believe when we consider that besides Washington and his aides, there was a large household staff who had to be provided with living and sleeping quarters. We believe that Washington commandeered two rooms in the small house for himself. He used one room, probably on the rear of the ground floor, as an office. His other room was an upstairs bedroom. Washington certainly had his black body servant Billy Lee with him. John Laurens mentions in his correspondence that he had a personal servant at Valley Forge named Shrewsberry (also referred to as Berry) who was also a black slave.[12] The other aides in all likelihood also had at least one personal servant. The stalwart Mrs. Elizabeth Thompson was there as well with her staff of cooks, maids, and washerwomen. Martha Washington joined her husband at Valley Forge on February 10, 1778. She arrived with at least one servant, which further taxed the living space.

When you add up the number of people on the headquarters staff the little Potts house was too small to have possibly held all of them. Where did all these people live and work? The answer is that it is believed that a large, temporary, log structure was built onto the back of the house. This structure was probably used as an office and dining area during the day and provided additional sleeping quarters for the headquarters staff at night.[13] It is also speculated that a number of temporary huts were also built near the house to further accommodate the large headquarters staff. Evidence for the construction of a log building onto the back of the Potts house, and other structures nearby, comes from the fact that a soldier named Gideon Savage kept a diary, which mentions that he worked at Washington's quarters for several days during mid-January 1778.[14] Savage worked as a carpenter before joining the army.

The winter lull in the fighting was a time for planning and reorganization. Commenting on this, Tench Tilghman wrote to a merchant friend from Valley Forge, "Winter Quarters is to us, what a stoppage of Navigation used to be to you. Rather an increase of Business in the way of Papers, Pens and Ink."[15] Washington arrived at Valley Forge with a superb personal staff headed by his capable military secretary, Robert Hanson Harrison. The general's aides-de-camp were John Fitzgerald, Alexander Hamilton, Richard Kidder Meade, and John Laurens. Tench Tilghman was there with the title of assistant secretary.[16] He continued to serve as a volunteer and was, in all likelihood, proud to serve the new nation without any salary. Completing Washington's military family were the two officers of the Commander in Chief's Guard, Capt. Caleb Gibbs and Lt. George Lewis. Both men were special aides. Peter Presley Thornton, who had been named an extra aide-de-camp by Washington in September 1777, also may have been at Valley Forge. Thornton served as an aide for only a short time, and it is not known exactly when he left Washington's service.

Other officers at Valley Forge pitched in to help keep up with Washington's workload. Historians have identified drafts of letters in the handwriting of Lt. Henry P. Livingston, of the Commander in Chief's Guard and Lt. Samuel Shaw of the 3rd Continental Artillery. Shaw ended the war as an aide to General Knox.[17] A handwriting analysis of the letter drafts prepared for Washington's review at the time shows that Peregrine Fitzhugh was among those who assisted at headquarters. He was the son of Washington's longtime friend, Col. William Fitzhugh. Young Fitzhugh served as a gentleman volunteer at the time while he sought an officer's commission. He was appointed as an aide-de-camp to Washington later in the war. An examination of the drafts and finished letters written from Valley Forge shows that Tench Tilghman wrote about a third of Washington's letters. Robert Hanson Harrison and John Laurens were next in line in the amount of correspondence they prepared for Washington's signature. Alexander Hamilton arrived at Valley Forge on January 20, 1778. Hamilton was ambitious and talented, and Washington took advantage of him, of necessity, along with the other workhorses on his staff at this time (Tilghman, Harrison, and Laurens). These four men produced many of the important drafts and finished letters for Washington's signature during this critical period of the war. Besides drafting letters for Washington, the aides also wrote numerous orders, notes, and memoranda, which they signed, "by order of His Excellency." In addition, because there was no simple mechanical means of reproducing a document, the aides had to write out copies of letters.

At Valley Forge we also have the usual examples of Washington using his aides-de-camp for his personal business. This practice was acceptable and one of the functions of a general's aide. The general sent, for example, one of his best horsemen, Richard Kidder Meade, to meet Martha Washington's coach and escort her to Valley Forge. In another instance, Washington instructed his nephew George Lewis to retrieve his household goods from Newtown, Pennsylvania: "I wish you to have every part, and parcel of my Baggage removed from New Town to this place. . . . I ought to have a good deal there. among other things a Bed; end Irons, Plates, Dishes, and Kitchen Utensils."[18] The baggage arrived at Valley Forge a week later.

Several of Washington's aides were absent on official business for long periods of time during the Valley Forge encampment. Sending his aides on challenging assignments with ever-increasing responsibilities was part of Washington's management style. In early February, John Fitzgerald was sent with letters to Virginia and probably did not return to Valley Forge until May 1778.[19] But Hamilton was dispatched on what was probably the most important mission delegated to one of the aides during this period of the war. His assignment started before the army arrived at Valley Forge. Washington instructed Hamilton to travel to General Gates's headquarters in Albany, New York, and tell him to send the bulk of his forces to reinforce the Grand Army at Valley Forge. Washington specifically selected Hamilton for this delicate mission: "I have thought proper to appoint you to that duty" the general told his young aide-de-camp. His Excellency's choice of Hamilton for this important mission shows the confidence that he had in him. Washington gave Hamilton a long letter of instruction on October 30, 1777, the essence of which was:

You are so fully acquainted with the two principal points on which you are sent, namely the 'State of our Army and the Situation of the Enemy' that I shall not enlarge on those heads. What you are chiefly to attend to, is to point out, in the clearest and fullest manner, to Genl. Gates, the absolute necessity that there is for his detaching a very considerable part of the Army at present under his command to the reinforcement of this.[20]

Hamilton, accompanied by Captain Gibbs departed that same day (October 30) for Gates's headquarters. Hamilton wanted two of Gates's three brigades released, but Gates only agreed to give him one. In an apologetic letter explaining the situation, the young aide wrote the commander in chief,

I arrived here yesterday at Noon and waited upon General Gates immediately on the business of my mission . . . all I could effect was to have one Brigade dispatched . . . I found myself infinitely embarrassed [and] was at a loss how to act. I felt the importance of strengthening you as much as possible, [but] on the other hand, I found insuperable inconviences in acting diametrically opposite [to] the opinion of a Gentlemen [Gates], whose success have raised him into the highest importance . . . I am afraid what I have done may not meet with your approbation as not being perhaps fully warranted by your instructions; but I ventured to do what I thought right, hoping that at least the goodness of my intention will excuse the error of my judgment.[21]

Gates pretended cheerful compliance with Hamilton's mission but tried to take advantage of his perceived youth and inexperience by giving him his smallest and weakest brigade. Hamilton was not fooled and he demanded that the devious Gates hand over better troops. Writing to Gates on November 5 the young aide let his wishes be known:

By inquiry, I have learned that General Patterson's brigade, which is the one you propose to send is, by far, the weakest of the three now here . . . When I preferred your opinion to other considerations, I did not imagine you would pitch upon a brigade little more than half as large as the others; and finding this to be the case I indispensably owe it to my duty, to desire in His Excellency's name, that another brigade may go instead of the one intended. [Hamilton, a twenty-two-year-old aide-de-camp then told Gates, a major general,] As it may be conducive to dispatch, that Genl. Glovers brigade should be the one; if agreeable to you; you will give directions accordingly.[22]

Lieutenant Colonel Hamilton arrived at Valley Forge in late January 1778. He returned to find his friend Laurens lobbying his father for permission to raise a regiment of black slaves for the army. Hamilton shared Laurens's idea of allowing blacks to earn their freedom by serving in the army. Individual blacks were already serving in the manpower-starved American and British armies. Laurens probably got inspiration to promote his plan from his knowledge of a scheme proposed by Gen. James Varnum from Rhode Island. Varnum wrote Washington on January 2, 1778, explaining that he wanted to raise a black regiment from his home state: "It is imagined that a Battalion of Negroes can be easily raised there."[23] Washington gave his tacit approval to the plan.[24] Rhode Island in particular was interested in offering bounties to owners to permit their slaves to enlist with the promise of freedom at the end of the war.[25] Laurens must have been aware of Rhode Island's plan to raise a black regiment because he drafted a letter for Washington to Gov. Nicholas Cooke of Rhode Island promoting the idea.[26] It will be recalled that Laurens probably got his reformist ideas about slavery from his days in Geneva where there was considerable criticism of the institution. He returned home passionately opposed to slavery. Ironically, Laurens's liberal European education had been financed from the profits of his father's vast slave labor plantations in South Carolina and Georgia. Aware of the opportunity to give slaves their freedom through military service, young Laurens wanted to raise a regiment of men of fighting age from his father's South Carolina plantations. He wrote his father with his ideas from Valley Forge on January 14, 1778:

> I barely hinted to you, my dearest Father, my desire to augment the Continental Forces from an untried Source—I wish I had any foundation to ask for an extraordinary addition to those favors which I have already received from you I would sollicit you to cede me a number of your able bodied men Slaves, instead of leaving me a fortune. [Laurens went on to explain that his idea would] . . . advance those who are unjustly deprived of the Rights of Mankind [and] . . . reinforce the Defenders of Liberty with a number of gallant Soldiers.[27]

Surprisingly, John Laurens's proposal was given serious consideration by his father. Henry Laurens's position on slavery had undergone a gradual but steady change, from being an importer of African slaves in the 1750's to being an advocate of universal emancipation by the time of the American Revolution. Henry summed up his compassionate but pragmatic position concerning slavery in one of the letters he wrote to his son while he was attending school in Europe:

> . . . I am devising means for manumitting [freeing] many of them & for cutting off the entail of Slavery—great powers oppose me, the Laws & Customs of my Country, my own & the avarice of my Coun-

try Men—What will my Children say if I deprive them of so much Estate? . . . I will do as much as I can in my time & leave the rest to a better hand.[28]

Lieutenant Colonel Laurens pursued the subject of raising a black regiment with a persistence, even going so far as to describing to his father the uniform that his black regiment would wear: "if you should give me leave to execute my black project, my uniform will be a white field (faced with red) . . . a Color which is easiest kept clean and will form a good Contrast with the Complexion of the soldie."[29]

John's tenacity forced his father to give him a decision, and in the end the practical side of Henry Laurens prevailed and he squashed his son's humanitarian idea. Henry wrote his son with his opinion of raising a black regiment in a letter dated February 6, 1778:

> . . . the conclusion that your whole mind is enveloped in the Cloud of that project, is unavoidable—if any good shall arise from a prosecution of it—the merit will be solely yours—for now, I will undertake to say there is not a Man in America of your opinion. . . . You want a Regiment that's certain, go to Carolina & I'll warrant you will soon get one, I Will venture to say, sooner than any other Man of my acquaintance—you will have many advantages—in raising a Regiment of White Men.[30]

For the moment at least, young Laurens dropped his idea of organizing black troops. But he regularly returned to this project. For example, in March 1779 he wrote his father again on the subject and concluded his letter by saying: "As a soldier, as a Citizen, as a Man . . . I am interested to engage in this work . . . and I would cheerfully sacrifice the largest portion of my future expectations to its success."[31]

Hamilton was an enthusiastic supporter of his friend's efforts to enlist black troops. He supported Laurens's "black scheme" but wrote him concerning the stiff opposition the idea faced: "Prejudice and private interest will be antagonists too powerful for public spirit and public good . . . Even the animated and persuasive eloquence of my young Demosthenes will not be able to rouse his countrymen from the lethargy of voluptuous indolence, or dissolve the fascinating character of self interest."[32]

Washington was the consummate politician who successfully eluded the touchy issue of arming black slaves. Writing to Henry Laurens on the subject in late March 1779, Washington said, "this is a subject that has never employed much of my thoughts." He felt the policy of arming slaves was a moot point, unless the enemy set the example. Moreover, to arm some of the slaves, he said would produce discontent among those remaining in servitude. Washington steered clear of the slavery issue throughout his life, but he occasionally revealed his feelings on the subject to his closest friends. One example is a 1794 private letter he wrote to Tobias Lear. In this letter Washington told his secretary and friend that he was selling off land to make the remainder of his days more tranquil and free from cares. "Besides these," Washington said, "I have another motive which makes me earnestly wish for the accomplishment of these things, it is indeed more powerful than all the rest, namely to liberate a certain species of property which I possess, very repugnantly to my own feelings; but which imperious necessity compels."[33] Washington probably began to meditate on the morality of slavery during the Revolutionary War. One influencing factor was the courageous service of black soldiers in the Continental Army. Another was his close association with members of his military family who detested the institution. During their numerous discussions with Washington, Laurens, supported by his friend Hamilton, must have persuaded their commander to reflect on the evils of slavery.[34]

Washington approached Congress at this time asking permission to add additional aides beyond the four allowed to him.[35] We know that he lobbied at least one member of Congress, Elbridge Gerry, about enlarging his personal staff. The general wrote Gerry in December 1777,

> I shall be obliged to you for recollecting what I mentioned respecting some additional Aids; I find, especially at times; the multiplicity of writing, and other business too great for those I have. Congress may be assured I do not want to run the public to any unnecessary expence on this Acct. and that I shall be as sparing as possible in my appointments under the Indulgence they may give.[36]

His Excellency's lobbying was effective because on January 3, 1778, Congress informed Washington that he could "appoint such a number of aids de camp, as he may, from time to time, judge necessary."[37] They told him that he should try to select his aides from among the regimental officers in the army. Washington served at the sufferance of Congress, and he wrote back assuring them that he would use his new authority with economy and "not appoint more, at any time, than shall be necessary and essential to advance the public interest." He added that he would appoint his aides from among the officers in the army "if circumstances will allow it."[38]

Washington added only one person to his staff during 1778. The new man was James McHenry, and he was a doctor by profession. McHenry was born in Ballymena, County Antrim, Ireland, on November 16, 1753. He was the son of Daniel and Agnes McHenry, and following what was apparently a good education in Dublin, he immigrated to America on his own as a young man in about 1771 and settled in Baltimore. His family followed him a year later and together they established an import business.[39] The family business prospered while young McHenry continued his education at Newark Academy (today the University of Delaware) throughout 1772, after which he was apprenticed to Dr. Benjamin Rush in Philadelphia to study medicine. McHenry was studying with Dr. Rush when the war began. He dropped his studies soon after the war started and hurried to Cambridge, Massachusetts, to volunteer for military service and was assigned to the army's medical staff.[40] According to one story, McHenry was impressed by Washington and "followed his idol to the camp at Cambridge to serve as a volunteer surgeon."[41] On August 10, 1776, McHenry was named surgeon of the 5th Pennsylvania Battalion commanded by Col. Robert Magaw.[42] McHenry's battalion was stationed at Fort Washington, where he was captured when the fort surrendered to the British on November 16, 1776.[43] Ironically, November 16 was his birthday. McHenry was held prisoner in New York City following his capture. He was paroled on January 27, 1777, and exchanged on March 5, 1778. The Continental army was camped at Valley Forge at the time of McHenry's exchange. He apparently returned to the army soon after his release because the artist Charles Willson Peale recorded in his diary that he painted McHenry's miniature at Valley Forge on April 26, 1778.[44] McHenry resumed his duties as a surgeon because Dr. Rush addressed a letter to him on May 17, 1778, as "Senior Surgeon of the Flying Hospital, Valley Forge."[45]

When and how James McHenry first came to Washington's attention is not known. It is possible that Dr. Rush introduced him. We know that the general knew McHenry by early 1777 through their exchange of letters concerning the treatment of sick and wounded American soldiers who were British prisoners of war. McHenry was on parole at the time and caring for his fellow captives. In one letter to Washington he described conditions in a house assigned by the British for the care of American sick and wounded:

> . . . Exclamations for drink and food, from such as had the strength left to speak—the groans of the dying—the looks of the dead that lay mixed with the living—and the insufferable impurity of the house, made up altogether a scene more affecting and horrid than the carnage of a field of battle wherein no quarters is given.[46]

McHenry joined Washington's staff as an assistant secretary on May 15, 1778, while the army was at Valley Forge. He was mentioned in the general orders for that day, "James McHenry, Esquire, is appointed as Assistant Secretary to the Commander in Chief and is to be respected and obeyed as such."[47] Up to this point in his military career, McHenry was an army surgeon. Surgeons were civilians working for the army. They did not hold any rank or wear uniforms. It is probable, however, that McHenry wore a uniform following his appointment to Washington's staff because he held the implied rank of lieutenant colonel so long as he served as one of the commander in chief's aides. McHenry said in a letter written in 1780 that he was serving as a volunteer (assistant secretary) on Washington's staff "without any emolument."[48]

Another aspect of McHenry's appointment is the possibility that he was invited to join Washington's military family because he was a doctor who could care for the headquarters staff. McHenry seems to have been a competent doctor by eighteenth-century standards. Capt. Alexander Graydon, who was captured with him at Fort Washington, spoke highly of him saying that McHenry cared for him when he suffered from an attack of quinsy.[49] The idea of Washington purposely selecting a doctor for his headquarters staff is interesting, especially since there was another doctor, David Cobb, who was appointed Washington's aide when McHenry transferred to Lafayette's staff. This theory runs into trouble, however, when we look at the dates; McHenry left headquarters sometime in August 1780 and Cobb was not appointed until June 15, 1781, almost one year after his fellow doctor's departure. Also, there is no known documentation to show that McHenry or Cobb were selected as aides-de-camp because they were doctors. There is a surviving letter in which McHenry prescribed a diet for Alexander Hamilton who was apparently suffering from bowel problems. McHenry's advice to his fellow aide included the following:

> Water is the most general solvent the kindliest and the best assistance in the process of digestion. I would therefore advise it for your table drink. When you indulge in wine let it be sparingly. Never go beyond three glasses. . . . [McHenry closed his letter with one of his charming phrases that makes his personal correspondence so interesting to read,] You will then be your own councellor in diet for the man who has had ten years experience in eating and its consequences is a fool if he does not know how to choose his dishes better than his Doctor.[50]

For the first months following McHenry's appointment, he wrote much of the tedious headquarters correspondence. This was not uncommon because every new aide-de-camp or secretary was given the bulk of the routine work by the older hands.[51] Washington seemed happy in his selection of McHenry, and there is a charming reference concerning his relationship with his chief: "McHenry's easy and cheerful temper was able to bear the strain which we suppose must sometimes occur between two persons thrown so closely and so constantly together in a position of social equality and military inequality."[52] From all accounts McHenry had an easy disposition, good sense of humor, and willingness to work hard. He became one of Washington's favorite Revolutionary War aides-de-camp and a lifelong friend.

While many men wanted to be appointed as Washington's aides-de-camp, there were some instances where the general's invitation was declined. Two of the best documented cases of officers refusing Washington's solicitation happened during the Valley Forge encampment. One of the men who turned down Washington was Henry Lee. Perhaps better recognized as "Light Horse Harry" Lee, he was a Princeton graduate, class of 1773. Lee is famous as a Revolutionary War partisan fighter, governor of Virginia, and the father of Robert E. Lee. His invitation to become Washington's aide-de-camp occurred in March 1778 while the army was encamped at Valley Forge. The invitation came from Hamilton who met with Lee and asked him, on behalf of General Washington, to join the headquarters staff. Lee thought over the offer finally writing His Excellency on March 31, 1778, explaining that he was very flattered by the invitation but was, "wedded to [his] sword."[53] Washington accepted Lee's refusal graciously and replied the following day,

> By your favor of yesterday I am made acquainted with the feelings of your mind on the subject of my proposal communicated to you by Colo. Hamilton, the undisguised manner in which you express yourself cannot but strengthen my good opinion of you. . . . I entreat you to pursue your own inclinations, as if nothing had passed on this Subject, and to be assured of the good wishes of, Dear Sir Yours &ca.[54]

The second person that we know about who turned down Washington during the Valley Forge encampment was Maj. Peter Scull of Pennsylvania. Scull is particularly interesting because he was apparently much admired by Washington who wanted him on his staff.

Peter Scull was the grandson of Nicholas Scull, the great surveyor general of Pennsylvania.[55] Peter Scull was born and raised in Reading, Pennsylvania, where he was practicing law at the outbreak of the Revolution. He was one of the officers recommended by Washington in November 1777 for the post of adjutant general of the army. His Excellency described Scull as "a Young Man, but an Old Officer and very highly spoken of, for his knowledge of service, strictness of discipline, diligence and correctness. He early was Brigade Major to General Thompson."[56]

In December 1777 Scull apparently had returned to his Reading home while the army was encamped under extreme hardships at nearby Valley Forge. Scull wrote Washington on December 27 requesting that he be allowed to resign from the army. Washington discouraged him, telling him in a letter dated January 5, 1778, "It is no time for officers of merit in which class I consider you, to leave the Army. I know the service has been less honorable and attended with more distressing circumstances than I could have wished. These I hope will be in great measure shortly removed."[57] Scull renewed his plea in a letter to Washington dated January 7, 1778. Excerpts from this letter are included to show this young officer's excellent writing ability:

> At the time I made the request I was conscious, Sir, that there was some impropriety in doing it but that an inevitable distress was the alternative. I am not possessed of an independent fortune and what little I have is much impaired by the continuance in the army . . . I ask Your Excellency's indulgence for having been thus minute with respect to the situation of my private Fortune. I have been more explicit on that head to show that my conduct has not proceeded from any sinister views but altogether from motives of economy.[58]

This time Scull's resignation was accepted and he began looking for new employment in the harsh wartime economy. He tried to get the job of secretary to the newly formed Board of War.[59] Washington, however, was not finished courting Scull for his personal staff. On March 20, 1778, the general invited him to come to headquarters at Valley Forge, "—As I want to see you upon particular Business."[60] Scull met briefly with Washington but the general was not able to convince him to join his family. Following their meeting, Washington wrote to one of Scull's friends, Maj. Gen. Arthur St. Clair, with another invitation for Scull to join the headquarters staff:

> The place I had in view for him was in my own family; assistant Secretary. The good character given me of this Gentn., added to the favorable opinion I had imbibed of his abilities, and prudent deportment, makes this a desirable object; and I should think myself fortunate in the success of it, provided he could be brought into the Office with his own entire consent.
>
> The pay will be Sixty Dollars and four Rations a Month. His expenses trifling, as he will have the use of my Table and be found forage for his Horses.[61]

St. Clair must have contacted Scull with the offer because the young lawyer wrote Washington a letter on April 14, 1778:

> General St. Clair has been so obliging as to inform me that he is empowered to offer me the post of Assistant Secretary in your Excellency's Family. I do assure your Excellency without the least affectation that I want words to convey to you an adequate idea of my sensations on this occasion. I would wish to make your Excellency sensible how gratefully I receive this fresh instance of your favorable opinion & how extremely my feelings are hurt to find my situation and late connections in the commercial line render it totally impracticable for me to embrace so favorable, so desirable an object. . . . But when I reflect that a large and young family of brothers and sisters are dependent on my industry for support, the tyes of humanity and affection require me to relinquish what in other circumstances, it would be my utmost ambition to obtain.[62]

Scull finally got a job in November 1778 as secretary to the Board of War. He must have done a creditable job, because he was considered for the post of secretary to the American minister plenipotentiary to France the following year. He lost that job but was hired as an "additional secretary to the minister" and departed some time in October 1779 for Europe on the frigate *Confederacy* sailing from Philadelphia. He never reached France because on December 4, 1779, Peter Scull died aboard ship and was buried at sea will full military honors.

As the winter dragged on at Valley Forge, General Washington was becoming increasingly concerned about the welfare of his army, but contrary to popular belief, there is no evidence that he made frequent inspection tours of the encampment. His Excellency left this task to his officers, especially the officers of the day, one of whose functions was to tour unit encampments and make reports.[63] There is a popular story that Washington was sometimes seen riding around the perimeter of Valley Forge with General Duportail, the French engineer. According to the tale Washington did not speak French and Duportail spoke very little English. The story goes on that John Laurens accompanied them as translator.[64] Lacking evidence to substantiate this tale it must be reduced to the status of a legend or myth. In fact the latest evidence is that Duportail spoke English.[65] In addition, we know that Washington spent much of his time at Valley Forge with a large delegation from the Continental Congress called the "Committee at Camp," and he had no time to tour the encampment with Duportail or anyone else.[66]

Washington faced several problems at Valley Forge, the most serious of which was that the army seemed close to dissolution due to a lack of food and clothing. This resulted in a feverish work pace at headquarters as Washington drove his aides hard to write the letters and orders that would produce action to get his army fed and clothed. There are a few references to the hectic activity at headquarters during this period. One is a letter written by Adj. Gen. Timothy Pickering from Valley Forge that includes, "at head-quarters, there is a continual throng, and my room, in particular, (when I was happy enough to get one) was always crowded by all that came to head-quarters on business."[67] Another indication of the heavy work load at headquarters is a letter from Valley Forge on March 26, 1778, written by an officer who knew Hamilton: "Col. Hamilton is so hurried that he has not yet had time to write to you.—He looks like Death!!!"[68] Laurens gives us another glimpse of the activity at Washington's Valley Forge headquarters. He stole a moment to write his father on a personal matter on January 3, 1778, saying, "I have taken the liberty of writing to you my dear father . . . I have been obliged to do it in a hurry, and in a small, noisy, crowded room."[69]

What went wrong at Valley Forge? Whatever else, the inclement weather was not the major factor. The winter that Washington's army spent at Valley Forge was not particularly severe for the eastern region of Pennsylvania in the eighteenth century.[70] Some observers are quick to blame Thomas Mifflin, Washington's former aide-de-camp for the crisis. Mifflin was the quartermaster general during the previous summer and fall, and his neglect of his duties is blamed in part for the shortages of food, animal fodder, and warm clothing at Valley Forge. But was the calamity at Valley Forge Mifflin's fault? Certainly his disinterest in his job was a contributing fact but it is unfair to focus on Mifflin as a cause of the crisis. The shortages at Valley Forge were actually the result of an accumulation of errors including the last minute decision to winter there, the indifference of the local Quaker and German farmers to the outcome of the war, and the fact that eastern Pennsylvania had been a war zone for almost six months prior to the winter encampment during which the British and American armies had exhausted the local food supplies. Poor sanitation at Valley Forge also led to an outbreak of contagious diseases in the American encampments. While the general orders stressed the need for cleanliness, many of the soldiers did not understand the importance of proper sanitation, and the officers failed to enforce the orders. There was also a severe shortage of fodder, and dead, unburied animals added to the stench and filth. In addition, the camp's drinking water became contaminated, which helped spread diseases among the cold and undernourished soldiers. Medical knowledge was primitive by modern standards, especially concerning contagious diseases.[71] Smallpox, dysentery, and typhus broke out at Valley Forge, which accounted for the staggering death toll. The soldiers who got sick were taken to nearby crude and dirty (by today's standards) hospitals. If they were not seriously ill beforehand, exposure to a variety of ontagious diseases in their weakened conditions at the hospitals soon made them victims. It is estimated that 1,700 of the soldiers who wintered at Valley Forge died in the hospitals that had been established in nearby towns such as Lancaster, Reading, and Yellow Springs. However, there is no evidence that anyone froze or starved to death at Valley Forge. There is no documentary evidence that anyone was buried at Valley Forge, with the exception of one soldier who was forced to dig his own grave before he was executed as a spy.

This brings us to the role of Thomas Mifflin in the catastrophe. His quartermaster department, whose responsibilities included transportation, was barely functioning at the time, and there were not enough wagons to deliver food and clothing to the troops. This department was disorganized long before the main army arrived at Valley Forge. As we have already seen, Mifflin was made quartermaster general early in the war. He approached his new job with enthusiasm, but by the summer of 1777 he was frustrated and worn-out from his efforts. Congress's indecision and neglect were to blame as quartermaster operations fell apart particularly in the critical area of transportation. Exhausted and frustrated, Mifflin abruptly went to his country home near Reading, Pennsylvania, in July 1777 claiming he was sick, leaving assistant quartermasters to run his department.[72] He finally sent his resignation to Congress on October 8, 1777. Congress did not even acknowledge his resignation until a month later after which they asked him to carry on until a replacement could be named. Mifflin agreed but failed to honor his pledge. He continued to neglect his duties as the campaign of 1777 was winding down and the army was preparing to go into winter quarters at Valley Forge.[73] Mifflin could have done better but the blame for the sufferings of the army at Valley Forge rests with the meddling and inaction of Congress. The result of their stagnation was grim. Washington informed his civilian bosses a few days after arriving at Valley Forge that the army was on the verge of starvation: "this Army must inevitably be reduced to one or other of these three things. Starve, dissolve, or disperse."[74]

One reason for Mifflin's unexpected departure from the quartermaster department was his growing dislike of Washington. The two men had worked well together at the start of the war as fellow delegates to the Continental Congress. Mifflin was selected by Washington to be his first aide-de-camp and then as the army's first quartermaster general. Despite Mifflin's promotion to major general in February 1777, he was excluded from Washington's inner circle of advisors. He became angry with Washington during the summer of 1777, when in his opinion, the commander in chief refused to commit the main army to the defense of Philadelphia.[75] Mifflin also believed himself to be a great military leader, deserving a line command in the army. Washington apparently did not share that opinion insisting that Mifflin continue to serve as quartermaster general. In addition, Washington had criticized some of Mifflin's decisions as quartermaster. On May 15, 1777, for example, Washington wrote Mifflin to return to headquarters and do his job: "As your continuing at Philadelphia was founded on the application of Congress, to answer a beneficial purpose; If it has been effected . . . I wish you to repair immediately to Head Quarters."[76] In another instance, Washington criticized an appointment that Mifflin had made: "Mr. Morris, in my opinion, is by no means qualified for such an Office. He is a very young Man, and cannot have had any experience in the line to which he is promoted. I therefore, fear, that the Solicitation of his Friends and not your own choice has influenced you."[77] Mifflin's wounded vanity must have been common knowledge because it is mentioned in a private letter written by Gen. Nathanael Greene from Valley Forge on January 3, 1778: "it is said he is disgusted with the general for not paying such mighty deference to him as his vanity leads him to think himself entitled to."[78]

As a young officer in the French and Indian War, Washington had criticized his civilian superiors. But he was a savvy politician by the outbreak of the American Revolution, and he knew that criticism and confrontation did not work. Experience had taught him patience and the need for a good working relationship with the Continental Congress no matter how slow or incompetent they appeared to be. As historian Philander D. Chase said, "Washington simply had to grit his bad teeth and muddle through."[79] Washington's strategy was to provide Congress with information and then press that paralyzed body to take action. He set his aides to work at Valley Forge composing numerous letters to members of Congress, state governors, and other politicians, telling them of the ghastly conditions at Valley Forge, and urging them to take immediate action to alleviate the great sufferings of "their" army.

Besides their official duties, Washington's aides wrote personal letters to influential family members and friends describing the situation at Valley Forge and encouraging action. Hamilton wrote his friend and confidant, Gov. George Clinton of New York, on February 13, 1778, with this blistering account of conditions in camp:

By injudicious changes and arrangements in the Commissary's department, in the middle of a campaign, they have exposed the army frequently to temporary want, and to the danger of a dissolution, from absolute famine. At this very day there are complaints from the whole line, of having been three or four days without provisions; desertions have been immense, and strong features of mutiny begin to show themselves. It is indeed to be wondered at, that the soldiery have manifested so unparallelled a degree of patience, as they have. If effectual measures are not speedily adopted, I know not how we shall keep the army together or make another campaign.[80]

John Laurens wrote his father about the situation at Valley Forge in this personal letter dated February 17, 1778:

We have lately been in a most alarming situation for want of provisions—the Soldiers were scarcely restrained from mutiny by the eloquence and management of our officers—those who are employed to feed us, either for want of knowledge or for want of activity or both, never furnish Supplies adequate to our wants— . . . by extraordinary exertions, by scraping frozen distant scanty magazines & collecting with parties, we have obtained a temporary Relief; and have hopes that the representation of our late distress to several persons of influence and authority in different States will procure us such further supplies as will save us from the disagreeable necessity of dividing the Army into Cantonments . . . The Carcases of Horses about the Camp, and the deplorable leanness of those which still crawl in existence speak the want of forage equal to that of human food—[81]

Washington was fortunate that there were a number of delegates to Congress nearby. They were living near Valley Forge at Washington's request to confer with him about reorganizing the army and preparing for the 1778 campaign. Called the Committee at Camp, they arrived at Valley Forge at the end of January and resided about two miles west of the encampment, at an estate called Moore Hall. The delegation included Gouverneur Morris from New York who was a great admirer of Washington. The member of the committee who is of greatest interest to this narrative, however, is Joseph Reed, Washington's former military secretary and confidant. Reed, who had been elected as a Congressional delegate from Pennsylvania, was chairman of the committee sent to meet with the commander in chief. Given Washington's notorious tactfulness, the subject of Reed's disloyalty during the 1776 New Jersey retreat was probably never discussed during their time together at Valley Forge.

Always on the lookout for good writers, Washington recruited members of the committee to pitch in at headquarters. Gouverneur Morris worked on a passionate address to the states asking that they raise cattle for the army while

Joseph Reed drafted a letter to Thomas Wharton, Jr., the president of Pennsylvania's supreme executive council, dated March 7, 1778, concerning the army's need for forage and wagons.

The Committee at Camp quickly became absorbed in the army's supply problems. With their help, Washington intervened in the operations of the various departments only to the extent of making sure that the immediate needs of the army were met. The huge responsibilities of the quartermaster department were not a matter to be dealt with by delegates to Congress, Washington's aides-de-camp, or line officers. The position needed an experienced senior officer with extensive knowledge of organization and administration. Reed worked with Washington to convince the brilliant organizer Gen. Nathanael Greene to take charge of the paralyzed quartermaster department.[82]

Washington's aides did everything they could to help the half-naked, hungry patriot army survive in those bitter Pennsylvania hills. An examination of the unpublished *George Washington Papers,* available on microfilm from the Library of Congress, reveals a flood of orders, memoranda, and letters written by Washington's aides, often at the general's direction, during the winter at Valley Forge.[83] Their communications were clear, often ordering specific action and always carrying the weight of the commander in chief's authority: "His Excellency desires you . . . ," "His Excellency received last night your favor of Yesterday. He thanks you much for your viligence & exertions, and wishes you to continue them . . . ," "It is his Excellency's desire that you repair immediately . . . ," "His Excellency desires me to let you know . . . ," "His Excellency is of opinion that this matter should be minutely inquired into."

Tench Tilghman's administrative experience was put to good use at Valley Forge. He was involved, for instance, in coordinating a massive foraging campaign during February 1778 that prevented the army from starving. Among the letters and orders that Tilghman wrote during this period was one to Lt. Col. Clement Biddle on February 15, 1778, urging him to find forage and send it to Valley Forge:

> His Excellency desires that you would extend your Views beyond your present Circle of foraging . . . that you could send some persons further back, impress every Carriage that can be found and send them forward to Camp loaded with Forage . . . if some is not got in soon it will come too late so I fear we shall not have a Horse left alive to eat it. You know our distress and I am sure you will endeavor to alleviate it.[84]

In desperation, Washington sent Tilghman to Trenton, New Jersey, to help find food and forage. Writing from Trenton, Tilghman told Col. Charles Stewart on February 18, 1778,

> I must inform you in the fullest and plainest terms that I very much fear whether the Army can be kept together. . . . His Excellency has

sent me over to get a true state of the Magazines . . . For Gods sake exert yourself to forward every Barrel of Pork in the Neighborhood of Potts Town immediately to Camp, and I shall be glad that you will inform me by Express, as quick as possible what quantity may be expected . . . I am going down to Bordentown now and I shall be back tomorrow and shall expect to find a letter from you.[85]

Another problem facing Washington was his ability to keep reconnaissance parties out looking for any movement by the British toward Valley Forge. Washington's headquarters correspondence from the period includes numerous orders and letters written by his aides pertaining to patrols in the countryside. A typical example is a letter written by Richard Kidder Meade to Maj. John Jameson:

Hd Qrs, Feby 15th 1778, His Excy requests that you will let him know, at least once a week what is passing in your quarter . . . but particularly within this Day or two, as we have heard the Enemies Horse have ventur'd rather higher up the Country than we supposed, and could not but conjecture they had some design, of which we are entirely ignorant. you will therefore please not to fail writing punctually.[86]

Adding to Washington's worries at Valley Forge was speculation that some army officers and members of Congress were plotting to replace him as commander in chief with Horatio Gates, who was the darling of Congress after his victory at Saratoga. Thomas Mifflin was one of Gates's admirers. Mifflin's resentment towards Washington is evident in a letter he wrote Gates on November 17, 1777:

If you had remained with the Army we might have opposed but could have counteracted the deep rooted System of Favoritism which began to shoot forth at New York [a reference to the 1776 campaign] & which has now arrivd to its full Growth & maturity. Repeated Slights & unjustifiable Arrogance combined with other Causes to drive from the Army those who would not worship the Image & pay an undeserved Tribute of Praise & Flattery to the great & powerful.[87]

The existence of a plot to replace Washington with Gates remains one of the mysteries of the American Revolution. But Washington and his supporters were convinced of its existence and moved quickly to crush it. Washington's military family were particularly active in supporting their beloved commander and squashing what historians have labeled "The Conway Cabal."[88]

The Conway Cabal is named for Gen. Thomas Conway, an Irishman who had been a colonel in the French army. He came to America to heighten his prestige in France (as did Lafayette, von Steuben, and other European officers). Because of his military experience and reputation, Conway was promptly commissioned a brigadier general by the Continental Congress. Conway was the most junior of the army's twenty-four brigadiers, but he was a gossipy critic of Washington's military abilities and he found a ready audience among some members of Congress. Conway's friends in Congress advanced his career by promoting him over the other brigadiers to the rank of major general on December 13, 1777. Congress further stirred up the officer corps by promoting one of Gates's favorites, Col. James Wilkinson, to the rank of brigadier general over the heads of many senior officers. As a final gesture to antagonize Washington, Conway was named by the Board of War as the army's inspector general, with orders to bring order and discipline to the ragtag army encamped at Valley Forge.

Helping to fuel the situation was talk, related by one of Washington's supporters, that Colonel Wilkinson had been overheard boasting in a tavern that Conway had written Gates, "Heaven has been determined to Save your Country; Or a weak general and bad counsellors would have ruined it."[89] Washington confronted Conway with this story. He denied using the expression. Gates accused Alexander Hamilton of rifling through his papers when left alone in Gates's room during his mission to Albany. Gates alluded to Hamilton when he wrote the commander in chief on December 8, 1777, "by detecting a wretch who may betray me."

John Laurens was particularly active in writing his father about the shadowy plot. Henry Laurens had recently been elected president of the Continental Congress. They had a mutual father-son loving relationship and Henry trusted his son implicitly. He encouraged his son to write frequent and detailed letters from his vantage point at army headquarters as an aide-de-camp to the commander in chief. These letters supplemented the official reports he received and helped Henry Laurens form his opinions and act on them. Young Laurens admired Washington and defended him against Conway in a devastating confidential letter he wrote to his father from headquarters at Valley Forge, January 3, 1778. John told his father about Conway's reputation in the army, "that Gen Conway was charged with cowardice at the battle of German Town, and that a Gentleman of Rank and Reputation desired to be called upon as an evidence.[90] It is notorious that he disobeyed his orders, and that he was for a considerable time separated from his Brigade." John Laurens then got to the heart of the assumed plot in which Conway was involved: "He has weight it seems with a certain party, formed against the present Commander in chief, at the head of which is Gen Mifflin. His own preposterous Panegyricks [panegyrizing] of himself, and the influence of this Junto have probably gained him the extraordinary promotion, which has convulsed the army." Laurens continued his thundering attack, "My private opinion is, Conway never meant to act as Inspector Gen, or to carry his new Grade of Major General into the Field— but that his Vanity being amply gratified by his exaltation, not only above the Brigadiers but even the Major Generals—he was desirous of retiring to a more

lucrative and less dangerous Employment in the service of the States at home."
Laurens closed his assault with a kind thought about his father's health and his
heavy responsibilities as president of the Continental Congress: "I hope it will
find you perfectly relieved from your Old Eemy, the Gout and in condition to
save American from her most dangerous Enemies."[91] Henry Laurens had been
an early admirer of Washington and his son's letters reinforced his support for
the general.

Hamilton also worked behind the scenes against Conway through his confidant and friend, governor George Clinton. He wrote Clinton on February 13,
1778, with a fiery assault on the advancement of Conway and Wilkinson:
"They have disgusted the army by repeated instances of the most whimsical
favoritism in their promotions." Referring to Conway, Hamilton gave this mar-
velous description of the feckless Continental Congress to his powerful friend:

> They have not been able to summon resolution enough to withstand
> the impudent importunity and vain boasting of foreign pretenders; but
> have manifested such a ductility and inconstancy in their proceedings,
> as will warrant the charge of suffering themselves to be bullied, by
> every petty rascal, who comes armed with ostentatious pretensions of
> military merit and experience. [Hamilton closed his letter by men-
> tioning the supposed plot to oust General Washington,] You and I had
> some conversation when I had the pleasure of seeing you last with
> respect to the existence of a certain faction. Since I saw you, I have
> discovered such convincing traits of the monster, that I cannot doubt
> its reality in the most extensive sense . . . Have you heard any thing of
> Conway's history? He is one of the vermin bred in the entrails of this
> chimera dire, and there does not exist a more villainous calumniator
> and incendiary.[92]

Governor Clinton replied to Hamilton's seditious letter on March 5. A
small portion of his reply is included to show his interest in what Colonel
Hamilton was telling him and the close relationship that Washington's young
aide-de-camp enjoyed with the governor of New York:

> I have received your Favour of the 13th Feb'y last. . . . I can hardly
> steal a Moment to write to my Friends tho their Letters always afford
> me the greatest Pleasure. May I then hope Sir that you will continue
> to write me frequently tho I should not prove a very punctual Corre-
> spondent . . . I take for granted that Military Men burn Confidential
> Letters for fear of accidents as soon as they are read.[93]

Many historians have concluded that there was no organized plot to dis-
place Washington. Historian Lee Boyle gives a good summary of our understanding of the so-called Conway Cabal: "Whatever the facts were, they were

lost in the tempest which ensued as Washington loyalists rallied around him and colonels and brigadiers fumed about unfair promotions."[94]

While the controversy over the Conway Cabal blew over, there were still other problems to tackle. Grievances by officers that had been suppressed by the preoccupation of an active campaign quickly came to the surface once the army settled in at Valley Forge. The winter encampment had hardly begun when an alarming number of officers requested furloughs or submitted their resignations. While Washington was working with the Committee at Camp to reorganize the army and reduce the overall number of officers, he was staggered by the rash of resignations. Tench Tilghman wrote a personal letter to Congressman Robert Morris describing the flood of resignations coming from Valley Forge. Tilghman's letter is dated February 2, 1778: "No sooner had we sat down in winter quarters, than what was expected began to appear. The Officers, having gone thro' the fatigues and dangers of the campaign, came in crowds to resign their Commissions." Tilghman explains that many refused to remain in the army under any circumstances, "some were quieted by the indulgence of Furloughs to go home and see into the situation of their families."[95]

Some 576 officers are believed to have left the army during the Valley Forge encampment.[96] While it is likely that a lot of malcontents and incompetents were among those who resigned, Washington did not want to see the wholesale resignation of his officer corps. The general brought into play the considerable writing skills of his aides to help stem the flow of resignations. In one example Col. Edward Stevens who commanded the 10th Virginia Regiment requested a leave of absence, which was denied. Unwilling to endure the hardships at Valley Forge, he submitted his resignation. On January 24, 1778, John Fitzgerald responded to Stevens as follows:

> His Excellency has received your Favor of this date with your commission inclosed which I am ordered to return to you & at the same time to inform you, that He will not in future receive the Resignation of any Colonel without the approbation of Congress thereon.
> . . . The Genl is sorry to find that when leave of Absence is not immediately granted upon application, be the Circumstances what they will, officers should think themselves justifiable in laying down their Commissions and leaving the service of their Country; it having been his constant study to gratify every Officer as far as he could do it consistent with the safety of the Army.[97]

When Lt. Col. Lott Brewster of the 3rd North Carolina Regiment offered his resignation on March 14, 1778, he got a reply from Washington's aide Richard Kidder Meade who kept Brewster at his post on a technicality. This situation is interesting to our story because it shows the complexity of administering the Continental Army. What happened at the time was that Washington agreed to plan to reorganize all the North Carolina regiments in the Continental

Army (the North Carolina Line) by reducing the number of regiments (and thus the number of officers necessary) while filling out the remaining regiments. As a result of this shake-up, a number of North Carolina officers lost their posts or were sent home on recruiting duty. Brewster remained on active duty with North Carolina troops at Valley Forge where it was understood that he had volunteered to stay and his presence was required and necessary.

Washington was constantly involved in reorganizing the Continental Army to make it a more effective fighting force but these changes required an enormous amount of administrative paperwork by his small personal staff.

> Agreeable to my promise I informed His Excelly of your determination to resign your Commission, and expected to have found you in the House, [headquarters] and give you his answer verbally, but that not being the case, I take this method of communicating the General's answer to you, which is as follows. "That the reduction of your Regts, [North Carolina regiments] or at least the stay of the officers who Command them, being a voluntary act, and all those officers necessary to be present with their respective Regt." He will not consent to your going, without very sufficient reasons, and those, too, are to be given in writing.[98]

The winter encampment at Valley Forge had a positive side. One of them began on February 23, 1778, when an obscure German officer who called himself the Baron Friedrich Wilhelm August Heinrich Ferdinand von Steuben arrived at camp. Promenading as a former general in the service of the king of Prussia, von Steuben was knowledgeable in military matters. He was warmly received by Washington and the army gave this foreigner the name that he would be known in history, Baron von Steuben. Von Steuben spoke only German and French, but fortunately aides Tilghman, Laurens, and Hamilton spoke French. Laurens and Hamilton apparently took von Steuben under their wing. Laurens described his first encounter with the baron in a letter to his father dated February 28, 1778:

> I have since had several long Conversations with the Baron Steuben, who appears to me a man profound in the Science of war, and well disposed to render his best services to the United States;—in an interview between him and the General, at which I assisted in quality of Interpreter, he declared that he had purposely waved making any Contract with Congress previous to his having made some acquaintance with the Commander in chief, in order that he might avoid giving offence to the Officers of the Army, and that the General might decide in what post he could be most useful.

Lieutenant Colonel Laurens became one of von Steuben's greatest supporters and he wrote his father in this same letter, "I think he would be the properest man we could choose for the Office of Inspector General . . . as he seems to be perfectly aware of the disadvantages under which our army has labored from short inlistments [*sic*] and frequent changes . . . he will not give us the perfect instructions absolutely speaking, but the best which we are in condition to receive."[99]

General Gates wrote von Steuben about his friendship with Washington's aides in a letter dated March 25, 1778: "I have particular pleasure in the favorable reception you met with at the Army, His Excellencys politeness, & that of the Gentlemen of his Family must have been most agreeable to you; Col: Hamilton & Col: Laurens, who are both masters of the French Language, must be most agreeable acquaintance."[100]

Von Steuben was shocked by the deplorable condition of the army and how ill-prepared it was to resume campaigning in the spring. After conferring with Nathanael Greene, John Laurens, and Alexander Hamilton, three men whom he said were "officers of merit, who gave me every satisfaction," von Steuben began to compose a simplified drill manual that could be taught to the army before fighting resumed.[101] He showed his ideas to the general's aides "who made alterations they deemed advisable."[102] Von Steuben dined frequently with Washington and his aides perhaps during which it was agreed that he should institute his new system of drill as soon as possible. Hamilton and Laurens translated von Steuben's work from French to English after which copies were written out. Von Steuben's manual was apparently an ongoing work that was not finished until the baron started drilling the troops. Within days, von Steuben was teaching 120 men selected from the Commander in Chief's Guard his new and simplified manual of arms. At his first meeting with the troops, very few understood the commands that von Steuben was giving them in French, German, and broken English. Capt. Benjamin Walker, of the 2nd New York Regiment, spoke French and offered to translate for him. Von Steuben later remarked about Walker's help, "If I had seen an angel from Heaven, I should not have been more rejoiced."[103] When the baron became exasperated at the clumsy efforts of the trainees, however, he bypassed Walker and reverted to a multilingual tirade to express his displeasure. Benjamin Walker became von Steuben's aide-de-camp and eventually joined Washington's military family as an aide in 1782.

The heavy workload at headquarters apparently continued into the late winter because John Laurens wrote his father from headquarters on March 25, 1778, "I have long anxiously desired to see you—but the unabating flow of business in the Generals family restrained me from asking leave—two of our Gentlemen are appointed Commissioners to meet General Howe at German Town, for negotiating the exchange of prisoners—their absence will render the presence of the rest more than ever necessary."[104] The event that Laurens was referring to took place in late March 1778 when Washington appointed a delegation to negotiate an exchange of prisoners with the enemy. The general selected his secretary, Robert Hanson Harrison, aide Alexander Hamilton, and former aide William Grayson for the mission. They were joined by Elias Boudinot, who was commissary general of prisoners. The British delegation was headed by Col. Charles O'Hara.

Prisoner exchanges during the American Revolution were a complicated issue because Great Britain viewed the colonists as rebels. They did not recognize American independence or the sovereignty of the United States. Because of this, prisoner exchanges were individually negotiated one-time gentleman's agreements between two military commanders who pledged their personal honor that all parts of the agreement would be faithfully executed. Washington's appointment of two of his aides-de-camp (Harrison and Hamilton) and one former aide (William Grayson) to represent him on this delicate mission showed his confidence in his staff. The two sides agreed to meet at Germantown, Pennsylvania. The British removed their garrison from the town, and no troops, except a military escort of fourteen men for each side, were to be present while negotiations were in progress. The two teams of negotiators met for the first time on March 31, 1778. Nothing of consequence was concluded, so they met again the following day. At the second meeting, lawyers Harrison and Grayson took the offensive. They wanted a prisoner exchange backed by the word of the British government, not a personal pledge by General Howe. The British delegation said they could only offer a exchange secured by their commander's word of honor. The Americans withdrew. Another meeting was arranged in Newton, Pennsylvania, on April 6. This time Hamilton, a future lawyer, drew up a lengthy draft calling for a cartel for the exchange of prisoners.[105] A cartel was a general treaty that, in this situation, would establish the terms and conditions for all future prisoner exchanges. The Newton negotiations continued for several days but were deadlocked as the Americans continued to insist upon a prisoner exchange endorsed by the government of Great Britain.

On April 11, both sides realized that the talks were deadlocked and they broke off negotiations. During the time they spent together, however, the British and American officers met socially and they became friendly with one another. They frequently dined together as a break from their tedious discussions. There had been several drinking bouts in which Colonel Grayson had reportedly drunk the British officers under the table.[106] When the two sides had their final meeting, Colonel O'Hara, the chief British commissioner, declared that if any of the American delegates were captured, the British commissioners would make sure they were well treated. On the other hand, if one of them were ever taken prisoner by the Americans, they would call upon Colonels Harrison, Hamilton, and Grayson to assist them. The two sides agreed and they parted company. At the surrender of the British army at Yorktown three years later, General Cornwallis claimed illness and Colonel O'Hara, his second in command, delivered up his sword on the parade ground to the Americans.

O'Hara immediately called out for Colonel Hamilton whom he recognized among the American officers. Hamilton came forward. "Now sir," said O'Hara, "perform your promise." Hamilton kept his word and made sure that O'Hara was well treated as a prisoner of war.[107]

The coming of spring brought great changes in the fortunes of the rebellion. On May 21, 1778, Gen. Charles Lee, second in command of the Continental Army, arrived at Valley Forge after being exchanged for Major General Prescott.[108] There was an elegant dinner for Lee upon his return and he was paid the highest military honors. Lee was an experienced officer who had made important contributions at the start of the war. As we shall soon see, however, his arrogance was to be his downfall.

The spring of 1778 also brought the great news that France had signed a treaty of alliance with the rebellious colonists. Upon learning the news, Washington wrote Henry Laurens, president of the Continental Congress, "no event was ever received with a more heart felt joy."[109] The French army and navy of King Louis XIV would be coming to the aid of the Americans.

The Grand Army celebrated the alliance on May 6, 1778. John Laurens wrote his father the following day describing the celebration at Valley Forge. He said that the day began with a divine service, after which the army lined up in battle formation. Once in line, "Three salutes of artillery, thirteen each, and three general discharges of a running fire by the musquetry, were given in honor of the king of France, the friendly European powers, and the United American States. Loud huzza!"[110] The British government had a different response to the news of the French alliance; they rushed a peace commission to Philadelphia to try to end the war. Their mission was a failure because the Americans insisted upon independence as a condition for peace, so the war continued. While in Philadelphia, the commissioners tried to bribe Joseph Reed to help them.[111]

The Grand Army soon abandoned Valley Forge, never to return. The winter encampment there, however, remains a symbol of the suffering and hardship of the thousands of men who brought about America's independence. The winter at Valley Forge was a great moment for Washington's aides, who performed brilliantly to help keep the army from disintegrating. But they were not alone. Every man who stayed at Valley Forge contributed to the survival of the army and to the winning of independence.

CHAPTER SIX

The Campaign of 1778

My three brother aids gained themselves great applause by their activity and bravery, while the three secretaries acted as military men on this occasion, and proved themselves as worthy to wield the sword as the pen.

John Laurens to Henry Laurens[1]

D uring May 1778 American spies reported unusual activities in Philadelphia to Washington's headquarters at Valley Forge. They said that British officers in the city were hastily retrieving their dirty laundry from washerwomen. Other intelligence reports stated that all the vessels on the stocks had been burned and that over 100 British ships had set sail from the city's waterfront docks.[2] It was evident from the information reaching Valley Forge that the British were preparing to evacuate the Quaker City. In response, Washington dispatched Gen. William Maxwell with the New Jersey Brigade (four regiments with a battery consisting of two pieces of artillery) to reinforce the New Jersey militia who were mobilizing for the defense of their state.

The possession of Philadelphia proved to be a hollow victory for the British. Unlike the seizure of a great European capital like Paris or London, the capture of the rebel capital had not toppled the American government; the fledgling Continental Congress had run off to the frontier village of York, Pennsylvania, where they continued to meet in a wayside tavern. Frustrated and under censure from the home government, Gen. Sir William Howe resigned as commander in chief and was replaced by Maj. Gen. Sir Henry Clinton.

General Clinton faced serious problems when he accepted command of the Crown forces in May 1778. The war had taken a turn for the worse for the British with the entry of France as an American ally. The arrival of France escalated the conflict from a colonial insurrection to a world war. British warships and troops had to be diverted from the thirteen colonies for operations elsewhere leaving an insufficient number of troops left to defend both Philadelphia and New York. Since New York was the more important of the two, the decision was made to evacuate the Quaker City without delay.

There were not enough ships to evacuate all the Crown troops and Loyalists in Philadelphia. Clinton's solution was to send his sick soldiers, Loyalists, and as much military equipment as could be crammed into the available ships and send them off to New York. He would personally lead his best troops across New Jersey to New York along with 1,500 wagons with rations, ammunition, a hospital, and other necessary military stores.

On June 18, 1778, the last Crown troops were ferried across the Delaware River to New Jersey. With everyone safely across, General Clinton started marching with his magnificent army across New Jersey, looting and pillaging along the way. He purposely moved slowly to lure Washington to come out of Valley Forge to fight. Clinton reasoned that once he reached New York City, he would lose part of his army per his instructions from London. Clinton wanted to fight while his army was strong enough to defeat Washington's Grand Army in one great battle and possibly end the war if an opportunity presented itself. Washington was informed of Clinton's movements and was suspicious of his intentions. Reports reached him that the enemy's baggage train of 1,500 wagons stretched out for over ten miles and was a tempting target. Washington decided to shadow Clinton and await further developments. He knew that Clinton was headed for New York City, but he did not know the enemy's route. On June 20, Clinton's army reached the village of Mount Holly where they camped for the night. From the outset of Clinton's march, the New Jersey militia undertook a campaign to harass his army by destroying bridges and felling trees in its path. Finding drinking water became a problem for the British as the weather turned savagely hot, and the Americans destroyed wells ahead of Clinton's slowly advancing column. On the afternoon of June 23, 1778, Clinton's army arrived at the village of Crosswicks, New Jersey, where they camped for the night. On the same day, Washington arrived at Hopewell, New Jersey, about twenty miles away. Concerned that the enemy might turn and try to engage him, Washington dispatched at least one reconnaissance party to scout ahead for defensible sites. The party was made up of his chief engineer, General Duportail, accompanied by aide John Laurens. On June 23, Laurens wrote Washington, "By General Duportails leave I inclose a rude Sketch of the Roads and principal points."[3]

Washington stayed at Hopewell for two days to rest his troops and wait to see the direction Clinton's army would take to reach New York City. From Hopewell, Washington dispatched additional troops to join the militia in harassing the enemy: Col. Daniel Morgan with his 600 riflemen and Capt. Caleb Gibbs with eighty men from the Commander in Chief's Guard.[4] Morgan and Gibbs joined the New Jersey militia, commanded by Gen. Philemon Dickinson, and Maxwell's New Jersey Brigade, who were already skirmishing with Clinton's slowly moving columns.

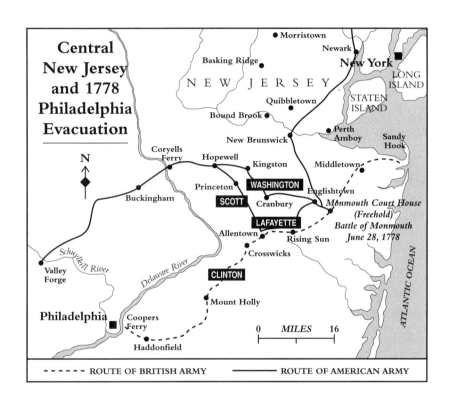

Central New Jersey and 1778 Philadelphia Evacuation

N

Morristown

Basking Ridge

Newark

New York

LONG ISLAND

N E W   J E R S E Y

Quibbletown

STATEN ISLAND

Bound Brook

Perth Amboy

Sandy Hook

Coryells Ferry

New Brunswick

Hopewell

Middletown

Kingston

Princeton

WASHINGTON

Englishtown

Buckingham

SCOTT

Cranbury

Monmouth Court House (Freehold)
Battle of Monmouth
June 28, 1778

LAFAYETTE

Allentown

Rising Sun

Schuylkill River

Crosswicks

Valley Forge

Delaware River

CLINTON

ATLANTIC OCEAN

Philadelphia

Coopers Ferry

Mount Holly

0   *MILES*   16

Haddonfield

- - - - - ROUTE OF BRITISH ARMY   ——— ROUTE OF AMERICAN ARMY

Washington continued to shadow Clinton's army watching and waiting for some opportunity to present itself. There was the political need to have the semblance of a fight, especially since he had ordered the New Jersey militia to slow down and harass the British instead of allowing the Redcoats to quickly retreat across the state to New York City. Meanwhile Clinton's army had only traveled forty miles since abandoning Philadelphia almost a week before. Dr. James McHenry was among those who were baffled by the enemy's slow pace. He wrote in his journal after arriving in Hopewell, "The seventh day since the evacuation of Philadelphia and the enemy tent near Allen's Town. This gives rise to a conjecture that their slow movement is not the consequence of obstructions—broken bridges &c., but that it proceeds from a desire to give us battle."[5]

Washington called a council of war at his headquarters in Hopewell, on June 24, at the farmhouse of John Hunt. His Excellency asked his senior officers if they should fight the British or let them pass unmolested to New York. A heated debate followed with the majority of the officers opposed to bringing on a battle. Charles Lee was strongly against attacking Clinton, advising instead that Washington should build a "bridge of gold," to expedite the march of the British across New Jersey. Based on what he heard at the council, Washington decided not to risk a potentially disastrous general engagement with the enemy. Hamilton was angered by their passiveness and criticized the council's decision in a personal letter:

> When we came to Hopewell Township, The General unluckily called a council of war, the result of which would have done honor to the most honorab[le] society of midwives, and to them only. The purport was, that we should keep at a comfortable distance from the enemy, and keep up a vain parade of annoying them by detachment.[6]

Despite his decision not to attack, Washington was drawn towards Clinton's retreating army and the possibility that some opportunity for action would arise. He ordered another detachment, four battalions, made up of 1,500 "picked men" to join the New Jersey militia, Maxwell's Continentals, and Morgan's riflemen who were already harassing the enemy.[7] These 1,500 men were immediately dispatched from Hopewell under the command of a Virginia general named Charles Scott. Washington camped in Hopewell until the morning of June 25, when he advanced his main army closer to the enemy. The Grand Army marched to the village of Kingston, where they halted to rest from the intense heat of the day. It was here that a courier found General Washington with the news that Clinton's army had taken a road that would take them through Monmouth County and the village of Monmouth Courthouse (which was also called Freehold). It was now clear to the Americans that the British were headed for Sandy Hook, on the New Jersey coast, where the Royal Navy would rendezvous with them and transport them the rest of the way to New York. However, to reach Sandy Hook, the Crown forces would first have to cross the open farmland of Monmouth County, which offered opportunities for the Americans to harass the long enemy column of troops and wagons. Washington would have to act quickly to take advantage of the situation, for once Clinton's army was past Freehold they would be in a hilly area and better able to defend themselves. His Excellency already had almost 4,000 men nipping at Clinton's long column; a force composed of 800 New Jersey militia, 1,000 from Maxwell's New Jersey Brigade, Daniel Morgan's 600 riflemen, 80 men from the Commander in Chief's Guard, and 1,500 troops commanded by General Scott.

During his stop at Kingston on the afternoon of June 25, 1778, Washington ordered an additional 1,000 men into the foray, commanded by Gen. Anthony Wayne, "and sent the Marquis de la Fayette to take command of the whole advanced Corps . . . with orders to take the first fair opportunity of attacking the Enemy's Rear."[8] This brief quotation from Washington's orders gives us some important information. First, Washington designated all the troops skirmishing with Clinton as the advance corps. Secondly, Lafayette's orders were to attack the enemy's rear; Washington never intended to fight a pitched battle with Clinton's army.

The commander in chief also dispatched Hamilton on June 25 to accompany the advanced corps to gather information on the enemy's movements and send the information back to headquarters. Washington probably also wanted Hamilton to offer any assistance he could to Lafayette. They had become good friends by this time and Washington made a good choice by assigning Hamilton to Lafayette. Why did the commander in chief pick Hamilton from among his aides for this important assignment? Obvious reasons were that he was young and energetic: the assignment required physical stamina. Another was that he spoke French and could easily talk with Lafayette. But the compelling reason for selecting Hamilton for this job was that Washington could count on him to use good judgment in dealing with Lafayette and keep headquarters informed of what was happening. Some historians have concluded that Hamilton instructed Washington how to deploy his forces at Monmouth based on his first-hand knowledge of the terrain and military situation. This is incorrect. Hamilton's function was to act as Washington's eyes and ears and report back to his commander. Hamilton may have been asked by Washington to give his opinion or offer his advice based on what he had seen. The battlefield decisions were made by Washington based on information provided by Hamilton and others.

After ordering Wayne into the foray, assigning the advanced corps to Lafayette, and sending Hamilton out to reconnoiter, Washington resumed his march beyond Kingston. He proceeded another five miles to the banks of Lawrence Brook where he ordered a halt at Long Bridge Farm.[9] Washington wanted to move closer to the enemy to support Lafayette and the advanced corps. To accomplish this, he undertook a night march with the main army from Long Bridge Farm to the village of Cranbury, where they arrived on the morning of June 26. Clinton's army was encamped on some high ground only twelve miles away at Freehold. Washington received the decisive report from Hamilton, at Cranbury on the evening of June 26.

> The result of what I have seen and heard, concerning the enemy, is, that they have encamped with their van a little beyond Monmouth Court House, and their rear at Manalapan's river, about seven miles from this place. Their march to day has been very judiciously conducted;—their baggage in front, and their flying army in the rear with a rear guard of one thousand men about four hundred paces from the main body. To attack them in this situation, without being supported by the whole army, would be folly in the extreme.[10]

Whatever happened next, Washington knew he had to move closer to the enemy to support the advanced corps. Gen. Charles Lee, second in command of the Continental Army, had previously declined Washington's offer to lead the advanced corps. When the main army reached Cranbury on June 26, however, Lee changed his mind and told Washington he wanted the command of the corps. Lee outranked Lafayette and Washington gave his senior lieutenant the command. Lafayette was disappointed but agreed to the change. For good measure, Washington gave Lee 300 additional men, commanded by his former aide-de-camp, Col. William Grayson. Grayson commanded two understrength regiments and a battery of two guns.

Lee took over command of the advance corps from Lafayette at the village of Englishtown on June 27. The corps numbered 5,000 men, including artillery and a few mounted troops, and was camped only three miles to the west of Clinton's army at Freehold. Washington moved forward with the main army to Manalapan Bridge (located in present-day Monroe Township, New Jersey) that same day to support Lee. His Excellency's position was six miles west of Freehold and three miles from Lee's corps at Englishtown. Although he had moved closer to Freehold, Washington was too far away from the scene of action to support Lee with the main army if Lee got into trouble.

While there was intense activity in the American camp on June 27, Clinton was allowing his army a day of rest at Freehold. He used this lull to have provisions cooked and issued to his troops for the final leg of their march. One more hard push and his army would reach the seacoast at Sandy Hook and the protection of the Royal Navy. Clinton was also stretching out his stay in the open farmlands of central New Jersey to entice Washington into battle.

Washington rode to Lee's headquarters at Englishtown on the evening of the twenty-seventh for a final conference. Washington told his second in command to attack the enemy the following morning, "on their march."[11] At the same time, he would advance with the main army to support Lee if necessary. Thus the stage was set for the longest and most confusing battle of the American Revolution, one in which Washington's aides-de-camp would constantly be in the center of the action.

Colonel Grayson's 300 men were the first to move out the next morning, leaving their campsites at Englishtown at dawn on Sunday, June 28. Lee followed with the rest of the advanced corps an hour later. Washington began his promised advance from Manalapan Brigade with the main army at 8:30 A.M. Charles Lee was an intelligent and courageous officer. Lacking mounted troops to scout the enemy's positions, he thought it would be best to deploy his troops as events unfolded.[12] Lee was a poor communicator, however, and his "wait and see" strategy was never conveyed to his subordinates.

As Lee's troops advanced toward Freehold from the west, Sir Henry's baggage train was already underway and moving slowly east toward the coast. As planned, the lethal part of Clinton's army, the flying army of 10,000 commanded by Lord Cornwallis, slowly departed the village after the baggage train was on its way.[13] Cornwallis knew that the Americans were nearby.

The ensuing action took place in a relatively small area; about one square mile of cultivated farmland. The terrain consisted of soft, rolling hills with several morasses (swampy lowlands sometimes forded by simple wooden bridges), defiles (a narrow gorge or pass), and hedgerows (fences reinforced with pruned saplings). There were also a number of hilltops, which dominated the area. The landscape was dotted with farmhouses. There were many apple orchards and the fields were planted with wheat and corn. While most of the land was cleared farm fields, the rolling terrain and occasional wooded areas made it difficult to see very far, even with a telescope. This resulted in both sides constantly scouting to determine the position, strength, and movements of their opponent. The Americans had a small force of cavalry commanded by Washington's former aide-de-camp, Stephen Moylan. Moylan and his troopers, however, were pursuing Clinton's wagon train, leaving the Americans attacking Clinton's rear guard with few mounted troops. Interestingly, Moylan's second in command was Anthony Walton White, the young New Jersey gentleman whose rich father had lobbied so hard in 1775 to get his son appointed as one of Washington's aides-de-camp.[14]

Lacking mounted troops, Washington used his aides to reconnoiter, and they were riding to and from the scenes of action throughout the day.[15] As Lee's troops were moving forward, a small party of officers on horseback rode out in front to scout. These intrepid Americans were led by General von Steuben, attended by his aides-de-camp (one was Benjamin Walker, who would later join Washington's staff). Von Steuben and his suite were joined by John Laurens, who had been riding alone reconnoitering for the commander in chief. Together, they rode close to the village, stopping on a bald hilltop from which they could look down on Freehold. They were spotted at about 7:00 A.M., however, by British officers near the village. The British were particularly drawn to the glitter of metal on the chest of one of the American officers; General von Steuben was wearing his European decorations.[16] Orders were given to Lt. Col. John Simcoe, commander of a tough Loyalist corps called the Queen's Rangers, to cut off the American reconnoitering party.

Simcoe took twenty mounted soldiers and forty infantryman, and tried to get behind the little group of Americans. His plan failed when two mounted militia scouts were flushed from cover but got away. Then Simcoe's horsemen began chasing a militia patrol who they pursued straight into the muskets of two regiments of Hunterdon County militia posted behind a hedged fence. Von Steuben was probably alerted by all the commotion and fled ahead of Simcoe's party. He jumped his horse over the hedged fence, losing his hat but keeping his freedom. Laurens mentioned this incident in a letter to his father dated July 2, 1778:

> Genl Steuben, his Aids and your son narrowly escaped being sur-
> rounded by the british horse, early on the morning of the action—we
> reconnoitered them rather too nearly, and Ld. [Lord] Cornwallis sent
> the Dragoons of his guard to make us prisoners—Gen Clinton saw
> the barons star and the whole pursuit was directed at him—but we all
> escaped—the dragoons fearing an ambuscade of Infantry.[17]

Lieutenant Colonel Laurens watched Simcoe's men return to the village and join the rear guard of the British column, which was leaving the village and moving east toward the coast. Laurens and his party quietly left the shelter of the woods and rode back to Lee's corps. The colonel quickly wrote Washington a note describing what had happened and the news that the British were leaving Freehold: "the two columns of the enemy were only as I apprehend two Regiments [Simcoe's American rangers] marching by files [in a single line, one behind the other; movement in this manner was usually because of rough terrain], to envelop the party of Cavalry with which I was reconnoitering—have retired from the woods into which they were gliding on our right and left—their advanced videts have been withdrawn, and the whole appears to be moving off."[18] James McHenry mentioned this incident in his diary: "The Baron Steuben and Col. Laurens reconnoiter. Find the encampment up [the British were preparing to move] and their rear formed at the court house. They appear ready to march. Gen. Lee informed of this by Col. Laurens."[19]

Lee attempted to surround the British rear guard as it was preparing to leave Freehold. Fighting began at about 10:00 A.M. One American soldier with General Scott reported, "It was ten or eleven o'clock before we got through these woods and came into the open fields. The first cleared land we came to was an Indian cornfield. . . The sun shining full upon the field, the soil of which was sandy, the mouth of a heated oven seemed to me to be but a trifle hotter than this ploughed field; it was almost impossible to breathe."[20] Once Lee's attack was underway, Cornwallis turned around his entire army to reinforce his rear guard. Lee's force was soon outnumbered; he had 5,000 troops including militia, while Cornwallis had 10,000 including dragoons and some of the best regiments in the British Army. Washington was too far away with the 8,000 men of the main army to give Lee any assistance. Although army surgeon Samuel Adams was not on the battlefield until later in the day, his diary gives a good explanation of this opening phase of the battle: "At about 8:00 A.M., a scattering fire began was kept up for some time, and reinforcements were sent on both sides, and the action with various success for some time: but the enemies main body being nearer the seat of Action than ours [the village of Freehold] their numbers in the field soon exceeded ours & obliged our people to retreat about two miles."[21] Meanwhile, the heat and humidity were increasing.[22]

Lee retreated to the Ker farmhouse (also spelled in various accounts of the battle as the Kerr or Carr house), which lay near a wooded area west of Freehold. There was confusion during this retreat and General Scott's four battalions became separated from the rest of Lee's corps. It was approaching 11:00 A.M. and the temperature soared to well above ninety degrees with uncomfortably high humidity. On such days, the local people would find some shade and wait out the heat of the day. But the two armies were already locked in combat, with each British soldier wearing heavy woolen clothing and carrying sixty pounds of equipment. Water was in short supply and the troops were, "ready to sink under the heat and fatigue of the day."[23]

At about 11:00 A.M., Washington heard artillery firing from the direction of Freehold. He ordered one of his aides, Richard Kidder Meade, to ride toward the village, locate General Lee and find out what was happening.[24] At about the same time General Clinton was also out reconnoitering, accompanied by two of his aides-de-camp. Clinton emerged from a bend in a road to see a lone American officer riding toward him on a magnificent black horse. The American officer stopped and began to move forward as if he wanted to speak with them when one of the British officers drew a pistol and fired it at the lone rebel horseman. The shot missed as the American immediately bolted away to safety.

Almost a year later, a captured British officer named Capt. Thomas Anburey was conversing with three of Washington's aides. The conversation turned to horses and one of the aides, Richard Kidder Meade spoke proudly of his fine horse. Meade told how his horse had saved his life at the battle of Monmouth when he was surprised by a party of British officers, one of whom fired a pistol at him. Anburey knew this story from a fellow British officer and asked Meade if his horse was black. Meade said it was but did not know that one of the three British officers was Gen. Sir Henry Clinton, the British commander in chief. If he had known it, said Meade, "I would have made a desperate effort to take him prisoner."[25]

As noon approached, Washington was still two miles from Freehold but, "pressing hard to come up with the Enemy."[26] Washington and his army were approaching the unpainted Presbyterian Meeting House (known today as Tennent Church). A few large trees towering above the building offered some shade from the intense heat. Gravestones stood on either side of the church building. A dirt road led from the meetinghouse toward Freehold with rail fences on either side to partition the various farms. The sounds of battle could be heard in the distance. Eight thousand Continental troops marching in column from Englishtown were behind Washington and his aides. Among them were Gen. William Woodford's Virginia and North Carolina regiments.[27] There were also three Pennsylvania regiments commanded by George Weedon. Connecticut men were on the scene commanded by Jedediah Huntington. There were also troops from Massachusetts led by John Glover who, in 1775, had helped Joseph Reed and Stephen Moylan outfit the cruisers of "Washington's Navy." Many of the troops marching with Washington toward Monmouth had stood by him during the winter at Valley Forge. They were trained in the new manual of arms devised by von Steuben and were eager to fight.

Washington was on horseback, in front of his troops, wearing his blue and buff uniform. As usual, he wore an elegant military cocked hat. Upon the upright left brim of his hat was a black and white cockade. His shoulder epaulets each bore three stars, the symbol of his rank as commander in chief of the army. Accompanying him was his body servant, Billy Lee. Billy was well mounted and probably armed with a carbine and a pair of pistols.[28] Also at Washington's side at this point in the battle were his aides Harrison, Fitzgerald, Tilghman, and McHenry. They were wearing similar uniforms to their chief except that they wore two plain gold epaulets to identify them as lieutenant colonels. They were also wearing green ribands to identify them as aides-de-camp to the commander in chief. Completing this military turnout, Washington and his aides were each probably armed with a sword and a pair of pistols in saddle holsters. These weapons were more for display than for serious fighting; the commander in chief and his aides were not expected to engage in close combat.

As Washington was passing the meetinghouse (about 11:45 A.M.) three of his aides, Laurens, Hamilton, and Meade, were away on reconnaissance. Suddenly Hamilton rode up from the direction of the sounds of battle to report that Lee's corps was in trouble. Fitzgerald listened as Hamilton told Washington of the importance of throwing part of the army to the right along a road that the British could use to outflank the American positions. Gen. Henry Knox, who had also been out scouting arrived on the scene to confirm Hamilton's recommendation. Washington took their advice and ordered Gen. Nathanael Greene with a brigade of Virginia troops and four cannons to occupy this flank. This decision would prove decisive later in the day when Greene occupied a strategic hilltop known as Combs Hill.

While Greene's troops were moving off, a lone fifer appeared on the road coming from Freehold. Robert Hanson Harrison recalled that the young fifer,

> appeared to be a good deal frighted. The General asked him whether he was a soldier belonging to the army, and the cause of his returning that way; he answered, that he was a soldier, and that the Continental troops that had been advanced were retreating. [Harrison commented that His Excellency was,] exceedingly surprised, and rather more exasperated, appearing to discredit the account, and threatened the man, if he mentioned a thing of the sort, he would have him whipped.[29]

Washington and his aides advanced another fifty yards when they intercepted several other soldiers who were retreating. Washington still could not believe that Lee was in trouble, especially since he had not heard any firing, except for a few cannons, for some time. Harrison and Fitzgerald offered to go ahead and find out what was happening. His Excellency agreed and the two men rode off. Somewhere in the midst of the confusion, Washington may have come across Colonel Grayson, leading his exhausted regiment.[30] There is no record of any exchange of words between Washington and Grayson, who had spent many pleasant hours together in prewar Virginia discussing politics and hunting foxes. Now they were together in the midst of a great and confusing battle. Grayson had been in the morning action east of Freehold and was now retreating with his troops in the general confusion. He must have been exhausted after tense hours of marching and countermarching with his regiment in the oppressive heat. Grayson's men remained on the battlefield until at least 12:45 P.M., after which they probably returned to Englishtown.[31]

Washington continued his slow advance at the head of the main army. Tilghman was riding next to him when they intercepted several regiments approaching from the direction of Freehold. The retreating soldiers were all worn out and His Excellency ordered them into a nearby woods to rest. None of their officers knew what was going on and Washington "was exceedingly alarmed, finding the advance corps falling back upon the main body." Among the officers coming off the battlefield was Lt. Col. David Rhea of the 4th New Jersey Regiment. His family's farm was nearby. Tilghman spoke with Rhea, who told him "that he knew the ground exceedingly well, and that it was good ground, and that, should General Washington want him, he should be glad to serve him."[32] Tilghman thanked Rhea for his offer and rode on with Washington.

Up ahead, aides Fitzgerald and Harrison had not ridden very far when they met with "many scattering troops." Soon after, they came upon other troops retreating, some in tolerable good order, others in great confusion. None of the officers they met seemed to know what was happening. Among the retreating troops was Col. Matthias Ogden from New Jersey. Ogden left the College of New Jersey early in the war to join the Continental Army. He was an experienced combat officer by the time of the battle of Monmouth. Harrison asked him why Lee's corps was retreating, to which the exasperated Ogden gave his famous reply, "By God! They are flying from a shadow."[33]

As Harrison and Fitzgerald rode closer to the village they came across General Lee sitting on horseback near a fence and watching the British advance. The enemy were about a half a mile away. One of Lee's aides, Captain Mercer, told Fitzgerald that "we were all very much deceived, and that instead of finding a covering part as was expected, the enemy's whole force was drawn up to receive them." Harrison and Fitzgerald rode past Lee to get a closer look at the enemy. They were in a grain field where they met the last of the retreating American troops from Colonel Stewart's regiment. Several

American officers were with them, including Gen. Anthony Wayne, who was part of Lee's corps. As Harrison and Fitzgerald were talking with Wayne, British light infantry and grenadiers emerged from a nearby wood and came rushing toward them. The Americans quickly retreated to escape being captured. The commander in chief had to be warned how close the enemy were! Harrison and Fitzgerald turned their horses and rode back to find Washington.

Meanwhile, General Lee, who was retreating at the head of Varnum's Brigade, met Washington in the middle of the Rhea farm. This is another of the famous moments of the American Revolution. Dr. James McHenry, was at His Excellency's side at this moment and later reported what happened. According to McHenry, Washington demanded to know why Lee's corps was retreating. General Lee hesitatingly replied, "Sir. Sir." Washington repeated the question a second time. McHenry could not clearly hear the answer, "but can just remember the words confusion, contradictory, information, and some other words of the same import. The manner, however, in which they were delivered, I remember pretty well; it was confused, and General Lee seemed under an embarrassment in giving the answer."[34]

Moments later Fitzgerald found Washington and reported what Harrison and he had seen and that "some great exertions must be used, as the enemy were pressing on."[35] It was now about 12:15 in the afternoon. Washington had moved closer to Freehold, in the fields of the Rhea farm, trying to organize Lee's retreating troops. The general met the regiments commanded by Cols. Walter Stewart and Nathaniel Ramsay going in the opposite direction. These two regiments were still intact and part of Lee's corps. Washington ordered them into a nearby forested area known as the Point of Woods. A note written by McHenry described what happened next.[36] McHenry wrote, "I was at General Washington's side when he gave his orders to Colonels Stewart and Ramsay." He said that Washington called them to his side, and taking Ramsay by the hand, "Gentlemen, said he to them, I shall depend on your immediate exertions to check with your two regiments the progress of the enemy till I can form the main army." According to McHenry, Colonel Ramsay said, "we shall check them." Ramsay and Stewart took up positions in the wood and awaited the enemy. Washington next ordered Lee to organize a defensive line with the remnants of his corps. At this moment, according to historian and gossiper George Washington Parke Custis, Hamilton jumped from his horse and, drawing his sword, looked up to Washington and said, "We are betrayed; your excellency and the army are betrayed, and the moment has arrived when every true friend of American and her cause must be ready to die in their defence." Washington was amazed at this outburst and pointing to his young aide's horse, commanded, "Colonel Hamilton, get back on your horse."[37]

Washington rode back with several of his aides toward the main army. He realized that he had to move his troops into a defensive position, but he did not know where to establish his lines. Tilghman told Washington he had spoken to a New Jersey officer a short time before who said he was familiar with the area. Washington told Tilghman to bring the officer without delay. Tilghman returned with David Rhea, and on Rhea's advice, His Excellency gave orders to deploy the main army on the ridge of a hill that faced toward Freehold. This position was on the Perrine farm. The general's aides moved rapidly among the troops to help form a line of battle. Meanwhile, Lord Stirling wheeled his fieldpieces onto the ridge to support the infantry. Hamilton said that Washington "directed the whole with the skill of a Master workman. He did not hug himself at a distance and leave an Arnold to win laurels for him,[38] but by his own presence, he brought order out of confusion."[39]

Lee regained command of part of his corps (about 700 men) and formed a defensive line behind a hedgerow at the edge of the Rhea farm. On the other end of the farm, Gen. Sir Henry Clinton was on the scene directing his troops. At about 12:45 P.M., Clinton rushed Lee's hastily formed defense line at the hedgerow with some of his best troops: the 16th Light Dragoons, 1st and 2nd Grenadiers, and the Brigade of Guards. Hamilton was helping defend the hedgerow when his horse was wounded. He said that as a result he fell from his horse and "was considerably hurt. This and previous fatigue obliged me to retire."[40] Not surprisingly, Washington's other daredevil aide John Laurens was also helping to defend the hedgerow. Although he was not injured in the fighting, Laurens had his horse killed from under him and he was grazed by a musket ball.[41]

As Clinton was charging the hedgerow, Stewart and Ramsay burst from their concealed position in the woods with their regiments and counterattacked. "These officers performed what they promised," wrote McHenry. "Colonel Stewart was early wounded and carried off the field. Colonel Ramsay maintained the ground he had taken till left without troops. In this situation he engaged in single combat with some British dragoons, nor yielded till cut down by numbers, and left for dead in the field. It may not be superfluous to add, that this important service, which arrested the progress of the British army and gave time to the Commander in Chief to bring up and assign proper positions to the main army, was gratefully remembered on his accession to the Presidency of the U.S.; he appointed Colonel Ramsay to the civil office of Marshal, and afterwards to a place of more profit in the customs."[42]

The intense fighting at the hedgerow lasted only a few minutes; Lee's troops were quickly outflanked and retreated to the safety of the main army, which had moved into battle formation at the Perrine farm. The ridge of the Perrine farm would prove to be the scene of action for the dramatic climax to the battle. The action resumed when the British moved up to the abandoned hedgerow, brought up cannons, and started a fierce artillery duel with the Americans on the ridge that lasted for several hours. "Our artillery answered theirs with the greatest vigor," John Laurens later wrote.[43] Despite the terrific noise and smoke, three-quarters of a mile separated the two armies and there was little damage done to either side. Meanwhile, Clinton sent several regiments with some light artillery to slip around the Americans' left flank. The Americans' right flank had been probed but found solidly defended by General

Greene's artillery on Combs Hill, who had "balcony seats" overlooking the British artillery positions below.

General Scott's men had rejoined the fighting and were in front of the main army's position on the ridge of the Perrine farm. When he saw that the British were retreating, Washington ordered the regiments of Cols. Joseph Cilley and Richard Parker to counterattack the flanking British regiments. Cilley and Parker were supported by accurate firing from Lord Stirling's artillery. This was followed up with a charge made by three American regiments led by General Wayne. John Laurens described the late afternoon action in a letter to his father: "The grenadiers showed their backs and retreated every where with precipitation. . . .We advanced in force and continued masters of the ground; the standards of liberty were planted in triumph on the field of battle. We remained looking at each other, with the defile between us, till dark, and they stole off in silence at midnight."[44] Cornwallis rejoined the wagon train, which was already well ahead, and the farmer's fields west of Freehold finally fell silent. McHenry said that the army slumbered that night near the battlefield with their weapons at the ready. He joined Washington and the other aides under a large tree near the battlefield.[45] Lafayette was with them and he shared a cloak with Washington as protection against the night air. The two of them talked about General Lee's behavior that day on the field until exhaustion set in and they fell asleep.[46]

The retreating British troops were shadowed the next day by a detachment of light dragoons under the command of the acting chief of cavalry, Stephen Moylan. Moylan was joined during the night of June 29 by Lt. Col. Anthony White, who arrived on the scene with additional horsemen. Daniel Morgan and his riflemen also joined in the pursuit of Clinton's force. Tench Tilghman wrote the order that sent Morgan after the British.

> Monmouth Town, June 29, 1778,
>   As it is probable that the enemy is exceedingly harassed with the heat of the weather and the fatigue of the engagement yesterday. His Excellency desires that you will press upon their rear and pick up all that you can. You will follow them as far as you can consistent with the safety of your party.[47]

The Americans continued to skirmish with Clinton's army all the way to the coast. McHenry mentioned this in a letter he wrote dated, "Head Quarters, English Town, 30 June, 1778, 8 o'clock A.M. Col. Morgan, with his corps of light troops, and Col. Moylan's dragoons are still handing on the enemy, and waiting to see them safely a ship-board."[48] McHenry saw Lee after the battle. According to McHenry, Lee was talking with a number of gentlemen saying, "it was mere folly or madness, or words that conveyed to me a meaning of that kind," [to fight the British,] where they possessed so great a superiority in cavalry."[49]

Thus ended the longest battle of the American Revolution. The battle of Monmouth proved to be the coming of age of the Continental Army. They used the new tactics they learned from Baron von Steuben at Valley Forge and had stood up to some of the best regiments of the British Army. Washington probably had a total force of 15,000 at Monmouth, while Clinton commanded 20,000, but not everyone was on the battlefield at the same time. For instance, Morgan's 600 light infantrymen never got into the battle, while "small contingents of New Jersey militia were wandering about aimlessly."[50] Hamilton wrote about the behavior of the aides during the battle in a letter to Elias Boudinot:

> What part our family acted let others say. I hope you will not suspec[t] me of vanity when I tell you that one of them Fitzgerald, had a slight contusion with a Musket ball, another, Laurens, had a slight contusion also—and his horse killed—a third, Hamilton, had his horse wounded in the first part of the action with a musket ball. If the rest escaped, it is only to be ascribed to better fortune, not more prudence in keeping out of the way.[51]

General Washington and his followers knew that they had to portray the battle of Monmouth as a victory. The reason for this was that the fortunes of war had treated Washington badly in 1777 and men in Congress and the army were questioning his competency to command. A poor performance at Monmouth might have triggered a move in Congress to remove Washington as commander in chief. It was therefore important to make the battle appear to be a victory for Washington, no matter what the actual circumstances were. Washington's report to Congress proclaimed the battle to be an American victory. The commander in chief said, "We forced the Enemy from the Field and encamped on the Ground."[52]

No one worked harder than Hamilton and Laurens to support Washington's version of the battle.[53] They used the British dead and wounded left behind on the battlefield to explain why Monmouth was an American victory. They stated that some American reports said there were 800 dead or wounded Crown troops found on the battlefield after the fighting ended. The general's two aides reasoned that Clinton's army had carried off a large number of additional casualties. They added in deserters and concluded that the British had lost 2,500 men during the campaign; a devastating loss.

McHenry also did his part to make the battle of Monmouth appear to be a big victory for his chief. Writing two days after the battle, he made his own creative calculations about the British losses:

> General Clinton, by this march through the Jerseys, must have weakened his army full 2500. The desertions before we crossed the Delaware amounted to 428.—Since we entered the Jerseys we may

set down 200 more; and it is moderate, I assure you, to calculate for 400 taken down by the march, and 100 actually dead from fatigue. Near some little brooks we have found a dozen of their soldiers in this condition. In particular their route since the action is marked with such melancholy spectacles. To this we may add 30 or 40 killed in their different skirmishes with our militia and flying parties.—Now, allowing the usual number of wounded for one that is killed, and I believe it will coincide pretty nearly with the above calculation.[54]

To complete their crafting of the battle of Monmouth as a victory for Washington, his friends had a convenient scapegoat to explain why His Excellency failed to win a decisive victory. Gen. Charles Lee was the perfect victim. Not only was Lee a tailor-made target, but he was a troublesome subordinate and this was the perfect opportunity to get rid of him. Lee's truculent nature played right into the hands of Washington's supporters. On June 30, 1778, Lee wrote Washington a disrespectful letter.[55] In his letter Lee gave Washington's friends all the ammunition they needed to railroad him into taking the blame for the failure to win a decisive victory over the British. Lee wrote Washington,

> From the knowledge I have of your Excellency's character, I must conclude that nothing but the misinformation of some very stupid, or misrepresentation of some very wicked person, could have occasioned you making use of so very singular expressions as you did on my coming up to the ground where you had taken post; they imply'd that I was guilty either of disobedience of orders, of want of conduct, or want of courage; your Excellency will therefore, infinitely oblige me by letting me know on which of these three articles you ground your charge . . . I have a right to demand some reparation for the injury committed, and, unless I can obtain it, I must, in justice to myself, when this campaign is closed retire from a service at the head of which is placed a man capable of offering such injuries.

Lee went on to say that Washington was getting bad advice from the men around him, calling them "those dirty earwigs who will forever insinuate themselves near persons in high office."[56]

Lee demanded a court-martial to clear his name and Washington obliged him by having him put under arrest. His Excellency's loyal aides used this opportunity to assert that Lee was responsible for failing to make the battle of Monmouth a clear-cut American victory. Here are examples of the aides' expert handiwork at railroading Lee.

James McHenry wrote Congressman Elias Boudinot on July 2, 1778, with a brief account of the battle in which he criticized Lee's generalship of the advance corps:

I sincerely congratulate you on the signal success of our armies on the fields of Monmouth the 28 Ultimo—Had matters been conducted that morning agreeable to the system for attack it is more than probable that their whole army would have been routed. Every thing was in a fine tune for a total defeat—their men fatigued, murmuring and in a state of uncertainty as to their destination—with their leaders much alarmed and discouraged by uncommon desertions—An inquiry is now on foot, into the cause of the advanced corps recoiling. Gen. Lee who had the command is under arrest.

McHenry went on to praise the conduct of his fellow aides-de-camps during the battle:

I am happy to have it in my power to mention the merit of your friend Hammy [Hamilton]—He was incessant in his endeavors during the whole day in reconnoitering the enemy, and in rallying and charging.—But whether he or Col. Laurens deserves most of the commendation is somewhat doubtful.—both had their horses shot under them, and both exhibited singular proof of bravery. They seemed to court death under our doubtful circumstances and triumphed over it as the face of war changed in our favor. . . .—Colonel Fitzgerald and Colonel Meade claim the greatest encomiums—The former received a slight contusion. Even the Secretaries [a reference to Harrison and Tilghman] caught the general contagion, and had the audacity to put themselves in places of danger, and to share some of the honors of the day.[57]

On the same day that McHenry wrote Boudinot, Laurens wrote his father a letter in which he also blamed Lee for denying the Americans a great victory at Monmouth: "it is evident to me that Mr. Clinton's whole flying army would have fallen into our hands, but for a defect of abilities or good will in the commanding officer of our advanced corps. His precipitate retreat spread a baneful influence every where."[58]

Lee was brought to trial on July 4, 1778 (six days after the battle), on three charges: (1) "disobedience of orders, in not attacking the enemy on the 28th of June, agreeable to repeated instructions," (2) "making an unnecessary, disorderly, and shameful retreat," and (3) "disrespect to the Commander in Chief."[59] Lee pleaded not guilty to all three charges and said that he would represent himself at his court-martial. All of Washington's aides, Harrison, Hamilton, Fitzgerald, Laurens, Meade, McHenry, and Tilghman, gave damaging testimony against Lee.[60] There is no known documentation that links Washington in a conspiracy to railroad Lee. It seems out of character for him to have supported such a plot. But, after receiving Lee's disrespectful letter, Washington made no move to interfere with his aides' efforts to defame Lee's reputation.[61] Typical of the testimony the general's military family gave against Lee were

Lieutenant Colonel Laurens's comments. Laurens said that he was with Lee in
the morning when Fitzgerald rode up with a note from His Excellency asking
Lee to explain what was going on. Laurens testified that he saw Fitzgerald
deliver the note to Lee who read it and "answered that he really did not know
what to say."[62]

Meade's testimony supported what Laurens had said regarding Lee's men-
tal confusion during the morning phase of the battle. Meade said he was with
Washington early in the morning when they heard artillery and small arms fire
coming from Freehold. Washington told Meade to find General Lee and find
out what was happening. Meade said he found Lee and testified about their
exchange of words.

> Question: Did you hear General Lee give any orders to his troops
> while you were with him?
> Answer: None
> Question: What was General Lee about when you came up with
> him?
> Answer: He was sitting on his horse, doing nothing that I saw.[63]

John Fitzgerald said that he was with Lee on the battlefield during the critical morning fighting for about a half hour, during which time he "heard no
orders given, nor saw any plan formed or adopted for checking the progress of
the enemy."[64]

In his injurious testimony, Hamilton told the court that when he found
Lee's corps retreating, they "seemed to be marching without system or design,
as chance should direct; in short, I saw nothing like a general plan or combined
disposition for a retreat." When questioned by the court if he heard Lee give
any orders on the battlefield, Hamilton responded, "I recollect to have heard
General Lee give two orders; at both times he seemed to be under a hurry of
mind." Hamilton damaged Lee further when he responded to the question,
"Did General Lee, to your knowledge, advise General Washington of his
retreat?" Hamilton replied, "He did not, to my knowledge."[65]

Lee handled his own defense at his court-martial. He tried to discredit
Laurens when he asked the young man if he had ever seen combat before. Laurens snapped back with a devastating retort, "I have been in several actions; I
did not call that an action [referring to the battle of Monmouth], as there was
no action previous to the retreat."[66]

Lee attacked Hamilton's credibility by describing how the young aide-de-
camp, "flourishing his sword," exclaimed to Lee on the battlefield, "my dear
General, and I will stay, and we will all die here on this spot."[67] He criticized
the testimony given by Washington's other aides, saying,

> To Colonel Fitzgerald's, and more particularly to Colonel Harrison's
> evidence, I can say nothing; the whole is one tissue of negatives,

opinions and comments upon opinions of those who had seen nothing and knew nothing, collected gradually through all the successive ranks of the army, from fifers up to Colonels; . . . They suppose I issued no orders, because they did not hear me issue orders.[68]

One of Lee's defenders was Maj. John S. Eustace, his loyal friend and former aide-de-camp. At the close of the trial, Eustace charged loudly in the presence of many officers that he thought Colonel Hamilton was perjured at the trial. Later Eustace wrote to his old commander,

I met Hambeton [a purposeful misspelling] the other day in company with the favorite Green [Gen. Nathanael Greene] the Drunkard Stirling, [Gen. William Alexander] and their several classes of attendants—He advanced towards me . . . with presented hand—I took no notice of his polite intention, but sat down, without bowing to him or any of the clan . . . he then asked me if I was come from Camp—I say'd shortly, no, without the usual application of SIR, rose from my chair—left the room and him standing before the chair. I cou'd not treat him much more rudely—I've repeated my suspicions of his veracity on the tryall so often that I expect the son of a bitch will challenge me when he comes.[69]

Hamilton never challenged Eustace to a duel, but Eustace's career, and that of Lt. Col. Eleazer Oswald, another fine officer who also defended Lee at his court-martial, were ruined. Was this coincidence or were Washington and his friends punishing those officers who came to Lee's defense? Historian Dr. Mark Lender is an expert on the battle of Monmouth and he summarized the role of Washington's aides-de-camp in managing the smear campaign against General Lee: "Successful senior commanders always have relied on talented subordinates, and in crafting so sweeping a victory from the Battle of Monmouth, Washington was genuinely blessed in this regard. Chief among these young men were Hamilton and Laurens." Lender concluded that Hamilton and Laurens were also responsible for making Lee the scapegoat to explain the absence of a decisive American victory. Commenting on the two aide's involvement in railroading Lee, Dr. Lender said, "A prejudicial account of Lee's confrontation with the commander in chief had spread throughout the army by the evening of the 28th [the day of the battle]. . . . This was the doing of Hamilton and Laurens. They did their best to encourage these feelings, even hinting to all who would listen that Lee's conduct may have involved actual treachery."[70]

The court-martial judges gave their verdict on August 12, 1778. They found Lee guilty of "disobedience of orders, in not attacking the enemy on the 28th of June, . . . of making an unnecessary, and in some few instances, a disorderly retreat," and "disrespect to the Commander in Chief." The president of the court-martial, General Lord Stirling, then read the punishment, "The Court do sentence Major-General Lee to be suspended from any command in the armies of the United States of North America, for the term of twelve months."[71]

Congress had to confirm the verdict and Lee angrily hurried off to Philadelphia to lobby for a reversal. Lee had every reason to be enraged. He had marched in the early morning of June 28, 1778, expecting to engage the small rear guard of Clinton's army, amounting perhaps to 2,000 men. Instead he was quickly overwhelmed by 8,000 elite troops against his 5,000. We now understand that Washington was also at fault for being too far away to support Lee's advance corps when it got into trouble.

Following the battle of Monmouth, Washington marched his army to the lower Hudson River valley to watch Clinton's army, which had safely returned to New York City. As they were traveling through northern New Jersey, Washington stopped to see the falls of the Passaic River, accompanied by his suite. McHenry left a record of this agreeable excursion in his journal. He described how the party crossed an old bridge, "very much out of repair," over the Passaic River and about a half mile beyond they came upon the great falls. He wrote that the falls plummeted "into a large basin, where it loses all its rage and assumes the polish of a mirror." Writing further, he said the falling water produced

> a fine spray, that issuing from the cleft appears at a distance like a thin body of smoke, while viewed in the sunshine from the edge of the chasm it exhibits a beautiful rainbow. . . . But I was interrupted by a call from the General, . . . I found the General & suite seated under a large spreading oak tree—within view of the spray diversified by a beautiful rainbow.
>
> A fine cool spring bubbled out most charmingly from the bottom of the oak. The traveling canteens were immediately emptied, and a sudden repast spread before us consisting of cold ham—tongue—and excellent biscuits. With the assistance of a little spirits we composed some grog—over which we chatted away a very cheerful hour, and then took leave of the friendly oak—its refreshing spring—and the meek falls of Passaic.[72]

The general rode on with his retinue to the village of Paramus where he made his headquarters for a few days. It was at this point that John Laurens left headquarters on an important assignment. A French fleet commanded by the Count d'Estaing had arrived in the waters near New York City. Laurens, who spoke French, was sent by Washington to act as a liaison between the allies. Lafayette wrote d'Estaing on July 14 , 1778, welcoming him to America and introducing Laurens in the most flattering terms,

> Allow me here to introduce to you Colonel Laurens, General Washington's trusted aide-de-camp and son of the president of Congress.

He is a young man of wit, learning, and the greatest patriotism. You will greatly please the general and Congress by receiving him with distinction and that will have many good effects. You may speak to him in confidence of anything that you consider proper to communicate to General Washington; it is as if you were speaking to the general himself, who shares with him his most important secrets.[73]

Laurens was with the French when D'Estaing agreed to participate in a campaign to recapture Newport, Rhode Island. The British had seized the town in late 1776 and were using it as a naval base. The American forces at Newport were commanded by Gen. John Sullivan who was reinforced with two veteran brigades under the command of Lafayette. Maj. Caleb Gibbs also participated in the campaign, probably leading a contingent from the Commander in Chief's Guard. Laurens stayed with D'Estaing to help coordinate the allied attack. General Sullivan wrote to d'Estaing early in the campaign mentioning Laurens, "I Should be happy to have your advice & opinion upon the operations which Col. Laurens will Instruct your Escy how to forward."[74]

Despite the efforts of Laurens, there was friction between Sullivan and D'Estaing that contributed to the poor coordination that marked the campaign. Then, the arrival of a Royal Navy squadron off the coast resulted in a naval action in the waters near Newport on August 10–12. Following an indecisive engagement at sea, D'Estaing abandoned the siege and sailed off to Boston at midnight on August 21 to repair his ships and rest his troops. Sullivan was furious, but he could not easily withdraw and fought the British on August 29. Laurens commanded a unit of light infantry in this indecisive action. He was mentioned in Sullivan's report to Congress as one of the officers "who behav'd with great Gallantry." The Americans ended the hapless siege of Newport, and Laurens returned to headquarters. He was only back there a short time before getting involved in another escapade: challenging Gen. Charles Lee to a duel.

The duel had its origins in General Lee's inflammatory character and clever (but imprudent) pen. Lee managed to ruin his chances of Congress disapproving the sentence of his court-martial by talking and writing too much, and especially by criticizing Washington. Lee's activities at this time included publishing a pamphlet entitled, *Vindication to the Public,* in which he defended his behavior at Monmouth and attacked the hostile witnesses at his court-martial. Washington's two young firebrands, Hamilton and Laurens, were soon in the thick of the war of words. Laurens was in Philadelphia in early December 1778 when he wrote his alter ego Hamilton about Lee's wheezy pamphlet:

You have seen, and by this time considered, General Lee's infamous publication . . . The ancient secretary [Robert Hanson Harrison] is the Recueil of modern history and anecdotes, and will give them to us with candor, elegance and perspicuity. The pen of Junius is in your hand; and I think you will without difficulty, expose, in his defense, letters, and last production, such a tissue of falsehood and inconsistency, as will satisfy the world, and put him for ever to silence.[75]

On December 5, 1778, Congress confirmed the verdict of Lee's court-martial: "Resolved That the sentence of the General Court [Martial] upon Major General Lee be carried into execution."[76]

The congressional confirmation of Lee's court-martial was not the end of the affair. The impetuous and proud Laurens said that he had been informed on good authority "that General Lee had spoken of General Washington in the grossest and most opprobrious terms of personal abuse" and demanded an explanation.[77] Lee answered that if Lieutenant Colonel Laurens was desirous of reviving the ancient custom of *pro vidua* (the ancient custom where monks, old women, and widows were allowed a champion), he should consider himself as obliged to conform.[78] Laurens demanded satisfaction by challenging Lee to a duel. Lee's reply is a fascinating example of the gentleman's code of conduct at the time: "To Colonel John Laurens, December 22d, 1778 . . . I will do myself the Honour of meeting you attended by a Friend with a brace of pistols to-morrow [at] 1/2 past 3.p.m." Lee then set the meeting place at "a little on the Philad. Side of the four mile stone a very convenient piece of wood, where unless it should rain I will do myself the honor of meeting you."[79] Lee was an experienced duelist while Laurens and his friend Hamilton had probably menaced several people with the prospect of a duel, but neither had ever fought one. We know that Hamilton once got angry with a clergyman named William Gordon and threatened to challenge him to a duel.

An eighteenth-century duel was an elegant ritual adhering to a strict code of conduct. Each gentleman selected a person (Lee's reference to a "Friend" in his letter of acceptance to Laurens) to act as his second. The opponents' seconds adhered to the prescribed ritual by going through the motions of trying to reconcile the adversaries' differences. Once this rite had been dispensed with, the duel could proceed. A surgeon was normally present. Hamilton, of course, was asked by Laurens to be his second and Lee selected his former aide-de-camp, Maj. Evan Edwards, to accompany him.

The duelists and their seconds met on the afternoon of December 23, 1778. Laurens agreed to pistols. Although distinctive dueling pistols began to make their appearance in the 1760s in Europe, none were known to be in America at the time of the Revolution. Lee mentions in his note to Laurens of December 22 that he will bring a "brace of pistols" for the duel. This implied a pair of matched pistols, usually of small caliber, probably owned by Lee or Edwards, his second.[80] These fine pistols were seldom used on a daily basis because they were expensive and had elaborate decorations. General Lee was an excellent marksman and proposed that they advance toward each other and that each would fire at a time and distance he thought proper. Laurens agreed and the pistols were loaded by Hamilton and Edwards and handed to the duelists.

Laurens and Lee approached one another with their loaded weapons until only five or six paces separated them. The short distance between them can be explained because of the small caliber of the pistols they were using. The two duelists were at point-blank range when the snap of pistol locks made the quiet forest suddenly resound with the sound of gunfire. Both men had fired simultaneously. The air was thick with powder smoke as Lee cried out that he was hit. Laurens was untouched and rushed toward his antagonist, followed by Hamilton and Edwards. At first they thought that Lee, who had fallen to the ground, was mortally wounded. However, the wound proved to be minor; he had been grazed on his right side and wanted to continue the contest, which meant reloading the weapons for another shot. The seconds protested saying that the affair should end. But Lee insisted on resuming the deadly game and Laurens voiced his acceptance. Hamilton and Edwards conferred again in private and jointly declared that honor had been satisfied and the duel was over. Both parties returned to town and Lee later declared that Colonel Laurens's conduct on the occasion was perfectly genteel, and as such had obliged him to entertain an "odd sort of respect for him."[81] It was also gossiped that Lee "intends to have another Pop as soon as he recovers."[82] Hamilton and Edwards as the seconds published the usual report of the event, pronouncing that after the two gentlemen met, "their conduct was strongly marked by all the politeness, generosity, coolness and firmness, that ought to characterize a transaction of this nature."[83]

There was no further dueling but the factious General Lee continued to fight back with an attempt to denigrate Washington's reputation. Several months later, a Baltimore newspaper printed an article written by Lee, criticizing Washington's generalship. Lee pulled an unpleasant skeleton from the closet when he wrote of Washington's poor judgment in failing to evacuate Fort Washington before it was overrun by the British in November 1776. Lee mentioned Joseph Reed as one of the people who knew of Washington's blunder. Reed had just been elected the president of the Pennsylvania Executive Council, the equivalent of Pennsylvania's governor, and was upset to have this nasty episode haunt him again. Prior to his election he served as a volunteer aide-de-camp to Washington, without pay, and apparently assisted him during the Monmouth campaign.

With his political career on the ascent, Reed had to distance himself from his former confederate Charles Lee, who was out of favor and a troublemaker. Washington and his supporters were the undisputed military leaders of the Revolution and Reed must have cursed himself more than once for his poor judgment in questioning Washington's abilities during the 1776 campaign.

Reed's solution to his problem was to publish a letter addressed "to the public" dated July 14, 1779. In this letter he explained that his name was alluded to as a person who had a low regard for General Washington's abilities. Reed then gave his latest spin on the embarrassing events of November 1776 and his secret correspondence with Charles Lee that had cost him his friendship with Washington,

In the fall, 1776, I was extremely anxious that Fort Washington should be evacuated; there was a difference in opinion among those whom the General consulted, and he hesitated more than I ever knew him on any other occasion, and more than I thought the public service admitted. Knowing that General Lee's opinion would be a great support to mine, I wrote to him from Hackinsack, stating the case, and my reasons, and I think urging him to join me in sentiment at the close of my letter . . . I have now only to add, that though General Washington, soon after, by an accident, knew of this circumstance, it never lessened the friendship which subsisted between us.[84]

Reed's political career survived this nasty incident while Lee became a forgotten man. Through the efforts of his friends Washington had emerged from the battle of Monmouth as the unquestioned American military leader for the rest of the war. No one was ever appointed to replace Charles Lee as second in command of the Continental Army. In 1780, Congress removed him from the army entirely. He died a bitter and forgotten man before the end of the war.

The battle of Monmouth proved to be the last battle fought by the Grand Army in the north. Unable to defeat the Americans but unwilling to give up, the British switched their efforts to conquering the southern states. Washington's main army remained in the north planning and probing for an opportunity to retake New York City, which never happened. His army would not fight again until the siege of Yorktown, Virginia, in the autumn of 1781.

The Monmouth campaign also marked a big change in Washington's staff because John Fitzgerald, the general's acquaintance and aide-de-camp, resigned from the army soon after the battle. Fitzgerald was wounded at Monmouth and was probably exhausted from his two years of continuous service. He returned to Alexandria to resume his business career. Soon after returning home, he placed an advertisement in the local newspaper promoting his business and offering malaga and catalonia wines, pepper, olives, sweet oil, white wine, vinegar, and brown Irish linens for sale. Fitzgerald also held part interest in a brewery. He married Jane Digges, of Prince George County, Maryland, on June 2, 1779. Fitzgerald continued to aid the rebel cause through his business connections. In one episode Gov. Thomas Jefferson asked him to arrange for cloth and shoes to be sent to Virginia soldiers captured by the British. In 1783 following the end of the war Fitzgerald was elected the mayor of Alexandria and resumed his friendship with Washington who returned to his nearby home. Fitzgerald is regularly mentioned in Washington's diary as a guest at Mount Vernon. For example, the general wrote in his diary on January 18, 1786, "Colo. Fitzgerald called here on his way from Dumfries & dined."[85] At about this time Thomas Jefferson wrote Washington from Paris asking the general to recommend an American to a French business friend. Washington suggested Fitzgerald, saying,

I shall now proceed to mention a person in whose skill and integrity, Monsr. Coulteaux may, I think, have the fullest confidence; and tho' I am precluded in some measure from doing by being told that it is required that he should be an American born; I shall still venture to name a Gentleman who is a native of Ireland—Colo. John Fitzgerald. The active Services of this Gentleman during the War, his long residence in the Country and intermarriage in it (with one of the most respectable families, Digges of Maryland) all entitle him to be considered as an American. The laws of this Country know no difference between him and a native of America. He has besides been bred to trade, is esteemed a man of property and is at present engaged in the former in Alexandria.[86]

When Washington became president, he appointed Fitzgerald as the local collector of customs. Fitzgerald was also involved with Washington in one of the general's pet projects, which was building a canal around the rapids on the Potomac River. Named the Potomac Company, the plan never succeeded. Fitzgerald survived the battlefields of the American Revolution only to succumb to the perils of operating his own business. He was forced to declare bankruptcy in December 1799 and was dead a month later.

PART THREE

VICTORY AT LAST

1779–83

Washington started the war by recruiting men with limited military experience to serve as his aides-de-camp. As the war progressed, however, he was able to find meritorious aides from the officer corps. These new men elevated the professionalism of the general's staff because they combined the outstanding qualifications of Washington's earlier aides (intelligence, good writing skills, capability of independent action, discretion, and a willingness to work hard) with considerable military experience. Typical of the talented officers who joined Washington's military family during the second half of the war were Benjamin Walker (the French-speaking New York officer who helped von Steuben at Valley Forge), David Humphreys (aide to General Putnam), Richard Varick (aide to General Schuyler, deputy muster master general of the Northern Department and aide to General Arnold), and William Stephens Smith (a line officer said to have seen action in 120 engagements during the war). These new men gradually replaced a number of the general's most praiseworthy aides who left his service to advance their military careers or return to civilian life.

This period also saw a change in British strategy from fighting for control of the northern states to an effort to conquer the south. A powerful British force, however, remained at New York for the defense of that city, which occupied Washington's Grand Army, while other British and American forces struggled for control of the South. In the fall of 1781 Washington rushed his army to Yorktown, Virginia, to take advantage of a favorable set of circumstances that proved to be the decisive event of the American Revolution.

CHAPTER SEVEN

The War Moves South
July 1778–December 1780

*There have been no military transactions in this quarter since my
last worth mentioning.*

Alexander Hamilton to John Laurens,
March 30, 1780[1]

Following the June 1778 battle of Monmouth, Washington moved the Grand
Army north of New York City looking for some favorable opportunity to
engage the enemy. The city was stoutly defended by a large British land and
naval force. The arrival of the first French warships and troops in mid-July
1778 held great prospects that resulted in a joint Franco-American campaign
against British-held Newport, Rhode Island. But as we have already seen, the
campaign failed miserably, and the Continental Army settled in for their fourth
winter of the war at Middlebrook, New Jersey. Washington and his staff
arrived at the encampment, located in a well wooded area in the foothills of the
Watchung Mountains, on the evening of December 11, 1778, and immediately
went to work to provide huts for the enlisted men. The general rented rooms in
a new house that was owned by a wealthy Philadelphia fabric importer named
John Wallace. The Wallace house is still standing in the modern town of
Somerville, New Jersey. Washington stayed at the Wallace house with his
aides-de-camp only long enough to get the winter cantonment organized. He
was asked to confer with Congress and on December 21, 1778, the general
rode off for Philadelphia taking Harrison, Hamilton, Meade, Laurens, and
Tilghman with him. McHenry and Gibbs remained behind. The whereabouts
of the other member of the general's staff, Capt. George Lewis, was a mystery
even to his uncle George Washington. Lewis commanded the mounted unit of
the Commander in Chief's Guard and was a special aide-de-camp. The general
located his nephew and reprimanded him for being absent and demanded he
immediately return to headquarters:

. . . that these things reflect much discredit upon you as an Officer, and involve me in the censure, for the natural presumption is, that such indulgences are the effect of partiality proceeding from our connexion . . . Immediately upon receipt of this Letter you will, I expect, join your Regiment and give that constant attendance on duty, which is to be expected from a good Officer.[2]

Lewis returned to duty but resigned to marry Catherine Daingerfield, who was fifteen years old at the time. They were married on October 15, 1779. The couple resided at a plantation called "Marmion" in King George County, Virginia, where Lewis became a gentleman planter and land speculator. George and Catherine had three children, two sons and a daughter. Washington's rancor towards his nephew was not enduring. Captain Lewis and his family were regular visitors to Mount Vernon after the war. Lewis briefly returned to active military service during the 1794 Whiskey Rebellion. He died on November 13, 1796, at his plantation.

Washington and his aides were absent from Middlebrook for six weeks. Their visit to Philadelphia proved to be a busy time. A considerable amount of business was conducted by the general during his meetings with Congress. They resulted in the drafting of numerous letters and orders for His Excellency's review and signature. Probably following Washington's lead, whatever free time that the aides had seemed to be occupied with necessary socializing. Tilghman mentioned his busy schedule in a letter to his friend and fellow aide Dr. McHenry written from Philadelphia:

> Dear Mac
> I suppose you think we must be, by this time, so wedded to sweet Philada. that it will break our hearts to leave it. Far from it I assure you my Friend. I can speak for myself, and I am pretty certain I can answer for all, when I say, that we anxiously wait for the moment that gives us liberty to return to humble Middle Brook. Philada. may answer very well for a man with his pockets well lined, whose pursuit is idleness and dissipation. But to us who are not in the first predicament, and who are not upon the latter errand, it is intolerable. We seem to work hard, and yet we do nothing; in fact we have no time to do anything and that is the true reason a great assembly do so little. A morning visit, a dinner at 5 o'clock—Tea at 8 or 9—supper and up all night is the round die in diem. Does not the Republic go on charmingly?[3]

On December 29, 1778, an important vote was taken in Congress regarding a proposed plan to invade Canada. Following Washington's counsel, the delegates voted to abandon the idea. On that day, while Washington was deliberating with the members of Congress, a determined British army broke through the American defenses of Savannah, Georgia, and captured that city. The loss of Savannah was the harbinger of a new British strategy in the war, based on seizing control of the southern states. Washington returned to the Middlebrook encampment with his aides on February 5. However, Harrison and Meade did not return with him. They took the opportunity of a lull in the fighting in the North to return to their Virginia homes for brief visits. Their absence was mentioned in a letter Washington wrote to Lafayette on March 8, 1779, while the marquis was in France:

> Nothing of importance has happened since you left us, except the Enemy's invasion of Georgia, and possession of its capital [Savannah]. . . . The American Troops are again in Hutts; but in a more agreeable and fertile country, then they were in last winter at Valley Forge; and they are better clad and more healthy, than they have ever been since the formation of the Army. . . . Harrison and Meade are in Virga. [Virginia]; all the other Gentn. of my Suit join most cordially in tendering their best respects to you.[4]

John Laurens was stunned by the news from Georgia and the realization that South Carolina was the next target of the British offensive. He wanted to return home to join in the defense of South Carolina and got Washington's permission to take a leave of absence. Washington wrote to South Carolina's governor John Rutledge in March 1779 explaining the situation:

> Lieutenant Colonel Laurens, who will have the honor of delivering you this, has served two Campaigns in my Family in quality of aide De Camp. . . . Though unwilling to part with him, I could not oppose his going to a place where he is called by such powerful motives, and where I am persuaded he will be extremely useful. I have therefore given him leave of absence 'till a change of affairs will permit his return, when I shall be happy to see him resume his place in my family.[5]

The new British offensive in the South offered an opportunity for Laurens to renew his crusade to enlist black slaves into the army. By early 1779 the northern states were actively enlisting slaves to meet their troop quotas. Washington's main army was desperate for manpower and voiced no disapproval as blacks arrived to fill the ranks. There was also little opposition to use black soldiers from the Continental Congress, and following the fall of Savannah, Congress seemed ready to take the unprecedented step of recommending slave enlistments to the southern states. Before Colonel Laurens left the Wallace house, he and his friend Hamilton formulated a strategy that would bring about their dream of black slaves winning their freedom through military service. Laurens decided to stop at Philadelphia en route to South Carolina to see if he could get Congress to support a plan of recruiting slaves into the ranks of the southern army. Hamilton helped by writing a letter on March 14 to his friend John Jay, then president of Congress. Hamilton explained their plan for enlisting the slaves in this letter which included the thought provoking phrase, "to give them their freedom with their muskets":

> Col. Laurens, who will have the honor of delivering you this letter, is on his way to South Carolina, on a project which I think, in the present situation of affairs there, is a very good one and deserves every kind of support and encouragement. This is to raise two three or four battalions of negroes; with the assistance of the government of that state, by contributions from the owners in proportion to the number they possess. . . . He wishes to have it recommended by Congress to the state; and, as an inducement, that they would engage to take those battalions into Continental pay. . . . I have not the least doubt, that the negroes will make very excellent soldiers, with proper management; and I will venture to pronounce, that they cannot be put in better hands than those of Mr. Laurens. . . . An essential part of the plan is to give them their freedom with their muskets. This will secure their fidelity, animate their courage, and I believe will have a good influence upon those who remain, by opening a door to their emancipation.[6]

Laurens's departure reduced Washington's staff to Tilghman, Hamilton, McHenry, Gibbs, and Lewis. But Harrison and Meade returned from their leaves of absence in Virginia shortly after Laurens's departure for South Carolina. As planned, Colonel Laurens stopped at Philadelphia where he found unexpected support for his scheme to raise black troops. Favoring his plan were the South Carolina delegates to Congress, William Henry Drayton and Henry Laurens (Colonel Laurens's father). Also favoring the plan was Gen. Daniel Huger, who had been sent north by South Carolina's governor John Rutledge to entreat Congress to send military aid to help defend their state.[7] With its funds and manpower exhausted, Congress felt it was time to sanction the arming of black slaves and use them to fill the ranks of the depleted Continental Army.[8] On March 29, 1779, with an elated John Laurens present, Congress resolved, "That it be recommended to the states of South Carolina and Georgia, if they shall think the same expedient, to take measures immediately for raising three thousand able bodied negroes." Following Laurens's and Hamilton's idea, Congress also suggested that the blacks be formed into separate battalions "according to the arrangements adopted for the main army, to be commanded by white commissioned and non commissioned officers." Congress agreed to make provision for paying the slave owners a sum of not more than a thousand dollars for each man they supplied to the army. And finally, Congress resolved, "That every negro who shall well and faithfully serve as a soldier to the end of the present war, and shall then return his arms, be emancipated and receive the sum of fifty dollars."[9]

To help Laurens in his mission, they gave him the additional prestige and authority of a Congressional commission as a lieutenant colonel.[10] As previously noted up to this time Laurens held the implied rank of lieutenant colonel as one of the commander in chief's aides-de-camp. Upon learning of Laurens's achievements in Philadelphia, Hamilton wrote to congratulate his friend: "I am pleased with your success, so far, and I hope the favorable omens, that precede your application to the [South Carolina] Assembly may have as favorable an issue."[11]

Laurens was exhilarated with Congress's approval of his plan and hurried to South Carolina with the slave soldier resolution in hand. For good measure, the president of the Continental Congress, John Jay, gave Colonel Laurens an impressive letter of introduction addressed to Gen. Benjamin Lincoln who commanded all American troops in the South. Jay's letter, dated "Philadelphia, 31st March, 1779," helps explain the ease with which Laurens was given the command of troops during the time he served in the South.

> You will receive this from the Hands of Lt Colonel Laurens. This Gentleman's Zeal for the American cause & his Bravery in support of it, have induced Congress to honor him with the Commission he now holds. His Excellency General Washington has, in compliance with the Colonel's Request, consented to his joining in the defense of his native State & it would be very agreeable to Congress that he should have a Command suitable to his Rank. . . . Permit me to recommend him warmly to your Attention, and to assure You that I am of the Number of those, who, from public, as well as personal Considerations, are sincerely disposed to promote his Welfare & Honor.[12]

Laurens arrived in Charleston to find his home state already threatened by a British assault launched from their newly conquered base at Savannah. He rushed to the field headquarters of Gen. William Moultrie who commanded a 1,000-man force composed mostly of unsteady militia that was blocking the British advance towards Charleston. Laurens volunteered to lead the withdrawal of some rear guard troops who were in danger of being overrun by the enemy. Moultrie agreed and Laurens went off with a detachment of 250 men to escort the rear guard back to camp. Moultrie would shortly learn that it was hazardous to give John Laurens an independent command with the enemy nearby. Anxious for glory on his native soil, Laurens ignored Moultrie's orders and combined his 250-man detachment with the rear guard troops and crossed the Coosawhatchie River in search of the enemy. After finding them, he led his inexperienced troops in a reckless, unnecessary charge. The British bested him by carefully deploying their men and artillery. Within moments, two Americans were killed and seven wounded. Laurens's horse was shot from under him, and he was wounded in the right arm. Moultrie heard the distant gunfire at his headquarters and assumed it was Laurens's detachment skirmishing with the enemy while escorting the rear guard back to camp. Back on the battlefield, the wounded Laurens was forced to withdraw. His battered troops followed making a hasty retreat to Moultrie's encampment. Upon his return the wounded Laurens told Moultrie, "Sir, your men won't stand." The veteran Moultrie was furious. He replied that Laurens was at fault for recklessly exposing the troops under his command to enemy fire.[13] While some army officers felt Colonel Laurens was an irresponsible combat officer, many civilians thought differently of him and admired his battlefield courage and bravery. His father Henry adored him and wrote him from Congress (in Philadelphia) on May 30, 1779, upon hearing the news that he had been wounded in the defense of Charleston: "My Dear Son & beloved fellow Citizen. I most heartily congratulate with my Countrymen in general on your escape from death in an action with the Enemy . . . The slaughter of your horse & the record on your arm, testify that your journey to So. Carolina was not calculated merely for pleasureable amusements."[14]

The arrival of American reinforcements to South Carolina forced the British to withdraw back to Savannah. However it was only a matter of time before they would launch another invasion of South Carolina. The situation was now ripe for John Laurens to present the recommendation of Congress to arm slaves to defend the southern states. John had been elected to the South Carolina House of Representatives early in 1779 as an acknowledgment of his war efforts. This appointment gave him easy access to the state's legislators. Young Laurens presented Congress's proposal at the first session of the South Carolina House of Representatives, which met in July 1779.[15] The response from his fellow legislators was a howl of protest. They felt not only abandoned by the Continental Congress but mocked and insulted by its recommendation to arm black slaves. The cry in the legislature was for Continental troops and not schemes to give guns to their slaves. Christopher Gadsden, a member of the legislature wrote a friend after hearing the proposal: "We are much disgusted here at the Congress recommending us to arm our Slaves, it was received with great resentment, as a very dangerous and impolitic Step."[16] The only surprise was that Laurens received a few votes of support from members of the legislature.

Colonel Laurens remained in South Carolina despite the contemptuous outcry given his proposal to raise black troops and he took an active part in the defense of his home state. He participated in a failed Franco-American effort to retake Savannah. The allies ran into unexpected stiff resistance at Savannah and abandoned the enterprise on October 18, 1779, after suffering heavy losses. The greatest storyteller of the American Revolution, Mason Locke Weems, said that Lieutenant Colonel Laurens "raged like a wounded lion" when he was ordered to retreat from Savannah. As he turned to go, Laurens looked down on his fallen men and exclaimed, "Poor fellows, I envy you." Then he hurled his sword on the ground and retired from the field of battle.[17]

Laurens seemed inexhaustible. Following the allied debacle at Savannah, he made a brief trip north to plead for reinforcements for the defense of South

Carolina. He was in Philadelphia on November 20, 1779, where he conferred with members of Congress. Laurens then rode to Washington's headquarters for a brief visit. He returned to Philadelphia for additional meetings with Congress and then back to Charleston where he arrived on January 11, 1780, a month before the British launched a new assault against the city. As predicted, the British came in force to seize Charleston; 8,500 troops supported by warships. They lay siege to the city in February 1780 as the Americans fought back from behind their defenses. It was reported that Lieutenant Colonel Laurens threatened to run his sword through the first civilian who suggested that the city surrender.[18] But Charleston surrendered to the British on May 12, 1780, after a long siege. Almost 5,500 American defenders laid down their arms including Colonel John Laurens. The fall of Charleston proved to be the worst American defeat of the Revolution.

While fighting was raging in the South, the Continental Congress was waging its own war to keep the infant nation's economy afloat. By 1779 their paper money was practically worthless, valued at about one cent on the dollar. Congress decided to control inflation by regulating prices, which made matters worse. It seemed the war would go on forever, and people were losing confidence in the ability of the Continental Army to win a decisive victory. In June 1779 Washington moved his army to West Point on the Hudson River. This post was about fifty miles north of British-held New York City. As fighting was raging in the South, Washington remained with the Grand Army in the Hudson River Valley, looking for some favorable opportunity to retake New York City. A French diplomat visited the Americans' camp a few months later, in September 1779. He mentioned Washington's personal staff in one of his letters, which included a flattering assessment of Hamilton:

> Washington's family is quite worthy of its head, his aides-de-camp are very pleasant, and the greatest of unity exists amongst them. One of them, Mr. Hamilton, is noticeable for having more diligence than the rest. If courage, assiduity, and penetration, mingled with a few traces of ambition, can raise a man above his equals, in a nascent republic, some day you will hear of him.[19]

It was rare for Washington's army to winter twice in the same place during the war. The lengthy winter cantonment of the army, which included many horses and oxen, tended to exhaust the food supply of the surrounding countryside for years. The army also cut down many of the trees in the area to build huts and provide firewood. The strategic location of Morristown, New Jersey, however, drew Washington to return to the region for a second winter encampment.

Troops began to arrive at Morristown in late November 1779. Washington reached the village from West Point with his military family in the midst of a severe hail- and snowstorm on December 1, 1779. This storm was only an introduction to the harsh winter that lay ahead. In fact, the winter of 1779–80 was probably the worst winter of the eighteenth century. More than twenty snowstorms devastated the Morristown area with unremitting ferocity while six-foot snowdrifts blocked the few roads into the area, threatening the army's supply line. The army probably would not have survived similar weather conditions at Valley Forge two years earlier. But by the time of the second Morristown encampment, the army was better organized and more experienced to maintain itself through the winter. For his second winter cantonment at Morristown, Washington rented a portion of the spacious mansion owned by the widow of Jacob Ford, Jr. Mrs. Ford moved into two rooms in the house with her four young children. Other senior officers found quarters in private homes nearby. The junior officers and common soldiers built huts and spent the winter a few miles south of Morristown in a farming area known as Jockey Hollow.

Washington settled into the Ford mansion with his entourage of aides-de-camp, personal servants, household servants, laundresses, cooks, and grooms. Two cooks were probably employed full time to feed Washington, his aides, and the multitude of servants. There were familiar faces among Washington's military family at Morristown: Robert Hanson Harrison, Tench Tilghman, Alexander Hamilton, Richard Kidder Meade, and James McHenry. John Laurens returned briefly from South Carolina with dreadful tales of bloody fighting. He convinced Washington that South Carolina was in a more defenseless position then the commander in chief had realized. With the approval of Congress, Washington ordered the entire Virginia Line to march south as reinforcements.[20] The Virginia troops departed Morristown over a three-day period, from December 9–11. Having accomplished his mission, Colonel Laurens left Morristown to return to South Carolina. Washington wrote Gen. Benjamin Lincoln a few days after Laurens had left.

> I shall take the liberty in my turn of referring you to Colo. Laurens for a minute account of our circumstances and situation, and I am happy in having the testimony of so able a judge and so good a Man to witness that the utmost has been done by me to afford relief to the quarter [South Carolina] which so loudly and with so much reason calls for assistance.[21]

Washington's nephew, twenty-year-old George Augustine Washington, was also at headquarters at this time serving as a gentleman volunteer. He was the son of the general's youngest brother, Charles. George Augustine was well liked by his uncle and it is probable that he lived and worked for a time with his aides-de-camp. Nephew George is frequently mentioned by historians as one of Washington's aides-de-camp, but he was not. The evidence shows that there is no known reference of George Augustine being appointed as an aide-de-camp in the general orders of the army, the journals of the Continental Congress, or Washington's letters or orders. While he composed letters for his uncle at headquarters, there were other gentlemen volunteers, officers, and visiting government functionaries who were similarly and temporarily pressed into service without being appointed as official aides-de-camps. Another piece of evidence against George Augustine's appointment was a letter his uncle wrote to Gen. William Woodford from Morristown on December 18, 1779. This letter mentions young George's "temporary duties" at headquarters. Washington wrote Woodford, "My Nephew George Augustine Washington (Son of Charles) seems to have a warm desire to enter the Service." His Excellency continued, "I shall keep him for some time doing the duty of Ensign in my guard at least till he can be made somewhat acquainted with his duty as an officer."[22] George Augustine was subsequently mentioned in the general orders for April 27, 1780, which stated that he had been commissioned as an ensign in a Virginia regiment. The same general orders refer to him as temporarily serving in the Commander in Chief's Guard: "Congress having been pleased to appoint George Augustine Washington an Ensign in the second Regiment of Virginia, he is to do Duty in the Commander in Chief's Guards until further Orders."[23] Other work apparently was soon found for this laudable young man because he was mentioned in a letter dated August 2, 1780, as being an aide-de-camp to the marquis de Lafayette.[24] He was frequently absent from the army because of illness, however, and it is believed that he suffered from consumption. George Augustine remained on Lafayette's staff until May 1782 when he left because of ill health and never returned to the army. Following the war, he married Martha Washington's niece Frances Bassett. The newly-weds moved into Mount Vernon where nephew George helped his uncle operate his vast estate. He managed Mount Vernon during Washington's presidency until illness forced him to retire. George Augustine Washington died from consumption on February 5, 1793, at the age of thirty-four.

The Ford mansion was several miles from the army's encampment at Jockey Hollow. Because of this security problem a large number of guards protected the house. The Commander in Chief's Guard composed the core of the security force surrounding headquarters, and they were housed close to the mansion. Elijah Fisher was a member of the Guard, and his journal mentions arriving at Morristown on December 4, 1779, "where Head Quarters was and Piched our tents." On December 9, "we finished our huts and leit our tents and mooved into them."[25] There were guards stationed at every door of the mansion. We do not know how many sentries surrounded the Ford mansion while it was used as headquarters, but one British spy reported that there were 500 men guarding the house. The British launched one attempt during the winter to kidnap Washington. They sent 500 calvarymen from Paulus Hook (a section of modern Jersey City) to raid Morristown and capture him, but cold weather and ice turned them back before they ever had a chance to test the security surrounding the Ford mansion.[26]

The mansion was a typical house of the Georgian period with a large center hallway. The house had two stories. Washington and his aides occupied two downstairs rooms and the entire second floor. It is believed that the aides occupied the large front room on the left as you entered through the front door. Their office doubled as the dining room. It was probably furnished with a large table that the aides used as a work area during office hours. They cleared the table in time for the servants to set up the table for the big 3:00 P.M. dinner meal. This table was part of the headquarters baggage and was made up in sections, which could be added or removed, depending on the number of people invited to dinner.[27]

Washington's private office was in a rear corner room of the lower level of the house. A window in his room had been removed and the space enlarged to make a doorway. The army probably built a large log building that butted up against the side of the mansion and the new doorway to Washington's office. The log building was used as an office during the day and sleeping quarters at night. A visitor typically entered the mansion through the log building. He was met by a headquarters officer of the day who was stationed there. This officer probably belonged to the Commander in Chief's Guard. He would determine the visitor's business and direct him accordingly. If someone had an appointment with His Excellency, the officer could take the visitor from the log building, through the doorway cut in the wall, directly into Washington's office. The aides were too busy to deal with casual visitors and they worked undisturbed in their front room in the mansion. Couriers also entered headquarters through the log building and perhaps waited there until their dispatches had been delivered. If necessary a courier could stay in the log building until a reply had been prepared by Washington or one of his aides. Washington must have consulted with particular aides about specific matters depending on their abilities and his need for help. A clue to the high volume of work coming from the Ford mansion was the large quantity of office supplies being consumed by Washington and his military family. We have one letter from the general written in 1780, saying that, "I am totally out of Writing paper, Wax and Wafers." He asked for the "quick delivery of twenty-four reams of pretty good quality paper" and a suitable supply of wax and wafers.[28]

There were the usual retinue of servants living at the house. In fact, we know the number of servants with Washington and his aides at one point at the Ford mansion because it is mentioned in a letter. Washington wrote to Gen. Nathanael Greene from the house on January 22, 1780, "nor is there a place at this moment in which a servant can lodge with the smallest degree of comfort. Eighteen belonging to my family and all Mrs. Fords are crowded together in her kitchen and scarce one of them able to speak for the colds they have caught."[29] This figure of eighteen servants for the general and his military family would have included at least one personal servant for each of his aides-de-camp. Some of the aides may have had more than one servant using, for example, one to attend to their personal needs and a second one to take care of their horses and saddles. Washington probably had three retainers including Billy Lee. The military family's dependable housekeeper, Mrs. Elizabeth Thompson, was also at the Ford mansion. As the senior female employee in the household she supervised the cooking, washing, and cleaning of the house. She was probably assisted by two cooks, a washerwoman, and two kitchen helpers. Martha Washington joined her husband at Morristown and she must have brought two or three slave servants to wait on her.

Washington had a large upstairs bedroom reserved for himself and his wife. The aides shared the remaining two bedrooms sleeping on their folding camp beds. If there were overnight visitors to the house, they would have shared the bedrooms with the aides. The arrival of important visitors probably required the aides to move their sleeping quarters out of the house to the log office building.[30] It is believed that there was another large log buildings constructed in the grounds of the Morris mansion. It was probably a kitchen used for cooking food for the headquarters staff.

There was a lighter side to camp life at Morristown. In one incident, James McHenry mentions that his fellow aide, Richard Kidder Meade, wanted to read a private letter he had received away from "profane eyes." Seeking privacy, he thrust himself up a chimney to read his letter.[31] Meade apparently repeated this act to keep his fellow aides from seeing his personal correspondence. McHenry loved to write poetry and he spent some spare moments writing verse while wintering at Morristown. One of the charming poems he wrote at Morristown illustrates the warm comradeship that existed among the general's staff. Note that McHenry particularly mentions his friendship with Hamilton. They were good friends and McHenry loved to be in his company. The aides were probably spending their nights in the log office building when the poem was written.

A Morning Scene in a Hut

Now through the camp the morning gun resounds:
now, noisy Gibbs the nightly watch relieves
Up, up, my sons! Grave Harrison exclaims,
(A learned clerk and not unknown to fame
and forth displays large packets unexplored.
Tilhman [Tilghman], accustom'd to the well known voice,
pulls up his stockings smiling, and preludes
his daily labor with some mirthful stroke
But falls, like, down without inflicting pain.
Kidder of gentle soul, and courage true,
and dearly lov'd by all for worth most rare,
such as in times of yore fill'd Bayards breast,
uprose, to plead for others longer sleep.

> But nought might smooth the ancients care-worn brow
> he restless still would pace the hut & still
> on Ham [Alexander Hamilton] and Henry [James McHenry]
>   call; congenial pair
> who in rough blankets wrapped snor'd loud defiance
> to packets hugh [huge], to morning gun & Gibbs!
> For oft in gamesome mood, these twain combin'd
> to tease Sectarius through him they pris'd
> next to the chief who holds the reins of War [a reference to
>   Washington].[32]

Martha Washington's presence at the Ford mansion presented an opportunity for socializing. Other officers' wives and family members visited Morristown that winter including Elizabeth Schuyler, the daughter of Washington's friend Gen. Philip Schuyler. Washington mentions her being at camp in a letter to her father dated January 30, 1780: "Your fair daughter, for whose visit Mrs. Washington and myself are greatly obliged."[33] Elizabeth was twenty-three years old at the time. Tench Tilghman met her briefly earlier in the war and recorded this impression: "I was prepossessed in favor of this young Lady the moment I saw her. A brunette with the most good natured lively dark eyes I ever saw, which threw a beam of good temper and benevolence over her whole Countenance."[34]

We do not know when or where Alexander Hamilton met Elizabeth Schuyler. It appears likely they became acquainted during her visit to Morristown in 1780. There is, for instance, a reference to the general's aides-de-camp taking her and her cousin, Catherine Livingston, on a winter sleigh ride. Elizabeth probably stayed with her relatives, Dr. John Cochran and his wife, who were quartered just down the road from the Ford mansion at the home of their friend Dr. Jabez Campfield.[35] She apparently started seeing Hamilton socially during the early part of February 1780 and they became engaged in April. The young couple decided to get married the following December at her parents' mansion in Albany. Hamilton had been thinking about getting married for some time. When his best friend John Laurens was in South Carolina the previous year, Hamilton had asked him to find him a wife. Hamilton had jokingly given his friend his requirements:

> And Now my Dear as we are upon the subject of wife, I empower and command you to get me one in Carolina. . . . Take her description— She must be young, handsome (I lay most stress upon a good shape) sensible (a little learning will do), well bred . . . chaste and tender (I am an enthusiast in my notions of fidelity and fondness) of some good nature, a great deal of generosity (she must neither love money nor scolding, for I dislike equally a termagent [termagant—a shrew]—

and an œconomist). . . . But as to fortune, the larger stock of that the better. You know my temper and circumstances and I will therefore pay special attention to this article in the treaty.[36]

Hamilton was fortunate that he found a wealthy woman whom he loved. He was an ambitious young man who had worked hard to achieve some success in his life. He had also made two excellent decisions in his life since the start of the Revolution. One was accepting Washington's invitation to be his aide-de-camp and the second was his decision to marry Elizabeth, which aligned him with the respectable and important Schuyler clan of New York.

News reached Morristown that the British had captured Charleston. The fall of the city further dampened American morale and sent the already depleted Continental currency notes into a deeper inflationary tailspin. Washington and his staff learned that Lieutenant Colonel Laurens was a prisoner of war, but unhurt. As was the custom, both sides moved to exchange captives but this procedure could take many months, sometimes years to negotiate. In the interim, officers were frequently afforded the courtesy of being put on their parole, promising on their word not to return to rejoin the fighting until they were exchanged.[37] There is a curious entry in the Journals of the Continental Congress for July 10, 1780, relating to Laurens's exchange: "Resolved, For special reasons that the Board of War do take the most speedy measures for the exchange of Lieutenant Colonel John Laurens, one of General Washington's family, and now a prisoner of war on parole."[38] Laurens was probably being afforded special treatment through the influence of his father. Whatever special efforts were made to try and quickly exchange Laurens unfortunately did not work. He was captured in May 1780 and had to wait to be traded as part of a general prisoner exchange that took place in early November of that same year. Laurens was luckier than some of the officers who were captured at Charleston who remained as prisoners on parole for almost two years.

Young Laurens was on parole when he set sail from Philadelphia on August 13, 1780, aboard the brig *Mercury.* He was accompanying his father, who was on the start of his mission to negotiate a treaty and a loan from Holland. The lieutenant colonel traveled as far as Fort Penn where he bid his father farewell and watched his ship continue downriver toward the open sea. The *Mercury* was in the midst of its Atlantic crossing when it was intercepted and captured by the HMS *Vestal,* a twenty-eight-gun frigate, off the coast of Newfoundland on September 3, 1780. Realizing that his ship was about to be boarded, Henry Laurens threw his official papers overboard but it was too late. They were retrieved by the British, who discovered his identity and mission.[39] Laurens was taken in chains to England where he claimed diplomatic immunity, which was ignored. He was interrogated and confined in the Tower of London on suspicion of high treason. Held in tight confinement Laurens was twice offered a pardon if he agreed to renounce his allegiance to America and join the British side. He refused both times. The Continental Congress tried every means to get Laurens released or exchanged but the British were unwilling to make a trade and continued to let him languish in prison. The only consolation from his miserable imprisonment was a brief visit from Martha Manning Laurens, his son John's wife. She brought along their daughter Fanny to meet her grandfather for the first time.

We must leave Henry Laurens in the Tower of London for the moment and proceed to the black deed that would prove to be the emotional low point for the American patriots during the eight years of the Revolution.

CHAPTER EIGHT

Hard Times
January–December 1780

There has just been unfolded at this place a scene of the blackest
treason . . .

Alexander Hamilton to Nathanael Greene[1]

By the beginning of 1780 the colonists had been fighting for independence for over five years with no prospect of victory in sight. American enthusiasm was waning and the financial manipulations of the Continental Congress finally brought about an economic collapse. Public credit had been exhausted, and the army was existing on a day to day basis. The loss of Charleston in May 1780 was followed by another catastrophic American defeat in the South when Gen. Horatio Gates, the hero of Saratoga, had his army smashed near Camden, South Carolina. After learning of Gates's defeat, Hamilton wrote his friend John Laurens a letter on September 12, 1780, which reflected the terrible state of the army, the new nation, and his personal frustrations. Laurens had been captured when Charleston surrendered and was a prisoner on parole at the time.

> Indeed, my Dear friend, to drop allegory, you can hardly conceive in how dreadful a situation we are. The army, in the course of the present month, has received only four or five days rations of meal, and we really know not of any adequate relief in future. . . . I hate Congress— I hate the army—I hate the world—I hate myself. The whole is a mass of fools and knaves; I could almost except you and Meade [Richard Kidder Meade].[2]

Washington faced mounting problems as the war staggered on, but he made the time to help Tench Tilghman who had served as a volunteer aide-de-camp for almost four years. The two men had also become close friends. The hardworking Marylander is referred to in correspondence as "Mr. Tilghman" and he signed his oath of allegiance at Valley Forge in May 1778 as "assistant secretary to his Excellency."[3] The probable explanation for Tilghman's long-standing volunteer status was his patriotic idea that he should serve without any salary. There are other examples of men refusing to accept money for their service in the Continental Army including Washington.

Tilghman continued to serve as a volunteer until Washington and other members of the military family probably insisted that he receive recognition for his hard work. The general orders for June 21, 1780, includes his long overdue appointment as an aide-de-camp, "Tench Tilghman Esqr. is Appointed Aide de Camp to the Commander in Chief and is to be obeyed and respected as such."[4] Washington, however, wanted him to benefit from the honor and advantages of being commissioned by Congress as a Continental Army officer. Robert Hanson Harrison wrote about his friend Tilghman's situation a few months after Tilghman's official appointment as an aide-de-camp: "There must be something done with respect to our worthy Tilghman."[5] Tilghman waited another year, however, before Congress would consider commissioning him.

The year 1780 also saw what proved to be an important addition to Washington's military family when Maj. David Humphreys arrived on the scene. He turned out to be one of the most colorful and interesting of Washington's aides. Humphreys was born in Derby, Connecticut, on July 10, 1752. He was the youngest son of the Reverend Daniel Humphreys, a Congregational clergyman and scholar and his wife, Sarah. David got his interest in literature and poetry from his father. His higher education was at Yale College where he graduated in the class of 1771.[6] His graduating class consisted of nine men. It was the custom in Connecticut that recent Yale graduates devote a few years to teaching in the local schools as a public service before pursuing other interests.

Yale graduates were sought after by the various Connecticut towns because they were educated young men who could be employed at low wages. Humphreys was no exception, and following graduation he accepted a position as a schoolmaster in the town of Wethersfield, Connecticut. In 1773 he took a new position as a private tutor at the Philipse Manor on the Hudson River. The wealthy Col. Frederick Philipse had eleven children for Humphreys to teach. Living in Philipse Manor gave Humphreys his introduction to aristocratic tastes and luxury, which he must have enjoyed because he loved pomp and wealth for the rest of his life. Humphreys also found the time to earn a master of arts degree from Yale in 1774. After the outbreak of war he volunteered as adjutant in the 2nd Connecticut Militia Regiment. To mark his transformation from scholar to soldier, he wrote this piece of verse, which will serve as our introduction to his weighty poetry: "Adieu thou Yale . . . Here ye the din of battle? Clang of arms?"[7]

Humphreys proved to be a talented and courageous officer, and he quickly rose through the ranks attracting the attention of Connecticut's celebrated Gen.

Israel Putnam. The young schoolmaster was appointed as Putnam's aide-de-camp and remained in the job until Putnam suffered a severe stroke in 1780. Humphreys already had an excellent reputation as a "pen-man" so he was quickly recruited by Gen. Nathanael Greene to serve as one of his aides. But Washington imposed his will and friendship upon Greene and had Humphreys transferred to his own staff.[8]

His appointment was mentioned in the general orders of the army for June 23, 1780: "Captain David Humphrys of the Connecticut Line is Appointed Aide de Camp to the Commander in Chief and is to be respected and obeyed accordingly."[9] Greene and Washington did not learn about Humphreys by chance. He was a self-promoter and he wrote patriotic verses during the lulls in the war. In the winter of 1779–80, Humphreys wrote a thunderous poem called *An Address to the Armies,* in which he praised the American cause and glorified its military leaders. The poem was published and the opportunistic Humphreys sent a copy to his hero, General Washington, who recognized a good wordsmith when he saw one.

Humphreys loved to celebrate in rhyme the events of the Revolution. His stirring patriotic poetry was popular at the time; however, it is platitudinous by modern standards. As way of introduction here are a few lines from a poem he is said to have written to a young lady while he was en route to take up his post as Washington's aide-de-camp,

> I go wherever the battle bleeds,
> To-morrow—(brief then be my story)—-
> I go to Washington and glory;
> His Aid-de-Camp[10]

Sensitive documents concerning strategy, troop locations and movements, the supply situation, unrest in the army, and spy operations were routinely handled at Washington's headquarters, and trustworthiness and confidentiality were necessary characteristics of the aides-de-camp. The general's aides also attended councils of war where military campaigns were planned. They were present at these meetings to keep minutes of what was discussed and write follow-up reports. Washington's aides also worked closely with him in the collection and distribution of intelligence information. There are numerous examples to show their involvement in this area. Tench Tilghman wrote General Sullivan from headquarters on May 30, 1777, saying, "The inclosed intelligence was transmitted to his Excellency Yesterday. It comes from a person of undoubted credibility and much intrusted by the Enemy."[11] Robert Hanson Harrison wrote Sullivan the following month acknowledging the receipt of intelligence from him: "His Excellency was favored with Yours of today. The Intelligence contained in it, agrees nearly with that which I transmitted last night." Alexander Hamilton instructed Stephen Moylan from headquarters, Valley Forge, April 3, 1778,

There is a certain Mr. Bankson, late of the Continental marines, who has a family in Princeton. We suspect him to be a spy to Mr. Howe [the British general Sir William Howe], though he offers himself as one of us. We wish to find out his true history. He left this camp the 24th March, on pretence of making a visit to his family, and is now returned with renewed offers of service. It is doubted whether he has not, in the mean time, been at Philadelphia. . . . take cautious methods to ascertain whether Bankson has been at home, since he left camp—how long—and when he left home—in short any thing that may throw light upon his designs.

Let him [General Washington] hear from you as soon as possible on the subject. Manage the business with caution and address.[12]

Both sides used encoded messages, and Congressman James Lovell was particularly effective at breaking enemy ciphers. Lovell wrote Washington on September 21, 1781, with the keys to breaking a British code.[13] Washington replied to Lovell on October 6, making it clear that his military secretary had access to what today would be called top secret information: "My Secretary has taken a Copy of the Cyphers, and by help of one of the Alphabets has been able to decipher one paragraph of a Letter lately intercepted going from Lord Cornwallis to Sir Henry Clinton."[14]

Historians have found evidence of extensive intelligence operations carried out by both the British and Americans during the war. Washington was relatively sophisticated in dealing with intelligence matters; he operated numerous spy rings, especially inside British-held New York City.[15] He used double agents, ciphers, invisible inks, and disinformation with great skill. We will probably never know the extent of his spy operations, because there is no record of most of his covert activities. Washington appointed Maj. Benjamin Tallmadge the director of his secret service in 1778.[16] Espionage operations, however, were supervised by Washington and his aides-de-camp. We have some American espionage documents written by Washington's aides that confirm their involvement in intelligence-gathering activities. One surviving document is a set of instructions for American spies in the handwriting of Washington with changes and additions made by Tilghman. This document, written in plain English, is dated September 1780, and reads in part:

INSTRUCTIONS FOR SPIES GOING INTO NEW YORK

Get into the City.

There, in the best manner possible, learn the designs of the Enemy. . . . Enquire whether the Transports are Wooding and Watering. Whether the Stores are moving from the City into them, and whether any Regimental Baggage is Imbarked. Enquire also, how the Enemy are off for Provisions; whether the Cork Fleet is arrived and the num-

ber of Provision Ships it consists of. . . . Whether the Merchants who
came from Europe and those who have been attached to Government
are packing up or selling-off their goods. Attend particularly to Cof-
fin and Anderson who keep a large dry good Store and supply their
Officers and Army.[17]

Also surviving is a letter written by Hamilton to Joshua Mersereau on
October 24, 1780. Mersereau lived in New Jersey and served as the American
deputy commissary of prisoners. He also secretly operated a spy network for
Washington.

> By intelligence just received from New York, we have reason to
> believe the enemy have some attempt in view by way of Staten
> Island, the execution of which will probably take place on thursday
> [*sic*] evening; if so the troops from New York will probably be past
> upon Staten Island thursday morning. The General wishes you to
> have [one] trusty person over on the Island, to ascertain, whether any
> troops do come from New York and whether there are any movements
> more than common among the enemy on the Island. . . .[18]

The British were carrying out similar clandestine activities. One specialty
was the printing of large quantities of counterfeit Continental notes to undermine the fledgling American economy. Both sides were also active in propa-
ganda campaigns, which included creating false letters that were purposely
allowed to fall into enemy hands. Another technique was to change captured
letters, which were then planted in newspapers to embarrass the enemy and
fuel dissent. A good example of this technique involved a genuine letter written by congressional delegate Benjamin Harrison to his friend George Washington. Harrison wrote from Philadelphia in late July 1775 with news and
gossip about what was happening in Congress. Harrison gave the letter to an
express rider who was captured en route to Washington's headquarters. The
British published Harrison's letter in a Boston newspaper adding the following
spurious paragraph within the authentic letter:

> As I was in the pleasing Task of writing to you, a little Noise occa-
> sioned me to turn my Head round, and who should appear but pretty
> little Kate the Washer-woman's Daughter over the Way, clean, trim
> and rosey as the Morning: I snatch'd the golden glorious Opportunity,
> and but for that cursed Antidote of Love, Sukey, I had fitted her for
> my General [Washington] against his Return. We were obliged to
> part, but not till we had contrived to meet again; if she keeps the
> Appointment I shall relish a Week's longer stay—I gave you now and
> then some of these Adventures to amuse you, and unbend your Mind
> from the Cares of War.[19]

This letter was also published in other British-controlled newspapers.

Another piece of false information spread by the British involved an exchange of prisoners in late 1778. This piece of misinformation is of particular interest because it involved two of Washington's aides-de-camp. General Washington appointed Robert Hanson Harrison and Alexander Hamilton as commissioners to negotiate a prisoner exchange on behalf of the Continental Army. The British fabricated a false letter written by their commissioners (Colonels O'Hara and Hyde) claiming that Harrison and Hamilton were only interested in the welfare of the American officers held in captivity and had no regard for the fate of the private soldiers. The counterfeit letter reads,

> Copy of a letter from Colonels O'Hara and Hyde,
> to Lieut. Colonels Harrison and Hamilton
> Amboy [Perth Amboy, New Jersey], December 12, 1778.

> . . . Every sense of honor, justice, and humanity, makes it impossible to acquiesce in a proposal which might lead to separate the officers from the private soldiers, by exchanging the former, and suffering the latter to remain in captivity—Companions in their more fortunate hours, they must be equally sharers of affliction; such cruel and unprecedented distinction, between men who have equally a claim upon the favor and protection of their country, we are certain, your own feelings, as officers and men, would condemn. You will consequently not be surprised, that we cannot assent to the partial mode of exchange proposed.

> We beg leave, therefore to acquaint you that we intend returning to New-York tomorrow, to make our report to Sir Henry Clinton. Let us flatter ourselves, that some expedient may be immediately embraced by both parties, upon such honorable, humane, and disinterested principles, as may give the most speedy and ample relief to every order of unfortunate men concerned.[20]

Besides spies, another important intelligence source were prisoners and deserters. Both sides interrogated captured prisoners and deserters for information. The importance of this activity in the American camp is indicated by the fact that the subject is included in one of Washington's first general orders. Washington arrived at Cambridge, Massachusetts, on July 2, 1775, to take command of the New England troops that were besieging British-held Boston. On July 4, only two days after his arrival, he issued a general orders that included instructions regarding prisoners and deserters: "All Prisoners taken, Deserters coming in, Persons coming out of Boston, who can give any Intelligence: any Captures of any kind from the Enemy, are to be immediately reported and brought up to Head Quarters in Cambridge."[21]

The practice of interrogating prisoners and deserters continued throughout the war. For example, writing from New York City on July 7, 1776, Washington reported to one of his senior officers, "Four prisoners that Fell into Our hands last week on a separate examination agree, that General Howe being Joined by some regiments from the West Indies and part of the Scotch Highlanders in his passage heither, has now about Ten Thousand men."[22] On September 18, 1776, Washington wrote John Hancock, "By a sergeant who deserted from the Enemy & came in this Morning, I find that their party was greater than I imagined."[23] Washington constantly repeated that he wanted prisoners and deserters brought to headquarters for questioning. In the general orders of November 4, 1776, he made this point clear: "All Deserters and Prisoners to be reported to the Brigadier of the troops to whom they come, or by whom they are taken, who is to send them to Head-Quarters, as soon as possible."[24] Washington attributes his November 1776 decision to move part of his army to defend New Jersey on information gained from prisoners and deserters that the British were preparing to invade that state.

Washington was a busy man with myriad responsibilities. He was too busy to interrogate every prisoner and deserter and there were no intelligence officers to handle the job for him. Besides, questioning prisoners and deserters required a person familiar with the current operations of the army who could decide what was important information that should be passed along to the commander in chief. The record is mute on who interrogated prisoners and deserters at headquarters but this task appears to be one of the catchall responsibilities of Washington's aides. It is unfortunate for us that they took the confidential aspect of their jobs seriously and there is no known account by any of the aides stating that they acted as interrogators.

Washington and his staff also studied captured documents looking for intelligence information. In one instance, Washington's secretary Robert Harrison wrote to prize agent Joshua Wentworth on January 14, 1776, thanking him for sending all the documents and letters found on captured enemy ships: "I am commanded by his Excellency to acknowledge the receipt of your favor of the 10th inst, with sundry Newspapers, packages &c,."[25]

The British also carried out covert operations to lure senior American officers to become spies or join the loyalist cause. They used money and promises of high rank in the British Army to entice American officers to desert. By 1780 Gen. Sir Henry Clinton and his ambitious young adjutant general, Maj. John André, were in secret contact with a senior American officer who was prepared to switch sides for money and a commission in the British Army. Here is the story of the treason of Benedict Arnold and the role that Washington's aides-de-camp played in it.

The scene of the action is the lower Hudson River. The Hudson is navigable by oceangoing ships for 150 miles into the interior of North America. The river flows straight for its entire length except for one point, about 60 miles north of New York City, where it makes an "S-shaped" turn. A ship has to maneuver slowly through this bend in the river, making it an easy target for shore artillery. It was at this curve in the river that the Americans built their "Gibraltar of America," a fortress that they named West Point.

Washington recalled years later that he was surprised when Maj. Gen. Benedict Arnold approached him in June 1780 with a desire to have command at West Point. Arnold was a courageous officer of "distinguished military talents."[26] There was a darker side to him, however, that was described by Mercy Otis Warren in her 1805 history of the Revolution: "Involved by extravagance, and reproached by his creditors, his resentment wrought him up to a determination of revenge for public ignomy, at the expense of his country, and the sacrifice of the small remains of reputation left, after the perpetration of so many crimes."[27] Washington offered Arnold the command of the Continental Army's light infantry, which was a post of great honor and prestige. His Excellency remembered Arnold's response to his generous offer: "Upon this information his countenance changed and he appeared to be quite fallen, and, instead of thanking me or expressing any pleasure at the appointment, never opened his mouth. I desired him to go on to my quarters . . . and I will meet him there soon. He did so."[28]

Arnold followed Washington's advice and went to headquarters, where he ran into Tench Tilghman. Arnold knew that Tilghman was one of the general's most influential aides. He took Tilghman aside and told him that the wound he had received at the battle of Saratoga had not healed properly and would not permit him to ride a horse for any length of time. Arnold repeated that he wanted command of West Point. Tilghman later told his chief of his discussion with Arnold. Arnold was America's foremost combat officer and Washington admired him for his courage and initiative. Although disappointed with his request, he decided to grant Arnold his wish and gave him command of West Point.[29]

Washington had a small personal staff at this point in the war, consisting of his military secretary Robert Hanson Harrison and aides-de-camp Alexander Hamilton, Richard Kidder Meade, Tench Tilghman, and David Humphreys. Caleb Gibbs was also on the general's staff. He had been promoted to major and continued as the officer in charge of the Commander in Chief's Guard. His Excellency departed his headquarters in northern New Jersey on September 18, 1780, to attend a conference with the French Army's senior officers at Hartford, Connecticut. He took Harrison, Hamilton, Meade, and Tilghman with him. Washington probably wanted Hamilton and Tilghman with him to translate. Humphreys remained behind, perhaps because he was the newest of the general's aides.

Washington and his suite arrived on September 21 at Hartford where the conference took place over the next two days with the comte de Rochambeau, chevalier de Ternay, and other senior French officers. His Excellency left Hartford on September 23 to return to New Jersey, accompanied by his aides plus Gens. Henry Knox and the marquis de Lafayette. Their entourage included Lafayette's aides James McHenry (Washington's former aide who had recently transferred to Lafayette's staff as a volunteer aide-de-camp) and George Augustine Washington (the general's nephew).[30] General Knox was also there with Capt. Samuel Shaw, who was one of his aides. The general was scheduled to stop at West Point on his return trip to inspect its fortifications and confer with Arnold.

On the same day that Washington and his suite left Hartford, three militiamen near the village of Tarrytown, New York, on the lower Hudson River stopped a stranger who was trying to cross through to the British lines. The militiamen did not know at the time that the man standing before them was Maj. John André, General Clinton's adjutant general. André thought that he was at a British outpost, but realizing his error he gave his name as John Anderson, a merchant who was in the Hudson Valley on business for General Arnold. He showed the militiamen a pass from Arnold, but by then they were suspicious and decided to search the young civilian. They looked through his clothing and found nothing suspicious and were about to let him go when one of them, John Paulding, said that they should look inside his boots.[31] André protested but they made him sit down and took off his boots. Inside they found papers. "Hastily scanning them, Paulding exclaimed, My God! He is a spy!"[32]

Washington spent the night of September 23 at Litchfield, Connecticut, where he and his entourage were entertained at the home of Gen. Oliver Wolcott. He spent the following night at Fishkill, New York, where he dined with M. de Luzerne, the French minister, who was en route to Newport, Rhode Island, where the French expeditionary force had its headquarters. Washington was up early on the morning of September 25 to continue his trip with an inspection tour of West Point.[33] The general rode for several hours, as was his habit, before stopping for breakfast, which was scheduled to take place at Arnold's headquarters. Aides McHenry and Shaw rode ahead to make sure everything was ready for Washington's arrival.[34] McHenry and Shaw arrived at the Robinson House, which Arnold used as his home and headquarters, to find Arnold sitting at his breakfast table. He greeted them warmly, and invited them to sit down and join him. They were chatting pleasantly when a courier arrived with important dispatches. Arnold read them while his guests talked and ate. McHenry recalled later that Arnold had a fleeting moment of embarrassment as he was reading one of the communiqués. The general excused himself saying he had to attend to urgent business at West Point but would return within an hour. He darted out of the room, went upstairs for a few moments, returned downstairs, quickly went outside, and mounted a horse that was waiting for him and galloped away. When Washington and his suite arrived, they were surprised to be greeted by one of Arnold's aides-de-camp, Maj. David Solebury Franks.[35] Franks was from Montreal and had been Arnold's business associate before the war. He made apologies for his general who he said had gone across the river to West Point to prepare for His Excellency's visit. As a major general, Arnold was authorized two aides-de-camp. His senior aide was Col. Richard Varick, who was in his bed with fever in a small room on the first floor of the house. Varick had only been on Arnold's staff for six weeks, having arrived from his New Jersey home on August 13. Mrs. Arnold, the former

Peggy Shippen, was also absent. She was in her bedroom upstairs with their six-month-old son. Peggy was a beautiful young woman, half Arnold's age, whom the general had recently married.

Breakfast was served but neither Arnold nor his wife made an appearance. It was assumed that Arnold was involved in some urgent business at West Point and would meet Washington when he crossed the river. Mrs. Arnold remained in her bedroom, claiming she was "indisposed." Having finished breakfast, Washington and his suite went down to the Hudson River and were rowed across to West Point on a barge. Hamilton stayed behind at the Robinson House, which became Washington's makeshift headquarters. The house was quiet when a dispatch rider rode up with a thick packet addressed to General Washington. Hamilton routinely took the package, decided not to open it, and put it aside to give to Washington when he returned from his inspection tour.

The barge returned from West Point in the afternoon with Washington and his party. Hamilton expected to see Arnold among them and was surprised that he was not there. In fact, no one had seen Arnold all day. Washington thought it strange but was certain that his old comrade would soon make his appearance with an explanation. His Excellency retired to the bedroom that had been reserved for his use to freshen up before dinner. Hamilton gave him the bundle of papers that had arrived during his absence. Historian Douglas Freeman says that Robert Hanson Harrison was also in Washington's room at the time.[36] A minute or two later, Hamilton came dashing out of the room. He burst into Lafayette's bedroom telling him that he must go to his His Excellency immediately. Hamilton and Lafayette raced back to Washington's room. They found him standing in the middle of the room with the contents of the dispatch opened, his hands trembling and with tears in his eyes: "Arnold has betrayed us! . . . Whom can we trust now?"[37]

Arnold's treason had been uncovered only through the miraculous capture of André, who had gone up the Hudson from New York City on the Royal Navy sloop of war *Vulture*. André's mission was to meet with Arnold to arrange for the British capture of West Point. He was rowed ashore around midnight on September 21, and the two conspirators met along the west bank of the Hudson. During their meeting, Arnold gave André vital information about the fortifications at West Point and the disposition of its garrison. In return, Arnold was promised money and a commission as a general in the British Army. Meanwhile, downriver, another drama took place as American shore artillery fired on the *Vulture*. The ship dropped farther downriver to get out of range. Arnold convinced the young British officer that it was best for him to change into civilian clothing and return on horseback through Westchester County to British-held New York. Among the dispatches that Arnold had received at breakfast was one informing him that a British spy had been captured with detailed sketches of the West Point defenses and a pass signed by Arnold. The dispatch said that these incriminating documents had been forwarded to General Washington. Arnold knew that his role in the plot would be quickly uncovered and he had to escape. When he galloped away from his house that morning he rode down to the river where his barge was waiting for him. He ordered the crew to row him to the *Vulture,* which was waiting for André. The crew followed their commander's baffling order and rowed him to the safety of the British warship.

Having discovered Arnold's treason, Washington ordered Hamilton to ride downriver to try and intercept Arnold's barge at the American outpost at King's Ferry. McHenry went with him.[38] When they arrived at King's Ferry, they discovered that Arnold was already on board the *Vulture.* Arnold sent a flag of truce to King's Ferry with a letter addressed to Washington. Before returning to the Robinson House with Arnold's letter, Hamilton took the initiative to write a note to Gen. Nathanael Greene alerting him to the situation:

> There has just been unfolded at this place a scene of the blackest treason, Arnold has fled to the Enemy. André the British Adjt Genl is in our possession as a Spy. This capture unraveled the mystery. West Point was to have been the Sacrifice . . . I advise your putting the army under marching orders, and detaching a brigade immediately this way.[39]

Hamilton and McHenry returned to the Robinson house where they gave Arnold's letter to Washington. Arnold wrote his former commander in chief, "I have ever acted from a Principle of Love to my Country, since the Commencement of the present unhappy Contest between Great Britain and the Colonies, that same principle of Love to my Country Actuates my present Conduct, however it may appear Inconsistent to the World."[40]

By the evening of September 25, Washington realized the extent of Arnold's treason and that a British attack on West Point might already be underway. He quickly dispatched a series of orders to redeploy the garrison and send for reinforcements. The bulk of the drafts of the orders sent are in the handwriting of Robert Hanson Harrison. One of the orders, written to Col. John Lamb, was written by Capt. Samuel Shaw (Knox's aide).[41] There is no explanation why Harrison composed almost all of the orders. The other aides may have been occupied with other vital business, such as helping organize the troops at West Point. Or they may have been copying Harrison's drafts into finished copies to be carried by civilian dispatch riders, mounted infantry, or light dragoons to the various army posts in the Hudson highlands. Since time was critical and treason was in the air, Washington may have told Harrison what he wanted to say to each recipient.

Here is a summary of the orders that Harrison drafted on the evening (September 25, 1780). Writing to Col. James Livingston, Washington said, "Sir; I wish to see You here immediately and request that You will come without the least delay."[42] To Lt. Col. Ebenezer Gray, commander of the 6th Connecticut Regiment, "From some intelligence I have received I think it necessary that the

Regiment at present under your command should march without a moments delay."[43] To Col. Nathaniel Wade, "General Arnold is gone to the Enemy . . . command of the Garrison [West Point] for the present devolves on you. I request you will be as vigilant as possible, and as the Enemy may have it in contemplation to attempt some enterprise, even to night, against these Posts, I wish you to make immediately after receipt of this, the best disposition you can of your force."[44] To Lt. Col. John Jameson, "I wish every precaution and attention to be paid to prevent Major André from making his escape . . . He had better be conducted to this place by some upper road rather than by the route thro Crompond [the village of Compound, New York, which was near enemy lines]."[45] To Maj. Caleb Low of the Massachusetts militia who was stationed nearby, "You will pleased to march early to morrow morning with all the Militia under your command and proceed to the Landing opposite West point."[46] To Maj. Gen. Nathanael Greene, "I request that You will put the Division on the left in motion as soon as possible. . . . The Division will come on light, leaving their heavy baggage to follow. . . . Transactions of a most interesting nature and such as will astonish You have been just discovered."[47] To William M. Betts, the assistant deputy quartermaster general at Fishkill, New York, "It is my wish from some matters which have just occurred, to call the Militia employed in cutting Wood to Fishkill, where they will receive frther orders."[48]

We now know that Arnold's wife Peggy was implicated in the plot from the beginning. She had in fact, encouraged her husband in his anger over affronts to his seniority in the American army and in his plan to betray his country for money. But all this was unknown as Hamilton wrote his fiancée Elizabeth describing what happened when he returned from his failed mission to catch the traitor and joined Washington for an interview with Mrs. Arnold:

> when on my return, I saw an amiable woman frantic with distress for the loss of a husband she tenderly loved—a traitor to his country and to his fame, a disgrace to his connections. It was the most affecting scene I ever was witness to. She for a considerable time intirely [sic] lost her senses. The General went up to see her and she upbraided him with being in a plot to murder her child; one moment she raved; another she melted into tears, sometimes she pressed her infant to her bosom and lamented its fate occasioned by the imprudence of its father in a manner that would have pierced insensibility itself.

In danger of being executed as a spy herself, Peggy Arnold gave the greatest performance of her life for Washington's benefit, as Hamilton, who was present, continued to relate the incident: "All the sweetness of beauty, all the loveliness of innocence, all the tenderness of a wife and all the fondness of a mother showed themselves in her appearance and conduct. . . . She instantly fell into a convulsion and he [Washington] left her in that situation."[49]

Gen. Sir Henry Clinton was shaken when he received the news that Major André had been captured and accused of being a spy. Young André was one of his favorite officers, and Clinton had warned him not to remove his uniform during his secret mission to meet with Arnold. André arrived at Washington's headquarters under heavy guard on the morning of September 26. Hamilton described the sequence of events that followed in a letter to his friend Laurens:

> André was, without loss of time, conducted to the headquarters of the army, where he was immediately brought before a board of General Officers to prevent all possibility of misrepresentation, or cavil on the part of the enemy. The board reported that he ought to be considered as a spy, and, according to the laws of nations, to suffer death . . . [50]

The court decided that André should be hanged as a common spy. Hamilton visited André during his final days of captivity. He wrote to Laurens about the young British officer who was very much like them in his ambition and devotion to his cause,

> Never, perhaps, did a man suffer death with more justice, or deserve it less. . . . His education was handsome; his address easy, polite and insinuating. By his merit he had acquired the unlimited confidence of his general [Sir Henry Clinton] and was making a rapid progress in military rank and reputation. But in the height of his career, flushed with new hope from the execution of a project the most beneficial to his party, that could be devised, he was at once precipitated from the summit of prosperity and saw all the expectation of his ambition blasted and himself ruined.
>
> . . . I congratulate you my friend on our happy escape from the mischiefs with which this treason was big. It is a new comment on the value of an honest man [John Paulding].[51]

André made a big impression on Hamilton because he wrote his fiancée about him, "I wished myself possessed of André's accomplishments for your sake; for I would wish to charm you in every sense."[52] Richard Kidder Meade wrote a friend on the day after André's execution that the pain he felt on that occasion proved to him that he was not suited for public service. "Poor André, the British adjutant general, was executed yesterday, nor did it happen my dear Sir without the drop of a tear on my part."[53]

Washington and his military family occupied the DeWint House at Tappen, New York, while the André affair was played out to its sad conclusion. Tradition says that Washington could have witnessed the execution from his headquarters but he ordered the shutters of the house closed and stayed inside with some of his aides to avoid seeing André hang.

What happened to Arnold's two aides, David Solebury Franks and Richard Varick? Washington knew Varick and felt that he had no knowledge of Arnold's plot. Shortly after the treason was uncovered, Washington asked Varick to take a walk with him outside the Robinson House. As they strolled together, Washington told Varick that Arnold had gone over to the enemy. The general told Varick that he and Franks were not suspected of being involved with Arnold, but they must consider themselves as being under arrest and give up the keys to their personal baggage. Varick understood and proceeded to tell Washington everything he know about Arnold's strange behavior and unexplained absences. Varick and Franks were cleared of complicity in the Arnold plot by a court of inquiry in November 1780. Unfortunately, their mere association with Arnold was a blight on their future careers. Washington liked Varick, however, and soon came to his rescue.

While the general was considering helping Varick, he lost the services of Richard Kidder Meade and Robert Hanson Harrison. It happened in October 1780 when Meade took a leave of absence to return to his Virginia home to get married. He departed headquarters in company with Harrison, who was going home to Virginia for a short visit to see his two young daughters. The two aides stopped in Philadelphia for four days en route, where Harrison took the time to write Hamilton a letter describing conditions in the city: "The most flattering attentions have been paid to Meade & myself and such as would not permit us to progress before, unless we have shown ourselves entirely disregardless of the great world." Harrison reported meeting with another former aide, Col. William Grayson, who was serving in Congress: "Grayson says this is the best Congress we have had since the first." They also saw "our Dear [John] Laurens. . . . Our Finances are almost entirely deranged and there is little or no money in the treasury. . . . I hope we shall by Christmas have some Cloathing from the W. Indies, if the moth have not destroyed it. . . . My love to the rest of the family."[54]

Washington's former extra aide-de-camp, John Walker, was also serving in Congress, and he met Meade and Harrison when they passed through Philadelphia. Walker wrote his friend Gen. George Weedon from Philadelphia on October 24, 1780, mentioning their visit: "In a few days you will probably see Colo. Meade. He & old Harrison are now here on their way to Virga. From them you will hear many things which it might not be altogether proper to commit to a Letter."[55] Meade and Harrison may have told Walker some of the chilling details of Arnold's treason or the unrest in the army, stories which Walker felt were best not put into writing.

Once back in Virginia, Meade married Mary Fitzhugh Grymes Randolph, the widow of William Randolph of "Chatsworth." It was Meade's second marriage. But Meade's honeymoon was cut short by an invasion of Virginia by Benedict Arnold, now wearing the uniform of a British general. Arnold led Crown troops on a rampage through the Old Dominion.[56] After escorting his new wife, mother, and about twenty other women and children to safety,

Meade returned to help General von Steuben try to stop Arnold with a small force of Continentals and militia. He wrote his friend Hamilton back at headquarters about how unprepared Virginia was to repel the invasion and that the traitor had

> really been here & with shame be it said marched 25 miles & back without having a single musket fired at him. . . . You possess a heart that can feel for me; you have a female too that you love. I was reduced at one period to entreat, threat, kiss, but all to no purpose; her fears were for my safety, mine not hers. . . . Was it not cruel my dear fellow that my matrimonial enjoyments should have been interrupted thus soon; not more than one month had passed when the damned invasion separated us and we have yet to meet again. . . . If we meet not again my dear Hamilton as Brother aids, I still flatter myself that in the course of time we shall meet as the sincerest of friends.[57]

Meade got caught up in the defense of Virginia and never returned to Washington's headquarters from his leave of absence. He probably commanded Virginia troops until the end of the war. Following the war, he returned to farming.

During this period Tilghman was Washington's only aide. Hamilton was at Albany for his marriage to Elizabeth Schuyler, McHenry was serving as Lafayette's aide-de-camp, and Harrison and Meade were in Virginia on leave. Washington made his headquarters during this period of the war at the home of William Ellison in New Windsor, New York. Overworked and for a time ill, Tilghman nevertheless, working alone composed almost the entire correspondence from Washington to the comte de Rochambeau at headquarters that winter, as well as several other lengthy and significant documents for Congress.

Hard times continued to plague the infant nation as 1780 drew to a close. Tilghman summarized the effects of the economic crisis on the army in the letter he wrote to his fellow Philadelphia businessman and friend Robert Morris on December 22, 1780:

> To be candid with you, I do not think the Contest ever stood upon more critical ground than at present . . . until the Army can be regularly cloathed—paid and fed by the means of a substantial Medium, we are only lingering out the time of our own dissolution. Can Men be expected to serve without provision, without Cloathing, without pay? Of the last, we have had none since March and no prospect of any. Two things will save us, and that speedily—a sufficient permanent Army, and a foreign loan in aid of our own Resources.[58]

Despite the depressing times, there were still things to celebrate. One of them occurred on December 14, 1780, when Alexander Hamilton married

Elizabeth Schuyler. The Schuylers were of Dutch ancestry and in keeping with the Dutch custom of home weddings, the couple exchanged vows in the drawing room of the bride's parents' home, and in the presence of only a few relatives and friends. Dr. James McHenry, Hamilton's admirer and friend, apparently was the only person attending the wedding from Hamilton's side.[59] Elizabeth's aunt Gertrude and her husband Dr. John Cochran were present to witness the culmination of the courtship that had its start at their Morristown, New Jersey, house ten months earlier. The happy event was crowned by a poem that McHenry wrote to his friend the next day:

> . . . And now would friendship's voice prevail
> To point the moral of the tale.
> Know then, dear Ham [Hamilton], a truth confest
> Soon beauty fades, and love's a guest.
> Love has no settled place on earth;
> A very wan'rer from his birth;
> And yet who happiness would prove,
> Like you must build his hopes on love,
> When love his choicest gifts has giv'n
> He flies to make another heav'n;
> But as he wheels his rapid flight
> Calm joys succeed and pure delight.
> Faith adds to all: for works we're told
> Is love's alloy, and faith the gold.
>
> . . . All these attendants Ham are thine,
> Be't yours to treat them as divine;
> To cherish what keeps love alive;
> What makes us young at sixty five.
> What lends the eye its earliest fires;
> What rightly managed still inspires.[60]

Hamilton thanked McHenry in a note he sent a few days later:

I think you Dear Mac for your poetry and your confidence. The piece is a good one—your best. It has wit, which you know is a rare thing. I see by perseverence all the ladies may be won. The Muses begin to be civil to you, in spite of Apollo and my prognosis.

You know I have often told you, you wrote prose well but had no genius for poetry. I retract.

Adieu.[61]

CHAPTER NINE

The Varick Papers

I take this first opportunity to signifying my entire approbation of the manner in which you have executed the important duties of recording Secretary.

George Washington to Richard Varick[1]

George Washington acquired the habit of keeping good records as a teenager when he was befriended by Robert Dinwiddie, who was the royal governor of Virginia at the time. Dinwiddie taught his young protégé the importance of keeping accurate records. As he grew older, Washington became a busy businessman and learned to further appreciate the value of maintaining good records. As a result, besides all the work involved in writing letters and orders, Washington insisted on good record keeping when he was commander in chief of the Continental Army. Lacking any other office staff or assistance, his aides-de-camp were obligated to devote some of their time to the administrative details of making copies of outgoing correspondence and filing all incoming and outgoing documents.

At the beginning of the war, the system for recording outgoing correspondence was to copy it into cheap bound books called letter or copybooks. Documents were classified into two vague groups: Official and private. The handwriting of all the early aides appears in these copybooks. Letters were neatly copied at first, but as the army got bigger and Congress piled more responsibilities upon Washington, the headquarters workload increased and the letter books became a mess as documents were copied into them in great haste. The copybook method proved hopelessly slow and was abandoned at the end of October 1776 in favor of keeping drafts of letters and orders. Every document was now on a separate sheet of paper that was folded and docketed for inclusion in the headquarters papers. "Docketing" was a notation on the folded document, which identified its contents and was visible when the papers were filed. In addition to outgoing documents, there were many thousands of miscellaneous incoming documents that were also recorded and filed at headquarters. These papers included troop returns, reports, rosters, inventories, lists, estimates, vouchers, warrants, invoices, bills, receipts, payrolls, ledger accounts, commissions, oaths of allegiance, passes, leaves of absence, and discharges. All these documents were kept in large leather-covered trunks that served the same purpose as modern filing cabinets. There were no specifications for these trunks, which were purchased from various commercial sources as and when they were needed. It is believed that stacks of these trunks accompanied Washington's headquarters everywhere it went throughout the Revolutionary War. The trunks were the responsibility of the Commander in Chief's Guard, who loaded them onto wagons as part of the headquarters baggage. The trunks were numbered according to their contents and after a while the aides knew what type of correspondence was held in each of them. The trunks had no compartments or special interiors. Papers were placed inside them in bundles, which were filed by subject and date. Documents of similar type were bundled together inside a piece of paper, which was labeled with the contents of the packet. Each packet was tied with a piece of red ribbon to keep its contents together. This simple system was surprisingly efficient. The aides probably worked surrounded by open trunks of correspondence. If, for example, Washington wanted to see a copy of a troop return from 1775, his aides could find the document in the files and bring it to him. When records were no longer believed to be needed, they were shipped off to be stored probably at army depots at Reading or York, Pennsylvania. The exception were copies of Washington's outgoing letters and orders, which stayed with his headquarters baggage under lock and key and protected by the Commander in Chief's Guard.

Washington recognized the archival value of his letters and orders and the need to organize and preserve them. He described the problem, and proposed a solution, to Congress in a letter dated April 4, 1781:

> The business that has given constant exercise to the Pen of my Secretary: and not only frequently, but always, to those of my Aides de Camp, has rendered it impracticable for the former to register the Copies of my Letters, Instructions &ca. in Books; by which means valuable documents which may be of equal public utility and private satisfaction remain in loose Sheets; and in the rough manner in which they were first drawn.
>
> [In the same letter the general proposed a solution to the problem.] Unless a set of Writers are employed for the sole purpose of recording them it will not be in my power to accomplish this necessary Work—and equally impracticable perhaps to preserve from injury and loss such valuable papers; but to engage these without the sanction of Congress I have not thought myself at liberty.
>
> The business now, must be performed in some quiet retreat . . . It must be done under the Inspection of a Man of character in whom

entire confidence can be pleased, and who is capable of arranging the papers, methodizing the register. Such an one, with as many clerks as can be employed to advantage.[2]

Congress approved of Washington's idea and the general began to look for a person he could trust to supervise the organization and copying of his head-quarters papers. He focused his search on Col. Richard Varick, the New York lawyer, who had been Benedict Arnold's aide-de-camp. Despite his long asso-ciation with New York City and state, Richard Varick was born in Hackensack, New Jersey, on March 25, 1753. His parents were Johannis (John) and Jane Dey Varick and their son Richard was one of six children who survived to adulthood.[3] The Varick family could trace their ancestry back to young Richard's great-grandfather, Jan Varick, who immigrated to New York in about 1687 from Holland. Richard's membership in the colonial aristocracy however was based more on his mother's bloodline. She was born Jane Dey, the daugh-ter of the wealthy New York merchant Dirick Dey. Little is known about Richard's childhood or early education. Surviving letters show that he studied Latin, French, and other traditional subjects with private tutors. Young Varick is sometimes mentioned as a graduate of King's College, New York. This is incorrect and based largely on the fact that he served as a trustee of the univer-sity for nearly thirty years.[4] Varick began to study law sometime in late 1771 under the direction of John Morin Scott, one of New York City's most success-ful lawyers. Varick, who was eighteen years old at the time, was one of several clerks employed by Scott to assist him with his busy law practice. They per-formed routine legal duties while studying law under his direction. Scott's clerks had a heavy workload because their boss was active in land speculation and a leader in the Sons of Liberty. Varick was admitted to the New York Bar (October 1774) after clerking for the traditional three years. He must have been an outstanding student because he was offered a partnership in Scott's lucrative law practice after his acceptance to the Bar. Varick accepted the offer and practiced law with Scott for eight months, until the outbreak of the Revo-lution. Influenced by Scott, Varick joined the city's elite volunteer militia bat-talion at the start of the war. On June 28, 1775, Varick was commissioned as a captain in the newly organized 1st New York Regiment, which drew many of its officers from the city's militia battalion.[5] He was twenty-two years old at the time with very little military experience. Young Varick's tenure as a field officer lasted only three days because on July 1, 1775, he was appointed Maj. Gen. Philip Schuyler's secretary.[6] John Morin Scott is credited with getting his young law partner this desirable appointment.[7] Varick was busy from the start of his new position because Congress had given Schuyler command of the Northern Department of the Continental Army with orders to seize Canada.[8] Schuyler left New York City on July 4, 1775, with Varick and the rest of his staff, heading for Fort Ticonderoga, which he decided to use as a base of oper-ations to launch his assault on Canada. His suite stopped briefly in Albany, Schuyler's home town. It was here that Schuyler and Varick met Col. Benedict

Arnold for the first time as he was passing through Albany following his successful but controversial military service in upper New York state. This threesome (Schuyler, Arnold, and Varick) would remain political allies and friends until Arnold's treason in 1780.

Schuyler was under pressure from Congress for action, and he launched his poorly equipped and undermanned Canadian invasion from Fort Ticonderoga in August 1775. The general accompanied his small army but he was soon stricken with a severe case of gout and rheumatism forcing him to return to his Albany mansion with Varick in tow. Schuyler was an expert administrator who devoted much of his time to trying to keep his army supplied, leaving the field operations to his subordinates, who eventually included Horatio Gates and Benedict Arnold. Schuyler's army was in serious trouble by the summer of 1776. The American invasion of Canada had failed, and the British were pursing the retreating Americans back across the border. The talented and obviously well-organized Varick was in Albany doing three jobs: personal secretary to Schuyler (who like his acquaintance Washington was a workaholic) and unofficial quartermaster for the forts held by the Northern Army, which he combined with being the Northern Army's deputy muster master general.[9] Varick's function as deputy muster master general came with a promotion to the rank of lieutenant colonel that was arranged for him by Schuyler as a reward for his hard work.[10] Meanwhile at Fort Ticonderoga, Arnold was frantically building a fleet to stop the British advance down Lake Champlain. With a crisis at hand, Varick was given the additional job of finding Arnold shipbuilding materials and men. Varick worked frantically at his new task. He contacted government functionaries and businessmen throughout New York and neighboring states pleading with them to rush materials and workmen to Arnold. Somehow Arnold's flotilla was built, armed, and manned. He sailed out onto Lake Champlain and fought the British on October 11, 1776, at the battle of Valcour Island. Although Arnold was defeated he scored a tactical victory because his fleet delayed the British assault long enough to send them scurrying back to their Canadian bases for the winter.

Varick faced his next crisis the following month. On November 18, 1776, he was at Fort Ticonderoga when Lt. Col. Anthony Walton White challenged him to a duel. It will be remembered that White had served briefly at Washington's headquarters early in the war. Following his unsuccessful bid to get an appointment as one of Washington's aides-de-camp, White returned to New Jersey where he was commissioned as a lieutenant colonel in one of that state's new Continental regiments. White's regiment was assigned to the Northern Army where he got into trouble with Schuyler over allegations that he had looted the upstate New York home of Sir John Johnson. Varick said that he was working quietly when White barged into his room and accused him of making insulting remarks about White's character related to the ransacking of Johnson's home. White challenged him to a duel, and drew his sword on the spot and lunged toward Varick. The unarmed colonel sidestepped the thrust and fled the scene. White was arrested but managed to escape. Search parties found him sitting upon a tree stump outside Fort Ticonderoga armed with two loaded pistols and three swords. White said that he was sitting there waiting for Varick from whom he demanded satisfaction. White faced a court-martial but his friends intervened and arranged for his transfer to the 4th Continental Dragoons.[11]

The spring of 1777 saw a new and more serious invasion of New York state by the British under the command of Gen. John Burgoyne. His army captured Fort Ticonderoga, and Schuyler was blamed for the disaster. Gates replaced Schuyler in early August 1777. Varick was bitter over the change in command and wrote about it to a fellow officer: "Genl. Gates is a happy man to arrive at this Moment when Genl. Schuyler had just paved the way to Victory."[12] Varick was present during the Saratoga campaign, but apparently did not participate in any combat. He applauded Arnold's actions during the campaign while criticizing Gates. For example, writing to Schuyler on September 22, 1777, following the fighting on Bemis Heights, Varick said, "This I am certain of: Arnold has all the credit of the action . . . Had Gates complied with Arnold's repeated desires, he would have obtained a general and complete victory over the enemy."[13] Arnold further antagonized Gates by welcoming twenty-four-year-old Varick to his headquarters along with two other young admirers of Schuyler: Matthew Clarkson, the scion of a distinguished New York mercantile family, and Clarkson's nineteen-year-old cousin Maj. Henry Brockholst Livingston, the son of the governor of New Jersey. Gates's sycophant James Wilkinson called them the "New York gang."[14]

Varick continued to serve as deputy muster master general of the Northern Department in the reorganized muster department until January 12, 1780, when the department was abolished by Congress. He decided to return to his father's home in Hackensack and resume his law career. The colonel wrote his mentor Schuyler outlining his plans: "I shall as soon as conveniently I can, set myself down to Books and attempt to recover the little Law & Practice I possessed & which five years avocations have almost erased from my memory."[15] Varick returned home to find that the British had recently raided Hackensack destroying many of its homes. He felt obligated to join the Bergen County militia and serve on patrol every other night. Adding to his frustrations was his feeling that he was serving with an amateur military outfit, and only fear of his neighbors' opinions kept him from leaving town. Dramatic relief from militia duty arrived in August 1780 in the form of an invitation from Gen. Benedict Arnold to become his aide-de-camp and military secretary.[16] Arnold made the offer shortly after he was given command of West Point:

> I am in want of a secretary, having within a few days been appointed to this command. General Schuyler informed me yesterday that he believed it would be agreeable to you, as the duty would engross only a part of your time and leave a considerable time for you to prosecute your studies if you choose [Arnold knew from Schuyler that Varick was trying to brush up on his legal studies in preparation for resuming his practice]. . . . As this has the appearance of a quiet post, I expect Mrs. Arnold will soon be with me.[17]

Varick replied on August 7, 1780, accepting Arnold's offer, and he arrived at West Point a week later. Arnold's activities aroused some suspicion from Varick and the general's other aide-de-camp, David Franks. But Varick admired Arnold and believed that he was doing some illegal trading with merchants in New York City. On the day that Arnold's treason was uncovered Varick was sick in bed with a fever. About noon, Franks appeared outside Varick's window whispering to him that a spy (André) had been captured and Arnold had acted strangely when he received the news. Varick told Franks that he was "injuring a gentleman and friend of high reputation and that it was uncharitable and unwarranted even to suppose it."[18] Varick was as shocked as everyone else when he found out that Arnold was a traitor.

Although Varick was cleared of any involvement in the Arnold treason plot, he remained the object of suspicion.[19] He appealed to General Washington for help by asking him to publish the findings of his court-martial along with a certificate as to his character. Washington refused on the grounds that he had neither the money nor the authority to take such action. But, in a show of confidence, Washington invited Varick to join his military family, and take the responsibility of arranging, classifying, and copying all the headquarters correspondence and records. These files included many confidential documents, and Varick's appointment was probably partially intended to show the commander in chief's faith in the colonel. There was a similar situation early in the war when Washington helped young Edmund Randolph of Virginia. Washington confirmed Varick's appointment in a letter dated New Windsor, New York, May 25, 1781: "Sir: By Virtue of the Authority committed to me by Resolution of the Honbl. Congress of the United States of America, I do hereby appoint you my recording Secretary at Headquarters." Washington knew Varick by reputation to be a talented and capable administrator. He also had some previous firsthand experience with Varick who had worked at headquarters for a few weeks in 1779 as the officer in charge of the Muster Department.

The general told Varick how he wanted his headquarters papers organized. His instructions are interesting because they show the variety of letters and orders being drafted by his aides. Washington instructed Varick to divide his correspondence into six categories:

1. All letters to Congress, Committees of Congress, the Board of War, individual members of Congress in their public Characters, and American Ministers Plenipotentiary at Foreign Courts.
2. All letters, Orders, and Instructions to Officers of the line, of the Staff, and all other Military Characters.
3. All letters to Governors, Presidents and other Executive of States, Civil Magistrates and Citizens of every Denomination.
4. Letters to Foreign Ministers, Foreign Officers, and subjects of Foreign Nations not in the immediate service of America.

5. Letters to officers of every Denomination in the service of the Enemy, and to British subjects of every Character with the Enemy, or applying to go in to them.
6. Proceedings of Councils of War in the Order of their dates.[20]

Washington further instructed Varick that he was to employ clerks "who write a fair Hand, and correctly, . . . and that there may be a similarity and Beauty in the whole execution all the writing is to be upon black lines equidistant [these black lines were ruled sheets, which were laid under the papers and served as a guide for the clerks]."[21] Washington also told Varick to make all the books the same size.

The project started in July 1781 and continued until it was completed in December 1783. Varick proved to be an intelligent and innovative manager. He worked in the village of Poughkeepsie, New York, with his clerks who were George Taylor, Jr., Oliver Glean, Edward Dunscomb, Zachariah Sickels, Peter Hughes, and John J. Myer.[22] Trunk loads of documents were delivered to them under escort by members of the Commander in Chief's Guard. Varick and his team started with documents from the beginning of the war and neatly copied all of Washington's letters and general orders into their new books. His clerks used several sources to create their copies. They tried to work from "retained" copies of a letter or order if they found one in the headquarters files. These were carefully written copies of letters and orders, which were made before the finished letters (called the "fair" or "sent" copies) were signed and dispatched to their addressee. If there was no "retained" copy, they used the final draft of the document, which had been kept for the files. Once Varick's clerks caught up with the old records, they were forwarded corrected drafts of newly written letters and orders, which they copied into their letter books.

Varick must have had a considerable amount of the headquarters files at any given time because he was regularly asked to send documents or copies back to headquarters. For example, Tench Tilghman wrote Varick on August 12, 1781, "Be kind enough to look among the papers between the 20th of December, 1776 and the middle of January 1777 and endeavor to find either a letter of appointment or recruiting Instructions to Col Saml. B. Webb. If you find them be pleased to make an exact Copy—certify it, and send it to me by return of the Bearer. It is wanted to settle a dispute of Rank."[23]

We know that Washington also sent copies of his personal letters to Varick for inclusion in the records. The general wrote Varick in this regard on October 2, 1783, "Enclosed are my private letters for registering. As fast as they are entered, return to me by the weekly mail, because references to them are frequently necessary; do the same thing with the public Letters." In this same letter, Washington reminded Varick to protect the correspondence in his possession, "As the Letters which are handed to you now, contain sentiments upon undecided points; it is more than ever necessary that there should be the strictest guard over them, and the most perfect silence with respect to their contents."[24]

Colonel Varick and his team of clerks created forty-four large volumes, each of which was 300 pages or more. In these volumes, known today as the *Varick Transcripts,* the colonel and his staff copied nearly every official letter and order written by Washington during the war. The books were classified and indexed according to Washington's instructions. Varick proudly delivered the complete set of letter books to His Excellency at the close of the war and then, having completed his mission, resigned from the army. Varick wrote Washington on November 18, 1783, "bidding a happy Adieu to public Services & return to the pleasant, tho fatiguing, Amusement of a City Lawyer."[25] The project cost the Continental Congress between $10,000 and $15,000, which was a considerable sum of the money at the time. Commenting on the cost Washington said he was "fully convinced that neither the present age or posterity will consider the time and labour which have been employed in accomplishing it unprofitably spent."[26]

The completed transcripts were a tribute to Varick's excellent organizational skills. Washington warmly thanked him for his "care and attention" to the project in a letter dated January 1, 1784:

The public and other Papers which were committed to your charge, and the Books in which they have been recorded under your inspection, having come safe to hand, I take this first opportunity of signifying my entire approbation of the manner in which you have executed the important duties of recording Secretary, and the satisfaction I feel in having my Papers so properly arranged, & so correctly recorded.[27]

The Varick Papers survive to this day and are among the treasured possessions of the Library of Congress and an important reference source for scholars.

Washington did a great service to Varick by giving him the job of transcribing the headquarters papers. His connection with Washington and his meritorious work cleared his reputation and he was able to pursue a brilliant postwar career. Varick was appointed the recorder of the City of New York soon after the war ended.[28] The recorder was the second in command of the city's government (the equivalent of today's deputy mayor) as well as its chief legal counsel. The colonel's connection with New York City was further cemented when he married Maria Roosevelt in 1786. She was the youngest daughter of Isaac Roosevelt, a leading New York merchant. Varick was ten years older than his bride; Richard was thirty and Maria was twenty at the time of their marriage. They had no children and Maria outlived her husband by ten years. Varick rendered additional service to New York state by helping to codify its statutes (in 1786 with Samuel Jones), then as speaker of the Assembly (1787–88) and attorney general (1788–89). He did these jobs while he continued to serve as recorder.

Varick was appointed mayor of New York City in 1789 by New York's Federalist governor George Clinton.[29] He held this post until 1801 when he was swept out of office by the Jeffersonian Republicans. Varick was involved in various business projects including the development of Jersey City, New Jersey, which lay just across the Hudson River from Manhattan. In 1817 he was one of the appraisers of the Erie Canal. His estate was valued at over $500,000 when he died. This was an enormous sum of money for the time, representing Varick's investments in New York City, Albany, and Jersey City properties, mortgage obligations, and stocks in banks, turnpikes, and canals.

Varick was an old-fashioned colonial aristocrat whose ideas included a responsibility to serve the public good. He generously gave his time and money to a number of worthwhile activities including twenty-nine years of service as a trustee of Columbia University in addition to his leadership in the American Bible Society and the American Sunday School Union. Varick's great attachment however was to the Society of the Cincinnati. When the society was organized many people attacked it as a military elite that would undermine republican institutions. But the society took a fraternal direction and was America's first patriotic organization. Varick was one of its charter members, and he was active in the society's charitable works. He served as the president of its New York state chapter from 1806 until his death. He was also present when the remnants of the Continental Army officers corps assembled in 1825 during Lafayette's tour of America.

Realizing that he was coming to the end of his life, Varick made an emotional trip to visit Mount Vernon in May 1831. He returned to his summer home in Jersey City where he died a few months later on July 30, 1831. Varick was seventy-nine years old when he died. His funeral took place in New York City and was a huge affair. His body was transported from Jersey City to New York where it was met by a large military escort. Numerous members of the Society of the Cincinnati attended his funeral wearing badges of mourning and expressing their sentiments in a formal statement, which read in part, "That his courtesy and kindness to the members, his liberality to such of the descendants of deceased members as needed it, and his attachment to this Institution can never be forgotten."[30] One of his pallbearers was Col. John Trumbull, the artist, one of General Washington's last surviving aides-de-camp. Some of the aged veterans may have recalled what Colonel Varick's mentor and friend, Maj. Gen. Philip Schuyler, said about him in 1780 when Varick was implicated in Arnold's treason: "That I reflect with satisfaction on the propriety of that Gentleman's conduct in every point of view; that I had such entire confidence in his attachment to the Glorious Cause we are engaged in, that I concealed nothing from him, and never once had reason to repent that I reposed so much trust in him."[31]

On November 9, 1783, Washington wrote out orders to Capt. Bezaleel Howe to take an escort of twenty-four soldiers and deliver his personal belongings, including his headquarters papers, to Mount Vernon.[32] With his usual flair for organization and attention to detail, the general ordered six strong trunks "well clasped and with good locks" for the safe transportation of his papers.[33] He kept his headquarters papers at Mount Vernon along with his other public and private correspondence during his lifetime and provided for them in his will: "To my nephew Bushrod Washington I give and bequeath all the papers in my possession, which relate to my Civil and Military Administration of the Affairs of this Country."[34] The United States acquired Washington's papers from his heirs in the nineteenth century. Washington's letters and orders have been carefully preserved and published four times since his death in 1799.[35] The letters written by his aides-de-camp have not enjoyed the same scholarly benefits. The wartime letters and orders of Alexander Hamilton are the most complete record we have from one of Washington's aides. They were published as *The Papers of Alexander Hamilton.* Hamilton's wartime letters and orders, however, represent only a fraction of the output of Washington's personal staff. It is estimated that his aides-de-camp wrote 5,000 official letters and orders during the American Revolution, which bear their own signatures. While their letters often concerned routine matters, they are still an important part of the historical record of the Revolutionary War.

The personal letters that Washington's aides wrote during the war often make fascinating and significant reading, but unfortunately they are scattered throughout private and public collections. Here is an excerpt from a personal letter written during the war by Tench Tilghman to his father describing the evacuation of Brooklyn Heights following the American defeat at the battle of Long Island:

> Head Quarters N. York, 3 September 1776
>
> Honored Sir
>
> I have attempted to write to you several times since our Return from Long Island, but have been as often interrupted by the vast hurry of Business in which the General is engaged. He is obliged to see into, and in a Manner fill every Department, which is too much for one Man—Our Retreat [from Long Island] before an Enemy much superior in Numbers, over a wide River, and not very well furnished with Boats certainly does Credit to our Generals. The thing was conducted with so much Secrecy that neither subalterns or privates knew that the whole Army was to cross back again to N. York, they thought only a few Regiments were to go back. General Howe has not yet landed upon this Island [Manhattan], but I imagine something of that kind is in Agitation, as the Fleet drew nearer and nearer, they are now about long Cannon Shot from the Battery, but no firing on either side. . . . we must leave our heavy Cannon behind us in Case of Retreat, but I don't know that that will be any loss, as we never used them to much advantage.[36]

It is unfortunate that the correspondence of Washington's aides-de-camp has never benefited from a project like the *Varick Transcripts.*[37]

CHAPTER TEN

The Siege of Yorktown
January–November 1781

*Nothing but want of exertion can possibly blast the pleasing
prospect before us.*

General Orders of the Army, September 6, 1781[1]

The year 1781 started off with a bang. On January 1 at about 9:00 P.M., a mutiny broke out among the Pennsylvania troops wintering near Morristown, New Jersey. An estimated 1,300 men paraded under arms, refusing to obey their officers. They killed one who tried to stop them. The following day, the mutineers marched in a body toward Philadelphia, demanding back pay and a redress of other grievances. They brought six cannons with them to help make their point.

Army headquarters at the time was at the home of William Ellison, a two-story house a few miles north of West Point.[2] It became a hive of activity at the news of the mutiny. Washington, with the help of Gen. Anthony Wayne, managed to quell the rebellion after promising the mutineers satisfaction. Within a month, however, the commander in chief found himself dealing with a one-man mutiny within his own staff.

Lt. Col. Alexander Hamilton was unhappy and wanted a field command. He vented his frustration in a letter to his confidant John Laurens, dated Morristown, January 8, 1780. Hamilton told his best friend that his request for a command had been denied by Washington who needed his ready pen at headquarters:

I am chagrined and unhappy but I submit. In short Laurens I am disgusted with every thing in this world but yourself and a very few more honest fellows and I have no other wish than as soon as possible to make a brilliant exit. . . . All the Lads embrace you. The General sends his love. Write to him as often as you can.[3]

On February 16, 1781, Hamilton's pent-up frustrations got the better of him. On that day, headquarters was bustling as usual. Washington's office was short staffed with both Robert Hanson Harrison and David Humphreys away. The confrontation started as Hamilton was leaving the general's office, which was located on the second floor of the Ellison house. As he was going down the staircase, he met Washington coming the other way. The general stopped Hamilton and told him that he wanted to see him immediately. Hamilton acknowledged the order but continued downstairs to deliver a letter to Tench Tilghman. After completing his mission, Hamilton turned around and started for the staircase and Washington's office. He was stopped en route, however, by Lafayette who conversed with him briefly concerning army business. As he reached the top of the stairs, Hamilton found his boss pacing on the upstairs landing. Upon seeing Hamilton he said in an unpleasant tone, "Colonel Hamilton, you have kept me waiting at the head of the stairs these ten minutes. I must tell you, Sir you treat me with disrespect." Hamilton claimed he was calm but decisive when he replied, "I am not conscious of it Sir, but since you have thought it necessary to tell me so we must part." Washington, who was accustomed to respect from his subordinates, fired back, "Very well Sir if it be your choice."[4]

Hamilton ran downstairs and poured out his outrage to his friend Lafayette. Hamilton believed that not more than minutes had elapsed from the time he passed Washington on the stairs and their confrontation. In less than an hour Tilghman was trying to calm Hamilton down. Washington had sent him to talk with Hamilton. Tilghman said that His Excellency had great confidence in Hamilton's abilities, integrity, and usefulness, and he would like to have a forthright conversation with him to heal their differences, which had surfaced in a moment of passion. Hamilton told Tilghman "that a conversation could serve no other purpose than to produce explanations mutually disagreeable . . . However, I did not wish to distress him or the public business, by quitting him before he could derive other assistance by the return of some of the Gentlemen who were absent." Washington did not pursue the matter further and thanked Hamilton for his offer to remain on his staff until Harrison and Humphreys returned. Historian John C. Fitzpatrick has given age as the reason for the encounter: "Washington seems to have displayed some of the petulance so usual with advancing years and Hamilton the quick resentment of hot youth."[5]

Colonel Hamilton wrote to his friend Dr. James McHenry shortly after his run-in with Washington. McHenry seems to have been aware of his friend's frustrations at headquarters when he received Hamilton's letter, which was dated New Windsor, New York, February 18, 1781: "I have, Dear Mac, several of your letters. I shall [soon] have time enough to write my friends as often as they please. The Great man and I have come to an open repture. . . . He shall for once at least repent his ill-humor. Without a shadow of reason and on the slightest ground, he charged me in the most affrontive manner with treating him with disrespect." Hamilton then gave McHenry an account of the incident which revealed that he apparently was the only aide working at headquarters at the time: "I wait till more help arrives. At present there is besides myself only Tilghman, who is just recovering from a fit of illness the consequence of too close application to business [Hamilton claimed that Tilghman got sick because he was overworked]."[6]

Hamilton wrote his father-in-law, Philip Schuyler, two days later with a more detailed account of his confrontation with Washington. "Since I had the pleasure of writing you last an unexpected change has taken place in my situation. I am no longer a member of the General's family." Hamilton described his confrontation with Washington and then stated, "I always disliked the office of an Aide-de-camp as having in it a kind of personal dependance. I refused to serve in this capacity with two Major General's at an early period of the war [Nathanael Greene and Henry Knox]." But despite what had passed between them, Hamilton admitted his genuine admiration for Washington:

> The General is a very honest man. His competitors have slender abilities and less integrity. His popularity has often been essential to the safety of America, and is still of great importance to it. These considerations have influenced my past conduct respecting him, and will influence my future. I think it is necessary he should be supported.[7]

Washington should have appointed Hamilton to a line command long before their confrontation, as he had done for several of his other aides-de-camp. But it seems that the general wanted Hamilton's energy and skills at headquarters and kept him chained to his writing desk beyond his time. It is to Washington's credit that his break with Hamilton was not permanent. Hamilton had entered the general's military family as a young college student with few prospects, but he left as a man with a growing reputation and a wide circle of influential friends. But despite his progress, the general could have ruined Hamilton's career at this point. Washington was the foremost American of the day and was well on the way to becoming a world figure. Hamilton was a West Indian immigrant and a comparative nobody. Instead of hurting Hamilton's career, however, Washington helped him. With the general's intervention his former aide got his wish in July 1781 when he was given a command in the elite Corps of Light Infantry. Hamilton was thrilled and wrote his adoring wife with the news.

> Camp near Dobbs Ferry, New York, July 10, 1781.
> The day before yesterday, my angel, I arrived here, but for the want of an opportunity could not write you sooner. . . . Finding when I came here that nothing was said on the subject of a command, I wrote the General a letter and enclosed him my commission. This morning Tilghman came to me in his name, pressed me to retain my

commission with an assurance that he would endeavor by all means to give me a command nearly such as I could have desired in the present circumstances of the army. . . . I consented to retain my commission and accept my command.[8]

On July 31, 1781, the general orders of the army made Hamilton's new line command official: "The Light Companies of the first and second regiments of New York with the two companies of York Levies . . . will form a Battalion under command of Lieutenant Colonel Hamilton and Major Fish."[9]

Within a month, another dedicated and important member of Washington's military family left the general's service. On March 25, 1781, Robert Hanson Harrison resigned as military secretary.[10] There are conflicting stories about the reason and the date of his resignation. We know that he had been absent for part of 1780, apparently living in Baltimore and looking for a new wife.[11] Previous to this, in October 1779, Harrison had also been away attending to important family business. His father had died and Harrison went home to settle the estate. He journeyed on this trip as far as Philadelphia with Richard Kidder Meade. Continental currency had become so deflated that the trip and stay in Philadelphia cost them $3,628.00. Harrison left Meade in Philadelphia and continued to his father's home in Maryland. Harrison had two brothers, and their father had provided in his will that "all his lands . . . be equally divided betwixt his three well beloved sons, Robert, William and Walter." Besides being the eldest of three sons, Robert Hanson Harrison was a lawyer, and he took most of the responsibility for the supervision of his father's affairs. Harrison's own finances were a mess because of his long absence from home. At about the same time (March 1781) he was offered the post of chief judge of the General Court of Maryland. The position carried not only a high honor, but a large and secure income as well as allowing him to be close to his daughters. The offer was too tempting to pass up and Harrison resigned from Washington's staff.

Harrison returned briefly to headquarters where he took the time to write a beautifully crafted farewell letter to his friend Hamilton, dated, "New Windsor, March 26th: 1781." The complete letter is included because it is a splendid example of Harrison's polished writing style:

I came here, My Dear Hamilton, on Friday night to bid adieu to the General, to you and to My other Friends as a military man, and regret much that I have not had the happiness of seeing you. Tomorrow I am obliged to depart, and it is possible our separation may be for ever. But be this as it may, it can only be with respect to our persons, for as to affection, mine for You will continue to my latest breath. This event will probably surprise you, but from your knowledge of me, I rely you will conclude at the Instant, that no light considerations could have taken me from the Army, and I think I might safely have rested the matter here. However, as the friendship between us gives you a claim to something more, and as I am not indifferent about character and shall be anxious to have the esteem of All who are Good & virtuously great, I shall detail to you, My Friend, the more substantial reasons, which have led to my present conduct. I go from the Army then, because I have found, on examination, that my little fortune, earned by an honest & hard industry, was becoming embarrassed—to attend to the education of my Children, to provide, if possible, for the payment of a considerable sum of Sterling money & Interest, with which I stand charged, on account of the Land I lately received from my Honoured Father, for equality of partition between myself & two Brothers, to save a house which he had begun & and which without instant attention would be ruined, or at least greatly injured, to provide, if possible, for the payment of taxes, which far exceed any profits I can make from my Estate, and because the State of Maryland, in a flattering manner, have been pleased to appoint me to a place, very respectable in its nature, corresponding with my former and very interesting to my whole future life & support. They have appointed me to the Chair of their Supreme Court. Those, my Friend, are the motives to my present resolution. My own feelings are satisfied on the occasion, tho I can not but regret parting with the most valuble acquaintances I have, and hope they will justify me most fully to you My Hamilton, especially when you consider, besides, the time I have been in service & the compensation I have received. I wish sincerely I had been sooner apprised of the good intentions of the State towards me, for reasons which will occur to you. They were but very lately known & I was not sooner possessed of them than I communicated the matter (that I should leave the Army) to the General, having found on enquiry it was only in my power to accept the Offer of the Chair or decline it forever, as the filling it had became a measure of immediate necessity, and there were other Gentlemen, both of ability & merit, who had been mentioned for it & who would probably have willingly accepted it You are now to pardon me for this long relation, so very personal. You must do it, as what I owed to your friendship produced it, and as it is my hope & wish to stand fair in your opinion & esteem.

I proceed to tell you, that I live in Charles County Maryland, where I should be peculiarly happy to see you; but as I can have but little hopes of being gratified in this, let me have the next pleasure to it, the favor of a Letter now & then, in which write of matters personally interesting to yourself, as they will be so to me. Present me most respectfully to your Lady, to General & Mrs. Schuyler. My best wishes attend you all.

Adieu Yrs in haste Most affy Rob:
H: Harrison[12]

Robert Hanson Harrison was an American patriot. Despite his poor health and pressing family obligations, he worked tirelessly behind the scenes for the American cause. He was never in the limelight and sought no glory or recognition for his efforts. While he spent most of his time sitting behind a desk, there is also the vision of him mounted on his powerful black mare riding with Washington toward the sound of gunfire at the battle of Monmouth. Washington said of him: "That his whole conduct . . . has been marked by the strictest integrity and the most attentive and faithful services, while by personl. bravery he has been distinguished on sevl. occasions."[13] That Harrison was an intelligent man of great abilities is proven by the fact that he left his obscure post at headquarters to accept an invitation to become chief justice of Maryland.

So three of Washington's most experienced aides-de-camp departed his family during 1781: Harrison, Hamilton, and Meade. The general moved quickly to fill the vacancies with Jonathan Trumbull, Jr., Dr. David Cobb, and William Stephens Smith. These three new men led fascinating lives and are worthy of our attention. Since we have already been introduced to other members of the Trumbull family of Connecticut, we will begin with Jonathan Trumbull, Jr.

When Washington lost the valuable services of Robert Hanson Harrison, he cast about for an outstanding writer to replace him. As he had done sometimes in the past when he needed help, Washington turned for assistance to the talented Trumbull family of Connecticut. That state's governor, Jonathan Trumbull, was the patriarch of the family and one of Washington's staunchest allies. When the general was desperate for men or food during the war, his best hope was to turn to Governor Trumbull, whom he purportedly called, "Brother Jonathan."

Governor Trumbull had four sons, all of whom played an active role in the Revolution. We briefly met his eldest son Joseph who was the first commissary general of the Continental Army. Joseph resigned from this post in the spring of 1777 under pressure from a meddling congressional committee. He afterward served on the newly established Board of War, but he was exhausted and sick from his endless hard work on behalf of the American cause. Joseph became seriously ill in the spring of 1778 and died on July 23, 1778, at the age of forty-one.

We also know the governor's youngest son, John, who was the artist and Washington's aide-de-camp for nineteen days during 1775. Another son, Daniel, was an army contractor during the war. It was Governor Trumbull's namesake, Jonathan Trumbull, Jr., who is of interest to us now because he replaced Harrison as Washington's military secretary. Jonathan, Jr., was born on March 26, 1740, in Lebanon, Connecticut. He entered Harvard College at the age of fifteen and graduated in 1759. Jonathan continued his education at Harvard, earning an M.A. degree in 1762. He gave the valedictory oration at the Harvard graduation that year. Following his formal education at Harvard college, Jonathan worked as a merchant and entered local politics. He was elected to the Connecticut legislature in 1774 and served as a member of that body until

1775. When the Revolution started, Jonathan sided with the rebels and was appointed paymaster general for the Northern Army, taking post on July 28, 1775, and resigning July 29, 1778. He gave up this office when his elder brother Joseph died to help settle his estate. Jonathan, Jr., was next unanimously elected as the first comptroller of the treasury, a post that he held until April 1779. He resigned from this post and returned to civilian life, which included another term in the Connecticut legislature (1779–80), until he received the following flattering invitation from Washington dated April 16, 1781:

> Sir: Colo. Harrison who has acted as my Secretary since the beginning of 1776 has accepted an honorable and profitable Civil appointment in the State of Maryland and is gone to enjoy it. The circle of my acquaintance does not furnish a character that would be more pleasing to me as a successor to him than yours; I make you the first offer therefore of the vacant Office and should be happy on your acceptance of it.
>
> The pay is one hundred dollars pr. month; the Rations that of a Lieutt. Colonel in the Army. . . . The Secretary lives as I do, is at little expense while he is in my family, or when absent on my business, and is in the highest confidence and estimation from the nature of his Office.[14]

Jonathan, Jr., accepted Washington's offer and his appointment was included in the general orders of June 8, 1781: "Jonathan Trumbull, Esqr., Junior, is appointed Secretary to the Commander in Chief and to be respected accordingly."[15] He served as Washington's military secretary until the end of the war.

Jonathan Trumbull, Jr.,'s career following the Revolution was impressive. He was reelected to the Connecticut Assembly in 1788 and served as its speaker of the house. Trumbull was next named a member of the Connecticut convention that ratified the United States Constitution and subsequently elected to represent his home state in the United States House of Representatives for the First, Second, and Third Congresses (March 4, 1789, to March 3, 1795). Trumbull was the speaker of the house during the Second Congress. Following his three consecutive terms in Congress, Trumbull was elected to the United States Senate where he served from March 4, 1795, to June 10, 1796, when he resigned to accept the post of lieutenant governor of Connecticut. He was elected governor by a huge majority of the voters in 1797 and reelected governor for an astounding eleven consecutive terms. Jonathan Trumbull, Jr., died in office on August 7, 1809.[16]

The second man to join Washington's military family in 1781 was Dr. David Cobb who was appointed an aide-de-camp on June 15, 1781. Cobb was thirty-three years old at the time. He was the son of Thomas Cobb, a prosperous merchant of Bristol County, Massachusetts. Young Cobb was another Harvard

College graduate, class of 1766. Following college, he studied medicine in Boston "under the instruction of Dr. Perkins, a celebrated physician of that day."[17] Cobb was practicing medicine in Taunton, Massachusetts, when the war broke out. His early service to the American cause included civilian posts in the newly organized Massachusetts government and service as a surgeon in a state regiment. But, as an early biography of Cobb states, "He sought for more active duties and was impatient to share the perils and the glory of the camp . . . he assumed the sword, and entered the army in 1777."[18] Cobb was commissioned a lieutenant colonel in Henry Jackson's Additional Regiment on January 12, 1777. This understrength regiment was consolidated with two others, and ordered to harass the rear of General Clinton's army during the Monmouth campaign of 1778. There is no record that Cobb participated in the battle of Monmouth, however, and he was probably at Englishtown with the "foot sore" soldiers who were left behind to guard the unit's baggage. Cobb continued to serve in his regiment through another reorganization in 1780 from which it emerged as the 16th Massachusetts. This regiment disbanded at New Windsor, New York, on January 1, 1781, at which time Cobb transferred to the 9th Massachusetts, where he served until his appointment as Washington's aide-de-camp on June 15, 1781.[19] Cobb's appointment is mentioned in the general orders for June 15, 1781: "David Cobb, Esqr. Lieutenant Colonel of the 9th Massachusetts regiment, is appointed Aide-de-camp to the Commander in Chief and is to be respected and obeyed accordingly."[20]

The third replacement to Washington's staff in 1781 was Lt. Col. William Stephens Smith. Colonel Smith probably led the most lamentable life out of all of the general's thirty-two aides. As a means of introduction, here is how one of his kindest biographers summarized his life: "Colonel William Stephens Smith . . . In 1776, an ardent and gifted youth tendering his sword in defense of the liberties of his country; in 1876, an unmarked grave in a rural hamlet in Central New York. Between, a life of more than usual dramatic and historic interest."[21] When Smith was appointed as Washington's aide-de-camp on July 6, 1781, he was a young and promising officer with a brilliant education, excellent war record, and bright future. Washington mentioned Smith in a letter to James Duane dated December 26, 1780, naming him, "one of the best Battalion Officers of the whole line."[22]

William Stephens Smith was born in New York City on November 8, 1755. His father, John, was a wealthy New York merchant who owned homes in the city as well as a country seat in what is now the Throgs Neck section of the Bronx. His mother was Margaret Stephens Smith and his grandfather was Capt. John Stephens, a Royal Navy officer killed in action on board a man-of-war at Cartagena in 1741. Captain Stephens's wife, Belinda Bush Stephens, lived to be ninety years old. Like many other members of the Smith clan, she remained loyal to Britain during the Revolution.

William Stephens Smith, was the eldest of a family of four sons and six daughters. He graduated from the College of New Jersey in 1774. After college, Smith studied law with Samuel Jones in New York City where he was living when the Revolution started. His matriarchal grandmother, Belinda Bush Stephens, did everything she could to prevent her grandson from joining the American army, but to no avail. According to a story told by the marquis de Chastellux, Smith enlisted as a common soldier in the Continental Army to hide his decision from his Loyalist family. Chastellux said, "Being one day on duty at the door of a General Officer [John Sullivan of New Hampshire], he was discovered by a friend of his family, who spoke of him to that General Officer." Chastellux wrote that when Sullivan learned that the sentry at his door was a gentlemen, he immediately invited the young solder to dinner, "but he answered that he could not quit his duty; his corporal was sent for to relieve him, and he returned to his post after dinner. A few days only elapsed before this general officer, charmed with his zeal and his inclinations, made him his aide-de-camp."[23] Smith was appointed General Sullivan's aide-de-camp on August 15, 1776, with the rank of major. This was the start of one of the most remarkable combat records of any officer in the American Revolution. It began when Smith was captured with Sullivan at the battle of Long Island in August 1776. He managed to escape and was invited to join the staff of Gen. Nathanael Greene. Serving under Greene, Smith was wounded at the battle of Harlem Heights in September. The wounded major was taken by his parents to their home on Throgs Neck to recover, but the family had to flee to escape the fighting when the British landed there in a move to outflank the American positions on upper Manhattan Island. Despite his wounds, Smith helped delay the British advance into Westchester County. It was said that he and seven men destroyed the bridge connecting Throgs Neck with the mainland, which compelled the enemy to land further up Long Island Sound.[24] Gen. Sir William Howe eventually made the Smith mansion on Throgs Neck his headquarters during this campaign. Meanwhile Major Smith rejoined Washington's Grand Army and next saw action at the battle of White Plains on October 28. He subsequently fought at the battle of Trenton on December 26, where legend has it that he helped Colonel Rall, the wounded commander of the Hessian troops, from his horse to surrender to General Washington. It is probable that Washington appointed Smith as a lieutenant colonel in Col. William Raymond Lee's Additional Regiment (of Massachusetts) in part because of his gallantry at Trenton.[25] The next step in Smith's brilliant military career requires us to unravel the complicated origins of a consolidated unit, which included Lee's Regiment, that was designated as Jackson's detachment.

Smith's appointment in early 1777 was in one of the sixteen new regiments (called Additional Regiments) authorized by Congress in late 1776. These sixteen regiments were not numbered but were known instead by the name of their colonels. Smith's superior, Colonel Lee, apparently was unsuccessful in recruiting men for his new regiment because it marched with two other understrength additional regiments from Massachusetts, designated Henley's (named for Col. David Henley), and Jackson's (for Col. Henry Jackson).

Lt. Col. David Cobb (another future aide to Washington) was an officer in Jackson's Regiment at the time. Lee's detachment was commanded by Smith, and it joined the main army in Pennsylvania sometime in mid-November 1777 with smallpox among its men.[26] Washington's letter to Gen. William Heath, who commanded in Boston, dated December 17, 1777, tells the story and explains what happened next to Smith and his detachment:

> I was not less surprised than mortified to find the fine detachment of Men that came forward under Lt. Colo. Smith rendered intirely use-less for this Campaign by my Orders not being attended to [Washing-ton wanted recruits inoculated against smallpox before they joined the main army]. By the time they reached the Camp the small pox broke out upon them, which obliged me to send the whole into the Hospital, as those who were well were not more than sufficient to nurse the sick.[27]

Smith's Massachusetts men were sent to Lancaster where it was hoped the sick would recover while the healthy men were inoculated against smallpox. Cobb mentions this in a letter to his commander, Col. Henry Jackson, who apparently was still in Massachusetts trying to raise additional men for his regiment. Cobb's letter is dated December 16, 1777: "The Regt, you know are gone to Lancaster for Inoculation."[28] The health of the detachment apparently improved by late winter because Smith issued the following orders in Lan-caster on March 6, 1778: "As the Detachments from Colo. Lee, Henly & Jack-son's Regts will probably march soon for Camp [Valley Forge] . . . it is recommend to the Officers to put their affairs in such a situation that they may be ready to march at the Shortest Notice."[29] Smith commanded the men from these three undermanned regiments in Lancaster throughout the winter, and after they joined the main army at Valley Forge. The three understrength regi-ments remained consolidated, and identified as Smith's detachment until the arrival of Col. Henry Jackson on the scene in May 1778 at which time Smith became second in command of what was identified as Jackson's detachment.[30]

Smith and Cobb, who were both high ranking officers in the unit, must have known each other before they joined Washington's military family. While Cobb was stationed behind the lines at the battle of Monmouth on June 28, 1778, however, Smith was in the midst of the daylong fighting. At Monmouth, Jackson's detachment was assigned to Gen. Charles Lee's advance corps where Smith once again proved his leadership and courage as he rallied his troops in the face of a determined enemy attack. Smith next participated in the abortive attempt to recapture Newport, Rhode Island, in August. His incredible service record continued as commanding officer of Spencer's New Jersey Regiment in Gen. John Sullivan's expedition against the Iroquois Indians in 1779 and the battle of Springfield, New Jersey, in 1780. Smith was next attached to the Corps of Light Infantry, commanded by the marquis de

Lafayette. In the general orders for August 5, 1780, Smith was appointed Inspector "and will consider the Light Infantry in his Department."[31] In January 1781 he was appointed Lafayette's adjutant and inspector. When Washington asked Lafayette to recommend officers for the post of adjutant general of the army, the Marquis responded on November 28, 1780, with several recommendations, one of which was Colonel Smith. Lafayette said, "Colonel Smith has been by me wholly employed in that line and I can assure you that he will perfectly answer your purpose."[32] Smith served as Lafayette's adjutant and inspector from January 1781 until he joined Washington's staff as an aide-de-camp in July 1781. The General Orders of the Army for July 6, 1781, mention his appointment: "Lieutenant Colonel William S. Smith is Appointed Aide-de-camp to the Commander in Chief and is to be respected accordingly."[33]

One other person was added to Washington's personal staff in 1781, Peregrine Fitzhugh, who was appointed an extra aide-de-camp. While Fitzhugh was a worthy officer, he probably owed his appointment to Washington's sense of obligation to young Peregrine's father, Col. William Fitzhugh. The elder Fitzhugh was one of Washington's best friends. He had helped Washington advance his military and political career in the years prior to the Revolution. For instance, when young George wanted to be appointed as an adjutant general in the Virginia militia, it was Colonel Fitzhugh who used his influence to get him the appointment. In 1759 Fitzhugh moved to Calvert County, Maryland, where he was active in state politics and remained friendly with Washington. The colonel approached Washington in 1778 asking him to help his son Peregrine obtain a commission as an officer in the Continental Army. Washington could not refuse his old friend, and he promptly wrote George Baylor (his former aide-de-camp) who commanded the 3rd Continental Dragoons, as follows:

> If there is a vacant Cornetcy in your Regiment, I should wish it reserved for Mr. Peregrine Fitzhugh Son of Colo. Fitzhugh of Patuxent in Maryland, a young Gentleman strongly recommended to me by his father.[34] He is now here [Valley Forge], but will go over to Major Clough [Maj. Alexander Clough, second in command of Baylor's dragons] and receive proper instructions from him, to fit him for command. Should your Regiment be full, be pleased to speak to Colo. Bland and desire him to reserve a Cornetcy in his, for Mr. Fitzhugh.[35]

In Washington's defense, the appointment Colonel Fitzhugh sought for his son was as a junior officer with little authority. The young man was probably worthy of the minor appointment anyway. Unfortunately for Peregrine, Baylor had a vacancy in his regiment. Washington wrote Peregrine's father from Valley Forge on June 8, 1778, with the news of his son's appointment in Baylor's dragoons. The general wrote his old friend, "I have given him a Cornacy in Baylor's Regiment of light Dragoons, with which he seems to be pleased, and I have not a doubt will do honor to himself and the Corps, as he is spirited, possesses a fund of good sense, and good humor which cannot fail of rendering him agreeable to the Regiment he is going into; the Officers in which being all Gentlemen."[36]

Young Fitzhugh was soon promoted to lieutenant and was caught in the surprise attack on Baylor's dragoons in New Jersey on the night of September 28, 1778. Fitzhugh was one of the officers lucky enough to survive "Baylor's Massacre" but he was wounded in the action and taken prisoner. He was exchanged two years later on October 25, 1780. What I believe happened is that following Peregrine's release, Washington felt obligated to help him. He could not appoint Peregrine as one of his aides-de-camp without attracting criticism that he had increased his staff to give a job to his friend's son. I feel that his solution was to give a vague title to Peregrine, which could mean anything. Thus, Peregrine Fitzhugh's confusing appointment was announced in the general orders for July 2, 1781: "Peregrine Fitzhugh, Esqr, Lieutenant in the third regiment of Dragoons is appointed an Extra Aid de camp to the Commander-in-chief and to be respected accordingly."[37] I believe this public announcement counters any argument that Washington was trying to hide Fitzhugh's appointment to his staff or that the use of the term "extra aide-de-camp" was an attempt to confuse. There is no known response from any member of Congress complaining of Fitzhugh's appointment as Washington's aide.

Peregrine Fitzhugh served as an aide-de-camp for only a few months. He resigned in late October 1781 to be married.[38] If he had remained longer on Washington's staff, and proved useful, he may have been promoted from an extra aide-de-camp to aide-de-camp. Following his resignation from the army, Fitzhugh became a farmer on Kent Island, Maryland. Facing financial difficulties in the years following the Revolution, he held a bankruptcy lottery in Annapolis, Maryland, in 1793 after which he moved to Geneva, New York, in 1799.[39] A few years later he moved again, this time to Sodus, New York, where he died on November 28, 1811.

Peregrine Fitzhugh was a worthy officer, but he owed his aide's appointment to his father's connection with Washington. The general occasionally used his influence to secure a junior commission for a relative, friend, or son of a friend. Perhaps the most conspicuous example of this was the appointment of his old comrade Dr. James Craik to the Continental Army medical department. The general was careful, however, not to help anyone get a post who he thought might embarrass him with incompetence or neglect of duty.

On another political front in the first part of 1781, Washington renewed his effort to get Congress to give Tench Tilghman a commission as a lieutenant colonel. Tilghman had joined Washington's military family as a volunteer aide in August 1776 and was appointed Washington's aide-de-camp in June 1780. His 1780 appointment by Washington gave him the rank of lieutenant colonel under the authority given the general earlier in the war by Congress. But that did not satisfy Washington. He wanted Tilghman to be commissioned as a lieutenant colonel by Congress with his rank retroactive to April 1777. Washington wrote Gen. John Sullivan on May 11, 1781, concerning Tilghman's situation. Sullivan was a member of Congress at the time.

> This Gentn. came out a Captn. of one of the light Infy. Companies of Philadelphia, served in the flying Camp in 1776. In August of the same Year he joined my family and has been in every action in which the Main Army was concerned. He has been a zealous Servant and slave to the public, and a faithful assistant to me for near five years, great part of which time he refused to receive pay. Honor and gratitude, Interests me in his favor, and makes me sollicitous to obtain his Commission. His modesty and love of concord, placed the date of his expected Comn. at the first of April 1777, because he would not take rank of Hamilton and Mead, who were declared Aids in Orders (which he did not choose to be) before that period, altho' he had joined my family and did all the duties of one from the first of Septr. preceeding.[40]

Congress finally took action on Tilghman's behalf. His commission was one of several issues addressed at the Board of War meeting of May 22, 1781, that pertained to Washington's aides-de-camp. The Board resolved, "That Tench Tilghman, esq. receive the commission of lieutenant colonel in the line of the army and take rank from the 1st April, 1777."[41] The Board's use of the term "in the line of the army" is important. It meant that Tilghman held a regular (official) commission from the Continental Congress. Prior to the Board of War's resolution, Tilghman held the "implied" rank of lieutenant colonel in his capacity as an aide-de-camp to the commander in chief. This meant that another officer had to follow an order from him as the personal representative of the commander of the army. Tilghman, however, had no authority beyond his function as the commander's aide. For example, he had no authority to command troops in combat.

The second item of interest to us from the Board of War meeting of May 22, 1781, is that they commissioned Dr. James McHenry as a major. The Board's resolution reads: "That Dr. James McHenry receive the commission of major in the army of the United States, to take rank from the 30th of October last." As McHenry was an aide-de-camp to Maj. Gen. the marquis de Lafayette at the time he was authorized to hold the rank of major. Only aides to the commander in chief were ranked as lieutenant colonels. McHenry, like Tilghman, was being rewarded with a Continental Army commission, which gave him unquestioned authority in his rank and made him eligible for promotion. It also qualified him for any land grants or pensions that Congress might bestow to veteran officers.

The Board's third dictate gave Washington and the commanders of the northern, southern, and western armies (called departments) the explicit authority to allow their aides to command troops. The board ruled:

That officers not annexed to any line, serving in the family of the Commander in Chief, and those serving as Aids-de-camps with other general officers, retain the rank they now hold, and shall be eligible to command upon detachments when the Commander in Chief, or commanding officer of a department, shall think proper.[42]

Beyond these administrative changes, there was little worth reporting from Washington's main army during the first part of 1781. With money in short supply only limited military operations were possible. There was not even enough money to pay the officers and men. When financier Robert Morris wrote his seemingly wealthy friend Tench Tilghman to invest in a new bank, he got a surprise answer dated June 24, 1781, in which Tilghman asked his friend Morris for a loan: "Paper Money of all kinds has become useless, that I must beg the favor of you to send me twenty or thirty dollars in specie by Doctor Craik who accompanies Mrs. Washington as far as Philadelphia."[43] As the summer of 1781 began the American situation looked grim, but the situation changed when Col. John Laurens arrived from France with shiploads of money and military equipment.

Laurens had been captured when Charleston surrendered to the British in May 1780, and remained a prisoner on parole until his exchange in November of that same year. Following his repatriation, Laurens was offered a congressional assignment as a special envoy to assist Benjamin Franklin in securing desperately needed military supplies and hard currency from France. Congress selected Laurens for this important mission because they wanted to send a Continental Army officer to France who could give their ally an up-to-date report on the war and the condition of the American army. Laurens responded to Congress's invitation by graciously recommending his friend Hamilton for the job, as being "superiorly qualified in every respect." But Hamilton was not sufficiently known to Congress and Laurens finally accepted the posting, which bore the imposing title of special minister to France. Upon hearing the news of Laurens's mission, Lafayette wrote him a letter of introduction to his wife.

The person who will give you this letter, my dear heart, is a man I love very much, and I would like you to have a close acquaintance with him. His is the son of President Laurens, who has recently been put in the Tower of London. He is a lieutenant colonel in our service and an aide-de-camp to General Washington. He is sent by Congress on a special mission to the French court. I know him very well during the first two campaigns, and his honesty, his openness, and his patriotism have made me particularly attached to him. . . . treat him as a friend of the family. He will tell you all that has happened during our campaign, our present situation, and all the details that may concern me.[44]

As we saw from the fate of Henry Laurens's mission to Holland, a voyage across the Atlantic Ocean was a dangerous undertaking for any American during the war. Colonel Laurens risked the voyage, sailing from Boston on February 13, 1781, aboard the frigate *Alliance,* commanded by the famous Capt. John Barry. When the British learned of his mission they told his father, who was their prisoner, that he would receive milder treatment if he would convince his son to abandon his assignment and return home. The elder Laurens scorned the proposal and remained a prisoner. Colonel Laurens's ship reached the French port of L'Orient without incident (other than being struck by an iceberg) on March 9, 1781. The colonel learned after arriving in L'Orient that the marquis de Castries, minister of the marine, was in the area en route to Brest to supervise the sailing of a French naval squadron commanded by the count de Grasse destined for the West Indies. Laurens found the minister and in a brief meeting he stressed the importance of French naval supremacy in American waters. Laurens's account may have influenced Castries to give de Grasse latitude in his orders, which allowed him to cooperate with the Americans at Yorktown later that year.[45]

Laurens proceeded to Paris where he settled into his mission of assisting Franklin in securing additional loans from France. Young Laurens proved impatient and "pressed his demands with more pertinacity and less regard than is usual in diplomatic intercourse."[46] After six weeks of what seemed fruitless meetings and interviews, Laurens boldly called upon the comte de Vergennes, the French minister of foreign affairs, demanding weapons, clothing, ammunition, and money for the American cause. Vergennes replied, "Colonel Laurens, you are so recently from the Head Quarters of the American Army, that you forget that you are no longer delivering the order of the Commander-in-Chief, but that you are addressing the minister of a monarch."[47] With that the audience ended.

Despite his rebuff and Franklin's warnings, Laurens decided that he would present his case directly to King Louis XVI. His opportunity came when he was invited to attend one of the king's levees. When the "Special Minister of the United States of America" was announced, Laurens entered the private apartment where the king was standing with his ministers and other dignitaries. The young colonel, renowned for his reckless bravery, bowed to the king but instead of moving along, advanced toward the monarch. He saluted the king and handed him his memorial. Laurens's action was unprecedented but Louis did not flinch and immediately passed the paper to the marquis de Segur, the French minister of war, who put it in his pocket.[48] The French gave the Americans a gift of six million livres through Franklin's efforts.[49] Laurens was able to secure an additional ten-million-livre loan from the Dutch that was underwritten by the French. The elated Laurens spent his final weeks in France gathering arms, ammunition, clothing, and equipment for the American army. He departed France at the end of May 1781 abroad the frigate *La Resolute* with money and in the company of two ships carrying much needed military supplies. Laurens arrived safely back in Boston on August 25, 1781, just over six months from the date of his departure. He promptly invested part of the French money in bills of exchange. The balance was carried by oxcarts under heavy guard to Philadelphia. Laurens now returned to army headquarters and Washington's family.

Critics claimed that Colonel Laurens's mission to France was a success because the French court was already favorably disposed to provide aid to the Americans. Benjamin Franklin quietly noted later that the young man's impetuous manners towards the French court "gave more offence than I could have imagined."[50]

Laurens's wife, whom he had married while he was a law student in England, probably went to France to see her husband. There are romantic accounts of their reunion and Laurens's first meeting with his four-year-old daughter, "Fanny" (Frances Eleanor). These same storytellers say that the colonel planned to bring his family to America. However, he returned home alone leaving his wife behind in France, where she died later that year. We know something of his daughter's later life. She apparently stayed with her mother's family in England until she went to America accompanied by members of the Laurens family who were living in Europe at the time. The *South Carolina Gazette and Public Advertiser* mentioned their arrival in Charleston in its May 14, 1785, issue: "Wednesday last Mrs. Laurens (widow of the late James L. Laurens, Esq. [the brother of Henry Laurens]) Miss Patty Laurens & Miss Polly Laurens (daughters of the Hon. Henry Laurens, Esq.) Miss Fanny Laurens (only child of the brave Col. John Laurens) and others arrived here from London, in the ship Olive Branch, Capt. Angus."[51] Fanny remained in Charleston for a number of years before returning to England, where in 1795 she married Francis Henderson. Henderson was a Scottish merchant described as a "little ugly man." They had one child, a son, whose name was Francis Henderson, Jr., born in 1800. A year later the couple separated and Francis got custody of his son. Fanny remarried in England, this time to James Cunnington. The couple had no children. Frances Laurens Henderson Cunnington died in 1860 at the age of eighty-three. Her son from her first marriage, Francis, Jr., graduated from the University of Edinburgh in 1819. He never married, was an alcoholic, and died in 1847.[52]

By September 1781, Washington's military family had undergone several major changes of personnel and now consisted of: Jonathan Trumbull, Jr., in the position of military secretary, with aides-de-camp Tench Tilghman, John Laurens, David Humphreys, Dr. David Cobb, and William Stephens Smith. Peregrine Fitzhugh was an extra aide-de-camp. They were all with Washington the following month for the siege of Yorktown, Virginia, the campaign that proved to be the climax of the American Revolution. Four former members of Washington's staff were also at Yorktown. They were Hamilton, McHenry, Moylan, and Gibbs. Hamilton was there serving proudly as a lieutenant colonel commanding a regiment of light infantry. He owed his coveted appointment to Washington and was finally going to have an opportunity to lead troops in combat. Dr. James McHenry was also there. He was serving as a volunteer aide-de-camp to his friend Lafayette.[53] Stephen Moylan, who had been a great help to Washington early in the war as a temporary secretary and aide-de-camp, was also at Yorktown commanding the 4th Continental Dragoons, popularly known as "Moylan's Horse." And finally, Maj. Caleb Gibbs was present at the siege commanding light infantry. An interesting irony to the Yorktown campaign was the presence of Lt. Col. Francis Barber. He was Hamilton's first teacher when he arrived in America. Colonel Barber commanded light infantry at Yorktown and joined his former student for what proved to be one of the decisive operations of the siege.

The siege of Yorktown had its origins in the British conquest of Georgia and South Carolina in 1780. The British offensive in the South threatened Virginia, which had largely escaped the war to-date. In November, 1780 General von Steuben was put in charge of helping Gov. Thomas Jefferson organize Virginia's defenses. Von Steuben found an apathetic and confusing military situation and asked Governor Jefferson to help him find experienced military men to join his personal staff. Among the men Jefferson contacted was Washington's former aide-de-camp John Walker. Jefferson wrote his neighbor and friend on January 18, 1781, "Baron Steuben, being very much unacquainted with Virginia's laws, customs, resources, and organization . . . has desired we will prevail on some gentlemen acquainted with these to be of his family . . . Searching about for such a person we cast our eyes on you, and hope you will undertake the office."[54] Walker agreed to help and there are references to his activities during this period. For example, Walker wrote Governor Jefferson from Williamsburg on March 8, 1781, "The Baron has desired me to send you the inclosed papers in order to shew you and the Legislature of Necessity of giving more Energy to the Militia Laws of this State."[55]

The British launched a devastating raid against Virginia in late 1780 led by the high traitor Benedict Arnold.[56] Virginia needed help and General Washington rushed 1,200 Continental troops to the beleaguered state. These reinforcements were commanded by Lafayette whose personal staff included Washington's former aide-de-camp Dr. James McHenry.[57] Sir Henry Clinton countered by reinforcing Arnold with 2,000 troops commanded by Maj. Gen. William Phillips, who assumed overall command of British forces in Virginia. Meanwhile, in complete defiance of his orders from General Clinton in New York, Cornwallis brought his army of 1,500 up from North Carolina to rendezvous with the British troops in Virginia.[58] Phillips died of fever in Petersburg, Virginia, on May 13, which put Arnold back in command. Cornwallis, however, arrived a week later and, as senior officer, took over from Arnold. Arnold returned to New York while additional troops arrived to further reinforce Cornwallis. Thus were the circumstances that put Cornwallis in Virginia in late May 1781, commanding a sizable army of 7,500 troops. He sent his forces raiding as far west as Charlottesville, but by early August, he was in the Tidewater region of Virginia at the York River port of Yorktown ready to rendezvous with the Royal Navy.

General Washington watched the alarming situation in Virginia following a strategy conference in Connecticut with his French counterpart, the viscount de Rochambeau. Washington and Rochambeau reasoned that if French admiral de Grasse could bring his fleet to Chesapeake Bay and Lafayette's army was reinforced with troops and artillery, the allies could trap Cornwallis at Yorktown. On August 19, 1781, Washington and Rochambeau began to march their troops toward the York. Washington and his army reached Philadelphia on August 30, 1781. We have an idea of what he and his entourage looked like on the march from an eye-witness account:

> As I walked on the road alone, for I ever loved solitary rambles, ascending a hill suddenly appeared a brilliant troop of cavaliers, mounting and gaining the summit in my front. The clear autumnal sky behind them equally relieved the dark blue uniforms, the buff facings, and glittering military appendages. All were gallantly mounted—all were tall and graceful, but one towered above the rest, and I doubted not an instant that I saw the beloved hero. I lifted my hat as I saw that his eyes turned to me, and instantly every hat was raised and every eye fixed to me . . . I still think of the blue and buff of Washington and his aids, their cocked hats worn sidelong, with the union cockade, their whole equipment as seen at that moment, was the most martial of anything I ever saw.[59]

Washington was very apprehensive about the success of the operation as he left Philadelphia. Its success depended on the arrival of de Grasse's fleet. The general and his suite were passing through the town of Chester, Pennsylvania, in the afternoon of September 5, 1781, when they were intercepted by a courier with an urgent dispatch from Gen. Mordecai Gist, who commanded at Baltimore.[60] Washington hurriedly broke the seal of the message, unfolded it, and read with unrestrained joy that de Grasse had come! His fleet blockaded Chesapeake Bay. In the general orders issued the following day, Washington shared the glorious news with his army. While florid language appears in the general orders throughout the war, the orders for September 6, 1781, were probably drafted by David Humphreys because of their particularly oratorical style:

> Head Quarters, Head of Elk [Maryland], September 6, 1781
> It is with the highest pleasure and satisfaction the Commander in Chief announces to the Army the arrivals of the Count de Grasse in the Chesapeake with a very formidable Naval and Land force; at the same time he felicitates them on this auspicious occasion he anticipates the glorious Events which may be expected from the combined

Operations now in contemplation . . . The General calls upon all the gallant Officers, the brave and faithful soldiers he has the honor to command to exert their utmost abilities in the cause of their Country and to share with him (with their usual alacrity) the difficulties, dangers and glory of the present Enterprize.[61]

Washington rode ahead of his troops, crossing the Potomac River into Virginia late on Sunday, September 9, 1781. He traveled late into the night with Humphreys and reached Mount Vernon, tired but elated to be home. He had not seen his estate for almost six and a half years, having lived all that time in various private homes and tents. Washington spent a few wonderful days at Mount Vernon acting as host to Rochambeau and the other French generals. The tension of the previous weeks was somewhat relieved, because the 3,000 French troops that de Grasse brought with him were already landed and cooperating with Lafayette's Continentals and militia. Washington departed Mount Vernon on September 12 to join the allied army that was collecting against Cornwallis. Washington's high-living, spendthrift stepson, John Parke Custis (called Jack or Jacky by his relatives), accompanied the general. He was Martha Washington's only son from her first marriage and principal heir to the large Custis estate. Jacky was twenty-eight years old at the time and married to Eleanor (Nelly) Calvert. They had four children including George Washington Parke Custis. Jacky wanted to see something of the war and his stepfather reluctantly agreed to allow him to accompany him to Yorktown. Custis is frequently mentioned as one of Washington's aides-de-camp but he was classified as a volunteer aide-de-camp or "gentleman volunteer." There is no known record of him ever being appointed as one of Washington's aides.[62]

September had been a fortuitous month for the allies. De Grasse's fleet had driven off a Royal Navy squadron sent to rescue Cornwallis, guaranteeing the allies at least temporary naval superiority in the region. Then on September 10, Admiral Barras's squadron arrived from Newport, bringing the big French siege guns necessary to smash Corwallis's defenses and force him to surrender.[63] The main allied army was at Williamsburg, a short distance away from Yorktown.

At 5:00 on the morning of September 28, the allies left Williamsburg arriving within a mile or two of Yorktown by nightfall. Washington's military secretary, Jonathan Trumbull, Jr., kept a diary of the campaign, and his entry for September 28 described the event: "the army commences its march from Williamsburg and approaches within two miles of York Town. The enemy on our approach make some shew of opposition from their Cavalry, but upon our bringing up some field pieces and making a few shot, they retire, and we take a quiet position for the night." Trumbull wrote that Washington and his military family slept on the open ground that night under the stars: "The General and family sleep in the field without any other covering than the canopy of the heavens and the small spreading branches of a tree, which will probably be rendered venerable from this circumstances for a length of time to come."[64] Washington Irving described the scene in his biography of the general: "Washington and his staff bivouacked that night on the ground in the open air. He slept under a mulberry tree, the root serving for his pillow."[65]

The following evening Cornwallis received a dispatch from Clinton in New York, informing him that a relief expedition was preparing to sail. Upon receipt of this news, Cornwallis abandoned his outer works during the night of September 29 and withdrew his troops within the town, believing that he could make a better defense from his inner fortifications in the week or so that it would take reinforcements to arrive. Trumbull recorded what happened the next morning when the allies realized that the British had abandoned their outer defenses: "[September] 30, In the morning it is discovered that the Enemy have evacuated all their exterior works, and retired to the interior defence near the town. We immediately take possession of . . . the Enemies Redoubts, and find ourselves very unexpectedly upon very advantageous ground."[66]

Washington established his headquarters in tents behind the siege lines.[67] At the start of the siege, the allies had 16,000 soldiers facing 7,500 Crown troops bottled up at Yorktown. Cornwallis, however, had veteran regiments with him and they evolved into a classic eighteenth-century siege conducted according to a strict plan developed by Sebastien le Prestre de Vauban (1633–1707) and refined by others. Before Vauban, sieges were disorganized affairs, often with high casualty rates among the besiegers. But Vauban changed all that when he wrote his book, *A Manual of Siegecraft and Fortifications,* which was the result of experiences gained in forty-eight separate sieges—forty of which he personally directed as chief engineer and none of which failed. Siege craft was a science with success almost guaranteed if the techniques prescribed by Vauban followed. The idea was to dig a series of trenches toward the defender's walls and move up artillery protected by infantry. That is exactly what happened at Yorktown.

The Americans had little experience conducting a siege, and they got their first lesson at Yorktown from French engineers. First men and materials were gathered out of view and range of the defender's guns. A number of winding approach trenches were dug toward Yorktown stopping at the edge of the effective range of artillery fire, which was about 1,000 yards. All the work was done at night and the diggers were protected against an enemy sortie by infantrymen. Once these approach trenches were completed, another set of trenches was dug at a right angle to the approach trenches. These new trenches were much bigger; twelve to fifteen feet wide and about seven feet deep. The new trenches faced the enemy and were called the first parallel. Heavy artillery was moved into the first parallel, and began firing shells into Yorktown around the clock.

Work on the first parallel started on the night of October 6. It was a dark and cloudy night with a gentle rain; perfect weather for the dangerous business at hand. Tench Tilghman kept a journal of the siege and he left us a record of its start: "The 6th, at night the trenches were opened between 5 and 600 yards from the enemy's works and the 1st parallel run—commencing about the centre of the enemy's works . . . The enemy kept up a pretty brisk fire during the night but as our working parties were not discovered by them, their shot were in a wrong direction."[68] Some 1,500 men dug the approach trench and first parallel that night. The next day McHenry wrote a friend, "This seiging work is very serious business. We go on however very briskly. Last night we broke ground upon our first parallel and this morning we are under cover; but we shall not open our trenches for some days. When we do it, it will be with about eighty pieces of cannon and mortars."[69] The allies constructed the first parallel on October 7 and 8. At 3:00 P.M. on October 9, allied gun batteries opened fire on the town.[70]

As the first parallel was being constructed, Washington gave Laurens temporary command of a battalion of light infantry while he continued to serve as one of the general's aides. Washington probably gave Laurens this opportunity as a reward for his long and hard service. Laurens's line command was included in the General Orders of the Army for October 8:

> Head Quarters before York, Monday October 8, 1781
> The Regiment lately commanded by Colonel Scammell is to be formed into two Battalions, one to be commanded by Lieutenant Colonel Huntington and Major Rice: the other by Lieutenant Colonel Laurens, Aid to the Command in Chief and Major Cummings.
> Lieutenant Colonel Laurens will join his corps whenever it mounts the Trenches.[71]

Work was begun on the second parallel on the night of October 11. Tilghman wrote in his journal, "11th, Fire from all the Batteries continued—2 transport vessels fired by hot shot and burnt. The French Bomb Battery of 6 mortars opened—The night of the 11t the 2d parallel was opened within 300 yards of the enemy's Works."[72] The second parallel could not be extended all the way to the York River on the right because two British redoubts stood in the way. The engineers agreed that the outposts had to be reduced before the second parallel could become effective. It was decided that the fortification closest to the river, designated Redoubt Number 10, would be attacked by the Americans, while Redoubt Number 9 would be assaulted by the French. Everything was ready for simultaneous attacks on the night of October 14. As men hurried through the lines to prepare the assault, a squabble arose over who should lead the attack on Redoubt Number 10. Lafayette had named his aide, the chevalier de Gimat, to lead the American attack, but Hamilton protested, claiming that he was the senior officer of the day and should be given the command. Washington settled the argument by giving the command to Hamilton.[73]

The assault commenced at 8:00 P.M. on the evening of October 14. Rockets went screaming into the air to signal the attacks. Hamilton's light infantry ran forward silently with their muskets unloaded and bayonets fixed. They were preceded by a detachment of pioneers carrying axes, and sappers and miners armed with explosives.[74] The job of these specialized troops was to open a path through the obstructions such as abatis and fraises that surrounded the redoubt.[75] The men racing across the open ground toward the redoubts could hear musket firing from their left; this was a feint whose purpose was to confuse the British into believing that an attack was being made in another sector of the British lines. Colonel Laurens was part of the assault team, his mission was to take the rear of the redoubt with two companies of light infantry and cut off the enemy's retreat. When the British realized that an attack was underway, they opened fire with all the artillery they could bring to bear.

As Hamilton's men reached the redoubt, a sentry called a challenge. When there was no reply the British fired a volley. Hamilton and his infantrymen did not wait for the pioneers to clear gaps in the obstructions. They pushed them aside or tore them down with their bare hands and scrambled over the earthen walls. The redoubt was soon taken by his men at the point of the bayonet. The French had a similar success in taking Redoubt Number 9, though their attack was made with loaded muskets.

Washington was an excited spectator to the storming of the two redoubts. According to Dr. James Thacher, Washington was observing the attack from an exposed position in the midst of the British artillery fire. Lieutenant Colonel Cobb, one of his aides-de-camp was at his side and as the story is told, "Cobb was solicitous for his safety and said to his excellency, 'Sir, you are too much exposed here. Had you not better step a little back?' 'Colonel Cobb,' replied his excellency, 'if you are afraid, you have liberty to step back.'"[76]

Cornwallis finally made a sortie against the second parallel, and Tilghman reported the incident: "the night of the 15th the enemy made a sortie—They entered one of the French and one of the American unfinished Batteries and spiked 6 Cannon with the points of Bayonets, which made them to be unspiked with ease, they left 7 or 8 dead and 6 prisoners—the French had four officers wounded and twenty men killed and wounded—We had one Sarjt. Mortally wounded."[77] Tilghman's next entry describes the event that sealed the fate of Cornwallis and his army: "October 16th. Compleating 2d parallel—Several Batteries upon it opened, which galled the Enemy much."[78]

At about 10:00 A.M. on the morning of October 17, a British drummer appeared on the parapet of the Yorktown fortifications and beat a parley.[79] He went unheard in the din of the shelling until he was seen by allied infantrymen and then by the gunners. One by one the batteries fell silent until all that could be heard was the sound of the drummer. Then a British officer came out of Yorktown holding a white handkerchief over his head. He passed a letter to the allies from General Cornwallis. Tench Tilghman described the long awaited event in his journal:

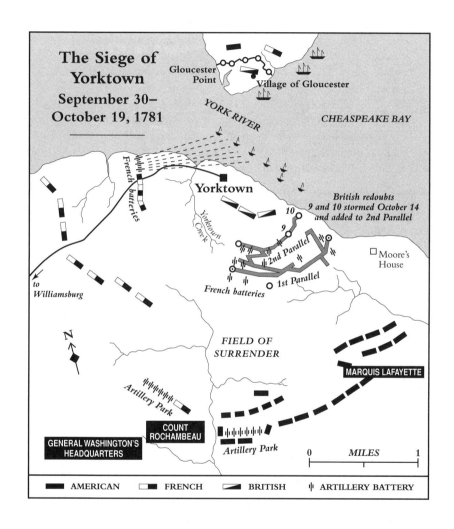

The Siege of Yorktown

September 30–October 19, 1781

Gloucester Point

Village of Gloucester

YORK RIVER

CHEASPEAKE BAY

French batteries

Yorktown

Yorktown Creek

10

9

British redoubts 9 and 10 stormed October 14 and added to 2nd Parallel

Moore's House

2nd Parallel

French batteries

1st Parallel

to Williamsburg

N

FIELD OF SURRENDER

MARQUIS LAFAYETTE

Artillery Park

Artillery Park

GENERAL WASHINGTON'S HEADQUARTERS

COUNT ROCHAMBEAU

0   MILES   1

AMERICAN   FRENCH   BRITISH   ARTILLERY BATTERY

In the morning [October 17, 1781,] Lt. [Gen.] Cornwallis put out a letter requesting that 24 Hours might be granted to Commissioners to settle terms of Capitulation for the surrender of the posts of York and Gloster. The General [Washington] answered that two Hours only would be allowed to him to send out his terms in writing. He accordingly sent them out, generally as follows, that the Garrisons should be prisoners of War, the German & British Soldiers to be sent to England and Germany. The Customary honors of war—preservation of private property—&.[80]

Time was critical for the allies because favorable news about the British relief expedition from New York would encourage Cornwallis to hold out. Washington promptly appointed Colonel Laurens and the viscount de Noailles (Lafayette's brother-in-law) as the allied commissioners to meet with Cornwallis's representatives to work out the terms of surrender.

The commissioners met on October 18 at the house of Augustine Moore, a plantation home near the York River just behind the allied lines. Lt. Col. Thomas Dundas and Maj. Alexander Ross were Cornwallis's representatives. After much discussion, a rough draft was made of the terms of the British surrender. Laurens and Noailles stipulated that the British and German troops at Yorktown must surrender as unconditional prisoners of war. But the most galling condition of the surrender was the stipulation that the Crown troops must march out of Yorktown with their flags cased and stipulations about the music their bands could play. This may have been insisted upon by Laurens in retaliation for the British stipulating the same conditions when General Lincoln surrendered Charleston the previous year. Historian and storyteller Alexander Garden reported the subsequent dialog between Ross and Laurens:

[Colonel Ross spoke first] "This is a harsh article."—"Which article?" said Colonel Laurens—"The Troops shall march out, with colours cased, and drums beating a British or a German march."

"Yes, Sir," replied Colonel L, with some sang froid, "it is a harsh article."

"Then, Col. Laurens, if that is your opinion, why is it here?"

"Your question, Col. Ross, compells an observation, which I would have suppressed.—You seem to forget, Sir, that I was a capitulant at Charleston—where Gen. Lincoln, after a brave defense of six weeks' open trenches, by a very inconsiderable garrison, against the British army and fleet, under Sir Henry Clinton and Admiral Arbuthnot, and when your lines of approach were within pistol-shot of our field works, was refused any other terms for his gallant garrison, than marching out with colours cased, and drums not beating a British or a German march."—"But," rejoined Col. Ross, "my Lord Cornwallis did not command at Charleston." "There, Sir," said Col. Laurens, "you extort another declaration. It is not the individual that is here considered—it is the Nation. This remains an article or I cease to be a Commissioner."[81]

Nothing more was said about this condition of surrender; the article stood, and the Crown troops marched out of Yorktown on October 19 with their flags cased, playing melancholy British and German tunes.[82]

Washington gave Tench Tilghman the honor of delivering his dispatch to Congress announcing the American victory at Yorktown. This was probably the greatest honor that Washington granted to any of his aides during the war. The dispatch was addressed to Thomas McKean, who was the president of the Continental Congress at the time. The victory message was drafted by Trumbull and the fair copy written by Humphreys. Here is the text of the message that Tilghman carried to Philadelphia:

> To The President of Congress, Head Quarters near York,
> October 19, 1781
>   Sir; I have the Honor to inform Congress, that a Reduction of the British Army under the Command of Lord Cornwallis, is most happily effected . . . Colo Tilghman, one of my Aids de Camp, will have the Honor to deliver these Dispatches to your Excellency; he will be able to inform you of every minute Circumstance which is not particularly mentioned in my Letter; his Merits, which are too well known to need my observations at this time, have gained my particular Attention, and could wish that they may be conored [honored] with the Notice of your Excellency and Congress.
>   Your Excellency and Congress will be pleased to accept my Congratulations on this happy Event.[83]

Tilghman was still recovering from a fever (probably malaria) but he would not pass up this prestigious assignment. He was weak and flushed when he left camp and sailed down the York River in a small boat. The boat ran aground in Chesapeake Bay, and precious time was lost until it was floated off the following morning. More delays came as the wind died down and the boat could make no headway. Meanwhile, Tighman's fever returned, but he was determined to complete his mission. Unwilling to wait any longer for a favorable breeze, he went ashore on Maryland's eastern shore at the town of Rock Hall and persuaded someone to lend him a horse. He halted often to change horses, shouting to astonished farmers and workmen along his route, "Cornwallis is taken, Cornwallis is taken!" Sometime before dawn on October 24, Tilghman rode into Philadelphia, shaking with chills and fever. With the aid of a night watchman, he aroused McKean at his home and gave him Washington's dispatch. The old German watchman resumed his rounds, bellowing in the streets, "Past dree o'clock—und Corn-val-lis is ta-gen." The bells at the

State House (now called Independence Hall) began to ring, while Congress met later in the day to celebrate the great news from Yorktown. Tilghman was so ill that he was put to bed, but he had no money and a collection was taken up among the congressmen to pay for his room and board. Congress declared a day of national thanksgiving and voted Colonel Tilghman a horse, saddle, bridle, and elegant sword. He spent several days in bed before he was well enough to return to headquarters.

George Washington Parke Custis told his own version of Tilghman's mission in his *Recollections and Private Memoirs of Washington,* published in 1860. In the Custis version Tilghman vaulted into the saddle at Yorktown and galloped north with his dispatch. Custis said Tilghman rode all night,

> At length there is a cry—"He comes! he comes!" and merging from a cloud of dust, a horseman is seen at headlong speed. He plies the lash and spur; covered with foam, with throbbing flank, and nostril dilated to catch the breeze, the generous horse devours the road, while ever and anon the rider waves his cap, and shouts to the eager groups that crowd his way, "Cornwallis is taken."[84]

Following Tilghman's arrival in Philadelphia, Custis said, "there arose a joyous cry that made the very welkin tremble. The tories, amazed and confounded, shrunk away to their holes and hiding-places, while the patriotic whigs rushed into each other's arms, and wept for gladness."[85]

General Washington gave his aide David Humphreys the honor of following Tilghman to Philadelphia with the British flags captured at Yorktown. Humphreys's entry into Philadelphia was noted in the diary of a citizen of the city:

> November 3, 1781, This afternoon the British colors, twenty-four in number, taken from Lord Cornwallis, were brought to this city by Colonel Humphreys, aide to his Excellency. At the Schuylkill they were met and escorted into the city by our City Light Horse, commanded by Captain Sam Morris, and delivered to Hon. Thomas McKean, President of Congress, at the State House. At night the house of the French Minister was illuminated to a great degree.[86]

Following Cornwallis's surrender, Washington turned his attention to a personal tragedy. He had reluctantly agreed to allow his stepson, John Parke Custis, to participate in the Yorktown campaign as a gentleman volunteer. Custis became critically ill at Yorktown with what was then called camp fever.[87] He was taken thirty miles away to Eltham, the home of Col. Burwell Bassct, who was married to Martha Washington's sister Anna Maria. The Bassett and the Washington families had close social ties, and George Washington had been a frequent visitor to Eltham before the war. Custis died there on November 5,

1781. Washington was at Custis's bedside when he died.[88] The general did what he could to console his beloved wife in the loss of her only son.

Within a week of the British surrender at Yorktown Alexander Hamilton had resigned from the army. He went to Albany, New York, to be reunited with his wife and study for a career as a lawyer. Hamilton was admitted to practice as an attorney in July 1782 following which he opened a law office in New York City. He had meanwhile been appointed by Robert Morris as receiver of Continental revenues for the State of New York, and in November 1782 he was elected as one of New York's representatives to the Continental Congress.

By the end of the siege of Yorktown, Stephen Moylan was exhausted and in poor health. He joined Hamilton in resigning his commission after Yorktown and returned to Philadelphia to rebuild his merchant business. He had married during the war and probably also wanted to spend some time with his new wife, Mary Ricketts Van Horne, of New Jersey.[89] The couple was married on September 12, 1778, and they had two surviving daughters named Maria and Elizabeth Catharine.[90] Moylan was breveted as a brigadier general in 1783 and subsequently honored in 1793 with an appointment as a major general in the Pennsylvania militia. He had been among the first volunteers to join the army from outside New England. He served Washington faithfully in the early days of the war as muster master general of the Continental Army, military secretary *pro tem,* aide-de-camp, and quartermaster general. When he became president, Washington rewarded Moylan by first offering him the position of United States marshal of Pennsylvania, which he declined, and later, in 1793, offering him an appointment as United States commissioner of loans for the State of Pennsylvania, which he accepted. Moylan served in this position until his death on April 13, 1811. He was remembered as a gentleman of the old school, a man of honor who devoted himself to American independence. His obituary appeared in the Philadelphia *American Daily Advertiser* a few days after his death.

> Died on Saturday morning last, in the 74th year of his age, after a lingering illness, General Stephen Moylan of this City; Commissioner of Loans for the State of Pennsylvania. He served with distinction in the American army during the whole of the Revolutionary War, and few of his illustrious associates enjoyed a larger share of the favor and friendship of the Commander-in-Chief. . . . The singular tenderness of his nature, the active benevolence of his feelings, the candor and uprightness and generosity of his disposition, the mildness and urbanity of his manners, attached to him by the strongest ties of affection and respect not only the members of his own family, but all those who formed the numerous circle of his friends.[91]

Despite his other accomplishments during the Revolution, Stephen Moylan is best remembered as the man who commanded the intrepid 4th Continental Light Dragoons, forever etched in history as Moylan's Horse. Several of

Stephen Moylan's brothers—James, John, and a half brother named Jasper—were also active in the American cause during the war.[92] Stephen's brother James went to France early in the war, and his commercial firm was named the American prize agents in the French port of L'Orient. James was responsible for refitting and improving the Continental Navy sloop *Ranger* commanded by John Paul Jones and the frigate *Alliance* commanded first by Pierre Landais and later by John Barry. James obtained the old French merchant ship *Duc de Duras* in 1778 and remodeled her as a warship for John Paul Jones. Renamed the *Bonne Homme Richard* and armed with forty guns, she is probably the best known American warship of the Revolutionary War. On March 22, 1781, Stephen Moylan wrote General Washington, "My brother James has sent you a case of claret. He prays your Excellency would pardon the liberty and accept it as a small mark of veneration he had for your exalted character."[93] The other brother, John, was appointed clothier-general of the Continental Army in 1781. Stephen's half brother Jasper was an ensign in the Philadelphia militia.

Following Yorktown, Lord Cornwallis became an American prisoner of war, and Lt. Col. John Laurens was named the American captain general of prisoners. The Continental Congress finally had their hands on someone important enough to exchange for Laurens's father, who was still imprisoned in London. Cornwallis was permitted to return to England on parole while Benjamin Franklin, operating from Paris, arranged an exchange of Lord Cornwallis for Henry Laurens. Some members of Congress were opposed to a quick exchange, because of Cornwallis's "cruel and barbarous" conduct while in America.[94] But, Congress's wish to get their former president and "Honorable Commissioner to the Seven United Provinces" released from prison prevailed and the exchange took place in April 1782. After recuperating with some relatives in southern France, Henry Laurens, or "Tower Henry" as he was being called, was named one of the American Peace Commissioners and joined Franklin and John Jay in Paris. He arrived to find negotiations to end the war were already well underway.

CHAPTER ELEVEN

Waiting For Peace
November 1781–December 1783

It appears to me, Hamilton, to be no longer either necessary or a
duty, for you and I to go on to sacrifice the small remnant of time
that is left us. We have already immolated largely on the alter of
liberty.

James McHenry to Alexander Hamilton,
August 11, 1782[1]

The siege of Yorktown did not end the American Revolution, and the war lingered on for two more years. This final phase of the conflict, however, saw little fighting except for continued stiff resistance from the Loyalists who refused to accept the fact that there was little hope of a British victory. Within a few weeks of receiving the news of Cornwallis's surrender, the British opened unofficial peace talks with Benjamin Franklin in Paris. As the delicate negotiations moved forward it was critical for the Americans to maintain the semblance of what Washington called a "respectable army." During this period, the Continental Army made its principal encampments along the lower Hudson River at West Point and New Windsor, New York. Washington established his headquarters nearby at the Hasbrouck House in Newburgh, New York.[2] His personal staff had changed considerably from a few years before. Gone were many of the familiar faces including Robert Hanson Harrison, Alexander Hamilton, Richard Kidder Meade, Tench Tilghman, John Laurens, and James McHenry. But their replacements were no less competent. When Washington arrived at Newburgh, his military family was composed of Jonathan Trumbull, Jr., David Humphreys, Dr. David Cobb, and William Stephens Smith. Two additions were made to the staff in this closing phase of the Revolution: Hodijah Baylies and Benjamin Walker. These last two appointees were professional soldiers and a far cry from the civilians such as Joseph Reed, Thomas Mifflin, and John Trumbull whom Washington had appointed at the start of the war.

Hodijah Baylies joined Washington's staff with an impressive education and military record. He was born in Uxbridge, Massachusetts, on September

17, 1756, making him twenty-six years old when he joined the general's family.[3] Baylies had an impressive college education, which consisted of an A.B. (today's bachelor of arts) from Harvard College (1777) and an A.M. (master of arts) from Harvard (1781). He was commissioned a lieutenant in Jackson's Additional Continental Regiment in March 1777. He was then appointed an aide-de-camp to Gen. Benjamin Lincoln in 1777 and promoted to the rank of major. Baylies served as General Lincoln's aide during the 1780 siege of Charleston and was captured when that city surrendered to the British on May 12, 1780.[4] Baylies was exchanged on November 8, 1780, and decided to return to Harvard to get the above mentioned A.M. degree. He was subsequently invited to join Washington's staff, probably at the urging of General Lincoln. Baylies accepted the invitation and was appointed an aide-de-camp on May 14, 1782. His appointment appeared in the General Orders of the Army for that date. The announcement reads, "Major Bailies is appointed an Extra Aide-de-camp to the Commdr. In Chief, and is to be respected accordingly."[5]

Baylies served as Washington's aide-de-camp until the end of the war, resigning his commission on December 23, 1783. He married one of General Lincoln's daughters, Elizabeth, on June 23, 1784. In that same year he went into business with his father-in-law operating a flour mill near Hingham, Massachusetts. Hodijah and Elizabeth had at least four children: William, Edmund, Amelia, and Benjamin. Baylies held several minor government positions during Washington's presidential administration, largely through his father-in-law's influence. He died in Dighton, Massachusetts, in 1842.

General Washington's other "post Yorktown" appointment was Benjamin Walker. Walker was born in England in 1753, and not much is known about his early life except that he attended the Blue-Coat School in England, which was a prestigious private school, and that he was "brought up for the counting-house."[6] He immigrated to New York City sometime before the outbreak of the Revolution. At the start of the war he was commissioned a second lieutenant in the 1st New York Regiment in August 1775, promoted to first lieutenant on February 24, 1775, and named a captain in the 4th New York on November 21, 1776.[7] Walker first appeared in this narrative during the 1777–78 winter encampment at Valley Forge when he helped Baron von Steuben translate his drill manual from French into English. Von Steuben later appointed the New Yorker as his aide-de-camp on September 3, 1778, fondly nicknaming him "Le Petit Walker."[8] It was said that Von Steuben frequently relied on Walker's cool temper and sound judgment to keep him out of trouble. The success of Von Steuben's reforms in the Continental Army were due in part to his "indefatigable and able aid-de-camp."[9] Von Steuben repaid his friend Walker's kindness in many ways. Von Steuben taught Walker how to play chess, and the tradition is that Walker later taught the game to Martha Washington.[10]

A fellow Continental Army officer left us a flattering description of Walker: "He had not received a brilliant, but a solid education; he was master of the French language, and gifted by nature with a clear head and sound judgment. He was brave, intelligent, honest and true. I enjoyed his friendship to the time of his death. He was beloved and respected by all who knew him, and the baron, particularly, was much attached to him."[11]

There was an incident where Walker was especially helpful to Von Steuben in writing a letter. Following the 1778 battle of Monmouth, Gen. Charles Lee insulted Von Steuben (among others) in a pamphlet. Lee mentioned Von Steuben as a "very distant spectator" to the battle. The proud German was incited by the affront and wanted to challenge Lee to a duel. Walker apparently wrote the challenge in French for his commander. We can picture Von Steuben in a rage, pacing the floor of his headquarters composing his challenge to Lee, who spoke French, while his aide Walker picked over the numerous oaths to write the formal challenge.[12] "Le Petit Walker" delivered the missive to Lee, who backed down, claiming he had not questioned von Steuben's courage, only his "forwardness" in testifying against him at his court-martial. Von Steuben accepted the explanation and the matter was closed. Walker was appointed Washington's aide on January 25, 1782, while His Excellency was visiting Philadelphia. The general orders for that date includes his appointment: "Captain Benjamin Walker, of the 2d New York Regiment is appointed Aid de Camp to the Commander in Chief and is to be respected and Obeyed accordingly."[13]

What seems like a large headquarters staff at the close of the war becomes logical when we realize that Washington's aides were often absent from camp. Washington wrote to Maj. Hodijah Baylies from Newburgh on January 8, 1783, in this regard. The general was angry with Baylies's extended leave and the fact that headquarters was shorthanded. Note that Washington had informed Baylies that he wanted three aides-de-camp present at headquarters at all times.

> You will recollect upon our first arrival in quarters [the Hasbrouck House in Newburgh], I proposed to the Gentlemen of my family to accommodate themselves by agreement as to the time of their absence, in the most convenient manner, leaving a sufficient number which I expected would be three at Head Qrs. to have the duties performed . . .
>
> Colonels Cobb, Trumbull, Tilghman, who could no longer wait your return and yourself are, in consequence, now absent; the three former I suppose for the greater part or whole of the Winter; the extension therefore of your absence agreeably to your request, would continue to impose the business of and confinement to the Office very unequally upon the two remaining Gentlemen . . .
>
> I have only to remark farther, that notwithstanding some Officers of the Army have supposed, there was nothing, or at least very little to be done in Winter Quarters, yet for my own part, I must confess I have never found it so, but on the contrary have frequently had as much business to be done by myself and Aides in that Season as in any part of the Campaign.[14]

Benjamin Walker remained on Washington's staff until the end of the war, when he established himself as a business broker in New York City. His post-war career included an appointment by President Washington to the coveted post of Naval Officer of Customs for the Port of New York.[15] He married "a young Quaker lady, who resided in the State of New York," and they lived in a house in Maiden Lane, in New York City. When his old commander and good friend Baron von Steuben became impoverished, Walker showed him every kindness and invited the old general to move in with him. The baron lived with the Walkers for a long time, and Walker managed his former commander's modest business dealings. When Von Steuben died, he bequeathed half of his property to Walker.

The Walkers moved to upstate New York in 1797, following Benjamin's appointment as agent of the Earl of Bute's estate in western New York.[16] They settled in Old Fort Schuyler, which was later renamed Utica.[17] Walker was elected to the United States House of Representatives as a Federalist in 1801 from Oneida County, New York. He declined to accept renomination when his term expired. Benjamin Walker died on January 13, 1818, in Utica. Walker is best remembered as the young officer who stepped forward to assist Baron von Steuben explain his new drill to a squad of soldiers at Valley Forge. It was said that after Von Steuben had exhausted his rich store of German and French oaths, he would call upon Walker to curse for him in English, "Viens, Walker, mon ami, viens, mon bon ami, sacre', God dam de gaucheries of dese badauts je no puis plus, I can curse dem no more!"[18]

The last two years of the American Revolution, following the surrender of Cornwallis at Yorktown, are frequently ignored by historians. It was an eventful period, however. Among the episodes that took place during this closing phase of the war was Colonel John Laurens's renewed efforts to enlist and arm a regiment of black slaves. Despite their defeat at Yorktown, the British continued to hold Charleston and the Americans feared that they would try to keep it and other territory they still occupied as negotiations got underway to end the war. Colonel Laurens decided this was a good time to make a fresh approach to the South Carolina legislature offering to raise a regiment of blacks to assist in the defense of the state and help retake Charleston. Young Laurens wrote Washington on December 10, 1781, outlining his plan. The general responded on February 18, 1782, encouraging his former aide-de-camp to pursue his dream: "I know of nothing which can be opposed to them with such a prospect of success as the Corps you have proposed should be levied in Carolina . . . Believe me, My dear Laurens, I am convinced, under all circumstances, of your unbounded zeal in the service of your Country."[19]

Colonel Laurens's plan failed to be adopted, and he thought of attempting to pursue his dream of a regiment of blacks in Georgia. He wrote Washington of his failure in South Carolina on May 19, 1782. The frustrations of almost eight years of war are evident in Washington's reply to young Laurens,

I must confess that I am not at all astonished at the failure of your Plan. That spirit of Freedom which at the commencement of this contest would have gladly sacrificed every thing to the attainment of its object has long since subsided, and every selfish Passion has taken its place; it is not the public but the private Interest which influences the generality of Mankind nor can the Americans any longer boast any exception; under these circumstances it would rather have been surprizing if you had succeeded nor will you I fear succeed better in Georgia.[20]

The relative obscurity of John Laurens in South Carolina history was probably because of his strong attitude of antislavery.[21]

While fighting in the northern states had virtually ceased following the 1781 victory at Yorktown, Washington faced a new and dangerous problem within his army. His officers and men were angry over the lack of pay, clothing, and food. The general summarized the situation in a letter to his former aide James McHenry written on October 17, 1782: "the patience, the fortitude, and long and great sufferings of this Army is unexampled in History; but there is an end to all things, and I fear we are very near one to this."[22] The growing discontent among the officers finally came to a head on March 15, 1783. At the time the Continental Army was camped a few miles west of the Hudson River at New Windsor, New York, where it awaited the end of the war and disbandment. On March 10 an anonymously printed notice was circulated through camp urging the officers to meet to decide what to do to get Congress to give them their back pay. A second notice advised the officers to take matters into their own hands. Washington was worried over this dangerous situation and requested a meeting with representatives of his officer corps at the "New Building" (also called "the Temple") on Saturday, March 15. It is probable that one or more of the general's aides-de-camp accompanied him to this meeting. The traditional account of what happened was written by his aide David Cobb in a letter addressed to Timothy Pickering on November 9, 1825. Upon investigation however, it was discovered that Cobb was seventy-seven years old when he wrote a secondhand report of an event that happened forty-two years before: "I was not present at the meeting of the officers in the Temple at Newburgh in March, 1783; but within a fortnight after, I joined the family at head-quarters, where the circumstances of that meeting and the anonymous letters were the subjects of our frequent conversations." Cobb then proceeded to give his account of the meeting, based on information he got from Jonathan Trumbull, Jr., the general's secretary who probably was there. Cobb told the story of how Washington addressed his officers and began to read a letter from a member of Congress. His Excellency faltered while trying to read it and while holding the letter in one hand, he took out a pair of spectacles from his coat pocket with his other hand. Washington had never worn his glasses in public before and according to Cobb's story, told his officers, "Gentlemen, you will permit me to put on my spectacles, for I have not only grown gray, but almost blind, in the service of my country. This little address, with the mode and manner of delivering it, drew tears from many of the officers."[23]

Cobb reported that Washington ended his speech with an impassioned plea to his officers, "you will by the dignity of your conduct, afford occasion for posterity to say, when speaking of this glorious example you have exhibited to mankind, Had this day been wanting, the world had never seen the last stage of perfection, to which human nature is capable of attaining." Washington's speech squashed the movement, and the army somehow continued to stagger along until the end of the war.

Washington was restless and bored as he too waited for the signing of the peace treaty that would bring the conflict to an end. Some relief came when he was invited to confer with the Continental Congress, which was meeting at Princeton, New Jersey, at the time. He quickly accepted the offer, and left Newburgh for Princeton on August 18, 1783, accompanied by his wife, and his three aides-de-camp (Humphreys, Cobb, and Walker). They were escorted by a small military guard consisting of twenty-four men commanded by Lt. Bazaleel Howe.[24] The general's party included the usual retinue of servants, whom Washington referred to as "domesticks." Washington arrived in Princeton on August 24 and made his headquarters at the home of Judge John Berrien in nearby Rocky Hill. The house, which Judge Berrien named "Rockingham," was rented by Congress and suitably furnished for Washington's stay.[25]

To provide a diversion during his stay at the Berrien house, Washington decided to find out if a story he had heard from the local residents was true. The tale was that the nearby Millstone River could be set on fire by disturbing the mud at its bottom, and then holding burning paper or straw a little above the surface of the water. Thomas Paine was also visiting Princeton at the time and was interested in everything. Paine heard the story and got into an argument with Humphreys and Cobb over the possible causes of this alleged phenomenon. It was decided that they would all go out onto the river the next night to make their own experiments.

The following night a boat was launched on the river with Washington, Paine, Gen. Benjamin Lincoln (who was visiting Princeton and invited along), Cobb, and a few soldiers with poles to stir up the bottom. Humphreys and Walker were sick and could not join the scientific river excursion.[26] Sure enough, when the mud at the bottom was disturbed by the poles, gas bubbles rose fast. Paine reported, "I saw the fire take from General Washington's light and descend from thence to the surface of the water." The experiment went on for sometime until everyone returned to shore.[27] Paine referred to this incident later in his book on the causes of Yellow Fever.[28]

Finally, in late October the long awaited treaty of peace was announced, ending the war. Washington traveled to New York City via West Point accompanied by Humphreys, Walker, and Cobb. In New York, he bade farewell to his officers on December 4, 1783, at Fraunces Tavern. At this final meeting, his Excellency filled a glass of wine and addressed his officers, "With a heart full of love and gratitude I now take leave of you: I most devoutly wish that your latter days may be as prosperous and happy as your former ones have been glorious and honorable."

Washington continued to Annapolis, where the Continental Congress had moved, to resign his commission.[29] As the general traveled toward Annapolis, congratulatory letters from the towns and cities along his route came pouring into headquarters. The general felt that each had to be answered, and his aides apparently were responsible for drafting his eloquent and patriotic replies. The language is characteristic of the eighteenth century and fitting for the joyous occasion. Here are excerpts from two his congratulatory responses. The first one is dated December 6, 1783, and addressed to the New Jersey legislature. The draft is in the handwriting of David Humphreys.

> Gentlemen: I want Words to express the heart-felt pleasure I experience on receiving the congratulations and plaudit of so respectable a Body, as the Legislature of the State of New Jersey. . . .
>
> I am now to bid you a long farewell, and to recommend, you Gentlemen, and the State whose welfare you are appointed to superintend, to the indulgent care of Heaven. May unanimity and wisdom ever prevail in your public Councils! May Justice and liberality distinguish the Administration of your Government! And may the Citizens of New Jersey be completely happy in the practice of Industry economy and every private Virtue.[30]

David Cobb drafted another reply for Washington in response to a congratulatory letter received from the people of Hackensack, New Jersey: "In retiring from the field of Contest to the sweets of private life, I claim no merit, but if in that retirement my most earnest wishes and prayers can be of any avail, nothing will exceed the prosperity of our common Country, and the temporal and spiritual felicity of those who are represented in your Address."[31]

On December 8, the general reached Philadelphia where he took a few moments to write a note to share his happiness with his former aide Dr. James McHenry, who was a Congressman at the time:

> After seeing the backs of the British Forces turned upon us, and the Executive of the State of New York put into peaceable possession of their Capital, I set out for this place. On Monday next I expect to leave the city, and by slow traveling arrive at Baltimore on Wednesday, where I will spend one day and then proceed to Annapolis and get translated into a private Citizen.[32]

David Cobb left the general at Baltimore to return home. Humphreys and Walker wanted to remain and escorted Washington to Annapolis. They stood behind their commander in chief on December 23, 1783, when he resigned his commission. Washington's resignation as commander of the army was a milestone in the political development of the United States. By handing back the commission they gave him eight years earlier and peacefully divesting himself of all authority to return to private life, Washington acknowledged the supremacy of the civilian government over the military. His former aide Dr. James McHenry, who was seated among the other members of Congress during the historic ceremony, wrote his fiancée the best account of the resignation ceremony:

> The General's hand which held the address shook as he read it. When he spoke of the officers who had composed his family, and recommended those who had continued in it to the present moment to the favorable notice of Congress he was obliged to support the paper with both hands. . . . he proceeded to say in the most penetrating manner, "Having now finished the work assigned me I retire from the great theater of action, and bidding an affectionate farewell to this August body under whose orders I have so long acted I here offer my commission and take my leave of all the employments of public life."
> . . . So many circumstances crowded into view and gave rise to so many affecting emotions. The events of the revolution just accomplished—the new situation into which it had thrown the affairs of the world—the great man who had borne so conspicuous a figure in it, in the act of relinquishing all public employments to return to private life—the past—the present—the future—the manner—the occasion—all conspired to render it a spectacle inexpressibly solemn and affecting.[33]

Although Alexander Hamilton was a New York representative to Congress at the time, he did not attend its sessions for a whole year starting from October 1783. He was therefore not present in Congress when Washington resigned his commission. There are also accounts that Tench Tilghman stood at Washington's side when he resigned his commission. The origin of this often repeated story apparently is a nineteenth-century biography of Tilghman written by his grandson Oswald Tilghman.[34] It seems plausible that Tilghman was present in the room because Washington journeyed through Baltimore, where Tilghman lived, on his way to nearby Annapolis where Congress was sitting. Oswald, however, gave no evidence to support his story, and lacking any substantiated eyewitness account this touching story must be classified as a legend. John Trumbull, Washington's nineteen-day aide, painted the scene of Washington resigning his commission. The original is in the Yale University Art Gallery, and a large copy, executed by Trumbull, is in the rotunda of the United States

Capitol. Trumbull claimed he created this painting based on extensive research. His rendition of the scene shows Humphreys and Walker standing just behind Washington but Tilghman is not present. The other men in uniform in the painting were spectators to the event. They were all Maryland officers identified as Gen. William Smallwood, Gen. Otho Williams, Col. Samuel Smith, and Col. John E. Howard.[35] James McHenry, who was there, was not included in Trumbull's painting.[36]

Washington was eager to return home after eight years of war. He left Annapolis quickly, and his two aides-de-camp asked to ride with him. Washington was honored to have them as his escort, and the little entourage arrived at Mount Vernon in time for Christmas.

Back at Mount Vernon, Washington warmly responded to a congratulatory letter he received from his former military secretary Jonathan Trumbull, Jr. Washington told him, "Every thing My Dear Trumbull will come right at last . . . After having passed with as much prosperity as could be expected, through the career of public Life, I have now reached the goal of domestic enjoyment; in which state, I assure you I find your good wishes most acceptable to me."[37]

Humphreys and Walker stayed as Washington's guests for a few pleasant days of good food and soft beds. They set out to return to their homes on December 28, 1783. Unexpectedly, Washington advanced each of them one hundred dollars to help them pay their expenses home.[38] It is easy to visualize these two young men, clad in their faded blue and buff uniforms trotting away from Mount Vernon. They may have stopped their horses when they reached the gate to turn around to take a final look at the house. They turned to see the vast lawn covered with snow, beyond which lay the great house. And maybe they saw the tall figure of their commander in chief framed in the doorway, waving farewell to them.[39]

PART FOUR

POSTWAR
AMERICA

Following the end of the war, many of Washington's aides-de-camp went on to serve the new nation with distinction. The next chapters follow their lives through postwar America. We will also see how George Washington dominated these early years of the republic.

It would appear that Washington was isolated living at Mount Vernon, but a number of correspondents, including some of his wartime aides-de-camp, wrote him frequently, making him one of the best informed men in America. His former aide Benjamin Walker, updated him on political events and gossip from the nation's temporary capital in New York City. David Humphreys, "the Connecticut poet," wrote his former commander from New England with news including the 1786 Shays' Rebellion. Edmund Randolph, another former aide and governor of Virginia at the time, was also a regular correspondent. His neighbor and wartime aide William Grayson was serving in Congress and wrote Washington with news of the activities of that body. For example, Grayson wrote Washington from Congress on May 27, 1785: "The Ordinance for the disposal of the Western territory was pass'd three days ago, & I take the earliest opportunity of inclosing you a copy."[1]

As we follow the lives of Washington's aides into postwar America, we should remember that the young nation faced serious problems. The thirteen colonies had reluctantly banded together in 1775 to face their common enemy and win their independence. They eventually formed a union late in the war called the Articles of Confederation that united them into a league of friendship. Some of Washington's former aides served in Congress under the Articles of Confederation: James McHenry, Alexander Hamilton, Thomas Mifflin, and William Grayson. But Congress was little more than a loose knit council in which each state retained so much power that the central government was ineffectual. The voluntary cooperation that was envisioned under the Articles never took place as the states put their sovereignty ahead of national interests.

The inability of the new nation to act unilaterally also weakened its prestige abroad and encouraged the British to retain military outposts in the Northwest Territory in violation of the Treaty of Paris. Adding to the nation's problems was an uprising of combative farmers in western Massachusetts in 1786 (Shays' Rebellion). The farmers were losing their land in court because they were unable to pay their taxes in hard currency. They demanded that Massachusetts print paper money to pay the public debt as other states were doing. Shays' Rebellion helped convince many of the men who had worked to achieve independence that the voluntary association of the states under the Articles of Confederation was not working and that a strong federal government had to replace it.[2]

George Washington was an early and vocal nationalist. In fact, the Continental Army that he commanded was a nursery for nationalism as men from the different states learned to work together toward a common goal. Washington probably spent many quiet evenings during the war in the company of his talented aides-de-camp discussing the merits of a strong central government. Many of them shared his opinion and worked with him after the war in the Federalist movement.

In 1787 a meeting of all the states was called for the purpose of amending the Articles of Confederation. The delegates met in Philadelphia during that summer, and representatives from all the colonies, except Rhode Island, participated in what became known as the Constitutional Convention. Washington was one of the Virginia delegates, and he was elected chairman of the convention. His fellow Virginia delegate and former aide Edmund Randolph, took the lead and spoke out early in their deliberations. "Look," he said, "are we not on the eve of war?, which is only prevented by the hopes from this Convention."[3] He then shook the delegates by proposing a new national government, composed of executive, judiciary, and legislature branches. This was the famous Virginia Plan, which became the basis for the summer-long deliberations that led to the creation of the United States Constitution. Among the provisions of the Constitution was the federal government's authority to raise taxes, issue currency, and control interstate commerce.

The individual states had to ratify the Constitution, and its adoption was uncertain as each state convened at a convention to decide the issue. William Grayson was opposed to the Constitution declaring at Virginia's ratification convention, "We are yet too young to know what we are fit for."[4] In the end, the states ratified the Constitution, and Washington was elected the first president. He served two terms as president and was succeeded by John Adams. In the election of 1800, Thomas Jefferson defeated Adams to become the third president. Washington, however, the revered Cincinnatus, continued to be the leading American until his death in 1799. With his passing, the remaining members of his military family gained added prestige because of their close association with the man who was the symbol of eighteenth-century America.

CHAPTER TWELVE

Different Paths

Every thing, my dear Trumbull, will come right at last as we have often prophesied.
> George Washington to Jonathan Trumbull, Jr.
> January 5, 1784[5]

When the Revolution ended, Washington became a private citizen who held no public office and dispensed no patronage. His influence remained far-reaching, however, and his recommendation would be helpful to anyone seeking a government position. Washington claimed that he had made it his policy not to assist anyone who wanted a job with the government. He explained his position in a letter dated August 31, 1785, to Dr. John Cochran, the wartime director general of the Continental Army's military hospitals. Cochran asked Washington to help him secure a government job to which the general replied, "I took up an early determination not to hazard the mortification of a refusal . . . and to this resolution I was further prompted by the numberless applications with which it was impracticable, and in many instances would have been improper, for me to comply."[6] Washington was also swamped with a variety of other requests following the end of the war. He wrote his former aide-de-camp David Humphreys on this subject from Mount Vernon on February 7, 1785:

> Enquiries after Dick, Tom, and Harry who may have been in some part, or at sometime, in the Continental service. Letters, or certificates of service for those who want to go out on their own State. Introductions: applications for copies of Papers; references of a thousand old matters with which I ought not to be troubled, more than the Great Mogul, but which must receive an answer of some kind, . . . if I do not change my course, I shall certainly sink under it.[7]

But Washington's wartime aides were exceptions whom the general seemed happy to help. The beginning of his assistance was probably a remark he made on December 23, 1783, at his resignation ceremony. It will be remembered that Washington went to Annapolis, Maryland, where Congress was meeting, to resign his commission as commander in chief of the Continental Army. His two remaining aides-de-camp, David Humphreys and Benjamin Walker, accompanied him. They stood behind their commander as he returned his commission to Congress and made a brief speech. In his short address to Congress, Washington first acknowledged the assistance of all of his aides-de-camp during the war: "I should do injustice to my own feelings not to acknowledge in this place the peculiar Services and distinguished merits of the Gentlemen who have been attached to my person during the War. It was impossible the choice of confidential Officers to compose my family should have been more fortunate." Washington then made an appeal to Pres. Thomas Mifflin and the members of Congress to provide employment for aides Humphreys and Walker: "Permit me Sir, to recommend in particular those, who have continued in Service to the present moment, as worthy of the favorable notice and patronage of Congress."[8] Humphreys in particular wanted a government job and we will see how his association and friendship with Washington helped him.

David Humphreys spent seven years of his life in the Continental Army during the Revolutionary War. Following Washington's resignation ceremony and speech, President Mifflin took Humphreys aside and told him, "if any thing should occur to me in consequence of what had just been suggested in favor of the Gentlemen of General Washington's family who had continued with him to that moment, that I would communicate it to him in a Letter." In plain language, Congress would try to satisfy Washington's request to find government positions for his remaining aides-de-camp. Humphreys returned to Connecticut with an uncertain future before him. He delayed taking any action concerning a career because he felt certain that, based on Washington's request, he would receive a government post. He wrote Washington asking him to write Congress on his behalf. Washington not only complied, but wrote a beautiful letter for his wartime aide. Washington's letter dated January 14, 1784, addressed to Thomas Mifflin, the president of the Continental Congress reads in part, "Having devoted the last Seven or Eight years to the Service of his Country, he is desirous of continuing in the walk of public life, although he is ignorant, as I also am, of the Offices which Congress have to bestow and may think him competent to." Washington then suggested several positions that he felt the young war hero was qualified to hold and said, "For his ability, integrity, punctuality, and sobriety I can fully answer. If I have gone too far, Congress will please to excuse it; and attribute the error to my wishes to serve a worthy character."[9] Humphreys was first mentioned in Congress in February 1784 for consideration as either undersecretary in the Department of Foreign Affairs or deputy secretary to Charles Thomson. A short time later, however, when a plum job became available, Humphreys's name was mentioned for the post. The position was secretary to the Commission for Negotiating Treaties of Commerce with Foreign Powers. This long-winded title translated into a job in Paris as secretary to Benjamin Franklin, John Adams, and Thomas Jefferson who were appointed to negotiate trade agreements with European countries.[10] Humphreys interviewed with Jefferson for the job in Philadelphia. The two men had first met each other the previous December when Humphreys had accompanied Washington to Annapolis to resign his commission. The day before the resignation ceremony Congress hosted a dinner in Washington's honor at Mann's Tavern in Annapolis. Congressman Jefferson and aide-de-camp Humphreys were among the invited guests. They may have chatted during the course of the evening, especially since they shared a common interest in literature. After an elegant dinner Jefferson and Humphreys raised their glasses with the other "distinguished guests" in thirteen toasts beginning with "to the United States" and ending with "to the long health and happiness of our illustrious general." The pleasant circumstances of their first meeting surely helped Humphreys's chances for the job. Colonel Humphreys received Jefferson's recommendation and was formally elected to the secretary's position by Congress on May 12, 1784. James Monroe was a congressman at the time and he wrote to Gov. Benjamin Harrison of Virginia, "I have also the pleasure to inform your excellency that Colo. Humphrey[s] is appointed secretary to the commission. By this the States not only engage in their service a gentleman who merits this attention, but comply with their engagement to the late commander in chief by providing for one of those who attended his person till his retreat from publick life."[11]

Humphreys accepted the position without hesitation and packed his bags for Paris. Franklin and Adams were already there, and it was arranged for Jefferson and Humphreys to travel to France together on a ship sailing from New York City. In preparation for his new post, however, Jefferson went to New England to discuss business opportunities for the new nation in Europe. While he was in Boston, Nathaniel Tracy, a wealthy New England merchant, offered him free passage to Europe on one of his ships. It was too tempting an offer to refuse and Jefferson sailed from Boston on Tracy's ship the *Ceres.* Humphreys followed about two weeks later on the *Courier de l'Europe,* sailing out of New York.

This must have been an exciting moment in Humphreys's life. He loved literature and art and was on his way to France, the cultural center of the western world, as a representative of the new United States of America. We can visualize Humphreys relaxing on deck and unfolding to read again the affectionate letter Washington had written him prior to his departure for France:

> My Dr. Humphreys: I very sincerely congratulate you on your late appointment. It is honorable, and I dare say must be agreeable. . . . It only remains for me now to wish you a pleasant passage, and that you

may realize all the pleasures which you must have in expectation. It cannot be necessary to add how happy I shall be at all times to hear from you . . . Mrs. Washington adds her best wishes for you, and you may rest assured that few friendships are warmer, or professions more sincere that mine for you.[12]

The voyage was the first Atlantic crossing for Humphreys who used the time writing an epic poem about his trip. Here is an excerpt from Humphreys's epistle:

On board the *Courier de l'Europe*, July 30, 1784

Yet what would all avail to prompt the smile,
Cheer the sad breast, or dull hour beguile;
If well-bred passengers, discreet and free,
Were not at hand to mix in social glee?
Such my companions—such the muse shall tell,
Him first, known once in war full well,
Our Polish friend, whose name still sounds so hard,
To make it rhyme would puzzle any bard; . . .[13]

Sever'd from all society but this,
Half way from either world we plough th' abyss;
Save the small sea-bird, and the fish that flies
On yon blue waves, no object meets my eyes . . .[14]

Jefferson arrived in Paris on August 6, 1784, six days after landing at Le Havre. Humphreys followed, reaching the French capital ten days later. The American Commission for Negotiating Treaties of Commerce with Foreign Powers held their first meeting in Paris on August 30, 1784. Present were the three ministers—John Adams, Benjamin Franklin, Thomas Jefferson—and David Humphreys, as the commission's secretary.[15] The young war hero already enjoyed a friendship with Washington, and his post in France gave him the opportunity for additional patronage from three of America's most important and influential statesmen. Washington helped his former aide ease his way into French society by writing glowing letters of introduction on his behalf.[16] Typical of these is Washington's note to the marquis de Chastellux: "permit me to recommend Colo. Humphreys, who is appointed Secretary to the Commission, to your countenance and civilities while he remains in France; he possesses an excellent heart, and a good understanding."[17] Washington also wrote a letter of recommendation to Jefferson on Humphreys's behalf: "In him you will find a good scholar, natural and acquired abilities, great integrity, and more than a share of prudence."[18]

Humphreys got a warm welcome from Jefferson. Both were culturally minded and eager to experience everything that Paris had to offer. They accompanied each other to see the sights of the city. This relationship was also an important career opportunity for Humphreys because Jefferson, who was forty-one years old at the time, was a rapidly rising American statesman and anyone associated with him would likely benefit from his patronage and prestige. Among their shared social activities were dinner parties with Jefferson's fellow commissioner John Adams. Adams was living in Paris with his wife Abigail and their nineteen-year-old daughter Abigail Amelia who was nicknamed "Nabby" by her affectionate parents. Humphreys was a thirty-one-year-old bachelor at the time. He arrived on the scene to find Miss Adams stubbornly in love with a brilliant and wealthy young Boston lawyer named Royall Tyler. Her parents knew Tyler and believed him to be frivolous and insincere. There was also gossip in Boston that Tyler had fathered a illegitimate child while he was a student at Harvard College. John and Abigail Adams reluctantly allowed their daughter to become engaged to Tyler with the provision that she accompany her parents to Europe. They hoped a long stay overseas would cool their daughter's infatuation, or at least give Tyler a chance to establish himself in his profession. Nabby was promptly introduced to Humphreys. Her first impression of him was that he was too "soldier like." On her second meeting with him she remarked in her diary that he was "a sensible man, I believe, but his address is not agreeable." Humphreys later presented her with a copy of one of his poems. She was surprised to learn that he was a poet and noted in her diary, "Col. Humphreys has taken the most effectual means of gaining my good opinion; no more reflections upon the stiffness of his manner must proceed from me."[19] Their romance never got off the ground, however, because Humphreys was a pompous windbag.

More important to Humphreys than his failed romantic overtures to Nabby Adams was that his relationship with Jefferson was not flourishing. The "Connecticut poet" tried to build a good relationship with his new chief and at one point gave him a signed copy of John Trumbull's epic work, *McFingal*.[20] But Jefferson and Humphreys had different personalities. Jefferson was relaxed and easygoing while Humphreys was formal and military. In addition, Humphreys was a distinguished Continental Army officer, which made Jefferson ill at ease. He had an embarrassing wartime record as governor of Virginia. The state's defenses were in a shambles when Benedict Arnold staged his devastating raids through the state in 1780, and Jefferson was frequently blamed for the debacle. Jefferson was also accused of cowardice for running away and hiding when British dragoons came looking for him at his home outside of Charlottesville, a story Jefferson's political enemies delighted in retelling for the rest of his life. But Jefferson was brilliant, and his political career continued to ascend. He was named to succeed the ailing Benjamin Franklin as the American minister plenipotentiary to France. As American minister to the French court, Jefferson accompanied by Humphreys, attended the king's weekly reception, which was followed by a dinner with the diplomatic corps. Humphreys loved the grandeur of these events while Jefferson was disgusted by their pomposity.

Humphreys's prospects of becoming one of Jefferson's inner circle diminished further when William Short (1759–1849) arrived on the scene. Short was Jefferson's Virginia neighbor and protégé. He was twenty-five years old at the time and a graduate of the College of William and Mary (class of 1779). After college, Short studied law under Jefferson's direction and, at his mentor's urging, opened his practice in Charlottesville, near Jefferson's mountaintop home. Jefferson wanted his young protégé to join him in Europe and created a position for him as his personal secretary. Jefferson's greatest biographer, Dumas Malone, compared Short to Humphreys: "This slim Virginian had none of the stiffness or pomposity of the poetic Colonel; he had social grace and fell into the little American circle with ease."[21] In time, Short replaced Humphreys in Jefferson's inner circle in Paris.

Although Humphreys's relationship with Jefferson had stalled, he still enjoyed the friendship and patronage of Washington, the most important and admired American of the time. The two men often exchanged letters while Humphreys was in France. Humphreys kept his old commander informed of events in France. In one of his letters, dated Paris, January 15, 1785, Humphreys set the stage for the next episode in his life. In this letter he first suggested that Washington write an account of his service in the Revolution. Humphreys said,

> I have expressed in several of my letters to you, my dear General, my ardent desire to see a good history of the Revolution, or at least of those scenes in which you have been principally concerned; I have suggested your undertaking it yourself, and I cannot help repeating, that to travel over again those fields of activity at leisure in your study would be a rational amusement . . . Such a work by having truth, instruction & public utility for its objects would make the evening of your day more precious in the eyes of future ages . . .
>
> [Then Humphreys offered to collaborate with the general in writing an account of his life.] If however you should decline the task, & if ever I shall have leisure and opportunity, I shall be strongly tempted to enter on it, more with the design of rescuing the materials from improper hands or from Oblivion, than from an idea of being able to execute it in the manner it ought to be done.[22]

The work of the Commission for Negotiating Treaties was due to expire in May 1786, at which time Humphreys realized that he would be unemployed. With no other prospects in Europe, he decided to return home. He departed France in mid-April 1786. Jefferson wrote him an amiable letter of recommendation and bade him farewell. Jefferson never disliked Humphreys; the problem was that their personalities were incompatible to permit a close friendship. The colonel made a fast voyage home and arrived in New York City on May 19, 1786. Humphreys spent twenty-one months in Europe and, according to his kindest biographer, "returned . . . with added grace of manner and polish of speech; but with the same strong patriotism and desire for America's glory as when he had fought in her battles."[23]

After spending a few days in New York, Humphreys left to visit his family and friends in Connecticut. He then went to live with General and Mrs. Washington at Mount Vernon while he decided what to do next with his life. Washington genuinely liked Humphreys and wanted his help answering his numerous and widespread correspondents. Despite Washington's retirement to Mount Vernon, Humphreys saw that his former commander was "the focus of political intelligence for the new world."[24]

Following his arrival at Mount Vernon, Humphreys was surprised and thrilled when Washington asked him to proceed with his biography. Humphreys leaped into the project, reviewing drafted manuscript pages with the general for historical accuracy. The book was interrupted, however, when Humphreys learned that he had been elected to serve in the Connecticut assembly. He left Mount Vernon and returned to his native state to assume his new duties. The colonel continued to correspond with his patron and friend whom he kept informed particularly about Shays' Rebellion in Massachusetts. In one of his letters describing the situation, Humphreys said, "you will have seen by the public papers that every thing is in a state of confusion in Massachusetts."

Washington replied, "For God's sake, tell me what is the cause of all these commotions: do they proceed from licentiousness, British influence disseminated by the Tories, or real grievances which admit of redress."[25] Militia had to be called out to suppress the rebellion, and the event frightened many men who saw the infant nation on the brink of chaos. The insurrection was led by Daniel Shays, a destitute farmer who had risen to the rank of captain in the Continental Army during the Revolutionary War. Wielding muskets and pitchforks, Shays and his followers closed the local courts and threatened to raid the federal arsenal at Springfield. David Humphreys and Dr. David Cobb helped suppress the uprising. Humphreys commanded a regiment of Connecticut militia during the insurrection while Cobb was a Massachusetts militia general and a judge in the local Court of Common Pleas in Taunton, whose courthouse was threatened by the rioters. Confronted by the mob Cobb is reported to have replied, "I will hold this court, if I hold it in blood. I will sit as a Judge or I will die as a General."[26] In another version of this story, when Judge Cobb saw the mob gathered outside his courthouse, he ran to his home, which was nearby, and told his wife: "Mother, bring out my old regimentals. Damme I'll sit as a judge, or die as a general."[27] The rioters dispersed but in another account they returned more determined than ever to close Cobb's court and destroy the tax records. Cobb responded by bringing up a cannon, which he ordered to be placed in front of the courthouse. He had the gun loaded with canister shot (grapeshot) and told an artilleryman to stand by with a lighted match while he shouted back at the mob, "If you want these papers you must come and take them, but I will fire on the first man that crosses the line."[28] The mob withdrew and no further attempts were made against Cobb's courthouse. Cobb went on to become a member of the Massachusetts house of representatives (1789–93) and served as its speaker. He was next elected to the United States House of Representatives (1793–95), after which he moved to the Maine district of Massachusetts where he was engaged in agricultural pursuits. Cobb returned to public office as a representative of the eastern district of Maine in the Massachusetts Senate, in 1802, and served as the senate's president. He was elected as the lieutenant governor of Massachusetts in 1809 and was later appointed to the state's board of military defense during the War of 1812. In 1817 Cobb returned to Taunton, Massachusetts, where he died on April 17, 1830.[29]

Washington's former aide David Humphreys was also busy following the suppression of Shays' Rebellion. Back home in Connecticut, Humphreys completed his biography of Gen. Israel Putnam, "Old Put" as he was known, the popular Revolutionary War folk hero from Connecticut. Humphreys was his aide-de-camp until the old general suffered a paralytic stroke in December 1779, forcing his resignation from the army. It was said that Humphreys got a large portion of the material for his book from the lips of the aging general, to which he added his own recollections. Humphreys's *Life of General Putnam* was published in 1788. This obscure little book proved to be the highlight of Humphreys's literary career.

In 1786, both Humphreys's mother and father died suddenly within a short time of one another. Humphreys was particularly depressed by the death of his father, "a capable scholar and much beloved by the Congregational church," and by September 1787 he wanted to return to the pleasant surroundings of Mount Vernon and the company of his "Dear General."[30] Washington warmly invited him to return in a letter dated October 10, 1787, in which he told his former aide, "With great pleasure I received the intimation of your spending the winter under this Roof . . . The only stipulations I shall contend for are, that in all things you shall do as you please."[31]

Back at Mount Vernon, Humphreys resumed work on his biography of Washington and managed to draft some pages as well as a summary. It included this intriguing excerpt:

> The first conversation which General Washington ever held with any person on the question of his accepting or refusing the Office of the President of the United States was with the Author of this work. The General had then resolved to decline accepting the Office, from a persuasion it was not necessary, as he believed that there were others better able than himself to perform the duties of it. After a conversation of four hours they separated, the General receiving the counsel that it was proper to postpone his ultimate determination as long as the circumstances would allow without detriment to the public cause. For

several months afterwards they scarcely failed one day of conversing on the same subject or subjects connected with it. From a variety of considerations & correspondences the General became convinced that it was his indispensable duty to accept the Presidency.[32]

Humphreys lived at Mount Vernon from November 1787 until April 1789. Washington's generous invitation for Humphreys to live with him is an example of his concern for the welfare of his former aides-de-camp. Some observers believe that Washington's warm and lasting friendship with Humphreys and several of his other aides was because the general had no children of his own. These people assert that Washington's military family became his substitute children. I don't think Washington ever consciously thought about it. He genuinely loved some of his wartime aides, particularly Tilghman, Harrison, Hamilton, and Humphreys and remained close to them after the war. But he also looked upon some of them, especially Hamilton, Randolph, and Humphreys, as vigorous young leaders of the new nation, and he sought out their opinions to balance out the advice he received from his older friends.[33] Washington also took advantage of Humphreys's extraordinary writing skills during his extended stay at Mount Vernon. When Washington returned from the 1787 Constitutional Convention, Humphreys helped him compose letters to various political leaders explaining the new Federal Constitution and urging them to support its adoption by the various states.[34]

By the start of 1789 it was evident that Washington would be elected the first president of the United States. Upon the news of his election, Humphreys escorted the president-elect to New York, arriving at the capital on April 23, 1789. After Washington assumed office, Congress authorized him to have a staff of four secretaries. His senior secretary was Tobias Lear followed by Humphreys who was next in rank. Because of his experience abroad and his love of haughty formality, Humphreys was put in charge of ceremonies and official protocol. Humphreys hovered over President and Lady Washington's formal levees. He orchestrated them to be an imitation of the king of France's receptions that he had attended in Paris with Jefferson. Humphreys was his usual stiff and portentous self at these affairs. It was said that at Washington's first levee, Humphreys aped the French court by throwing open the doors and in a loud voice announcing, "the President of the United States." Washington was shocked by this silly display of European pomp and told Humphreys not to do it again. "Well," said Washington, "you have taken me in once, but by God you shall never take me in a second time."[35]

Shortly after he became president, Washington arranged for Humphreys to be appointed to a temporary committee to negotiate a border dispute between the Creek Indians and the State of Georgia. He returned from this mission to resume his duties as one of President Washington's secretaries. New employment was soon found for the colonel when Secretary of State Jefferson persuaded Washington to use the opportunity of a threatened war between Spain and England to secure American rights of navigation on the Mississippi River. Humphreys was secretly dispatched to Madrid in July 1790 to work with William Carmichael, the American minister to the court of Spain. His mission was probably the best kept secret of Washington's first administration and was known to only a few people. Six months later Washington informed the Senate of Humphreys's mission explaining that he had first been sent to Spain as a "person in a private character, full acquainted with the present state of things here, to be the bearer of written and confidential instructions . . . which could not be conveyed in Writing." Washington further explained that Humphreys had instructions to continue to Portugal: "The Court of Lisbon had, on several occasions, made the most amicable advances for cultivating friendship and intercourse with the United States. The exchange of a diplomatic character had been informally, but repeatedly suggested on their part."[36] Humphreys remained in Portugal and was officially appointed as America's first minister resident to "her faithful Majesty the Queen of Portugal" by President Washington on February 21, 1791. As a result of this appointment, Humphreys is acknowledged as the United States' first ambassador.[37] He remained at this post until 1796, during which time he was the senior American diplomat in the Mediterranean region and at the center of American negotiations with the Barbary pirates.

American involvement with the Barbary pirates is one of the great stories in American history. It starts just after the Revolution, when merchant ships flying the United States flag were sailing into the Mediterranean Sea in search of new markets. American ships no longer had the protection of the Royal Navy and were easy prey for the warships of the Turkish controlled city-state of Algiers. The first American ship seized was the schooner *Maria,* which was boarded by the Algerian pirates on July 25, 1785, while sailing peacefully off the coast of Portugal. America had an insignificant navy and United States ships could be taken with little fear or consequences. Early efforts to negotiate with the Algerians failed while Humphreys, the senior American diplomat in the region, arranged for relief funds for the growing number of American sailors being held as slaves for ransom by Dey Hassan Bashaw, the ruler of Algiers. Humphreys even wrote to the editors of New England newspapers suggesting that the ransom money be raised through a lottery. In 1793 President Washington instructed Colonel Humphreys to personally take charge of the negotiations. He was authorized to offer $800,000, to the Dey, in ransom for the prisoners and obtain a guarantee of safe passage for American ships. Humphreys's offer was rebuffed before he arrived in Algiers; the Dey demanded $2,435,000, and Humphreys returned to Lisbon. Homesick and frustrated, Humphreys decided to return to America for a visit. He arrived in Newport, Rhode Island, in February 1795, and announced his arrival to the new secretary of state Edmund Randolph (another of Washington's wartime aides-de-camp). Randolph was furious when he learned that Humphreys had returned home without permission, despite the colonel's insistence that he had returned "to state verbally the real situation of things with regard to the Barbary States; and to receive your ultimate orders."[38] But Humphreys was warmly received by President and Mrs. Washington who prevailed upon the general's former aide-de-camp to go to Paris and seek French government assistance in dealing with the Algerians. Humphreys sailed for Europe in April, 1795, aboard the United States Navy brigantine *Sophia* with full authority to negotiate a "Treaty of Amity and Commerce" with Algiers and the other Barbary States.[39] The French were secretly unwilling to help, however; the Algerian pirates seemed a simple expedient to keep the Americans and other small nations from trading in the Mediterranean. As the senior American diplomat in the region, Humphreys eventually approved a deal with Dey Bashaw in September 1795 that provided a payment of $642,500 in gold for peace and ransom, plus an annual tribute of $21,600.[40] The United States agreed to throw in a new 36-gun frigate as a gift for the Dey's daughter. This humiliating episode aroused the indignation of the United States, which, in 1794, began construction of six warships, including four 44-gun super frigates, in response to the blackmail of the Barbary pirates.[41]

The Algerian episode provided one benefit for Humphreys; it introduced him to his future wife. Colonel Humphreys was using a British merchant banker, John Bulkeley & Son, to accumulate the gold ransom payment demanded by Dey Bashaw. John Bulkeley, the owner of the firm, lived in Lisbon with his daughter whose name was Anne Frances. Humphreys probably met Bulkeley's daughter during the course of his business with her father. Anne and David fell in love and were married in Lisbon in 1797. When Humphreys wrote Washington of his marriage, the general replied warmly from his retirement at Mount Vernon, "I offer my congratulations, with all the sincerity and warmth you can desire; and if ever you should bring Mrs. Humphreys to the U. States, no roof will afford her and you a more welcome reception than this."[42] But Humphreys would never see his old commander in chief again. In 1797 Humphreys was appointed the American minister to Spain. He was at his post in Madrid when he learned that Washington had died. Humphreys's ornate writing style was in perfect form when he wrote Martha Washington a lengthy and beautiful letter of condolence that included these thoughts:

Madrid, February 22, 1800

. . . Too long was I an inmate of your hospitable family, and too intimately connected with the late illustrious head of it, not to share in the poignancy of your distress for the death of the best of husbands. . . . While a grateful country offers to you the joint tribute of sympathetic tears, I am encouraged to hope that the solitary condolences of an absent friend will not be unseasonable or unacceptable. Accept, then that pledge of my sincere affection and respect for you.

[Humphreys then mentioned the death of Martha's son, John Park (Jackie) Custis, who became ill and died at the siege of Yorktown in 1781.] . . . When, nearly nineteen years ago, you were bereaved by death of a dear, an only son, after having mentioned the superior motives for a resignation to the dispensations of the Deity, I attempted to adminster some consolation, by showing that the lenient hand of time might mitigate the severity of grief, and that you had still the prospect of enjoying many good days on earth in the society of the best of friends, as well as in beholding your grandchildren happily established in life, as a comfort for your more advanced years. Highly favored have you been by Providence, in the uninterrupted fruition of those felicities, until the late fatal stroke, which has removed, all you held most dear forever from this world. Having lived long enough for himself, and long enough for glory, he has gone before us from these mutable scenes of trouble to the mansions of eternal rest.[43]

Humphreys remained as the American minister to Spain through the administration of John Adams. When Thomas Jefferson was elected president in 1800, all the old Federalist officeholders were swept out of office. Although Jefferson respected Humphreys, the aging Revolutionary War veteran was recalled from Spain to be replaced by a Jeffersonian Republican. But before he left Spain, Humphreys turned his creative mind and boundless energy to the idea of cultivating merino sheep in America. This breed of sheep are desirable because of the fine quality of their fleece, which is soft yet strong, easy to dye, and resistant to insects. Humphreys called the merino sheep that produced this excellent wool "as valuable a race of sheep as any in the world."[44] The Spanish government maintained the strictest regulations over the merinos and prohibited exportation under penalty of death. Political unrest in Europe and Humphreys's knowledge of sheep farming gained while living abroad made it possible for him to bring some of these worthy animals to America. He described his exploit in a dissertation he delivered in 1802:

> Convinced that this race of sheep, of which I believe not one had been brought to the United States until the importation by myself, might be introduced with great benefit to our country, I contracted with a person of the most respectable character, to deliver to me, at Lisbon, one hundred, composed of twenty-five rams and seventy-five ewes, from one to two years old. They were conducted, with proper passports, across the country of Portugal by three Spanish shepherds, and escorted by a small guard of Portuguese soldiers.[45]

Humphreys had friends and political connections in Spain and Portugal who made his project possible. He made the Atlantic crossing with his flock aboard a sloop appropriately named *Perseverance,* which safely arrived in Connecticut with most of his merinos intact and healthy. His timing was perfect, because the foreign wool supply was cut off by an embargo and an insatiable demand for Humphreys's merinos quickly developed. In 1806, he sold a ram and two ewes for $300. Merino mania swept Connecticut and in 1810 he was paid $1,500 each for rams and ewes.[46] Most of the early pedigree sheep in America came from Humphreys's original flock of 100 merinos.

The raising of sheep stimulated the establishment of woolen mills, and again Humphreys led the way. He purchased a fulling mill already in operation in Derby, Connecticut.[47] The spinning and weaving were done at the homes of the inhabitants throughout the area. Using this primitive system, Humphreys began producing fine broadcloths on a modest scale. The section of Derby where the fulling mill was located was renamed Humphreysville around 1806. The town was given its modern name of Seymour in 1850. Having been told that the best cloth in the United States was made by Humphreys, Pres. Thomas Jefferson ordered enough fabric from his former secretary to make a coat, declaring that "homespun is become the spirit of the times . . . it is a duty to encourage it by example." Jefferson is believed to have worn his new coat for the first time on New Year's Day, 1809.[48] Humphreys visited England looking for ways to expand his woolen business. He met John Winterbotham, who was successfully manufacturing woolen cloth in Manchester. Humphreys struck up a deal with Winterbotham, who came to Humphreysville to become a partner with Colonel Humphreys and Capt. T. Vose in a woolen mill called T. Vose & Company. The mysterious Mr. T. Vose turned out to be married to a daughter of Humphreys's brother.

Humphreys's mill prospered, and he moved to Boston, where, according to his biographer, "he and Madam Humphreys dispensed an elegant and generous hospitality admit the society of eminent and congenial friends." The colonel divided his time between his fashionable home on Olive Street in Boston and his woolen mill in Humphreysville. The aging Humphreys was honored with an appointment as a general in the Connecticut militia and reelected to the Connecticut State Legislature (1813–14). Mr. Winterbotham's daughter remembered meeting Humphreys when she was a little girl. She recollected that he was a grandly handsome man, who kept up the old traditions in his habits and appearance:

> I remember him in a blue coat with large gold buttons, a buff vest and lace ruffles around his wrists and in his bosom. His complexion was soft and blooming like that of a child, and his gray hair, swept back from the forehead, was gathered in a cue behind and tied with a black or red ribbon. His white and plump hands I recollect well, for whenever he met me they were sure to ruffle up my curls, and sometimes my temper . . .
>
> . . . Colonel Humphreys took great interest in the discipline and education of the apprentice boys attached to the factory. Seventy-three of these boys were indentured, I have been told, at the same time from the New York almshouse, and others from the neighboring

villages. For these he established evening and Sunday-schools, with competent teachers: and indulged his military tastes by uniforming them at no light expense as a militia company, drilling them himself.[49]

It was said that when he was an old man, Humphreys liked to talk about the days when he was a young officer in the Revolutionary War. One of the stories he told was the day (September 15, 1776) when the British invaded Manhattan Island:

> So critical indeed was our situation and so narrow the gap by which we escaped, that the instant we had passed, the enemy closed it by extending their line from river to river. Our men, who had been fifteen hours under arms, harassed by marching and countermarching in consequence of incessant alarms, exhausted as they were by heat and thirst . . . could have made but feeble resistance.[50]

Humphreys died on February 21, 1818. It was said that he seemed to be in good health until shortly before his death and was staying at the fashionable Butler's Tavern in New Haven.[51] Humphreys was a gentleman to the end; with the usual courtesy that distinguished all of his actions, he escorted a lady friend to her carriage and stood with his hat in his hand until she drove off. He then returned to the room from which he had led her, lay down on a sofa, and died.[52] His lawyer friend John Trumbull wrote his epitaph: "To sum all titles of respect in one—There Humphreys rests—belov'd of Washington."[53]

What became of Col. William Stephens Smith, who was Washington's aide toward the end of the War? Smith saw considerable combat experience prior to joining Washington's staff. In fact, it was said that Smith saw action in 120 engagements with the enemy. The Continental Army was reduced in size following Yorktown and the opening of formal negotiations to end the war. Smith took a leave of absence from Washington's staff in the spring of 1782 to participate in a joint French-Spanish attack on the British-held island of Jamaica. The invasion never took place and, in the meantime, Washington downsized his headquarters staff as part of the overall reduction of the army. Washington, however, found Smith employment as a commissary of prisoners, and he was appointed to this post in September 1782. Washington added to Smith's responsibilities later that year by ordering him to take command of the Continental Army post at Dobbs Ferry, New York (located on the lower Hudson River), which was close to British-held New York City and the only site of regular and official communications between the Americans and the British. This posting was actually a cover for Smith to gather intelligence for Washington about the movement of British troops in the New York area.[54] Washington needed reliable intelligence because he planned to attack the British encampments on northern Manhattan Island if the peace negotiations failed. Typical is a letter from Washington dated December 22, 1782, in which the commander in chief asks Smith to "ascertain the number of Vessels in the fleet destined for England; and whether there are any Men except Invalids on board."[55]

Because of his close proximity to the British in New York, Smith's responsibilities were extended to include arrangements for the British evacuation of Manhattan Island. On May 8, 1783, Washington appointed Smith one of the three American commissioners to supervise the final evacuation of the British from New York City. Smith and his fellow commissioners were charged with preventing the British from removing American property from the city, particularly slaves. Smith won high praise for his efforts. Despite the fact that Smith was performing other duties for Washington late in the war, he is considered to have been the general's aide-de-camp until the war ended in December 1783.

Following the victory, Smith lobbied unsuccessfully to secure a post in the small peacetime army. He was also occupied with organizing the New York Chapter of the Society of the Cincinnati and contemplated returning to his study of law.[56] A great opportunity, however, was soon presented to Smith by Congress, who appointed him as secretary to John Adams, the newly appointed American minister to Great Britain.

Colonel Smith arrived in Paris in April 1785 with dispatches from Congress that included the official appointment of John Adams as America's first American minister to Great Britain. Adams spent the next three weeks concluding his business in France and getting ready for his new assignment. He left Paris on May 20, 1785, accompanied by his wife, daughter, Colonel Smith, and two servants, and arrived in London later that month to take up his new post. Smith was thirty years old at the time and unmarried. When Adams presented his credentials at the English court, the heroic Colonel Smith was at his side. The two Americans were shocked to see the traitor Benedict Arnold at court, dressed in the uniform of a British officer.

Adams's daughter Nabby was twenty years old when she arrived in London with her parents, still in love with Royall Tyler. She wrote him often but he failed to answer any of her letters. Gossip reached her that he had publicly displayed some of her love letters to his friends in Boston. In addition, stories from home told of Tyler's alleged immaturity, instability, and spendthrift habits. At this point, much to the delight of her parents, the suave Colonel Smith entered their daughter's life.

Smith was a ladies' man; tall, dark, and handsome, with boyish blue eyes, an elegant dresser with a charming personality. He was a graduate of the College of New Jersey with a decent but undistinguished family background. He also had a magnificent war record as a Continental Army line officer and the prestige of having served as an aide-de-camp to General Washington. He particularly distinguished himself at the 1778 battle of Monmouth, where he maintained discipline of his regiment during the disorganized retreat of General Lee's advance corps. Anti-American feelings ran high in London in 1785 (not surprisingly), and the heroic Colonel Smith was seen accompanying Nabby and her mother to the theater or shopping in his chariot.[57] He joined them at dinner parties given by the few Americans living in London at the time. Nabby's letters home to her younger brother John Quincy Adams began to include frequent references to Colonel Smith—"Monsieur le Colonel," as she liked to call him. Colonel Smith swept Nabby off her feet with the enthusiastic backing of her loving parents who were also charmed by this genuine hero of the Revolution. Mrs. Adams was enthralled by Smith, writing her son John Quincy about him, "He appears to be a man of an independant spirit, high and strict sentiments of honour, Much the Gentleman in his manners and address."[58] Nabby broke off her understanding with Tyler, who passionately replied that he had written her often and that he still loved her, and would cross the Atlantic to make his case in person. Nabby was ready to give him a second chance and her sympathetic father shared his daughter's feelings, but her strong-willed mother prevailed, telling her daughter to forget Tyler, especially with the dashing Colonel Smith on the scene. Smith recognized Mrs. Adams as an ally and wrote her a formal letter on December 29, 1785, requesting permission to court her daughter. Smith wrote Mrs. Adams in the second person saying, "I cannot postpone informing her [Mrs. Adams], tht her Amiable Daughter, is the only Lady of my acquaintance, either in Europe or America, that I would connect myself with for Life." Smith commented on his lack of a profession to Mrs. Adams saying, "that I have some claim to indulgence on that point; having sacrificed that important Period of my Life in my Country's Service which others have (perhaps more wisely) spent in their private concerns and arrangements."[59] The Adamses permitted the courtship and the young couple became engaged. At Smith's insistence, they were quickly married and their wedding took place on June 12, 1786. Ten months later, in April 1787, John and Abigail became grandparents for the first time when Nabby gave birth to a boy who was named William Steuben Smith. A second son whom they named John Adams Smith followed in 1788. They had a third son named Thomas Hollis Smith who was born in August 1790, but died in infancy.

When John Adams wanted to meet with Thomas Jefferson in London, he sent Colonel Smith to escort Jefferson to England. The two men became friends en route and began to correspond with each other. Among the letters that Smith received from Jefferson, two include well-known and often quoted excerpts. The first involved an accident on September 18, 1786, in which Jefferson dislocated his right wrist. It is probable that this happened while he was vaulting a fence in the company of Mrs. Maria Cosway. Jefferson wrote Smith after the incident: "How the right hand became disabled would be a long story for the left to tell. It was by one of those follies from which good cannot come, but ill may."[60] Jefferson's second famous comment to Smith appeared in a letter written in 1787. Upon learning about Shays' Rebellion, Jefferson wrote the colonel, "What signify a few lives lost in a century or two? . . . The tree of liberty must be refreshed from time to time with the blood of patriots and tyrants.

It is its natural manure." In another incident, when British booksellers refused to sell an unexpurgated version of David Ramsay's *History of the American Revolution,* Smith and Jefferson arranged for its sale in Paris. Colonel Smith was also cultivating other important relationships. People in America were interested in what he had to say from London, and his correspondents included the influential politician Rufus King (1755–1827). Smith wrote King a letter dated, "W.S. Smith, Leicester Square, London, July 25, 1787," in which he offered his appraisal of Britain's attitude toward the newly independent United States: "They still continue to attempt the great career of national importance and have almost persuaded themselves that the Separation of America from this country is very immaterial to them." The Colonel followed this with a poem of his own composition:

> They sink the sense of shame in Public pride,
> Nor feel the shaft that trembles in their side;
> They'll neigh, until some treaty's dreadful blast
> Makes them to groan—and then, they'll groan their last.

"You must excuse this sudden Dash at imitation [continued the colonel]— I could not stop my pen—By the public papers which accompany this, you will note the meeting of the Parliament and the King's Speech."[61]

Despite his impressive acquaintances, elegant manners, and good education, it soon became evident to John and Abigail Adams that their son-in-law had no particular career in mind by which to support his wife and family. Colonel Smith had studied law in New York before the Revolution, but was disinterested in pursuing this vocation further. He told his father-in-law that he was certain that his grateful nation would provide him with lifetime employment. In the spring of 1788, John and Abigail Adams returned from England to their home near Boston. Smith and his family followed them to America, arriving in New York City in May 1788. They moved in with the colonel's mother, who lived in nearby Jamaica, Long Island. After returning home, John Adams was elected vice president under the new constitution, and he moved to New York City with his wife to assume his new duties. Meanwhile Colonel Smith lobbied for a position in the new federal government. President Washington rewarded Smith for his wartime service by appointing him the United States Marshal for the New York district. Smith was appointed to this post on September 26, 1789.[62] The colonel held this position until December 1790, when he suddenly asked Washington for a leave of absence to attend to urgent private affairs in England. Smith's business involved the collection of some family debts and the sale of land and bank stocks for several wealthy New York merchants. Smith may also have been on a secret mission for Alexander Hamilton to improve commercial relations between Britain and the United States. In March 1791, while Smith was still in England, President Washington appointed him the supervisor of revenue for the district of New York.[63] Smith remained in this job until February 1792 when he resigned the position to return to Europe with his wife and children on another of his speculative ventures. Smith had put on a considerable amount of weight since his lean days as a Continental Army offi- cer, and his departure for England was delayed when he came down with what was described as a bilious complaint, brought on by his fondness for food and drink. Once back in Britain, Smith sold land in America to British investors and engaged in other "money making pursuits," which he later said were never suited to his genius or ambition. The colonel also visited France during this trip, writing his friend Thomas Jefferson upon his return to New York in February 1793: "I left Paris on the 9th of November & have the satisfaction to inform you, that your friends there are well, and pursuing attentively the interests of that great & rising Republic."[64] Despite President Washington's patronage, it became increasingly apparent to John and Abigail Adams that Colonel Smith was not the prize that he at first appeared to be. The colonel turned out to be an idle dreamer, spendthrift, and gambler: the embodiment of the worst that the Adamses had feared in Royall Tyler. Indicative of his behavior, in 1795, Smith decided that he would build a home on Manhattan Island modeled after Mount Vernon. On March 25 he purchased twenty-three acres on the banks of the East River, an area where several prominent New York families were also building country homes. Smith grandly named his new estate, "Mount Vernon on the East River," and began construction of a elegant mansion and outbuildings on the property.[65] The project was beyond his means, and he was forced to sell off the partially built mansion house to William and Mary Burrows within a year of starting construction. When the Burrowses put the estate up for sale the follow- ing year, the property was described in a newspaper advertisement as twenty- three acres of land, "on which premises is the frame of a superb house erected by Colonel Smith last spring." A subsequent owner, William T. Robinson, com- pleted the mansion and carriage house. The property, however, continued to be associated with Colonel Smith and was nicknamed "Smith's Folly" long after his brief ownership. The mansion was destroyed by fire in 1826, but the stone carriage house survived and is preserved as the Mount Vernon Hotel Museum and Gardens.

Smith's career next turned to land speculation in upstate New York, which was the get-rich-quick rage at the time. He purchased six townships in what are now the counties of Madison and Chenango, New York. John Adams was president at the time, and the colonel was trading on his father-in-law's name to borrow money for his land speculation. His reckless spending habits, according to one of his sympathetic early biographers, was "stimulated to unnatural excess by the exciting events of the Revolutionary war."[66] Smith lost money on his various New York real estate schemes and was heavily in debt. He went into hiding in 1797 to escape his creditors, abandoning his wife with a family that now included a young daughter named Caroline Amelia (born in 1795). Nabby withdrew, ashamed of her "mortifying situation." She shipped her two sons off to her Great-aunt Elizabeth in New Hampshire where they would be out of the reach of their father's influence. The colonel remained incommunicado for eight months in upstate New York but returned to New York City early in 1798 to try to settle with his creditors.

The colonel loved his wife and children, but he was a gambler, opportunist, and dreamer who believed he was always on the verge of financial triumph. When Adams was elected president he was pressured by his wife to find a government job for their hapless son-in-law. Adams reluctantly agreed and in 1798 tried to get the Senate to confirm Smith as the army's adjutant general while the nation was preparing for possible war against France. The Senate scoffed at this recommendation, dismissing Smith as a bankrupt failure with some senators probably voting against Smith as a means of striking a personal blow against the president. Adams felt humiliated by his son-in-law. He wrote his wife that "nothing disgraced me so much as this man." Smith was finally given the lowly command of a regiment, with the understanding that he could keep his wife with him. They lived together in a log hut in Plainfield, New Jersey, near Smith's troops, with John Adams writing his wife that his son-in-law's pay "will not feed his dogs."[67]

Despite his gaming, hunting, and quick money schemes, Smith was not villainous or unpatriotic. President Adams finally got the Senate to give his son-in-law a lucrative job as the surveyor of customs for the Port of New York.[68] The president did this in the last days of his administration with the support of Alexander Hamilton, whose real intent may have been to embarrass Adams. Smith was removed from office early in 1806 and sent to prison on charges of unpaid debts and allegations that he was helping organize a filibustering expedition to liberate Venezuela from Spain in violation of United States law.[69] The colonel protested that he was innocent and that Jeffersonian politicians had rigged the indictment against him. Nabby stood by her husband. She moved onto the prison grounds, living with him in a tiny cottage until he was acquitted of the criminal charges in July 1806 because of insufficient evidence. Smith's eldest son, William Steuben (who displayed unmistakable signs of having been cut from the same cloth as his father), was involved with his father in the plot to liberate Venezuela. He was captured by the Spanish and almost executed.

Smith was unemployed and penniless after his release from prison. In 1807 the Smiths finally parted: Nabby went to live at her parent's home in Massachusetts while Colonel Smith fled to a remote part of upper New York State to escape his creditors. He lived in upstate New York with some relatives who had settled there. Everything was quiet for a while, then Smith suddenly reappeared in January 1808 insisting that his wife return with him to the newly established town of Hamilton, New York, where he was living. Nabby agreed but left her sons in the care of her aging parents.

The situation seemed settled for a while until Abigail received a letter from her daughter reporting that she had breast cancer. Her mother consulted with the best physicians in Boston and all agreed that Nabby must come to Boston at once for treatment. She resisted saying that she was reluctant to leave her husband but the truth was probably that Amelia feared that the doctors would put her under the knife. In the end, she made the difficult trip and after examining her, the doctors agreed that a mastectomy was necessary. The gruesome operation was performed in her parents' home. There was no anesthesia at the time, and Nabby was conscious through the surgery. It was so horrible that her mother and father never talked or wrote about it. Nabby survived the ordeal, and Colonel Smith was permitted to visit his wife briefly, at which time he announced that his wife and daughter could stay with her parents indefinitely. But Smith returned in July 1812 to once more claim his family. Reluctantly, they accompanied him to Lebanon, New York, where he was campaigning to be elected to the House of Representatives as a Federalist. To everyone's surprise, he won the election. He took whatever money was left when he went off to Washington, D.C., to take his seat in the Thirteenth Congress (March 4, 1813–March 3, 1815), leaving his wife and daughter destitute in a remote area of upstate New York promising to return with his reputation and fortune rebuilt.

During her husband's absence in Washington, Nabby began to suffer excruciating pains that she at first attributed to rheumatism. It became evident, however, that her cancer had returned and she was dying. Her final wish was to die in her father's house, and she summoned her youngest son John from New York City, where he was a successful lawyer. With her son's help, she made the jolting trek across 300 miles of trails and crude roads to her father's home. She lived only two weeks after returning home. Her mother was too distraught even to be with her stricken child, but John Adams remained at his daughter's bedside, comforting her until the end. Nabby died on August 15, 1813, at the age of forty-eight. Colonel Smith arrived just before she died. His grief was so great that even John Adams relaxed his scorn for his pathetic son-in-law. Smith returned to Washington to serve out his term in Congress, but he failed to get reelected.

Colonel Smith spent the remaining three years of his life as an exile in upstate New York, sponging off his brothers. He retained his bravado and charm to the end, adopting the guise of a heroic Revolutionary War veteran. Smith died on June 10, 1816, at the age of fifty-nine of "liver complaints," leaving debts in the then staggering amount of $200,000, beating Thomas Jefferson who died with debts of $100,000. The colonel's only daughter, Caroline Amelia, was at his bedside when he died. When John Adams learned of Colonel Smith's death, he wrote his son John Quincy Adams, "Be to his virtues ever kind, to his faults a little blind. The world will never know all the good or all the evil he has done."[70] The colonel was buried in Sherburne, New York, where a monument was erected at his burial site in the 1880s that bears the following inscription:

Here Lie
The
Mortal Remains
Of Col. Wm. S. Smith
Who died at Lebanon
June 10, 1816,
Aged 59 years
In the War of
Independence
He fought in twenty-two Battles
Served as aide to
Gen. Washington
Who always held him in
Affectionate Esteem[71]

Col. William Stephens Smith and his wife Abigail Amelia had three sur-viving children. Their oldest son, William Steuben Smith, married Catherine Johnson, but they had no children. He died in 1850. Their second son, John Adams Smith, was a lawyer who eventually moved to Hamilton, New York, where he practiced law. He never married and died in 1825. Their only daugh-ter, Caroline Amelia, grew into a beautiful and charming woman who was said to bear a striking resemblance to her mother. She married John Peter DeWindt, of Fishkill-on-Hudson, New York, and they had eight children. Caroline Amelia died in a terrible tragedy. She was a passenger on the steamboat *Henry Clay,* which caught fire and burned on the Hudson River on July 28, 1852.

CHAPTER THIRTEEN

Closing Scenes

I have been employed for the last ten months in rocking the cradle
and studying the art of fleecing my neighbors.
Alexander Hamilton to the marquis de Lafayette,
November 3, 1782[1]

Although Washington was happy to remain in contact with his wartime aides-de-camp, and help them where he could, there were exceptions. One was Caleb Gibbs, who was the officer in charge of the Commander in Chief's Guard with additional duties as a special aide-de-camp. He was wounded in the ankle at the siege of Yorktown, and resigned from the army in June 1784. Gibbs was a favorite among his fellow aides during the war, he was liked for his intelligence and good humor. Laurens mentioned him in a letter to Hamilton, "I am afraid I was so thoughtless as to omit my remembrances to Gibbs in the last Letter. Tell him that I am always his sincere well wisher and hope to laugh with him again before long." Gibbs seemed to have had great promise along with the respect of Washington and his fellow aides, but he did not go far in civilian life. Following the war he became a businessman in Boston. In 1787 Gibbs married Catherine Hall and they had five children including a son whom they named Alexander Hamilton.[2] Gibbs proved to be a failure at business. According to one source, "his character is very low in Boston, that he is looked upon as a trifler."[3] When he heard that his former commander had been elected president of the United States, Gibbs wrote to congratulate him and asked for a government job: "It is with your Excellency, from whence will originate many appointments under the New Government; and in the distribution of which, may an old servant flatter himself that he shall not be forgotten."[4] Failing to get a response, Gibbs wrote Washington again a few months later telling him about his wife and large family, which included "an aged Worthy Grandmother who I have maintained . . . ever since I left the

Army."[5] Washington finally appointed Gibbs to a clerkship at the Boston Navy Yard in December 1794. Gibbs was unhappy with this position, however, and solicited his old commander for a more lucrative post as late as 1798, but to no avail. Gibbs died on November 6, 1818, at the Boston Navy Yard.

At first glance, Gibbs's appointment as the clerk at the Boston Navy Yard seems like a minor appointment, but some investigation revealed that President Washington had generously rewarded his former aide. Gibbs was actually the naval storekeeper at the yard, which was an important job that included the distribution of naval stores. A naval storekeeper was needed in Boston because it was one of the centers of the Navy's frigate-building program; the USS *Constitution* was built there. We do not know what Gibbs's yearly salary was, but there is a record that his assistant was paid $600 per year, which was a good salary for the time. We can assume that Gibbs was paid considerably more in his supervisory capacity. Gibbs's position also provided him with a $250 annual housing allowance. There was an incident that shows the respect that Gibbs enjoyed from his close association with Washington. It happened in 1816, when the secretary of the navy stepped in to settle a dispute between Gibbs and the commandant of the navy yard. Without discussing the merits of the case, the secretary told the commandant to accord Gibbs his attention and indulgence "as far as may be consistent with public duty," because Gibbs was an honored Revolutionary War veteran.[6]

Washington may have avoided Gibbs, but he snubbed Joseph Reed and Thomas Mifflin, both of whom had fallen out of favor during the war. Reed, the brilliant Philadelphia lawyer, was Washington's first military secretary while Mifflin, a Quaker businessman, was his first aide-de-camp. Both men lost Washington's patronage and friendship during the war: Mifflin because of his bungling as quartermaster general and suspected leadership in the Conway Cabal and Reed for his criticism of Washington's mismanagement of the 1776 campaign. Both men managed to achieve political prominence without Washington's support, however. Who knows what high public office Reed, in particular, could have achieved had he retained Washington's good will and friendship?

There is one situation where Washington helped Reed. It happened late in the war when Reed's political enemies accused him of disloyalty, saying that he had contemplated going over to the British side in 1776 when the Revolution seemed doomed.[7] They pointed out that Reed had English relatives (his wife and her family) and reminded the voters of his early efforts to reconcile England and America. Reed's quick-tempered and sometimes suspicious nature helped fuel these unfounded charges. He appealed to his former commander to testify to his patriotism. Washington came to Reed's defense, although his response was cold and formal:

> Not knowing the particular Charges which are alledged against you, it is impossible for me to make a specific Reply, I can therefore only say in general Terms, that the Employments you sustained in the Year

1776, and in that period of the Year, when we experienced our greatest Distress, are a proof that you was [were] not suspected by me of Infidelity or Want of Integrity.[8]

In 1784, Reed was reelected to Congress, but ill health prevented him from serving. He died the following year at the age of forty-four.

Washington was disappointed with Joseph Reed, but he apparently detested Thomas Mifflin, his first aide-de-camp. Washington was angry over Mifflin's inattention to his job as quartermaster general of the army, and believed he was one of the ringleaders in the so-called Conway Cabal. Following his resignation as quartermaster general, Mifflin was elected to a succession of important public offices. He was a delegate to the Continental Congress, serving as the president of that body from December 13, 1783, until June 3, 1784. Mifflin was elected governor of Pennsylvania in 1790. This was the highest public office that he would achieve. Dr. Benjamin Rush also despised Mifflin, writing a friend with his opinion of him when he learned of his appointment as governor:

This day Gen. Mifflin was elected Governor of Pennsylvania. This man was known to be of a very immoral character. He had lived in the state of adultery with many women during the life of his wife, and had children by some of them, whom he educated in his own family. It is said his wife died last summer of a broken heart in consequence of this conduct towards her. Besides this vice, he was much addicted to swearing and obscene conversation. His political character was as bad as his moral. He had deserted his friends and joined with the men who slandered them. He was wholly dissipated and given to low company. His popularity was acquired by the basest acts of familiarity with the meanest of the people. He avoided the society of gentlemen and cherished that of the mechanicks. He lived beyond his income, and was much in debt.[9]

Mifflin served as the governor of Pennsylvania from 1790 to 1799. Unlike Dr. Rush, Washington was too politically astute to openly criticize his former aide, but he steered clear of him. Mifflin died on January 20, 1800.

If Washington ignored Reed and Mifflin, and found Gibbs annoying, he doted on a number of his former aides, including Humphreys, McHenry, Smith, Fitzgerald, and Meade. Indicative of this was a 1786 letter to McHenry, who was living in Baltimore at the time, in which Washington said, "Why will you not make a small excursion to see an old acquaintance. It is unnecessary I hope to assure you of the pleasure it would give."[10] Tilghman, Harrison, and Hamilton probably held a special place in Washington's heart and mind. They were the three master craftsmen who had served him during much of the war. Of the three he admired Hamilton's intelligence and ambition but theirs was not a warm relationship. But for the other two, Tilghman and Harrison, there was openhearted praise and friendship.

Tench Tilghman served the longest of any of Washington's aides. He joined the commander's military family as a volunteer aide-de-camp on August 8, 1776, staying on the job until mid- to late-December 1782 when he took a leave of absence. With the war almost over, he probably never returned to headquarters. Tilghman and Washington wrote each other often. Historian Dumas Malone said of their correspondence, "Washington's letters to and about him constitute a most unusual acknowledgment of friendship, of valued services, and a high eulogy of patriotic devotion."[11] My favorite letter from Washington to Tilghman was written at Newburgh, New York, on April 24, 1783. As background, with the war about to end Washington felt obligated to remain with the army but was anxiously awaiting news of a peace treaty so he could go home. Washington wrote his friend Tilghman,

> No Man, indeed, can relish the approaching Peace with more heart felt, and grateful satisfaction than myself. A Mind always upon the stretch, and tortured with a diversity of perplexing circumstances, needed a respite; and I anticipate the pleasure of a little repose and retirement. It has been happy for me, always to have Gentlemen about me willing to share my troubles, and help me out of difficulties. To none of these can I ascribe a greater share of merit than to you.
>
> I can scarce form an idea at this moment, when I shall be able to leave this place. . . . But as I now see the Port opening to which I have been steering, I shall persevere till I have gained admittance. I will then leave the States to improve their present constitution, so as to make that Peace and Independency for which we have fought and obtained, a blessing to Millions yet unborn.[12]

Tilghman married his cousin, Anna Maria Tilghman (the daughter of the patriarch Matthew Tilghman), on June 9, 1783. They settled in Baltimore where Tench returned to his mercantile activities in partnership with Robert Morris. Their main business was importing European goods and exporting American tobacco. Washington made Tilghman his business agent in Baltimore, which was close to Mount Vernon. Baltimore had been a sleepy seaport at the start of the Revolution but had developed as an important business center by the war's end. Washington wrote Tilghman on a variety of matters, calling upon his former aide to assist him with a host of business and personal matters. Not unusual was Washington's request written on August 11, 1784: "Shall I, for this reason, ask the favor of you to give me a short detail of the internal construction of the Green House at Mrs. Carrolls?"[13] Although Tilghman was doing business with Washington, the two men were also friends. On one occasion, Washington wrote his former aide ordering some wine to be shipped to his plantation, ending the letter with a heartfelt toast: "I hope to drink a Glass of it with you at Mount Vernon 'ere long."[14]

Tilghman led a quiet life, enjoying a successful business and a happy marriage. He was not active in politics. The long war and the hardships he had suffered took their toll on his fragile health and he lived only three years beyond the end of the war. Tilghman died on April 18, 1786, at the age of forty-two, leaving behind his pregnant wife and a young daughter. The daughter born posthumously was named Elizabeth Tench (1786–1852), and she married Col. Nicholas Godsborough of Talbot County, Maryland. Tilghman's elder daughter, Anna Margaretta (1784–1812), married, to the utter confusion of historians and genealogists, her cousin, whose name was Tench Tilghman. He was identified by the name of his plantation, "Hope." They had a son whom they also named Tench. Colonel Tilghman's wife, Anna Marie, lived for another fifty-two years after her husband's death, and died at the age of eighty-eight on January 17, 1843. She said that the greatest tragedy of her life was the premature death of her husband, whom she loved dearly.

Washington was saddened by Tilghman's untimely death. He wrote to Thomas Jefferson soon after, calling his extraordinarily competent, modest friend, and aide-de-camp a pillar of the Revolution who had "as fair a reputation as ever belonged to a human character."[15] Others who knew him held him in similar high regard. Robert Morris, who was associated with Tilghman in business wrote Washington, "You have lost in him a most faithful and valuable friend."[16]

Following Tilghman's death, his father James wrote Washington with a proposed inscription for his son's monument. The general replied on December 4, 1786, "The inscription intended for the Tomb of my deceased friend meets my entire approbation; for I can assure you Sir, with much truth, that after I had opportunities of becoming well acquainted with his worth, no man enjoyed a greater share of my esteem, affection and confidence than Colo. Tilghman."[17]

The inscription, which can still be seen on Tilghman's grave, reads:

IN MEMORY OF
Col. Tench Tilghman
Who died April 18, 1786
In the 42nd year of his age,
Very much lamented
He took an early and active part
In the great contest that secured
The Independence of
The United States of America
He was an Aide-de-Camp to
His Excellency General Washington
Commander in Chief of the American Armies,
And was honored
With his friendship and confidence,
And
He was one of those

Whose merits were distinguished
And
Honorably rewarded
By the Congress
But
Still more to his Praise
He was
A good man.[18]

Tench Tilghman was a modest and industrious man who enjoyed the confidence and good will of Washington and his entire military family. There was no better patriot in the Continental Army than him.

Robert Hanson Harrison served the second longest on Washington's staff next to Tilghman. He was at the general's side from November 6, 1775, to March 25, 1781, a total of just under six years. Harrison resigned to devote time with his two daughters who were raised during the war by his sister-in-law and to accept the post of chief justice of the General Court of Maryland. Washington and Harrison kept up their friendship, and Harrison was a regular guest at Mount Vernon after the war. When Washington was elected president, he nominated Harrison to be an associate justice on the newly established United States Supreme Court. His nomination was confirmed by the Senate; however, Harrison declined to serve. His former fellow aide-de-camp and friend Alexander Hamilton wrote him on November 27, 1789, urging him to accept the post:

> After having labored with you in the common cause of America during the late war, and having learned your value, judge of the pleasure I feel in the prospect of a reunion of efforts in this same cause; for I consider this business of America's happiness as yet to be done. . . . If it is possible, my dear Harrison, give yourself to us. We want men like you. They are rare at all times.[19]

Harrison formally declined his appointment to the Supreme Court on January 21, 1790, because of his failing health. He died a few months later, on April 2, 1790. In 1825, the elderly marquis de Lafayette made a sentimental return trip to America. While in America, the sixty-eight-year-old Lafayette wrote a letter to one of Harrison's daughters with his memories of her father:

> On my first joining headquarters early in 1777 I found Col. Robert Harrison acting as the intimate friend, the first aid de camp and Secretary of the Commander in Chief, whose confidence has proved most useful to General Washington, to the army, to the country and the cause. . . . I have had continued and peculiar opportunities to witness the great and daily services rendered by Col. Harrison; the trust Gen-

eral Washington reposed in him; the high esteem the tender attachment which Col. Harrison reciprocated, by the most affectionate devotion to his bosom friend.[20]

Washington appointed three of his Revolutionary War aides-de-camp to his presidential cabinet. They are probably the best known of Washington aides: Alexander Hamilton, Edmund Randolph, and Dr. James McHenry. Even as he grew older, Hamilton maintained the same slim appearance, handsome face, and chestnut hair brushed back loosely as he had when he was Washington's youthful aide-de-camp. His friend Robert Hanson Harrison had named him the "little lion" and he remained so throughout his life. Hamilton probably would have married for money and influence, and he was fortunate to find both in a woman he loved.[21] After the war he went on to become a lawyer, congressman, leading proponent of the Constitution, secretary of the treasury in Washington's cabinet, general in the army in the undeclared war with France, and leader of the Federalist party. General Washington shielded his former aide throughout Hamilton's galvanizing career particularly during the 1797 uproar over his affair with Maria Reynolds.[22]

In 1798 Washington wrote Pres. John Adams on behalf of Hamilton. In the letter, Washington referred to Hamilton as his "principal and most confidential aid." This statement has led historians to believe that Hamilton was the most important of Washington's wartime aides. Washington, however, was writing a letter of recommendation on behalf of Hamilton in which it was natural for him to overstate the qualifications of his friend in an effort to help him get an important job. Washington liked Hamilton and thought him to be a talented and ambitious man. He gave his opinion of Hamilton in this same letter to Adams: "By some he is considered as an ambitious man, and therefore a dangerous one. That he is ambitious I shall readily grant, but it is of that laudable kind which prompts a man to excel in whatever he takes in hand. He is enterprising, quick in his perceptions, and his judgement intuitively great."[23]

Hamilton was fascinated by power. But he was not the calculating schemer that some historians have portrayed him to be. In 1804, Hamilton was mortally wounded in a duel fought with Col. Aaron Burr who he had served with briefly at headquarters in 1776.

Another of Washington's wartime aides who served in his presidential cabinet was Edmund Randolph. Young Randolph left headquarters in October 1775 to escort his uncle Peyton Randolph's body to Virginia for burial. Edmund was swept into Virginia politics and never returned. The highlights of his career after resigning as Washington's aide-de-camp were: Delegate to the Virginia Convention (which drafted the Virginia Constitution and encouraged independence from Britain), first attorney general of Virginia, mayor of Williamsburg, delegate to the Continental Congress (1779, 1781–86), governor of Virginia, and Virginia delegate to the Constitutional Convention. Randolph's participation in the Constitutional Convention of 1787 is particularly interesting because as the governor of Virginia, Randolph was the titular head of his state's delegation. He is remembered for introducing the Virginia Plan on the third day of the Convention. This plan proposed replacing the Articles of Confederation with a constitution that would create a strong national government. Randolph is also remembered for being obstinate and refusing to sign the finished document. He was particularly wary of creating a one-man executive. He eventually supported the Constitution and urged its adoption by the Virginia Ratification Convention of 1788, to which he was a delegate. Washington was friendly with Randolph throughout the period (he handled much of Washington's personal legal work after the end of the Revolutionary War) and nominated him to be attorney general (appointed February 2, 1790) in his presidential administration. This was followed by his appointment on January 2, 1794, as secretary of state when Jefferson resigned that post. As secretary of state Randolph was instrumental in bringing about a treaty with Spain providing for free navigation of the Mississippi River. The long association between these two men, which had started when Randolph was Washington's aide-de-camp, ended abruptly in 1795. The breakup came as a result of an intercepted letter from a French diplomat saying that Randolph was fishing for a bribe. The evidence against Randolph was weak, but President Washington confronted his old friend in the presence of his cabinet, accusing him of treason. As Washington impatiently listened, Randolph denied the charges. Randolph promptly resigned as secretary of state, writing the President, "This, Sir, as I mentioned in your room, is a situation in which I cannot hold my present office, and therefore I hereby resign it. . . . I here most solemnly deny that any overture ever came from me which was to produce money to me . . . and that in any matter, directly or indirectly, was a shilling ever received by me."[24] The charges against Randolph proved false. Still fuming weeks later over Washington's mistrust and short temper, Randolph wrote his friend James Madison, "I feel happy at my emancipation from an attachment to a man who has practiced upon me the profound hypocrisy of a Tiberius, and the injustice of an assassin."[25] This unfortunate incident ended Randolph's career in public life. He moved to Richmond where he resumed his law practice, which included successfully defending Aaron Burr in his 1807 treason trial. Randolph's departure from twenty years of public service had one good effect, which was to give him time to spend with his wife and family. He had married Elizabeth Nicholas in 1776, and they had four surviving children, one son and three daughters. Edmund named his son Peyton in honor of the uncle who had helped him get a post as Washington's aide-de-camp. Young Peyton married "the celebrated beauty," Maria Ward in 1806. There was a second son, named John Jennings Randolph, but he died in infancy. His daughters were named Susan Beverly (after one of Edmund's sisters), Edmonia Madison, and Lucy Nelson. All three daughters eventually married. Daughter Susan married Bennett Taylor, Edmonia married Thomas Lewis Preston, and Lucy married one of her father's law students, Peter Vivian Daniel, who later became a United States Supreme Court Justice. Edmund's childhood sweetheart and wife Elizabeth died in 1810. The couple had been married in Williamsburg in the midst of the Revolution. Following Elizabeth's burial, Edmund wrote his children reflecting on his thirty-three years of married life: "I am fully aware that I must have caused her some pains but in all those instances her sufferings recoiled upon myself with tenfold vengeance because I knew that she had felt them. Innumerable were the instances in which I have returned home dissatisfied with some of the scenes of the day abroad, and found an asylum in her readiness to partake of my difficulties and make them her own."[26] Randolph's health deteriorated following his wife's death, and he was unable to practice law. His devoted children took care of him and he spent the last years of his life writing a history of Virginia that was never published. Edmund Randolph died on September 13, 1813, while visiting a friend in Frederick County, Virginia. He was buried in the graveyard of a nearby chapel, and his tombstone reads: *"Edmund Randolph. Aide de Camp to Gen. Washington. Secretary of State U.S. Governor of Virginia."*[27] Randolph was sixty years old at the time of his death, which went largely unnoticed in the press because he had been politically exiled by Washington years earlier. But Washington had done the new nation a great service during the Revolutionary War when he appointed Randolph as one of his aides-de-camp. Randolph's brief tenure as Washington's aide was his ticket into the American patriot ranks, which benefited from his considerable talents.

This brings us to Dr. James McHenry, the third of the former aides-de-camp to serve in Washington's presidential cabinet. McHenry was the army surgeon who was appointed aide-de-camp while the army was wintering at Valley Forge. He transferred from Washington's staff in August 1780 to serve as an aide-de-camp to Lafayette and resigned from the army following the victory at Yorktown. After returning to civilian life, McHenry was elected to the Maryland Senate. In May 1783, while serving in the Maryland Senate, McHenry was also appointed as a Maryland delegate to the Continental Congress.[28] He began attending its sessions in June 1783 following Congress to Princeton, New Jersey, where it moved for its own safety after a mutiny of the troops of the Pennsylvania Line. Congress's move to Princeton gave McHenry the opportunity to visit nearby Philadelphia to see his friend John Caldwell, who was a merchant in that city. He became acquainted with Caldwell's sister Margaret ("Peggy") during his visits, and he fell passionately in love with her. McHenry also knew Peggy's stepfather, Capt. William Allison. Young McHenry was placed under Captain Allison's care when he first arrived in America in 1772.[29] McHenry was a superb letter writer, and his six month courtship of Peggy Caldwell, which started in mid-July 1783, included dozens of beautiful love letters that must have swept the young woman off her feet. Here is a little excerpt from one of McHenry's best love letters to Peggy, written on Monday morning, October 13, 1783:

As I was looking at your letter I perceived on the wafer [wax seal] a little circle that appeared to have been made by the edge of your thimble. You will laugh perhaps, when I tell you, that the discovery of this little circle gave me more pleasure than I could have received from a view of the impression of the finest seal in the world. I instantly associated with the thimble that made it, the finger it had often embraced, and I kissed the little circular impression, as I would have kissed the little hand to which the thimble belonged. Good morning my Peggy.[30]

James McHenry married Peggy Allison Caldwell on January 8, 1784. He continued to serve in Congress until December 1785, after which he returned to Baltimore to resume his mercantile business and serve in the Maryland Senate from 1781 to 1786. In 1787 he was named as one of Maryland's representatives to the Philadelphia Convention that met from May through September, and from whose deliberations came the Constitution of the United States. McHenry took little part in the debates, although he strongly supported the adoption of the Constitution. He returned to his home state to take an active role in Maryland's ratification of the Constitution and continued to be active in local politics. McHenry earned his living as a merchant in his family's Baltimore business but his passion was politics. He was a dependable political ally to Washington and shared his old commander's opinion that the nation needed a strong central government. McHenry remained on good terms with many of his other wartime connections including Benjamin Rush, Alexander Hamilton, and the marquis de Lafayette. McHenry idolized his former fellow aide-de-camp Hamilton whom he tried to imitate. For example, McHenry wrote Hamilton in August 1782, "Write me then what you are doing—what you have done—and what you intend to do, that I may endeavor to follow your example. And be full, for I really intend to be wise, and you shall be my Apollo."[31]

In 1790, McHenry became extravagantly wealthy when he inherited the estate his father and younger brother had compiled as merchants and landowners in Baltimore.[32] His new found wealth gave him the freedom to indulge his love of politics. He served additional terms in the Maryland House of Representatives and Maryland Senate. In 1796, McHenry was offered the cabinet position of secretary of war by President Washington. The post was offered to him only after three other men had turned down the position. Washington mentioned the circumstances of McHenry's appointment and his subsequent performance as secretary of war in a confidential letter to Alexander Hamilton written in 1798: "I early discovered after he entered upon the Duties of his Office that his talents were unequal to great exertions, or deep resources. In truth they were not expected: for the fact is, it was a Hobson's choice."[33]

McHenry served his old commander in chief faithfully, and fortunately he faced nothing more challenging than the administration of a small peacetime army and navy. When John Adams became president, he hesitated changing Washington's cabinet appointments, including McHenry's, for fear that he would be criticized for questioning the wisdom of the Father of the Country. He soon realized, however, that McHenry was intensely loyal to his political rival Alexander Hamilton. Adams denounced McHenry for his subservience to Hamilton, finally firing him from his cabinet in May 1800. That was the end of McHenry's political career. He retired to his estate near Baltimore, which he had named "Fayetteville" in honor of his friend and former commander the marquis de Lafayette. He lived there as a leisured gentleman with his wife and their four surviving children, Daniel William (born 1786), Anna (1788), John (1791), and Margaretta (1794). Their eldest son, Daniel William, married Sophia Hall Ramsay, the daughter of Col. Nathaniel Ramsay, McHenry's long-standing friend. These two Revolutionary War veterans had seen action together at the battle of Monmouth where McHenry had overheard Washington tell Ramsay to delay the British advance long enough for the main army to organize a defense line. There must have been some interesting table talk when McHenry and Ramsay got together on June 23, 1812, for their children's wedding! McHenry's other son John married Juliana Elizabeth Howard. She was the daughter of Col. John Eager Howard, another one of Dr. McHenry's wartime friends. These two old soldiers probably first met each other in 1776 when Howard was a young captain in the Maryland Flying Camp and McHenry was the surgeon of the 5th Pennsylvania Regiment.

McHenry was a staunch Federalist, and when Thomas Jefferson's Republican party came to power, they accused McHenry of mismanagement of the War Department. Nothing came of the accusations, however, and the charges were dropped. Although he was trained as a doctor, McHenry never practiced medicine again after his appointment as Washington's aide-de-camp during the winter encampment at Valley Forge. There is no evidence that medicine interested him much, or that he was especially good at it. He wrote poetry, but none of his poems were ever published. His appointment as secretary of war was the highest public office he achieved. But McHenry had an extraordinary talent for making friends. People were attracted to his kindness, intelligence, and devotion. He seemed to understand that he was not cut out to be a great leader and was content just being a political insider and friend to many of the prominent men of his day. He died peacefully at his estate on May 3, 1816, at the age of sixty-six. His wife wrote affectingly about him after his death:

> In May 1816, my dearest and best earthly friend was taken from me . . . Here we come to the end of the life of a courteous, high-minded, keen-spirited, Christian gentleman. He was not a great man, but he participated in great events and great men loved him, while all men appreciated his goodness and the purity of his soul. His highest titles to remembrance are that he was faithful to every duty and that he was the intimate and trusted friend of Lafayette, of Hamilton and of Washington.[34]

Emily Stone Whiteley tells a delightful tale about Richard Kidder Meade. One day in 1799, young George Washington Custis said he was met in the fields surrounding Mount Vernon by a pleasant-looking gentleman, who inquired in which direction he would be likely to meet General Washington who was, according to his custom, riding somewhere about the estate. Custis gave the stranger the information, adding: "You will meet, sir with an old gentleman riding alone, in plain dark clothes, a broad brimmed white hat, a hickory switch in his hand, an umbrella with a long staff, which is attached to his saddle-bow; that personage, sir, is General Washington." The stranger, much amused at the description, answered with a good-humored smile, "Thank you, thank you, young gentleman; I think if I fall in with the General, I shall be rather apt to know him." The dignified gentleman addressing Custis was Richard Kidder Meade. He was fifty-three years old at the time and a prosperous Virginia farmer. Meade found his old commander, and the two men rode across the fields together. When they came to a gate, Meade insisted that he must open it for his companion to pass; he was still the general's aide-de-camp and must be allowed to wait on him.[35] Washington and Meade may have talked that day about the 1,000 acres that Meade was farming in western Virginia. His land turned out to be so rich and valuable that he named his plantation "Lucky Hit." Washington had encouraged Meade to buy the land on what had been the Virginia frontier. Perhaps the two old soldiers also talked about that hot June day over twenty years before when they had fought the flower of the British Army at the battle of Monmouth. The ride and conversation that Meade and Washington enjoyed together in 1799 across the fields of Mount Vernon was the last time that Meade would see his old commander alive. Washington died suddenly after a brief illness on December 14, 1799. Meade lived another six years, dying in 1805 of what his doctors described as gout aggravated by the hardships of military life.

What happened to John Laurens, Washington's young and dashing aide-de-camp, who first appeared in our narrative in the fighting around the Chew House at the battle of Germantown in 1777? Following the siege of Yorktown, he joined Gen. Nathanael Greene's army in South Carolina, where he played an important part in driving the British from the backcountry of his home state. The war was almost over, and Laurens seemed destined to become a national leader. His reputation had grown; during the siege of Yorktown it was known that he gave quarter when he could, thus setting a humane example that other officers would follow. He favored leniency toward Tories and renewed his plan to raise black troops. In addition, he was one of the best-educated young men in America.

Hamilton treasured Laurens and believed his friend would be one of the great leaders of postwar America. When Hamilton was appointed a delegate to the Continental Congress in July 1782, as the war was ending, he urged Laurens to quit the army and join him there:

Peace made, My Dear friend, a new scene opens. The object then will
be to make our independence a blessing. To do this we must secure
our union on solid foundations; a herculean task and to effect which
mountains of prejudice must be leveled! Quit your sword my friend,
put on the toga, come to Congress. We know each others sentiments,
our views are the same; we have fought side by side to make America
free, let us hand in hand struggle to make her happy.[36]

Laurens probably never got to read Hamilton's letter. The British continued to occupy Charleston late in the war and were sending foraging parties into
the countryside to seize rice. In August 1782 the British sent a foraging party in
armed boats and schooners to the region around the Combahee River south of
Charleston, which offered more prospects for provisions than the area around
the city. Laurens's small unit was part of the troops commanded by Brig. Gen.
Mordecai Gist detached to oppose the invaders. Laurens was ordered by Gist to
garrison a small redoubt with 50 infantrymen and one piece of artillery. In violation of his orders, Laurens went in search of the British. This was not the first
time in his military career that Laurens had disobeyed orders to pick a fight
with the enemy. Loyalist spies alerted the British to Laurens's movements, and
they prepared an ambush for him. At sunrise on August 27, 1782, Laurens was
riding at the head of his 50 men on a road near the banks of the Combahee. He
saw an enemy picket and went after them when 140 British soldiers, who had
been hiding in the high fennel grass, arose as one and delivered a murderous
fire. Laurens escaped the volley, but he knew that he either had to surrender or
fight his way out of the ambush. "His brave spirit could not brook the former,
and leading the way, he made an energetic charge," which was as futile as his
slave soldier scheme. The British fired another volley at the charging Americans led from the front by Laurens. As the volley struck, he suddenly fell from
his horse, his midsection torn by enemy bullets, and was probably dead before
his body hit the ground. Laurens's men turned, fleeing in confusion with the
enemy in pursuit. American reinforcements, attracted by the gunfire, arrived a
short time later and reorganized what was left of Laurens's command. Together
they counterattacked and forced the enemy to retreat to their boats. Laurens
was buried that same day on the nearby plantation of a Mrs. Stock, with whose
daughters he had spent the previous evening in cheerful conversation. The
British made no further attempts to procure supplies from the countryside and
evacuated Charleston a few months later.

Learning of what had happened, General Greene announced Laurens's
death in the general orders to his troops: "The army has lost a brave officer and
the public a worthy citizen." At the same time, however, Greene wrote privately
to a fellow officer, "Poor Laurens has fallen in a paltry little skirmish. You know
his temper, and I predicted his fate. The love of military glory made him seek
it."[37] Other officers who knew Laurens shared Greene's opinion. Alexander

Garden, an officer in Lee's Legion said, "There was a quixotic spirit in this young officer which could not be disciplined into the dull route of military utility."[38] Gen. William Moultrie gave his opinion in his journal: "Colonel Laurens was a young man of great merit and a brave soldier, but an imprudent officer: he was too rash and impetuous."[39] Washington was more prudent in his comments about Laurens, telling historian William Gordon, "in a word, he had not a fault that I ever could discover, unless intrepidity bordering upon rashness could come under that denomination; and to this he was excited by the purest motives."[40] Hamilton was devastated by the news of his friend's untimely death and told General Greene, "His career of virtue is at an end. How strangely are human affairs conducted that so many excellent qualities could not ensure a more happy fate? . . . I feel the loss of a friend I truly and most tenderly loved, and one of a very small number."[41] To Lafayette he wrote, "Poor Laurens; he has fallen a sacrifice to his ardor in a trifling skirmish in South Carolina."[42]

Even the *Royal Gazette* newspaper in British-held Charleston paid honor to Laurens:

> By accounts from the country we learn, that Mr. John Laurens, a Lieutenant colonel in the rebel army, and son of Mr. Henry Laurens, now in London; was lately killed near Combahee river, in attempting to impede the operations of a detachment of his Majesty's troops.
>
> When we contemplate the character of this young gentlemen, we have only to lament his great error on his outset in life, in espousing a public cause which was to be sustained by taking up arms against his Sovereign. Setting aside this single deviation from the path of rectitude, we know no one trait of his history which can tarnish his reputation as a man of honor, or affect his character as a gentleman.
>
> . . . While we were thus marking the death of an enemy who was dangerous to our Cause from his abilities, we hope we shall stand excused for paying tribute at the same time to the moral excellencies of his character—Happy would it be for the distressed facilities of those persons who are to leave this garrison with his Majesty's troops that another Laurens could be found.[43]

Henry Laurens learned of his son's death while he was recuperating in Bath, England, from his long imprisonment. Laurens senior had agreed to act as one of the American representatives to negotiate a treaty of peace with Britain, and he received a letter from John Adams on November 12, 1782, summoning him to come to Paris. In this same letter Adams relayed the melancholy news of Henry's eldest son's death concluding, "Our Country has lost its most promising Character." Henry was devastated by the news. Returning to America in August 1784, he was worn out and frail from years of public service and his imprisonment in the Tower of London. He came home to find his plantations ruined by the war, but most of all he seemed unable to recover from his grief over the death of his oldest and most promising son. Soon after his return home, Henry Laurens had his son's body brought from Mrs. Stark's plantation and reburied at his Mepkin plantation on the Cooper River. Ironically his son had survived the great battles of Germantown, Monmouth, and Yorktown only to be killed in an insignificant skirmish in the closing months of the war. Henry Laurens's health deteriorated, and he withdrew from public life. His loving daughter Martha called for doctors to treat her ailing father. Eventually the great Dr. David Ramsay was called in on the case.[44] He was the brother of the famous Col. Nathaniel Ramsay, the American officer who had been seriously wounded and captured at Monmouth, but only after keeping his promise to Washington that "we shall check them." David Ramsay shared his brother's fiery revolutionary spirit. He served in the Revolutionary War as an army surgeon and was captured when Charleston surrendered to the British in 1780. The doctor was one of the staunchest rebels captured at Charleston and the peculiar object of the vengeance of the enemy who imprisoned him in St. Augustine, Florida, for a year before permitting him to be exchanged. Besides being a physician, David Ramsay was also a statesman and historian. He served as a South Carolina representative to the Continental Congress (1782, 1783, 1785, and 1786), and in 1785 published his first book, *The History of the Revolution of South-Carolina: From a British Province to an Independence State.* Ramsay began working on a new book during his tenure as a delegate to the wheezy Continental Congress. He was bored and occupied his time talking to all the great generals and politicians living in or passing through New York where Congress was meeting at the time. Ramsay returned to Charleston with his extensive notes and was involved with writing a history of the American Revolution when he was asked by Martha Laurens to treat her ailing father.

Dr. Ramsay did what he could to help Henry Laurens, but the cheerless statesman's health continued to decline.[45] Meanwhile, Ramsay fell in love with Martha, who was much younger than he was. He had been married twice before, but both of his wives had died. Martha was a bright and inquisitive young woman and the brilliant Dr. Ramsay, with his interests in medicine, politics, and history, was a perfect intellectual match for her. Martha returned his love, calling him the "Main Spring of all my earthly happiness," and they were married on July 28, 1787.[46] Ramsay went on to finish his new book, which was the first history of the American Revolution written by an American. *The History of the American Revolution* was published in Philadelphia in 1789.[47] His book is a classic, and Ramsay is accredited with exceptional insights as a historian.[48] In 1807 Ramsay followed with his biography of George Washington *(The Life of George Washington: Commander in Chief of the Armies of the United States of America),* which brought him additional fame.

David and Martha Ramsay lived happily at their home at 92 Broad Street in Charleston. They had eleven children, eight of whom lived to maturity. They named one of their sons Nathaniel (1801–82) in honor of the doctor's brother who had fought so valiantly at Monmouth. Martha died in 1811 after a short illness, and David was murdered four years later by a deranged tailor named William Linnen. Ramsay's books about American history remained popular, and a boy on the frontier named Abraham Lincoln read his *Life of George Washington*. Lincoln probably also read Ramsay's history of the American Revolution, which was a popular book at the time. Ramsay praised John Laurens in his books as a champion of equality. Here is Ramsay's description of Colonel Laurens from his *History of the American Revolution*:

> The British sometimes sallied out of their lines for the acquisition of property and provisions, but never for the purpose of conquest. In opposing one of these near Combehee Lieutenant Colonel John Laurens, an accomplished officer of uncommon merit, was mortally wounded. Nature had adorned him with a large proportion of her choicest gifts, and these were highly cultivated by an elegant, useful and practical education. His patriotism was of the most ardent kind. The moment he was of age, he broke off from the amusements of London, and on his arrival in America, instantly joined the army. Wherever the war raged most, there was he to be found. A dauntless bravery was the least of his virtues, and an excess of it his greatest foible. His various talents fitted him to shine in courts or camps, or popular assemblies. He had a heart to conceive, a head to contrive, a tongue to persuade, and a hand to execute schemes of the most extensive utility to his country, or rather to mankind, for his enlarged philanthropy knowing no bounds, embraced the whole human race. This excellent young man, who was the pride of his country, the idol of the army, and an ornament of human nature, lost his life in the 27th year of his age, in an unimportant skirmish with a foraging party, in the very last moments of the war.[49]

The death of John Laurens extinguished one of America's most active early opponents to slavery. His friend Alexander Hamilton was among those who carried on Laurens antislavery work. Hamilton was among the sponsors who, in 1785, founded the New York Society for Promoting the Manumission of Slaves. But his deceased friend was the real antislavery firebrand. Henry Laurens accurately predicted the bloody climax of the slave issue when he wrote Hamilton following his son's death: "at present the Number of wretched Slaves, precarious Riches, is our greatest Weakness—but alas! these Southern States are not at this moment in a disposition to be persuaded tho' one should rise from the dead—God forbid our conversion by too long a Delay, shall be the Effect of a direful Struggle."[50]

CHAPTER FOURTEEN

Conclusion

I am from my station, Master of the most valuable Secrets of the
Cabinet and Field.
                    Tench Tilghman to his brother William Tilghman[1]

I began my investigation of Washington's Revolutionary War aides-de-camp with no preconceived ideas. My goal was to uncover their names and backgrounds, and the scope of their wartime activities. What I discovered is that thirty-two men served as aides to Washington, and that they tended to share a common background of wealth, privilege, and education. I learned that they were all recruited by Washington primarily for their ability to write well and constantly. They were the men behind the scenes, working under Washington's close supervision, who drafted the thousands of letters and orders of the Revolutionary War that today are among the sacred writings of American history.

As I learned about these talented men, I could see how they made it possible for Washington to stretch his prerogative of a few personal assistants to create a brilliant headquarters staff that rendered him valuable assistance throughout the Revolution. Going further into the subject I arrived at another interesting conclusion: Washington had a warm relationship with some of his aides, such as Reed, Tilghman, Harrison, Hamilton, Laurens, Humphreys, (Jonathan) Trumbull, Jr., and perhaps Moylan. I believe that I am on firm historical ground when I say Washington took these men into his confidence. For example, Tilghman wrote to his brother in 1781, "I am from my station, Master of the most valuable Secrets of the Cabinet and Field."[2] It only seems logical to believe that Washington would have been interested in what these intelligent and well-informed men had to say on a variety of administrative issues including the organization of the Continental Army. I searched for the proof but I was unable to discover the necessary evidence in their correspondence or the letters written by the high ranking officers of the Continental Army. The documentation that shows that Washington's principal aides acted in an advisory role will probably never be found because the general was a secretive person and his aides shared his belief in confidentiality. It is unfortunate for posterity that none of Washington's aides thought of earning notoriety, and money with a tell-all book about what they did at headquarters. I cannot help but look at the impressive public offices these men held during the closing years of the war and in postwar America, and wonder what additional assistance they provided Washington besides their secretarial duties. Here is a list of the positions held by Washington's aides, noting that some of them had a record of long public service, and appear on the list in several places: Three cabinet officers in the administrations of Presidents Washington and Adams (Hamilton, McHenry, and Randoph); four state governors (Randolph, Jonathan Trumbull, Jr., Reed, and Mifflin); three United States senators (Grayson, Jonathan Trumbull, Jr., and John Walker); four members of the United States House of Representatives (Cobb, Benjamin Walker, Smith, and Jonathan Trumbull, Jr.); one speaker of the House of Representatives (Jonathan Trumbull, Jr.); one president of the Continental Congress (Mifflin); two delegates to the Constitutional Convention (Hamilton and McHenry); six delegates to the Continental Congress (Grayson, McHenry, Hamilton, Reed, Mifflin, and Randolph); a mayor of New York City (Varick); a diplomatic representative to Spain and Portugal (Humphreys); and a nomination as an associate justice of the United States Supreme Court (Harrison).[3] The list would be unwieldy if I included every elected office and appointment these men held during their lifetimes.

While many of Washington's wartime aides made it on their own, the general seemed eager to assist those who sought his patronage. When Washington became president in 1789 he helped some of his former aides with government jobs; Baylies and Fitzgerald were appointed customs collectors; Benjamin Walker was named naval officer of the Port of New York; Moylan was made commissioner of loans in Philadelphia; Smith was appointed federal marshal and later supervisor of revenues in New York, and Gibbs was made clerk of the Boston Navy Yard. A handful of Washington's wartime aides did not seek high public office or patronage following the war. They were content to pursue their professions and enjoy a quiet family life. Counted in this group are Tilghman, Webb, Cary, and Meade. Even if they were never helped directly by their old commander in chief they benefited from their close association with him. Washington praised his former aides-de-camp during his lifetime. Their stature and prestige seems to have increased after his death because of their close connection with the American Cincinnatus.

The aides also risked their lives in battle and undertook difficult assignments. From this common bond close and lasting friendships developed. While all the aides seemed to be friendly with each other, there apparently was an intimate inner circle at headquarters composed of Harrison, Tilghman, Hamilton, McHenry, Laurens, Gibbs, and Meade. Their personal letters to each other are full of affection and good humor. Hamilton and Harrison were particularly close friends while McHenry adored Hamilton. But the closest bond among the aides was probably between Hamilton and Laurens. Their frequent exchange of letters during the war is extraordinary in terms of the intensity of their relationship and the lofty subjects they discussed. Laurens was more reserved than Hamilton in expressing his emotions. In April 1779 for example, Laurens was on his way to South Carolina when Hamilton wrote him, "Cold in my professions, warm in my friendships, I wish, my Dear Laurens, it might be in my power, by action rather than words, to convince you that I love you. I shall only tell you that 'till you bade us Adieu, I hardly knew the value you had taught my heart to set upon you."[4]

Laurens's letters to Hamilton were more subdued but still filled with warm sentiments of friendship. Laurens wrote Hamilton late in the war,

> I am indebted to you, my dear Hamilton, for two letters; the first from Albany, as masterly a piece of cynicism as ever was penned, the other from Philadelphia . . . in both you mention a design of retiring, which makes me exceedingly unhappy. I would not wish to have you for a moment withdrawn from the public service; at the same time, my friendship for you, and knowledge of your value to the United States, make me most ardently desire, that you should fill only the first offices of the Republic.[5]

Hamilton is the most complicated of Washington's aides to understand. He was brilliant and a natural leader. But Hamilton's friend and fellow aide John Laurens had the potential to outshine him. It is unfortunate that Laurens was killed at the age of twenty-seven because he might have been an explosive force in American history. Laurens's leadership in the budding antislavery movement had important implications. Writing from Valley Forge in February 1778 Laurens said this about slavery: "I have long deplored the wretched State of these men and considered in their history, the bloody wars excited in Africa to furnish America with Slaves—the Groans of despairing multitudes toiling for the Luxuries of Merciless Tyrants."[6] We can only wonder what this young crusader from South Carolina might have accomplished had he lived.

Who was Washington's most important aide-de-camp? It is impossible to say because he had a different relationship with each of them based on their personalities and abilities. Also, Washington was astute in his impartiality. But we can narrow down the list to four men who were Washington's most important wartime aides: Robert Hanson Harrison, Tench Tilghman, Alexander Hamilton, and David Humphreys. Each of them was equally important to Washington but in different ways. Washington was a brilliant executive who knew how to match the men on his staff with the job that had to be done. Harrison was a thirty-five-year-old lawyer with two children when he joined Washington's staff. He filled a vital bureaucratic role for the general that included keeping the headquarters running while Washington was away. Harrison was also one of the best at conveying into writing what Washington wanted to say. Washington utilized Harrison's writing skills by having him draft much of his important official correspondence. Harrison, for example, drafted many of the letters that conveyed Washington's sentiments and intelligence reports to the Continental Congress.

Tilghman was probably Washington's best all-around aide-de-camp. He was not as brilliant as Harrison or Hamilton but he apparently was able to handle any task Washington gave him. Tilghman functioned well both behind a desk and on assignment in the field. He also had a good personal relationship with Washington who apparently liked working with him. Both Harrison and Tilghman were dependable hard workers whom Washington recruited from among the leading families in America. Neither seemed overly ambitious or felt it necessary to show initiative to enhance their reputations. Hamilton was the opposite. He was ambitious and took a lot of initiative. Hamilton clearly had superior leadership and intellectual abilities to Harrison and Tilghman. Hamilton did his share of letter writing and copying at headquarters, but Washington seems increasingly to have used this exceptional young man for important military and political missions.[7] Harrison, Tilghman, and Hamilton served the longest among all the aides, and were the foundation of Washington's headquarters staff.[8]

The fourth person to be included in Washington's inner circle was David Humphreys. He joined the headquarters staff in 1780, and came the closest to being Washington's protégé. Washington's letters to and about Humphreys are unique in their praise and sincere expressions of friendship. A good example is when Humphreys wrote his old commander asking his help to get a government appointment. The request came at a time when Washington was being inundated by requests from other former officers who wanted him to help them with one thing or another. Washington balked at helping most of them, but he responded promptly and warmly to Humphreys's request:

> My Dear Humphrys:
> Be assured that there are few things which would give more pleasure than opportunities of evincing you the sincerity of my friendship, and disposition to render you services at any time when it may be in my power. . . . I feel very sensibly the obligations I am personally under to you for the aid I have derived from your abilities, for the cheerful assistance you have afforded me upon many interesting occasions, and for the attachment you have always manifested towards me. I shall hold in pleasing remembrance the friendship and intimacy which has subsisted between us, and shall neglect no opportunity on my part to cultivate and improve them . . .[9]

There is another incident that illustrated Washington's fondness for Humphreys. He once sent the general a pair of shoe buckles from Spain as a gift. Washington thanked his former aide for the present saying, "I receive the Buckles (which are indeed very elegant) as a token of your regard and attachment; and will keep, and wear them occasionally for your sake."[10]

We know that Washington honored Tilghman and Humphreys in a unique way. The Continental Army and French officers who served in the Revolution established a fraternal organization, which they called the Society of the Cincinnati. They wore a badge, which included the image of an eagle (the badges were called Eagles), to identify themselves as members. The Eagles followed a basic pattern but were custom-made to the taste and budget of their owners. A number of beautifully crafted Eagles were made in France including eight that were ordered by Washington in late October 1783. He kept one for himself and probably gave the others as gifts to his wartime aides-de-camp.[11] We know that he gave one of the Eagles to Tilghman who acknowledged its receipt in a letter to Washington dated June 7, 1784. In this letter, Colonel Tilghman thanked him for the gift saying, "I pray your Excellency to accept my warmest and most grateful thanks for this distinguishing mark of your attention and regard."[12] Humphreys was another recipient of one of Washington's Eagles. He mentioned it in a long-winded Fourth of July speech he gave in 1804: "This medal of the Society of the Cincinnati, General Washington caused to be procured in France and he gave it to me as a present with his own hand."[13] The other recipients of Washington's coveted Eagles remain unknown.[14]

Another group of aides who impressed me were Washington's prewar Virginia acquaintances. They were Harrison, Meade, Grayson, and Fitzgerald. These men came to headquarters, rolled up their sleeves, and went to work for their neighbor and friend. Worthington Chauncey Ford's list of Washington's aides-de-camp included Martha Washington.[15] While there is evidence that she rendered some small assistance in her husband's office, I wondered why Ford included her on his list. I believe that Ford wanted to acknowledge her valuable contribution to the smooth operation of the domestic side of the army's headquarters. She was at headquarters during every winter cantonment of the Continental Army, and the general loved to have her at his side. She doted on her husband and his military family, and was concerned about their health and welfare. She shared her husband's work habits, devoting long hours to the efficient management of the domestic operations of his headquarters. Her grandson remembered "her admirable management of her servants and households, going through every department before or immediately after breakfast." The domestic side of Washington's headquarters operations operated smoothly when Martha was around. Theirs was also a great love affair about which unfortunately we know very little. They were frequently together in the company of the general's aides, but not one of them is known to have recorded a word of what passed between the general and his wife.

The Founding Fathers disguised the fact that Washington ultimately won the war with a professional army of common soldiers recruited from the lower ranks of colonial society. The officer corps was frequently staffed with middle-class men who saw military service as a means of ascending the social and economic ladder. Most had no training before they became officers and did not have ready access to a written code of conduct. While the officers can be partially excused for their lack of experience and an intense need to defend their honor, the fact remains that there were 593 courts-martial proceedings against American officers during the American Revolution.[16]

Where then did the patriotism come from that sustained the American cause throughout the Revolutionary War? At the top, Washington stands alone in terms of his resolution and sacrifice. The intensity with which he employed his considerable skills and experience, and risked his life and fortune in the struggle is lost to us because he was not interested in posing as a man of the people. His personality and bearing conveyed an impression of aloofness. But he was emotionally wrapped up in the conflict, and especially concerned about the welfare of the officers and common soldiers who served under him. Besides Washington there was a group of dedicated officers, common soldiers, and statesmen who became the backbone of the rebellion. Washington's aides-de-camp rest squarely within this inspiring group. Historian John C. Fitz-patrick called them "the most remarkable group of young men to be found in the history of the United States."[17]

I emerge from this project with a profound respect for the men who served as aides-de-camp to George Washington during the American Revolution. I hope I have rescued them from obscurity, and showed how they worked unselfishly on behalf of American independence. They played a role at head-quarters the extent of which we will probably never know. They behaved like gentlemen throughout the war and helped give Washington a dignity that was even acknowledged by the enemy. Washington's aides-de-camp were an extension of his greatness for they were the means by which he was able to communicate the nobility of his person and ideas.

POSTSCRIPT

If you have enjoyed reading this book you may be interested in visiting some of the sites that are associated with Washington's aides-de-camp. Although Washington occupied many houses as his headquarters during the Revolution only a handful are still standing, unaltered, and open to the public. There are three jewels among them that include restored interiors that show how they may have looked when they were occupied by Washington and his aides. These three houses are the Hasbrouck house in Newburgh, New York, the Ford mansion in Morristown, New Jersey, and the Issac Potts house in Valley Forge, Pennsylvania.

I also recommend that my readers visit the site of the important 1778 battle of Monmouth. Located in central New Jersey near the town of Freehold, it is the best preserved battlefield of the American Revolution. The state of New Jersey is doing a superb job of restoring the area to look as it did on the day of the battle. Don't try to read about the battle because the few books on the subject have incorrect information or miss pieces of the story. Historians are only now piecing together an accurate account of what happened at Monmouth, and it is best to take one of the park-sponsored guided tours. Eventually there will be a tour road through the battlefield park with historic markers along the way to tell the story of what was the longest and most complicated battle of the Revolution.

The boyhood homes of aides Samuel Blachley Webb (Wethersfield, Connecticut) and David Humphreys (Derby, Connecticut) are also open to the public. A warehouse and office owned by John Fitzgerald are part of a waterfront restaurant called "The Seaport Inn" in Alexandria, Virginia. The home that Alexander Hamilton built in New York City, which he named "The Grange," is also a museum. The carriage house from the estate that aide William Stephens Smith planned to build along the East River in Manhattan is a museum called the Mount Vernon Hotel and Gardens. It is tucked away in the heart of Manhattan, and a pleasant place to take a breather from the hectic pace of New York City.

NOTES

PREFACE
1. Richard K. Showman and Dennis R. Conrad, eds., *The Papers of General Nathanael Greene* (Chapel Hill: University of North Carolina Press, 1976–), 1:263.
2. Emily Stone Whiteley, *Washington and His Aides-De-Camp* (New York: Macmillan, 1936).
3. John C. Fitzpatrick, *The Spirit of the Revolution* (Boston: Houghton Mifflin, 1924), 60–86; Gerald Edward Kahler, "Gentlemen of the Family: General George Washington's Aides-de-Camp and Military Secretaries" (master's thesis, University of Richmond, 1997). There is also a lengthy but flawed account of Washington's aides in Broadus Mitchell, *Alexander Hamilton: Youth to Maturity, 1755–1788* (New York: Macmillan Company, 1957), 105–16. The only other creditable information that I found on the subject was a brief article of 1881 written by Berthold Fernow, "Washington's Military Family," *Magazine of American History* (August 1881): 81–83.

CHAPTER 1
1. George Washington to Lt. Col. Joseph Reed, January 23, 1776 W. W. Abbot et al., eds., *The Papers of George Washington,* Revolutionary War Series (Charlottesville, Virginia: 1985–), 3:173 (cited hereafter as *Papers of Washington).*
2. George W. Corner, ed., *The Autobiography of Benjamin Rush* (Princeton, New Jersey: Princeton University Press, 1948), 113. Dr. Benjamin Rush's autobiography is the origin of this story. Rush said he heard it from Patrick Henry. Douglas Southall Freeman, Washington's greatest biographer, commented about the story, "This is second-hand—Doctor Rush's recollection of what [Patrick] Henry told him, but it has the ring of sound money on the historical counter."
3. George Smith, *An Universal Military Dictionary* (London: J. Millan, 1779), 2.
4. Gates, for example, introduced into the fledgling American army the use of printed forms to help him get accurate reports of the number of men in each regiment. See general orders dated July 12, 1775, *Papers of Washington,* 1: 107. An excellent explanation of the function of the adjutant general in the Continental Army can be found in Charles H. Lesser, ed., *The Sinews of Independence: Monthly Strength Reports of the Continental Army* (Chicago: The University of Chicago Press, 1976), xii–xiv.
5. An example of Washington's problems with the department system is found in his letter to James Mease, head of the Clothier General Department, written from Valley Forge on April 17, 1778, "Scarcely a day passes, but I am either applied to by different Officers for cloathing, or by persons for payment or some Business in the Cloather Generals department . . . In a word your absence and the incompetency of a Clerk, to answer the various applications that are daily making, throws a load of business upon me which ought to be the burthen of your own Shoulders." John C. Fitzpatrick, ed., *The Writings of George Washington* (Washington, D.C.: U.S.

Government Printing Office, 1931–44), 11:269 (cited hereafter as *Writings of Washington*).

6. The most famous example of the breakdown of the army's department system occurred during the relatively mild winter of 1777–78. The army spent this winter at Valley Forge. The serious shortages of food and warm clothing at Valley Forge was mostly caused by a collapse in the army's department system. The army had food and clothing in nearby depots but lacked the wagons, all-weather roads, and experienced personnel to get the supplies to Valley Forge. But despite these problems there is no evidence that a single soldier died at Valley Forge from starvation or exposure.

7. An example of Washington's mentioning a shortage of line officers can be found in his March 1778 letter to Maj. Gen. John Armstrong, "there having been so many resignations to late that the Regiments are in general thinly Officered." See *Writings of Washington*, 11:158.

8. Fitzpatrick, *Spirit of the Revolution*, 60.

9. Worthington Chauncey Ford et al., eds., *Journals of the Continental Congress, 1774–1789* (Washington, D.C.: Government Printing Office 1904–14), 2:102 (cited hereafter as *Journals of Congress*). On June 21, 1775, Congress authorized Washington to have three aides-de-camp. Major generals were allowed two aides.

10. Historians sometimes refer to Washington's military secretary as his "personal secretary" or "private secretary." While both terms are descriptive of the job, they were not used at the time of the Revolution. Washington tended to identify this person as his secretary.

    Congress made an exception and allowed major generals, acting in a separate department, to have a secretary. Maj. Gen. Philip Schuyler, for example, who commanded the Northern Department, was permitted to have a secretary. See ibid., 2:94.

11. Smith, *An Universal Military Dictionary*, 3.

12. *Writings of Washington*, 10:378.

13. Christopher Hibbert, *Redcoats and Rebels: The American Revolution through British Eyes* (New York: W. W. Norton, 1990), 60.

14. Ibid., 44–45.

15. The tradition of gentlemen volunteers was already well established in both the British Army and the American forces during the colonial wars that preceded the American Revolution. Washington served as an extra volunteer aide on Gen. Edward Braddock's staff in 1755.

16. The term "military family" was in common use in both the British and by the Americans during the Revolution. George Washington's Revolutionary War aides-de-camp used the term regularly to describe themselves. As an example, aide-de-camp Alexander Hamilton wrote to a former fellow Washington aide from Morristown, New Jersey, on March 13, 1777, "The family are all well; and hope soon to see you here, at the head of your bloody myrmidons." Harold C. Syrett, ed., *The Papers of Alexander Hamilton* (New York: Columbia University Press, 1961–87), 2:206 (cited hereafter as *Hamilton Papers*). Washington used the term as well, for instance in a letter written on November 6, 1783, "As the Gentlemen who are now remaining of my family, propose to honor me with their Company to my Home in Virginia." and also a letter to Lafayette written on May 4, 1781, "Mrs. Washington and the rest of my (small) family which at present consists only of

Tilghman and Humphrey join me in cordial salutations." See *Writings of Washington,* 27:232 and 22:32.

Commenting on the term, historian James Thomas Flexner said, "It was the usage in the American as well as the English army to refer to a general's aides as his 'family.'" *The Young Hamilton* (Boston: Little, Brown, 1978), 137. The term was sometimes also used to include all officers attached to a general. For example, in describing a visit to Washington's headquarters, a French officer wrote,"the Aides de Camp, Adjutants and other officers attached to the General, form what is called his family." Marquis de Chastellux, *Travels in North-America in the Years 1780, 1781, and 1782.* (London: G. G. J. and J. Robinson, 1787), 1:113 (cited hereafter as *Travels in North-America*).

17. An example is in a letter wrote on January 19, 1783, "Humphrys and Walker who are the only Gentlemen of the family, with me at present." See *Writings of Washington,* 26:30. Another example can be found in a letter Washington wrote to Col. George Gibson on March 11, 1778, which includes, "The Doctor that you have in Custody called at Head Quarters when he came out of Philada. and some of the Gentlemen of my Family say he told them the same story that he did to you." See *Writings of Washington,* 11:65. Washington's aides referred to themselves in the same way. Aide Samuel Blachley Webb, for example, wrote Washington on April 1, 1777, closing his letter by saying, "With my most Respectfull Compliments to your Lady, and Gentlemen of the family." See *Papers of Washington,* 9:45.

18. Washington said, for example, in his December 23, 1783, address to Congress, "It was impossible the choice of confidential Officers to compose my family should have been more fortunate." See *Writings of Washington,* 27:284. In a letter to Congress dated January 14, 1784, Washington refers to his wartime aides as, "those Confidential Officer[s] who had attended me." Ibid., 27:300.

19. Gerald Edward Kahler, "Gentlemen of the Family," 14

20. *Papers of Washington,* 3:282–83.

21. Ibid. 2:263.

22. Herbert T. Wade and Robert A. Lively, *This Glorious Cause* (Princeton: Princeton University Press, 1958), 235. Hodgkins retired from the Continental Army as a captain in the 15th Massachusetts Regiment.

23. *Hamilton Papers,* 2:455.

24. J. Watson Webb, *Reminiscences of Gen'l Samuel B. Webb of the Revolutionary Army* (New York: Globe Stationery, 1882), 135.

25. Bernard C. Steiner, *The Life and Correspondence of James McHenry* (Cleveland: Burrows Brothers, 1907), 25–26.

26. James McHenry, *Journal of a March, a Battle, and a Waterfall: Being the Version Elaborated by James McHenry from His Diary of the Year 1778* (Greenwich, Connecticut: privately printed, 1945), 1.

27. *Writings of Washington,* 1: xiv.

28. L. G. Shreve, *Tench Tilghman: The Life and Times of Washington's Aide-de-Camp* (Centerville, Maryland: Tidewater, 1982), 119–20 .

29. Philander D. Chase, letter to the author.

30. *Writings of Washington,* 2:458–60. The draft is in the writing of Tench Tilghman.

31. Steiner, *Life and Correspondence of James McHenry,* 27 n. Sometimes a number of aides had to be employed to make fair copies of a letter or document that was

being distributed to a number of different people. Such letters were called "circular letters."

32. Washington and his aides knew all about how to care for quill pens. Our modern word "pen" comes from the Latin word *penna,* meaning feathers. Most quill pens were made from goose feathers. A goose could provide six good feathers from each wing. Of these twelve quality writing quills, six were right hand and six were left hand. A quill could last forever if it was properly cared for. After the quill was cut (which was an art in itself) the tip was dried and sometimes dipped in hot sand to make it as hard as steel. There were silver and gold tips (called points) available at the time but they were expensive. The technique of writing with a quill was to press lightly on the pen. Ink was commonly sold as a powder, which was mixed with water. The ink used in colonial America was often made from oak galls, which were the knotlike growths on trees, mixed with iron sulphate and gum arabic.

33. Green possibly became the traditional color for baize writing surfaces because it was a comfortable color to look at. The most common use of baize today is a pool table playing surface. The word is derived from French *baie* meaning bay-colored.

34. Surviving documents from the Revolutionary War era, which were drafted in shorthand, include examples written by Arthur Middleton, who was a member of the Continental Congress. Middleton's shorthand characters have been identified as coming from a textbook on the subject entitled: *LaPlume Volante: Or the Art of Short-Hand Improv'd.* It was published in London in 1707. See Paul H. Smith, ed., *Letters of Delegates to Congress, 1774–1789,* (Washington, D.C.: Library of Congress, 1976–98), 18:89, (cited hereafter as *Letters of Delegates*).

35. *Papers of Washington,* 2:607. In a letter to Col. (later Gen.) Alexander McDougall, Washington further emphasized the need for letters of recommendation, "It is exceedingly necessary for every Person, appearing the character of a Gentleman, & not personally known, to bring Letters of Introduction from those that are, otherwise, a proper attention cannot be paid to them." See ibid., 2:343–44.

36. Ibid., 1:58–59.

37. Ibid., 1:365 n. 1.

38. Ibid., 2:450.

39. Ibid., 1:365.

40. Ibid., 1:59 n, and 2:249; also Francis Heitman, *Historical Register of Officers & the Continental Army* (Washington, D.C.: Rare Book Shop, 1914), 585. White was commissioned a lieutenant colonel in the 3rd New Jersey Regiment on January 18, 1776. His regiment was assigned to the Northern Army commanded by Major General Schuyler. White apparently was in trouble because he wrote Schuyler from Albany, New York, on September 16, 1776, "I have remained at this place by your order, for a long time in the most disagreeable situation.—The pain and anxiety to have my Character as an officer and Gentlemen impeached, I assure you Sir, I can much better feel than express.—I told you every circumstance attending the Plunder of Johnson Hall," [the home of a Loyalist in upstate New York] that I was acquainted with from any criminal act or intention concerning the same my conscience acquits me and I must therefore beg of you Good Sir to give me up the author, if any, that accuses me of more than I confided to you. I desire him to produce his evidence and also to order a General Court Martial that I may be either condemned or acquitted." (Emmet Collection Rare Books and Manuscripts Division, Center for the Humanities, Astor, Lenox, and Tilden Foundations, New York

Public Library.) White ultimately lost his commission for conduct unbecoming an officer. However, he was appointed a lieutenant colonel in the 4th Continental Light Dragoons on February 15, 1777, through the influence of his friends and family. White commanded the 1st Continental Dragoons later in the war.

41. Washington to Timothy Pickering, September 9, 1798, *Writings of Washington,* 36:431.
42. Martha Washington visited her husband at his headquarters frequently and for long periods of time during the Revolution. The amount of work she did at headquarters is a matter of speculation among George Washington scholars to date. Five headquarters documents have been found in Martha's handwriting. For example, she drafted a letter to John Moylan in 1781 concerning the issuing of clothing. Other isolated examples of her writings may be discovered. However it is safe to say that her clerical services at her husband's headquarters were occasional.
43. Worthington Chauncey Ford and Herbert Putnam, eds., *Aids and Secretaries to Gen. George Washington* (Washington, D.C.: U.S. Government Printing Office, 1906), 3, 5.
44. Ford and Putnam, *Aids and Secretaries to Gen. George Washington,* 5. The purpose of Ford's book was to show facsimile reproductions of Washington's aides' handwriting. In his introduction, Ford said, "So much doubt has existed on the names of those who served in the military family of General Washington as aides and secretaries, and so great is the interest attaching to the assistance given by them to the General in the preparation of his dispatches, that the following list has been prepared."

CHAPTER 2

1. Kenneth R. Rossman, *Thomas Mifflin and the Politics of the American Revolution* (University of North Carolina Press, 1952), 45.
2. The term "half-pay officer" existed in the British Army well before the time of the American Revolution. It meant that an officer had been retired by the government, for example if his regiment had been eliminated, but he was given half his salary for life as a pension. Officer's commissions were purchased in the British Army at the time. The buying and selling of commissions was another way to provide a pension for an officer; he could sell his commission when he retired or otherwise left the service.
3. George Washington was believed to be one of the three wealthiest men in America. The other two were Charles Carroll of Maryland and Henry Middleton of South Carolina. See Richard M. Ketchum, *Saratoga: Turning Point of America's Revolutionary War* (New York: Henry Holt, 1997), 10.
4. *Journals of Congress,* 2:94. As a means of comparison regarding salaries, Washington was offered a salary of $500 per month for his pay and expenses, which he refused. Major generals received $160 and the adjutant general was paid $125. The chief engineer received $60 per month and his assistants were paid $20 per month. John Adams was one of the members of the Continental Congress who complained about what he felt were high salaries for the army officers, "The pay which has been voted to all the officers, which the Continental Congress intends to choose, is so large, that I fear our people will think it extravagant and be uneasy."
5. Ibid., 2:102

6. Among the men recommended to Washington for his staff at this time were Joseph Trumbull whose patrons were Congressmen Silas Deane, Eliphalet Dyer, and Roger Sherman. Robert Treat Paine, a Massachusetts delegate to Congress championed William Tudor. John Hancock recommended William Bant and John Adams suggested Jonathan William Austin. See *Papers of Washington,* 1:8–9, 11–12 n. John Adams also apparently recommended Tudor, who was a law student at the time. Adams wrote Tudor from Philadelphia on June 20, 1775, "I have taken the Liberty to mention you to General Washington for his secretary, which is a very genteel Place." See *Letters of Delegates,* 1:517.

7. *Letters of Delegates* 1:529. John Adams's high regard for Mifflin is evident from his correspondence. Writing to his wife Abigail on May 29, 1775, from Philadelphia, for example, Adams said, "Mr. Mifflin a Major. He ought to have been a Genl. for he has been the animating Soul of the whole." See L. H. Butterfield et al., eds., *Adams Family Correspondence* (Cambridge: Belknap Press of Harvard University Press, 1963–), 1:207.

8. Andrew Oliver, ed., *The Journal of Samuel Curwen* (Cambridge, Massachusetts: Harvard University Press, 1972), 1:7. Washington also knew Thomas Mifflin socially before his appointment as his aide-de-camp.

9. John Adams was among those who accompanied Washington to the outskirts of Philadelphia. Adams was a vain, opinionated, tactless man with a deep-rooted persecution complex. After escorting Washington on the start of his trip to Boston, Adams wrote, "Such is the pride and pomp of war, I, poor creature, worn out with scribbling for my bread and for my liberty, low in spirits and weak in health, must leave others to wear the laurels which I have sown; others to eat the bread which I have earned; a common case."

10. John F. Roche, *Joseph Reed: A Moderate in the American Revolution* (New York: Columbia University Press, 1957), 65–66.

11. William B. Reed, *Life and Correspondence of Joseph Reed* (Philadelphia: Lindsay and Blakiston, 1847), 1:105–6.

12. *Papers of Washington,* 1:335–36.

13. George H. Moore, *The Treason of Charles Lee* (New York: Charles Scribner, 1859), 27. Moore gives no source for this quote. Washington also had a low regard for Ward's military abilities.

14. Charles Lee, *The Lee Papers* (New York: New York Historical Society, 1871–74), 1:207 (hereafter cited as Lee Papers). Lee included this comment in a letter dated September 19, 1775, to his friend, Dr. Benjamin Rush. The title "His Excellency" was often used for high ranking persons, including governors, and was not necessarily pretentious at the time.

15. This title was not unique to General Washington in eighteenth-century America. Other important people were addressed with the same title. The governor of Rhode Island is still referred to as "His Excellency."

16. *Papers of Washington,* 1:49–50. The first General Orders were in Joseph Reed's writing.

17. At the time, a master's degree required no formal study and was available to any alumnus who paid the prescribed fee and presented a dissertation at commencement at least three years after receiving his bachelor's degree.

18. There was no law school in America when Joseph Reed decided that he wanted to become a lawyer and reading law with an attorney was the accepted way to join

the profession. Even after the first law school was established in America by the celebrated attorney Tapping Reeve in 1773 in Litchfield, Connecticut, many men continued to learn law by working for an attorney. There was formal legal training available in London at the Inns of Court and wealthy Americans studied law there. The colonists who studied law in England were considered the elite of their profession in America.

19. Reed, *Life and Correspondence of Joseph Reed,* 1:116.
20. "Distinguished courtesy" is a term coined by historian Douglas Southall Freeman to describe Joseph Reed. See Douglas Southall Freeman et al., *George Washington: A Biography* (New York: Charles Scribner's Sons: 1948–57), 3:460.
21. Reed, *Life and Correspondence of Joseph Reed,* 1:118.
22. Butterfield et al., *Adams Family Correspondence,* 1:166.
23. *Papers of Washington,* 1:54.
24. While the duties of the quartermaster general varied during the course of the war, his general responsibilities were the procurement and distribution of supplies other than food and clothing. Washington's authority to appoint the quartermaster general is included in a letter from John Hancock dated July 24, 1775, "The appointment of a Quarter Master General, Commissary of Musters, and a Commissary of Artillery is left to you, the Congress not being sufficiently acquainted with persons properly qualified for these offices." See *Papers of Washington,* 1:165.
25. Ibid., 1:372.
26. Ibid., 1:132.
27. Theodore Sizer, ed., *The Autobiography of Colonel John Trumbull* (New Haven: Yale University Press, 1953), 22.
28. *Papers of Washington,* 1:177.
29. Ibid., 1:309.
30. Ibid., 1:147.
31. Ibid., 1:372. Thomas Jefferson was Edmund Randolph's second cousin.
32. John J. Reardon, *Edmund Randolph* (New York: Macmillan, 1974), 22.
33. Peyton Randolph apparently died from an illness known at the time as "the dead palsy." The term was used in a letter Congressman Henry Lee wrote to Washington on October 23, 1775, describing Randolph's death, "our good old Speaker Peyton Randolph Esqr. went yesterday to dine with Mr. Harry Hill, was taken during the course of dinner with the dead palsey, and at 9 oClock at night died without a groan." See *Papers of Washington,* 2:218.

    The term "palsy" has its origins in Middle English and means paralysis. When the paralysis was accompanied by involuntary tremors the malady was called "the shaking palsy." The "dead palsy" meant paralysis with no tremors. What probably happened was that Henry Lee witnessed Peyton Randolph suddenly collapsing with loss of consciousness followed shortly by death. In modern medical terms Randolph probably suffered a fatal heart attack.
34. Peter Force, ed., *American Archives* (Washington, D.C.: 1837–53), 5th ser., 3:902.
35. On March 25, 1776, Congress resolved, "That a deputy muster master general be appointed for the southern department. The ballots being taken and examined, Mr. Edmund Randolph, was elected. Resolved, That Mr. E. Randolph, be empowered to appoint two deputy muster masters under him, one for North Carolina, and the other for South Carolina and Georgia." See *Journals of Congress,* 4:236. This was

an important post because Congress correctly believed that the British were preparing to attack the southern colonies. Randolph had to resign the post the following month and the reason is stated in the *Journals of the Continental Congress* for April 26, 1776. "Edmund Randolph, who was appointed deputy muster master general of the Southern department, having been chosen by the citizens of Williamsburg, to represent them in Convention, and an ordinance having been passed, excluding all persons holding any military post of profit from a seat therein, begged leave to resign his office: Resolved, That the resignation of Mr. Randolph be accepted." See ibid., 4:311.

A muster master was an inspector who reviewed "troops under arms." He counted men and horses and reported on their condition and the condition of their weapons and accoutrements. There were regional muster masters and a muster master general of the army. This office was also called commissary general of musters. The position, which had its origins in medieval England, was abolished later in the Revolutionary War.

36. *Papers of Washington,* 1:109–10.
37. Ibid., 1:110.
38. Ibid., 2:283.
39. Ibid., 3:339.
40. Ibid., 2:444.
41. George Athan Billias, *General John Glover and His Marblehead Mariners* (New York: Henry Holt and Company, 1960), 73 , 213, 214 n. 2.
42. Martin I. J. Griffin, *Stephen Moylan* (Philadelphia: privately printed, 1909), 34.
43. *Travels in North-America,* 1:141–42.
44. *Papers of Washington,* 1:385. Washington appointed Moylan muster master general on August 11, 1775, and his appointment was mentioned in the General Orders for that date.
45. Ibid., 2:90–91. The two additional schooners armed by Reed, Glover, and Moylan were named the *Franklin* and the *Hancock.*
46. Nathan Miller, *Sea of Glory: The Continental Navy Fights for Independence, 1775–1783* (New York: David McKay, 1974), 66.
47. Ibid., 67.
48. Ibid.
49. *Papers of Washington,* 2:106–7.
50. Ibid., 2:135 n. 5.
51. Edward W. Richardson, *Standards and Colors of the American Revolution* (Philadelphia: University of Pennsylvania Press, 1982), 91. This is a popular and reliable general history of the flags of the American Revolution. A more detailed account of the Washington cruiser flag can be found in Richard Frothingham, *History of the Siege of Boston* (Boston: Little, Brown, 1903), 261–62.
52. *Papers of Washington,* 2:251–52.
53. Washington Irving, *Life of George Washington* (New York: G. P. Putnam & Co., 1856–59), 2:81.
54. *Papers of Washington,* 3:172.
55. Ibid., 2:443.
56. Ibid., 4:115.
57. Ibid., 2:444–46.

58. Ibid., 2:448–49. Nathanael Greene from Rhode Island had a more kindly view of New Englanders and attributed Washington's low opinion of them to being unfamiliar with their ways. To Samuel Ward, Sr., on December 18, 1775, Greene wrote: "But his Excellency as you Observe has not had time to make himself thoroughly Acquainted with the Genius of this People. They are Naturally brave and spirited as the Peasantry of any Country, but you cannot expect Veterans of a Raw Militia from only a few months service. The common People are exceeding Avaricious; the Genius of the People is Commercial from the long intercourse of Trade." Showman and Conrad, *The Papers of General Nathanael Greene,* 1:163–64.

59. *Papers of Washington,* 3:89.

60. John Posey was Washington's neighbor. His son, Thomas Posey, was a lieutenant colonel in the Continental Army.

61. *Papers of George Washington,* Colonial Series, 8:252–54.

62. Lund Washington to George Washington, Mount Vernon, October 29, 1775, in *Papers of Washington,* 2:256.

63. *The Journal of Nicholas Cresswell* (New York: Dial, 1924), 19.

64. I found that the connections among George Washington's family, friends, business associates, and war cronies are only limited by the amount of time a person is prepared to devote to researching the subject. As an example, one of Robert Hanson Harrison's daughters, Sarah, married Adam Craik who was the son of Washington's good friend Dr. James Craik (1730–1814). James Craik was the chief physician and surgeon of the Continental Army.

65. *Papers of Washington,* 2:308. The evidence that Harrison began working as Washington's aide is a letter of certification the general wrote on March 25, 1781, which reads in part, "I certify that Robt. H. Harrison Esqr. Lieutt. Colo. In the Continental Army entered the Service in the month of October 1775 as one of my Aid de Camps." See *Writings of Washington,* 21:377.

66. *Papers of Washington,* 2:407. According to Washington scholar Douglas Southall Freeman, Washington recruited Harrison for his military family discharge the less important if necessary duties of aide. See Freeman, *George Washington,* 4:18.

67. *Papers of Washington,* 3:172.

68. Ibid., 3:283.

69. *Journals of Congress,* 4:33–34.

70. *Papers of Washington,* 3:215.

71. Ibid., 2:448.

72. Ibid., 3:172. At Washington's request, Congress raised the salary of his military secretary to $100, in an effort to induce Reed to return to headquarters. William Palfrey referred to this salary increase in a letter he wrote from New York in the spring of 1776, "Coll. Read [Reed]is expected in Town every Moment to resume his office of Secretary, his Salary is increas'd to 100 dollars @ month, and he is allow'd two assistants." See *Lee Papers,* I:476.

73. W. T. Baxter, *The House of Hancock* (Cambridge, Massachusetts: Harvard University Press, 1945), 241–42, 250. Palfrey's nineteenth-century biographer gives this explanation of the association between John Hancock and William Palfrey, "In the summer of 1764, Thomas Hancock died, leaving his large estate to his nephew John, then twenty-seven years of age. The young heir, whose education had been such as rather to qualify him for the conspicuous part he was destined to act in soci-

ety, than for the management of an extensive business, saw the expediency of securing the aid of some one distinguished for the kind of ability, which it was no discredit for himself not to possess in a high degree. His choice fell on the subject of
this memoir, who in October, engaged with Mr. Hancock on a salary, stipulating 'to
be allowed liberty to do his own business.'" See J. G. Palfrey, *Biography of William
Palfrey,* ed. Jared Sparks, *The Library of American Biography,* ser. 2, 3:343.

74. William Palfrey, The Memorandum Book of William Palfrey of Boston in New
England, 1771 Massachusetts Historical Society, Boston. Palfrey's journal reference to wearing clerical garb possibly means that he wore plain clothing for this
occasion compared to everyone else present who was elegantly dressed. Palfrey
used metaphors in his writing that support this idea.

75. *Papers of Washington,* 2:476–77.

76. Ibid., 2:497.

77. Ibid., 3:282–83.

78. Ibid., 3:339. Lee's comment about needing Palfrey's services, "particularly if I am
detach'd to Canada," refers to the fact that Palfrey knew the French language. His
wife was French and he was eventually selected as the American consul to France.
Palfrey's nineteenth-century biographer, J. G. Palfrey said that William Palfrey
learned French as a child.

79. The fact that Lee selected Palfrey to serve on his personal staff is interesting. Lee
was a difficult person to get along with. He was a brilliant, educated person with
strange habits and tastes. After meeting him for the first time the perceptive Abigail Adams wrote, "General Lee looks like a careless hardy Veteran . . . The Elegance of his pen far exceeds that of his person." One of Lee's early biographers,
Sir Henry Bunbury, said that he was "a fast friend, but a bitter enemy." Gen. Philip
Schuyler called him a sloppy and unwashed eccentric. But Palfrey seemed to get
along with Lee. He must have been an exceptional person and a capable aide-de-
camp to befriend the usually belligerent Lee.

80. *Papers of Washington,* 3:284 n. 2.

81. Ibid., 4:95.

82. *Letters of Delegates,* 3:561.

83. *Lee Papers,* 1:475–76.

84. Ibid., 2:122.

85. Apparently Palfrey was highly regarded by the delegates to Congress. Writing six
months after Palfrey's departure from Philadelphia and with no news of his ship's
arrival in France, delegate James Lovell wrote on June 14, 1781, "We believe
nothing favorable to him at this day. I am distressed for his amiable Family as well
as sincerely afflicted at the Loss of him. He would have repaired our tattered
Affairs in France and have raised a Character of Honesty & Ability in mercantile
Transactions for the Public." See *Letters of Delegates,* 17:319.

86. *Papers of Washington,* 3:413.

87. Sizer, *Autobiography of Colonel John Trumbull,* 23–24.

88. *Papers of Washington,* 3:489–90.

89. Julian P. Boyd et al., eds., *Papers of Thomas Jefferson* (Princeton: Princeton University Press, 1956–), 13:199–200.

90. John Jay (1745–1829) had a long and distinguished public career that included
service as chief justice of the United States between 1789–95. He was considered

a serious candidate for president until his popularity plummeted as a result of the treaty he negotiated with Britain, which is known as Jay's Treaty.

91. Art historian James Thomas Flexner commented about Trumbull's commission from Congress to paint the four murals for the Capitol, "His most valuable assets proved to be the Revolutionary scenes he had painted as a young man. . . . The figures were to be life-size, a scale that had given the one-eyed painter difficulty even in his best days; those days were far behind him. Yet he painted with energy and, as each monstrosity was completed, further lined his pockets by exhibiting it throughout the country to patriotic crowds." See James Thomas Flexner, *History of American Painting, 1760–1835: The Light of Distant Skies* (New York: Dover, 1969), 163–64. Trumbull painted the portraits of the French officers who appear in his painting at Thomas Jefferson's Paris home. Jefferson made the arrangements when Trumbull visited Paris in 1787.

CHAPTER 3

1. Fitzpatrick, *Spirit of the Revolution,* 76–77.
2. William S. Baker, *Itinerary of General Washington* (Philadelphia: J. B. Lippincott, 1892), 36–37. Washington was accompanied on his journey from Cambridge to New York by aides Palfrey and Moylan and adjutant Gates. Washington followed the coastline in order to supervise the embarkation of his troops to New York City. The general's other two aides, Harrison and Baylor, escorted Martha Washington, her son John Parke Custis and his wife Eleanor to New York by a safer inland route through Hartford.
3. *Papers of Washington,* 3:340.
4. The Continental Army was the official name of the army under the control of the Continental Congress: it did not include state troops and militia although they frequently operated with the Continental regiments. George Washington was commander in chief of the Continental Army. However, Continental troops sometimes operated far from his immediate control, such as in northern New York state, Canada, and the southern states. In addition, state troops and militia were under state control. To clarify this confusing situation, the term Grand Army or main army was used during the Revolution to identify all the troops under Washington's immediate command, be they Continental regiments, state troops, or militia. Congress used the term Grand Army to identify the main army as early as June 16, 1775, when they resolved, "That there be one quarter master general for the grand army, and a deputy, under him, for the separate army." See *Journals of Congress,* 2:94.
5. *Papers of Washington,* 4:112–13.
6. *Journals of Congress,* 4:311.
7. Ibid., 5:418. The General Orders of the army dated June 21, 1776, announced Congress's decision to the army, "The Honorable Continental Congress have been pleased to give the rank of Lieutenant Colonel, to the Aids-du-Camp of the Commander in Chief, and to his principal Secretary. Also the Rank of Major to the Aids-du-Camp of the Majors General." See *Papers of Washington,* 4:61.
8. *Journals of Congress,* 7:197. On March 24, 1777, Congress resolved, "that the pay of aides de camp be equal to that of other officers of their rank." A few weeks later (April 1, 1777) Congress authorized that the pay of the secretary to the commander in chief was to be increased to 100 dollars per month "and that Colonel

Harrison, the present secretary, be allowed that pay from the time of his appointment to that office." See ibid., 7:216.

9. *Papers of Washington,* 3:448–49.

10. *Letters of Delegates,* 10:109. The letter quoted was written by Robert Morris to Gouverneur Morris.

11. *Papers of Washington,* 3:244–45.

12. Ibid., 4:310.

13. Holly A. Mayer, *Belonging to the Army: Camp Followers and Community during the American Revolution* (Columbia, South Carolina: University of South Carolina Press, 1996), 171. Gibbs continued to manage the household staff until 1780 when he left headquarters for another assignment. Washington searched for a replacement but without success. He wrote to the Board of War about his problem and they appointed John Loveday to the position.

14. Heitman, *Register of Officers In the Continental Army,* 246.

15. *Letters of Delegates,* 10:109. Morris's letter about Gibbs is dated June 16, 1778.

16. Author Carlos E. Godfrey states that Lewis returned to headquarters on May 1, 1777. See Carlos E. Godfrey, *The Commander-in-Chief's Guard* (Washington, D.C.: Stevenson-Smith, 1904), 205. However, Godfrey is not a reliable source; page 26 of his book, for example, is the source of the preposterous story of the 1776 plot by disloyal members of the Commander in Chief's Guard to poison Washington's dish of green peas. We have some clues from other sources to Lewis's whereabouts and approximate return to headquarters. Clothier Gen. James Mease wrote Washington from Philadelphia on April 12, 1777, "Capt. Lewis has recived all the necessaries in my department that he wants & is indeed very handsomely equipt; he proposes in a few days to set out for Head Quarters if no disappointment happens." See *Papers of Washington,* 9:140. Washington did not know where Lewis was on May 3, 1777, because he wrote Captain Gibbs (who was in Philadelphia at the time) from Morristown, "neither have I heard any thing of Captn Lewis (or his Troop) whom I desired might come on to this place." See *Papers of Washington,* 9:330.

17. Fred Anderson Berg, *Encyclopedia of Continental Army Units* (Harrisburg, Pennsylvania: Stackpole Books, 1972), 135.

18. *Papers of Washington,* 9:236.

19. See Godfrey, *Commander-in-Chief's Guard,* 20.

20. *Writings of Washington,* 37:277.

21. *Papers of Washington,* 4:113.

22. Ibid., 3:475.

23. The term "marquee" was used at the time of the American Revolution to describe any type, style, or manner of construction of a large tent used by an officer. The *Oxford English Dictionary (OED)* defines the term as, "a large tent, as an officer's field tent or one used as a public entertainment, exhibition or like." The *OED* cites an interesting use of the word from a 1758 issue of the *London Chronicle,* "General Abercombie would not suffer any of the officers to carry any chests, beds, or markees with them." See J. A. Simpson and E. S. C. Weiner, ed. *Oxford English Dictionary* New York: Oxford University Press, 1989), 9:394.

24. Of the three tents, two survive and are displayed in large hermetically sealed glass chambers in museums. The outer lining of Washington's sleeping tent is at Valley

Forge, and the inner layer of this tent is at Yorktown. His complete dining marquee, also known as the headquarters tent, is in the Smithsonian Institute.

25. *Papers of Washington,* 3:428–29.

26. Ibid., 3:538.

27. American quartermasters and other department heads and their assistants may have abused the system but their chicanery was minor in comparison with what was going on in the enemy camp. A good example of profiteering by the British involved the procurement of wagons for use by their army. The British Treasury sent a civilian employee to America named Francis Rush Clark who was in charge of the wagons used to haul provisions to General Howe's army. Clark was an expert on the construction and maintenance of wagons. He modified the heavy wagons brought from England, reducing their weight so they could operate on the crude American road system. General Howe became bored by Clark and his tedious talk of wagons and carts. His proposals were also ignored by the British commissary staff who preferred to make money by supplying the army with wagons that they leased or purchased at low prices from local farmers. After securing wagons cheaply from the harassed farmers, the commissaries cheated the government by selling the vehicles to the army at huge markups and pocketing the profits. Clark saw what was happening and wrote, "private emolument has been more attended to than publick good." Similar scams and corrupt practices were present in every department.

28. Rossman, *Thomas Mifflin and the Politics of the American Revolution,* 94.

29. James L. Kochan, "'as plain as blue and buff could make it': George Washington's Uniforms as Commander-in-Chief and President, 1775–1799," (*Catalog of the 44th Washington Antiques Show,* 1999), 53–4. Also see *Papers of Washington, Colonial Series,* 10:173–74.

30. All known portraits of Continental Army generals show them wearing blue and buff uniforms with the exception of a 1783 portrait of Joseph Reed who is wearing a blue regimental coat with red facings. The Reed portrait was painted by Charles Willson Peale.

31. Worthington Chauncey Ford, ed., *Correspondence and Journals of Samuel Blachley Webb* (New York, 1893–94), 1:168 (cited hereafter as *Correspondence of Webb*).

32. Benjamin Walker to von Steuben, March 10, 1780. Friedrich Kapp, *The Life of Frederick William Von Steuben* (New York: Mason Brothers, 1859), 617

33. W. M. Gilmore Simms, ed., *The Army Correspondence of Colonel John Laurens in the Years 1777–8* (New York: Bradford Club, 1876), 119 (cited hereafter as *Army Correspondence of Colonel John Laurnes*). Dimity is a strong linen fabric that resembles corduroy.

34. Tench Tilghman's uniform is complete except for the waistcoat (vest), which does not match the buff color of the facings of the regimental coat and breeches. The waistcoat however is of a style worn during the Revolutionary War. Tilghman's uniform becomes more important when we realize that only a few articles of clothing worn by American officers during the Revolutionary War are known to exist today. Besides Tilghman's uniform there are a regimental coat and waistcoat owned by Col. Peter Gansevoort of New York and a regimental coat worn by Thomas Pinckney of the 1st South Carolina Regiment. The Smithsonian Institution has a uniform worn by Washington; however, it was made sometime after the Revolution.

35. According to eighteenth-century usage, a military riband was a three-to-six-inch wide strip of material, generally made of silk or some other expensive fabric, visible across the chest and sewn along the edges. This was not to be confused with a ribbon, which was a piece of civilian costume such as a hair ribbon. The General Orders of the Army for July 14, 1775, include, "The General Officers and their Aids-de-Camp, will be distinguished in the following manner. The Commander in Chief by a light blue Ribband, wore across his breast, between his Coat and Waistcoat. The Majors and Brigadiers General, by a Pink Ribband wore in the like-manner. The Aids-de-Camp by a green ribband." *Papers of Washington,* 1:115.

36. *Writings of Washington,* 3:399 n.

37. Washington apparently stopped wearing a riband sometime in mid- to late-1779. We know this from a comment by the French diplomat the marquis de Barbe-Marbois who noted in September 1779 that Washington formerly "wore a wide blue ribbon [but] He has given up this scarcely republican distinction."

38. John Laurens to Henry Laurens, November 6, 1777. Philip M. Hamer et al., eds., *The Papers of Henry Laurens,* (Columbia: University of South Carolina Press, 1968–), 12:31 (cited hereafter as *Laurens Papers).*

39. *Writings of Washington,* 19:22. The General Orders of the army for June 18, 1780, specified that "The Aides de Camp . . . of the Major Generals and Brigadier Generals to have a green feather in the Hat: Those of the Commander in Chief a White and Green." However, this regulation may have been codifying a practice that was already in use.

40. Gibbs and Lewis are always identified by Washington as officers in the Commander in Chief's Guard. Historian John C. Fitzpatrick called them "special aides" and lacking any better terminology, I will follow his example. See John C. Fitzpatrick, "The Aides-De-Camp of General George Washington," *Daughters of the American Revolution Magazine* 57, no. 1 (January 1923): 7.

41. *Papers of Washington,* 5:61. Alexander Counter Harrison is a misspelling, the General Orders should read Alexander Contee Hanson.

42. Webb's middle name is frequently misspelled Blatchley. This error appears, for example, in the entry for Webb in Mark M. Boatner, *Encyclopedia of the American Revolution* (New York: David McKay, 1966), 1178. The correct spelling of Webb's middle name is Blachley.

43. *Papers of Washington,* 3:407.

44. Margreta Swenson Cheney, *A Family of Patriots: The Webbs and the Deanes* (pamphlet, privately printed, 1979).

45. *Papers of Washington,* 3:537–38.

46. *Correspondence of Webb,* 1:xxviii–xxix.

47. *Journals of Congress,* 4:380.

48. Allen Johnson et al., eds., *Dictionary of American Biography* (New York: Charles Scribner's Sons, 1928–36), 8:230.

49. Surprisingly, the great Washington scholar Douglas Southall Freeman incorrectly identified Cary. He said that Cary was from Peartree, in Warwick Colorado, Virginia, and was approximately of the age of his distant kinswoman, Sally Cary Fairfax. See Freeman, *George Washington,* 4:124 n. 52.

50. Clifford K. Shipton, *Sibley's Harvard Graduates Biographical Sketches of Those Who Attended Harvard College in the Classes of 1761–1763* (Boston: Massachusetts Historical Society, 1970), 15:371.

51. It is interesting to think that one of Washington's aides was a former British officer. However, the facts do not confirm this story. There is no record of an officer
named Cary in the published lists of officers in the 14th Regiment between 1764
and 1772. In fact no officer with the name Cary was found in any of the British
Army regimental lists for the period.

52. *The Life of Esther De Berdt: Afterwards Esther Reed* (Philadelphia: C. Sherman,
1853), 212–13.

53. Robert J. Taylor, ed., *Papers of John Adams* (Cambridge: Belknap Press of Harvard University Press, 1979–), 3:103.

54. Ibid., 3:104.

55. *Correspondence of Webb,* 1:175 and Clifford K. Shipton, *Biographical Sketches of
Those Who Attended Harvard College* (Boston: Massachusetts Historical Society,
1970), 371, state Cary married Anna Phillips on July 12, 1771. There is no reference to her death. On page 372 Shipton says, "having lost his first wife, he married
Anna, daughter of Cornelius P. Low about 1792."

56. *Correspondence of Webb,* 1:175–76.

57. Emmet Collection.

58. Aaron Burr was first introduced to General Washington in a note from John Hancock at the start of the war. Hancock wrote Washington: "Philadelphia, 19 July,
1775 . . . Mr Ogden [Matthias Ogden who had an active service record during the
Revolution] & Mr. Burr of the Jerseys . . . Visit the Camp not as Spectators, but
with a View of Joining the Army & being Active during the Campaign." Ogden
and Burr were associated together at this point in the war because they grew up
together in the house of Burr's uncle in Elizabeth, New Jersey. Washington
received a second letter of introduction about Burr because His Excellency wrote
the influential Lewis Morris on August 4, 1775, "I have been favored with your
Letter of the 18th Ulto by Messr Ogdan [Ogden] and Burr, & wish it was in my
power to do that justice to the merits of those Gentlemen which you think them
entitled to—whenever it is, I shall not be unmindful of your recommendations."
See *Papers of Washington,* 1:132 and 240.

59. See Nathan Schachner, *Aaron Burr* (New York: Frederick A. Stokes, 1937), 45.
Schachner says that Burr's brief service on Washington's staff was satisfactory.
"Whatever ill-feeling or dislike there may have existed between the two," according
to Schachner, "necessarily arose at a later date."

60. *Papers of Washington,* 4:72.

61. Roche, *Joseph Reed: A Moderate in the American Revolution,* 80.

62. *Papers of Washington,* 3:429.

63. Reed, *Life and Correspondence of Joseph Reed,* 1:182. Charles Pettit (1736–1806)
served as secretary to New Jersey governor William Livingston. He subsequently
served as assistant quartermaster general from March 2, 1778, until he resigned
this post on June 20, 1781. He declined the post of quartermaster general of the
Continental Army when it was offered to him. Pettit was also a Pennsylvania delegate to the Continental Congress.

64. *Papers of Washington,* 4:310. Washington scholar Douglas Southall Freeman commented on Reed's absence and Harrison's appointment as military secretary,
"Washington had not ceased to miss him, and, indeed, had found nobody to fill
completely the place Reed had occupied. . . . Robert H. Harrison, who still was

growing in usefulness though not yet wholly adequate was made official Secretary to the Commander-in-Chief on May 16." Freeman, *George Washington,* 4:105–6.

65. *Journals of Congress,* 5:419. There is a curious entry in the *Journals of the Continental Congress* dated March 1, 1776. Reed was on a leave of absence from headquarters at the time and living back home in Philadelphia. Washington was at Cambridge, Massachusetts, in early March and still commanding his small navy. The *Journal* entry reads, "Resolved, That an addition of 34 dollars per month be added to the pay of Joseph Reed, Esq. the secretary to General Washington, on account of the extraordinary services at present attending that office, by reason of the General's direction of the naval department." See *Journals of Congress,* 4:180. It appears that Washington found an excuse to get Congress to increase Reed's salary as an inducement for him to return to headquarters. This pay increase was granted several months prior to Reed's appointment as adjutant general.

66. *Papers of Washington,* 5:31.

67. Christopher Ward, *The War of the Revolution* (New York: Macmillan, 1952), 1:209.

68. Ibid., 209.

69. *Papers of Washington,* 5:246.

70. Ibid.

71. *Correspondence of Webb,* 1:153.

72. Henry P. Johnston, *The Campaign of 1776 around New York and Brooklyn* (Brooklyn: Long Island Historical Society, 1878), 97.

73. Historian Douglas Southall Freeman wrote that Lieutenant Brown said at this point, "I am very sorry and so will be Lord Howe that any error in superscription should prevent the letter being received by General Washington." See Freeman, *George Washington,* 4:139. Freeman gives a detailed account of this incident on pages 138–40.

74. Reed, *Life and Correspondence of Joseph Reed,* 1:204–5.

75. Edward H. Tatum, Jr., ed., *The American Journal of Ambrose Serle* (San Marino, California: Huntington Library, 1940), 35. According to a delightful story in James Thacher's military journal, this second letter was addressed to: "George Washington, Esq., &c.&c.&c." It was hoped, recounted Thacher, that this title would remove all difficulties, "as the three et ceteras might be understood to imply everything that ought to follow. To this the general replied, that though it was true the three et ceteras might mean every thing, it was also true they might mean any thing, . . . and declined receiving the letter; adding that he should absolutely decline any letter directed to him as a private person, when it related to his public station." See James Thacher, *The American Revolution, from the Commencement to the Disbanding of the American Army: Given in the Form of a Daily Journal* . . . (Hartford: Hurlbut, Kellogg, 1861), 50–51 (cited hereafter as *Military Journal*). Thacher's book was originally published in 1823 as *A Military Journal during the American Revolutionary War, from 1775 to 1783.*

76. *Correspondence of Webb,* 1:156.

77. Reed, *Life and Correspondence of Joseph Reed,* 1:214.

78. *Papers of Washington,* 5:462.

79. *Journals of Congress,* 5:613. Congress seemed to be reasonably responsive to Washington's requests for more staff assistance throughout the course of the war.

80. *Papers of Washington,* 6:116.

81. Hugh Blair Grigsby, *The History of the Virginia Federal Convention of 1788* (Richmond: 1890–1891), 2:146, 148. See also Joseph Horrell, ed., "New Light on William Grayson: His Guardian's Account," *Virginia Magazine of History and Biography* (October 1984): 423–43.

82. William Grayson's mother, whose maiden name was Monroe, was the sister of Spence Monroe, who was the father of Pres. James Monroe. See D. R. Anderson, "William Grayson: A Study in Virginia Biography of the Eighteenth Century," *Richmond College Historical Papers* 2, no. 1 (June 1917): 75.

83. Ibid., 76

84. *Papers of Washington,* 4:44. Lee's comments about Grayson are in a letter to Washington dated Williamsburg, April 5, 1776. Lee was ordered south by the Continental Congress to help organize the defenses of the southern states and met Grayson when he was passing through Virginia en route to Charleston, South Carolina.

85. Boyd, et al., *Papers of Thomas Jefferson,* 1:287. "Hampton" refers to a battle fought between British forces sent to destroy Norfolk, Virginia, and Virginia militia on October 24–25, 1775.

86. Dumas Malone, ed., *Dictionary of American Biography* (New York: Charles Scribner's Sons), 5:525.

87. Anderson, "William Grayson: A Study in Virginia Biography," 75.

88. Charles Homer Bast, "Lieutenant-Colonel Tench Tilghman—The Portrait of an Aide" (master's thesis, University of Virginia, 1937), 19.

89. Matthew Tilghman is sometimes called the "Patriarch of Maryland." He had a long and distinguished career of public service. Tilghman served as a member of the Maryland provincial legislature prior to the Revolution. He declined a seat on the Governor's Council but later accepted a post on the rebel Provincial Committee of Correspondence and the first Council of Safety in 1775. He also headed every Maryland delegation to the Continental Congress from 1774 to 1776. Although he was not present in Philadelphia when the Declaration of Independence was signed, Tilghman was an early supporter of American independence. He was elected president of the Maryland Constitutional Convention in 1776 and later elected to the newly established Maryland Senate in 1776. He was reelected in 1781, serving as its president in 1782. Tench Tilghman eventually married his uncle Matthew's daughter.

90. Shreve, *Tench Tilghman,* 42.

91. John Stockton Littell, ed., *Memoirs of His Own Time with Reminiscences of the Men and Events of the Revolution by Alexander Graydon* (Philadelphia: Lindsay & Blakiston, 1846), 123 (hereafter cited as *Graydon: Memoirs of His Own Time*). This book was originally published as *Memoirs of a Life Chiefly Passed in Pennsylvania: Within the Last Sixty Years . . .* (Harrisburg, Pennsylvania: John Wyeth, 1811).

92. The Flying Camp was a temporary mobile reserve created by Congress in July 1776 as part of the defense of New York City. It was composed mostly of militia and state troops from Maryland, Pennsylvania, and Delaware who volunteered for active service for a short period of time. The Flying Camp ceased to exist toward the end of 1776 as the enlistments of its men expired.

93. As an example, Washington's diary entry for May 25, 1775, reads, "Dined at Mr. Tilghman's & spent the Evening at the City Tavern." See Donald Jackson and

Dorothy Twohig, eds., *The Papers of George Washington: The Diaries of George Washington,* (Charlottesville: University Press of Virginia, 1976–79), 3:331. The upper class, or "better sort," as they were called, was made up of a limited number of families. They knew each other and worked together on business deals especially to spread the risks involved in speculative ventures. Common interests brought Washington in contact with the Tilghman family including Tench Tilghman's father James. James was a passive Loyalist who kept a low profile during the Revolution. Another of James Tilghman's sons, Philemon, joined the Royal Navy at the start of the war. Descendants of the Tilghman clan include deputy United States marshal William "Bill" Tilghman who helped bring law and order to the Oklahoma Territory in the 1890s. Marshal Tilghman named one of his sons Tench.

94. As an example, Washington's diary entry for June 15, 1772, includes, "Mr. [James] Tilghman [Jr.,] & and Mr. Andrews came to Dinner & stayed all Night." See ibid., 3:114. Also, the entry for September 9, 1774, reads, "Dined at Mr. [James] Tilghman's & spent the evening at home." See ibid., 3:276.

95. In a letter to Gen. John Sullivan dated May 11, 1781, Washington mentioned when Tilghman joined his staff: "This Gentn. came out a Captn. of one of the light Infy Companies of Philadelphia, served in the flying Camp in 1776. In August of the same Year he joined my family." *Writings of Washington,* 22:71. The earliest known reference to his possibly being on Washington's personal staff is a letter dated August 8, 1776, from Washington to Gen. Hugh Mercer, which includes the following, "The Account given you by a Deserter as brought me by Mr. Tilghman." See *Papers of Washington,* 5: 633. The August 8 letter is not hard evidence of Tilghman's presence on the commander in chief's staff because it can also be interpreted that Tilghman was delivering a message from Mercer to Washington. The general often identified a letter by giving the name of its carrier.

96. Tilghman probably joined Washington's staff as a volunteer aide-de-camp sometime in early August 1776. He remained at headquarters until March 22, 1782, when he took an extended leave of absence and returned on August 11, 1782. He remained at headquarters until sometime in December 1782 when he took another leave of absence and, with the war almost over, apparently never returned. See Shreve, *Tench Tilghman,* 172–76.

97. *Writings of Washington,* 24:422. Washington's letter is dated: "Head Qrs., Newburgh, July 10, 1782." Tilghman eventually married the young woman, Anna Maria Tilghman, who was his first cousin.

98. Reed, *Life and Correspondence of Joseph Reed,* 1:216.

99. These American officers were Gen. John Sullivan, a prewar lawyer from Portsmouth, New Hampshire, and William Alexander, a wealthy New Jersey landowner and large-scale farmer who fancied himself as "Lord Stirling." Both men were captured that day by the British.

100. *Papers of Washington,* 6:140–42.

101. Shreve, *Tench Tilghman,* 66.

102. Roche, *Joseph Reed: A Moderate in the American Revolution,* 92.

103. Reed, *Life and Correspondence of Joseph Reed,* 1:231.

104. *Papers of George Washington,* 6:313.

105. Johnston, *Campaign of 1776 around New York and Brooklyn;* see appendix, 92, doc. 32.

106. Shreve, *Tench Tilghman,* 68.

107. Freeman, *George Washington,* 4: 193: Force, *American Archives,* 5:2, 1251.
108. William Heath, *Memoirs of Major-General Heath* (Boston: I. Thomas and E.T. Andrews, 1798), 60.
109. Johnston, *Campaign of 1776 around New York and Brooklyn,* 236–37. The nineteenth century produced a flood of claptrap histories of the American Revolution. This 1878 book is one of the few exceptions. It is accurate and packed with great stories. Among the handful of other important eighteenth-century books about the Revolution are Lyman C. Draper, *King's Mountain and Its Heros* (1881) and Washington Irving, *Life of George Washington,* 5 vols. (1855–59).
110. Showman, *Papers of General Nathanael Greene,* 1:300.
111. Irving, *Life of Washington,* 2: 353. This incident is one of the best-known stories about Washington's aides-de-camp, and I wanted to trace it to its source. Irving tells the story in his 1855 biography of George Washington and gives Alexander Graydon as his source. See *Graydon, Memoirs of His Own Time,* 174. Graydon gave a brief account of the affair at Kips Bay but he did not say that one of Washington's aides led the general to safety. In another early version of the story in James Thacher's military journal, Washington, "drew his sword and snapped his pistols, to check them; but they continued their flight without firing a gun; and the general, regardless of his own safety, was in so much hazard, that one of his attendants seized the reins and gave his horse a different direction." See *Military Journal,* 58. The word "attendants" could be interpreted as one of Washington's aides-de-camp or the general's black slave Billy Lee. In one of the earliest published accounts of the Revolution, historian David Ramsay recorded the incident as, "His aids and the confidential friends around his person, by indirect violence, compelled him to retire." David Ramsay, *The History of the American Revolution* (1789; Trenton, New Jersey: James J. Wilson, 1811), 1:392, reprint. Ramsay was not an eyewitness to the scene but is a generally reliable source. Another early history written by William Gordon explains that the incident "left the general in a hazardous situation, so that his attendants, to extricate him out of it, caught the bridle of his horse, and gave him a different direction." William Gordon, *The History of the Rise, Progress, and Establishment of the Independence of the United States of America,* 4 vols. (London: Charles Dilly, 1788), 2:327. Gordon was a great gossip and was not present at Kips Bay. Lacking any creditable eyewitness account of the incident, the story of Washington being led away from danger by one of his aides on the day of the battle of Kips Bay must be classified as "camp gossip."
112. David Humphreys, *An Essay on the Life of the Honorable Major-General Israel Putnam* (Hartford: Hudson and Goodwin, 1788), 133, 136–37.
113. Henry P. Johnston, *The Battle of Harlem Heights* (New York: Macmillan, 1897), 138.
114. For Washington's daily routine during the war see John Ferling, *The First of Men: A Life of George Washington* (Knoxville: University of Tennessee Press, 1988), 258–59.
115. Washington included an expense on October 2, 1776, "For mending 2 coats for the Coachman." See George Washington, Papers Presidential papers Series, microfilm, ser. 5, vol. 24, reel 116, Library of Congress (hereafter cited as George Washington Papers).
116. Ebenezer Austin was the steward of Washington's household between July 1775 and April 1776. He did not want to follow Washington to New York. The next

civilian to be hired as steward was Patrick McGuire who held the position until March 6, 1778, when he was dismissed. Washington wrote about McGuire in a letter to Thomas Wharton shortly afterward, "He was hired about twelve months ago, to act as steward in my family, in which station he continued until a few weeks past, when I was obliged to dismiss him. (and I have the greatest reason to believe, that during the whole time of his employ, he took every opportunity of defrauding me) He is given to liquor, and where he dares take the liberty, very insolent." See *Writings of Washington,* 11:268. Following Gibbs's departure from Washington's staff in 1780, John Loveday was hired as steward.

117. Mrs. Mary Smith was probably hired as Washington's headquarters housekeeper in April 1776, shortly after the general's arrival in New York City with his staff. She was replaced by Mrs. Elizabeth Thompson who started working for Washington on July 9, 1776. She was about seventy-three years old at the time and continued working as the headquarters housekeeper until December 1781. Washington usually had his own cook with him throughout the war. His name was Isaac and it is unknown if he was a slave or a free black.

118. Mabel Lorenz Ives, *Washington's Headquarters* (Upper Monclair, New Jersey: Lucy Fortune, 1932), 72. Ms. Ives places the kitchen of the Morris mansion in the basement. It is generally believed that the kitchens in colonial period homes were in separate buildings because of the danger of fire. However, historian Eric Olsen from Morristown National Historical Park explained that kitchens were put in separate buildings in the southern colonies because of the great amount of heat that comes from cooking and not the danger of fire. Northern homes had their kitchens whereever it was most convenient, including the basement.

119. Constance M. Griff, *The Morris-Jumel Mansion: A Documentary History* (Rocky Hill, New Jersey: Heritage Studies, Inc., 1995), 123.

120. *Military Journal,* 271–77.

121. When von Steuben arrived at Valley Forge in 1778 he commented about this situation, "The army was looked upon as nursery for servants, and every one deemed it his right to have a valet; several thousand soldiers were employed in this way." Kapp, *Life of Frederick William Von Steuben,* 116.

122. *Writings of Washington,* 23:450–52.

123. Mayer, *Belonging to the Army,* 171. Historians are just beginning to realize the importance of the use of soldiers as servants during the Revolutionary War. The Founding Fathers left us few clues on the subject and Ms. Mayer's book is the best study available to date on the practice of using common soldiers as personal servants.

124. John Womack Wright, *Some Notes on the Continental Army* (Cornwallville, New York: Hope Farm, 1962), 10.

125. *Travels in North-America,* 1:124.

126. *Writings of Washington,* 22:284 n. While it is possible that Washington might have discussed some specific matter with Scammell before or after dinner, it is likely that the general talked with him about army business at dinner. Scammell was a Harvard graduate with extensive combat and administrative experience. The dinner meal was a perfect opportunity to have an informal discussion with him concerning army business.

127. "Extracts from the Diary of Dr. James Clitherall, 1776," *The Pennsylvania Magazine of History and Biography,* 22, no. 4 (1898): 473.

128. For a description of the dinner meal at Washington's headquarters see *Travels in North-America,* 1:125–28.
129. One letter in the handwriting of Tench Tilghman illustrates how long the workday could be during the war. The letter is dated "Head Quarters Middle Brook [New Jersey] 22d June 1777 11 OClock P.M." It was written at Washington's direction and described recent military events to John Hancock, the president of the Continental Congress. The letter ends as follows, "His Excellency having been on Horseback from 3 OClock in the Morning and much fatigued, rather than disturb his Rest, I take the Liberty to close the Letter without his Name. I am Sir with the greatest Respect Yr most obt Tench Tilghman." See *The Papers of Washington,* 10:104–5.
130. S. A. Harrison, *Memoirs of Lieutenant Colonel Tench Tilghman* (Albany, New York: J. Munsell, 1876), 143.
131. *Papers of Washington,* Revolutionary War Series, 6:393–400.
132. The closest council of war prior to the date of Washington's letter to Congress took place on September 12. According to the notes taken at the meeting by Reed, the subjects discussed were the disposition of the troops and the number of men who should garrison Fort Washington. See ibid., 6:288–89.
133. *Travels in North-America,* 1:125–28. While General Washington spent quiet evenings talking with his aides and writing letters to Martha on the upper end of Manhattan Island, nightlife was much more exciting at Gen. Sir William Howe's headquarters on the lower end of the island. Howe kept an American mistress named Elizabeth Loring. She was a sensuous young woman described as a flashing beauty. Howe met her when he arrived in Boston early in the war and became infatuated with her. He quickly dispensed with her greedy husband by giving him a lucrative position, and openly took up with the man's wife as his mistress. Howe loved to drink, play cards, and talk with his army cronies late into the night with the beautiful Mrs. Loring at his side. The rebels celebrated the amour with various ditties including,

> Sir William he, snug as a flea,
> Lay all this time a snoring,
> Nor dream'd of harm as he lay warm,
> In bed with Mrs. Loring.

Sir Henry Clinton replaced Howe as commander in chief in 1778 bringing his own mistress to headquarters. Clinton apparently distrusted everyone, and seemed to be a lonely, neurotic widower. He hired an Irish housekeeper named Mrs. Mary Baddeley. The daughter of an Irish country gentleman, after running off with a carpenter, she came with him to America when he joined the army. Mrs. Baddeley presided over Clinton's teeming household for years, keeping a sharp eye on thirty servants and local tradesmen. "From her care alone" Clinton wrote "I saved at least ten thousand dollars." Clinton became infatuated with her and wanted her as his mistress. He appointed her husband a captain in the army and he, in turn, encouraged his wife in her liaison with Clinton. According to Sir Henry, "Though she admitted me to certain liberties, I never could prevail on her to grant the last—until resentment did what a warm attachment could not effect. She detected her husband in an intrigue with a common strumpet. She came to me directly and surrendered."

Captain Baddeley conveniently died of a camp fever later in the war. Mary Badde-ley remained Clinton's mistress until his death, bearing him many children. For information concerning Clinton's association with Mary Baddeley see William B. Willcox, *Portrait of a General: Sir Henry Clinton in the War of Independence* (New York: Alfred A. Knopf, 1962), 60, 174, 198–99, 454.

134. Governor Cooke of Rhode Island to Washington, December 11, 1775, in Force, *American Archives,* ser. 4, 4:235.

135. Ibid., ser. 5, 3:1065.

136. This letter is dated Paris, May 31, 1776. William James Morgan, ed. *Naval Documents of the American Revolution (*Washington D.C.: U.S. Government Printing Office, 1964–), 6:397–98.

137. This letter is dated Versailles, June 1, 1776. See ibid., 6:399–400.

138. *Papers of Washington,* 5:552–53.

139. *Journals of Congress,* 6:869–70. A brevet is a military term meaning a commission in an officer rank without pay.

140. Fitzpatrick, *Spirit of the Revolution,* 72.

141. Johnston, *Battle of Harlem Heights,* 219. Johnston identifies the author of the letter as Capt. Francis Hutcheson, assistant secretary to Sir William Howe. Hutcheson said, "General Washington town Residence is General Robertsons, on the top of which they display the Continental Colours."

142. *Papers of Washington,* 6:592–93.

143. Johnston, *Campaign of 1776 around New York and Brooklyn,* 270–71. Tilghman's reference to sinking ships was a wasteful American scheme to blockade the Hudson River with sunken ships on the Fort Washington—Fort Lee defense line.

144. Baker, *Itinerary of General Washington,* 53.

145. *Papers of Washington,* 7:80.

146. Ibid., 7:135.

147. There was no known effort organized to gather boats for the evacuation of the Fort Washington garrison even if there had been time to get them off Manhattan Island. Washington did not repeat this mistake and arranged for boats to be waiting to take his army across the Delaware River when he was retreating across New Jersey a few weeks later.

148. *Lee Papers,* 2:284.

149. Ibid., 2:283. Lee had written this letter to Reed before Lee received a dispatch from General Washington that Fort Washington had surrendered. Lee's estimate of 1,400 American troops at Fort Washington was inaccurate and far below the actual number.

The loss of Fort Washington proved to be Washington's worst defeat in the war. Embarrassed by the episode, he wrote historian William Gordon two years after the end of the conflict, claiming that he had ordered General Greene to evacuate Fort Washington on November 8, 1776, before the British surrounded it. Washington wrote Greene on November 8 about Fort Washington but never gave his lieutenant a direct order to abandon Fort Washington. See Washington to Gordon in *Writings of Washington,* 28:97–98 and Washington to Greene, in the same source, 6:257–58.

150. Heath, *Memoirs of Major-General Heath,* 88.

151. Force, *American Archives,* 5th ser. 3:779.

152. Ibid., 3:780.

153. Ibid., 3:781.

154. *Lee Papers,* 1:207

155. John Alden, *General Charles Lee* (Baton Rouge: Louisiana State University Press, 1955), 77.

156. *Papers of Washington,* 7:193–95.

157. Force, *American Archives,* 5th Ser. 3:793.

158. *Correspondence of Webb,* 1:172.

159. *Lee Papers,* 2:305–6.

160. Force, *American Archives,* 5th Ser. 3:921.

161. *Correspondence of Webb,* 1:172.

162. *The History of the Civil War in America by an Officer of the Army* (London: T. Payne and Son, 1780), 222.

163. Historian James Thomas Flexner commented that Lee had a propensity for sleeping in strange places (and with strange women). He had spent the night of December 12 some distance from his army in an inn kept by a widow. The next morning, he was lounging in his shirtsleeves when British light horse came galloping up. James Thomas Flexner, *George Washington in the American Revolution* (Boston: Little, Brown, 1967), 167.

164. William S. Stryker, *Battles of Trenton and Princeton* (Boston: Houghton, Mifflin, 1898), 107.

165. Robert C. Powell, ed., *A Biographical Sketch of Col. Leven Powell* (Alexandria, Virginia: 1877), 41–43.

166. Harrison, *Memoir of Lieutenant Colonel Tench Tilghman,* 148–49.

167. Ramsay, *History of the American Revolution,* 1:415.

168. The three British regiments at Princeton were the 17th, 40th, and 55th. The light dragoons were several troops of the 16th Light Dragoons. There was an important distinction between dragoons and light dragoons. Dragoons were mounted infantry that rode into battle on horseback and dismounted to fight. No dragoon regiments took part in the American Revolution. The official horse troops employed by both the Continental and British Armies were called light dragoons. They were trained to fight from horseback and their primary weapon was a long saber. Such mounted units were mostly employed for reconnaissance, communications, escort duty, and raiding.

169. George Washington Parke Custis, *Recollections and Private Memoirs of Washington, by His Adopted Son, George Washington Parke Custis: With a Memoir of the Author, by His Daughter, and Illustrative and Explanatory Notes, by Benson J. Lossing* (New York: Derby & Jackson, 1860), 191–92 (hereafter cited as *Recollections and Private Memoirs of Washington*). Fitzgerald told the story to Custis when he was an old man. There is an earlier detailed account of Washington riding in front of his troops during the battle of Princeton in Hannah Adams, *A Summary History of New England* (Dedham, Massachusetts: H. Mann and J. H. Adams, 1799), 374. The Hannah Adams narrative does not include Fitzgerald's account of the incident. There is also a delightful telling of this story in Irving, *Life of Washington,* 2:509. Douglas Southall Freeman, Washington's greatest biographer points out that Custis was prone to be theatrical but there probably was some foundation to the story. (See Freeman, *George Washington,* 4:354 n. 141). George Washington Parke Custis referred to himself as George Washington's adopted son. He was actually the son of John Parke Custis who was Martha Washington's son from her first marriage and not related or adopted by George Washington as his son. Histo-

rian Douglas Southall Freeman states that, "Stories of Washington's immediate adoption of the two younger children of Custis as his own are patently apocryphal." See Freeman, *George Washington,* 5:402.

George and Martha Washington did help raise George Washington Parke Custis who was plenty of trouble for them. As an example, they enrolled him at Princeton University and received a letter from the Rev. Samuel Stanhope Smith, president of the college, that contained disquieting reports on the boy. The exact nature of his misconduct at Princeton is not recorded, but Parke Custis wrote General Washington from college about the late contest with the passions and promised to reform. Washington wrote of his almost unconquerable disposition to indolence in everything that did not tend to his amusements. See Freeman, George Washington, 7:455.

170. There are eyewitness accounts that Washington was in the midst of the fighting at Princeton. Ens. Robert Beale of the 5th Virginia Regiment said "that the charge was made by Washington in person who carried the men." Maj. Appolos Morris wrote, "Washington was exposed to both firings for sometime." See William Dwyer, *The Day is Ours* (New York: Viking, 1983), 347–48.

171. *Recollections and Private Memoirs of Washington,* 222–23. There is another eyewitness account of Washington emerging unharmed at the battle of Monmouth. This account says, "The flight was conducted by our Great good General in person who was the whole time exposed to the fire of the artillery wch. was well served on both sides and did much Execution." See manuscript letter, Col. Otho H. Williams to Dr. Phil Thomas, June 29, 1778, in the Gen. Otho Williams Papers, Maryland Historical Society, copy from Michael Adelberg December 5, 1994, transcribed February 1995 by Garry Wheeler Stone.

172. John C. Miller, *Alexander Hamilton: Portrait in Paradox* (New York: Harper & Brothers, 1959), 2. There is conflict among historians whether Hamilton was or was not accepted to the College of New Jersey. Legend has it that Hamilton had a grudge against Princeton because the trustees had turned down his application because they would not agree to let him study independently, advancing from class to class at his own pace. King's College was more flexible and allowed Hamilton greater independence in his course of study.

173. Richard A. Harrison, *Princetonians, 1769–1775: A Biographical Dictionary* (Princeton, New Jersey: Princeton University Press, 1980), 500–501. The earliest account of this story is in Benson J. Lossing, *The Pictorial Field-Book of the Revolution* (New York: Harper & Brothers, 1860), 2:30. Dr. Hugh Mercer was a prominent American patriot and one of Washington's best officers. He also died heavily in debt to Washington. Mercer purchased Washington's Ferry Farm, located near Fredericksburg, Virginia, just before the start of the war. He agreed to pay for the property in five large and equal yearly installments. Mercer's debt was apparently paid by the executors of his estate.

174. *Correspondence of Webb,* 1:178–79.

CHAPTER 4

1. *Proceedings of the New Jersey Historical Society* 51, no. 3 (July 1933): 252; title changed in 1967 to *New Jersey History.*

2. Irving, *Life of Washington,* 3:2.

3. Humphreys, *An Essay on the Life of the Honorable Major-General Israel Putnam,* 154–55.

4. *Writings of Washington,* 6:495–96. These sixteen regiments are known as the Sixteen Additional Regiments.

5. *Papers of Washington,* 8:177–78.

6. Ibid., 9:35.

7. Ibid., 9:237.

8. Ibid., 9:299

9. Ibid., 7:456.

10. Congress resolved on January 1, 1777, "That a horse, properly caparisoned for service, be presented to Lieutenant Colonel Baylor, and that he be recommended to General Washington to be appointed to the command of a regiment of light horse [light dragoons]; and that he rank with Colonel Sheldon [Elisha Sheldon from Connecticut who was appointed Colonel, 2nd Continental Dragoons, on December 12, 1776] lately appointed to the same command, saving to Colonel Sheldon any preference which arises from the senior date of his commission." See *Journals of Congress,* 7:7. Congress had fled Philadelphia and was meeting in Baltimore at the time.

11. Washington to Baylor, March 4, 1778, *Writings of Washington,* 11:22. In this letter the general gave his former aide instructions concerning the purchase of horses for all the cavalry regiments in the Continental Army.

12. D. Bennett Mazur and Wayne Daniels, *Baylor's Dragoons Massacre, September 28, 1778: Excavation of the Burial Site* (pamphlet, 1968), 3, 9.

13. Kevin Wright, "Overkill: Revolutionary War Reminiscences of River Vale," *Bergen's Attic* (New Jersey, Bergen County Historical Society), 21, no. 2 (June 1994).

14. Irving, *Life of Washington,* 3:473.

15. Ibid., 3:472.

16. *Military Journal,* 150.

17. It is believed that the Bergen County Militia feared that the British would return and hastily buried Baylor's dead men in nearby abandoned tanning vats. The skeletal remains of six men were discovered in a 1967 excavation of the site along with buttons marked "BD" (Baylor's Dragoons). See Mazur and Daniels, *Baylor's Dragoons Massacre,* 10, 19.

18. Thomas Jones, *History of New York during the Revolutionary War* (New York: Printed for the New York Historical Society, 1879), 1:286. Accounts vary regarding the number of men in Baylor's regiment as well as the number killed and wounded in the British attack. One report is from an American surgeon named David Griffith who reported a month after the massacre that Baylor's regiment included 104 privates "out of which Eleven were killed outright, 17 were left behind wounded, 4 of whom are since dead, 33 are Prisoners in N York, 8 of them wounded, the rest made their escape." See Wright, "Overkill: Revolutionary War Reminiscences of River Vale," 3.

19. Moylan was given command of the 4th Continental Light Dragoon Regiment that was authorized by Congress on January 5, 1777. Moylan raised his regiment during the spring of 1777, recruiting his troopers from the Philadelphia and Baltimore area. His regiment was also called "Moylan's Horse."

20. Webb's Additional Regiment was reorganized in 1780 as the 9th Connecticut Regiment as an administrative move to help Connecticut satisfy its quota of troops.

21. Webb, *Reminiscences of Gen'l Samuel B. Webb* (New York: Globe Stationary and Printing, 1882). This book appears to be the earliest reference to Webb's unit being called the "Decoy Regiment" and purposely wearing enemy uniforms to apprehend spies. This story is a myth without substance. The wearing of British uniforms, or portions of British uniforms, was not uncommon and a necessary expedient for the improvised Continental Army. Attempts to dye captured scarlet uniforms were usually unsuccessful and resulted in bizarre, ugly colors.

There was one occasion when Washington suggested using Webb's scarlet uniformed troops to masquerade as British soldiers. The circumstance was a plot to kidnap British general Henry Clinton from the isolated New York City mansion that he was using as his headquarters. See Washington's letter to Brig. Gen. Samuel Holden Parsons dated March 5, 1778, which describes the scheme, *Writings of Washington,* 11:30. It was in a follow-up letter to Parsons, dated March 8, 1778, that Washington suggested using Webb's regiment to snag Clinton, "I will add a thought which has occurred since the writing of it [letter of March 8]; and which if the Scheme is practicable at all may add not a little to the success namely to let the Officers and Soldiers imployed in the enterprize be dressed in red and much in the taste of the British Soldiery. Webb's Regiment will afford these dresses." See *Writings of Washington* 11:51.

The author of this book, J. (James) Watson Webb, was one of Colonel Webb's sons. James was born in 1802 in Claverack, New York. After serving as an army officer, James became the owner and editor of a New York City newspaper. He was appointed minister to Brazil by President Lincoln in 1861 and served in that post until 1869. James also received notoriety when he fought a duel in Delaware in 1842. He was indicted by the grand jury of New York for leaving the state with the intention of giving or receiving a challenge. Webb pleaded guilty to the charge and was sentenced to two years imprisonment, but was immediately pardoned by the governor.

22. Q.M. Gen. Thomas Mifflin issued Webb the following order, "Headquarters, June 28, 1777, Col. Webb has his Excellency's, General Washington's Orders, to appropriate so much of the Scarlet Clothing, taken from the Enemy at Sea, as will be sufficient to cloath one Regiment."

23. *Papers of Washington,* 8:25. Washington included a comment in this letter that troubled me when I first read it. It reads, "If they can write a good Letter—write quick—are methodical, & diligent, it is all I expect to find in my Aids." This statement implies that Washington used his aides as clerks. However, it is important to understand the he made this comment in a letter dated January 9, 1777, just weeks after he accidentally uncovered one piece of the unflattering correspondence about him that was passing between Joseph Reed and Gen. Charles Lee. Washington was probably venting his frustrations with Reed's betrayal and decided he would be happier at that moment if he had a more distant relationship with his aides.

24. Ibid., 8:111.

25. *Writings of Washington,* 7:161.

26. Dumas Malone, *Jefferson the Virginian* (Boston: Little, Brown, 1948), 154. Malone says that Jefferson admitted to the charges in a letter to Robert Smith dated July 1, 1805.

27. John Walker is sometimes incorrectly mentioned as being from North Carolina. Francis Heitman makes this error in his usually accurate reference book listing officers who served in the Continental Army during the Revolutionary War. See Heitman, *Register of Officers of the Continental Army,* 565.
28. H. R. McIlwaine, ed., *Journals of the Council of the State of Virginia* (Richmond: 1931), 1:315.
29. *Papers of Washington,* 8:367.
30. Ibid., 8:437. Note that Washington used the unusual word marplot in his letter. It means a stupid, officious meddler, derived from a character named Marplot in a play called *The Busy Body* written by Susannah Centlivre (1669–1723).
31. Ibid., 8:474, 478. John Fitzpatrick identifies Walker's handwriting in letters written from headquarters later in 1777 and into 1778. See, for example, Washington to Hancock dated October 3, 1777, in *Writings of Washington,* 9:298–99. However, the editors of *Papers of George Washington* identify the handwriting of other aides in the late 1777–78 letters Fitzpatrick attributes to Walker. *Papers of Washington,* 8:80–81 n.
32. The *Journals of the Council of the State of Virginia* include the following resolution dated September 8, 1777, "Captain William Pierce was this Day employed by the Governor, with the advice of Council, to proceed to the American Camp, in order to perform Certain Services for the Safety of the State similar to what Mr. John Walker was employed in." See McIlwaine, *Journals of the Council of the State of Virginia,* 1:485. Washington wrote Governor Patrick Henry of Virginia on October 3, 1777, "I shall cheerfully communicate every piece of intelligence, particularly interesting to the State of Virginia, to Capt. Peirce, and any other of such Nature, that may be made public without injuring the Service. I therefore hope, that thro' him, you will be informed of every material occurrence in the Army." See *Writings of Washington,* 9:302. Washington apparently tolerated this annoying eavesdropping at headquarters as part of his policy of cooperating with the civilian authorities.
33. Heitman, *Register of Officers of the Continental Army,* 441.
34. *Journals of Congress,* 10:9.
35. H. R. McIlwaine, ed., *Official Letters of the Governors of the State of Virginia* (Richmond: Virginia State Library, 1926), 1:290, 294.
36. *Letter of Delegates,* 16:xxiv.
37. Boyd, *Papers of Jefferson,* 4:400.
38. Ibid., 5:108.
39. Ibid., 9:251. John Walker's daughter and only child was named Mildred. She married Francis Kinloch.
40. Kathryn Allamong Jacob and Bruce A. Ragsdale, ed., *Biographical Directory of the United States Congress, 1774–1989* (Washington, D.C.: U.S. Government Printing Office, 1989), 1996.
41. Malone, *Jefferson the Virginian,* 449.
42. Ibid,.
43. Ibid., 155.
44. Ibid., 451.
45. *Hamilton Papers,* 1:195. The *Hamilton Papers* contain only a portion of Washington's letter to Harrison with footnotes. The complete text with footnotes appears in *Papers of Washington,* 8:116–17. The unabridged text reveals that Harrison was ill

at the time and apparently convalescing in the Philadelphia area, "I am exceeding glad to hear you are getting better of your complaints, I would not wish you to come out too soon—that may only occasion a relapse which may add length of time to your confinement." Hamilton must have been in the Philadelphia area at the same time.

46. Custis, *Recollections and Private Memoirs of Washington,* 344–45. Custis promoted himself as George Washington's adopted son. Next to Mason Locke Weems, who invented the story of George Washington chopping down the cherry tree and praying in the snow at Valley Forge, George Washington Parke Custis gets the credit for creating more dubious and undocumented stories about George Washington than any other writer to date.

47. Historian Benson J. Lossing (probably best known for his *Pictorial Field-Book of the Revolution*) provided explanatory notes in Custis's *Recollections and Private Memoirs of Washington.* Lossing acknowledges Gen. Nathanael Greene's interest in Hamilton in one of his footnotes for which there is no supporting documentation offered. According to Lossing's footnote, "In March, 1776, Hamilton became captain of artillery in a New York regiment. In the summer following, General Greene's attention was one day arrested, as he was crossing 'The Fields' [now City Hall park] by the able movements of a company of artillery, commanded by a mere youth. It was Hamilton. Greene conversed with him a few minutes, and discovered evidence of extraordinary ability. He invited him to his quarters, cultivated his acquaintance, and introduced him afterward to Washington." (See Custis, *Recollections and Private Memoirs of Washington,* 342 n.) There is no mention of Hamilton during this period in Showman and Conrad, *The Papers of General Nathanael Greene.* Hamilton's biographer Broadus Mitchell gives a good summary of the situations in which Hamilton may have come to Washington's attention. (See Mitchell, *Alexander Hamilton: Youth to Maturity,* 104).

48. Miller, *Alexander Hamilton: Portrait in Paradox,* 21.

49. *Graydon: Memoirs of His Own Time,* 149.

50. Ibid., 275–76.

51. Some historians give Hamilton's year of birth as 1757. Much of the confusion over the year arises because he apparently lied about his age when he arrived in America. He made himself younger so he would not be embarrassed to enroll in a school where the other students were younger than him.

52. Lavien's name has also appeared in history books as Levin, LaVin, Levine, Lavine, and Le Vin, leading some in Nevis to conclude that he was Jewish. It's possible because seventy-five Jews lived in Nevis in the early 1770s. Rachel Faucett was born in 1729 in St. Croix. She was sixteen when she married Lavien and already had the reputation of being a prostitute. The marriage failed and Lavien brought action against Rachel for adultery. She was sentenced to jail in St. Croix and detained in a dungeon. Following her release, she fled to Nevis where she met James Hamilton. Rachel died in 1768, and James Hamilton died in 1799. The often repeated story that George Washington was Alexander Hamilton's father has been dismissed as nonsense by all reputable historians.

53. Jacob Ernest Cooke, *Alexander Hamilton* (New York: Charles Scribner's Sons, 1982), 1.

54. Francis Barber was a Greek scholar. He served as a Continental officer during the Revolution. It was perhaps due to Hamilton's intervention that Barber got to lead

a battalion under his former pupil's command in the celebrated nighttime assault against British-held Redoubt Number 10 at the 1781 siege of Yorktown.

55. King's College was founded in 1760. It occupied a plot in the colonial city of New York bordered by today's West Broadway, Murray, Church, and Barclay Streets. The campus was moved to 49th Street and Madison Avenue in 1857, and to its present site in the Morningside Heights section of upper Manhattan forty years later. The college building was used as a hospital during the American Revolution.

56. Hamilton is said to have studied medicine at King's College under the learned doctors Samuel Clossey and James Magrath. See Michael J. O'Brien, *Hercules Mulligan: Confidential Correspondent of General Washington* (New York: P. J. Kennedy & Sons, 1937), 45. Hamilton lived in Mulligan's house when he first arrived in New York City in 1772.

57. Custis, *Recollections and Private Memoirs of Washington,* 342; also Flexner, *Young Hamilton,* 77.

58. Flexner, *Young Hamilton,* 77.

59. Ibid., 147.

60. *Hamilton Papers,* 2:186. Duane included this comment in a letter he wrote Hamilton on September 23, 1779.

61. Flexner, *Young Hamilton,* 147. Flexner gives his source for this story as Harrison, *Memoir of Lieutenant Colonel Tench Tilghman,* 153.

62. Hamilton seems to have been the French language expert on Washington's staff at the time. Tilghman apparently translated a few letters for Washington from French to English. See, for example, *Washington Papers,* 5:552–53. There are a sufficient number of translations in Tilghman's writing to indicate that he knew French as opposed to making copies of letters that someone else had translated. Tilghman may have gained a working knowledge of the language at college. He graduated in 1761 from the College and Academy of Philadelphia (now the University of Pennsylvania). See Committee of the Society of the Alumni, *University of Pennsylvania: Biographical Catalogue of the Matriculates of the College* (Philadelphia, 1894), xxi, which lists William Creamer as a professor of French and German languages. Creamer was appointed in 1754 and retired in 1775. Whether or not Tilghman actually received instruction in French at college is another matter. Another possibility is that, as a merchant prior to the war, Tilghman may have learned some French particularly if he was doing business with any of the French islands in the West Indies. Latin and Greek formed the backbone of education at the time, but modern languages were not entirely neglected. Washington, for example, wrote his stepson Jacky Custis's tutor Jonathan Boucher in 1771, "To be acquainted with the French Tongue, is become a part of polite Education; and to a Man who has any idea of mixing in a large Circle, absolutely necessary." See *Papers of Washington,* Colonial Series, 8:425–26.

63. See Jonathan R. Dull, *A Diplomatic History of the American Revolution* (New Haven: Yale University Press, 1985), 63, 101. Deane was the stepfather of Washington's aide Samuel B. Webb.

64. Letter, William Arthur Oldridge Collection, Manuscript Division Library of Congress. Mamaroneck is a town in Westchester County along Long Island Sound. "Major Green" is John Green of the 1st Virginia Regiment. This officer is listed as being wounded at Mamaroneck on October 21, 1776. See Heitman, *Register of Officers of the Continental Army,* 260.

65. Force, *American Archives,* ser. 5, 3:740.
66. *Hamilton Papers,* 1:209.
67. Ibid., 1:241. Hamilton's report is dated "Head Quarters Morris Town, April 28, 1777."
68. *Writings of Washington,* 7:280.
69. The reference to Dalston appears in Brother Ronald E. Heaton, *Masonic Membership of Washington's Aides and Military Secretaries,* 17. The Drafton reference is from Kahler, "Gentlemen of the Family," 149.
70. Heitman, *Register of Officers of the Continental Army,* 387.
71. *Hamilton Papers,* 3:70.
72. Irving, *Life of Washington,* 3:5. Also see *Hamilton Papers,* 1:593.
73. *Proceedings of the New Jersey Historical Society* 51, no. 3 (July 1933): 250–53.
74. Eugene Parker Chase, ed., *Our Revolutionary Forefathers: The Letters of François, Marquis de Barbe-Marbois* (New York: Duffield, 1929), 114. It was popular in the colonial period to pass around skin-covered balls. Rounders and baseball existed at the time, but apparently with no formalized rules. It is believed that Washington and his aides were throwing around a ball for exercise and not playing some kind of game. The ball's size and shape are unknown.
75. *Graydon: Memoirs of His Own Time,* 277.
76. Thomas Fleming, *Duel: Alexander Hamilton, Aaron Burr, and the Future of America* (New York: Basic Books, 1999), 16.
77. *Hamilton Papers,* 1:225–26.
78. Mrs. Mercy [Otis] Warren, *History of the Rise, Progress, and Termination of the American Revolution* (Boston: E. Larkin: 1805), 1:370. Mrs. Warren wrote one of the first complete histories of the American Revolution. Her history was also one of the first books to be authored by an American woman. As an ardent patriot and the wife of the Revolutionary War governor of Massachusetts, she gained an introduction to many of the great American political and military leaders of the war. Early histories of the Revolution, like Mrs. Warren's, are overlooked by modern historians. However, I find them wonderful to read because the authors were frequently passionate eyewitnesses to the rebellion. They are also surprisingly accurate because they substituted scholarly research with their own recollections and interviews with the men and women who participated in the war.
79. *Papers of Washington,* 9:542.
80. Ibid., 9:606–7.
81. *Writings of Washington,* 8:247.
82. *Life of Esther De Berdt: Afterwards Esther Reed,* 294.
83. It is believed that Joseph Reed wrote his wife's epitaph, which reads:

In memory of Esther, the beloved wife of Joseph Reed,
President of this State, who departed this life
On the 18th of September, A.D. 1780, aged 34 years.
If to have the cup of temporal blessings dashed
In the period and station of life in which blessings
May be best enjoyed, demands our sorrow, drop a tear, and
Think how slender is that thread on which the joys
And hopes of life depend.

84. After reading their 1777 exchange of letters, historian Douglas Southall Freeman concluded that Washington forgave Reed and the two men resumed their former friendship. Freeman points out that in 1777 Washington was in favor of making Reed the "General of Horse." See Freeman, *George Washington,* 4:429 n. While Freeman is correct that Washington seems to have forgiven Reed, he never confided in him again or resumed their close friendship. Washington's correspondence with Reed, for instance, ceased at the end of the war.
85. Warren, *History of the Rise, Progress, and Termination of the American Revolution,* 1:370–73.
86. *Hamilton Papers,* 1:321. Hamilton's report is dated "Head Quarters Wilmington [Delaware], September 1st, 1777."
87. *Writings of Washington,* 9:22.
88. Ibid., 9:189.
89. See Boatner, *Encyclopedia of the American Revolution,* 869, and Edward McCrady, *The History of South Carolina in the Revolution, 1775–1780,* 319. Boatner's encyclopedia, originally published in 1966, remains one of the most popular reference books about the American Revolution. It is surprising to see that he incorrectly identifies Pinckney as one of Washington's aides-de-camp. A later reference work, Richard L. Blanco, ed., *The American Revolution, 1775–1783: An Encyclopedia,* 2:1305 has an article about Pinckney, which includes the same mistake, "By September [1777] he became a colonel and an aide to Washington."
90. There was no higher education available in the thirteen colonies south of William and Mary College located in Williamsburg, Virginia. As a result wealthy South Carolinians tended to send their young men to Europe, especially to Britain for advanced education. Charles Cotesworth Pinckney and John Laurens were typical recipients of the style of education given wealthy young South Carolinians.
91. John Laurens to Henry Laurens, January 23, 1778, *Laurens Papers,* 12:330.
92. The children of Henry and Eleanor Laurens in order of their birth dates were Henry (1753–58), John (1754–82), Eleanor, whose nickname was "Nelly" (1755–64), Martha nicknamed "Patsy" (1759–1811), Henry nicknamed "Harry" (1763–1821), James nicknamed "Jemmy" (1765–75), and Mary Eleanor nicknamed "Polly" (1770–94).
93. Gregory D. Massey, *John Laurens and the American Revolution* (Columbia: University of South Carolina Press, 2000), 21.
94. *Laurens Papers,* 11:228. Henry Laurens was an early and ardent American patriot. He was elected to the South Carolina provincial congress in 1775 and was later named its president. Laurens was also president of the colony's Council of Safety. When South Carolina's royal governor fled the colony, Laurens became South Carolina's chief executive based on his presidency of the Council of Safety. His participation in the early period of the American Revolution included helping to draft South Carolina's constitution (February 1776) and serving as a delegate to the Continental Congress.

Henry Laurens must have realized that his letters to John, filled with news about the war and patriotic remarks, only increased his son's desire to return home and join the army. For example, Henry Laurens wrote his son a letter on December 6, 1775, which included this patriotic passage, "we Shall rise again & although half naked, we Shall rise in the Splender of Freedom, who would not Submit to temporary Losses & inconveniences, upon a well founded prospect of recovering his Liberty & transmitting that inestimable Blessing to posterity." See *Laurens Papers,* 10:544.

95. Letter from George W. P. Custis to John S. Littell, Esq., dated: "Arlington House (a mansion in today's Arlington National Cemetery in Virginia near Washington D.C.), February 14, 1846." Published in *Graydon: Memoirs of His Own Time,* 472–76.

96. Flexner, *Young Hamilton,* 257. Flexner cites his sources for this quote in his footnotes as Sara Bertha Townsend, *An American Soldier: The Life of John Laurens* (Raleigh, N.C.: Edwards & Broughton, 1958) and David Duncan Wallace, *The Life of Henry Laurens: With a Sketch of the Life of Lieutenant Colonel John Laurens* (New York: G. P. Putnam's Sons, 1915).

97. Massey, *John Laurens and the American Revolution,* 71.

98. Heitman, *Register of Officers of the Continental Army,* 586.

99. *Papers of Washington,* 10:509.

100. *Letters of Delegates,* 7:469.

101. *Laurens Papers,* 11:428. Henry Laurens wrote this letter in Philadelphia to his business associate and friend John Lewis Gervais in Charleston, South Carolina. Gervais (1741–95) was of French Huguenot descent. He looked after Laurens's property interests in South Carolina while Laurens served in the Continental Congress. For information about Gervais see ibid., 4:331–32 n.

102. *Writings of Washington,* 9:60–61.

103. *Journals of Congress,* 8:592–93.

104. The General Orders for December 4, 1777, include, "Major General, The Marquis La Fayette is to take the command of the division lately commanded by General Stephen." See *Writings of Washington,* 10:138.

105. As a major general, Lafayette was authorized two aides-de-camp ranked as majors. In 1777, his aides were Jean-Joseph Sourbader de Gimat and Edmond Brice. Gimat was a French officer who accompanied Lafayette to America. In his memoir, Lafayette mentions Gimat as being his aide-de-camp at the battle of Brandywine (September 11, 1777). His other aide was Edmond Brice who is sometimes incorrectly identified as John Bryce or Edmond Price. He is incorrectly referred to as John Brice, for instance, in Heitman, *Register of Officers of the Continental Army,* 120. Heitman said Brice was from Pennsylvania, a captain lieutenant in the 4th Continental Artillery in March 1777 and appointed as a major and aide-de-camp to Lafayette in 1778. The facts are that Brice went to Europe to study painting and returned to America with Lafayette. He seems to have had no military experience prior to joining Lafayette's military family. We get a glimpse of his character from a letter Silas Deane wrote from Paris on March 16, 1777, to John Hancock. Deane said, "I send you for your entertainment, by Mr. Brice, a young gentleman of Maryland, whom I think deserving your notice, as a worthy sensible young man." See Stanley J. Idzerda, ed., *Lafayette in the Age of the American Revolution* (Ithaca: Cornell University Press, 1977–83), 1:33–4.

Another point of interest is that my reader will notice that the rank of "captain lieutenant" is mentioned in the above footnote. It technically meant a rank between a lieutenant and a captain. The term tended to be used by the artillery corps and sometimes honored an officer with special skills.

106. Idzerda, *Lafayette in the Age of the American Revolution,* 1:92, 101 n.

107. *Laurens Papers,* 11:547. Henry Laurens first met Lafayette in Bristol, Pennsylvania, on September 19, 1777. Lafayette was wounded in the battle of Brandywine and was en route to Bethlehem, Pennsylvania, to convalesce. Laurens was in Bristol after evacuating Philadelphia, which was in imminent danger of being captured by the British. Laurens and Lafayette traveled together, during which time they became friends. See Massey, *John Laurens and the American Revolution,* 75.

108. *Laurens Papers,* 12:31. A general engagement seemed likely on September 16 until the heavens interceded. The skirmishing that took place that day was named "the Battle of Clouds."

109. *Hamilton Papers,* 1:326.

110. The Journals of Congress for Thursday, September 18, 1777, read, "Adjourned to 10 o'Clock to Morrow. During the adjournment, the president [John Hancock] received a letter from Colonel Hamilton, one of General Washington's aides, which intimated the necessity of Congress removing immediately from Philadelphia: Whereupon, the members left the city, and agreeable to the resolve of the 14, repaired to Lancaster [a town in central Pennsylvania]." See *Journals of Congress,* 8:754.

111. John Adams Diary, September 19, 1777, in *Letters of Delegates,* 8:3.

112. Thomas J. McGuire, *Battle of Paoli* (Mechanicsburg, Pennsylvania: Stackpole Books, 2000), 60.

113. *Letters of Delegates,* 8:8.

114. *Travels in North-America,* 1:139.

115. *Graydon: Memoirs of His Own Time,* 473.

116. Custis, *Recollections and Private Memoirs of Washington,* 199. This was the same young man who had returned from Europe with John Laurens. After reaching America, White became a volunteer aide-de-camp to Gen. John Sullivan. White was mortally wounded trying to set fire to the Cliveden mansion (October 4, 1777) and died from his wounds on October 10. See Heitman, *Register of Officers of the Continental Army,* 586. Benson Lossing tells a story about White in his notes to Custis, *Recollections and Private Memoirs of Washington,* 199 n. Lossing said he visited Cliveden in the autumn of 1848 when the daughter of Judge Chew was still living there.

> She informed me that, several years after the war, and soon after her marriage, while a young man named White was visiting her father-in-law, the old gentleman, in relating incidents of the battle in Germantown, mentioned the circumstances that a Major White, an aid of General Sullivan, and one of the handsomest men in the continental army, attempted to fire the house for the purpose of driving out the British. He ran under a window with a fire-brand, where shots from the building could not touch him. He was discovered, and a British soldier, running into the cellar, shot him dead from a basement window. The young man was much affected by the recital, and said to Judge Chew, "That Major White, sir, was my father."

117. This description was in an anonymously written letter to George Clinton, October 5, 1777. See *Public Papers of George Clinton: First Governor of New York* (Albany, New York: 1899–1914), 2:372–73.
118. John Laurens to Henry Laurens, November 6, 1777, in *Laurens Papers,* 12:31.
119. Ibid., 11:548–49.
120. *Writings of Washington,* 9:313.
121. *Army Correspondence of Colonel John Laurens,* 93.
122. *Journals of Congress,* 5:418.
123. Ibid., 11:704.
124. Ibid., 13:388.
125. *Hamilton Papers,* 2:35–36.
126. Joseph Webb, Jr., (1749–1815) was a member of the Connecticut general assembly and a colonel in the Connecticut militia. He supplied General Washington with leather boots from his shoe manufactory during the war.
127. Worthington Chauncey Ford, ed., *Family Letters of Samuel Blachley Webb* (New York: 1912), 136.
128. *Correspondence of Webb,* 3:128–29.
129. Ibid., 1:153.

CHAPTER 5

1. Letter, John Reed Collection, Valley Forge National Historical Park. The letter is dated: "Valley Forge, Head Quarters, 2d. Feby. 1778."
2. Charles H. Lesser, ed., *The Sinews of Independence: Monthly Strength Reports of the Continental Army* (Chicago: University of Chicago Press, 1976), 55. The figure used is based on the number of officers and men, " present fit for duty and on duty" from the "General Return of the Continental Army Under the Immediate Command of His Excellency George Washington December 31, 1777." Subsequent returns taken throughout the winter at Valley Forge reveal a sharp reduction in the number of officers and men, "present fit for duty and on duty." The return for January 31, 1778, for example, shows just over 7,000 officers and men at Valley Forge. See ibid., 58–59.
3. Johann Kalb quoted in Freeman, *George Washington,* 4:565. Kalb (1721–80) is best known in American history as Baron de Kalb. He was a French officer who came to America with Lafayette and was appointed a major general in the Continental Army by Congress in September 1777. De Kalb was killed in the battle of Camden (August 10, 1780). There are nine cities or towns and six counties in the United States named de Kalb after him.
4. *Writings of Washington,* 10:180.
5. Ibid., 10:181.
6. *Laurens Papers,* 12:231.
7. "Military Papers of General John Cadwalader," *Pennsylvania Magazine of History and Biography* 32 (April 1908): 168.
8. Historian Lee Boyle compiled references to the weather on Christmas Day at Valley Forge from the diaries and journals of people who were at or near Valley Forge at the time. None of these sources mention a snowstorm on December 25, 1777. Here are examples of references to the weather. Dearborn, *Journals,* 119, "We have Not

so mery a Crismus as I have seen—the weather warm & Rayny." Smith, *Diary,* "it snowd a Little at Night." Waldo, *Diary,* 133, "the poor Sick, suffer much in Tents this cold Weather." Savage, *Diary,* "Cloudy and Some Snow." From nearby Darby, Pennsylvania, Peebles, *Journal,* "Very pleasant weather for the season."

9. *Writings of Washington,* 20:475.
10. Octavius Pickering, *The Life of Timothy Pickering* (Boston: Little, Brown, 1867), 1:199.
11. See Katherine B. Menz, *Historic Furnishings Report: Washington's Headquarters* (Valley Forge National Historical Park: National Park Service, 1989).
12. Massey, *John Laurens and the American Revolution,* 229.
13. Martha Washington wrote Mercy Otis Warren from Valley Forge on March 7, 1778, "the Generals apartment is very small he has had a log cabben built to dine in which has made our quarters much more tolarable than they were at first." See Joseph E. Fields, ed., *Worthy Partner: The Papers of Martha Washington* (Westport, Connecticut: Greenwood, 1994), 178.
14. Gideon Savage, *The Revolutionary War Diary of Gideon Savage* (privately printed).
15. Tench Tilghman to Robert Morris, February 2, 1778, John Reed Collection, Valley Forge National Historical Park.
16. Tench Tilghman is listed as "Assistant Secretary to his Excellency the Commander in Chief" in his oath of allegiance to the United States. He signed his oath at Valley Forge on May 12, 1778. Nellie Protsman Waldenmaier, *Some of the Earliest Oaths of Allegiance to the United States of America* (privately printed, 1944), 20.
17. Heitman, *Register of Officers of the Continental Army,* 354, 492. Shaw was sometimes mentioned as being invited to be an aide-de-camp to General Washington. However, I was unable to find any evidence to confirm this story. His journal, *The Journals of Major Samuel Shaw: The First American Consul at Canton with a Life of the Author by Josiah Quincy* (Boston: Wm. Crosby and H. P. Nichols, 1847) makes no reference to Shaw being invited to join the general's staff.
18. *Writings of Washington,* 10:290.
19. Washington wrote his stepson John Parke Custis on February 1, 1778, from Valley Forge, "We are in a dreary kind of place, and uncomfortably provided; for other matters I shall refer you to the bearer, Colonel Fitzgerald, who can give you the occurrences of the camp, &c., better than can be related in a letter." See ibid., 10:414. Fitzgerald apparently went to York, Pennsylvania, where the Continental Congress was meeting, prior to going to Virginia. Fitzgerald wrote Washington from York on February 16, 1778. See ibid., 10:528–29 note. The exact date that Fitzgerald returned to Valley Forge cannot be determined; however, he wrote a note from the encampment on May 24, 1778.
20. Ibid., 9:467.
21. *Hamilton Papers,* 1:353–54.
22. Ibid., 1:351–52.
23. Varnum to Washington, January 2, 1778, George Washington Papers, microfilm, reel 46.
24. Charles Patrick Neimeyer, *American Goes to War: A Social History of the Continental Army* (New York: New York University Press, 1996), 78, and Benjamin Quarles, *The Negro in the American Revolution* (Chapel Hill: University of North Carolina Press, 1961), 62. Rhode Island emancipated every slave who enlisted, the

state compensating the master. See Wallace, *Life of Henry Laurens,* 448 nn. Gen. James Mitchell Varnum (1748–89) was a 1769 graduate of Rhode Island College (today called Brown University) and was admitted to the bar in 1771. He was a lawyer at the outbreak of the war.

25. Mayer, *Belonging to the Army,* 167.
26. *Writings of Washington,* 10:257.
27. *Laurens Papers,* 12:305. The Laurens's fortune was built on slave labor and Henry Laurens's largest plantation was named "Mepkin," an estate of 30,000 acres on the Cooper River, a short distance above Charleston. John Laurens planned to recruit his first black soldiers from the Mepkin plantation.
28. Ibid., 11:224–25. This letter is dated: "Charles Town, August 14, 1776."
29. Ibid., 12:430. This text appears in a letter that John Laurens wrote from Valley Forge on February 9, 1778.
30. Ibid., 12:412–13.
31. Ibid., 15:65.
32. Alexander Hamilton to John Laurens, September 11, 1779, in *Hamilton Papers,* 2:166–67. Although Hamilton's comments were written over a year after Laurens first made his proposal to raise black troops, they are inserted at this point because they are a clear statement of Hamilton's support for raising black troops as well as a realistic appraisal of the opposition against the idea's adoption.
33. *Writings of Washington,* 33:358.
34. Historian John Ferling also identified Joseph Reed, Washington's first military secretary, as an ardent opponent to slavery. See John Ferling, *Setting the World Ablaze: Washington, Adams, Jefferson, and the American Revolution* (Oxford: Oxford University Press, 2000), 164.
35. The mandate for Washington to have four aides-de-camp is the congressional resolution of June 21, 1775, authorizing three aides and that of July 29, 1776, which stated "That the General be empowered to appoint another aid-de-camp." For the July 29, 1776, resolution see *Journals of Congress,* 5:613.
36. *Writings of Washington,* 10:200–201.
37. *Journals of Congress,* 10:15.
38. *Writings of Washington,* 10:286.
39. The family members who immigrated to America in 1772 are identified as James's father and mother (Daniel and Agnes) and their younger son named John. In the autumn of 1773, Daniel McHenry established himself in business in Baltimore under the company name of Daniel McHenry and Son. John went into business with his father while James pursued higher education. The McHenrys advertised their business as importers of cloth, hardware, groceries, spices, wines, teas, and spirits. Daniel McHenry's wife Agnes died on August 16, 1774, at the age of forty-six. See Steiner, *Life and Correspondence of James McHenry,* 1–2.
40. McHenry wrote out a will in Philadelphia on July 29, 1775, which reads in part,

> Being about to set off for the head Quarters in New England to serve as a volunteer, or Surgeon in the American Army, raised by order of the Continental Congress and Provincial Conventions, to defend the liberties of Americans and mankind, against the enemies of both And should the events of war number me with the dead, in

the name of the disposer of these and all other events, I will and bequeath by this writing, all my portion of earthly possessions in the manner following, . . .

See Steiner, *Life and Correspondence of James McHenry,* 4–5.

41. *Magazine of American History,* 7, no. 2: 96.
42. For many years before and after the American Revolution the military designation for doctor was "surgeon." Surgeons cared for wounds and amputated limbs and were respected members of society. There were also physicians at the time who dispensed medicine and treated common ailments.
43. McHenry was one of five surgeons captured at the fall of Fort Washington.
44. Menz, *Historic Furnishing Report,* 22, and Charles Coleman Seller, *Charles Willson Peale: Early Life* (Philadelphia: American Philosophical Society, 1947), 180.
45. Steiner, *Life and Correspondence of James McHenry,* 16.
46. McHenry to Washington, June 21, 1777, *Papers of Washington,* 10:97.
47. *Writings of Washington,* 11:389.
48. Letter from Dr. James McHenry to Gen. Nathanael Greene, Showman and Conrad, *Papers of Nathanael Greene,* 6:420.
49. *Graydon: Memoirs of His Own Time,* 244. Quinsy is an archaic medical term. The current term is peritonsillar abscess. It is a complication of an acute inflammation of the tonsils.
50. McHenry to Hamilton, September 21, 1778, Steiner, *Life and Correspondence of James McHenry,* 18.
51. *Writing of Washington,* 1:xliv-xlv.
52. *Magazine of American History,* 7, no. 2: 97.
53. Thomas Boyd, *Light-Horse Harry Lee* (New York: Charles Scribner's Sons, 1931), 32–34 and Noel B. Gerson, *Light-Horse Harry* (Garden City, New York: Doubleday, 1966), 56–59.
54. *Writings of Washington,* 11:198. The draft of Washington's letter to Lee is in the handwriting of John Laurens.
55. When I first came across the name "Scull" in researching this book, I knew I had seen this unusual name before. I realized that the name appears on a famous map of Philadelphia known to cartographers as "The Scull and Heap Map." Peter Scull turned out to be the grandson of Nicholas Scull, surveyor general of Pennsylvania, who with George Heap created a beautiful map of Philadelphia, which was first published in 1752. It is among the rarest and most desirable maps of colonial America. The Boston Public Library owns an orderly book kept by Peter Scull. It confirms that he was commissioned early in the war (July 17, 1775) as a second lieutenant in the Pennsylvania Rifle Battalion. See "How Washington Organized His Army" in *More Books—Bulletin of the Boston Public Library,* 2 nos. 4–5 (May 1927). After several promotions, Scull was named a major in Patton's Additional Continental Regiment in January 1777.
56. *Writings of Washington,* 10:80. Washington's letter was addressed to Richard Henry Lee who was a Virginia delegate to the Continental Congress. The general Thompson referred to was Gen. William Thompson who was appointed commander of the Pennsylvania Rifle Regiment on June 25, 1775, which was reorganized as the 1st Continental Regiment in January 1776. See Heitman, *Register of*

Officers of the Continental Army, 541, 487; also see Robert K. Wright, Jr., *The Continental Army* (Washington, D.C.: Center of Military History, United States Army, 1989), 100, 323.

57. *Writings of Washington,* 10:269. The draft of this letter is in the handwriting of Robert Hanson Harrison.

58. J. Bennett Nolan, *George Washington and the Town of Reading* (1931), 85. According to one source, Scull resigned his commission as a major in Patton's Additional Continental Regiment on January 1, 1778. See Heitman, *Register of Officers of the Continental Army,* 487.

59. The Continental Congress was overwhelmed with the endless details of the operations of its army. In June 1776 it created a Board of War with broad supervisory powers over the army, which included the power to "superintend the raising, fitting out and despatching of all such land forces as may be ordered for the service of the United Colonies." See *Journals of Congress,* 5:435. The board consisted of five members selected from Congress and army officers. Its control could be dangerous to Washington in the hands of his rivals and critics.

60. *Writings of Washington,* 11:109. The draft of this letter is in the handwriting of Tench Tilghman.

61. Ibid., 11:242.

62. Nolan, *George Washington and the Town of Reading,* 91.

63. The term "officer(s) of the day" was borrowed from the British Army. It was an administrative function and its specific duties were never clearly defined. The number of officers of the day depended on the size of an army and if there was a special event or need to exercise additional control over the troops. There were five officers of the day at Valley Forge until March 26, 1778; the number was reduced to four when the post of major general of the day was eliminated. However, this position was reinstituted before the army left Valley Forge. Duties of an officer of the day included inspecting the camp and making sure guards were posted and alert. If an army occupied a city or town the term "town major" was frequently used instead of officer of the day. However, the town major was a permanent post as opposed to the officer of the day who was appointed on a daily basis.

64. This story can be found in John F. Reed, *Valley Forge: Crucible of Victory* (Monmouth Beach, New Jersey: Philip Freneau, 1969), 19–20.

65. As early as April 23, 1778, there is a report from Duportail to Washington written as one might expect in John Laurens's hand, but with corrections in English by Duportail. This suggest that Duportail was able to read and write English. There is other evidence to suggest that while Duportail found communication in English time-consuming and difficult, he was by no means incapable of using the language.

66. Tench Tilghman wrote Lord Stirling on January 24, 1778, "As His Excellency is very busy preparing matters to lay before the Committee of Congress and Board of War, he commands me to acknowledge your Lordships favor of this day." See Fredrick R. Kirkland, ed., *Letters on the American Revolution in the Library of "Karolfred"* (New York: Coward-McCann, 1952), 46.

67. Pickering, *Life of Timothy Pickering,* 1:199.

68. George Fleming to Sebastian Bauman, March 26, 1778, Sebastian Bauman Papers, New York Historical Society.

69. *Army Correspondence of Colonel John Laurens,* 101–4.
70. See John B. B. Trussell, Jr., *Birthplace of an Army: A Study of the Valley Forge Encampment* (Harrisburg, Pennsylvania: Pennsylvania Historical and Museum Commission, 1979), 38.
71. Eighteenth-century medicine was so primitive, and the hospitals so dirty that we now know that sick soldiers had the best chance of recovering if they were put to bed in an isolated farmhouse, away from doctors, and fed nourishing food. Medical procedures of the period could kill the patient. As an example, Surgeon Samuel Adams was at the daylong battle of Monmouth, which took place on an extremely hot day in June 1778. Men were overcome with heat exhaustion and Adams reported: "bled a number that were over come with the heat." See diary, Samuel Adams, New York Public Library.
72. Victor Leroy Johnson, "The Administration of the American Commissariat during the Revolutionary War" (Ph.D. diss., University of Pennsylvania, 1941), 95.
73. Congress failed to appoint a successor to Mifflin until March 2, 1778.
74. *Writings of Washington,* 10:192.
75. Freeman, *George Washington,* 4:559.
76. *Papers of Washington,* 9:432.
77. Ibid., 9:556.
78. Showman and Conrad, *Papers of General Nathanael Greene,* 2:242–43. Greene was famous for saying, "No body ever heard of a Quartermaster in history."
79. Philander D. Chase in a letter to the author.
80. *Hamilton Papers,* 1:426.
81. *Laurens Papers,* 12: 456–58.
82. Nathanael Greene's appointment as quartermaster general on March 2, 1778, made a big difference. Under Greene's capable administrative skills, the supply situation improved dramatically through the spring of 1778.
83. The George Washington Papers are part of the Presidential Papers Series. The documents in this microfilm series are reproductions of the original manuscript material.
84. *Writings of Washington,* 10:464 n.
85. William A. Oldridge Collection, Manuscript Division, Library of Congress. Original in Houghton Library, Harvard University.
86. George Washington Papers.
87. *Letters of Delegates,* 8:314 n.
88. The word "cabal" comes from the French and means an intrigue carried out by a small group intent on the execution of a secret plot or scheme.
89. Lord Stirling (an American major general) in a letter to Washington dated November 3, 1777, George Washington Papers, microfilm, roll 45. Wilkinson was overheard by Maj. William McWilliams, Stirling's aide-de-camp, who reported the incident to Stirling. If Conway was denounced for making his alleged remark about Washington, just imagine the furor that would have resulted if the following excerpt of a letter written by Baron de Kalb had surfaced. De Kalb wrote a letter in cipher to a fellow French officer, the comte de Broglie, from Valley Forge, which included this harsh appraisal of Washington, "At the camp of Valleyforge, on the right bank of Schuylkill, twenty-two miles from Philadelphia, 25th December [1777]. He is indeed the most valiant, and upright man, with the best intentions and the soundest judgement; I am convinced he would do good work if he dared to take

more upon himself than he does; but he is indeed the weakest general and the most badly counselled by those who possess his confidence in the largest degree, and those are so many ignorant persons if they are not traitors. I am convinced that this positions [Valley Forge] unless he changes it will fulfill none of its objects; on the contrary, the troops will have no repose, it is too near the enemy, and on account of our weakness (the army has not now six thousand men to put under arms) being obliged to regulate our movements by them, we may expect to have no rest." See Benjamin F. Stevens, ed., *Facsimiles of Manuscripts in European Archives Relating to America, 1773–1783* (London: 1889–95), vol. 8, doc. 761.

90. Probably a reference to the fact that Conway was found asleep in a barn during the retreat from Germantown. This was, however, more the result of fatigue than cowardice. Ward, *War of the Revolution,* 1:371.

91. *Laurens Papers,* 12:245–46.

92. *Hamilton Papers,* 1:425–28.

93. Ibid., 1:436–37.

94. Letter to the author, April 22, 1997. Lee Boyle is the historian at Valley Forge National Historical Park. Whatever the facts, Washington remained convinced that there was a plot against him. Writing to Landon Carter on May 30, 1778, several months after the alleged plot had ended, Washington said, "That there was a scheme of this sort on foot, last fall, admits of no doubt; but it originated in another quarter; with three men [Maj. Gen. Gates, Mifflin, and Conway], who wanted to aggrandize themselves; but finding no support, on the contrary, that their conduct and views, when seen into, were likely to undergo severe reprehension, they slunk back, disavowed the measure, and professed themselves my warmest admirers." See *Writings of Washington,* 11:493–94.

95. John Reed Collection, Valley Forge National Historical Park.

96. Jeffrey D. Schnakenberg, "Officer Attrition in the Continental Army during the Valley Forge Encampment" (master's thesis, Temple University, 1994), 16.

97. William A. Oldridge Collection.

98. Ibid.

99. *Laurens Papers,* 12:483.

100. Gratz Collection, Historical Society of Pennsylvania, case 4, box 11.

101. Kapp, *Life of Frederick William Von Steuben,* 124.

102. Ibid., 124.

103. Reed, *Valley Forge: Crucible of Victory,* 41.

104. *Laurens Papers,* 13:35.

105. *Hamilton Papers,* 1:466. Hamilton's draft was a summary of the views of the American commissioners.

106. Elias Boudinot, *Journal or Historic Recollections during the Revolutionary War,* (Philadelphia: Frederick Bourquin, 1894), 45.

107. Ibid., 49.

108. On April 6, 1778, in anticipation of Lee's exchange, Washington's aide Richard Kidder Meade wrote General Greene, "I am commanded by his Excellency to desire that you will furnish Gen. Lee with a Good Waggon & Team to transport his Baggage up the Country—you will also be pleased to furnish two of the best Horses you have, both Waggon & Horses to be sent here early to morrow morning." See Gratz Collection, case 4, box 10. Lee was on parole in Philadelphia at the time.

109. *Writings of Washington,* 11:333. The French had been secretly assisting the Americans since the beginning of the war. According to popular belief, the American victory at Saratoga was responsible for France's decision to enter the war in 1778. However recent scholarship indicates that the timing of French entry into the war was due to the completion of their rearmament and the deterioration of their relations with Britain rather than the sudden news of Saratoga. See Jonathan R. Dull, *A Diplomatic History of the American Revolution* (New Haven, Connecticut: Yale University Press, 1985), 89–95.
110. *Army Correspondence of Colonel John Laurens,* 169.
111. *Travels in North-America,* 1:190. Also Roche, *Joseph Reed: A Moderate in the American Revolution,* 140–41. Chastellux said about this incident, "Mr. Reed, who is a sensible man and above all eager for popular favor, made a great clamor, published and exaggerated the offers that were made him." Robert Hanson Harrison commented about the peace commission in a letter dated April 23, 1778, to Timothy Pickering, "I wish the people, who are fond of peace and tired of War, may not be caught with the delusive bait now being hung out." (Pickering Papers, Massachusetts Historical Society, microfilm, roll 17 pp. 145–46a).

CHAPTER 6

1. *Army Correspondence of Colonel John Laurens,* 200. John Laurens included this comment in a letter he wrote to his father on July 2, 1778, four days after the battle of Monmouth.
2. *Writings of Washington,* 12:2 and *Army Correspondence of Colonel John Laurens,* 19.
3. George Washington Papers. Duportail and Laurens were sent by Washington to reconnoiter the Sourland Mountains, which are near Princeton, New Jersey. Laurens's report included, "Water is not very abundant, but might be sufficient for a short stay."
4. Godfrey, *Commander-in-Chief's Guard,* 60. Elijah Fisher was a private soldier in the Commander in Chief's Guard and kept a diary. His entry for June 23, 1778, reads, "Capt. Gibbs, Leut. Grimes, four Sarg. And four Corpl. And seventy-two men of the guard jined Col. Morgan's Party and went Down to the Lines and the rest of the guard went with the Baggage and Leut. Colsare had the Command and at four in the after noon We Left Mr. Haises (Hunt) and Marched all night and Mett with a good eal of Dificulty in giting along." See *Elijah Fisher's Journal While in the War for Independence* (Augusta, Maine: Badger and Manley, 1880), 9.
5. McHenry, *Diary of the Year 1778,* 4. Apparently this diary was privately owned in 1945 by Helen and Henry Flynt of Greenwich, Connecticut, who arranged for its publication.
6. *Hamilton Papers,* 1:510. Note that the term "detachment" was used by Hamilton. This was a commonly used military term at the time, which meant a number of men organized together to function for a short time. A detachment usually meant something smaller than a regiment.
7. The term "picked men" or "chosen men" had a specific meaning in the American army during the Revolutionary War. They were reliable soldiers who volunteered from various regiments for temporary duty. They were often given hazardous assignments such as the advanced guard of an army. The American "picked men"

were organized in an effort to copy the British Army's elite corps of light infantry. A permanent corps of American light infantry was assembled later in the Revolution and served with particular distinction at Yorktown in 1781.

8. *Writings of Washington,* 12:140–41.

9. Long Bridge Farm or Longbridge, as it was also called, is in South Brunswick, New Jersey. Washington selected this location because the large, well-managed farm could provide food and some shelter for his army.

10. *Lee Papers,* 2:424.

11. Ibid., 3:5, testimony of General Wayne at the Lee court-martial.

12. See comments of Lafayette in ibid., 3:11. As a major general, Charles Lee was authorized two aides-de-camp, but he apparently had five aides or volunteers with him at the battle of Monmouth. They were John Brooks, the marquis Francis de Malmedy (sometimes incorrectly identified as Colonel Malmedie), John Francis Mercer, George Lee Turberville, and Evan Edwards. These men were no slouches. John Francis Mercer, for example, was a graduate of William and Mary College whose subsequent career included being elected the governor of Maryland. His appointment was mentioned in the general orders of June 8, 1778, "Captn. John Mercer of 3rd. Virginia Regt. is appointed to act as Aide de Camp to Majr. Genl. Lee and is to be accordingly respected." See *Writings of Washington,* 12:35, and Thayer, *The Making of a Scapegoat:Washington and Lee* 36–37. Like Washington, Lee at Monmouth, lacked reliable mounted troops on the day of the battle and used his aides as scouts.

13. British historian Charles Stedman gave a clear explanation of Sir Henry Clinton's strategy, "The army marched in two divisions; the van commanded by general Knyphausen, and the rear by lord Cornwallis; but the whole of the baggage was now put under the care of general Knyphausen's division, that the rear division, under lord Cornwallis, which consisted of the flower of the British army, being disencumbered, might to ready to act with vigor, as circumstances should require. This arrangement being made, general Knyphausen's division marched in pursuance of orders at break of day on the twenty-eighth of June, whilst the other division, with which the commander in chief remained, did not move till near eight, that it might not press too close upon the baggage, which was so enormous as to occupy a line of march of near twelve miles in extent." Charles Stedman, *History of the American War* (London: 1794), 2:18–9.

14. White was appointed lieutenant colonel of the 4th Continental Dragoons (Moylan's) in February 1777. See Heitman, *Register of Officers of the Continental Army,* 585. However he apparently was commanding a party of mounted troops (mostly militia) that had been hanging on the British rear for several days prior to the battle. It is reasonable that White was in the battle of Monmouth. He joined Moylan on the night of June 29 at Richmond's Mill, three miles from Monmouth. White saw further action as part of Moylan's efforts to harass the British on their march from Monmouth to Sandy Hook following the June 28 battle. Washington's former intimate friend and military secretary, Joseph Reed, apparently also participated in the battle. He was probably serving as a volunteer with Moylan, who was his friend, or with a small group of volunteers from Philadelphia who were following Clinton's army as it crossed New Jersey. See Reed, *Life and Correspondence of Joseph Reed,* 1:368.

15. The term mounted troops is a generalization describing any soldier on horseback. At the time of the American Revolution, there were names given to identify specific types of organized mounted troops. At the time, the names were dragoon and light dragoon. Dragoons were mounted infantry who rode into battle and then dismounted to fight. There is no known reference to any dragoon unit participating in the American Revolution. Another class of mounted troops used by both the Continental and British Armies in the Revolution was known as light dragoons. They were trained to fight from horseback. They usually were armed with a carbine (a smoothbore weapon with a shorter barrel length and smaller bore than a musket), one or two holstered pistols (attached to the forward end of the saddle), and a saber. Light dragoons were mostly used for reconnaissance, communications, escort duty, and raiding. The term cavalry was used by the French to identify their version of light dragoons. During the later years of the war, especially in the South, light dragoons were often combined with light infantry and a few cannons to create a fast moving attack force called a legion.

16. As a former Prussian officer, Von Steuben had received military decorations that he was proud to wear. These decorations were commonly made of bright metal with enameled designs. Eighteenth-century decorations or the honor of being elected to some Order was often accompanied by a corresponding sash. The American army issued no decorations during the Revolutionary War. The British had a few, which were worn by officers.

17. *Laurens Papers,* 13:545–46.

    Benjamin Walker, who was one of Von Steuben's aides at the time, joined Washington's staff later in the war. Walker made it back to safety separately. According to one account, Von Steuben asked Walker if he managed to recover his hat. The alleged dialog reads, "How is this? I thought you were taken prisoner." "Oh, no," said Walker, "they were intent on the high prize [Von Steuben] and overlooked us." "Have you brought my hat?" "Oh, no, Baron we had not time." See John McAuley Palmer, *General Von Steuben* (Port Washington, New York: Kennikat, 1966), 189.

18. Videt is commonly spelled vedette. An eighteenth-century source of reference, *An Universal Military Dictionary,* published in London in 1779 defines vedette as, "a centinel on horseback, with his horse's head towards the place whence any danger is to be feared, and his carbine advanced, with the butt-end against his right thigh." There is an account of this incident in Col. J. G. Simcoe, *A History of the Operations of a Partisan Corps: Called The Queen's Rangers* (New York: Bartlett & Welford, 1844), 68–71.

19. McHenry, *Diary of the Year 1778,* 5.

20. George F. Scheer, ed., *Private Yankee Doodle: Being a Narrative of Some of the Adventures, Dangers, and Sufferings of a Revolutionary Soldier,* by Joseph Plumb Martin (Boston: Little, Brown, 1962), 126–27.

21. Samuel Adams diary.

22. The day of the battle of Monmouth, June 28, 1778, turned out to be the fifth day of a heat wave, which saw temperatures close to 100 degrees Fahrenheit each day.

23. Stedman, *History of the American War,* 2:20. Clinton's army was on its way to New York City and every soldier carried all his clothing and equipment. The Americans, on the other hand, were able to leave their regimental coats and much

of their personal gear at their camp at Englishtown where they planned to return after engaging Clinton's rear guard.

24. *Lee Papers,* 3:62.

25. Thomas Anburey, *Travels through the Interior Parts of American in a Series of Letters,* 2 vols. (London: William Lane, 1789), 2:380–81. Anburey was captured at the battle of Saratoga and reported talking with Colonels Meade, Laurens, "and another officer of General Washington's suit" in Charlottesville, Virginia, in April or May 1779. Anburey is a creditable source and there is no reason to doubt the authenticity of this story. This incident seems plausible and probably occurred sometime between 10:30 and 11 A.M. on the morning of the battle. Meade testified at Lee's court-martial that he was reconnoitering alone near the enemy on the day of the battle. Meade said at the trial, "I went on towards Monmouth Court-house[;] I observed the front of the enemy advancing towards the village[;] I attended as much as I could to discern their numbers when I found it not safe to remain there, and returned." This incident is believed to have taken place at the modern intersections of Burlington Road (today's Main Street) and Englishtown Road (modern State Highway 522) in what is presently downtown Freehold, New Jersey.

26. *Writings of Washington,* 12:127

27. Woodford was a Virginia plantation owner when the war began. He was taken prisoner at the surrender of Charleston, South Carolina, in 1780 and evacuated to New York City where he died in captivity on November 13, 1780. Woodford is buried in old Trinity Church Yard in New York. Woodford County, Kentucky, is named in his honor.

28. Custis, *Recollections and Private Memoirs of Washington,* 224. Also Fritz Hirschfeld, *George Washington and Slavery: A Documentary Portrayal* (Columbia: University of Missouri Press, 1997), 100–1, 108, 110–11. Billy Lee appears in the background in numerous paintings including a 1780 portrait of Washington painted by John Trumbull. He is also identified as the black servant in the popular painting *The Washington Family* completed by artist Edward Savage in 1796. See *George Washington and Slavery,* 96–98.

29. *Lee Papers,* 3:72. Tench Tilghman was also at Washington's side during this incident. Tilghman reported that Washington, "not believing the thing to be true, ordered the fifer under the care of a light-horseman, to prevent his spreading a report and damping the troops who were advancing." Ibid., 3:79–80.

30. While there is no record that Washington ever saw or talked with Grayson at Monmouth, Washington's military secretary, Robert Hanson Harrison, mentioned that he saw part of Grayson's regiment in the late morning retreating down the road from Freehold to Englishtown. See ibid., 3:72.

31. William Grayson resigned from the army in 1779 and returned home to practice law. He was later elected to the Virginia House of Delegates (1784–85 and 1788), the Continental Congress (1785–87), and was a delegate to the Virginia Constitutional Convention (1788). He opposed the adoption of the Federal Constitution which Virginia ratified by a narrow margin. The Anti-Federalists however dominated the Virginia General Assembly and they appointed Grayson and Richard Henry Lee, who was also opposed to the Constitution, as Virginia's first United States senators. Grayson was remembered for his sarcastic wit in the first Senate. When the senators discussed a title for the vice president, Grayson, who was annoyed with the aristocratic pretensions of John Adams, suggested he be called

"His Limpid Highness" or "His Superfluous Excellency." See R. A. Brock, ed., *The History of the Virginia Federal Convention of 1788,* by High Blair Grigsby (Richmond: Virginia Historical Society, 1890–91), 2:234. Grayson died in office on March 12, 1790, at his estate named "Belle Air" near Dumfries, Virginia.

32. *Lee Papers,* 3:80.
33. Ibid., 3:73.
34. Ibid., 3:78. Meade said that he returned from his morning reconnaissance just in time to hear the exchange of words between Washington and Lee that took place on the battlefield at about 12:15 in the afternoon. Meade said that he heard Lee tell Washington "that he was averse to an attack or a general engagement." See ibid., 3:64. Laurens rejoined Washington a short time later.
35. Ibid., 3:69.
36. *Magazine of American History* 3, no. 6 (June 1879): 363. This source is suspect and the location of McHenry's copy of Marshall's *The Life of George Washington* is unknown. Vol. 3, 473, in Marshall's book talks about the skirmishing that took place during the winter at Valley Forge. However, the facing page, 472, is the opening of the chapter about the Monmouth campaign and includes a summary of the events. P. 511 tells the story of the counterattack. Marshall said, "There he met Lee, to whom he spoke in terms of some warmth, implying disapprobation of his conduct. He also gave immediate orders to the regiments commanded by Colonel Stewart and Lieutenant colonel Ramsay, to form on a piece of ground which he deemed proper for the purpose of checking the enemy, who were advancing rapidly on them."
37. Custis, *Recollections and Private Memoirs of Washington,* 219. Washington's exact reply to Hamilton's outburst, according to Custis's undocumented version was, "Colonel Hamilton, you will take your horse." Charles Lee told this story differently. In his version, Hamilton's emotional outburst was directed at him. Colonel Hamilton, according to Lee, "flourishing his sword, immediately exclaimed, that's right, my dear General, and I will stay, and we will all die here on this spot." See *Lee Papers,* 3:200–201.
38. This is a reference to General Gates's behavior at the second battle of Saratoga. Hamilton felt that Gates was safely at his headquarters during the battle while his subordinate, Benedict Arnold, was in the midst of the battle commanding and rallying the troops. Gates took full credit for the American victory at Saratoga.
39. *Hamilton Papers,* 1:512.
40. *Lee Papers,* 3:61.
41. *Army Correspondence of Colonel John Laurens,* 197, and Massey, *John Laurens and the American Revolution,* 110.
42. *Magazine of American History,* no. 6 (June 1879): 355–63.
43. *Army Correspondence of Colonel John Laurens,* 197.
44. Ibid., 198.
45. Diary of the Year 1778, 8.
46. Idzerda, *Lafayette in the Age of the American Revolution,* 2:11.
47. William A. Oldridge Collection, (New York Public Library, D. Mayer Collection, transcription of original document).
48. Postscript to letter from: "James McHenry to George Lux, Esqr., Baltimore. June 30th, 1778." "The Battle of Monmouth," *Magazine of American History* no. 6 (June 1879): 355–56.

49. *Lee Papers,* 3:79.
50. Freeman, *George Washington,* 5:20 n.
51. *Hamilton Papers,* 1:513. Elias Boudinot was a New Jersey delegate to the Conti-
    nental Congress at the time. He was a friend of Francis Barber who ran the school
    that Hamilton attended soon after he arrived in America.
52. *Writings of Washington,* 12:128.
53. Mark Lender, "What Kind of Victory?, Washington, the Army, and Monmouth
    Reconsidered," in *An Account of the Action* (from Brandywine to Monmouth:
    March 14–16, 1997), Council of American Revolutionary Sites, Independence
    National Historical Park Visitors Center, *A Seminar on the Impact of the Revolu-
    tionary War on the Delaware Valley* Philadelphia: 65–67, 71–72.
54. James McHenry to George Lux, Baltimore, June 30, 1778; "The Battle of Mon-
    mouth," 355–63. McHenry was not alone in reporting high enemy losses. Many
    other American officers were using similar math to calculate British casualties at
    Monmouth. See Lender, "What Kind of Victory?," 65–67. There is no known accu-
    rate record of the number of killed, wounded, and missing for both sides in the bat-
    tle. The best guess for British losses is 67 killed in combat, 59 "died with fatigue"
    (died from heat exhaustion), 170 wounded, and 65 missing for total casualties of
    350. For the Americans, the best information we have is Washington's report to
    Congress following the battle in which he stated 69 American troops killed, 162
    wounded, and 132 missing. "Many of the missing dropped through fatigue and
    have since come in." See *Lee Papers,* 2:447. Using Washington's figure and assum-
    ing that 100 of the missing 132 soldiers "came in" it would place the total Ameri-
    can casualties at about 263.
55. Lee's letter was misdated July 1, 1778.
56. *Lee Papers,* 3:98–99.
57. Emmet Collection, microfiche roll no. 8, item 9294. Elias Boudinot (1740–1821)
    was an attorney from Elizabethtown (today's Elizabeth), New Jersey, and a member
    of the Continental Congress at the time of the battle of Monmouth. He had
    recently resigned his important position as American commissary of prisoners
    (who received and distributed enemy prisoners and attended to their needs) to
    serve in Congress. McHenry had picked his correspondent wisely to damage
    Charles Lee's reputation because Boudinot was one of the leaders of the American
    Revolution and his opinion was respected and carried great weight. Boudinot was
    a close friend of Alexander Hamilton.
58. *Army Correspondence of Colonel John Laurens,* 200.
59. *Lee Papers,* 3:2. Researching a book of this broad scope exposed me to numerous
    sources that I had heretofore never studied in depth. The most interesting was the
    208-page printed transcript of Lee's court-martial. This court-martial proceeding is
    one of the most interesting and accurate sources of information we have from the
    American Revolution. The first published account of Lee's court-martial appeared
    in a pamphlet published in Philadelphia by the printer and bookseller John Dunlop
    in 1778, the same year that the trial took place. There was great interest in the trial
    at the time and Dunlop capitalized on it by rushing a transcript into print. Dunlop's
    hastily prepared publication badly misspelled some names, which made it confus-
    ing to read. A second edition of Dunlop's pamphlet published in Cooperstown,
    New York, in 1823 repeated the errors. However, a more accurate record of the trial

was included in the *Lee Papers* published in 1873 by the New York Historical Society. I used the 1873 record of the trial as my reference source.

60. Lender, "What Kind of Victory?" 76–77. Since this groundbreaking seminar paper is obscure and difficult to obtain I will quote a few excerpts from it, "Most of the senior officers were staunchly loyal to the commander-in-chief, and none more so than Washington's military 'family.' Hamilton and Laurens went to work early on Lee. These attacks were as assiduous as they were insidious; they were also effective."

61. Ibid., 76. Here is another key passage from Lender's seminar paper, "Even junior officers, men hardly privy so soon to anything that senior generals might have said, recorded in their diaries that Lee was in disgrace or at least under a cloud; private letters told of the court martial with strong hints of Lee's guilt. This was the doing of Hamilton and Laurens."

62. *Lee Papers,* 3:52–53.

63. Ibid., 3:64.

64. Ibid., 3:70–71.

65. Ibid., 3:60.

66. Ibid., 3:56.

67. Ibid., 3:201.

68. Ibid., 3:201–2.

69. Robert Hendrickson, *Hamilton* (New York: Mason/Charter, 1976), 208.

70. Lender, "What Kind of Victory?" 76–78.

71. *Lee Papers,* 3:208.

72. McHenry, *Diary of the Year 1778,* 9–10.

73. Idzerda, *Lafayette in the Age of the American Revolution,* 2:106.

74. Otis G. Hammond, ed., *Letters and Papers of Major-General John Sullivan* (Concord: New Hampshire Historical Society, 1930–39), 2:150.

75. *Hamilton Papers,* 1:593.

76. *Lee Papers,* 3:277.

77. *Hamilton Papers,* 1:602.

78. *Journals of Major Samuel Shaw,* 55–56.

79. *Lee Papers,* 3:283.

80. There were no military pistols manufactured in America at the time of the Revolution. American and English officers purchased pistols with their own money. They bought pistols of a size and design that they liked and could afford. The finest pistols were made in England and were called box lock pistols. They had a barrel that unscrewed to allow the ball and powder to be loaded. Dueling pistols had a distinctive design; a matched pair of pistols with ten-inch octagonal barrels and sensitive hair triggers. Almost all existing dueling pistols show no indications that they were ever fired. They were owned for display and status. Dueling was already outlawed in most of the colonies by the time of the Revolution.

81. *Journals of Major Samuel Shaw,* 55–56.

82. Col. Robert Troup to Major General Gates, January 3, 1779. *Lee Papers,* 3:290.

83. Ibid., 3:285.

84. Ibid., 3:348–50.

85. Jackson and Twohig, *Papers of George Washington: The Diaries of Washington,* 6:265.

86. Boyd, *The Papers of Thomas Jefferson,* 2:387–88. Washington's letter to Jefferson is dated Philadelphia, May 30, 1787.

CHAPTER 7

1. *Hamilton Papers,* 2:303.
2. *Writings of Washington,* 14:105–06.
3. Steiner, *Life and Correspondence of James McHenry,* 25–26.
4. *Writings of Washington,* 14:219. Lafayette departed for France in January 1779 on a mission to raise money for the American cause.
5. Ibid., *Writings of Washington,* 14:245–46.
6. *Hamilton Papers,* 2:17–18.
7. The five Huger brothers from South Carolina were American patriots who served with distinction in the American Revolution to the everlasting confusion of historians. In chronological order of their age, oldest first, the brothers were Daniel, Isaac, John, Benjamin, and Francis. Adding to the ambiguity is that Daniel was the third generation of Hugers with the same name. Gen. Isaac Huger is commonly mentioned as being South Carolina's emissary to Congress. However Daniel Huger (1741–99) has been conclusively identified as the person sent to Philadelphia to implore Congress to send aid to South Carolina. For Huger's mission see James Haw, "A Broken Compact: Insecurity, Union, and the Proposed Surrender of Charleston, 1779," *South Carolina Historical Magazine* 96 (January 1995): 30–53.
8. Until this point in the war Congress had officially forbade the enlistment of blacks, whether slave or free, into the Continental Army. But the individual states were enlisting blacks to help fill their quotas while Congress ignored the practice. The army did not complain. They needed men and the blacks proved to be good soldiers.
9. *Journals of Congress,* 13:387–88. Also see *Letters of Delegates,* 12:242–44.
10. The text of the journals of the Continental Congress pertaining to Laurens reads,

> Whereas John Laurens Esq. who has heretofore acted aid de camp to the Commander in Chief, is desirous of repairing to South Carolina, with a design to assist in defence of the southern states: Resolved, That a commission of lieutenant colonel be granted to the said John Laurens, Esq. [The following text was inserted and then crossed out:] his rank to commence the 5 October, 1777, the time he entered into the war, appointed aid de camp by the Commander in Chief.

> Congress had previously offered Laurens a commission as a lieutenant colonel on November 5, 1778, "in testimony of his patriotic and spirited services as a volunteer." See *Journals of Congress,* 12:1105. However, he declined the offer on the following day and continued to serve as an implied lieutenant colonel on Washington's staff without any salary in keeping with his ideas of republic virtue. Laurens could afford to be a paragon of patriotic principles because his wealthy father kept him supplied with food, uniforms, horses, and black slaves to serve his every need.

11. *Hamilton Papers,* 2:37.

12. *Letters of Delegates,* 12:268.

13. William Moultrie, *Memoirs of the Revolution* (New York: Printed by D. Long-worth, 1802), 1:402.

14. *Letters of Delegates,* 12:554.

15. The exact date that Laurens proposed the raising of a black regiment is not known because the records of the first session of the South Carolina House of Representatives have not survived.

16. Richard Walsh, ed., *The Writings of Christopher Gadsden,* (Columbia: University of South Carolina Press, 1966), 165.

17. [Brig. Gen.] P. Horry [of Marion's Brigade] and M. L.[Mason Locke] Weems, *The Life of General Francis Marion* (1809; reprint, Philadelphia: Joseph Allen, 1845), 61.

18. Wallace, *Life of Henry Laurens,* 477.

19. Chase, *Letters of François, Marquis de Barbe-Marbois,* 119. The marquis was the secretary of the French legation at the time.

20. The Virginia troops sent south were commanded by Gen. William Woodford. They numbered 1,389 men present and fit for duty when they left Morristown. The Virginia troops arrived in time to participate in the defense of Charleston and surrendered with the rest of the American defenders on May 12, 1780. Woodford died in captivity on November 13, 1780.

21. *Writings of Washington,* 17:249.

22. Ibid., 17:284.

23. Ibid., 18:306.

24. Idzerda, *Lafayette in the Age of the American Revolution,* 3:124.

25. *Elijah Fisher's Journal While in the War for Independence*, 13. There was little uniformity to spelling at the time of the American Revolution, especially among the enlisted men. Fisher's journal has some of the most confusing name and place references of any journal I have seen. For example, Fisher identifies the American major general Lord Stirling as "Gen. Lord." New Brunswick, New Jersey, or Brunswick as it was also called at the time, is called "Brumsick" by Fisher. However, what makes Fisher's journal a classic is his identifying Major General Marquis de Lafayette as "General Marques" or the "Right Honorable Major. Gen. Delefialee."

26. Eric Olsen, "A Raid to Capture General Washington" (unpublished article). Mr. Olsen is the National Park Service historian at Morristown National Historical Park. A copy of his article is on file at the park library.

27. *Travels in North-America,* 1:125.

28. *Writings of Washington,* 19:321. Wafers were in common use at the time and used instead of sealing wax. They were disck made of fish oil and beeswax, which were packaged and sold in metal tins. The wafers were kept moist in the tin with oil and when a letter had to be sealed, a wafer was placed on the fold of the paper and pressed onto the paper with a metal seal. The more elaborate way of sealing a document with sealing wax and red tape was commonly reserved for use on legal documents.

29. Ibid., 17:423.

30. Perhaps the most prominent visitors to headquarters that winter were the French minister, Chevalier de la Luzerne, who was accompanied by a Spanish observer, Don Juan de Miralles Trailhon. They arrived with their retinues on April 18, 1780. A few days later Juan de Miralles was ill with a "pulmonic fever" (a medical term

at the time to describe what was probably a bacterial infection of the respiratory system, likely pneumonia) and he lay in an upstairs room of the Ford mansion. He died during the night of April 28, 1780, and was laid to rest in a Morristown churchyard with great ceremony.

31. *Hamilton Papers,* 2:288.
32. *McHenry, Diary of the Year 1778,* vii.
33. *Writings of Washington,* 17:468.
34. Shreve, *Tench Tilghman,* 51.
35. Dr. John Cochran was the physician and surgeon general of the army in the Middle Department at the time of the 1779–80 Morristown encampment. His duties required him to be with the army. He and his wife, who was Elizabeth Schuyler's aunt, were quartered at the Morristown home of Dr. Jabez Campfield who was also an army surgeon and probably Dr. Cochran's friend. Dr. Campfield's Morristown home is still standing today and known as the Schuyler-Hamilton House.
36. *Hamilton Papers,* 2:37.
37. Officers were generally exchanged based on seniority; the longest serving officers were exchanged first. The two sides argued constantly about how many lieutenants they would trade for a captain and how many common soldiers equaled a general. The situation was further complicated by agreeing on the value of a militia officer. An additional problem was that the British had no colonels serving in America. A colonel in the British Army was an honorary rank, the commander of a British regiment was a lieutenant colonel. An American regiment, however, was actively commanded by its colonel.

   When an officer was allowed parole in lieu of some harsher form of internment, it was understood that his movements were still restricted. A good example of this is a letter written by then adjutant Horatio Gates to a British officer who was a prisoner of war, "When his Excellency granted you the District of the town of North Hampton, & five miles round for your place of Confinement, he understood that Northampton & Hadley were towns like those to the Southward, of moderate extent; Since, upon better Information, he finds that each of those towns contain a District of a very large extend of Country, he directs me to acquaint you & desires you will acquaint all the Gentlemen upon their Parole at either of those towns, that they must keep themselves with the Legal Limits of the town they live in." (Horatio Gates to Lt. John Knight, January 24, 1776, Oldridge Collection.) The terms of Lt. Col. John Laurens's parole were that he was not to leave the state of Pennsylvania until exchanged.
38. *Journals of Congress,* 17:598.
39. It is surprising that the British were able to retrieve Laurens's official papers identifying him as one of the leaders of the Revolution and the purpose of his mission. It was common for diplomats traveling at sea to wrap their official papers and dispatches in lead plates, which could be thrown overboard to prevent them from falling into enemy hands.

CHAPTER 8

1. Alexander Hamilton to Gen. Nathanael Greene, September 25, 1780, *Hamilton Papers,* 2:440.
2. *Hamilton Papers,* 2:428.
3. Waldenmaier, *Some of the Earliest Oaths of Allegiance to the United States of America,* 20. Despite his volunteer status, Tilghman was probably regarded as an aide-de-camp to Washington soon after joining the general's personal staff, with that position's corresponding functional rank of lieutenant colonel. Heitman, for example, says that Tilghman was appointed an aide to Washington, and lieutenant colonel, on April 1, 1777. See Heitman, *Register of Officers of the Continental Army,* 543.
4. *Writings of Washington,* 19:51.
5. *Hamilton Papers,* 2:491. Harrison included this comment in a letter he wrote to Hamilton from Philadelphia on October 17, 1780.
6. David's father, Daniel Humphreys, was a graduate of Yale in the Class of 1732. David Humphreys entered Yale in 1767 at the age of fifteen and graduated in the Class of 1771.
7. Malone, *Dictionary of American Biography* 9:373.
8. In one of his poems, Humphreys mentions that he was an aide to General Greene: "Then now I aided in the following scene, Death daring Putnam—then the immortal Greene." See Samuel Orcutt, *The History of the Old Town of Derby, Connecticut* (Springfield, Massachusetts: Springfield, 1880), 594.
9. *Writings of Washington,* 19:56. Humphreys was appointed a lieutenant colonel by Congress on November 12, 1782. His commission was to date from June 23, 1780. For some unknown reason, Humphreys often omitted the "e" from his surname when signing letters. His name appears as "Humphrys."
10. *Magazine of American History* 7, no. 2: 97.
11. Hammond, *Letters and Papers of Major-General John Sullivan,* 1:347.
12. Joseph Lee Boyle, ed., *Writings from the Valley Forge Encampment of the Continental Army* (Bowie, Maryland: Heritage Books, 2000), 97. "Mr. Bankson's" full name was Jacob Bankson.
13. *Letters of Delegates,* 18:65. For a complete description of cipher codes used during the American Revolution see Ralph E. Weber, *Masked Dispatches: Cryptograms and Cryptology in American History, 1775–1900* (Fort George G. Meade, Maryland: National Security Agency, 1993).
14. *Writings of Washington,* 23:189–90.
15. One of Washington's best operatives in New York City was a tailor named Hercules Mulligan. He eavesdropped on the conversations of the British officers who were among his customers and reported anything interesting to Washington.
16. There is the traditional view of Tallmadge's role in Washington's espionage activities. However, he may have only been the equivalent of today's caseworker, handling the Culper ring, which spied for Washington in the New York City area.
17. *Writings of Washington,* 20:104–5.
18. *Hamilton Papers,* 2:488.
19. *Papers of Washington,* 1:148 n.
20. *Epistles Domestic, Confidential, and Official from General Washington* (New York: F. and C. Rivington, 1796), 112–13. This unusual book was composed largely of counterfeit and altered letters originally published by the British during

the American Revolution. These letters were republished as factual by Washington's political enemies during his second presidential administration to embarrass him and his supporters.

21. *Papers of Washington,* 1:55. Washington made his headquarters at the time at the home of Samuel Langdon, who was the president of Harvard College. Residing with him in the house were Gen. Charles Lee and Washington's small personal staff consisting of Joseph Reed and Thomas Mifflin. Langdon agreed to give Washington and Lee the use of his entire house, except for one room that he kept for himself.

22. *Papers of Washington,* 5:236.

23. Ibid., 6:333.

24. Ibid., 7:84.

25. Transcription of original manuscript letter in the Oldridge Collection. Oldridge cites the original as being in the George Washington Papers. A prize agent was appointed to take charge of captured enemy property (frequently ships) and sell them at auction. The prize agent was paid a percentage of the sale in lieu of a salary.

26. Ramsay, *History of the American Revolution,* 2:516.

27. Warren, *History of the Rise, Progress, and Termination of the American Revolution,* 2:458. Dr. David Ramsay, another early chronicler of the Revolution, gave an impassioned explanation for Benedict Arnold's treason in his 1789 history of the Revolution, "His love of pleasure produced the love of money, and that extinguished all sensibility to the obligations of honor and duty. Oppression, extortion, misapplication of public money and property, furnished him with the further means of gratifying his favorite passions. In these circumstances, a change of sides afforded the only hope of evading a security, and at the same time, held out a prospect of replenishing his exhausted coffers."

28. Flexner, *George Washington in the American Revolution,* 382.

29. Diary of Tobias Lear, private secretary to Washington, October 23, 1786, in Henry Steele Commager and Richard B. Morris, eds., *The Spirit of Seventy-Six* (New York: Harper & Row, 1975), 756–57.

30. McHenry resigned from Washington's staff sometime in August 1780. He had served as a volunteer assistant secretary on Washington's staff since May 1778 without pay. In addition, McHenry did not have a commission as an officer, and held the honorary rank of lieutenant colonel only so long as he served on the commander in chief's staff. Although informed of McHenry's position, Congress had done nothing on his behalf. McHenry viewed this inaction as a "dismission" and decided to seek a position where he might be useful to his country but escape "any uneasiness" that may arise from a continuation of Congress's neglect. See letter from Dr. James McHenry to Gen. Nathanael Greene dated October 21, 1780, in Showman and Conrad, *Papers of General Nathanael Greene,* 6:420. McHenry resigned from Washington's staff to accept a position as a volunteer aide-de-camp to his friend Lafayette.

In October 1780, shortly after McHenry joined Lafayette's staff, Greene asked McHenry to became one of his aides. Greene petitioned Congress to appoint McHenry as a major in the Continental Army in an effort to entice McHenry to join his staff. Congress voted against commissioning McHenry. See *Journals of Congress,* 18:992. McHenry was mortified at his rejection but Congress apparently voted against McHenry because they were concerned about the effect that such a promotion would have on the policy of advancement by seniority. Remember that McHenry held no rank in the Continental Army at this point in his military service. McHenry did not accept Greene's offer following this embarrassing incident and continued to serve as a volunteer aide to Lafayette.

31. Paulding found an exact report on the troops at West Point in André's boot, including a return of the ordnance at the post, summaries of confidential letters written by General Washington, and the position of the fort's field artillery. To honor John Paulding's moment in history, Paulding, New York, was named in his honor. Paulding and his two companions were lauded at the time not only for their capture of André, but because they refused the enormous bribe he offered them if they would let him go. Historians still speculate, however, about what these three men were actually doing on the road near Tarrytown.

32. Irving, *Life of Washington,* 4:123.

33. Baker, *Itinerary of General Washington,* 190–91.

34. Freeman, *George Washington,* 5:196. General Arnold's headquarters was in the home of Beverly Robinson, a Loyalist who had fled to New York. It was a large house about two miles south of West Point, and lay on the other side of the Hudson River. Historian Washington Irving described the setting of the house, "It stood in a lonely part of the Highlands, high up from the river, yet at the foot of a mountain covered with woods."

35. David Solebury Franks was a Jewish merchant living in Montreal when the war began. Franks broke with his Loyalist father when the Americans captured Montreal in 1775. He was Arnold's business associate prior to the Revolution. Franks was commissioned a major and Arnold's aide-de-camp in 1778. His later service to America included bringing the ratification of the peace treaty ending the war to Paris, on behalf of the Continental Congress in 1784. For a short time Franks acted as the vice consul at Marseille. He later turned to business and was an assistant cashier at the Bank of North America in 1791.

36. Freeman, *George Washington,* 5:200.

37. Flexner, *George Washington in the American Revolution*, 386. Flexner gives his source as Freeman, *George Washington,* 5:199, which is not correct. Freeman's description of Washington's discovery of the plot does not mention the general speaking these words. Washington Irving, however, has Washington speaking this famous line in his *Life of Washington,* 4:133,

> Whatever agitation Washington may have felt when these documents of deep-laid treachery were put before him, he wore his usual air of equanimity when he rejoined his companions. Taking Knox and Lafayette aside, he communicated to them the intelligence, and placed the papers in their hands. "Whom can we trust now!" was his only comment, but it spoke volumes.

38. Showman and Conrad, *Papers of General Nathanael Greene,* 6:312 n.

39. *Hamilton Papers,* 2:440–41. Greene was at Orange Town (today's Orangetown), New York, which is on the west bank of the Hudson River. Hamilton wrote this letter early in the evening. The dispatch rider must have crossed the river and ridden at breakneck speed to deliver it to Greene's headquarters because Greene issued

orders at 11 P.M. for the Pennsylvania division under his command to march immediately.

40. *Hamilton Papers,* 2:438–39.
41. *Writings of Washington,* 20:84.
42. Ibid.
43. Ibid., 20:86.
44. Ibid., 20:85.
45. Ibid., 20:86–87.
46. Ibid., 20:87.
47. Ibid., 20: 84–85.
48. Ibid., 20: 88.
49. *Hamilton Papers,* 2:441. The interview with Mrs. Arnold took place on September 26, the day following the exposure of the plot. She was permitted to return to her family in Philadelphia but was later banished by that city's Council of Safety. Reunited with her husband in London, she lived out her life there and died in 1804.
50. Note that Hamilton uses the term "board of officers" to describe the investigation that General Washington ordered to determine if André was a spy. There was no judicial system in effect at the time of the American Revolution to determine if a person was a spy and what his punishment should be. The guilt or innocence of a person and his fate were left to the officer in charge, in this case Washington, to determine. The commander in chief convened a Board of General Officers to examine André. Washington's instructions to the board, in the handwriting of Alexander Hamilton, state, "After a careful examination, you will be pleased, as speedily as possible, to report a precise state of his case, together with your opinion of the light, in which he ought to be considered, and the punishment, that ought to be inflicted." See *Writings of Washington,* 2:101. When the American spy Nathan Hale was captured by the British in 1776, the decision to execute him as a spy was made exclusively by Gen. William Howe, who was the British commander in chief. Hale was not tried or court-martialed.
51. *Hamilton Papers,* 2:465, 467.
52. Ibid., 2:449.
53. Whiteley, *Washington and His Aides-de-Camp,* 155–56.
54. *Hamilton Papers,* 2:490–91. Harrison wrote this letter on October 27, 1780.
55. Smith, ed., *Letter of Delegates,* 16: 258.
56. Gov. Thomas Jefferson called upon Meade to help defend Virginia shortly after Meade's return home. Writing Meade on January 4, 1781, Jefferson spoke of the "Unorganized State of our military system" and the need for experienced military men to defend Virginia. "Under this exigency," Jefferson wrote, "we have taken the Liberty of casting our eyes on yourself as most likely to fulfill our wishes." See Boyd, *Papers of Thomas Jefferson,* 4:305.
57. *Hamilton Papers,* 2:534–35.
58. Manuscript letter, Morristown National Historical Park, Morristown, New Jersey.
59. For an account of Hamilton's wedding see Mitchell, *Alexander Hamilton: Youth to Maturity,* 207–8. Phillip Schuyler had five daughters who grew to adulthood. Besides Elizabeth they were Angelica, Catharine, Margaretta, and Cornelia. All the Schuyler girls married, but apart from Elizabeth, they all eloped. The probable cause of their elopements was because their father was fussy about whom he would permit his daughters to marry. Schuyler liked Hamilton and was happy to

have the ambitious young man as his son-in-law. While there is no known account of the Hamilton-Schuyler wedding, tradition has it that Elizabeth's mother Catherine, who was a Van Rensselaer, had one of her family's famous wedding cakes (an elaborate and expensive fruitcake) made for the occasion. For anyone with a taste for history, here is the Van Rensselaer wedding cake recipe: $1\frac{1}{2}$ pounds browned flour, 2 pounds of dark brown sugar, $1\frac{1}{2}$ pounds of butter, 18 eggs, 6 pounds of raisins, 3 pounds of currants, 3 pounds of citron, 1 pound of candied orange and lemon peel, $\frac{1}{2}$ pound of almonds chopped fine, one ounce each of cloves, allspice, nutmeg, mace, and cinnamon, 1 cup of black molasses, 1 pint of best brandy, $\frac{1}{2}$ pint Jamaica rum, 1 teaspoon of saleratus (baking soda). This makes five three-pint pans, or two large and one small loaves. The recipe called for lining the pan with buttered paper and baking in a slow oven for six hours. The finished cake weighs about 12 pounds and will feed a large number of people. The recipe appears in Mrs. Morris Patterson Ferris, *Grandmother's Cake Basket* (1922).

60. Steiner, *Life and Correspondence of James McHenry,* 30.
61. *Hamilton Papers,* 2:524.

CHAPTER 9

1. *Papers of Washington,* Confederation Series, 1:2.
2. Fitzpatrick, ed., Writings of Washington, 21:411–12.
3. Much of the information about Varick's early life is from John George Rommel, Jr., "Richard Varick: New York Aristocrat," (Ph.D. diss., Columbia University, 1966).
4. King's College, located in New York City, was reopened as Columbia College (later renamed Columbia University) at the end of the Revolutionary War. A board of directors was empowered by the New York state legislature to operate the school. The school's board of directors was called the Trustees of Columbia College and Varick was appointed as one of its members. He served on Columbia's board from 1787 until 1810 when he was elected as its chairman. He served in this capacity until 1816.
5. Wright, *Continental Army,* 41.
6. Congress authorized major generals, acting in a separate department, to have a military secretary. As commander of the Northern Department, Schuyler was allowed to have a secretary. See *Journals of Congress,* 2:94. Schuyler's authority to have a paid military secretary is stated in Varick's warrant,

> The Honorable Continental Congress having appointed me [Schuyler] a Major General in their Army and confided the Military operations in the New York Department to my care, and allowed a Secretary thereto, and appointed a Salary for his services. I do therefore, in full confidence of your honor, integrity and abilities which are well know, as is also your attachment to the cause of American Liberty, hereby constitute and appoint you to be my Secretary; giving unto you full power and authority to do and transact all and every matter whatsoever appertaining unto said office.

Schuyler Family Papers, box 1, folder 1, item 14, Albany Institute of History and Art, Albany, New York.

ation:

Varick officially remained the captain of the 6th Company of the 1st New York Regiment until September 14, 1776, when he was forced to resign his commission. Certain critics pointed out that Varick was unfairly drawing double salaries and rations, as an officer in the 1st New York and military secretary to Schuyler. Varick's letter of resignation to Washington, of which the following is an excerpt reveals that he was forced to resign his captaincy. It also reflects his legal training, "The honourable the Continental Congress (by their resolution of the 11th July) informed the Hon. Major-General Schuyler that officers of their army are prohibited from holding more offices than one, I do, therefore, in obedience to the said resolve, hereby resign to your Excellency the company which I now have in the regiment of forces of the United States of America raised in the State of New York." See Force, *American Archives,* ser. 5, 2:335; also see T. W. Egly, Jr., *History of the First New York Regiment, 1775–1784* (Hampton, New Hampshire: Peter E. Randall, 1981), 6.

7. Schuyler was in New York City at the time, which explains how Scott was able to talk to him about appointing Varick as his personal secretary. Schuyler's aides-de-camp in 1775 were John McPherson and JamesVan Rensselaer (Schuyler's brother-in-law).

8. On July 20, 1775, Congress empowered Schuyler to "dispose of and employ all the troops in the New York department in such manner as he may think best for the protection and defense of these colonies." Note that Congress used the term New York department. See *Journals of Congress,* 2:194. The forces under Schuyler's command were also referred to as the Northern Army or the Northern Department. These terms: New York Department, Northern Army, or Northern Department were used interchangeably. See Wright, *Continental Army,* 41.

9. Varick's appointment as deputy muster master general was confirmed by the Continental Congress on September 25, 1776. His appointment reads, "That Richard Varick, late captain in Colonel M'Dougal's regiment [1st New York Regiment] which office he resigned, secretary to the honorable Major General Schuyler, be appointed deputy muster master general to the northern army." See *Journals of Congress,* 5:824.

10. Varick's promotion from captain to lieutenant colonel is cited as November 12, 1776.

11. Rommel, "Richard Varick: New York Aristocrat," 16–17. White was commissioned a lieutenant colonel in the 4th Continental Dragoons (Moylan's) on February 15, 1777.

12. Varick to Col. Joseph Ward, August 23, 1777, in Rommel, ibid. 28. The American situation in upper New York state had stabilized by the time Gates took command. The scorched earth policy implemented by Schuyler was working, and the British had already been defeated at Bennington and Fort Stanwix.

13. Ibid., 30.

14. James Kirby Martin, *Benedict Arnold: Revolutionary Hero* (New York: New York University Press, 1997), 370–371.

15. Rommel, "Richard Varick: New York Aristocrat," 50.

16. Although Arnold referred to Varick as his secretary, his official position was aide-de-camp. As a major general, Arnold was authorized to have two aides-de-camp but no military secretary. Only the commander in chief and officers commanding

a department (Schuyler for example) were sanctioned by Congress to have a military secretary.

17. Carl Van Doren, *Secret History of the American Revolution* (New York: The Viking, 1941), 285–86. Van Doren gives his source as Albert Bushnell Hart, ed., *The Varick Court of Inquiry to Investigate the Implication of Colonel Richard Varick in the Arnold Treason* (1907), 82.
18. Rommel, "Richard Varick: New York Aristocrat," 63.
19. At Varick's request a court of inquiry was convened on November 2, 1780, to review his conduct as Benedict Arnold's secretary. The president of the court was Col. Goose Van Schaick who reported the court's unanimous conclusion "that Lieutenant Colonel Varick's Conduct with respect to the base Peculations and Treasonable Practices of the late General Arnold is not only unimpeachable but think him entitled (throughout every part of his conduct) to a degree of Merit that does him great honor as an Officer and particularly distinguishes him as a sincere Friend to his Country." See Egly, *History of the First New York Regiment,* 170–71, and General Orders [of the Continental Army], November 16, 1780, in *Writings of Washington,* 20:359.
20. Ibid., 22:113–14.
21. *Writings of Washington* 22:114–15.
22. Ibid., 22:112 n.
23. Emmet Collection, item EM 9255. Tilghman's letter is addressed to: "Col. Varick at Doctor Tappans, Poughkeepsie."
24. *Writings of Washington,* 27:174–75.
25. *Papers of Washington,* Confederation Series, 1:3 n.
26. Ibid., 1:2.
27. Ibid.
28. New York City was devastated by seven years of British occupation during the Revolutionary War. The city was further damaged by two major fires (in 1776 and 1778). The New York state government appointed a council to run the city at the end of the war, which appointed Varick to his post as recorder of New York.
29. Kenneth T. Jackson, ed., *Encyclopedia of New York City* (New Haven: Yale University Press, 1995), 1226.
30. John Schuyler, *Institution of the Society of the Cincinnati, Formed by the Officers of the American Army of the Revolution, 1783: With Extracts, from the Proceedings of its General Meetings and from the Transactions of the New York State Society* 1886; reprint, 1998), 333.
31. Ibid., 332.
32. Bezaleel Howe was from New Hampshire and enlisted as a private early in the war. He was wounded at Stillwater, New York, during the Saratoga campaign of 1777 and commissioned a first lieutenant in June 1779. Howe was detached and assigned to the Commander in Chief's Guard on September 5, 1783, and promoted to captain by brevet on October 10, 1783. He enlisted in the small postwar army where he was promoted to major in 1794. Howe resigned from the army in 1796 and died in 1825. See Godfrey, *Commander-in-Chief's Guard,* 188–89.
33. *Writings of Washington,* 27:20.
34. Ibid., 1:xl.
35. Jared Sparks, a Unitarian minister and Harvard president, was the first to publish Washington's correspondence. He published twelve volumes between 1833 and

1837. Sparks, however, took some cavalier liberties with Washington's correspondence, often changing words or even whole sentences to suit his own stylistic tastes. The second publication of Washington's correspondence was edited by Worthington C. Ford and published between 1889 and 1893. Ford published a slightly longer and more accurate edition than Sparks. The next publication of the correspondence was overseen by John C. Fitzpatrick, librarian of the Congress, who edited thirty-nine volumes that were published between 1931 and 1944 as *The Writings of George Washington.* The fourth project was started in 1969 at the University of Virginia and is still going on. It is titled *The Papers of George Washington* and its goal is to accurately publish not only Washington's outgoing letters, orders, reports, proclamations, and addresses but also selected correspondence and other documents that he received during his lifetime.

35. Johnston, *Campaign of 1776 around New York and Brooklyn,* 85–86, doc. 29.
36. The *Varick Transcripts* include a few of the letters written by Washington's aides. However there is no explanation of how Varick chose the aides' letters that were copied or why he excluded some including many that were transmitting orders from the commander in chief.

CHAPTER 10

1. *Writings of Washington,* 23:94.
2. The William Ellison house no longer exists. Washington made his headquarters there from November 28, 1780, until June 24, 1781.
3. *Hamilton Papers,* 2:255.
4. Ibid., 2:564. Hamilton described his confrontation with Washington in a letter to his father-in-law, Philip Schuyler, written two days after the incident took place.
5. Fitzpatrick, *Spirit of the Revolution,* 81.
6. *Hamilton Papers,* 2:569.
7. Ibid., *Hamilton Papers,* 2:563–68.
8. Ibid., *Hamilton Papers,* 2:647.
9. Ibid., 2:658. "Major Fish" was Nicholas Fish.
10. Harrison's date of resignation is based on a letter of certification that Washington wrote on his behalf. See *Writings of Washington,* 21:377.
11. George T. Ness, Jr. "A Lost Man of Maryland," *Maryland Historical Magazine* 35, no. 4 (December: 1940), 322.
12. *Hamilton Papers,* 2:584–86. The term "Chair of their Supreme Court" in Harrison's letter is a mistake. There was no such court in Maryland. The error probably arose in copying Harrison's original letter. See Ness, "A Lost Man of Maryland," 324 n.
13. *Writings of Washington,* 21:377.
14. Ibid., *Writings of Washington,* 21:467. The draft of this letter is in the handwriting of Tench Tilghman.
15. Ibid., 22:181.
16. Jacob and Ragsdale, *Biographical Directory of the United States Congress, 1774–1989,* 1956.
17. Francis Baylies, "Some Remarks on the Life and Character of General David Cobb," *New England Historical and Genealogical Register* 18 (January 1864): 6.
18. Ibid., 7.

19. Heitman, *Register of Officers of the Continental Army,* 162; Wright, *Continental Army,* 215.
20. *Writings of Washington,* 22:216.
21. Marcuis D. Raymond, *The New York Genealogical and Biographical Record* 25, no. 4 (October 1894): 11.
22. *Writings of Washington,* 21:16.
23. *Travels in North-America,* 1:351–52. Chastellux knew Smith and said of him, "this young man is not only a very good soldier, but an excellent scholar." See ibid., 1:351.
24. Schuyler, *Institution of the Society of the Cincinnati,* 292. The British landed about 4,000 troops in the Throgs Neck section of the Bronx on October 12, 1776. The area was called Throg's Neck, Frog's Neck, or Throck's Point at the time of the Revolutionary War. Throgs Neck was separated at the time from the mainland by a marshy creek over which a bridge had been built. Author Schuyler credits Smith with destroying this bridge. The British were repulsed at Throgs Neck; however, they successfully landed a few days later at nearby Pell's Point and started marching inland.
25. Smith's promotion to lieutenant colonel is listed as January 1, 1777, which is a few days after the battle of Trenton. See Heitman, *Register of Officers of the Continental Army,* 508.
26. Washington mentions the arrival of these three regiments, consisting of a total of 350 men, in a letter to Congress dated November 23, 1777. See *Writings of Washington,* 10:101.
27. Ibid., 10:165.
28. Manuscript letter, Valley Forge Historical Society.
29. Lt. Col. Smith, Garrison Orders, March 6, 1779, National Archives, RG 93, microfilm 853, roll 3, 98.
30. See returns for the Continental Army for the months of December 1777 through May 1778 in Lesser, *The Sinews of Independence: Monthly Strength Reports of the Continental Army,* 54–69. Apparently there were never enough recruits raised in Massachusetts to allow the three regiments (Lee's, Henley's, and Jackson's) to operate independently. This problem is mentioned in a letter from an officer in Henley's regiment who resigned his commission to Gen. William Heath in Boston on March 10, 1778, "My Acceptance of the Appointment to the Lieutenant Colonelcy of Col. Henley's Regiment, was founded on the Prospect of the Regiment being soon raised. The Difficulties which have intervened & impeded the Completion of it, have been various, & at present are so far from being removed, that they now force conviction that the Recruiting the 3 additional Battalions assigned for this State is impracticable. This truth must doubtless have struck you, Sir, in a pointed Light, & I presume will lead his Excellency General Washington to incorporate the Battalions of Lee & Henley into one Regiment. Under the Circumstances mentioned, And the great Number of Officers who are without Men to command will render my retiring, of no Consequence to the Service." Lt. Col. William Tudor to William Heath, Washington Papers, microfilm, reel 47.
31. *Writings of Washington,* 19:322–23. Smith's appointment is vague and bewildering. It was probably an honorarium, a way of rewarding an outstanding officer.
32. Idzerda, *Lafayette in the Age of the American Revolution,* 3:233.

33. *Writings of Washington,* 22:333. For Smith's service record also see Heitman, *Register of Officers of the Continental Army,* 508.

34. A cornet is the most junior officer in a mounted troop. An eighteenth-century military dictionary defines a cornet as "the third commission officer in a troop of horse or dragoons, subordinate to the captain and lieutenant, equivalent to the ensign amongst the foot. His duty is to carry the standard, near the centre of the front rank of the squadron." See Smith, *An Universal Military Dictionary,* 67.

35. *Writings of Washington,* 11:339. Major Clough was bayoneted and taken prisoner during the surprise attack on Baylor's command, September 28, 1778. He died a few days later from his wounds.

36. Ibid., 12:37–38.

37. Ibid.,22: 323.

38. Peregrine Fitzhugh to George Washington, February 19, 1793, in *Washington Papers,* microfilm, reel 103.

39. Lotteries were popular in colonial America and they were sometimes used for private relief. All lotteries were authorized by state legislatures. In the case of people who could not pay their debts, which apparently is what happened to Peregrine Fitzhugh, their property—land, house, livestock, etc. would be put up as prizes, and the proceeds would go to pay off their debts. The state took a percentage of the money for allowing the lottery to take place. The debtor might also get something from the proceeds. Critical to the success of the scheme was the sale of all the authorized lottery tickets. For more information about lotteries in colonial America, see John Samuel Ezell, *Fortune's Merry Wheel: The Lottery in America* (Cambridge: Harvard University Press, 1960).

40. *Writings of Washington,* 22:71.

41. *Journals of Congress,* 20:541. Apparently it was Tilghman's wish to have his commission retroactive to April 1777 instead of August 1776 when he joined Washington's staff as a volunteer aide. Tilghman made this request because he did not want seniority in rank over his friends Hamilton and Meade, both of whom were appointed aides-de-camp and lieutenant colonels in March 1777.

42. *Writings of Washington,* 22:164. "A detachment" was an unspecified number of soldiers, but usually less than a regiment. The word "department" refers to the area of operation of the Southern, Northern, or Western armies. These forces were under Washington's command but had their own commanders because of their distance from Continental Army headquarters.

43. Transcription in the Oldridge Collection from the Papers of Robert Morris, Manuscript Division, Library of Congress.

44. Idzerda, *Lafayette in the Age of the American Revolution,* 3:309–10. Lafayette's letter is dated "New Windsor on the North River, February 21, 1781" and addressed to his wife, Adrienne de Noailles de Lafayette.

45. Massey, *John Laurens and The American Revolution,* 177–78.

46. *Magazine of American History* 7, no. 2: 95.

47. Alexander Garden, *Anecdotes of the American Revolution: With Additional Notes by Thomas W. Field* (Brooklyn: 1865), 3:14. This is a reprint of Garden's *Anecdotes of the Revolutionary War in America: With Sketches of Character of Persons the Most Distinguished, in the Southern States, for Civil and Military Service* (Charleston: A. E. Miller, 1822) and *Anecdotes of the American Revolution: Illustrative of the Talents and Virtues of the Heroes and Patriots, Who Acted the Most*

Conspicuous Parts Therein, 2nd ser. (Charleston: A. E. Miller, 1828). Garden served in Lee's Battalion of light dragoons and was an aide-de-camp to Gen. Nathanael Greene from March 1781 to the end of the war. Garden died in 1829. His source for this story was the recollections of Capt. William Jackson (a former aide-de-camp to Gen. Benjamin Lincoln) who was Laurens's secretary during his mission to France. Vergennes wrote Lafayette after this incident, "Mr. Laurens shows zeal, but I tell you in confidence that he did not express it in a manner suited to the nature of his mission. We did not take offense, because we attributed his behavior only to his inexperience in public affairs." See Idzerda, *Lafayette in the Age of the American Revolution,* 4:47.

48. Garden, *Anecdotes of the American Revolution: With Additional Notes by Thomas W. Field,* 3:15. Captain Jackson was also Garden's source for this charming story. Unfortunately Jackson tended to embellish his stories and it is doubtful that the incident he described to Garden ever took place. The Garden family have a unique place in world history because the gardenia is named after Alexander Garden's father, also named Alexander Garden (1730?–91), who contributed to the classification of New World plants.

49. Massey, *John Laurens and the American Revolution,* 178. Also see Leonard W. Labaree et al., eds., *The Papers of Benjamin Franklin* (New Haven: Yale University Press, 1959–), 35:28 n. This footnote details the gifts and loans arranged by Franklin and Colonel Laurens. Franklin made it clear that he was responsible for a gift of six million livres from the French. Franklin wrote Laurens's secretary, William Jackson, on July 6, 1781, "The Six Million [livres] was a free Gift from the King's Goodness (not a Loan to be repaid with Interest) and was obtained by my application long before Col. Lawrens's Arrival." See Labaree, *Papers of Benjamin Franklin* 35:224.

50. Robert M. Weir, "Portrait of a Hero," *American Heritage* 27, no. 3 (April 1976): 88. Historian Jonathan Dull summarized Laurens's mission to France as follows, "[American] Government finances were restored only through massive infusions of French money, obtained chiefly by Franklin (rather than by the blustering amateur diplomat Colonel John Laurens, sent to France to obtain supplies for the Continental army)." See Dull, *Diplomatic History of the American Revolution,* 119. Franklin angrily wrote Laurens's secretary William Jackson on July 6, 1781, regarding Laurens's mission to France, "What Col Lawrens really obtained, and a great Service I hope it will prove, was a Loan upon interest of ten Millions [livres], to be borrowed on the Credit of this Court [France] in Holland. I have not heard that this Loan has yet produced anything: and therefore I do not know that a single Livre exists or has existed in Europe of his procuring for the States." See Labaree, *Papers of Benjamin Franklin,* 35:225.

51. Townsend, *An American Soldier: The Life of John Laurens,* 249.
52. Massey, *John Laurens and the American Revolution,* 237.
53. McHenry apparently resigned from Lafayette's staff sometime in late 1780 or early 1781 and returned to civilian life. He resided in Baltimore where he became a member of the Maryland Board of War. Lafayette wrote him a personal letter on February 15, 1781, which included an offer to join his staff, "Every Body Says You Are Going to Get Into the Governor's Council. If You Quit the House for the field, I shall Be Very Happy to obtain the Preference in Your Military Employements, and Hoping You know My tender friendship and affectionate Regard for

You." See Idzerda, *Lafayette in the Age of The American Revolution,* 3:324. McHenry apparently accepted his friend's offer because he returned to Lafayette's staff as a volunteer aide in March 1781.

54. Boyd, *Papers of Thomas Jefferson,* 4:400.

55. Ibid., 5:101.

56. Arnold sailed from New York on December 20, 1780, with about 1,600 troops. This was his first assignment as a British officer.

57. James McHenry got his wealthy Baltimore-based merchant father, Daniel McHenry, to rally the businessmen in Baltimore to supply Lafayette's army for the Virginia campaign. See *In Grateful Remembrance . . . An Exhibition of Patraits Commemorating the Founding of the State and Nation, 1770–1788* (Annapolis: Maryland Commission on Artistic Property, 1976), 91. Lafayette's friend, Col. John Laurens, was in France at the time. Writing Lafayette on May 14, 1781, from Paris, Laurens said, "Your Friends have heard of your being gone against the Traitor Arnold, and are anxious to hear of your Success, and that you have brought him to Justice. Enclos'd is a Copy of a Letter from his Agent in England, by which the Price of his Treason may be nearly guess'd at. Judas sold only one Man, Arnold three Millions." See Labaree, *Papers of Benjamin Franklin,* 35:65.

58. Cornwallis scored a shallow victory against an American force led by General Greene at the battle of Guilford Courthouse on March 15, 1781. Cornwallis's army was exhausted and badly in need of supplies following this engagement. He marched his army to the coast, making his temporary headquarters at Wilmington, North Carolina. Cornwallis's march north into Virginia was in defiance of General Clinton's orders. But Clinton took no action because he was disgusted with Cornwallis's insubordination and was looking for an opportunity to resign.

59. William Dunlap, *The Diary of William Dunlap* (New York: 1903), 298.

60. Mordecai Gist was a tough Continental officer and ardent American patriot. He took his politics seriously naming one of his sons "Independence" and another "States Rights." His grandson, Brig. Gen. States Rights Gist, was a Confederate officer who was killed in action at Franklin, Tennessee, in 1864.

61. *Writings of Washington,* 23:93–94.

62. John Parke Custis is one of the men erroneously most frequently listed as being an aide-de-camp to George Washington. Commenting on the subject, historian Douglas Southall Freeman said, "In the absence of reference in diaries to Custis's presence at Yorktown, it might be assumed that nothing more than family tradition supported the statement of his son (George Washington Parke Custis) concerning Jack's service as aide-de-camp to the General-in-Chief. If Custis had been appointed formally to the staff, announcement almost certainly would have appeared in General Orders: but his presence at camp in an unofficial capacity is beyond dispute." See Freeman, *George Washington,* 5:401–2 n.

63. French siege guns were 16– and 24–pound artillery pieces, mounted on limbers that could be drawn by horses. These were large and heavy cannons that were difficult to maneuver, but necessary in a siege against fortified enemy positions such as the British built to defend Yorktown. The Americans had few of these large caliber weapons and were largely dependent on the French who brought a number with them when they came to America. See Harold L. Peterson, *Round Shot and Rammers* (New York: Bonanza Books, 1969), 54, 57.

64. Jonathan Trumbull, "Minutes of Occurrences Respecting the Siege and Capture of York in Virginia: Extracted from the Journal of Colonel Jonathan Trumbull, Secretary to the General, 1781." *Proceedings of the Massachusetts Historical Society* 14 (1876): 334.

65. Irving, *Life of Washington,* 4:356–57.

66. Trumbull, "Minutes of Occurrences Respecting the Siege and Capture of York," 335.

67. One of George Washington Parke Custis's more incredible stories is about Washington's sleeping tent, which was one of the three tents made for him in Philadelphia in early 1776. According to Custis, Washington's sleeping tent was always pitched in the yard of the various houses he occupied as his headquarters. "Within its venerable folds," Custis said, "Washington was in the habit of seeking privacy and seclusion, where he could commune with himself, and where he wrote the most memorable of his despatches in the Revolutionary war. He would remain in the retirement of the sleeping tent sometimes for hours, giving orders to the officer of his guard that he should on no account be disturbed, save on the arrival of an important express. The objects of his seclusion being accomplished, the chief would appear at the canvass door of the marquee, with despatches in his hand, giving which to his secretary to copy and transmit, he would either mount his charger for a tour of inspection, or return to the headquarters and enjoy social converse with his officers." See Custis, *Recollections and Private Memoirs of Washington,* 279–80.

68. Tench Tilghman, "Journal of the Siege of Yorktown: List of French Regiments; Terms of Surrender," Society of the Cincinnati Library, Washington. D.C.

69. Steiner, *Life and Correspondence of James McHenry,* 39–40.

70. *Writings of Washington,* 23:212.

71. Ibid., 23:198–99. Col. Alexander Scammell is mentioned as being one of Washington's aides-de-camp and therefore worthy of some comment. There is no known evidence that he served as an aide to Washington. Scammell was adjutant general of the army at one point in the war, which would have put him at headquarters and close to the commander in chief. Scammell was a Harvard College graduate (Class of 1769), after which he studied law. He saw extensive combat in the Revolution and was appointed the adjutant general in 1780. Scammell commanded light infantry troops at Yorktown. It is believed that he was shot in the back by a British soldier after he surrendered. Washington's military secretary, Jonathan Trumbull, Jr., mentions this in his diary entry for September 30, 1781, "Colonel Scammel, being officer of the day is cruelly wounded and taken prisoner while reconnoitering." He died of his wounds a few days later. His friend David Humphreys wrote an epitaph about him shortly after the British surrender at Yorktown, "Alexander Scammell, adjutant general of the American armies, and colonel of the first regiment of New Hampshire, while he commanded a chosen corps of light infantry at the successful siege of Yorktown, in Virginia, was, in the gallant performance of his duty as field officer of the day, unfortunately captured, and afterward insidiously wounded—of which wound he expired at Williamsburg, October 1781." See Lossing, *Pictorial Field-Book of the Revolution,* 2:309.

72. Tilghman, "Journal of the Siege of Yorktown."

73. Hamilton took his former teacher Francis Barber with him on the assault of Redoubt Number 10. Barber was promoted to colonel of the 2nd New Jersey regiment on January 7, 1783. After being in combat for almost the entire Revolution,

Barber was crushed to death by a falling tree on February 11, 1783, as the war was ending.

74. Pioneers were troops normally responsible for repairing roads and occasionally preparing fortifications.

75. An abatis is an obstacle created by a tangled mass of felled trees with their branches facing toward the enemy and as much intertwined as possible. Fraises were wooden poles set horizontally or at an angle on the sloping outer parapet wall. The fraises had sharpened points facing toward an enemy.

76. Thacher, *Military Journal,* 285.

77. Tilghman, "Journal of the Siege of Yorktown."

78. Ibid.

79. The term parley has its origins in the French verb "to speak," which is *parler.*

80. Tilghman, "Journal of the Siege of Yorktown."

81. Garden, *Anecdotes of the American Revolution,* 2nd Ser. 17–18. The alleged dialog between Ross and Laurens does not appear in Garden's earlier *Anecdotes of the Revolutionary War in America (1822).* A usually reliable reference source for books about American history, Wright Howes, *U.S. IANA* (New York: R.R. Bowker, 1962), calls Garden's 1828 history of the Revolution a "slightly altered" version of his 1822 book (p. 221). However, this is incorrect and Garden's 1828 book is completely different from his earlier 1822 history.

82. The story that the British and German troops played a tune called "The World Turned Upside Down" first appeared in Garden, *Anecdotes of the American Revolution,* 2nd ser., 18, and was repeated by later historians. European military tradition allowed a conquered force, who had fought gallantly, to march out of their works with their flags unfurled and their music playing one of the victor's marches. The British humiliated the Americans by refusing them these little honors at Charleston and Laurens apparently took the opportunity at Yorktown to return the insult. There is no known first handaccount that mentioned the specific tunes that were played by the British when they surrendered at Yorktown.

83. *Writings of Washington,* 23:241–43.

84. Custis, *Recollections and Private Memoirs of Washington,* 246.

85. Ibid., 246.

86. Jacob Cox Parsons, *Extracts from the Diary of Jacob Hiltzheimer of Philadephia* (Philadelphia: Wm. F. Fell, 1893), 46.

87. Camp fever was a general term used at the time for a variety of acute infectious diseases. Typically, a man like John Parke Custis lived a somewhat isolated life and did not have a strong resistance to contagious diseases. Once a communicable disease took hold of an American encampment, it spread quickly. One reason for this was that the American army was mostly composed of men recruited from isolated farms who had not built up any resistance to disease. In comparison, the British Army suffered less from infectious diseases because its common soldiers were more often recruited from urban areas where they had been exposed to disease and developed immunities.

88. Baker, *Itinerary of General Washington,* 247. In an article by Eldon G. Chuinard, *Journal of the American Medical Association* 236, no. 5 (August 2, 1976), the author states that by the time of the American Revolution, it was already recognized that soldiers were healthier on the move than they were in an encampment.

John Parke Custis fell victim to the diseases that tended to spread through armies when they stayed in one place for any length of time.

89. The marquis de Chastellux mentions meeting Mrs. Moylan in 1780. She was still living at her father's New Jersey home when Chastellux stopped at the house en route from Morristown to Philadelphia. Moylan was escorting the marquis and insisted they stop to meet his young wife: "We soon arrived at Colonel Moylan's, or rather at Colonel Van Horne's, his father-in-law. This manor, for the house resembles closely what is called 'a manor' in England, is in a beautiful situation; it is surrounded by some trees, the approach, is adorned with a grassplot[.] Mrs. Van Horne is an old lady[.] Her three daughters are not unattractive; Mrs. Moylan, the eldest, is six months advanced in her pregnancy; the youngest is only twelve years old, but the second is marriageable." See *Travels in North-America,* 1:150–53. The Van Horne house is the setting for several charming stories about the American Revolution. It is still standing in central New Jersey but devoid of its surrounding land. The house, clad in aluminum siding, sits on a tiny plot of ground. It is surrounded by an interstate highway on one side and a shopping center on another. Thousands of motorists speed by the house every day without an inkling of its role in the American Revolution.

90. Stephen Moylan's children were an unidentified child who was born dead in 1780, another unidentified child who died in infancy in 1795, and two daughters, named Maria and Elizabeth Catharine, who lived to adulthood. Maria married Samuel Fox. Moylan's second daughter, Elizabeth Catharine, married her first cousin William Moylan Lansdale in 1807.

91. Griffin, *Stephen Moylan*, 137. Moylan's wife, Mary Ricketts Van Horn Moylan, apparently died in 1794. We know this from a letter that Martha Washington wrote a relative on March 9, 1794, in which she mentioned Mrs. Moylan's death, "pore Mrs. Moylan (who you have seen out at mount vernon some years agoe) is dead with in this week— and has left two little girls to lement her loss." See Fields, *Worthy Partner: The Papers of Martha Washington,* 261. The Moylans were guests at Mount Vernon in 1785.

92. Stephen Moylan's father, John Moylan, was married twice. His first wife is identified as the countess of Limerick and they had four sons, Stephen, Richard, Francis, and James. This marriage also produced two daughters who became nuns in Ireland. John Moylan's second wife was named Mary and they had two sons named John and Jasper.

93. Griffin, *Stephen Moylan*, 140.

94. *Journals of Congress,* 23:753.

CHAPTER 11

1. Steiner, *Life and Correspondence of James McHenry,* 45.

2. The Hasbrouck house is still standing and open as a museum. It has been expertly restored and furnished to look as it probably did when it was used as Washington's headquarters. The rooms have a busy but organized appearance, which probably is the way they looked when they were occupied by Washington and his staff.

3. Ancestral File, Library of The Church of Jesus Christ of Latter-day Saints, Salt Lake City, Utah.

4. The surrender of Charleston was the worst American defeat of the Revolutionary War. It is perhaps the blackest chapter in the history of the Revolution as General Lincoln received little support from the civilian government or local militia during the siege.

5. *Writings of Washington*, 24:254.

6. Kapp, *Life of Frederick William Von Steuben*, 614.

7. Egly, *History of the First New York Regiment*, 16; Heitman, *Register of Officers of the Continental Army*, 564.

8. Kapp, *Life of Frederick William Von Steuben*, 608; Heitman, *Register of Officers of the Continental Army*, 564.

9. Kapp, *Life of Frederick William Von Steuben*, 615. Von Steuben is now thought by some historians to have been a homosexual. See for example, John Ferling, *John Adams: A Life* (Knoxville: University of Tennessee Press, 1992), 323.

10. Whiteley, *Washington and His Aides de Camp*. Writing his friend von Steuben toward the end of the war, Walker said, "We are here in the center of dullness. Head-quarters, you know, was always the last place in the world for mirth[.] I had two disciples at chess, Mrs. Washington and my colleague [David Humphreys], but unhappily one is thinking too much of her home, and the other is making verses during the game." Kapp, *Life of Frederick William Von Steuben*, 619.

11. Kapp, *Life of Frederick William Von Steuben*, 614. The officer who wrote this description was von Steuben's wartime secretary, Peter S. Duponceau.

12. Here are excerpts of von Steuben's challenge to Lee of December 2, 1778,

> It has come to my ears that in your defense [a reference to Lee's conduct at the battle of Monmouth] you have permitted yourself to make indecent Remarks about myself. If I were in my own Country, where my reputation has long been well established, I should contradict your Epigrams and call them lies—but I am a Foreigner here—you have offended me—I demand satisfaction. Captain Walker, who brings you this letter, will inform me of your decision. I am, Sir, Your very humble Servant, Le Baron de Steuben.

See Kirkland, *Letters on the American Revolution*, 1:57.

13. *Writings of Washington*, 23:464.

14. Ibid., 26:21. Washington wrote this letter on January 8, 1783. Note that he makes reference to (Col. Tench) Tilghman as still being a member of his staff, who had taken a leave of absence "I suppose for the greater part or whole of the Winter." This is consistent with the idea that Tilghman left Washington's service sometime in mid- to late-December 1782 to take a leave of absence for the winter. Tilghman did not return to headquarters for the balance of the war and there is no known reference to his resigning from Washington's staff.

15. Walker served in this post from March 21, 1791, to February 20, 1798. The position of naval officer of customs required no knowledge of ships or the sea. It was a political appointment. The 1789 Act of Congress that established the United States Customs Service provided for a Naval Officer of customs for a number of American seaports. His duty was to receive copies of all arriving ship's manifests and to establish the import duties on the cargo with the collector of customs after which a permit to enter the port would be granted.

16. Schuyler, *Institution of the Society of the Cincinnati,* 336.
17. Old Fort Schuyler is sometimes confused with another upstate New York fortress called Fort Schuyler, which was built at the site of present-day Rome, New York.
18. Kapp, *Life of Frederick William Von Steuben,* 615.
19. *Writings of Washington,* 24:4. The draft of this letter was written by David Humphreys.
20. Ibid., 24:421. The draft of this letter was written by Benjamin Walker with changes to the draft in Washington's handwriting.
21. See E. T. H. Shaffer, "The Rejected Laurens: A Carolina Tragedy," *South Carolina Historical Association* 1934): 21–23.
22. *Writings of Washington,* 25:269.
23. Pickering, *Life of Timothy Pickering,* 1:431. The earlier and more important record of Washington's March 15, 1783, address to his officers is a letter written by Maj. Samuel Shaw who apparently was present at the meeting. Shaw's letter is also the earliest known account of Washington's famous comment to his officers as he tried to read a letter to them from a member of Congress. According to Shaw, "His Excellency, after reading the first paragraph, made a short pause, took out his spectacles, and begged the indulgence of his audience while he put them on, observing at the same time, that he had grown gray in their service, and now found himself growing blind." See Josiah Quincy, *The Journals of Major Samuel Shaw: The First American Consulat Canton, with a Life of the Author* (Boston: Wm. Crosby and H. P. Nichols, 1847), 103–5. For an analysis of the differences between Cobb's and Shaw's account of this renowned story from the American Revolution, see Freeman, *George Washington,* 5:434–35 n.

    Maj. Samuel Shaw (1754–94) is sometimes mentioned as one of Washington's aides-de-camp. He was an outstanding artillery officer who served throughout the war. Shaw apparently served as a volunteer at headquarters as shown by lengthy recruiting instructions he drafted for Washington on January 13, 1777 (see *Writings of Washington,* 7:8 n). However there is no evidence indicating that Shaw was appointed to Washington's personal staff. He was appointed an aide-de-camp to Gen. Henry Knox during the Revolution and is remembered as a pioneer in opening trade with China in the years following the war. President Washington appointed him America's first consul to China. Shaw died at sea en route home from a trading voyage to the Orient.
24. On June 6, 1783, the noncommissioned officers and enlisted men of the Commander in Chief's Guard were granted furloughs. A temporary headquarters guard was formed of soldiers from the Massachusetts Line. They were replaced on June 16, 1783, by a detail from the New Hampshire Line. Some of them were mounted. They were commanded by Lt. Bazaleel Howe who was also from New Hampshire. Howe appears to have been an officer of merit. He enlisted as a private soldier in Reed's New Hampshire Regiment on April 23, 1775, a few days after the start of the war. Howe was promoted to second lieutenant in November 1776 and breveted captain by the Continental Congress on October 10, 1783. Congress was meeting at Princeton at the time, and Howe was on duty at Washington's headquarters at nearby Rocky Hill.

    The purpose of Captain Howe's detail was to provide some military appearance at Washington's headquarters. They also guarded the headquarters property and personal baggage of the general and his aides-de-camp. Their function, however, was not to act as a bodyguard for Washington.

25. The house was rented from Judge John Berrien's widow. On April 21, 1772, the judge invited some distinguished Princeton citizens to witness his will, immediately after which he committed suicide by throwing himself into the nearby Millstone River.

26. Washington wrote Maj. Gen. Henry Knox from Rocky Hill on September 23, 1783, "Humphreys and Walker have each had an ill turn, since they came to this place; the latter is getting about, but the other is still in his Bed of a fever that did not 'till yesterday quit him for 14 or 15 days. Mrs. Washington has also been very unwell as most of my domesticks and Guards have been and indeed now are." See *Writings of Washington,* 27:165.

There is no record of George Washington ever being sick during the entire eight years of the Revolution although his aides seemed to be ill on a regular basis. Washington was immune from smallpox, the greatest epidemic killer of the eighteenth century, which he contracted and survived as a teenager. While he was sometimes sick as a young man during the French and Indian War, he seemed to enjoy good health during the Revolution.

27. This evidently was a favorite sort of parlor trick at the Berrien house. On May 10, 1768, William Franklin, then governor of New Jersey, wrote to his father, Benjamin Franklin, that he had tried the experiment unsuccessfully in a creek near Burlington, in company with "Judge Berrien, who has often perform'd the Experiment with Success in Millstone River." See *Historic Structures Report, Rockingham,* 1:11A–20.

28. Until the late nineteenth century the prime source of disease was believed to be miasmas, which are poisonous gases given off by unhealthy environments. These included stagnant water, overcrowded slums, and rotting animal and vegetable matter.

29. Congress was meeting at Annapolis on a temporary basis. Dr. James McHenry was a delegate to Congress at the time and he explained Congress's imposing scheme in a letter he wrote from Princeton, New Jersey, on October 22, 1783, "Congress some time ago determined to fix their federal Town on the Delaware near Trenton. Yesterday they determined to erect a second federal Town on the Potomac near George Town: and to reside equal periods at Annapolis & Trenton till the buildings are completed. We adjourn the 12 of next month to meet at Annapolis the 26." See *Hamilton Papers,* 3:472–73.

30. *Writings of Washington,* 27:260–62.

31. Ibid., 27:239–40.

32. Ibid., 27:266.

33. *Letters of Delegates,* 21:221–22.

34. Harrison, *Memoir of Lieutenant Colonel Tench Tilghman,* 41–42. It is possible that Tilghman attended Washington's resignation ceremony in an unofficial capacity.

35. Key to painting *Resignation of General Washington,* Frick Art Reference Library, New York, New York.

36. McHenry is also missing from a later depiction of Washington's resignation painted by Edwin White in 1859. White's painting is on exhibit at the Maryland State House. A large canvas of Washington's resignation was also painted by the

English-born artist Robert Edge Pine. However Pine's painting was destroyed in a fire in 1803, and there is no surviving record of its appearance.

37. *Writings of Washington,* 27:294–95.

38. The touching story of Washington giving his aides expense money is untrue. Washington only advanced the money to them. He charged the expense to the government and was reimbursed shortly afterward. A voucher from the office of accounts dated Philadelphia, February 6, 1784, reads, "Cash paid his Aids De Camps vis Col. Humphreys, Cobb & Walker to defray their Expenses returning to their respective homes—100 Dollars each." Washington was scrupulously honest and must have given Cobb his $100 when they parted in Philadelphia en route to Annapolis. See George Washington Papers, microfilm, ser. 5, vol. 24, reel 117.

39. This story appears in Fitzpatrick, *Spirit of the Revolution,* 85–86.

PART 4 AND CHAPTER 12

1. *Papers of Washington,* Confederation Series, 3:64. The Land Ordinance of 1785 divided the Northwest Territory into townships that were then divided into lots to be sold to the public.

2. The importance of Shays' Rebellion in bringing about the Constitutional Convention and the adoption of a federal constitution was mentioned in a letter that David Humphreys wrote to Thomas Jefferson, then American minister to France. Humphreys letter is dated November 29, 1788, "The insurrection in Massachusetts was not without its benefits. From a view of the impotence of the general government, of the contempt in which we were held abroad & the want of happiness at home, the Public was thus gradually wrought to a disposition for receiving a government possessed of sufficient energy to prevent the calamities of Anarchy & civil war." See Mary A. Giunta, ed., *The Emerging Nation:A Documentary History of the Foreign Relations of the United States under the Articles of Confederation, 1780–1789* (Washington, D.C.: Superintendent of Documents, 1996), 3:888.

3. Catherine Drinker Bowen, *Miracle at Philadelphia* (Boston: Little, Brown, 1966), 38.

4. Ibid., 299.

5. *Papers of Washington,* Confederation Series, 1:12.

6. *Writings of Washington,* 28:240–41.

7. Ibid., 28:65.

8. Ibid., 27:284.

9. Ibid., 27:300–301.

10. See Elbridge Gerry to John Adams in *Letters of Delegates,* 26:685. As our narrative unfolds John Adams will become one of its central characters. My readers should be warned that John Adams was perhaps the unhappiest and most frustrated of the Founding Fathers. He was the second president of the United States, and lived to the age of ninety, but he was in deep depression during much of his adult life. In the opinion of some historians he was vain, opinionated, ill-tempered, tactless, and soured by a deep-rooted persecution complex. As an example, after accompanying George Washington on his journey to Boston in 1775 to take command of the Continental Army, Adams wrote, "Such is the pride and pomp of war, I, poor creature, worn out with scribbling for my bread and for my liberty, low in spirits and weak in health, must leave others to wear the laurels which I have sown; others to eat the

bread which I have earned; a common case." The best thing that happened to Adams was his marriage to his devoted and talented wife Abigail who sustained him throughout their long marriage. See Abraham Blinderman, "John Adams," *New York State Journal of Medicine* (February 1977).

11. *Letters of Delegates,* 21:616. For Humphreys' appointment see *Journals of Congress,* 27:375.
12. *Writings of Washington,* 27:414–15.
13. One of Humphreys' fellow passengers was Gen. Thaddeus Kosciuszko, the Polish military engineer who had helped the Americans win their independence.
14. Frank Landon Humphreys, *Life and Times of David Humphreys* (New York: G. P. Putnam's Sons, 1917), 1:310–11. If Humphreys' poetry seems tedious, it was. Critics of his work said, "In the writing of verse he was a persistent journeyman; he wrote it out with the same order and urbanity with which he carved the chicken for Washington's family at Mount Vernon." Or, "Most of Humphreys poetry is worthless, and innumerable examples might be cited of his foolish rhymes, pompous diction, and ridiculous subjects; yet he had a certain fluency and at times wit." See Johnson, *Dictionary of American Biography,* 9:375.
15. Giunta, *Emerging Nation,* 2:433.
16. Washington's introductions were sent to the marquis de Chastellux, comte d'Estaing, Benjamin Franklin, George William Fairfax, Thomas Jefferson, and Sir Edward Newenham. Some of these names may not be familiar. Chastellux was one of the French generals who came with Rochambeau to America. The comte d'Estaing was a French naval officer whose fleet aided the Americans during the Revolution. Benjamin Franklin was still in Paris at the time. George William Fairfax was Washington's former neighbor. He made an extended visit to England in 1773 and never returned. Washington gave Humphreys a letter of introduction to Fairfax: "I give you a letter to him also, in case you should go to England." See *Papers of Washington,* 27:415. Washington identified Sir Edward Newenham to Humphreys in a letter as an Irishman, "from whom I have lately received several very polite letters, and a pressing invitation to correspond with him. He has been a warm friend to America during her whole struggle, he is a man of fortune, of excellent (I am told) character; and may, if you should go to Ireland, be a valuable acquaintance." See ibid., 27:414.
17. Ibid., 27:413–14.
18. James M. Gabler, *Passions* (Baltimore: Bacchus, 1995), 19 n.
19. Ibid., 21.
20. This John Trumbull (1750–1843) was not the Connecticut-born artist of the same name who served as Washington's aide-de-camp for nineteen days early in the war. The John Trumbull who wrote the satirical poem *McFingal* was a lawyer from Hartford, Connecticut, who possessed a talent for verse and belles-lettres. *McFingal* was a 3,000-line mock epic satirizing British bungling during the Revolution. Trumbull had the distinction of passing the entrance exam for Yale College at the age of seven. However, his parents wisely kept him from attending Yale until he was thirteen. He was one of a group of writers who wrote long, forgotten patriotic poetry and prose that was popular in the 1780s. Known as the Hartford Wits or the Connecticut Wits, they included Trumbull, Timothy Dwight, and Joel Barlow. David Humphreys is frequently included in this group although his poetry

never achieved the same popularity as that written by the other members. See Albert E. Van Dusen, *Connecticut* (New York: Random House, 1961), 247.

21. Dumas Malone, *Jefferson and the Rights of Man* (Boston: Little, Brown, 1951), 9.

22. Humphreys, *Life and Times of David Humphreys,* 1:320–21.

23. Ibid., 1:321.

24. James Thomas Flexner, *George Washington and the New Nation* (Boston: Little, Brown, 1969), 89.

25. Freeman, *George Washington,* 6:70.

26. Baylies, "Some Remarks on the Life and Character of General David Cobb."

27. Edward F. Kennedy, Jr., *David Cobb: An American Patriot* (1982).

28. *Proceedings of the Massachusetts Senate on the Occasion of the Reception of the Portrait of General David Cobb* (Cambridge, Massachusetts: John Wilson and Son, 1882), 18.

29. Jacob and Ragsdale, *Biographical Directory of the United States Congress, 1774–1989,* 797.

30. W. C. Sharpe, *History of Seymour, Connecticut: With Biographies and Genealogies* (Seymour, Connecticut: Record Print, 1879), 54.

31. *Writings of Washington,* 29:287.

32. Rosemarie Zagarri, ed., *David Humphreys' Life of General Washington* (Athens: University of Georgia Press, 1991), 54.

33. Freeman, *GeorgeWashington,* 6:122–23. Freeman calculated that from January 1784 to April 1789 Washington wrote six letters to Hamilton, twelve to Humphreys, and fifteen to Randolph on various political issues.

34. Ibid., 6:129.

35. Dumas Malone, *Jefferson and the Ordeal of Liberty* (Boston: Little, Brown & Company, 1962), 56.

36. *Writings of Washington,* 31:219–21.

37. United States Senate Resolution 125, dated June 27, 1991, states in part, "Whereas on February 21, 1791, the Senate gave advice and consent to the nomination of David Humphreys as Minister Resident from the United States to her most faithful Majesty and Queen of Portugal; Whereas David Humphreys was a Connecticut son, decorated patriot, and close friend of George Washington; Whereas this appointment served as the opening chapter of United States diplomacy (Minister Resident being the direct precursor of Ambassador) Resolved, That the Senate extends congratulations to the towns of Derby and Ansonia, Connecticut, on the occasion of the bicentennial of the occasion of the appointment of David Humphreys as the United States' first Ambassador." See *Congressional Record,* 102nd Congress, 1st sess., June 27, 1991, no. 101.

38. Humphreys to Randolph, February 3, 1795, *George Washington Papers.*

39. Randolph wrote a circular letter to the Barbary Powers dated "Philadelphia, 30 March, 1795" that stated in part, "I have appointed David Humphreys, one of our distinguished citizens, a Commissioner Plenipotentiary, giving him full power to negotiate and conclude a Treaty of Amity and Commerce with you." Manuscript Circular to Barbary Powers, *George Washington Papers.*

40. Giunta, *Emerging Nation,* 3:909.

41. Four states made up the Barbary States of North Africa: Morocco, Algiers, Tunis, and Tripoli. Following the troubles with Algiers, the pasha of Tripoli blackmailed the United States with demands for tribute. In May 1801 the United States refused

to meet Tripoli's demands and sent a naval squadron into the Mediterranean under the slogan: "Millions for defense, but not one cent for tribute." The United States negotiated a peace treaty with Tripoli in 1805, and American naval squadrons continued to patrol the area.

42. *Writings of Washington,* 35:481. The date of Washington's letter is June 26, 1797.

43. Fields, *Worthy Partner: The Papers of Martha Washington,* 354–55.

44. David Humphreys, *The Miscellaneous Works of David Humphreys: Late Minister Plenipoteniary . . . to the Court of Madrid* (New York: T. and J. Swords, 1804) , 349.

45. Ibid. Another characteristic of merino wool is that it is easy to manufacture into cloth. With the idea of improving the woolen industry, the American minister to France, Chancellor Robert R. Livingston preceded Humphreys in importing merino sheep to America. However, Livingston only managed to get a pair of merinos smuggled from France in 1802 and they turned out to be mixed breed. Humphreys knew his sheep and brought the first full-blooded merinos to America. Another early importer of merino sheep was E. I. DuPont de Nemours of Delaware. See Silvio A. Bedini, *Thomas Jefferson: Statesman of Science* (New York: Macmillan, 1990), 393.

46. There is one story that when merino sheep mania was at its height, a woman in Humphreysville knocked her child in the head that she might raise a merino lamb in its stead. See Orcutt, *History of the Old Town of Derby, Connecticut,* 598. Stories about the prices offered or paid for merino sheep are legendary. In one account, " the price of merino bucks went up to $1,500 and a few were even sold as high as $3,000, and ewes sold from $1,000 to $1,500. John Bassett was offered $1,000 by Philo Bassett for a full blooded merino ewe lamb eight days old and refused to take less than $1,500. A few days after[,] it was killed by a fox. Two young farmers united to buying a buck at $1,500 and the same day it died by being choked with an apple. But such mishaps checked the speculation but little, and it rapidly extended throughout New England, Vermont in particular being quickly supplied with some of the merinos." See Sharpe, *History of Seymour, Connecticut,* 59.

47. A fulling mill, or carding mill as it was also called, was a colonial period term for a place where cloth was cleaned and thickened.

48. Dumas Malone, *Jefferson the President* (Boston: Little, Brown, 1974), 629.

49. Orcutt, *History of the Old Town of Derby, Connecticut,* 457.

50. Humphreys, *An Essay on the Life of the Honorable Major-General Israel Putnam,* 131–33.

51. Humphreys was a regular visitor to New Haven. The city was home to his alma mater (Yale College) as well as being the center of commerce in Connecticut.

52. Orcutt, *History of the Old Town of Derby, Connecticut,* 459.

53. Willard Sterne Randall, *Thomas Jefferson: A Life,* (New York: Henry Holt, 1993), 377 n. 32. Humphreys was buried in New Haven. He was as haughty in death as he was in life. His portentous tombstone reads, "David Humphreys, Doctor of Laws, Member of the Academy of Science of Philadelphia, Massachusetts, and Connecticut; of the Bath [Agricultural] Society, and of the Royal Society London. Fired with the love of country and of liberty, he consecrated his youth wholly to the service of the Republic, which he defended by his arms, aided by his counsels, adorned by his learning, and preserved in harmony with foreign nations. In the field, he was the companion and aid of the great Washington, a Colonel in the

army of his country and commander of the Veteran Volunteers of Connecticut. He went Ambassador to the courts of Portugal and Spain, and returning, enriched his native land with the true golden fleece. He was a distinguished Historian and Poet;—a model and Patron of Science, and of the ornamental and useful arts. After a full discharge of every duty, and a life well spent, he died on the 21st day of February, 1818, aged 65 years." Humphreys' wife, Mrs. Ann Frances Bulkeley Humphreys, outlived her husband. She remained a widow until December 1829, when she married Count Étienne Walewski, a veteran of the Napoleonic wars. She died in Paris in 1832.

54. *Writings of Washington,* 52:353.
55. Ibid., 25:455.
56. The Society of the Cincinnati was a fraternal and charitable organization of American officers who served for at least three years or were in the army when the Revolutionary War ended. The Society was named after the fifth-century B.C. Roman citizen soldier Lucius Quinitius Cincinnatus, whose behavior and accomplishments were held in high esteem by the Americans. National officers of the Society were elected in June 1783 and Washington was named as the organization's first president. A branch of the Society was organized in France in 1784. The Society was criticized by some Americans, including John Adams, who denounced it for its aristocratic pretensions and as a dangerous means of someday saddling America with a military dictatorship. Smith was elected vice president of the New York state chapter of the Society in 1794, having been secretary in 1790. He served as the chapter's president from 1795 through 1797. He was reelected president of the chapter in 1804. Smith has been erroneously mentioned as being the president of the national Society of the Cincinnati. See, for example, Smith's biography in Jacob and Ragsdale, *Biographical Directory of the United States Congress, 1774–1989.* The origin of this mistake seems to be a misleading entry in Johnson, *Dictionary of American Biography.*
57. A chariot was an ornate, four-wheeled carriage drawn by four, six, or even eight horses. It was the sports car of its day.
58. L.H. Butterfield et al., *Adams Family Correspondence,* 6:196. Mrs. Adams must have also been impressed by Thomas Jefferson's comments about Smith. Jefferson met him in Paris in 1785. He wrote his friend Mrs. Adams about Smith, "Your knowledge of him will enable you to judge of the advantageous impressions which his head, his heart, and his manners will have made on me." See ibid., 6:463.
59. Ibid., 6:508–9.
60. Thomas Jefferson to William S. Smith, October 22, 1786, Boyd, *Papers of Thomas Jefferson,* 10:478. Also see Andrew Burstein, *The Inner Jefferson* (Charlottesville: University Press of Virginia, 1995), 78.
61. Charles R. King, *The Life and Correspondence of Rufus King* (New York: G. P. Putnam's Sons, 1894–1900), 1:151.
62. The office of United States marshal was created by the first Congress in the Judiciary Act of 1789, the same legislation that established the federal judicial systems. The marshals were given extensive authority to support the federal courts within their judicial districts and to carry out all lawful orders issued by judges, Congress, or the president. In addition, at the time that Smith was a United States marshal, they were also the local representatives for the federal government. They took the national census, distributed presidential proclamations, collected statistical

information on commerce and manufacturing, and performed other routine tasks needed for the central government to function effectively.

63. The position of supervisor of revenue was established to collect liquor duties throughout the United States. Washington appointed Smith to the post for the State of New York. The job paid a salary of 800 dollars per year and a commission of $^1/_2$ percent. See *Writings of Washington,* 31:233–34.

64. Malone, *Jefferson and the Ordeal of Liberty,* 50.

65. Information on Smith's ownership of his Manhattan estate, and its subsequent sale can be found in I. N. Stokes, *The Iconography of Manhattan Island* (New York: Robert H. Dodd, 1928), 6:128. At the same time, Colonel Smith had a summer home at Eastchester in Westchester County, New York.

66. Raymond, *New York Genealogical and Biographical Record* 25 no. 4, (October 1894). After reviewing my impartial account of Colonel Smith's life, my readers may be interested in comparing it with an aggrandized account in Katherine Metcalf Roof, *Colonel William Smith and Lady* (Boston: 1929). This ludicrous book was written during the Colonial Revival period when American colonial history was romanticized.

67. Nabby's mother had misjudged Royall Tyler. He was grief stricken when Nabby broke off their relationship and went into seclusion. He wrote a play called *The Contrast,* which was performed in New York City in 1787. The main plot concerned an arranged marriage. It was a huge success and was repeated several times in quick succession after its premier. See Kenneth Silverman, *A Cultural History of the American Revolution* (New York: Thomas Y. Crowell, 1976), 558–63. Tyler eventually resumed his law practice. He married a young cousin of the Adamses, and in time became chief justice of the Vermont Supreme Court. He was universally loved and respected.

68. The surveyor of customs superintends and directs all customs inspectors within his district and the boats, "which may be provided for securing the collection of the revenue." The surveyor reports to the district collector of customs and the district naval officer. The surveyor of customs was paid a flat fee for every ship that entered a port in his district. As an example, he was allowed $3.00 "for all the services required by law on board any ship or vessel of one hundred tons and upward." See R. A. Stevens, ed., *An Act of Congress Establishing the United States Customs* (Salem, Massachusetts: 1989). Reprinted from the *Pennsylvania Packet and Daily Advertiser,* August 7, 1789.

69. Smith toured Europe when he was John Adams's secretary in the company of Francisco Miranda, a Spaniard who wanted to liberate the Spanish colonies in South America. Smith and Miranda remained good friends, and the patriotic colonel got involved in the Spaniard's foolish plots. The United States laws, which were violated, were the equipping of an American vessel (named the *Leander*) for hostile action against a nation with which the United States was at peace, and the enlistment of Americans for such a purpose. See Malone, *Jefferson the President,* 80–81.

70. Natalie S. Bober, *Abigail Adams: Witness to a Revolution* (New York: Atheneum Books, 1995), 218.

71. Raymond, "Colonel William Stephens Smith," *The New York Genealogical and Biographical Record,* xxv, no. 4 (October 1894).

CHAPTER 13

1. *Hamilton Papers,* 3:192.
2. Bradford Adams Whittemore, *Memorials of the Massachusetts Society of the Cincinnati* (Boston: 1964), 209. Alexander Hamilton Gibbs (August 2, 1791– March 5, 1827) became a merchant in Roxbury, Massachusetts. He married Ellen Mary Hatch in 1816 and they had four children.
3. Jackson and Twohig, *Papers of George Washington: The Diaries of Washington,* 1:381 n.
4. Ibid., 1:380.
5. Howard H. Wehmann, "To Major Gibbs with Much Esteem" *Prologue: Official Publication of the National Archives* (winter 1972): 231.
6. Tyrone G. Martin, *A Most Fortunate Ship: A Narrative History of Old Ironsides,* (rev. ed. Naval Institute, 1997), 179.
7. Reed was accused of conspiring with the enemy in an article that appeared in the *Independent Gazetteer,* a Philadelphia newspaper. The story was published on September 3, 1782, and was signed "Brutus." A pamphlet war ensued with Reed defending his patriotism. An account of the affair can be found in William S. Stryker, *The Reed Controversy* (1885), a pamphlet, which showed that Reed was confused with another Continental officer named James Read who defected to the British in late 1776.
8. *Writings of Washington,* 25:159–60. This letter was written on September 15, 1782. The draft is in the handwriting of Jonathan Trumbull, Jr., with changes made by Washington.
9. Corner, *Autobiography of Benjamin Rush,* 190.
10. *Writings of Washington,* 29:60.
11. Malone, *Dictionary of American Biography,* 18:545.
12. *Writings of Washington,* 26:358–59.
13. *Papers of Washington,* Confederation Series, 2:30.
14. *Writings of Washington,* 27:176.
15. *Washington's Letter Book,* 7:130.
16. *Graydon: Memoirs of His Own Time,* 277.
17. *Writings of Washington,* 29:101–2.
18. Shreve, *Tench Tilghman,* 199–200. Tench Tilghman's grave was moved from Baltimore to the Maryland shore. He is buried next to his wife in the town of Oxford in Talbot County, Maryland. An obelisk with the inscription written by his father and approved by Washington marks the grave site today.
19. Ness, "A Lost Man of Maryland," 329. Washington also wrote Harrison on September 28, 1789, urging he accept his appointment to the Supreme Court. Washington wrote his former aide-de-camp, "it has been the invariable object of my anxious solicitude to select the fittest characters to expound the Laws and dispense justice. To tell you that this sentiment has ruled me in your nomination to a seat on the Supreme Bench of the United States, would be but to repeat opinions with which you are already well acquainted; opinions which meet a just co-incidence in the public Mind." See *Writings of Washington,* 30:417.
20. Ness, "A Lost Man of Maryland," 334.
21. Alexander and Elizabeth Hamilton had eight children, six sons and two daughters. Their eldest son, Philip, born on January 22, 1782, was killed in a duel with

George I. Eaker on November 24, 1801. Their other sons were named Alexander (born in 1786), James Alexander (1788), John Church (1792), William Stephen (1797), and Philip II (1802, and named after his eldest brother who was killed dueling the year before). Their daughters were named Elizabeth (born in 1799) and Angelica (born 1784). Although Alexander Hamilton never graduated from King's College; three of his sons did: Alexander, James Alexander, and John Church. Hamilton's son Alexander married Eliza Knox, daughter of Gen. Henry Knox. For information about Hamilton's children see Allan McLane Hamilton, *The Intimate Life of Alexander Hamilton* (New York: Charles Scribner's Sons, 1911), 210–11.

22. In one of the first sex scandals in American political history, a newspaperman named James Callender exposed Hamilton's love affair with a young woman named Maria Reynolds. Callender's accusations included corruption charges against Hamilton. Hamilton confessed to having the tryst, but asserted that no financial improprieties occurred. The disclosure of the affair severely damaged Hamilton's reputation.

23. *Writings of Washington,* 36:460–61.

24. Freeman, *George Washington,* 7:297–98. Freeman died before completing this seventh and final volume of his biography of Washington. The summary of the breakup between Washington and Randolph was probably drafted by Freeman and appears on page 298, which reads, "The President's confidential adviser, his closest companion, his friend for twenty years, would be at his side no longer. Edmund Randolph was gone."

25. Moncure Daniel Conway, *Omitted Chapters of History Disclosed in the Life and Papers of Edmund Randolph* (New York: G.P. Putnam's Sons, 1888), 358–59. Tiberius was emperor of Rome from A.D. 14 to 37. He is remembered as a suspicious and tyrannical ruler.

26. Ibid., 388–89.

27. Ibid., 392.

28. McHenry was a member of the Continental Congress from 1783–85.

29. Steiner, *Life and Correspondence of James McHenry,* 1.

30. *Letters of Delegates,* 21:46.

31. *Hamilton Papers,* 3:129.

32. James McHenry's father Daniel died on November 3, 1782. His younger brother John, who never married, died on May 7, 1790, leaving James a fortune from the family importing business and investments in Baltimore real estate. See Steiner, *Life and Correspondence of James McHenry,* 2.

33. *Writings of Washington,* 36:394. McHenry served as secretary of war in the cabinets of Presidents Washington and Adams serving from January 29, 1796, to May 13, 1800. Washington appropriately uses the term "Hobson's choice" to describe his selection of McHenry as secretary of war. The term means an apparently free choice that offers no real alternative. The term comes from Thomas Hobson (1544?–1630) who was a carrier in Cambridge, England, who let out horses. It was said that while his stable had numerous horses for hire, he rotated his horses by putting the next available horse by the stable door. Customers had the choice of renting the horse nearest the stable door or leaving.

34. Steiner, *Life and Correspondence of James McHenry,* 615. Fort McHenry, in Baltimore harbor, which was made famous during the War of 1812, was named after James McHenry.

35. Whiteley, *Washington and His Aides-de-Camp,* 205.

36. *Hamilton Papers,* 3:145.

37. The account of Laurens's death including the quotation from Nathanael Greene is from Lossing, *Pictorial Field-Book of the Revolution,* 2:572–73.

38. Garden, *Anecdotes of the American Revolution: With Additional Notes by Thomas W. Field,* 1:59.

39. Moultrie, *Memoirs,* 1:402.

40. *Writings of Washington,* 28:95–97. Washington wrote Lafayette privately, acrimoniously informing him of the death of Laurens, "Poor Laurens is no more. He fell in a trifling skirmish in South Carolina, attempting to prevent the Enemy from plundering the Country of rice." See ibid., 25:281.

41. *Hamilton Papers,* 3:183–84.

42. Ibid., 3:193.

43. Wallace, *Life of Henry Laurens,* 490–91.

44. David Ramsay was born on April 2, 1749, in Lancaster County, Pennsylvania. He was a 1765 graduate of the College of New Jersey after which he studied medicine at the College of Philadelphia under the instruction of Dr. Thomas Bond. He then practiced medicine in Maryland for a year before moving to Charleston where he made his home for the rest of his life. He was an early and ardent American patriot.

45. Henry Laurens died in 1792. He was sixty-eight years old at the time of his death. Henry Laurens is the first known individual in the United States to request his own cremation. He was afraid of being buried alive and specified in his will that he be cremated. His body was wrapped in twelve yards of tow cloth, saturated in oil, and burned on the high bluff above the Cooper River at his Mepkin plantation. The awful sight of seeing their master burn was said to have greatly excited the plantation slaves. Following his cremation, his remains were gathered up and buried next to his son John.

46. Arthur H. Shaffer, *To Be an American: David Ramsay and the Making of the American Consciousness* (Charleston: University of South Carolina Press, 1991), 78.

47. Ramsay wrote in the preface to his book, "The materials for the following sheets were collected in the years 1782,1783, and 1786; in which years, as a member of Congress, I had access to all the official papers of the United States."

48. Thayer, *Making of a Scapegoat,* 88.

49. Ramsay, *History of the American Revolution,* 2:291.

50. *Hamilton Papers,* 3:607.

CHAPTER 14

1. Shreve, *Tench Tilghman,* 144.

2. Ibid., 144.

3. See for example, Fitzpatrick, *Spirit of the Revolution,* 60. Fitzpatrick said that six of Washington's aides held cabinet posts, which is not correct.

4. *Hamilton Papers,* 2:34–36.

5. Ibid., 3:120.

6. *Laurens Papers,* 12:392. The letter quoted is from John Laurens to his father Henry Laurens.

7. I saved my favorite George Washington Parke Custis anecdote about Washington's aides for the end of my book so that my readers could fully appreciate its absurdity. The story deals with Hamilton, and Custis's implication that he was the most important of Washington's aides. Note, however, the interesting reference to Billy Lee; there is always some truth in Custis's stories,

> In the memorable campaigns of 1777 and 1778, the habit at headquarters was for the general to dismiss his officers at a very late hour of the night to snatch a little repose, while he, the man of mighty labors, drawing his cloak around him, and trimming his lamp, would throw himself upon a hard couch, not to sleep, but to think. Close to his master (wrapped in a blanket, but "all accoutred" for instant service) snored the stout yet active form of Billy, the celebrated body-servant during the whole of the Revolutionary war.
>
> At this late lone hour silence reigned in the headquarters, broken only by the measured pacing of the sentinels, and the oft-repeated cry of "all's well;" when suddenly the sound of a horse-tramp, at speed, is borne upon the night wind, then the challenging of the guard, and the passing the word of an express from the lines to the commander in chief. The despatches being opened and read, there would be heard in the calm deep tones of that voice, so well remembered by the good and the brave in the old days of our country's trial, the command of the chief to his now watchful attendant, "Call Colonel Hamilton!"

Custis, *Recollections and Private Memoirs of Washington,* 345–46.

8. Tilghman probably deserves the honor of serving the longest of any of Washington's aides-de-camp. He joined the general's staff as a volunteer aide sometime in early August 1776 and served until March 22, 1782, when he took an extended leave of absence. Tilghman returned to headquarters on August 11, 1782, staying until sometime in December 1782 when he took another leave. There is no known record of his returning to headquarters or resigning as Washington's aide-de-camp. Harrison began serving as Washington aide sometime in October 1775 and probably resigned on March 25, 1781. These dates of service are based on a letter of certification that Washington wrote on Harrison's behalf. See *Writings of Washington,* 21:377. Hamilton was appointed an aide on March 1, 1777, and left headquarters, following his argument with Washington, sometime in April 1781. It becomes difficult to decide who was the longest serving aide to Washington if we take leaves of absences into consideration. But Tilghman probably served the longest, followed by Harrison and Hamilton.

9. Ibid., 27:299–300.

10. Ibid., 35:480. Humphreys sent Martha Washington a gift of a gold chain in 1797. She sent him a letter from Mount Vernon thanking him for the gift saying, "I wanted nothing to remind me of the pleasure we have had in your company at this place; but shall receive the chain, nevertheless as an emblem of your friendship & shall value it accordingly." See Fields, *Worthy Partner: The Papers of Martha Washington,* 304.

11. Minor Myers, Jr., *The Insignia of the Society of the Cincinnati* (Washington, D.C.: Society of the Cincinnati, 1998), 46.

12. Shreve, *Tench Tilghman,* 186.

13. D. Humphreys, *Valedictory Discourse: Delivered before the Cincinnati of Connecticut, in Hartford, July 4, 1804* (Boston: Gilbert and Dean, 1804), 36.

14. Many of Washington's aides-de-camp joined the Society of the Cincinnati. They were, in order of their dates of appointment to the general's staff, Thomas Mifflin, John Trumbull, George Baylor, Stephen Moylan, Caleb Gibbs, George Lewis, Samuel Blachley Webb, William Grayson, Alexander Hamilton, Richard Kidder Meade, Peter Presley Thornton, Tench Tilghman, David Humphreys, Richard Varick, Jonathan Trumbull, David Cobb, Peregrine Fitzhugh, William Stephens Smith, Benjamin Walker, and Hodijah Baylies.

15. Ford and Putnam, *Aids and Secretaries to Gen. George Washington,* 1906), 5.

16. James C. Neagles, *Summer Soldiers: A survey & Index of Revolutionary War Courts-Martial* (Salt Lake City, Utah: Ancestry Incorporated, 1986), 29.

17. Fitzpatrick, *Spirit of the Revolution,* 60.

BIBLIOGRAPHY

PRIMARY SOURCES

Manuscripts

Adams, Samual. Diary. New York Public Library.

Emmet, Thomas A. Collection. Rare Books and Manuscripts Division, Center for the Humanities, Astor, Lenox, and Tilden Foundations, Microfiche Rolls Nos. 7 and 8 New York Public Library.

Oldridge, William Arthur. Collection. Manuscript Division. Library of Congress.

Palfrey, William. The Memorandum Book of William Palfrey of Boston in New England, 1771. Massachusetts Historical Society, Boston.

Schuyler Family. Papers. Albany Institute of History and Art, Albany, New York.

Tilghman, Tench. Papers. Society of the Cincinnati Library, Washington, D.C.

Washington, George. Papers. Presidential Papers Series, microfilm. Library of Congress.

Books

Abbot, W. W., et al., eds. *The Papers of George Washington.* Revolutionary War Series, 11 vols. to date. Colonial Series, 10 vols. Confederation Series, 6 vols. Diaries, 6 vols. Charlottesville, Virginia: University Press of Virginia, 1985–.

Boyd, Julian, et al., eds. *The Papers of Thomas Jefferson.* Princeton, New Jersey: Princeton University Press, 1956–.

Chase, Eugene Parker, ed. *Our Revolutionary Forefathers: The Letters of François, Marquis de Barbe-Marbois.* New York: Duffield, 1929.

Chastellux, Marquis de. *Travels in North-America in the Years 1780, 1781, and 1782.* 2 vols. London: G. G. J. and J. Robinson, 1787.

Fields, Joseph E., ed. *Worthy Partner: The Papers of Martha Washington.* Westport, Connecticut: Greenwood, 1994.

Elijah Fisher's Journal While in the War for Independence. Augusta, Maine: Badger and Manley, 1880.

Fitzpatrick, John C., ed. *The Writings of George Washington.* 39 vols. Washington, D.C.: U.S. Government Printing Office, 1931–44.

Force, Peter, ed. *American Archives.* 4th and 5th ser. Washington, D.C.: 1837–53.

Ford, Worthington Chauncey, ed. *Correspondence and Journals of Samuel Blachley Webb.* 3 vols. Lancaster, Pennsylvania: Wickersham, 1893.

———, ed. *Journals of the Continental Congress, 1774–1789.* 23 vols. Washington, D.C.: Government Printing Office, 1904–14.

————, ed., *Family Letters of Samuel Blachley Webb.* New York: 1912.

Giunta, Mary A., ed. *The Emerging Nation: A Documentary History of the Foreign Relations of the United States under the Articles of Confederation, 1780–1789.* Vols. 1 and 2. Washington, D.C.: Superintendent of Documents, 1996.

Hamer, Philip M., et al., eds. *The Papers of Henry Laurens.* 15 vols. to date. Columbia: University of South Carolina Press, 1968–.

Hamilton, Allan McLane. *The Intimate Life of Alexander Hamilton.* New York: Charles Scribner's Sons, 1911.

Hammond, Otis G., ed. *Letters and Papers of General John Sullivan.* 3 vols. Concord: New Hampshire Historical Society, 1930–39.

Harrison, S. A. *Memoir of Lieutenant Colonel Tench Tilghman.* Albany, New York: J. Munsell, 1876.

Humphreys, David. *The Miscellaneous Works of David Humphreys: Late Minister Plenipotentiary . . . to the Court of Madrid.* New York: T. and J. Swords, 1804.

Idzerda, Stanley J., ed. *Lafayette in the Age of the American Revolution.* 5 vols. Ithaca: Cornell University Press, 1977–83.

King, Charles R. *The Life and Correspondence of Rufus King.* 6 vols. New York: G. P. Putnam's Sons, 1894–1900.

Labaree, Leonard W., et al., eds. *The Papers of Benjamin Franklin.* 35 vols. to date. New Haven: Yale University Press, 1959–.

Lee, Charles. *The Lee Papers.* 4 vols. New York: New York Historical Society, 1871–74.

Lesser, Charles H., ed. *The Sinews of Independence: Monthly Strength Reports of the Continental Army.* Chicago: University of Chicago Press, 1976.

Littell, John Stockton, ed. *Memoirs of His Own Time with Reminiscences of the Men and Events of the Revolution by Alexander Graydon.* Philadelphia: Lindsay & Blakiston, 1846.

McHenry, James. *Journal of a March, a Battle, and a Waterfall: Being the Version Elaborated by James McHenry from His Diary of the Year 1778.* Greenwich, Connecticut: privately printed, 1945.

Moultrie, William. *Memoirs of the American Revolution.* New York: Printed by David Longworth, 1802.

Reed, William B. *Life and Correspondence of Joseph Reed.* 2 vols. Philadelphia: Lindsay and Blakiston, 1847.

Simms, W. M. Gilmore, ed. *The Army Correspondence of Colonel John Laurens in the Years 1777–8.* New York: Bradford Club, 1867.

Smith, Paul H., ed. *Letters of Delegates to Congress, 1774–1789.* 25 vols. Washington, D.C.: Library of Congress, 1976–98.

Steiner, Bernard C. *The Life and Correspondence of James McHenry.* Cleveland: Burrows Brothers, 1907.

Taylor, Robert J., ed. *Papers of John Adams.* 10 vols. to date. Cambridge: Belknap Press of Harvard University Press, 1977–.

Thacher, James. *The American Revolution, from the Commencement to the Disbanding of the American Army: Given in the Form of a Daily Journal . . .* Hartford: Hurlbut, Kellogg & Company, 1861.

Walsh, Richard, ed. *The Writings of Christopher Gadsden.* Columbia: University of South Carolina Press, 1966.

Zagarri, Rosemarie, ed. *David Humphreys' Life of General Washington.* Athens: University of Georgia Press, 1991.

SECONDARY SOURCES
Books

Baker, William S. *Itinerary of General Washington.* Philadelphia: J. B. Lippincott, 1892.

Barnby, H. G. *The Prisoners of Algiers: An Account of the Forgotten American-Algerian War, 1785–1797.* London: Oxford University Press, 1966.

Baxter, W. T. *The House of Hancock.* Cambridge, Massachusetts: Harvard University Press, 1945.

Berg, Fred Anderson. *Encyclopedia of Continental Army Units.* Harrisburg, Pennsylvania: Stackpole Books, 1972.

Burstein, Andrew. *The Inner Jefferson.* Charlottesville: University Press of Virginia, 1995.

Cifelli, Edward M. *David Humphreys.* Boston: Twayne, 1982.

Conway, Moncure Daniel. *Omitted Chapters of History Disclosed in the Life and Papers of Edmund Randolph.* New York: G. P. Putnam's Sons, 1889.

Cooke, Jacob Ernest. *Alexander Hamilton.* New York: Charles Scribner's Sons, 1982.

Cooper, Helen A. *John Trumbull: The Hand and Spirit of a Painter.* New Haven: Yale University Art Gallery, 1982.

Cunningham, Noble E., Jr. *In Pursuit of Reason: The Life of Thomas Jefferson.* Baton Rouge: Louisiana State University Press, 1987.

DuPriest, James E., Jr. *William Grayson: A Political Biography of Virginia's First United States Senator.* Manassas, Virginia: Prince William County Historical Commission, 1977.

Egly, T. W., Jr. *History of the First New York Regiment, 1775–1784.* Hampton, New Hampshire: Peter E. Randall, 1981.

Elkins, Stanley and Eric McKitrick. *The Age of Federalism.* New York: Oxford University Press, 1993.

Farrar, Emmie Ferguson. *Old Virginia Houses Along the James.* New York: Bonanza Books.

Ferling, John. *The First of Men: A Life of George Washington.* Knoxville: University of Tennessee Press, 1988.

———. *Setting the World Ablaze: Washington, Adams, Jefferson, and the American Revolution.* New York: Oxford University Press, 2000.

Flexner, James Thomas. *George Washington in the American Revolution.* Boston: Little, Brown, 1967.

————. *The Young Hamilton.* Boston: Little, Brown, 1978.

Garden, Alexander. *Anecdotes of the Revolutionary War in America: With Sketches of Character of Persons the Most Distinguished, in the Southern States, for Civil and Military Services.* Charleston: A. E. Miller, 1822.

————. *Anecdotes of the American Revolution, Illustrative of the Talents and Virtues of the Heroes and Patriots, Who Acted the Most Conspicuous Parts Therein.* 2nd ser. Charleston: A. E. Miller, 1828.

Godfrey, Carlos E. *The Commander-In-Chief's Guard.* Washington, D.C.: Stevenson-Smith, 1904.

Griffin, Martin I. J. *Stephen Moylan.* Philadelphia: Privately Printed, 1909.

Harrison, Richard A. *Princetonians, 1769–1775: A Biographical Dictionary.* Princeton, New Jersey: Princeton University Press, 1980.

Harrison, S. A. *Memoir of Lieut. Col. Tench Tilghman.* Albany, New York: J. Munsell, 1876.

Hearn, Chester G. *George Washington's Schooners: The First American Navy.* Annapolis, Maryland: Naval Institute Press, 1995.

Heusser, Albert H. *In the Footsteps of Washington.* Paterson, New Jersey: Privately published, 1921.

Hibbert, Christopher. *Redcoats and Rebels: The American Revolution through British Eyes.* New York: W. W. Norton, 1990.

Horry, P., and M. L.Weems. *General Francis Marion.* 1809. Reprint, Philadelphia: Joseph Allen, 1845.

Humphreys, David. *An Essay on the Life of the Honorable Major-General Israel Putnam.* Hartford: Hudson and Goodwin, 1788.

Humphreys, Frank Landon. *The Life and Times of David Humphreys.* New York: G. P. Putnam's Sons, 1917.

Ives, Mabel Lorenz. *Washington's Headquarters.* Upper Montclair, New Jersey: Lucy Fortune, 1932.

Jackson, Kenneth T., ed. *Encyclopedia of New York City.* New Haven: Yale University Press, 1995.

Jacob, Kathryn Allamong, and Bruce A. Ragsdale, ed. *Biographical Directory of the United States Congress, 1774–1989.* Washington, D.C.: U.S. Government Printing Office, 1989.

Johnston, Henry P. *The Campaign of 1776 around New York and Brooklyn.* Brooklyn: Long Island Historical Society, 1878.

————. *The Yorktown Campaign and the Surrender of Corwallis, 178l.* New York: Harper & Brothers, 1881.

————. *The Battle of Harlem Heights.* New York: Macmillan, 1897.

Kapp, Friedrich. *The Life of Frederick William Von Steuben.* New York: Mason Brothers, 1859.

Kennedy, Edward F., Jr. *David Cobb: An American Patriot.* 1982.

Leiby, Adrian C. *The Revolutionary War in the Hackensack Valley.* New Brunswick, New Jersey: Rutgers University Press, 1962.

Life of Esther De Berdt: The Afterwards Esther Reed. Philadelphia: C. Sherman, 1853.

Malone, Dumas. *Jefferson and the Rights of Man.* Boston: Little, Brown, 1951.

Martin, James Kirby. *Benedict Arnold: Revolutionary Hero.* New York: New York University Press, 1997.

Massey, Gregory D. *John Laurens and the American Revolution.* Columbia, South Carolina: University of South Carolina Press, 2000.

Mattern, David B. *Benjamin Lincoln and the American Revolution.* Columbia, South Carolina: University of South Carolina Press, 1995.

Mayer, Holly A. *Belonging to the Army: Camp Followers and Community during the American Revolution.* Columbia: University of South Carolina Press, 1996.

Miller, John C. *Alexander Hamilton: Portrait in Paradox.* New York: Harper & Brothers, 1959.

Mitchell, Broadus. *Alexander Hamilton: Youth to Maturity, 1755–1788.* New York: Macmillan, 1957.

Morris, Richard B. *Alexander Hamilton and the Founding of the Nation.* New York: Dial, 1957.

Neagles, James C. *Summer Soldiers: A Survey & Index of Revolutionary War Courts-Martial.* Salt Lake City, Utah: Ancestry Incorporated, 1986.

Quatannens, JoAnne McCormick, comp. *Senators of the United States—A Historical Bibliography.* Washington, D.C.: U.S. Government Printing Office, 1995.

Quincy, Josiah. *The Journals of Major Samuel Shaw: The First American Consul at Canton, with a Life of the Author.* Boston: Wm. Crosby and H. P. Nichols, 1847.

Ramsay, David. *The History of the Revolution of South-Carolina.* 2 vols. Trenton, New Jersey: Isaac Collins, 1785.

———. *The History of the American Revolution.* 2 vols. 1789. Reprint, Trenton, New Jersey: James J. Wilson, 1811.

Reardon, John J. *Edmund Randolph.* New York: Macmillan, Inc. 1974.

Roche, John F. *Joseph Reed: A Moderate in the American Revolution.* New York: Columbia University Press, 1957.

Rossman, Kenneth R. *Thomas Mifflin and the Politics of the American Revolution.* University of North Carolina Press, 1952.

Schuyler, John. *Institution of the Society of the Cincinnati, Formed by the Officers of the American Army of the Revolution, 1783: With Extracts, from the Proceedings of its General Meetings and from the Transactions of the New York State Society.* 1886. Reprint, 1998.

Sharpe, W. C. *History of Seymour, Connecticut: With Biographies and Genealogies.* Seymour, Connecticut: Record Print, 1879.

Shreve, L. G. *Tench Tilghman: The Life and Times of Washington's Aide-de-Camp.* Centerville, Maryland: Tidewater, 1982.

Smith, George. *An Universal Military Dictionary.* London: J. Millan, 1779.

Turner, Jane, ed. *The Dictionary of Art.* New York: Grove Dictionaries, 1996. Internet edition, www.Groveart.com.

Van Powell, Nowland. *The American Navies of the Revolutionary War.* New York: G. P. Putnam's Sons, 1974.

Ward, Christopher. *The War of the Revolution.* 2 vols. New York: Macmillan, 1952.

Warren, Mrs. Mercy [Otis]. *History of the Rise, Progress, and Termination of the American Revolution.* 3 vols. Boston: E. Larkin, 1805.

Webb, J. Watson. *Reminiscences of Gen'l Samuel B. Webb of the Revolutionary Army.* New York: Globe Stationery, 1882.

Weber, Ralph E. *Masked Dispatches: Cryptograms and Cryptology in American History, 1775–1900.* Fort George G. Meade, Maryland: National Security Agency, 1993.

Whiteley, Emily Stone. *Washington and His Aides-de-Camp.* New York: Macmillan, 1936.

Whittemore, Bradford Adams. *Memorials of the Massachusetts Society of the Cincinnati.* Boston: 1964.

Wright, John Womack. *Some Notes on the Continental Army.* Cornwallville, New York: Hope Farm, 1962.

Wright, Robert K., Jr. *The Continental Army.* Washington, D.C.: Center of Military History, United States Army, 1989.

Pamphlets and Booklets

Account of the Action from Brandywine to Monmouth: A Seminar on the Impact of the Revolutionary War on the Delaware Valley, An. Philadelphia: Council of American Revolutionary Sites, Independence National Park Visitors Centers, March 14–16, 1997.

In Grateful Remembrance . . . An Exhibition of Portraits Commemorating the Founding of the State and Nation, 1770–1788. Annapolis: Maryland Commission on Artistic Property, 1976.

Proceedings of the Massachusetts Senate on the Occasion of the Reception of the Portrait of General David Cobb, February 23, 1882. Cambridge, Massachusetts: John Wilson and Son, 1882.

Magazine Articles

Anderson, D. R. "William Grayson: A Study in Virginia Biography of the Eighteenth Century." *Richmond College Historical Papers* 2, no. 1 (June 1917).

"Battle of Monmouth, The" *Magazine of American History* 3, no. 6 (June 1879).

Horrell, Joseph, ed. "New Light on William Grayson: His Guardian's Account." *Virginia Magazine of History and Biography* 92 (October 1984).

"How Washington Organized His Army." *More Books—The Bulletin of the Boston Public Library,* 2, nos. 4–5 (May 1927).

Kochan, James L. "'as plain as blue and buff could make it': George Washington's Uniforms as Commander-in-Chief and President, 1775–1799." *Catalog of the 44th Washington Antiques Show,* 1999.

Ness, George T., Jr. "A Lost Man of Maryland." *Maryland Historical Magazine.* 35, no. 4 (December, 1940).

Raymond, Marcuis D. "Colonel William Stephens Smith." *The New York Genealogical and Biographical Record,* xxv, no. 4 (October 1894).

Weir, Robert M. "Portrait of a Hero." *American Heritage* 27, no. 3 (April 1976).

Wright, Kevin. "Overkill: Revolutionary War Reminiscences of River Vale." *Bergen's Attic* (Bergen County, New Jersey, Historical Society) 21, no. 2, (June 1994).

Studies and Reports

Craig, Vera B., and Ralph H. Lewis. *Furnishing Plan for The Ford Mansion, 1779–80.* Morristown National Historical Park, 1976.

Griff, Constance M. *The Morris-Jumel Mansion: A Documentary History.* Rocky Hill, New Jersey: Heritage Studies, Inc., 1995.

Menz, Katherine B. *Washington's Headquarters.* Harpers Ferry Center, West Virginia: National Park Service, 1989.

Dissertations and Theses

Bast, Charles Homer. "Lieutenant-Colonel Tench Tilghman: The Portrait of an Aide." Master's thesis, University of Virginia, 1937.

Clancy, John J., Jr. "David Humphreys: A Forgotten American." Ph.D. diss., St. John's University, New York, 1970.

Johnson, Victor Leroy. "The Administration of the American Commissariat during the Revolutionary War." Ph.D. diss., University of Pennsylvania, 1941.

Kahler, Gerald Edward. "Gentlemen of the Family: General George Washington's Aides-de-camp and Military Secretaries." Master's thesis, University of Richmond, 1997.

Rommel, John George, Jr. "Richard Varick: New York Aristocrat." Ph.D. diss., Columbia University, 1966.

Schnakenberg, Jeffrey D. "Officer Attrition in the Continental Army during the Valley Forge Encampment." Master's thesis, Temple University, 1994.

Internet Sites Consulted

Encyclopedia Britannica (www.britannica.com)

Fourth Regiment of Continental Light Dragoons (Moylan's Horse) (www.reenactor.net/colonial/rev-units-amer.html)

George Washington Papers, Library of Congress (memory.loc.gov/ammem/amhome.html)

Historical Almanack for article about Edmund Randolph (www. history.org)

Military Analysis Network (www.fas.org)

Papers of George Washington, The (www.virginia.edu/gwpapers)

INDEX

NOTE: Page references in *italic* type indicate photographs or illustrations. The denotation *"pl."* followed by a number indicates a plate in the series between pp. 174 and 175.

A

Adams, Abigail Amelia "Nabby," 271, 283–84, 285–86
Adams, John, 17, 56, 108–9, 125, 271, 285
Adams, Samuel, 17
An Address to the Armies (Humphreys), 203
adjutant general office, 4–5
aides-de-camp, Washington's
 appointed to Washington's cabinet, 295–99
 confidentiality of, 306
 education of, 8
 four most important, 307–9
 friendship with Washington, 76–77, 305
 friendships among, 306–7
 and intelligence work, 203–7
 list of, 14–15
 at Monmouth, 165, 173, *pl.4*
 Mrs. Bland's account of, 115
 number of, expanded, 140
 pay of, 46
 as *pen-men*, 9–11
 personal use of, accepted, 136
 position created, 18
 positions held, after War, 306
 railroad Lee after Monmouth, 174–76
 rank issues, 36–37, 46, 128

relatives as, 25
role in letter-writing, 11–13
selection of, 6–7, 9–11, 25
trial period, 57–58
uniforms, 50–52
Algeria, 276–77
alphabet style, 18th cent., 12–13
André, John, 42, 209, 210, 213
Army. *see* Continental Army
Arnold, Benedict
 treason of, 208–12, 220–22
 in Virginia, 214–15, 243
Arnold, Peggy, 212
Articles of Confederation, 265–66
Artillery Corps, 5
Austin, Ebenezer, 48

B

Bant, William, 38
Barbary pirates, 276–77
Barber, Francis, 243
Barry, John, 241
Bashaw, Dey Hassan, 276–77
Baylies, Hodijah, 255–56, 257–58
Baylor, George
 about, 28–29
 an excellent horseman, 9
 Baylor's Dragoons, 99–102, 237–38
 use, as aide, 36

quarrels with Washington,
227–29
resigns after Yorktown, 253
warns Congress to leave
Philadelphia, 125–26
writing skills of, 10
at Yorktown, 156–57, 242–43,
247–48
Hancock, John, 17, 37–38, 39–40,
125
Hannah, 29, 30
Hanson, Alexander Contee, 55
Hanson, Dorothy, 35
Hanson, John, 55
Harlem Heights, battle of, 69–70
Harrison, Benjamin, 27, 205
Harrison, Richard, 35
Harrison, Robert Hanson
about, 34–36
after War, 294–95
cousin Alexander Contee
Hanson, 55
at defense of New York, 66–67
drafts West Point orders,
211–12
importance of, to Washington,
110, 307–8
named military secretary, 59
resigns, 230–32
takes leave of absence, 214–15
headquarters procedures, 12, 70,
72–78, 217–19
Heath, William, 81
Henry, Patrick, 3, 105
History of the American Revolution
(Ramsay), 283, 303
*History of the Virginia Federal
Convention of 1788*,
62–63
Hitchcock, Daniel, 90
Hodgkins, Joseph, 9–10

Hogeboom, Catherine, 129
Howe, William
at Brandywine, 124–25
captures Fort Washington,
82–83
at New York, 60–61, 66, 82–83
to Nova Scotia, 45
replaced by Clinton, 159–60
Humphreys, David
about, 202–3
and Barbary pirates, 276–78
on British in New Jersey,
97–98
death, 280
importance of, to Washington,
308–9
Life of General Putnam, 274
at New York, 69
in Paris, 269–72
and Shays' Rebellion, 273–74
on Washington's death, 277–78
as Washington's secretary
during Presidency, 275–76
woolen mill success, 278–79

J

Jameson, John, 212
Jay, John, 43, 191
Jefferson, Thomas
and Humphreys, 269–72
and Mrs. Walker, 104–5, 107
and Trumbull, 42–43
as Virginia governor, 243, 271
and William Smith, 282–83
Johnston, George, Jr.
appointed aide, 35, 103–4
at Trenton, 90
Johnston, George, Sr., 35
Jones, John Paul, 254

at Valley Forge, 148–49

Washington entreats to return,
37, 58

Reed, Martha (Patty), 23

Rhea, David, 169, 170–71

Rochambeau, viscount de, 244

Ross, Alexander, 250

Rutledge, John, 122

S

sanitation, 146

Saratoga, 128, 133

Savannah, 188–89

Schuyler, 129

Schuyler, Elizabeth, 198–99,
215–16

Schuyler, Philip, 18, 19, 84,
219–20, 221

Scott, Charles, 162, 172

Scott, John Morin, 219

Scull, Peter, 143–44

servants, in army, 71–72, 73,
196–97

Shaw, Samuel, 135–36

Shays' Rebellion, 266, 273–74

Short, William, 272

shorthand, 13

Shrewsberry (Berry), 135

sieges, 246–47

Simon, Simon, 14

slavery, 138–39, 189–90, 258–59,
304, 307

smallpox, 236

Smith, William Stephens

about, 234–36

idle and spendthrift career after
War, 284–87

and Jefferson, 282–83

marries Nabby Adams, 282

as secretary to Adams, 281–83

Smith, William Steuben, 285, 287

Society of the Cincinnati, 225, 309

South Carolina, 190–93

South Carolina, 42

spying, 7, 203–6

Stevens, Edward, 153

Stewart, Walter, 170, 171

Storrs, Experience, 9

Sullivan, John, 106, 179, 235

*Surrender of Lord Cornwallis at
Yorktown* (Trumbull), 43

swords, 52

T

Thacher, James, 71

Thomas, Margaret, 71

Thompson, Elizabeth, 71, 197

Thornton, Peter Presley, 118–19

Throckmorton, Sarah, 119

Tilghman, James, Jr., 65

Tilghman, James, Sr., 65, 293

Tilghman, Matthew, 65

Tilghman, Tench

about, 64–66

after War, 292–94

appointed aide, 201–2

carries Yorktown news to
Congress, 251–52

commissioned Lt. Col.,
238–39

importance of, to Washington,
110, 308, 309

in New York, 67

reports to New York
committee, 111–13

on Trenton, 90

uniform, 51, *pl.3*

at Valley Forge, 149–50

and Washington's resignation,
262–63